# Modern Architecture and Climate

# Modern Architecture and Climate

## Design before Air Conditioning

Daniel A. Barber

**Princeton University Press**
Princeton and Oxford

For Felix and Clarissa Daisy

It is likely—bordering on certain—
that the existential interests of
future men and women will focus
on technical images.
— Vilém Flusser

What is proper to every event is
that it brings the future that will
inherit from it into communication
with a past narrated differently.
— Isabelle Stengers

# Contents

# Modern Architecture and Climate

### The Barcelona Lotissements

In 1931, Le Corbusier and his atelier designed a block of apartments as part of a larger urban plan for Barcelona.[1] The apartments had much in common with familiar projects by the Swiss-French architect, such as his Pessac development of 1920–24 or his houses for the Weissenhof Siedlung in 1927 (see figure 1.11). The Barcelona apartments, referred to simply as Lotissements (French for "subdivision," though with a sense of the British "allotments" or garden plots) were grouped in blocks of two or four, each unit a thin three-story structure. These blocks were, in most cases, mirrored along the axis of a centralized staircase that was partially open at the roof, serving as ventilation shaft and light well. The ground floor had an open court living space, set behind a single hinged door that tucks into the side and out of the way. In most drawings of the project, the ground floor façade is shown open, creating the kind of indoor/outdoor space also characteristic of Le Corbusier's *jardins suspendus*—though here remarkably more social and community oriented. This ground floor was double height in the back; a remarkable move that opened the downstairs *jardin* to the day-lit staircase, inducing ventilation through the court and taking advantage of natural illumination (figure 0.2; figure 0.3).

In these configurations of the living space—visible in section—the importance of light, air, and a relationship to the sun emerge as a crucial theme in Le Corbusier's oeuvre, and, as this book will describe, in modern architecture before the advent of air conditioning.[2] This specific temporal and technical framing suggests a different analytic framework for architectural history, one that treats as its object the spatial, climatic, and material inter-relationships of a building. Le Corbusier's Lotissements were, if not the first, a significant early instance of a kind of social and technical approach to the design of a building façade that sought to acclimatize the interior, architecturally, and thereby to improve the quality of life that would happen within.

The façade is rendered as a mechanism of climatic mediation. It both integrates this project into the history of architectural modernism (laying out a recognizable architectural past and future) and opens it up to a more general history of design methods, material innovations, and attention to systems. A history of architecture and climate. Although the Barcelona project was never built, the drawings the studio produced presented new graphic means by which a climatically active façade system could be understood and reproduced; it initiated decades of discussion about climate design methods. These discussions, and their resonance to the present, are the subject of this book.

The Barcelona apartments sat on the fringe of the Plan Macia, a larger urban redevelopment project typical of Le Corbusier's urban work of the period, and was developed with the Catalan collaborative GATCPAC (figure 0.4).[3] The larger project was framed by the theme of "une maison, une arbre": that an essential aspect of a house was to have a tree as part of the yard; again, the "allotment" aspect. Each house was to have had a tree planted for it, often more than one. As shown in the initial drawing from the archives, the roof was also planted, an elevated garden space (figure 0.5).

Above the ground floor interior patio, the second floor, as the initial plan shows, had a kitchen and a dining area as well as a deep balcony—one similar to those in the better known Immeuble Villas of 1922. The third floor had three bedrooms: a large one at the back for the parents; a smaller one, without a window, for the "garçons"; and another small room for "jeunes filles" open to the end of the hallway and the terrace. On both of the upper two floors there were small terraces at the front, with a wire mesh balustrade. The rear stair continued to a raised area on the roof, a lantern, perhaps best seen in the model. The lantern operated as a large exhaust flue for the staircase/ventilation shaft. It was also a sun room and provided access to the planted roof terrace. In an early drawing (figure 0.5), a figure walks atop

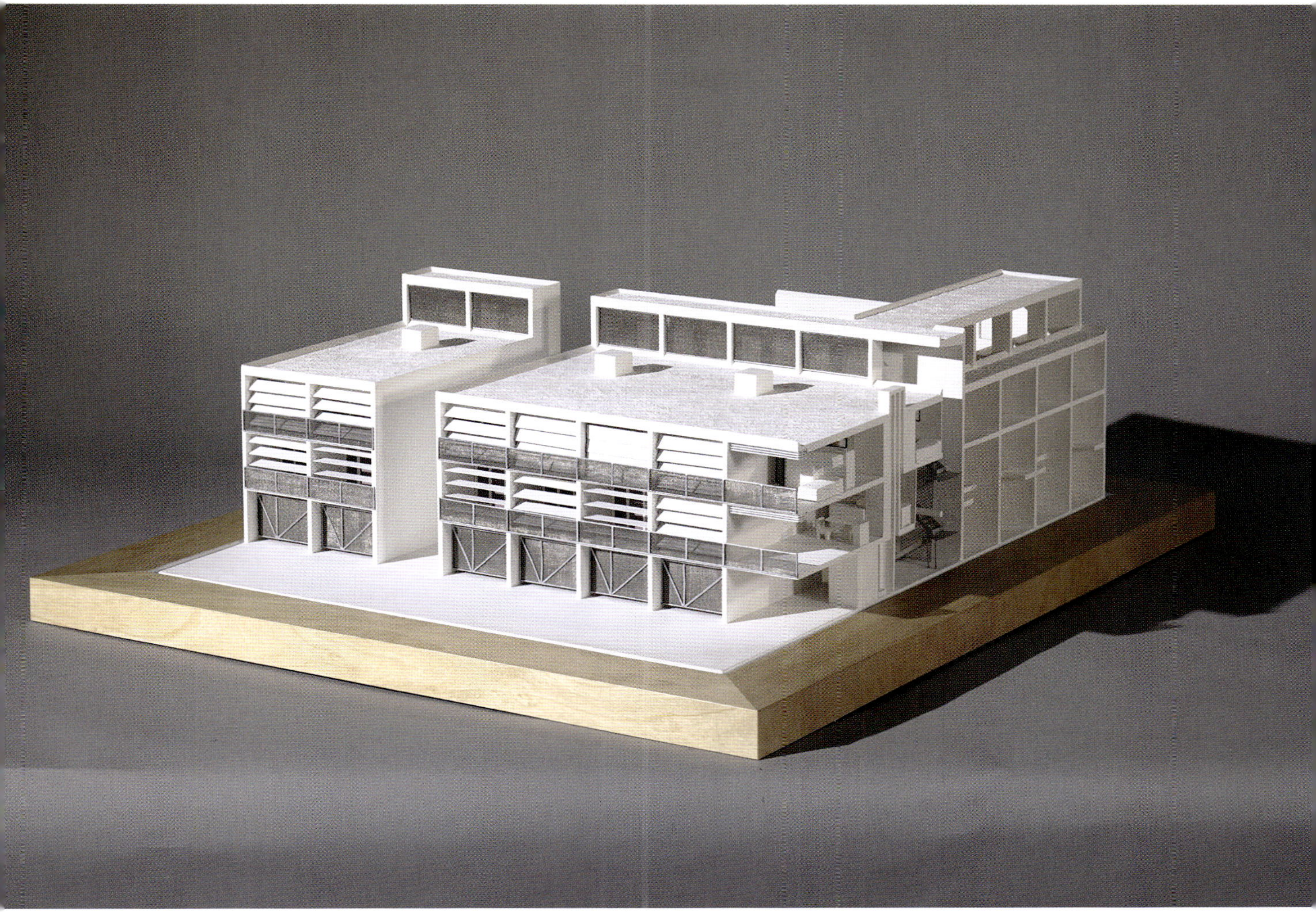

0.1 Le Corbusier, Lotissement, Barcelona, 1931 (project). Model from 2002, made by the Cité de l'architecture et du patrimoine, Paris.

BARCELONE, LOTISSEMENT 1933

(Le projet définitif)

Le coin de lotissement

0.2 Le Corbusier, Lotissement, perspective, from the *Oeuvre complète, 1929–1934*.

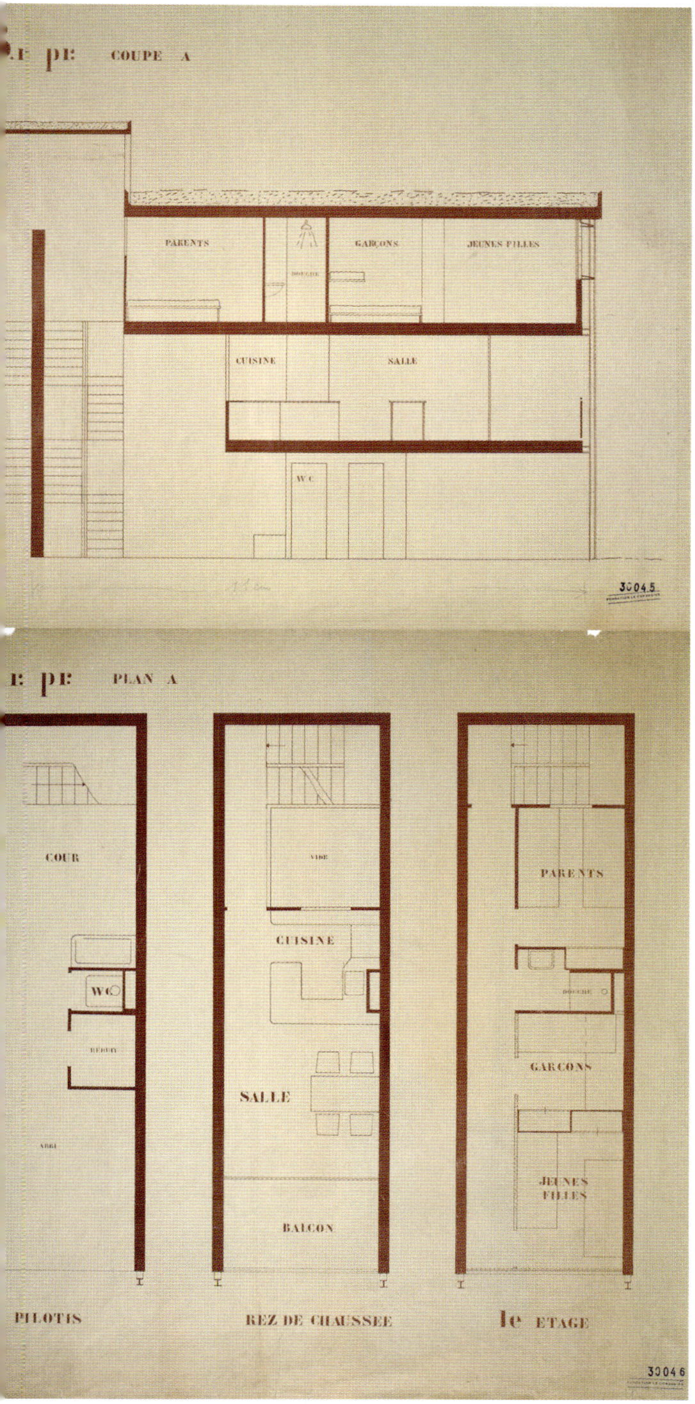


0.3 Le Corbusier, Lotissement plan and section.

the lantern space, seeming to be catching butterflies. In most later representations, the top of the lantern is more functional (for ventilation and climatic management) than habitable.

Louvers on the façade of the second and third floor—lining the balcony off the dining area and the young girl's bedroom—were proposed to provide seasonal shade. Drawings and models of the project indicate that the deep terrace at the second floor and the thinner terrace on the third (not really occupiable given the louver system) both had shading devices set back just behind the vertical plane of the façade—the shading system was embedded in the architecture, in the thickness of the façade itself rather than on top of or outside it. The "la façade" elevation in the *Oeuvre complète* (figure 0.6) indicates that at the bedroom floor the louvers could seal the window off from light; the living floor has some gaps between the louvers, allowing daylight in most conditions.

Both floors had sets of four large louvers. They were operable, and could be moved together according to four settings: tilted up, tilted down, vertical (closed), or horizontal. Adjustments would be made according to seasonal and diurnal patterns of the sun. Schematically, at least, the Lotissement project sketches out the *first principle* of emergent climatic design methods: an adjustable shading system at the façade, keyed to the specific microclimate on the exterior and the volumetric and material details of the interior, has the capacity to modify the daylight and thermal conditions of that interior, and to make it more comfortable year-round. The façade is in this sense embedded both in the interior (the architecture) and the exterior (the climate); it mediates, mitigates, and negotiates. The bioclimatic architecture of the 1950s would later elaborate on this principle, insisting not only on a carefully articulated façade system, but also that the façade for each elevation be treated differently, according to the precise dynamics of solar exposure.

After the site-specific façade, a *second principle* of climate design methods: the section drawing is essential to understanding these façade-based manipulations. The façade section drawing in the *Oeuvre complète* (figure 0.6) shows the louver system on the second floor as a series of X marks, representing the in-between, diagonal states; on the third floor a central vertical line bisects a series of horizontals—they are open and/or closed. This was an early exercise significant to the historical developments being

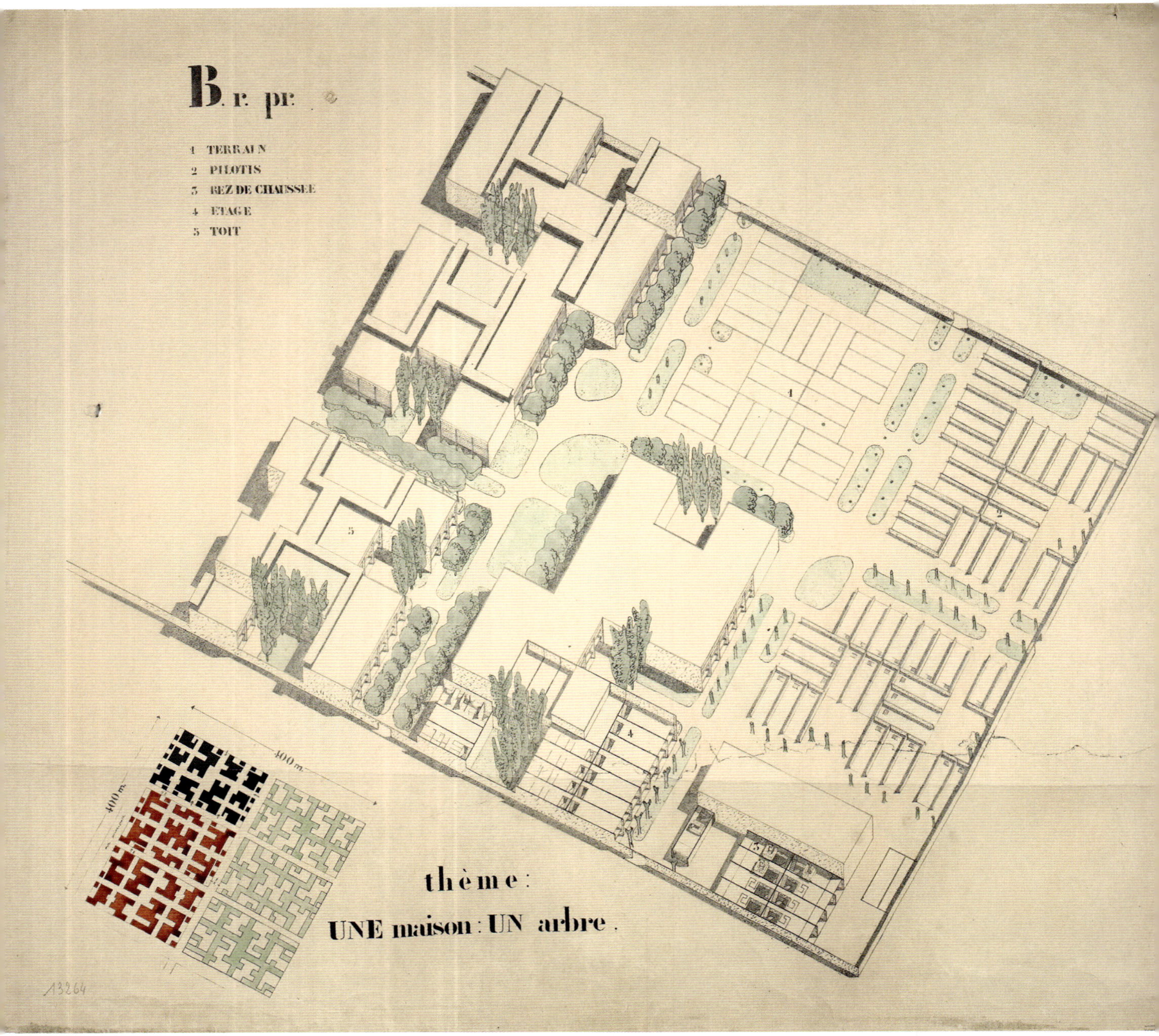


0.4 Le Corbusier, Lotissement block plan.

0.5 Le Corbusier, Lotissement concept drawing, c. 1931.

0.6 Le Corbusier, Lotissement plan and section from the *Oeuvre complète 1929–1934*, indicating the daylit staircase and the façade.

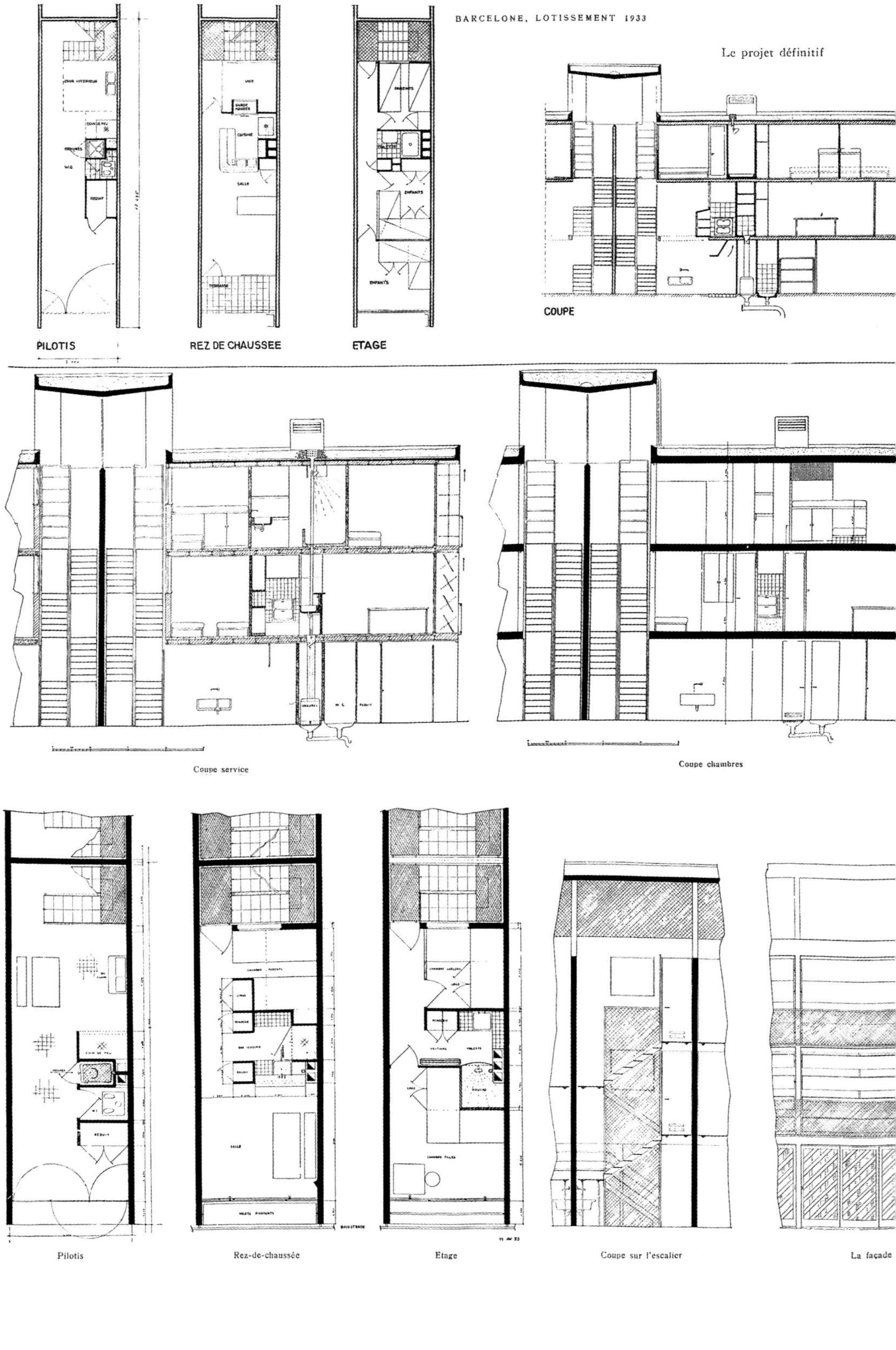

traced in this book: the expression, in graphic form, as technical image, of a carefully designed façade shading system, distinct for each program and orientation it faced. The variability of the façade, read as a media event, suggests a new relationship between cultural patterns and social practices, on the one hand, and the design of interactions with the façade, on the other.

Although the louvers themselves vary in detail, the mechanism to move them is uniform across the floors. The second and third floor façades are represented differently in an attempt to suggest the dynamism of the overall system—that it had multiple states of rest, that it could be adjusted in order to alter the experiential conditions of the interior—against the option of illustrating one setting and thereby giving the impression of their being one, or one preferred, state. The climatic façade section aims to map alternatives, to represent conditions across multiple settings, in relationship to season and daylight, and as a means to suggest both the building's flexibility and the general presumption of a building system that *changes*. Modern architecture, in this important sense, was challenged, before air conditioning, by the dynamic systems implications of the building as climate mediator. The X and bisected horizontal line work together, graphically, virtually representing this dynamism in the façade system, and reflecting the social life envisioned within: A life of comfort, the house as a platform for sociability, health, and progress.

In the Barcelona project, the façade is a media device, in a way both material and symbolic. The premise of a dynamic, site-specific façade invited new terms for representation—of the building, of the humans inside it, of the environment and the patterns of the geophysical world that surrounded it. Articulating a distinction from this world of geophysics, of *nature*, is of course part of the broad ambition of architecture: to delimit the social from the natural. The porous boundary of the shaded façade offers new material terms—"an environmental filter," as it will be called it in 1957—and new symbolic terms for understanding how humans live inside the built environment. The exchange between material experimentation and design representation will intensify in subsequent years and through subsequent projects; the façade, as media, is the primary element for experimentation in climatic modernism and, in section, the primary aspect of design representation.

Climate can only be understood through representation. The façade is a technical system for cultural engagement with the natural world that explicates a social relationship to climate, represents it. It is a liminal space between the interior and the exterior, between the building's program and the region's climate; it contains both. The façade is drawn (literally) as a means to indicate a specific cultural relationship to climate, a refined approach to the porous line of distinction between the civilized interior and the less predictable world outside. The line of the façade was theorized across the development of architectural modernism. The complexity of this interior/exterior relationship, the significance of the line that divided it, was experimented with and materialized as a new kind of image—technical images that conceptualized the thermal interior and aimed to optimize the conditions of this interior according to perceptions of health and productivity, of culture and progress, and of a universal norm. The sectional drawing of the façade is an emblem, then, for how a range of media reflected ideas about architecture and climate, and for how to render those ideas in built space, to bring specific thermal conditions into being. The building façade is both a screen on which to watch environmental change and an industrial-material system from which to produce it.

The Lotissements were relatively undeveloped as an architectural project. However, they set out a premise for the proliferation of design ideas and methods that became a significant thread in architectural modernism over the next few decades. It is in this sense an epochal, recursive project, an object from the past that describes a relationship to climate with unanticipated relevance to the present and the future.

## At the Right Place

*Modern Architecture and Climate* tells the history of shading devices, brise-soleil, louvers, screens, fins, jalousies, and other attempts to control the way that the sun enters the building by architectural (rather than mechanical) means. It surveys the midcentury tumult around energy, politics, technology, and design and documents—through diagrams, sections, photographs, collages, and other media—to describe a complex cultural apparatus intending to make sure that, as Victor Olgyay put it, "interception of the energy happens at the right place"—solar radiation is deflected at the façade, before it enters the building.[4] A simple yet, as will be shown, epochal imperative to focus design innovation in the context of radiation, thermodynamics, and geophysics. This book is a history of the façade being seen as the right place to engage in climate. The façade was a mechanism of climatic mediation and environmental management, from the early 1930s in the sectional drawings of Le Corbusier to the elaborate methodological diagrams of the Olgyays in the 1950s and early 1960s. This is a history of the façade as media and of the brise-soleil as a cultural technique—as a mediating device, selectively blocking the sun, and as a media device, rendering visible specific cultural relationships to climate patterns, as those relationships and patterns change over time.

It is also a history of how modern architecture was formulated, initially, as a strategy of climatic adaptability. Developments of modernism were a means to induce a way of living (*l'esprit nouveau*, in Le Corbusier's phrase) in which the building was the essential medium through which to construct adaptable conditions of comfort according to regional and seasonal vagaries—even though, at many junctures, this premise of adaptability was overwhelmed by an insistence on normative conditions, especially in the context of architecture's relationship to economic development and the global spread of capital. These multiply implicated architectural strategies, as climate-sensitive methods, are themselves premediations, again on material and symbolic terms, and at times an inversion of the structured dependence on fossil fuel that accelerated in the postwar period.[5] The dynamic façade in this sense reflects a different architectural past, one in which the profligate use of fossil-fueled HVAC (Heating, Ventilation, and Air Conditioning) systems, behind delicate glass façades, is seen as one of many threads in the historical development of architecture, across a timeline rich in variety and sensitivity of design methods.

The sectional exploration of the façade precipitated and developed alongside methods for conceptualizing the designed interior as a space of thermal optimization. The planetary interior emerged as a conditioned space of social inhabitation—a space of control for commerce and the processing of the global economy, a space of consistency and rationalization, of the working stiff and the man in the gray flannel suit, of the conditioned domestic interior, static as a space of tradition. Ideas and methods relative to thermal consistency and variability were initially seen to be activated through architecture—that is, by design methods rather than through mechanical systems. Elaborate techniques and systems were developed to account for climate as part of the design of the building, including especially the relationship between the volume of the interior, the precise microclimatic location of the site, and shading devices on the façade, as mediator. This same accounting for climate—the volumetric considerations, the concept of the "comfort zone," the general notion of regulating the interior—was later pursued through mechanical HVAC systems, working off the regulatory parameters established through nonmechanical means.

Put slightly differently, the conceptualization of the thermal interior initially developed through careful coordination between design elements, knowledge of climatic patterns, and assumptions about inhabitants' resilient capacity to adjust to different thermal conditions; this same aspiration for achieving thermal balance was then integrated into mechanical systems, modeling processes, and regulatory structures that, by contrast, were seen to be universal and everywhere applicable, able to produce an identical climate anywhere and across time. In this sense the International Style (despite the suspicion with which this term is generally accorded today) was in fact quite bold and effective—modern architecture, to a significant and underanalyzed extent, was about the delivery of a certain kind of managed thermal space, initially through design and then as part of the proliferation of air conditioning around the world. This book tells the story of climate as a project for design, just before air conditioning.

It is also about how the global imperative for the rendering normative of the built interior, when read through architectural-climatic media of the period surrounding World War II, provides evidence for the unintentional acceleration of the destabilization of climate systems.[6] Climate-methodological images, the aspirations for new ways of living that they sought to represent, and the buildings that they produced instigated and reflected new desires. They sought to articulate the possibility of a new kind of social and economic life, consistent across the unevenness of climate and of capitalist development.

This is a complicated set of connections that is also remarkably simple. Technical images and shading devices led to new ways of conceptualizing the thermal interior; these conceptual models became the object of regulatory mechanisms and mechanical systems intended to normalize the interior conditions around the globe. The focus is on the *architectural* methods (that is, rather than *mechanical* methods) that were developed to conceptualize and condition this planetary interior. The focus is also on how, by placing climate in the center of the historical trajectory of architectural modernism, a new perspective emerges relative to the role of seemingly "peripheral" regions and practices. Modernity is here less a promise of progressive liberation and more a framework for analyzing architecture's role in the project of economic development, with some interest in the prospects for new kinds of architectures, and new kinds of development, now that fossil-fueled modernity's promise has sharply faded.[7]

The façade is essential, though of course it is only one of many elements of a building that determines the thermal conditions of the interior—the roof, relationship to the ground, siting, volume of enclosed spaces, among numerous other factors, are taken into consideration when assessing a building's thermal condition. The façade is, for the purposes of this book, representative of these other factors. This is in part because it is often designed to represent the public or urban face of the building, and in part because sectional drawings of the façade emerge, in the archives revealed through the episodes that follow, as crucial to disciplinary articulations of specific aspirations relative to architecture and climate. While numerous other kinds of image production, especially the integrative diagram, also proliferate and also become important sites for tracing these threads, the façade section is the essential tool for reconceiving architectural value according to climatic performance.

## From the Brise-Soleil to the Planetary Interior

*Modern Architecture and Climate* is divided into two parts. The first, "The Globalization of the International Style," narrates the growth of climatic modernism in relationship to architectural innovations from the 1920s to the 1940s. The first chapter looks at Le Corbusier's engagement with climate to understand the historical development of shading and also to assess how the significance of climate as an aspect of modern architectural history has been clouded in the historiography. The second chapter looks to the proliferation of the brise-soleil in Brazil, emphasizing how climatic modernism developed in relationship to the political, social, and economic modernization programs of that country—and thereby figures a broader relationship between architecture, risk, and development. The third chapter examines a series of tests for these modern architectural strategies: first, Richard Neutra's so-called Planetary Test for postwar reconstruction in Puerto Rico, and then a different kind of geopolitical hedge in the American embassy building program in the Middle East, Africa, Southeast Asia, and elsewhere in the 1940s and '50s. The story all along is tightly focused on the images that are produced, the context for their dissemination, and the analytic relevance of these media practices to understanding climate and environment, as they are emerging as socially relevant categories.

The second part, "The American Acceleration," focuses on American design-methodological discussions of climatic modernism after World War II. Here, the technical image—its figures, its tropes, its dissemination, its technicity—was organized more precisely around a capacity for instrumentally applying a set of methods to a given building project—or, better, toward the development of a universal system for architectural-climate analysis. The project was no longer simply to construct new spaces, seemingly appropriate to an expanding industrial modernity, but to develop disciplinary methods that restructured the relationship between architecture and climate so as to better inhabit the planetary interior. These methods were explored diagrammatically. The images produced premediate and prefigure conceptions of conditioning and environmental management that would emerge in subsequent decades. They also render in sharp relief the developmentalism embedded in architecture's transformations over this period, embedded with patterns of racial and economic injustice in processes of industrialization, modernization, and growth.

Chapter 4 (the first in part two) tells the story of the Climate Control Project, a collaboration between *House Beautiful* and the Technical Education Office of the American Institute for Architects. The purpose of the project was to "communicate to the architect the complexities of climate completely in images" and involves a number of significant developments in the design of the thermal interior and its representation.[8] An unexpected mix of interdisciplinary climate thinkers—anthropologists, meteorologists, physicians, decorators, astronomers, historians, photographers, a large number of architects—got involved in the effort. Chapter 5 looks at the intensification of climate-design methods in labs and conferences, especially at the Princeton Architectural Laboratory in the mid-1950s, where Victor and Aladar Olgyay performed their research, wrote their books, and built the Thermoheliodon—perhaps the last, certainly the most ambitious, nondigital architectural-climatic modeling device. They drew a large number of diagrams attempting to articulate a careful, technically astute method for correlating a building to its climatic surround. The last chapter, "Conditioning" examines the hybrid building types that emerged in the 1950s as a transition toward mechanical acclimatization of the interior, in the context of the increasing regulation of interior space by the American Society of Heating, Refrigeration and Air-Conditioning Engineers (ASHRAE), founded in 1959, and as a passage toward reliance on fossil fuels. In the conclusion, the planetary interior is discussed as a site for contested modes of building and living, and as a space of politics.

In some ways, this book has already been written—written and rewritten a number of times over the past few decades, as architects and historians have struggled to insert issues of energy, environment, and climate into the mainstream of architectural discourse. Many of the climatic façades in Brazil (the concern of chapter 2) were collected at the end of Victor and Aladar Olgyays' *Solar Control and Shading Devices*, published in 1957 (itself an important reference in chapter 5). James Marston Fitch's book *American Architecture and the Environmental Forces That Shape It* (discussed in chapter 4), the 1974 revision of his 1947 text ("Environmental" was added in the later version) begins with a lament that architects had not effectively (if at all) taken up the environmental challenges and opportunities that sat right in front of them. Not to mention the complicated ways in which Reyner Banham's *Architecture of the Well-Tempered Environment* (1976) was received in the field and the vicissitudes of its historiographic treatment since.[9] Further, numerous texts have been written and illustrated with examples of best practices in terms of the energy-efficient technologies available in the present. At a number of junctures since World War II, the question of how architects can integrate their practices with scientific knowledge of the biosphere has come to the fore, been debated, and, haltingly, emerged as a framework for design intervention.

And yet, this discussion could not be more timely. Conditions have, of course, changed since the 1930s, and the 1960s—the climate has changed, scientific knowledge of climate has changed, and the tools of the architect have changed, all beyond recognition. The way that historians consider the relationship of scholarship to practice and culture has also undergone provocative transformation—a number of writers have recently discussed how uncertainty about the future has disrupted familiar patterns and methods of historical scholarship.[10] This book operates at the intersection of careful, theoretical elaboration of architectural-historical complexities and the urgency of the climate crisis. While I am attentive to the substantive distinctions between previous eras and our own—architects of the period under analysis knew nothing of the consequences of carbon emissions—I am also sensitive to the unexpected relevance of these marginalized forms of architectural knowledge.

Indeed, the hoped for effect of this book, of the discussion of architecture and climate more generally, is this: by rescripting the historical narrative of architectural modernism, other futures will be seen to be possible. As part of a wider arrangement of social and environmental forces, this text aims to enjoin architects, scholars, and others toward engagement with climate as a central aspect of architecture culture and the building industry. As Isabelle Stengers has recently written, "What is proper to every event is that it brings the future that will inherit from it into communication with a past narrated differently."[11] The histories here presented, and the broader project of the environmental history of architecture to which they relate, reframe the terms by which we consider a given architectural phenomenon to be seen as a *historical* event—a building, a drawing, an idea—in order to narrate the past differently, drawing out threads that have been concealed, so as to communicate with, pose trajectories for, an as yet undetermined future. In this sense I humbly aspire to, at best, open this discussion of histories and possible futures, of the techniques of climate management, to further contributions of scholars, architects, and others interested in the techno-cultural challenges of mitigating and adapting to climate instability. Which is to say: in light of the unintended consequences of the global proliferation of HVAC systems since the mid-1950s—carbon emissions, lifestyles rooted in burning fossil fuels, global warming, threats of species extinction—this history of nonmechanical practices is also about possible futures.

This is a history focused on the future, because it is likely that aspects of the built environment of tomorrow will resemble and reassemble elements of this relatively recent past—in the sectional treatment of the façade, in the reconceptualization of thermal comfort, in the cultural capacity for adaptation, in the recognition of new entanglements between architecture, politics, and social patterns that play out in the planetary interior. The cultural absorption of shading devices and climatic strategies sit just below the surface—just behind the façade—of more familiar narratives of architectural modernism; what began in Barcelona suggests an elaborate thread of architectural activity, rich in its interconnections, its object of study, and its relationship to contemporary questions.

## Environmental Media

Weather can be experienced; we need media to understand climate. Buildings can be experienced; we need media to understand architecture. Media is both general and specific—though the term as used here is not the media that plays out through journalism, radio, television, and the public sphere, or not exclusively. Media, for the purposes of this book, initially, is a means of cultural communication and reflection—images, their production, dissemination, and analysis, that provide insight into the methods and perspectives of historical agents.[12]

Media is evidence, more broadly, for cultural approaches to concepts such as climate. The narrative of *Modern Architecture and Climate* follows the emergence of the technical image—an image seen as an instrumental device, a technique, for changing the sociobiotic relationship. Technical images will be mapped, in this book, across a thirty-year transition from the vaguely experiential to the precisely scientific; from a humanist, romantic version of nature as a site for balance and harmony, to a data-driven understanding of climate as a realm of the chaotic and barely predictable, rethinking the position of humans and habitats within it. The façade's liminality will similarly be seen to register an architectural approach that is increasingly informed by new kinds of expertise.

Climate methods in architecture emerge through media, reimagining the future as a space of speculative investigation.[13] Analyzing these images, and framing the façade as a form of media itself, allows for analysis and interpretation of cultural norms and aspirations. The category of "environmental media" relevant in this period encompasses those images, devices, and other processing systems that seek to operate on the distinction between environmental knowledge and social practice. Architecture, in this sense, is both a material and a symbolic substrate for a range of new ideas about social engagement with climatic patterns.

*Reconceptualizing "Environment"*

Many of the concerns and questions that drove the development of modern architecture focused on the environment, even though this term was generally not in use.[14] As part of their thinking about new ways of building in the world—new materials, novel organization for social activities—modern architects imaged and imagined the environment as both obstacle and opportunity. They did so as a matter of course, and earlier than most other professionals who have since become concerned with it. While much of this concern was related to seemingly quotidian issues of placement on site, or the orientation of windows, there were also sophisticated discussions of, for example, access to light and air, isolating pedestrians from automobiles and their pollution, materials and their efficiency, prefabricated construction methods, and other careful means of considering the effects of the environment on design, and of design projects, as they aggregated, on environmental health. Many of the innovations around materials and design methods that were essential to the articulation of the principles of modern architecture were also arguments for a different relationship between social patterns and the uncertainty and unpredictability of environmental conditions—if not yet on a planetary scale.

In order to draw out the specificity of this conjuncture of architecture, media, and climate, the focus of this book is on those practitioners and writers who self-consciously sought to produce a new way of thinking about architecture's relationship to the geophysical systems that affect a given site. This drew on knowledge of both the geophysical conditions of the exterior, broadly conceived as climate, and the interior space that was produced in relationship to it, understood as a thermal interior. New kinds of images were needed to explore, understand, and communicate the novel terms, forms, and technologies that could best operate on these two conditions—the climate and the thermal interior—and their interconnections.

The intersection of architecture, media, and climate brings to the foreground a conception of the environment as instrumental—it is of interest as a system, as a means to develop operational approaches to human life—and sees planetary systems as subject to engagement, manipulation, and optimization. Many histories and contemporary discussions approach the concept of environmentalism with a focus on increased scientific knowledge of ecosystems—at a local, regional, and planetary scale—as this knowledge intensified from around the 1920s; other histories examine a range of bureaucratic and countercultural social movements that sought to renew "nature" as a site of cultural value, through legislation or protest.[15] The emergence of climatic modernism developed along this same historical continuum and in relationship to a number of these threads and other related historical patterns; however, it does so with a different emphasis, and with different ends.

The environmentalism of the climate-design methodologist was not one of land ethics, of "nature" as a site for reflection, or of an experimental ground for modeling peak ecological conditions. Architects instead sought to analyze how physiological norms, social behaviors, and atmospheric patterns were intertwined, and how the built environment could optimize these interconnections in producing spaces for habitation and work. It was a question of gathering data and minimizing risk. This was, importantly, not called "environmentalism" in any substantive fashion—the project was not one of social transformation; it is only from the present perspective that one can recognize these ideas, methods, and actions as aspects of a project for socioenvironmental change. Rather, the focus was on the capacity of applied scientific knowledge and material strategies to alter, and, hopefully, improve the relationship of societies to their surroundings. This aim operated experientially, at the scale of the individual—the inhabitant of the house, the worker in an office building—and at the scale of the population, where data and technical knowledge abstracted the techniques and the ends of improving quality of life. (The so-called comfort zone, which will be the subject of much discussion in the latter half of this book, was the figure conceptualized to model the experience of the interior according to optimized data sets.)

This is not to say, at this stage, that such efforts were successful on the terms as they were proposed. The means and ends of climatic analysis are significant as process: they opened up a new realm for architectural ideas and methodological application. "Climate" was and is a site for knowledge production in architecture that, in different ways across the decades under discussion here, provided access to a constellation of interconnections between scientific, technological, and bureaucratic innovations and the wide-ranging social transformations that these were seen to be in relationship to. At the limit, climate in architecture was, and is, a cipher: a way to talk about social collectives in their relationship to geography, economy, and politics, through the technical image.

This conception of environmentalism as applied knowledge is less about a concern for the seemingly inherent harmonies of the natural world and more about an interest in understanding the interaction of economies (social relationships to resources) and ecologies (uneven geographical and climatic conditions). This inflection of the sociocultural project of environmentalism reflects a broader disposition of the book, a sort of realpolitik that looks for historical knowledge according to contemporary use value, both techno-architecturally (how to build something) and historico-conceptually (how to think in relationship to history).

In this context the concept *architecture* has itself evolved, has been socially constructed in response to changing conditions in the world and changing knowledge about planetary systems. In much contemporary discourse, architecture is considered to be a process almost exclusively focused on cultural expression through creative form-making. Yet, the search for a novel form in and for itself is a relatively new phenomenon, indeed beginning in the debates of postmodernism just as this story of climatic creativity was ending. The architectural discourse of the past half century or so has naturalized the field as one that is focused on the formal to the exclusion of environmental, behavioral, or social, even though many architects, historians, and critics have operated otherwise.

There are other examples, other histories that underlay relational approaches to architecture. Lewis Mumford's urban histories and criticism, for example, drew strongly on the work of Patrick Geddes, whose formulation of paleotechnic and neotechnic—of a new realm of technological relationships and correlate social formations—was essential to Mumford's understanding of the political and economic relevance of the built environment.[16] Geddes, for his part, was influenced by the forest manager, governor of Vermont, and ambassador to Italy George Perkins Marsh, seen by many as an American protoenvironmentalist.[17] The environmental historians Ramachandra Guha and Joan Martinez-Alier have commented on this Marsh-Geddes-Mumford thread. Marsh, Guha, and Martinez-Alier write, posited "man as an 'active geological agent' who could 'uphold or degrade' but who was, one way or another, a 'disturbing agent,' who . . . overthrew the stabilities of existing arrangements and accommodations."[18] Balance or harmony where not substantive concerns; instead, regulatory methods to reduce human impact or to manage a resource came into play.[19]

Mumford, under Marsh's influence, as Guha describes it, recognized the ambivalence of technology relative to environmental stewardship, and emphasized the complexity and unpredictability of the consequences for the natural world and for societies and their political and economic frameworks. Mumford was concerned that concepts of the environment were conceptually inadequate as they did not consider individual and collective desire, the impact of social actions and activities on the ecosystem, and the complex feedback loops—between desire, economic production, and ecosystem management—that pertained. As Guha and Martinez-Alier summarized: "Like [John] Muir and [Aldo] Leopold, Mumford valued primeval nature and biological diversity, but unlike them, he focused simultaneously on cultural diversity and relations of power *within* human society, refusing to divorce individual attitudes to nature from their social, cultural, and historical contexts."[20] How nature is considered, or constructed, makes a profound difference in how the consequences of social actions are understood, configured, and rendered relevant.

Architecture, posed across this nexus of economies and ecologies, produces a distinct realm for discourse, a field of technical knowledge that seeks to adjust, reflect, and reconsider—in a word: *mediate*—the relationship between scientific knowledge of planetary systems and social means of expressing collective will relative to that knowledge. Architecture works toward new understandings of effective (in the sense of species continuation) means of engaging ecosystem conditions and behaviors, and is part of the cultural milieu that elaborates on, visualizes, and otherwise demonstrates these relationships. Again, the façade system is essential—as much for its architectural technicity as for its delimitation of the interior as cultural space, and further for its framing of the climatic exterior as a subject for scientific inquiry. Architecture operates as a material and symbolic intervention in the lifeworld, simultaneously interpreting this world through sophisticated visual technologies and intervening in it to alter and shape the conditions for future life.

This variety of environmentalism is less about "saving the planet," simply because the need was not yet present and identified—we are decades before Greenpeace, and all the geophysical knowledge and social awareness that modern environmentalism implies. Climatic modernism was about understanding how social and geophysical systems interact, and operating on those systems so as to alter them—most frequently, these alterations were framed as optimizations, and sought to simultaneously improve what were considered, in different historical contexts, to be ideal for both social opportunities (improving ways of life) and biotic opportunities (as a matter of course, not overcompromising the conditions of the planet that allow human life, and life in general, to persist). Such were the concerns of the climate methodologists, their precursors and successors.

None of these ambitions should be taken at face value—that is, these architectural-environmentalists had their own professional aims, biases, and sociocultural dispositions, and pressures from clients or institutions. This is not a story of triumph over the elements; rather, it is a story of identifying in climate a new object of history and a new subject of design practice, an interest in how design methods were refined for climate, and of the consequences of this expanded architectural discourse on the changing climate patterns of the past and the present.

It is also the story of a new kind of subjectivity—a narrative that reflects how individual desires have transformed in relationship to physiological and climatological changes. The concept of "comfort" is the important aspect here of the architectural-climatic discussion. Comfort is the ideal of all capitalist and induced forms of built developmentalism—relative to quality of life, to efficiency in the workplace, and such—and also the object of panic, the thing we can't let go of, the driver of so much of our climatic disruption. It is an epochal concept—it must be seen, that is, for the epochal transformations associated with it. The façade as media also shudders across this line of the Great Acceleration: the more comfortable we are, as a species, the more at risk we are, as a species. Architecture of the twenty-first century needs to be consumed with this fact.

Climate design methods of the 1950s encouraged inhabitants to interact differently with their façades and the spaces those façades helped produce, thereby activating a new relationship between inside and outside, and hence between societies and environments. It was dynamic, flexible, and, across a shorter time period, adaptable. Reconfigurable: able to be seen as operated on differently, to different effects. Not a static object. Climatic modernism, as with architectural modernism more generally, produced new subjects—new individuals with novel desires, newly sensitive to the thermal conditions of the interior. We have produced our air-conditioned selves through architecture. In this sense, architecture does not simply reflect a given social formation, but is generative, productive of new relationships.[21]

Architecture focused on climate is part, of course, of a biopolitical process. Biopolitics poses as its analytic object means of intervention in "the general system of living beings," offering, for better or worse, new ways of interacting with people, things, and spaces in a fashion that is resonant with the means and ends of climate design methodologists.[22] Michel Foucault also proposed to reconfigure the object (not just the subject) of historical analysis along the expanded terms just outlined, and under the figure of the "technical schema of this notion of milieu" that he described as "a kind of pragmatic structure . . . present in the way in which the town planners try to reflect and modify urban space." He described the milieu as a sort of given space of social formation: "The apparatuses of security work, fabricate, organize and plan a milieu . . . as [a] set of natural givens—rivers, marshes, hills—and a set of artificial givens—an agglomeration of individuals, of houses, etc. The milieu is a certain number of combined, overall effects bearing on a population."[23]

The concept of the milieu in Foucault—which cannot simply be translated as "climate," but is not unrelated—developed in relationship to Georges Canguilhem's treatise from 1948, translated as "The Living and Its Milieu." It is summary and canonical, organizing the concept as a means to understand both the history of its scientific articulation and the relationship between governance and environment the concept proposed. The sociotechnical concept of milieu relies on reflexivity, a definition of surroundings that necessitates a human agent as a point of reference, or, at least, this is how it was imagined by the evolving biological sciences: "The milieu on which the organism depends," Canguilhem writes, "is structured and organized by the organism itself," and further, "the environment he is supposed to be reacting to finds itself originally centered in and by him . . . therefore man's proper milieu is not situated in the universal milieu like a thing contained within its container. A center does not dissolve into its environment. A living thing does not reduce itself to an intersection of influences."[24]

The qualifying of architecture by "climatic," as in *climatic modernism*, is intended to be descriptive, a means to indicate the focus of a practice, an image, a building, and is projective—the project of the practice, the image, the building, was to operate on design and scientific knowledge so as to better coordinate (in a temporally, geographically, and conceptually bounded fashion) the relationship between people and things. Climate became a space of social analysis and optimization before it became the harbinger of a planetary society out of control.

### *The Technical Image*

The primary tactic of climatic modernism was the technical image—an image produced through technical means, that resonates across multiple realms of technologically informed sociobiotic engagements, and that speaks most clearly to those familiar with a given representational system. Technical images, especially in the cases at hand—the design-methodological diagrams of the climatic modernist—attempt to survey and understand economic and ecological interconnections and operate on them; they strive for sociobiotic improvements. They articulate an imaginary of the possible, albeit often overinvested in the promise of technology to resolve political debates.[25]

The category of the technical image is capacious. Vilém Flusser approached this category as not only images produced by technology—such as photographs or charts reliant on computational processing—but also as images, often on screens, that only existed through technological means. Technical images are made up of points: "on close inspection, all [technical images] prove to be envisioned surfaces computed from particles."[26] Most of the images explored in this book just barely predate, on Flusser's terms, the technical image proper; the concern of *Modern Architecture and Climate* is to investigate the transition *toward* technical images and their effects, and indeed of technicity and instrumentality more generally as they came to be embedded in diagrams and forms of climatic-architectural expertise. Data, concepts, and interconnections later processed through computation were here premediated, subject to diagrammatic correlation, and to an excess of misplaced assumptions and implicit intentionality that used images as tools to try to make sense of a world and its near-future possibilities. They seem naive, in contrast to the computational systems that they were essential to conceptualizing and creating. They are interesting not for their contemporary technical effectiveness but as evidence of attitudes and aspirations and the changing conditions of knowledge production.

The diagram is the primary technical image of climatic modernism—the sectional diagram even more so. Architectural interest in the relationship of design interventions to surrounding climatic conditions has long been expressed through diagrams—from Le Corbusier's sketch of the shading characteristics of the Immeuble Clarté in 1928 to any number of false color circulation drawings that aim to indicate the climatic performance of a newly designed building today. The diagram, as a "map of social forces," is an ideal visual medium for bringing together heterogeneous inputs and understanding their possible relations.[27] Diagrams seek to simultaneously provide coherent information and to process that information according to a possible future scenario. The diagram is, again, projective, seeking to articulate new possibilities and to do so in a generative fashion, allowing for multiple specific consequences from the general model simultaneously being analyzed and proposed.[28]

Concerns over site, orientation to the sun, and the relationship of materials to heat and humidity are all embedded in these methodological diagrams. Of course, a general understanding of climate was implicit in many vernacular or traditional conceptions of shelter. Much of what is being discussed here could be seen as an attempt to modernize (often without adequate technological means) this range of traditional practices, according to regional inflections. The diagram is in this sense the instrument of modernization, where ideas about absorbing previous tactics into contemporary strategies were drawn together. Architectural techniques intended to understand and communicate the relationship of a building to its climate not only on the specific terms of a regional practice but also according to a set of generalizable, universal principles.

Diagrams have long had a disciplinary role in architecture. Scholars have argued that the schematic, quasi-representational, and projective capacity of the diagram was essential to the turn toward architectural modernity. Anthony Vidler sees Jean-Nicolas-Louis Durand's drawings of universal building types at the end of the eighteenth century as generative of the modernist focus on function and abstraction.[29] Sven-Olov Wallenstein also cites Durand's drawings as transitional, moving the discipline from a focus on "expressing sense"—the aesthetic elaboration of contemporary thematics—to one whose task was to "find the optimal equation" amid a range of aesthetic, technological, and social (usually governmental) factors.[30] Others have emphasized how the diagram as an abstract figure was essential to the scientific management regimes that proliferated in the period of mass industrialization—organizing workflows, and also organizing human bodies, as factories, office towers, and suburbs were optimized through innovations in design and construction.[31]

The diagram has a specific history in the period of climatic modernism, one that highlights attempts to frame the image, and visualization more generally, as instigation toward certain kinds of human behavior. The use of visual tools to schematically bring together different kinds of social and natural forces intensified, from the late 1940s, in many fields of inquiry, from biology to engineering to behavioral science.[32] Architectural diagrams, though diverse in form and subject, tended to focus on the presentation of schematic ideas that can generate a variety of design solutions. Climate modernists were interested in assessing the relationship between a building and its climate and developed image-making methods that would help communicate new design principles to other architects. They used diagrams in an attempt to operate on the discipline, that is, in order to steer the field toward specific kinds of knowledge as they sought to develop new kinds of practice.

Many architectural-climatic diagrams took the novel figuration of social and biotic systems as their explicit subject. A new kind of image was being created, one that imagined new ways for humans to flourish according to increased knowledge of global ecological systems. Such diagrams were frequently proposed in a context that identified them as a means to instigate change, according to the aspirations that the image, however abstractly, sought to represent. In this form of disciplinary expansion—taking the climate into account—architectural diagrams did not precisely articulate a new ethico-political principle, nor did they rely on the purported truth-value of science to clarify proposals for behavioral change.[33] Neither strictly political, nor aesthetic, nor scientific, the diagram as technical image offered something new—an affective indication of collective desires for transforming sociobiotic relationships, at a moment when those relationships were not yet very well understood.

Technical images, Flusser proposed, tended to figure "relationships among things that no one would otherwise suspect." Although Flusser's focus, again, was on images that were produced through technical means—photographs and images on screens—he also saw in the visual production of information a new class of images intended to serve as models for action.[34] Thus a significant transition: from an aspirational diagram expressing desire to a computational or data-driven image that makes a claim to objective knowledge, and a precise intervention in the sociobiotic matrix. Caught in this transition, many diagrams of the climatic modernists attempted fact and aspiration; they tried to draw out of subjective experience some universal validity, and to produce a new image of the world in order to influence new kinds of expertise that could bring that worldview into being.

### *The Façade as Cultural Technique*

The images of the climatic modernists are technical in specific ways, in both content and form. Most are focused, either implicitly or explicitly, on the façade as the liminal condition of the built environment that clarifies and operates on the relationship between the thermal interior and the atmospheric system. These diagrams tend to focus on the specific technical condition that can best mediate between those two climates. This has already come up through the figure of the section—a diagram that reveals the unseen in the thickness of the façade and renders the façade according to its epochal profundity. The section attempts, with increasing sophistication, to posit the façade as a defining aspect of a specific character of built environment: for how it produced interior space, for how it expressed that production to a more general cultural field, and for how it generated—or accelerated the generation of—a specific relationship between social and biotic patterns, between the thermal regulation of the conditioned interior and the effects of emissions on the global climate.

The sectional diagram of the dynamically shaded façade is open to analysis and speculation. It is a media system. The façade section not only represents a given design proposal for a given site, it also operates in a generative fashion, reflecting and producing ideas about interior and exterior on cultural, conceptual, and material terms. It helps to reveal perspectives on the concept "nature" as they were constructed in a given time and place, and, reflexively, it reveals conceptions of the human in the priorities and aspirations for social transformation that can be read through the façade and the conditions it invokes.

"Every culture," as Bernhard Siegert writes, "starts with the introduction of distinctions, and techniques that process this distinction."[35] This inside/outside dynamic, mediated by the façade, has epochal consequences, in the sense that it allows for an understanding of developments that shift our perception of the historical and contemporary relationship between humans and their environment, between economies and ecologies. Siegert has traced the general significance of this liminality: the distinction between inside/outside; culture/nature (also: thermal interior/atmospheric system)—and its historic significance. "Culture" distinguishes itself from "nature" through media, understood as material and symbolic *cultural techniques* that process, activate, and emphasize this distinction.

The façade is one example; the building is an essential cultural location for processing these distinctions.[36] As Siegert clarifies, speaking directly to the terms of this book: "there is no such thing as *the* house, or the house as such, there are only historically and culturally contingent cultural techniques of shielding oneself and processing the distinction between inside and outside."[37] The concept and condition of the façade of climatic modernism is of a threshold that can be opened or closed and often contains a range of intermediate states.

As a dynamic register of the techno-social, architectural practices differentiate according to their approach to the façade, with historical vicissitudes of cultural approaches to climate evident in façade sections and other drawings. At stake is not simply the processing of distinctions itself, but how they gain significance, how the symbolic is rendered material through these approaches. Culture is revealed and produced through the articulation, visualization, and eventual habitation of a specific façade condition—or, really, the thermal interior that the façade produces. The façade—especially as rendered in section—distinguishes between the inside and outside, managing that divide, and also distinguishes one historical moment and set of cultural norms from another. Innovations in the façade are screens for understanding cultural relationships to climate; as a result, façades are useful for exploring cultural norms as they relate to carbon emissions and the ways of life they have offered.

The façade section speaks to both inside and outside. It communicates between the two, tracing a thin thread of culture that has been concerned with architecture and climate for many decades. This façade section depicts a palimpsest, a multilayered (literally) site for analysis of the past and the possible futures it contains. The perspective of cultural techniques allows for a view of the façade that recognizes its cultural expressivity—its elaboration, on architectural terms (either as project or built object) of a specific desired relationship between the inside and the outside. This set of desires transforms over the thirty years analyzed here: from one of a dynamic, operable, carefully designed shading system for selectively conditioning the thermal interior, to the façade as a tightly sealed membrane between interior and exterior, housing a fossil-fueled mechanical system. The façade is the medium of symbolic expression and the material condition by which humans have engaged with atmospheric systems, for better or worse.

This invocation of "the façade as media," or of "the shading device as cultural technique," is not simply to say that the façade mediates, or expresses, or articulates the desires of the liminal condition of the relationship between nature and culture, but also that the façade is epochal—an object of historical analysis and an agent of change on the conditions of history, change to the environmental conditions that allow for human life to persist, or not, on this planet. Although it was largely done without awareness of these eventual consequences, symbolic and material investment in the sealed façade—as distinct from the porous, dynamic façade of climatic modernism—has contributed significantly to the erosion of climatic stability and will continue to lead to atmospheric chaos, geographical displacement, and other forms of economic and political unrest, with increasing intensity. Architecture materially concentrates and symbolically represents, as media, collective desire on these terms, and the façade section suddenly becomes a political device, an essential battlefield for sociopolitical contestation. Architecture can render our desires meaningless or infuse them with hope.

## The Politics of Planetary Knowledge

This positing of the façade as media reads architecture for its environmental positioning—in relationship to its technicity and for the means by which it conditioned subjects for a different kind of cultural world. Another term of epochal significance: *conditioning*—how to prepare, practice, become adept at a set of usually muscular or physiological activities; or, how to mechanically transform an interior space into a pleasant thermal environment. Air conditioning is also people conditioning, culture conditioning, and bioproductive of a way of life that elicits specific attitudes and lifestyles, regulations, clothing, habits, and any other number of technological, material, and social path dependencies.

It is self-evident that air conditioning, and people conditioning, are realms for contestation and for the production of the future—they are sites for politics, however mediated and complex. In particular, the convergence of scientific knowledge about climate and its manipulation—albeit often abstractly, partially, or ineffectively—in buildings emerges as a realm of planetary contestation. Both the articulation of architectural modernism and the knowledge of climate systems were invested, if in different ways and through different means, in making claims at the scale of the planet. Modern architecture and climate science produced and reflected flows of knowledge and materials around the globe and also the emergence of global imaginaries.[38] The simultaneous development of shading devices and of atmospheric sciences was part of a new way of understanding the planet, the species, and a cultural means of mediating the two.

If the precise terminology of the International Style, as invoked by Philip Johnson and Henry-Russell Hitchcock in the 1932 exhibition of that name at the New York Museum of Modern Art, is itself historically delimited, it nonetheless suggests the importance of a universal framework to the innovations of architectural modernity.[39] The capacity to image and conceptualize planetary systems was an essential aspect of the postwar development of climatic knowledge as well—such data and models were significant to the more general postwar conception of the global.[40] Modern architecture and climate science both emerged from a handful of sites—Princeton, Oslo, Cambridge, Los Angeles. The climatological sciences also relied on the form and content of technical images.

At the intersection of these parallel histories of culture and climate lies this potent site of politics—of arguments focused on struggles for the improvement of life conditions. To frame a sense of politics as a means of articulating, through the built environment, a relationship between social and planetary systems is also to recognize the forms of exploitation embedded therein, in terms of human energy and of environmental resources.[41] Knowledge of climate patterns, as with that of the environment more generally, was a significant part of the colonial project.[42] Scientific encounter with unfamiliar geographies and unknown flora and fauna spurred colonial agents to understand their biodynamic conditions more rigorously, generally with the aim of more effective exploitation of resources and populations.

Modern architecture flourished first in authoritarian, colonial, and neocolonial contexts, and many of its innovations are caught up in ambivalent (at best) governmental strategies that offered new ways of life for some while intensifying the exploitation of others. In architecture and urban planning, this led to a wide range of hybrid formal systems and also to a more systematic understanding of the relationship of climate, among other environmental effects, on the material and spatial conditions of buildings. Other, more precise forms of climate knowledge also intensified.

How, then, does an analysis of climate intensify specific historical legacies relative to the universalist premise that sits at the heart of the modern architectural project? (And how has this ambition at the level of the masses, the people, the species returned, problematically, in contentious discussions around climate and carbon emissions?) In tracing design methods and technological devices as they migrated between the so-called centers and peripheries of twentieth-century culture, such questions will come to the fore. At the least, the framework of architectural modernism, its universal terms, however ambivalently detailed in the historical record, lays bare the concomitant formulation of a specific kind of subject. Modern buildings required "modern" inhabitants, conditioned for life in specific spatioclimatic configurations.

---

The sectional drawing of the Barcelona Lotissements provides an initial window into the emergence of climatic modernism. It was a specific type of architectural approach that is distinct from the larger swath of architectural and other modernisms and also reveals patterns endemic to these broader narratives, especially as they take purchase on the present. What began, or at least intensified, in Le Corbusier's project for Barcelona was a material system of climate management and also an architectural approach to absorbing geographic and cultural difference through technology. The technical image emerged as a site for political contestation by virtue of its articulation of the relationship between cultural desires and the experiential challenges of the environmental surround. Here the façade was media, operating as a means of processing and understanding distinctions between interior and exterior, between nature and culture, between cultures of expansion and contraction. Case studies on the façade as media—reflecting and enacting cultural priorities, and embedded in the politics of development and economic growth, form the evidentiary foundation of this book. The stories of architects, their designs and attempts to refine the relationship between the thermal interior and the vagaries of atmospheric systems, forms a history of how design was seen as a tool to improve quality of life—according to some, usually for others. It is also a history of how architects and others came to accept and attend to climate as an obstacle to be overcome, rather than a process available for dynamic cultural engagement. Today, again, many architects are designing dynamic façades—much more dynamic than heretofore, at times excessively so—in hopes of encouraging a cultural shift toward attentive forms of climatic engagement. *Modern Architecture and Climate* is thus both a history of these architectures and a preview of architectures yet to come.

# Part I

# The Globalization of the International Style

## The Climatic Basis of Modern Architecture

The writings, drawings, and buildings of Le Corbusier operate like a screen, selectively framing our view of the history and relevance of climatic modernism. As the Barcelona Lotissements project already begins to suggest, climate was essential to Le Corbusier's articulation of the principles of modern architecture in the interwar period and to their development after World War II. Buildings, texts, and diagrams indicate that Le Corbusier considered a flexible relationship to the climatic surround to be an essential aspect of the promise of modern methods and design ideas. Alongside a large number of architects of the period, most of the climatic modernists discussed in later chapters were, in one way or another, heavily influenced by Le Corbusier; for many, climate was an essential aspect of their master's work, and they saw themselves as developing his legacy on these terms. However, the voluminous historical literature on the work and influence of Le Corbusier has, with few recent exceptions, ignored this robust evidentiary thread.[1]

There are profound discursive obstacles to embracing the repositioning of architecture according to its relevance to environmentalist debates. Formalism, broadly considered, appears to resist the integration of architectural ideas into the constellation of cultural practices aiming to reconfigure social conditions according to environmentalist pressures. A history of architectural modernism with a focus on the production of novel form has, at risk of overgeneralizing, been the dominant narrative of relevance to debates in the field since the 1960s.[2] This was rendered explicit in Peter Eisenman's 1963 doctoral thesis at Cambridge, "The Formal Basis of Modern Architecture," which saw in the iterative manipulation of platonic solids the capacity to resolve the purported paradox of form and function.[3] Although only recently published, the ideas embedded in Eisenman's thesis, his insistence on the importance of modern architecture being almost exclusively in the formal tools that it engendered, have consumed significant aspects of architectural academia and, while less direct relative to professional activities, have conditioned the discussion of architecture since. Eisenman's project is a symptom of a wider turn away from social and political effects of architectural ideas and practices toward a widely embraced emphasis on the "autonomy" of architecture as a discipline—a premise that has, with a number of substantive exceptions, guided theory, pedagogy, and a number of practices for the last few decades.[4]

And yet, the history of architectural engagement with climate is robust. It offers tantalizing context for many familiar projects and ideas, and opens out to new ways of thinking about architectural engagement with technology, environment, and social conditions. At stake are the terms and

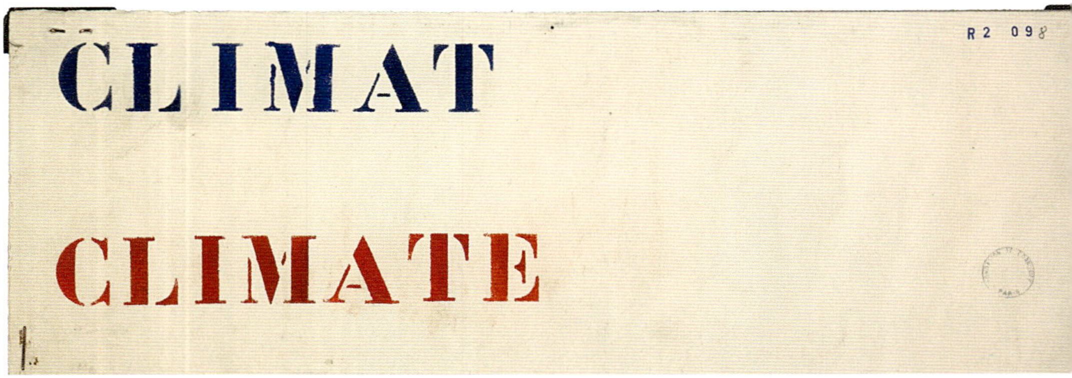


1.1 From the Le Corbusier archive.

# 1. Obstacles

means by which architecture is valued. The computational production of novel form is still seen by many historians, critics, and practitioners as the metric of value in the field—"innovation" in architecture tends to involve the production of heretofore unimaginable spatial experiences, generated through computational means and, at times, through collaboration with structural engineers or others. Concern over how those spaces and structures relate to the environmental conditions of the building is rarely discussed.

This may seem odd to those unfamiliar with architecture culture; indeed, it is something of an overstatement. There is extensive, elaborate, and excellent work occurring in architecture on technical questions in search of energy efficiency, though such questions rarely appear as central to the public value of a building. Think, for example, of the Pritzker Prize or high-profile building competitions, which until very recently tended to pay little attention to environmental questions. While there may be reasonable assumptions that some form of environmental metric should be in place to produce an architecture worthy of accolades, the terms of that metric are not always clear, and in any event, a building's success or failure, in the eyes of the architectural public, rarely relies on questions of climatic performance. While a comprehensive analysis of how architecture is valued—arguments about what, in fact, constitutes a substantive distinction in the context of differential evolution—exceeds the scope of the present volume, one of the essential claims of this book is that an alternative narrative of architectural innovation is available to inform such a criteria, one of direct relevance to questions about how to integrate form and performance, and as a means to shift the conception of architectural value in the present. New narratives can begin to suggest alternative legacies and emphasize new criteria for assessing architectural ideas and practices. The work of Le Corbusier, in its importance to claims of formalist lineage and in the richness of alternative historical threads that it offers, is here both obstacle and opportunity.

One of the effects of inserting climate into architectural histories is that it opens up a new set of events, and a new set of criteria, for understanding how that history has developed with relevance to the present. Emphasizing other *events*, as Isabelle Stengers suggests, can shift historical narratives, the legacies they imply, and the futures they offer an opening toward. This causal inversion, of a past rearticulated according to its relevance to possible futures, will continue to frame my approach to the effect of climate on the history of architecture. The ambition here is less to contribute to the scholarly literature on Le Corbusier and more to establish a historical ground from which to articulate the robust history of climatic modernism that followed from him.

The Barcelona Lotissement, already mentioned (see figures 0.1 to 0.6), represents an impasse and a transition. The façade as shading device was conceived as a means to temper the effects of the all-glass wall on the thermal interior. The Barcelona project was one of a number of such experiments in the 1920s intended to ameliorate the challenges faced by drawing the principles of European modernism into different climatic conditions. While Barcelona is, of course, in Europe, it was, for Le Corbusier and others, one of the southern ports among a select group of cities forming a consolidated ring of a specifically Mediterranean culture, with specific architectural needs. Other essential cities, most also of direct relevance to Le Corbusier's experiments in the period, included Marseille, Algiers, and Rome.[5] The Mediterranean basin thus embodied, in miniature, the climatic and lifestyle distinctions later encountered elsewhere. The climatic differences between the northern coast of Africa and the shores of Lake Geneva, for example, serve to emphasize how crucial climatic distinctions were to refining the design methods of interwar modernism—and how imbricated they were in the racialized and colonial frameworks of the period.[6] Barcelona was in this sense suggestive, if not representative, of a set of climatic and cultural challenges presented to the new architectural principles of modernism—challenges that would amplify the importance of the shading device and resonate across subsequent experiments in regions with more intensive climatic distinctions.

The Lotissements were a laboratory, a test site, for the paired strategies of the dom-ino diagram and the brise-soleil shading device, and for the paired principles of adaptability and normativity. A significant effect of *climate* as a historical and historiographic framework is the recognition that the purported potential of architectural modernism, in the years of its development and early expansion, was a capacity to produce a consistent interior across different regional, cultural, climatic, political, and economic conditions—as Le Corbusier indicated in a lecture in Buenos Aires in late 1929:

> Every country builds its houses in response to its climate. At this moment of general diffusion, of international scientific techniques, I propose: only one house for all countries. . . . The Russian house, the Parisian, at Suez or in Buenos Aires, the luxury liner crossing the Equator. . . . In winter it is warm inside, in summer cool, which means that at all times there is clean air inside at exactly 18°.[7]

The Athens Charter, similarly, insisted that every building should be oriented so as to receive at least two hours of direct winter sunlight.[8] The universalist, internationalist premise of modern architecture was, in this sense, the capacity to adapt the building to a given site and sociocultural condition, to use architectural means to adjust the building design toward a normative thermal interior. Conceptually, this interior was a space requisite for the elaboration of modernity—in the sense of social modernization and industrialization, and on both material and symbolic terms, as the deployment of modern strategies and techniques for the production of a universal space of life, work, and leisure—what Peter Sloterdijk later termed "the world interior of capital," emergent, as Sloterdijk notes, in the Crystal Palace of 1851. It was, by the 1920s, refined through a set of spatial, material, and technological strategies of adaptability and normalization.[9]

The geopolitical ramifications are significant. The climatic perspective also reveals that, despite its apparent affiliation with familiar tropes of metropolitan sophistication, the historical development of architectural modernism is really about an encounter with the dynamism of the so-called periphery—architecture became modern in the Global South. Or, better, the terms and tenets of architectural modernism were articulated in response to the challenges presented by other climates, other cultures, and as a result of strained colonial and metropolitan hegemony. Barcelona in 1931 was in this sense representative and transitional, a stand-in for a more elaborate interest in climates distinct from those of northern Europe—climates that would come to be seen, by Le Corbusier, as the site for architectural experimentation. These experiments in the capabilities of modernism, as a system of adaptation and normalization, then returned to the north once the concept of acclimatization was refined and applied through mechanical conditioning.

This periphery operated not only spatially but also temporally—as much as assumptions and presumptions were made about the geographic and climatic aspects of a given region and its culture, largely according to the presumed superiority of the metropolitan center, the emergence of modern architecture also depended on a host of complicated interrelationships with the vernacular and the traditional as cultural patterns purportedly inferior to those that followed. Climatic modernism consisted largely of attempts to formalize and render optimizable a range of building strategies that reach back millennia. Indeed, protection from the elements has long been a substantive aspect of the origin narratives of architecture; most cultures were, until the structured imperatives of industrialization, cultures of climatic adaptability. The thickness of walls, the use of earth-based thermally active materials, the deployment of screens, extended eaves, and other shading systems, and many other strategies intended to temper the interior at least in periods of climatic extremes. In part, the project of architectural modernity was to produce design techniques—universal or generally applicable—that could deploy new materials and strategies in order to provide the same, or better, thermal mitigation as these other, ongoing practices. In this sense, architectural modernism followed on the developments of various colonial architectures that regulated or rendered scientific the traditional practices that they sought to replace. That such vernacular or traditional strategies were less energy dependent, in both embodied and operating terms, is not insignificant to the present dilemma. More generally, here again, attention to climate reveals some of the broad complications and contradictions in the presumed progressive trajectory of modern architecture.

## Reorienting Modernist Icons

Climate was essential to Le Corbusier before the Barcelona project, even before the specific strategy of the shading device came to the fore. A number of his better-known projects attended to their solar orientation and climatic positioning—more generally, in Le Corbusier's work and that of many of his followers, an essential aspect of "the new architecture" was its capacity to manipulate design and materials so as to open for the inhabitant the experiential conditions of their atmospheric surroundings. The Villa Savoye (1928) and the Immeuble Clarté (1929), both discussed further on, were designed, in part, according to their relationship to the sun and according to the

1922 UNE VILLE CONTEMPORAINE

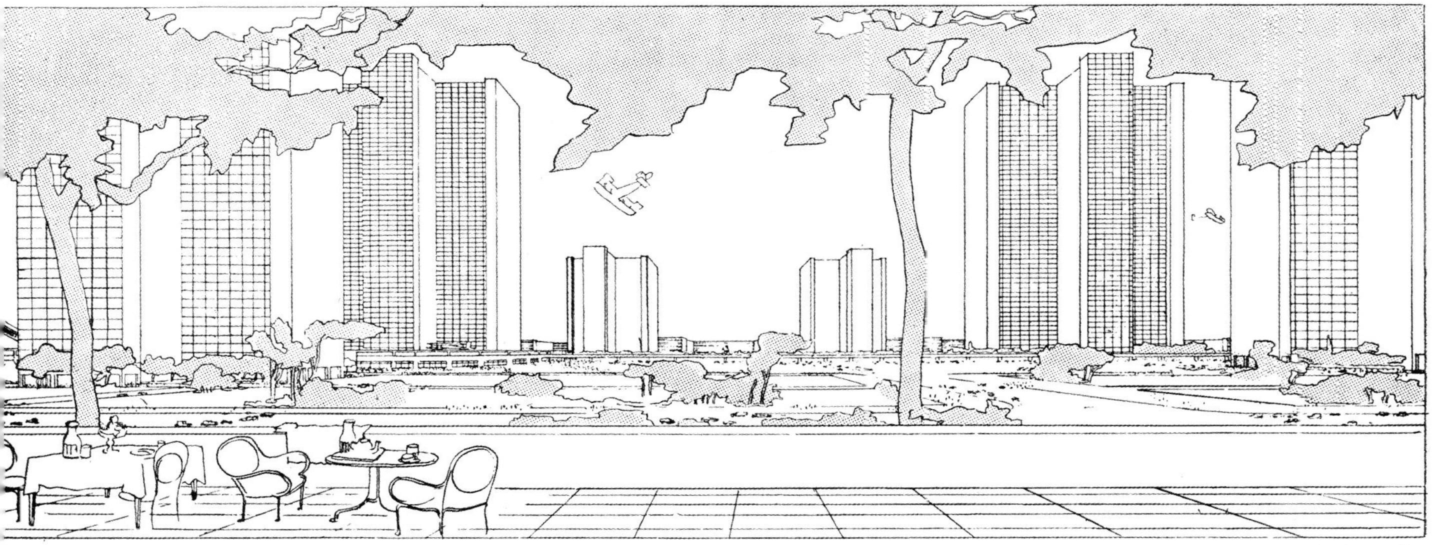

ne ville contemporaine: Le centre de la Cité vu de la terrasse de l'un des cafés à gradins qui entourent la place de la gare. On voit la gare entre les deux gratte-ciel de gauche, u élevée au-dessus du sol. Sortant de la gare, on voit l'autodrome filant à droite vers le Jardin Anglais. Nous sommes au centre même de la ville, là où la densité et la circulation nt les plus fortes. Les terrasses des cafés à gradins constituent les boulevards fréquentés. Les théâtres, salles publiques, etc., sont parmi les espaces entre les gratte-ciel, au milieu des arbres.

1.2 Le Corbusier, view of the Ville Contemporaine from an Immeuble Villa *jardin suspendu*, drawn in 1922, from the *Oeuvre complète, 1910–1929*.

means by which the built condition mediated and amplified the potential benefits of that relationship for seasonal heating and cooling.

Even further back, from the early 1920s, drawings of the Ville Contemporaine indicate the value placed on the façade's interface between social behaviors and planetary systems. Immeuble Villas—the multistory apartment blocks on the edges of the Ville Contemporaine—were drawn with a thick façade punctured by deep penetrating terraces (known as *jardins suspendus*) that served to provide each unit with outdoor space—thus, the means by which the apartment was to be seen as a "villa"—and also to shade the interior from direct summer sun (figure 1.2; figure 1.3). Later versions included apertures and interior shafts to induce ventilation, drawing the outside air through the living space.[10] The climatic concerns were general rather than scientific—orientation of the housing blocks relative to the sun was not a primary concern of the overall urban plan, nor were other issues such as the specifics of wind patterns or other climatic effects and inducements considered.

The basic strategy of deepening the façade to provide shading became a subject of much architectural elaboration. It was refined in the numerous Unités d'Habitation that Le Corbusier and his office built in the 1950s, which were celebrated for the ingenious combination of shading and programmatic amenity of the *jardins suspendus,* and also, later, criticized for inadequate attention to site orientation, thereby gesturing toward nuanced temperature control but falling short of fully achieving it. Many of the texts by climatic modernists of the 1950s began with discussions of the promise, and ultimate disappointment, of the Unité in Marseille—completed in 1952—in terms of these basic misconceptions of climatic performance (figure 1.4).[11]

Le Corbusier's ideas and built projects were, without doubt, essential to the articulation of architectural modernism—not in a vacuum, to be sure, but rather as representative of wider trends. On the one hand, climate was not an essential aspect of all architectural modernisms—many, if not most, celebrated principles of the early modernists did not take climatic issues into account. Imperatives concerned with reducing ornamentation, emphasizing volumetric design strategies, and the focus on new materials can be, and certainly have been, read without relevance to

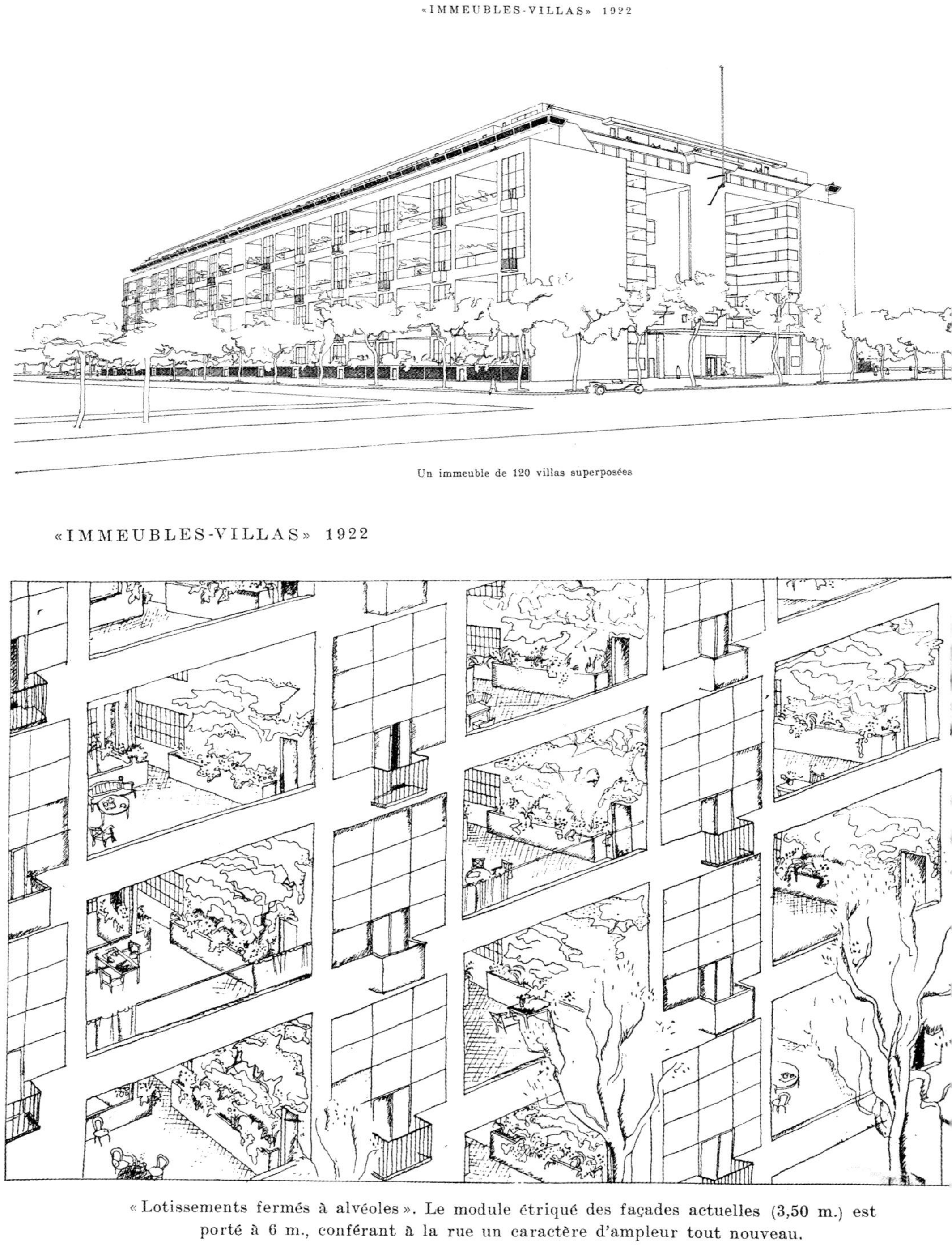


1.3 Le Corbusier, Immeuble Villas, 1922, from the *Oeuvre complète, 1910–1929*.

1.4 Le Corbusier, Unité d'Habitation, Briey, France, 1953.

concerns of climate adaptability; perhaps excluding ornamentation, most of these principles can be (and also, more recently, have been) read as available for productive engagement on these precise terms. On the other hand, Le Corbusier is atypical in taking on, as he did in the 1930s and '40s in particular, the importance of climate as a conceptual driver for design.

Although not as atypical as it might seem. Walter Gropius's "light and air diagram," for example, relied on a general understanding of climate in relationship to building height, orientation, and disposition on the site; Gropius's analysis settled on a relatively long spacing between mid-rise structures (figure 1.5).[12] The drawing, and the ideas behind it, were the subject of discussion at the 1930 meeting of the International Congress of Modern Architecture (CIAM) in Brussels; the meeting's topic was "Rational Land Development."[13] Somewhat more passively, Mies van der Rohe's Tugendhat House (1928) developed what the architect Colin Porteous calls an "opportunistic approach to taking advantage of fine climate" through the capacity for the glass wall on the southern façade to be pulled down into the basement by a mechanical system, opening up the living space to the exterior.[14] It would be specious—or, at least, the evidence is not being presented here—to claim either Gropius or Mies as substantive progenitors of architectural-environmental thinking; rather, these projects suggest a widespread, though largely vague and unscientific, interest in how modern strategies and materials can, through engagement with the exterior climate, change the experience of the interior.[15] Another iconic modernist, Frank Lloyd Wright, offers a somewhat more direct genealogical trace, albeit framed in the context of his general approach of a so-called organic relationship to site and interior plan arrangements. This is perhaps most evident in his Solar Hemicycle House, one of his Usonian Houses built in Wisconsin in 1946 (figure 1.6).[16] It plays out an arc, in plan, in order to take most advantage of changing solar

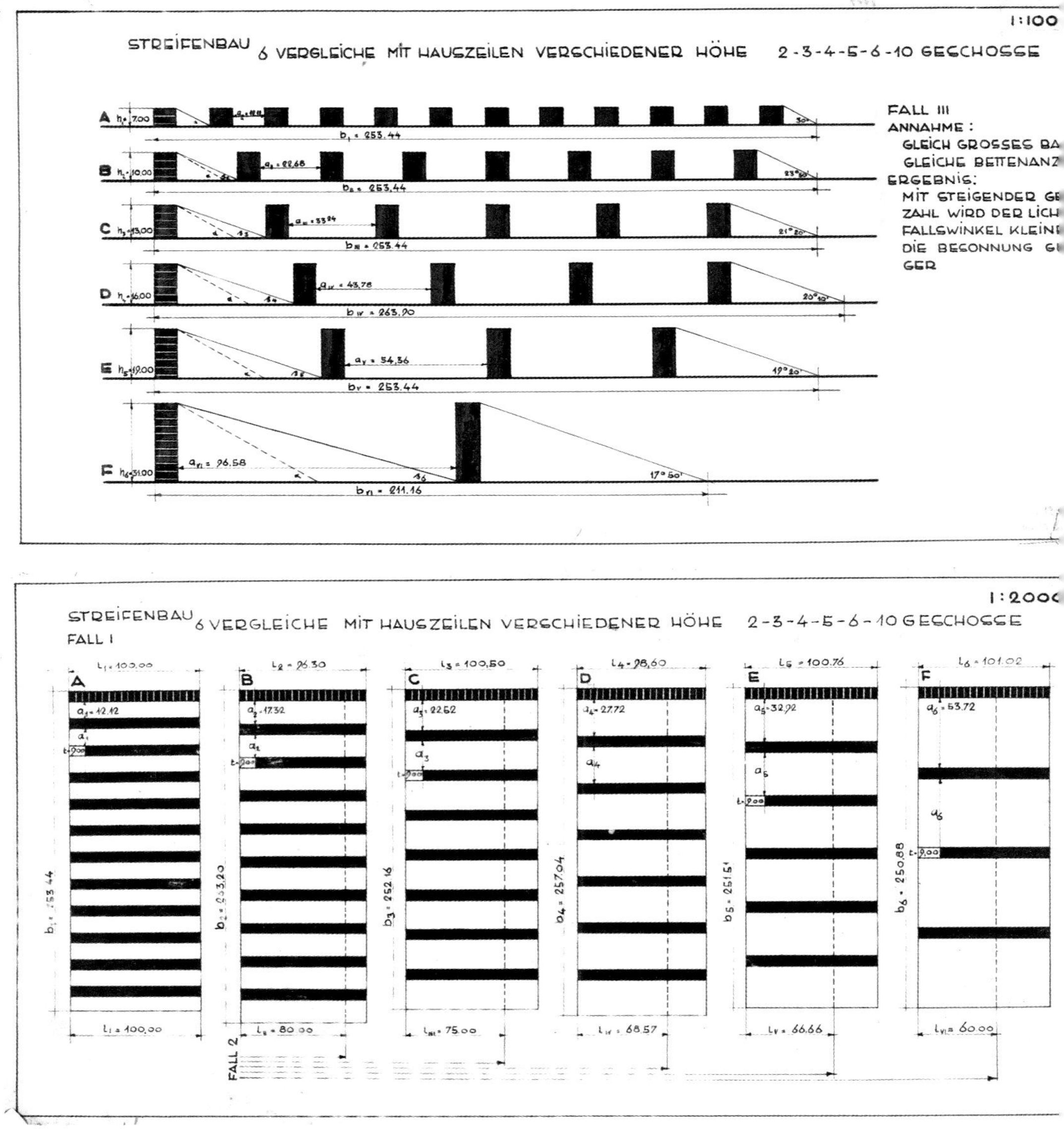


1.5 Walter Gropius, diagrams from "Houses, Walk-Ups, or High-Rise Apartment Blocks?" (1955 [1931]), Harvard Art Museums/Busch-Reisinger Museum, gift of Walter Gropius.

patterns and is built into a small berm to increase insulation.

Most of these proposals and buildings were intended to maximize solar insolation—the absorption of radiation so as to heat the interior—rather than to keep it out or carefully modulate it according seasonal variation.[17] The main concern in western and northern Europe, and in the United States, was heating, not cooling. Architectural knowledge of climate patterns, not to mention climate science, was piecemeal and circumstantial. All the same, these brief examples form a crack in the seemingly solid edifice of formal concerns as the context for architectural innovation, identifying the importance of climate, or at least geophysical systems, as a promising aspect of a more nuanced understanding of the field.

With Le Corbusier the concern is significantly more direct, albeit according to some variation across different periods of his career. "All modern architecture," he wrote, "has a mission to occupy itself with the sun."[18] He saw climate—the daily patterns of the sun, the regional patterns of weather—as essential to the development of a given design, and he saw the capacity of a building to manage climate as an important benefit of the new kinds of architecture that he tirelessly sought to promote. He made numerous drawings

1.6 Frank Lloyd Wright, Solar Hemicycle House, Middleton, Wisconsin, 1948.

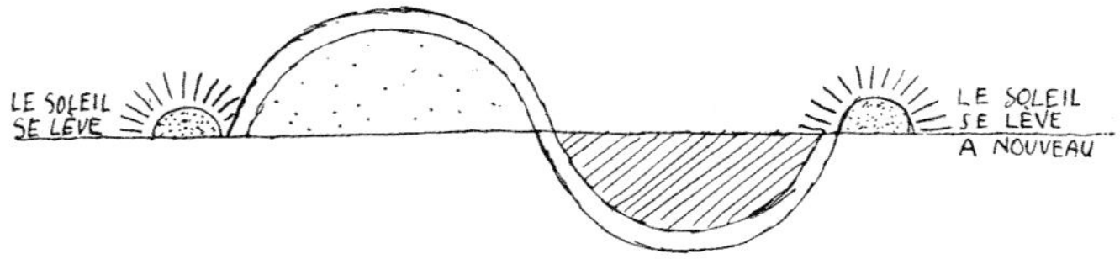


1.7 Le Corbusier, drawing of the solar cycle, which is the frontispiece to the *Oeuvre complète, 1934–1938*.

of a stylized rendition of the basic pattern of a solar path across the sky, often above the caption: "the sun rises, the sun sets, the sun rises again" (figure 1.7)[19] Many drawings of the buildings discussed further on, at least after 1936, were accompanied by sketches, off to the side or in the corner of the paper, indicative of this iconic horizontal *S* curve, a sort of emblem of attention to solar and climatic factors, however schematic or at times misconstrued. In the context of his broader influence on the development of modern architecture, Le Corbusier's interest in climate was significant, providing a substantive avenue for historical exploration. The relative lack of attention in the historical literature to this climatic legacy indicates some obstacles to historiographic clarification and necessitates a return to some familiar drawings and buildings in order to reconsider their possible impacts.

## The Dom-ino

Architectural investigations of climate played out through technical images as much as through buildings and were rooted in an early set of diagrams that generated a range of opportunities for architectural elaboration. Perhaps the most significant diagram in the early history of modern architecture was the dom-ino drawing, made by Le Corbusier in a number of iterations beginning in 1914 (figure 1.8). Although not explicitly climatic in origin or intent, it compresses into a single image the material and structural innovations of "the new architecture," and it also suggests the prospects for the modern building as a climatic technology.[20]

The basic premise was this: a structural steel frame held up a reinforced concrete floor plate. Because the steel frame bore the structural load of the building, masonry or stone walls, which heretofore were essential to hold the building up, were no longer necessary. The façade could instead be filled with glass, concrete, or other materials for expressive, affective, and climate management purposes. The dom-ino was, in many ways, the shift that ushered in the wave of experimental thinking that has come to be called modern architecture. The discussion in the field changed, slowly but inexorably, from concerns over the structural and expressive capacities of load-bearing walls to the freedom of design structural steel afforded.

Le Corbusier's "five points towards modern architecture" were articulated on these terms. These design principles, often said to have been realized in the 1928 Villa Savoye, included the open plan, the free façade, the horizontal window, the pilotis, and the roof garden or *jardin suspendu*. All are the result of the structural freedom allowed by the dom-ino idea. Numerous authors have recently sought to interpret all of the five points on environmental terms; at least four are relevant specifically to the building as a device of climate management. The liberation of the façade allows for its deployment as a filter for radiation; the open plan allows for volumetric determinations to also respond to solar incidence and other climatic patterns; and the horizontal window is, in this sense, representative of the debate around glazing that would later be overcome by Le Corbusier through the more general concept of the *pan de verre*—or wall of glass. The *jardin suspendu*, or elevated outdoor space, helps to bring together principles around leisure and the experience of the outdoors that many modernists saw as essential to the new ways of life their architecture could facilitate. This indoor-outdoor space was also a thermal buffer, in many cases, to reduce the impact of direct sun on the interior.

Some specialist historians, and their students and readers, are perhaps already feeling discomfited. Le Corbusier's life and work developed in a period when labeling him an environmentalist would be meaningless.[21] However, his concern for the relationship of the building to its climatic

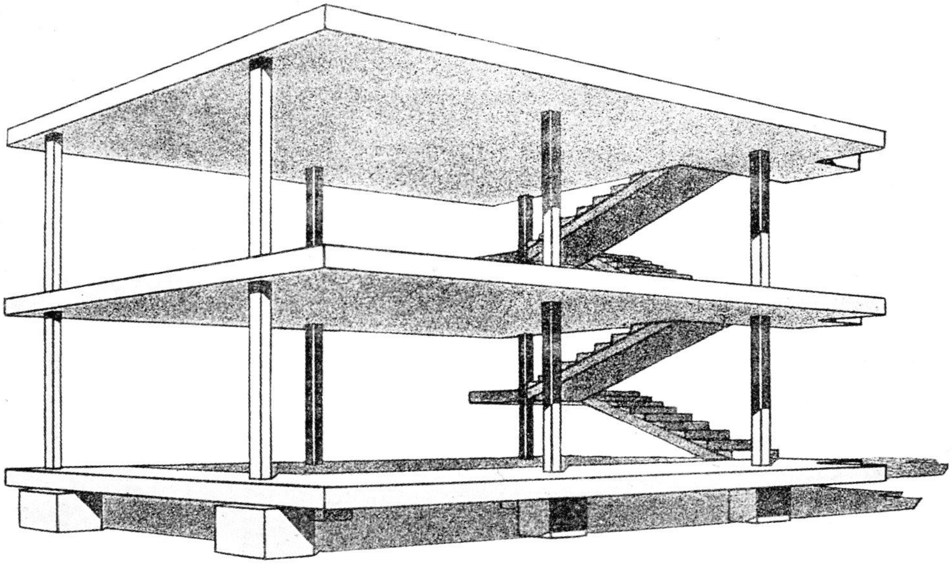

1.8 Le Corbusier, dom-ino diagram, 1914, from the *Oeuvre complète, 1910–1929*.

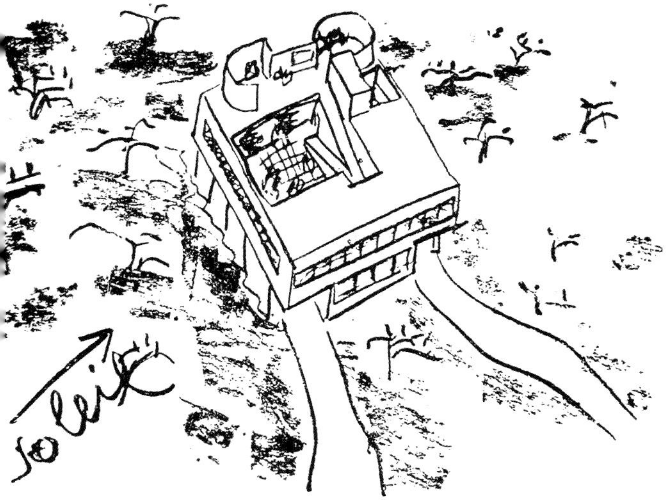


1.9 Le Corbusier, Villa Savoye, Poissy, France, 1928. Drawing with "soleil" arrow, from the *Oeuvre complète, 1929–1934*.

surround indicates the significance of a general approach to architectural modernism—one that sought to understand the conditions of the site, on a number of terms, and take them into account in deploying modernist strategies. Indeed, this is the point—Le Corbusier was not an environmentalist; rather, the project of modern architecture broadly construed was to engage with and rearticulate the complexity of issues we now address as "the environment."[22] All architecture is "environmental" in that it offers an opportunity to reconfigure the relationship between economies and ecologies, between people and their surroundings. It is more an issue of disposition—of how that relationship is imagined, and how it is seen to be malleable according to the specific flows of capital, materials, and ideas that inform a given project.

The *soleil* (sun) arrow pointing in to the *jardin suspendu* at the Villa Savoye, in a perspective drawing from 1928, is a meek symptom of this historical and historiographic complication (figure 1.9). Later photographs of the interior spaces as illuminated by the open access to the interior garden are a more robust indication that the ways of life imagined as essential to modernity—the cultural conditions of the *temps nouveaux*—were replete with a different relationship to the sun, the climate, and the body. Modern architecture was not just about new forms, materials, and structural principles, but about how these could together encourage new ways of living—better ways of

1.10 Le Corbusier, Villa Savoye, photographs of "sunlight on floors" and the roof garden, from the *Oeuvre complète, 1929–1934*.

living, it was hoped, in terms of sociability and health (figure 1.10).[23]

While the effects of these new times have long been interpreted relative to an interest, however compromised, in improving the lived conditions of the masses through spatiopolitical interventions, these new subjects were also conceived for their capacity to adjust to the mediated conditions of the thermal interior—to adapt, in their clothing, comportment, and in their relationship to the building, to seasonal changes in climate. In sum, the dom-ino diagram liberated the architect to explore new capacities for formal and material expression and opened up the built environment to a more intensive positioning as a biopolitical operation for the production of novel subjectivity, newly sensitive to climatic conditions.

The dom-ino was an idea, expressed in diagram, and not a built object or specific proposal. It was a generative project—one that could, and did, result in numerous, almost endless interpretations.[24] The combination of steel frame and concrete slab did not imply a specific building type, program, or site condition, but rather offered a set of parameters—as formula, device, assemblage, rule book—that could be interpreted and articulated in any number of ways. Le Corbusier distilled the ideas of a range of innovators in the field into an open yet formulaic approach to building with a new set of materials, anywhere. The dom-ino, as a historical agent, in this important sense, was not only generative of numerous possible built conditions but also makes clear the significance, the instrumentality, of the technical image as a generative device, as a means for producing different possible futures (figure 1.11).

A fundamental aspect of the dom-ino diagram was this embedded premise of adaptability. Modern architecture offered itself—argued according to these principles to clients, other architects, government agents, and experts—as an approach to building that could be adapted to a range of possible site conditions, building programs, and numerous other variables. While much was made, and

WEISSENHOF à STUTTGART 1927

*Façades*

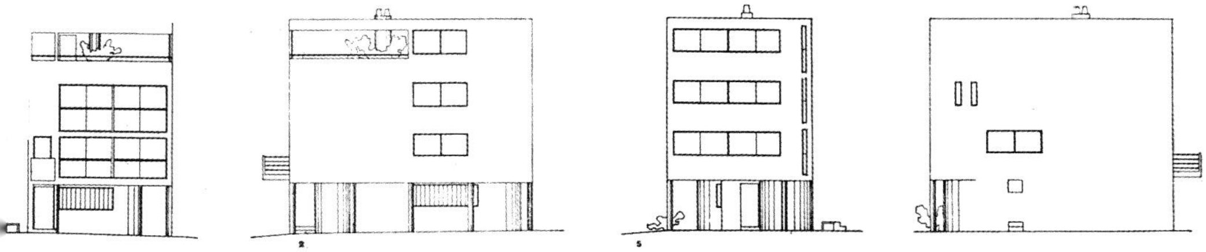

Sud Est Nord Ouest

« *Standardisation de l'élément fenêtre, à échelle humaine. Unité et ses combinaisons.* »

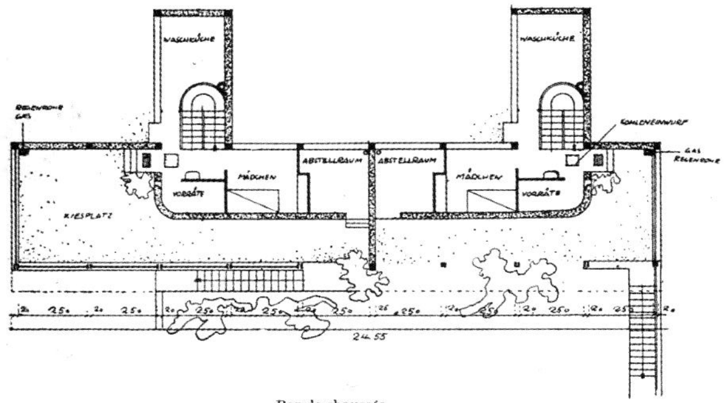

Rez-de-chaussée

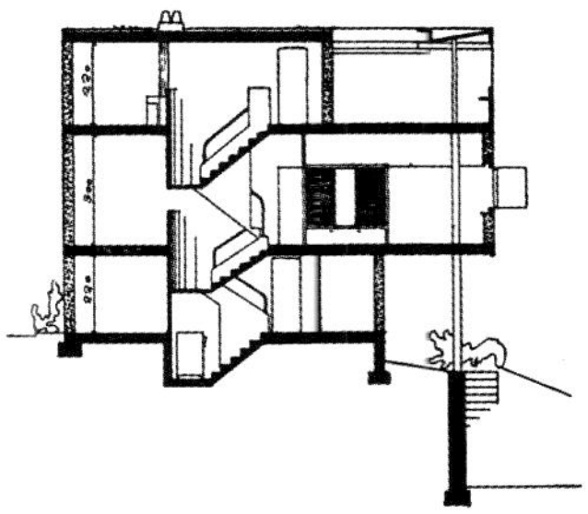

Coupe

1.11 Le Corbusier, House at the Weissenhof Siedlung, near Stuttgart, 1927. Elevations, plan, section, and photograph from the *Oeuvre complète, 1910–1929*.

has since been made, of the internationalist premise of these innovations, there is a hint already of an inversion in understanding this principle of universalism—in order to be universally applicable, the dom-ino did not propose one building type applicable everywhere but, rather, a set of generative principles that could be adjusted for any number of variable site conditions. Universalism was articulated, at least in part, as a premise of and process for regional adaptation.[25]

Architectural ideas conceived to have universal applicability were one aspect of a much wider set of cultural, economic, and governmental efforts to establish a certain kind of functional consistency across geographic and cultural space—if not precisely a universal space, and a universal way of life, then an imposed articulation of normativity. Which is to say, architectural modernism-as-universalism was such due to its capacity for regional inflection—more precisely, for adjusting the exterior, and the mediating condition of the façade, so that the interior could be consistent across time and space. Because of this regional adaptability, modern architecture first realized its promise outside the metropolitan center.

The formulation of universalism emerged from a very specific sociogeographic space. The buildings and interiors that were imagined and built across the Global South in the 1930s, '40s, and '50s, in other words, were based on a cultural, experiential, and thermal model of the Euro-American male, engaged in particular modes of commerce and industrial development, with very specific lifestyle habits, gender norms, and economic and labor relations, and embodying a very specific sense of culture (figure 1.12).[26]

Indeed, this bias of the universal is explicit in a parallel historical trajectory that, at this same time, was testing the physiological effects of conditioned space. The Carrier company, one of the innovators in the air-conditioning industry, began experiments to derive universal parameters for thermal comfort in the 1910s. Their experiments, in a controlled laboratory at Yale University, have been rehearsed in many contexts. They relied exclusively on shirtless, white males in their twenties as subjects. This illustrates, almost too conveniently, the limited conception of comfort that would develop in subsequent decades. As architects and engineers sought to bring such conditioned interiors into other climates around the globe, these limited parameters became articulated as the norm.[27]

Un Living-room

Un jardin-suspendu

Un jardin-suspendu

1.12 Le Corbusier, drawings of the lifestyle imagined in the interior/exterior space of the *jardin suspendu*, for the first Immeuble Wanner project, 1928, from the *Oeuvre complète, 1910–1929*.

1.13 Model of different louver orientations for brise-soleil façade attachments, from Olgyay and Olgyay, *Solar Control and Shading Devices*.

At risk of overgeneralizing: modern architectural strategies were proposed and received as a method for inserting a certain type of thermal interior—one that was seen to derive from and to be amenable to inhabitants from Euro-American metropolitan centers—into almost any climatic, social, or political condition. Articulated as universalist space, it was also a regime of materials, styles, and a more general built environmental condition that was recognizable to a political-economic position centered in western Europe or the United States, even though many, if not most, of the early examples were built elsewhere. The promise of modernism was, in no small measure, articulated as the capacity for design methods to bring a specific, and seemingly healthy, way of living from the center to the periphery, to the colony, and to the hinterlands. This promise was realized, in part, through experiments in those peripheral regions that were then reinterpreted for the Euro-American metropolitan centers, as will be seen in subsequent chapters.

It was not a question of adjusting the basic tenets of modernism to accommodate these new conditions; rather, it was a basic tenet of modernism, summarized through the dom-ino diagram, that it had a robust capacity for adaptation, a flexibility in approach that allowed it to be applicable as a tool of modernization, colonization, and globalization across the mid-twentieth century. Architecture became modern by mediating non-European climates and cultures, and by attempting through architectural means to make these climates and their inhabitants amenable to various forms of political and economic intensification.

## The Brise-Soleil

An excerpt from Le Corbusier's 1930 lecture in Buenos Aires addresses these general parameters, albeit cryptically. "Teach your children," he said to his audience, "that architecture is about sunlight on floors."[28] There are a number of interesting aspects to this elocution—first, as suggested in the ample wash of sunlight on the floors of the Villa Savoye (see figures 1.9, 1.10), one of the projects of Corbusian modernism was to encourage a new and purportedly more healthy relationship with the patterns of climate, especially relative to the path of the sun. That the intrusion of solar rays into the interior had a different experiential, thermal, and cultural valence in the Global South did not yet register for the Swiss-French architect, though it soon would.

Also of significance—"teach your children." Architectural modernism was projective, speculative, about the near future. Le Corbusier and others were focused on how integrating new principles and parameters into the built environment would construct, literally, a new world. The dom-ino was a generative device; Corbusian modernism, more generally, was focused on how the new ways of building could produce new subjects, newly conditioned to the experience of the city, of industrialization, and of the variables of climate as mitigated through the façade.

With such a universalist internationalism in mind, the shading device, or brise-soleil, emerged as the necessary correlate of the dom-ino idea (figure 1.13). One of the apparent conundrums, for historians of Le Corbusier, and of the so-called heroic period of modernism more generally, is his turn, in the late 1920s, away from purist, Platonic solids as the basis of design and toward a more

1.14 Le Corbusier, a *pan de verre* on a mid-rise residential block, from the *Oeuvre complète, 1934–1938*.

expressive, even regionalist approach. Here again, climatic effects are essential to understanding this set of events and to understanding the difficulty of their integration into narratives of modernism.

These narrative patterns revolve around the complications introduced by the dom-ino idea—in particular around the fact that once the façade was liberated from structural demands, it came to be filled with glass. Familiar architectural means to manage solar radiation, and to more generally use architecture to condition interior space, were confounded. Generally speaking, masonry and stone, often from the region of the building site, had offered thermal behaviors that glass and concrete do not. In hot climates, the thickness of the wall absorbed solar radiation during the day and released it to a cool interior in the evening; in cool climates that same thickness could offer some insulation for heat produced by a fireplace or other means. The use of stone and brick façades was not always carefully correlated to regional solar patterns, or sensitive to the changing demands placed on the interior; however, over the *longue durée* of architectural experimentation and expression, façade materials—from adobe to brick to quarried stone—mediated the climatic exterior to provide a set of interior thermal conditions relatively adapted, often without explicit theorization, to their use. This picture of vernacular-as-climatic-architecture would need to be addended with a discussion of domestic and labor habits, variabilities of clothing, and such, as will be suggested in later chapters. These forms, habits, and means for using materials were disrupted by industrialization and the innovations of architectural modernism. Indeed, this was one of the major effects of architectural modernism—a fundamental interruption of familiar patterns of climatic management, opening those patterns up for new kinds of technological engagement.[29]

Many other buildings and experiments could fill in this gloss on the continuities and disruptions between traditional practices embedded in specific cultures and the internationalist premise of modernism. Other writers have emphasized the transition from colonial adjustments to the liminal space between interior and exterior, looking at verandas, balconies, and extended eaves in this context.[30] Le Corbusier's Villa Baizeau, designed many times for a site in Carthage and finally built in 1928, builds on this tradition with its parasol roof, interior ventilation, and a series of alternating extended floor slabs to shade the façades and spaces below—the building became essential to the architect's self-referential typology of shading as developed right after World War II. Scholars have also noted the use of local stone in the partition walls of the Maisons Loucher (1929) and the extended eave in the roof of the Maison Erazzuris, planned for a coastal site in Argentina in 1930.[31] In many ways the discourse on climate here being traced can be seen as a fraught attempt to modernize traditional means for climate management—to technologize the louvers, screens, blinds, extended eaves, and many other techniques that have been used to shade interiors for centuries.

Perhaps even more significant than the basic gesture of the dom-ino—liberating the façade from structural demands—was the subsequent move of filling that façade with glass. It introduced numerous complications to the development of modern design methods. Indeed, there was much international debate among early modern architects regarding the amount, disposition, and technical characteristics of the glass that would be inserted into the now-open façade.[32] Previous limitations to the use of glass were also obviated by an abundance of supply, and a glass industry eager to expand its customer base; in general, until the early 1940s, this glass exhibited poor insulation qualities. The *pan de verre*—or wall of glass—in the early experiments arising from the dom-ino diagram, are antecedents of the curtain walls and all glass houses and towers—much more technologically sophisticated as insulating membranes—that developed later in the twentieth century (figure 1.14).

The *pan de verre* profoundly changed the thermal conditions of the interior, not necessarily for the better. In the third volume of the *Oeuvre complète*, published in 1946, Le Corbusier lamented the "problem" of the transparent envelope, indicating that by this time, because of the basic condition of overheating, the "hour of doom" was fast approaching for it.[33] The brise-soleil was needed to temper these effects, further clarifying modernism as a flexible means of building that could be adapted to different regional and social conditions. In combination, these two principles of modernism—the dom-ino and the brise-soleil—were essential to a new way of building and to a new way of living.

Much of the struggle with the *pan de verre* emerged through the design and construction of the Cité de Refuge de l'Armée du Salut—one of Le Corbusier's first large-scale buildings in France, with design work dating from 1929 (just after the construction of the Villa Savoye mentioned previously) (figure 1.15). The project was for temporary living spaces for homeless or otherwise economically disadvantaged individuals, initiated by the French office of the international Salvation Army. As has been detailed at length in the specialized literature, the Cité de Refuge was initially proposed to include specifications for what Le Corbusier termed a *mur neutralisant*—a wall that would neutralize the external conditions of the climate relative to their impacts on the interior. It was, indeed, with this neutralizing membrane in mind that Le Corbusier predicted the international consistency of buildings at a permanent 18°.[34]

The technological aspects of the *mur neutralisant* were ambitious—the *mur neutralisant* involved a double-skinned curtain wall on both of the long façades of the building, with an air space between the two layers of glass (figure 1.16). In the winter, the air space was to be filled with warm air in order to "neutralize" the cold air of the exterior; in the summer, the same space would be filled with cooled air, to prevent the warm air from entering. There were a number of what Reyner Banham later described as "Le Corbusier's obstinate environmental misapprehensions," relative to the physical capacities of cooling and warming interior space, evident in this plan.[35] Most problematic, the glass on each side of the air space offered little insulative capacity, so that when it was filled, for example, with warm air in the winter, that air simply radiated through the glass wall into the atmosphere, having little effect on the interior. When it was completed in 1928, the building was freezing in the winter and overheated in the summer (figure 1.17).

Both Banham and Kenneth Frampton discuss these misapprehensions at length. Frampton in particular sees them as essential to a second phase of Le Corbusier's career that involved a turn to a more expressive formal approach as well as

1.15 Le Corbusier, model of
Cité-Refuge de l'Armée du Salut,
Paris, 1928.

a reliance on passive shading technologies rather than technologically intensive conditioning systems.[36] Which is to say—the obstacle of climate, if nothing else, served to detour the work of Le Corbusier away from the purist principles of his early buildings (such as the housing complex at Pessac) and toward a more formally expressive approach to the inherent possibilities of new materials, programs, and technologies (such as the church at Ronchamp). Both historians also emphasize the challenges the architect faced in connection with the technological capacities of the French building industry and relevant regulatory agencies.

A generous interpretation of the failure of the *mur neutralisant* was that it resulted from an inadequate application of the principle of Le Corbusier's design: the mechanical system was too small to produce heated or cooled air adequate to the system, and the difficulties of constructing a fully sealed (that is, leak-free) curtain wall were also just being understood.[37] However, as Rosa Urbano Gutiérrez has documented, the basic principle of the system was misconstrued. She quotes a document from the archive in reference to a version of the system proposed for the Centrosoyuz in Moscow, in 1929, in which an American air-conditioning engineer, consulted by Le Corbusier, indicates that "the method would require, in order to heat and ventilate the building, four times as much steam and twice the mechanical power as would be necessary with methods currently employed in our country under comparable atmospheric conditions."[38]

Frampton points to these technological and bureaucratic barriers of the *mur neutralisant* as instrumental to what he sees as Le Corbusier's life-changing "loss of faith in the manifest destiny of the machine age" and a search for other means of activating the building as a system of climatic mediation—architectural means, rather than mechanical ones.[39] This new imperative is developed through the design of another structure, an apartment building in Geneva. The Immeuble Clarté, on the boards as the complications with the Cité building were becoming clear, used design means for tempering the thermal conditions of the interior. Although, arguably, the summer cooling demands of Geneva are not as significant as in other elevations and latitudes, the resultant design provides the opportunity for the diagrammatic elaboration of the brise-soleil as a principle of modern architecture, with impacts that will

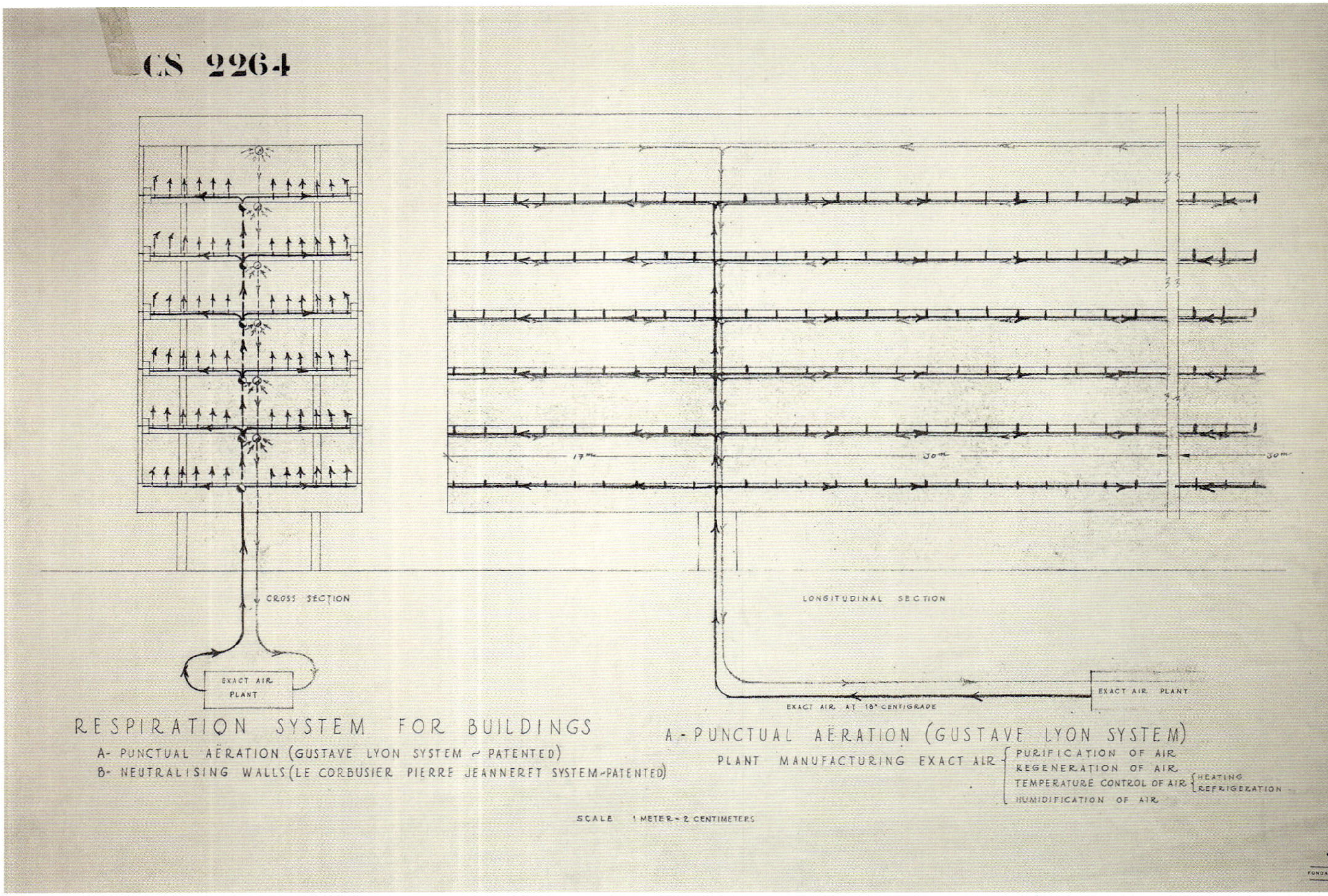


1.16 Le Corbusier, drawing of the "Respiration System for Buildings" proposed for the Cité-Refuge de l'Armée du Salut, Paris, 1927 and the Centrosoyuz, Moscow, 1928.

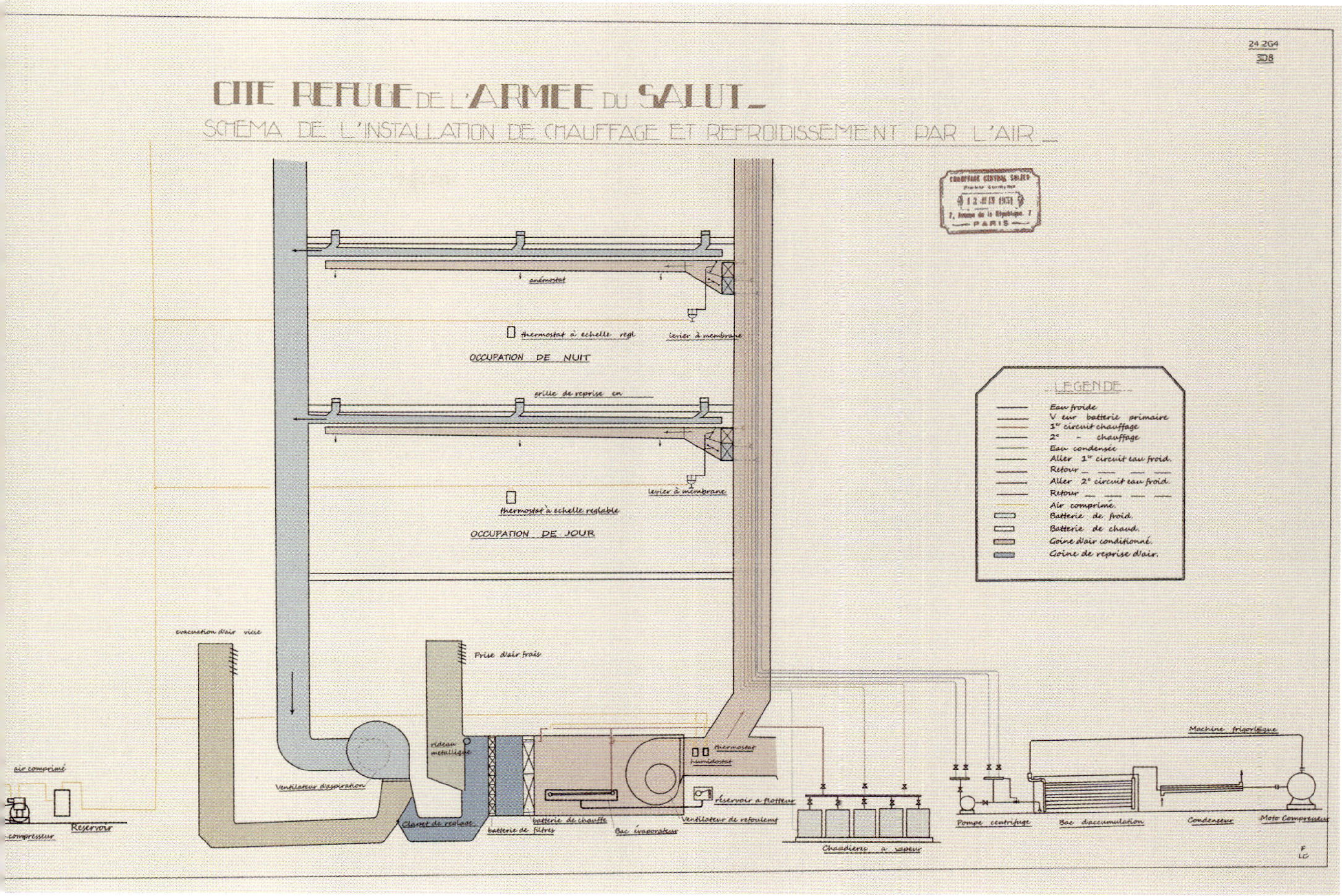


1.17 Le Corbusier, Cité-Refuge de l'Armée du Salut, heating and cooling scheme. Redrawn from the archive for clarity, 2019.

IMMEUBLE «CLARTÉ», GENÈVE 1930-32

Intérieur d'un immeuble locatif

Intérieur du même immeuble

La terrasse devant les appartements

Un living-room

1.18 Le Corbusier, interior images of the Immeuble Clarté, Geneva, 1930, from the *Oeuvre complète 1929–1934*.

1.19 Le Corbusier, Immeuble Clarté photograph of the façade.

resonate across subsequent decades and around the world (figure 1.18).

At the Immeuble Clarté, Le Corbusier did not attempt a mechanically sophisticated system. Instead, the building deployed a collection of low cost, user intensive, and visually dynamic sun-shading devices: balconies, external blinds, retractable awnings, and interior shutters blocked and modulated solar incidence (figure 1.19).[40] The effect on the interior was dramatic. The photographs that Le Corbusier published in the *Oeuvre complète* clarify and elaborate on the principles he had suggested for modern architecture's relationship to the sun, producing a comfortable living space that allowed for new ways of living in relationship to solar patterns.

His early sketch of the building indicates the effects of this shading system and is likely the first entry in a long series of technical images intended to clarify the principles of the brise-soleil and Le Corbusier's apparent invention of them. The drawing is divided into three parts. First, a top section that shows, on the left, the variation of the solar path—higher in summer (*été*) and lower in winter (*hiver*) (figure 1.20). To the right, a schematic section of the building, shows the extension of the balconies as shading devices, with rays from the summer sun being blocked and rays from the winter sun able to penetrate into the interior. The details of this schematic section are then clarified in the middle part of the drawing, where the purple lines of the balcony extensions are integrated into a more detailed rendering of the façade, with both horizontal and vertical divisions, the latter presumably mostly for privacy but also serving a secondary shading function. The third section of the drawing, on the bottom, shows the volume of the building in perspective, intended to demonstrate that this novel condition is only deployed on the façade that is most exposed to the sun. This basic principle of different treatments for different façades became a major principle of the bioclimatic design strategies proposed in later decades.

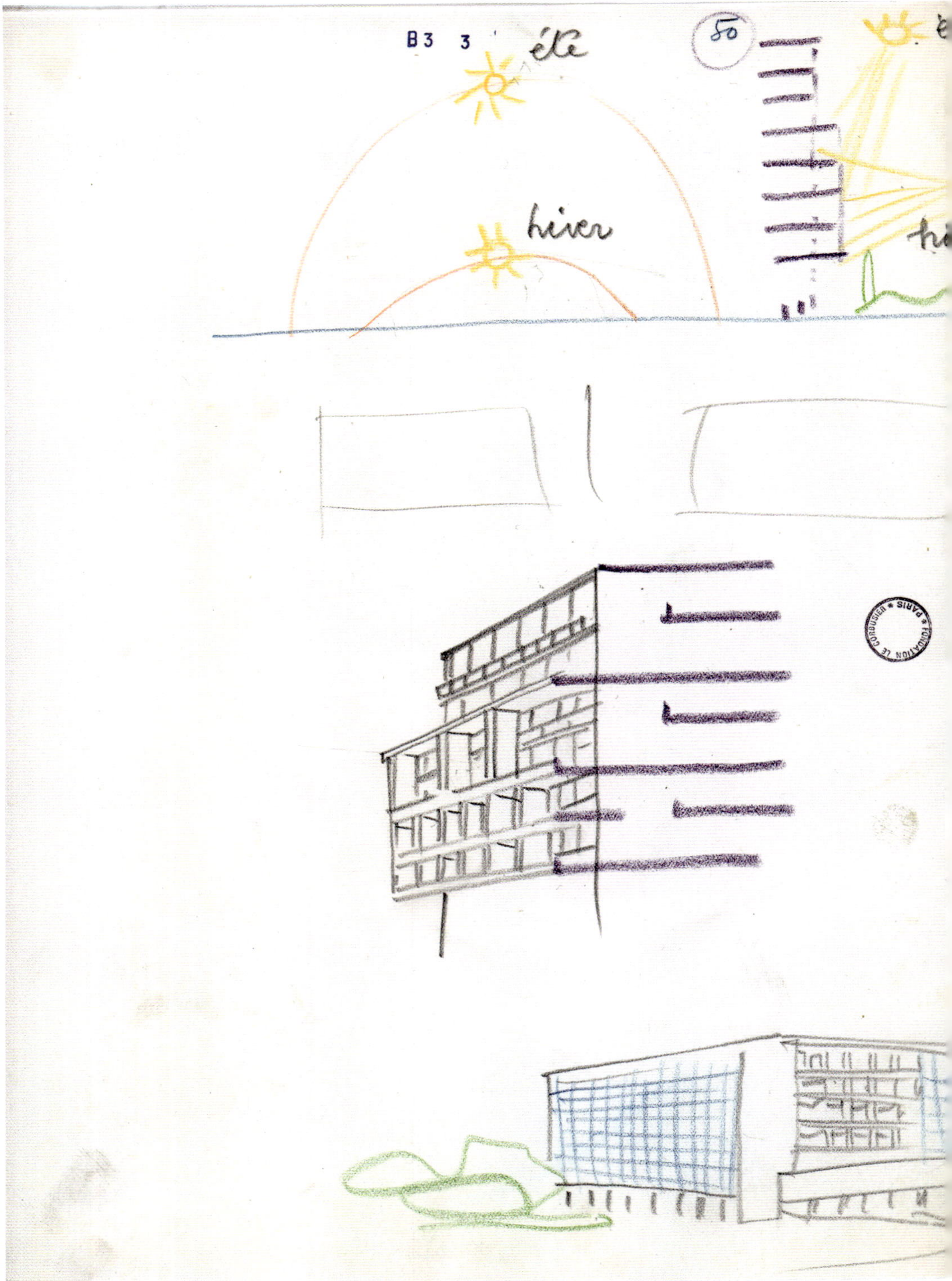


1.20 Le Corbusier, sketch indicating the principles of relationship between the façade shading system (brise-soleil) and the seasonal path of the sun, as applied at the Immeuble Clarté.

1.21 Le Corbusier, Cité-Refuge de l'Armée du Salut, after renovation with brise-soleil added, 1947.

Although much more than a brise-soleil, the basic principle was established. As part of the turn away from his faith in the machine age, Le Corbusier proposed architectural elements to manage those interior climatic conditions that the mechanical systems approach had proven too cumbersome to engage. Such a premise is not absolute. The Pavilion Suisse of 1931 contained a sort of middle ground, with mechanical roller shades allowing for selective protection from solar rays, but the turn toward designed façade elements, and away from mechanical conditioning, was, at least temporarily, definitive. As Banham summarizes the story: "however desperate its motivations, the brise-soleil is one of [Le Corbusier's] most masterly inventions, and one of the last *structural* innovations in the field of environmental management."[41] Banham also cites, as proof of the brise-soleil's technical and cultural effectiveness, the renovation of the Cité de Refuge in 1947, after it was damaged during the war. Double-paned insulated windows replaced the *mur neutralisant*, and an extruded grid was placed on the façade, what came to be called an egg-crate shading system, one of a number of typologies subject to elaborate exploration in the postwar period (figure 1.21).[42]

The historiographic and historical consequences are significant. Le Corbusier, prophet of the "machine for living," faced the limitations, however temporary, of a mechanical solution to the problem of the thermal interior. The platonic forms, and the social progressiveness and technological engagement they were seen to promise as part of the *esprit nouveaux*, were frustrated—other means were necessary to produce the architecture of the future. There were at least three essential effects: first, as Frampton has it, Le Corbusier would turn from a purist ideal to the more expressive gestures of his postwar career, his frustration with the possibilities of climate engineering leading, it seems, to a more general interest in the plastic opportunities afforded by the materials that he was exploring.

Second, the search for mechanical conditioning would continue in the work of Le Corbusier and elsewhere. The archives at the Fondation Le Corbusier are replete with reports and brochures concerned with early attempts to use mechanical systems to condition interior space (figure 1.22). Le Corbusier continued to collaborate with Gustave Lyon, an engineer he had worked with on the plan for the League of Nations competition and in conceiving the conditioning systems for the Cité de Refuge, the Centrosoyuz, and a number of other buildings in the late 1920s and early '30s. The two worked with the Saint-Gobain glass

CHAUFFAGE CENTRAL SULZER, SOCIÉTÉ ANONYME
7, Avenue de la République — PARIS
Téléphones: Oberkampf 83-50, 83-51, 83-52, 83-54 — R. C. Seine 64.318

SULZER

# CONDITIONNEMENT D'AIR

pour

**Théâtres, Cinémas, Salles de Réunion, Restaurants, Cafés, etc., Bureaux, Banques, Immeubles commerciaux, Usines**

Conditionnement d'air dans un bureau.
Introduction d'air à basse température par diffuseur breveté, placé au plafond et combiné avec le lustre sans risque de courant d'air.

## VENTILATION, CHAUFFAGE, RAFRAICHISSEMENT

suivant les besoins et d'après les conditions atmosphériques.

**Les installations Sulzer de conditionnement d'air**
assurent dans les locaux très fréquentés une ambiance favorable au bien-être des occupants.

SUCCURSALES:
BIARRITZ, BRUXELLES, LILLE, LYON, MARSEILLE, METZ, MULHOUSE, NICE, STRASBOURG

IX. 1931. - 200. Z No. 5705 P.

1.22 Brochure from the Sulzer Central Heating Company, 1931, in the Le Corbusier Archives.

laboratory on full-scale experiments in attempts to resolve the difficulties of the system.[43] Urbano Gutiérrez argues that much of Le Corbusier's later work involved a hybrid approach—a combination of shading techniques and versions of the *mur neutralisant*.[44] Le Corbusier's later work in India would intensify his interest in managing climate, leading to a number of collaborations with architects and engineers on these terms, and the development, in the early 1950s, of the *Grille Climatique* as a method of analyzing a building's socioclimatic relations.[45]

Urbano Gutiérrez also emphasizes that, however misconstrued and energy inefficient at the time, the *mur neutralisant* is essentially an early version of the double- and triple-skinned façades at the forefront of energy-efficient building practices developed since this period.[46] By the beginning of the 1950s the technology of insulated, glazed membranes, and of the mechanical systems that could condition the air inside them, had advanced considerably. The basic premise of using both façade and conditioning technology to isolate the building from its surroundings, and producing its own climate, has significant if unanticipated consequences for the future.

The third historical effect was the proliferation of brise-soleil and other shading strategies as part of the global dissemination of modern architecture of the 1940s and '50s—the paired interventions of the dom-ino and the brise-soleil allowed for an adaptive architectural approach to a range of climates and cultures, and they also allowed the more familiar principles of architectural modernism to flourish in the Global South.

## Adaptability and Normativity

While consolidating the premise of adaptability, the brise-soleil, as the necessary correlate of the dom-ino, also emphasizes the corollary concept of normativity. The dom-ino and the brise-soleil were paired innovations, one required the other—for what? The glazed, open, and carefully shaded façade aimed to produce a consistent thermal interior. An important aspect of modern architecture, in the midst of its development, was its purported capacity to produce a universal space for improving health and quality of life, for the normalization of ways of living. The production of a normative interior was essential to modern architecture's affiliation with a wide range of seemingly progressive associated trends—the production of a space for global commerce, for example, or the capacity for architecture to improve public health.

The premise of normativity suggests a wide range of transitions and dispositions that hover like a cloud over the development of architectural modernism and over the naturalization of many of its design tropes. Design ideas cannot be separated from political implications, especially when questions about climate and ways of life are kept in the foreground. The normative premise reveals an implicit, general approach of climatic determinism, in the midst of a wider ranging emergence of hegemonic cultural frameworks familiar to the theorization of globalization—frameworks in which the shaded façade operates, again, as a mediating device, and a transitional approach: clarifying dominant trends while also expressing new concerns.

Normativity, as the historian of science Georges Canguilhem argued in this same period, was essential to the conception of culture, and of civilization as such. Michel Foucault, introducing Canguilhem's text *The Normal and the Pathological* in its 1966 publication, wrote as follows: "people began to ask the West what rights its culture, its science, its social organization and finally its rationality itself could have to laying claim to a universal validity"—concerns of course since reflected in a wide-ranging effort to decolonize cultures and spaces.[47] These complications are played out in Le Corbusier's attempts to consolidate his ownership of the shading system as a technique of European modernism, disseminated to the periphery.

The concept of climatic determinism is essential here. Developed by numerous colonial and imperial scientists at the turn of the twentieth century, this attitude proposed that specific weather conditions are essential to the production of a specific kind of culture—with an emphasis on the purported excellence of the climate in the northern temperate zone. For European and American physiologists assessing the conditions of the colonies and the Southern Hemisphere, climatic conditions were determinant in a country's potential role on the world political and economic stage. "One of the reasons," as one such imperialist, Ellsworth Huntington, wrote in 1942, "for the rise of [one] nation [rather than others] in modern times is its control over climatic conditions: that nation which has led the world, leads the world, and will lead the world, is that nation that lives in a climate, indoor and outdoor, nearest the ideal" (figure 1.23).[48] An

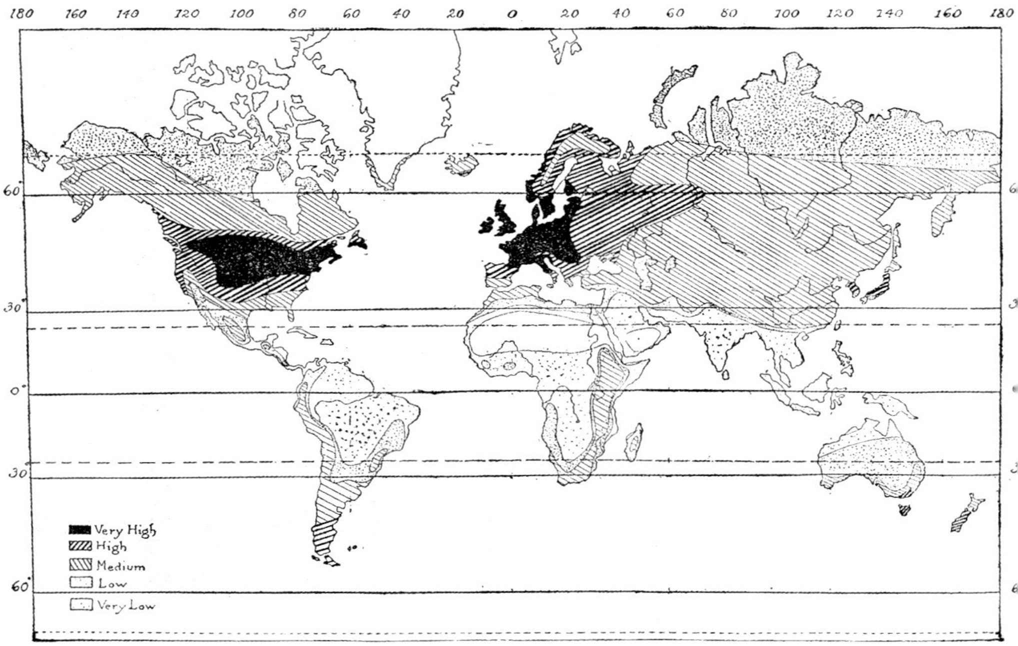


**Figure 43.** The Distribution of Human Health and Energy on the Basis of Climate

1.23 "The Distribution of Human Health and Energy on the Basis of Climate," from Ellsworth Huntington, *Civilization and Climate* (New Haven, CT, 1924).

ideal that was, needless to say, modeled on optimized European climates. The complex imposition of interior conditions reflecting the temperate climates of western Europe onto a range of regional variants was caught up, on the one hand, in attempts to improve health and eradicate disease and, on the other, with producing a "universal validity, tied," as Foucault put it, to "economic domination and political hegemony."[49]

Canguilhem's demystification of the pathological helps to clarify the intentions and intensity of this determinist notion. Nontemperate climates were seen as inadequate by the determinists, a pathology that was placed against a norm. Canguilhem, posing the maxim that "pathological phenomena are identical to corresponding normal phenomena save for quantitative variations," suggests that the normative emerges as essential for constructing notions of pathology, rather than the other way around. "Every conception of pathology," Canguilhem continues, "must be based on prior knowledge of the corresponding normal state, but conversely, the scientific study of pathological cases becomes an indispensable phase in the overall search for the laws of the normal state."[50] The conditions of a consistent thermal interior were, in this fashion, produced through experimentation in the Global South insofar as those experiments not only served to test design methods for thermal control but also helped to define the parameters of the normative interior. The aim—initially through shading systems and later through mechanical systems—was the construction of a planetary interior in which, it was imagined, thermal conditions were consistent enough to allow for a seamless globalization to emerge.

Architecture, and climatic modernism in particular, becomes an important medium through which claims of cultural value (civilization, western civilization, globalization) became mobile on these terms. The norm was thus constructed, literally, if not in fact imposed, through façade systems conditioning colonial interiors. "Strictly speaking," as Canguilhem concludes, "a norm does not exist, it plays its role which is to devalue existence by allowing its correction."[51] Whatever its other intentions, the elaboration of the brise-soleil encouraged the production of a normative interior on these terms.

This imperative was articulated diagrammatically in design methodology, before it was built. When Le Corbusier conceived of methods to produce a consistent thermal interior, he did so according to a vague though considered approach toward cultural distinctions based on climatic conditions. In his case, the premise of climatic determinism played out in part through the articulation of a specific Mediterranean culture, centered on a number of prominent cities lining the sea.[52] The climate of the Mediterranean was seen to be superior to others—in Huntington's map, the northern rim is classified as "Very High," the north of Spain as "High," and southern Spain and North Africa as "Medium." When he designed the Lotissement in Barcelona, Le Corbusier was seeking to articulate a design method appropriate to this climate—an architectural means to raise it from "High" to the pinnacle of "Very High." When he proposed an office tower in Algiers, on the northern coast of Africa, he similarly sought to extend the optimal climatic conditions—and its attendant norms—to the French colonies. A pattern that is repeated, from Le Corbusier's perspective, across the Global South, though the history of the shading device in Brazil, for example, frustrates this one-way-street model of historical change. The production of and the debates around the conditions of the thermal interior were in large part centered on this perception of precise climatic conditions for a western European notion of civilization.

## Evidence

On July 2, 1945, just as the war was ending, Le Corbusier participated in a small conference organized by the Centre National de la Recherche Scientifique (CNRS), concerned with "L'Urbanisme et l'Ensoleillement des Habitations" ("Urbanism and the Daylighting of Buildings").[53] The program included presentations on the physical properties and conditions of sunlight, on the physiological and biological consequences of solar incidence at both the urban and building scale, and on techniques for understanding solar absorption as a source of heat and of light. Le Corbusier presented last, focusing on the consequences of the above types of knowledge "sur l'Architecture et l'Urbanisme."[54] Sketching on the program for this seminar, he began to develop what would later be published as the "petit historique du brise-soleil" (see figure 2.7). It is an indication that he saw the development of the brise-soleil as significant to his historical legacy (figure 1.24).

For the purposes of this book, Le Corbusier's historical importance is not only for his formal interventions, as significant as they no doubt were; instead, the interest here reflects the broader context that the conference implies. Climate, however haltingly, had become a topic of architectural investigation; conversely, architecture began to be formulated, in the decades surrounding World War II, as an important aspect of climatic knowledge. Architectural concerns came to be visible to bureaucrats and technocrats concerned with the scientific knowledge of climatic patterns in new ways, just as architects, urbanists, policy makers, and manufacturers started to think about the building as a device for producing and managing a consistent global climate. Architectural discourse and practice became essential sites for experimentation in the relationship between climatic patterns and the daily life and habits of individuals. Design methodologies activated knowledge on the terms of, and for the application of—the testing of—climate science.

Le Corbusier's talk at the "l'ensoleillement" conference was published in *Techniques et Architecture* in January 1946 as "Problèmes de l'Ensoleillement: Le Brise-Soleil."[55] In it, he walks the reader through the basic premise of shading devices, emphasizing that they emerged as a necessary solution to the overheating characteristic of the *pan de verre*. The drawings begin with basic building types, and then the now-familiar schematic of the seasonal differences of the sun's path across the sky, followed by a brief discussion of the costs and benefits of different shading types (#12a–c on figure 1.24). He discusses the Villa Baizeau at Carthage (#3), where, again, a sort of tic-tac move in section brought the building mass behind protruding floors to allow for shading, and he continues with a sketch of the Barcelona Lotissement façade (#4), and then onto buildings in Algeria and Brazil. He summarizes his interventions as "solutions that are the first to allow modern life to flourish in complete freedom, in a country were the climatic conditions seemed to be imperatives that would impose themselves forever."[56]

In the *Techniques et Architecture* issue, Le Corbusier's article was followed by another presentation from the CNRS conference, a discussion of "Efficacité de l'Ensoleillement" by the engineer France Fradet (figure 1.25). This was likely the first instance of the publication of climate diagrams in the French architectural press. Indications of the solar path and shading charts for the latitude of Paris were accompanied by diagrams of suggested building heights and other design principles.[57] Climate discussions, and images at the interface of science, architecture, and conceptions of culture,

# PROBLÈMES DE L'ENSOLEILLEMENT

## LE BRISE SOLEIL

PAR

LE CORBUSIER

Conférence prononcée le 2 Juillet 1945, au Palais de Chaillot

*On serait en droit d'affirmer que l'histoire de la fenêtre est aussi celle de l'architecture, disons, du moins, d'une tranche des plus caractéristiques de l'histoire de l'architecture.*

*Je dessine la maison traditionnelle : elle est faite de murs portant des planchers; ces murs sont percés de fenêtres et ces fenêtres, pour des raisons diverses, ont été plus ou moins grandes à travers l'histoire.*

1 *On peut même prétendre que la grandeur des fenêtres était un signe de richesse, du moins d'opulence, peut-être bien de joie de vivre.*

*Percer les fenêtres dans un mur portant des planchers est un geste antagoniste à la fonction précitée : percer le mur de fenêtres, c'est l'affaiblir. Et l'on assistera à la lutte entre le plein et le vide au cours de l'histoire. Et la proportion s'établissant entre les pleins et les vides constituera une part plus déterminante qu'on ne croit de ce que beaucoup aiment à appeler les « styles ».*

*J'ai donc dessiné rapidement la petite maisonnette traditionnelle et tout à côté, l'immeuble Haussmann où l'ouverture des fenêtres atteint la limite du possible; pousser au delà serait dangereux.*

2 *Ceci est de la petite architecture. Voici p[...] exemple sur le plan de la plus grande [...]chitecture,*

3 *la grande ouverture de l'atrium de la m[...]son antique.*

4 *en 4, je dessine la petite fenêtre romane plein cintre et en 5,*

5 *la grande et magnifique fenêtre ogivale a[...] ses roses éblouissantes.*

6 *en 6, la fenêtre Renaissance avec ses m[...]neaux de pierre.*

7 *en 7, la fenêtre Louis XIV, Louis XV, Lo[...] XVI...*

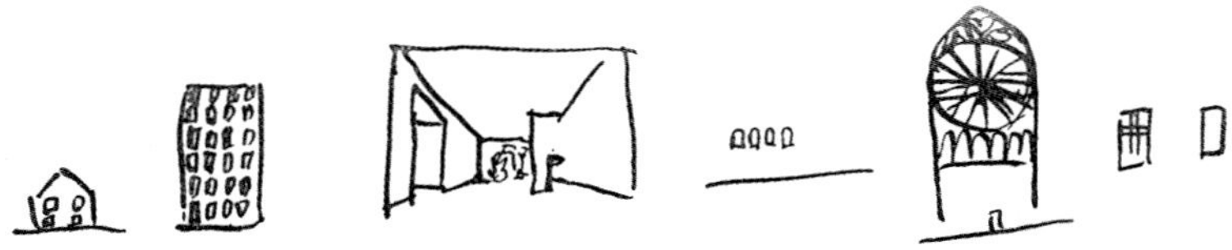

1 2 3 4 5 6 7

*Passons directement à aujourd'hui : nous disposons de l'acier et du béton armé; tout est transformé, c'est la coupe qui nous le révèle.*

8 *Voici la coupe d'un bâtiment moderne de bureaux, d'habitation ou de manufactures : on y voit des planchers superposés portés non par des murs mais par des poteaux.*

*Une bonne économie de la construction veut que les planchers portent en cantilever sur les poteaux, si bien que, d'un coup et subitement, le constructeur réalise ce rêve, réputé inaccessible, d'éclairer les locaux à 100 0/0.*

*Et dès lors, ce sont les planchers superposés qui* portent eux-mêmes *le mur, et ce mur peut être une membrane de verre, un «* pan de verre *». En 9, j'exprime diverses attitudes de ce pan de verre.*

9 *La solution 1 souligne la présence des planchers tandis que la solution 2 n'hésite pas à faire passer le pan de verre au devant des planchers; la solution 3 montre une mosaïque toujours possible de casiers du pan de verre où la plus grande fantaisie peut se donner libre cours.*

*Il va de soi que, désormais, se poseront de nouveaux problèmes : le chauffage des locaux, leur ventilation et surtout — ce qui sera le thème de cet exposé — les conditions de l'ensoleillement, de l'entrée bienfaisante du soleil en hiver, de l'entrée catastrophique du soleil en été. Ces conditions affectent l'habitant, qu'il soit le locataire d'un appartement, l'ouvrier derrière une verrière d'usine ou l'employé de bureau derrière sa fenêtre.*

*Je vais vous montrer une suite de petites découvertes successives qui m'ont permis de devenir et de demeurer ami du soleil et d'apporter, même à certains pays comme le Brésil et sous le soleil tropical, des solutions qui sont les premières à laisser s'épanouir en toute liberté la vie moderne dans un pays où des conditions climatiques impératives avaient institué des traditions qui semblaient devoir s'imposer à jamais; d'ailleurs, le mot employé ici — le brise-soleil — stipule qu'on s'est rendu maître d'un élément.*

*Mais revenons à notre bref historique le pan de verre est acquis et la lumière est 100 0/0; nous nous en sommes emparé a[...] joie estimant que c'était une chance inesp[...]rée. En 1933, le congrès C.I.A.M. d'Athèn[...] fixait ce point de doctrine fondamental : [...] matériaux de l'urbanisme sont le soleil, l'e[...]pace, la verdure. J'avais appelé ces ma[...]riaux :* « les joies essentielles » *et en les [...]corporant à la vie même de l'individu, a[...]traction faite bien entendu de toute situati[...] sociale, le problème cardinal de l'urbanis[...] se trouvait dès lors posé : donner à chac[...] le bénéfice des joies essentielles — sol[...] espace, verdure — et personne n'a osé, [...]puis, faire opposition à ce postulat.*

8 9



1.24 Le Corbusier, "Problèmes de l'Ensoleillement: Le Brise-Soleil," from *Techniques et Architecture*, January 1946.

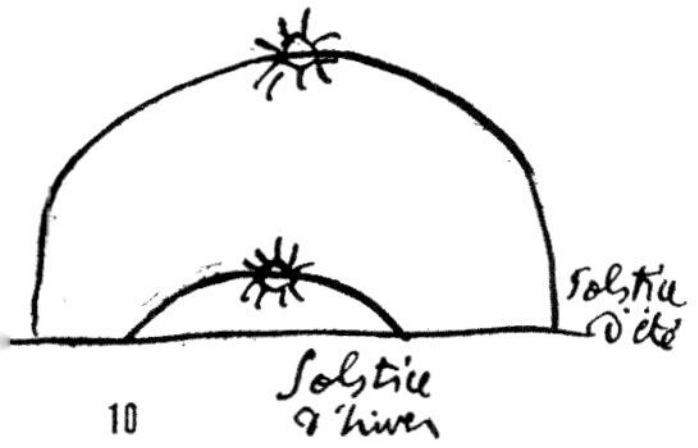

10

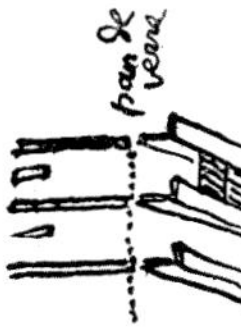

11

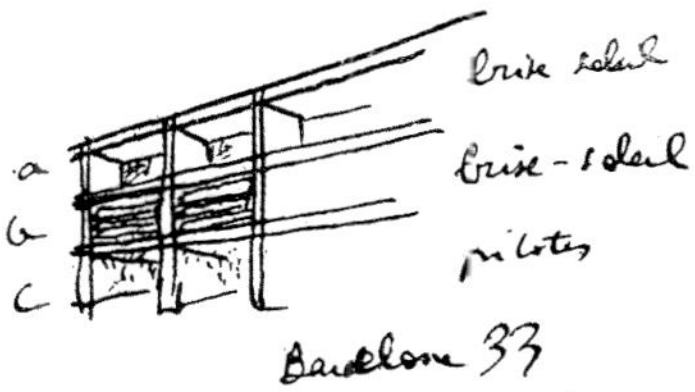

14

12

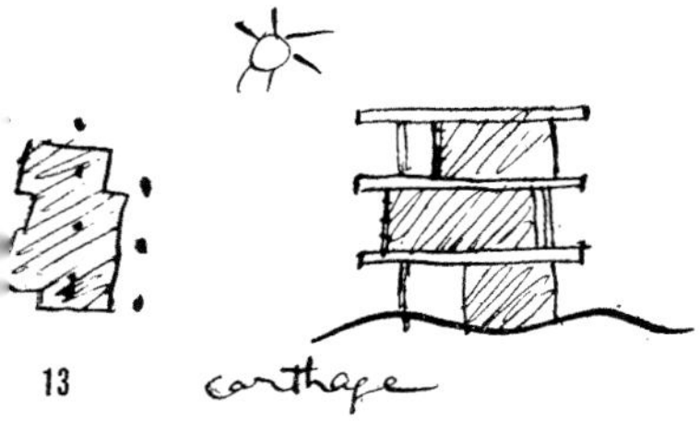

13

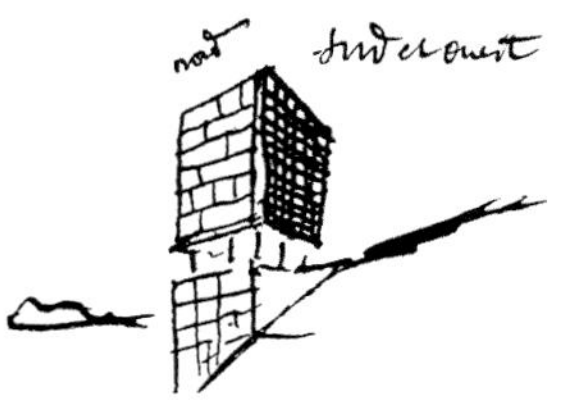


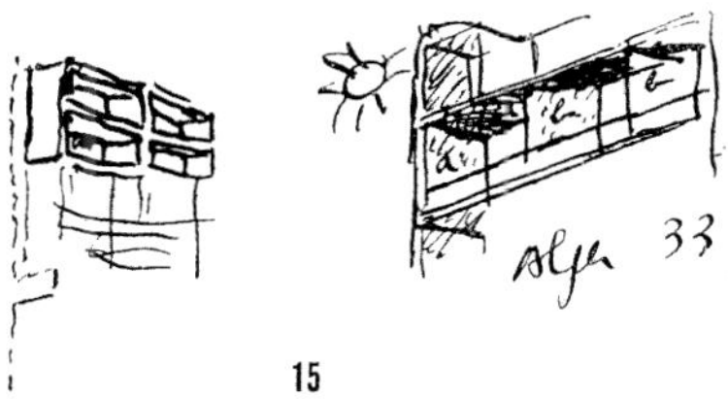

15

*Le soleil se lève, la lumière se répand, homme se réveille, il se met à agir : pen-r, travailler, etc... L'homme moderne qui énéficie par ailleurs des fruits irrécusables u progrès tels que le livre, le journal, l'ima-erie de toutes sortes, qui a appris à travail-r de ses doigts avec habileté, met à con-ibution incessamment ses yeux au cours de fournée; il a un besoin impératif de lu-ière solaire. Et celle-ci est une fonction irecte non seulement de sa joie de vivre ais du rendement de son activité. On peut ors bien dire : l'architecture consiste à nstruire des planchers éclairés. Bien-être utilité sont ainsi comblés.*

*Le jeu des saisons apportera une gamme uancée de bienfaits et de méfaits : au sols-ce d'hiver, le soleil est bas sur l'horizon et s rayons sont bienvenus à l'intérieur du gis où ils réchauffent moralement et phy-quement; les mi-saisons, printemps et au-mne, se satisfont fort bien d'un soleil doux la créature. Mais le solstice d'été et la ca-cule avec ses températures intenables ont it du soleil l'ami, un ennemi implacable; ces heures chaudes, le besoin d'ombre de-ent impératif : il faut obturer les fenêtres, faut « diaphragmer » le pan de verre.*

*Quels sont les moyens disponibles ? Ce sont s rideaux de tissu mince et épais superpo-s, les volets de diverses natures, intérieurs extérieurs, les écrans qui peuvent être des stèmes nouveaux à introduire dans l'éco-mie de la façade et de son pan de verre.*

*os premières constructions de 1921 à 1928 anifestèrent cette conquête du pan de rre par les étapes de la fenêtre horizontale mple, puis de la fenêtre horizontale dou-e, puis de la suppression définitive de allège. Et ce fut alors le pan de verre.*

*Mais dans l'immeuble « Clarté » de Ge-ève, baptisé ainsi par les usagers, nous ons amorcé instinctivement des travaux approche vers le brise-soleil. Je dessine les anchers, ils se prolongent au delà du pan verre par un balcon d'une assez forte illie d' 1 m. 50 muni de son parapet. Une emière ombre était provoquée; on y ajou-pour la canicule le complément de volets ulants installés au droit des parapets des balcons, créant ainsi des conditions très sa-tisfaisantes d'admission du soleil en hiver (soleil bas sur l'horizon) et d'obstacle au so-leil en été (soleil haut sur l'horizon) (11).*

*En 1932, l'immeuble de Molitor comportait une façade de verre intégrale; nous savions qu'il y ferait chaud à la canicule, mais baste! les Parisiens prennent leurs vacances à cette époque. Un barrage sérieux aurait été dressé par des volets roulants installés à l'extérieur de la façade. Il n'en fut pas fait ainsi volon-tairement; les volets roulants furent instal-lés à l'intérieur, maintenant ainsi la façade dans sa précise proportion de fer et de gla-ce, lui assurant sa dignité : nous n'admet-tions pas que chacun à sa guise, comme c'était le cas pour Clarté à Genève, pût ca-ricaturer, par une obturation purement acci-dentelle du pan de verre, une façade. Nous nous mettions en tort avec nous-mêmes, nous le savions. Nous l'avons voulu pertinemment ainsi afin qu'au moins, un pan de verre existât, intact, propre, et de bonnes propor-tions.*

CARTHAGE

*En 1928, le problème du soleil nous était impérieusement posé dans la construction d'une villa réalisée à Carthage.*

13 *L'ossature de la maison était complètement indépendante de la forme des locaux qui se trouvaient en retrait. Ainsi courait tout au-tour une partie plus ou moins profonde cons-tituant en fait des brise-soleil de diverses efficacités. Les locaux étaient éclairés par de grandes parois vitrées.*

*Je viens précisément d'avoir la visite du fils de notre client. Il me disait que la lu-mière, à l'intérieur des locaux, était admira-ble, affirmation intéressante à enregistrer à ce point de la démonstration puisqu'elle dé-montre que la visière constituée par le plan-cher supérieur de chaque étage et qui pour-rait être considérée comme un adversaire sé-rieux à l'introduction de la lumière, se trouve utilement compensée par le vitrage à 100 0/0 ouvert sur l'horizon.*

*En effet, le pan de verre fournit un afflux de lumière jusqu'ici inconnu, les solutions traditionnelles limitant à 20, 40 50 0/0 en général les surfaces éclairantes.*

BARCELONE

14 *A cette époque, à Barcelone, nous avions à dessiner de grands lotissements affectés à une main-d'œuvre de fortune venue des cam-pagnes : il s'agissait de paysans n'ayant eu aucun contact encore avec la vie citadine Le problème du soleil est impératif et s'étend sur de longs mois. Le logis fut aménagé pour assurer la fraîcheur dans les appartements et, sans que rien fût prémédité, les maisons furent munies de dispositifs qui devaient re-présenter plus tard des éléments de doctrine: en a, une profonde loggia — en b, des la-melles de béton formant jalousies et pivo-tant horizontalement — en c, la maison est surélevée sur un vide où l'ombre règne :*

*a constituait donc un premier brise-soleil;*

*b un autre brise-soleil et cela servirait plus tard;*

ALGER

15 *La même année, à Alger, le problème se posait à nouveau.*
*Un immeuble locatif construit de poteaux de béton portant plancher en cantilever, structure qui nous fournit quatre façades diversement exposées et par conséquent, te-nues de recevoir des formes du pan de verre appropriées. Au nord, et peut-être à l'est, nous pouvions conserver purement et simple-ment un pan de verre intégral, mais au sud et à l'ouest, il fallait installer un brise-soleil.*

*Celui-ci était fait d'alvéoles constituant des caissons d'environ 80 cms de profondeur sur 70 de hauteur environ, capables de pro-voquer une ombre efficace. Dispositif s'ins-tallant à quelques cms au devant du pan de verre et maintenu par un accrochage aux planchers qui faisaient saillie à chaque étage.*

*La difficulté résidait à l'ouest puisque le soleil le plus pénible est à l'heure du cou-chant car il projette des rayons lumineux horizontaux; notre brise-soleil s'avérait inef-ficace et devait être remplacé par des lames cette fois-ci verticales et disposées perpendi-culairement (a) ou obliquement (b) à la façade, le tout étant réglé par l'orientation de la façade. Les écrans ainsi créés cons-tituaient un prolongement architectural si-gnificatif, une espèce de balcon ou de loggia.*

BRÉSIL

*L'expédition de Rio de Janeiro en 1936 devait fournir l'occasion d'une expérimentation décisive : appelé par l'autorité pour établir, avec un comité d'architectes brésiliens de mes amis, les plans du palais du ministère de l'Education nationale et de la Santé publique, je vécus les conditions locales pendant des semaines. Le terrain choisi pour le bâtiment me parut inadmissible, enserré dans les lots étriqués d'une cité d'affaires mal dessinée qui multipliait l'effarant désordre des circulations automobiles. De plus, le paysage exceptionnel de Rio de Janeiro, avec ses prodigieuses montagnes échevelées de granit rose, ses végétations luxuriantes, sa mer partout présente, était aboli en ce lieu.*

16 *Je découvris à 200 m. de là, au bord de la mer, un terrain admirable; le palais pouvait s'étaler devant le site majestueux, ouvrant son pan de verre entier sur ce spectacle inestimable. Mes confrères brésiliens s'écrièrent : « Vous ne pouvez pas orienter votre façade ainsi, à Rio de Janeiro ! » — « Et pourquoi ? » — « A cause du soleil ! » Et de m'expliquer ses terribles ardeurs. Je riposte ; « Ne vous en faites pas, nous installerons devant le pan de verre un brise-soleil. » Et je dessine sur la feuille de plan, objet de la discussion, nos anciennes propositions pour Barcelone et pour Alger.*

*Huit jours avant mon départ intervint un contre-temps : le ministre, enchanté de son plan, est toutefois plein d'appréhension : il est persuadé que la politique s'en mêlant — si ce n'est le diable lui-même — le beau terrain lui sera contesté. Il me prie en conséquence d'adapter le projet au premier terrain envisagé; ce fut fait, tout en maintenant les mêmes principes architecturaux (17).*

17 *Les années passent, la guerre survient : 1945, une rumeur s'établit venue de Londres, des U.S.A. répétant : les Brésiliens ont fait des choses étonnantes. Des soldats et des officiers anglais et américains, si nombreux à me rendre visite, me le répètent constamment; en fin de compte, l'un d'eux m'administre la preuve sous forme du grand livre publié par le Museum of Modern Art de New-York, intitulé « Le Brésil bâti », ouvrage comportant d'innombrables photographies dont la moitié consacrée au folklore brésilien et l'autre à l'introduction au Brésil des méthodes nouvelles d'architecture : pilotis, pan de verre et brise-soleil.*

*Je dois reconnaître qu'hommage m'en est rendu. Voici ce qu'a écrit l'auteur du livre, Sir Philip Goodwin, chairman du département d'architecture au Musée d'Art Moderne :*

*« En 1936, Le Corbusier était invité à Rio « en qualité d'architecte consultant auprès « du groupe d'architectes chargés de cons- « truire le nouveau ministre de l'Education « nationale et de la Santé publique. Cet « édifice révèle fortement son influence mais « ce qui importe le plus, c'est qu'il a libéré « l'esprit créateur et creusé un gouffre sous « l'antique routine de la pensée gouverne- « mentale; tandis que le classique fédéra- « de Washington, l'archéologie de la Roya- « Academy de Londres et le classique na- « de Munich sont toujours triomphants, l- « Brésil a eu le courage de s'écarter de- « chemins faciles : le résultat a été que Ri- « peut s'enorgueillir de posséder le plu- « beau bâtiment gouvernemental de l'hémis- « phère occidental.*

*L'auteur précise encore : « Tandis qu- « l'impulsion permière venait du dehors, l- « Brésil prit de lui-même la tête; sa grand- « contribution originale à l'architecture mo- « derne est le contrôle de la chaleur et d- « rayonnement sur les surfaces de verre a- « moyen d'écrans extérieurs. L'Amérique d- « Nord a aveuglément ignoré la totalité d- « la question; en face du terrible soleil co- « chant de l'été, l'immeuble courant de bu- « reaux est comme une serre avec ses fe- « nêtres à guillotine à moitié fermées et san- « protection. Les pauvres employés de bu- « reau sont ou rôtis, tapis derrière d- « stores imperméables, ou étouffant sous l- « faible protection de stores vénitiens ineff- « caces contre le soleil qui brûle à travers le- « vitres.*

*« C'était une curiosité de voir comment le- « Brésiliens avaient traité ce très impor- « tant problème et ce fut là le motif ré- « de notre voyage ». (1).*

(1) *« Brazil Builds » The Museum of M- dern Art 11 West 53 Street N.York.*

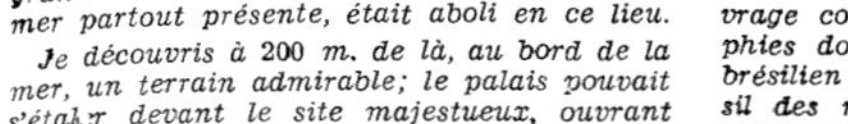

16

BRÉSIL

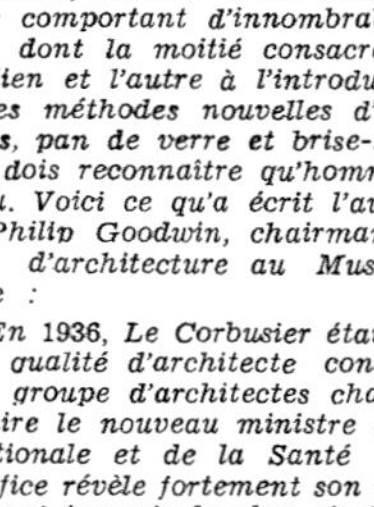

17

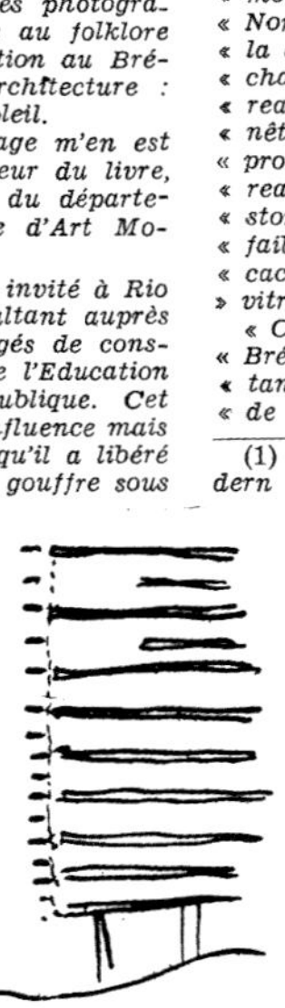

18

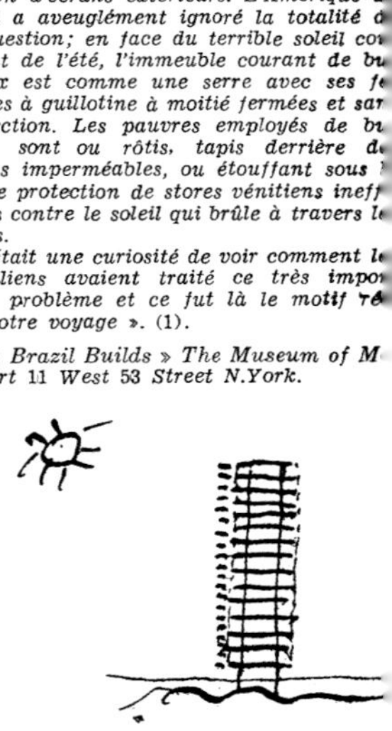

21

ALGER

20

19

ALGER

*1938 : je suis à Alger pour le gouvernement en tant que membre du Comité du Plan de la région d'Alger : urbaniser, c'est dresser dans l'espace des contenants capables de satisfaire aux fonctions qui s'opèrent à l'intérieur; par conséquent, c'est, en Afrique du Nord, tenir compte du soleil africain; c'est encore, partant du béton armé et de l'acier et de l'esprit neuf qui anime la colonie, chercher les formes architecturales sous lesquelles la vie moderne trouvera son compte.*

*Diverses études d'ailleurs m'occupent depuis dix années à Alger, entre autres (1937-38) une esquisse de palais de justice dont l'une des données est d'assurer une circulation aisée au sol, et l'autre, de tenir compte du soleil algérien et des reflets de la mer toute proche, l'ensemble devant s'intégrer dans une composition générale.*

*Voici le schéma de cette manifestation architecturale : tout d'abord, les pilotis qui élèvent les diverses salles du palais au niveau utile, laissant le sol disponible pour une circulation efficace des piétons et des automobiles, circulation séparée et classée; puis, les compartiments installés au devant des façades et qui constituent autant de brise-soleil appropriés. Vous en saisissez le principe, je n'insiste pas davantage.*

*Cette solution qui allait au devant d'une conclusion architecturale devait trouver une application architecturale significative lors de l'étude de la cité d'affaires d'Alger, bâtiment de 150 mètres de hauteur, dressé sur le bastion 14, au pied du boulevard Laferrière, dans le giron de la falaise et face à la mer et aux horizons magnifiques d'Alger.*

18 *La coupe a est sans ambiguité : on y lit à nouveau les planchers; on y voit le pan de verre apte à éclairer, dans les meilleures conditions, les innombrables bureaux et, devant le pan de verre, s'installe le brise-sole- fusionnant un système pur de constructio- et un élément incontestable d'architecture.*

19 *La figure 19 montre l'efficacité du bris- soleil à l'intérieur des bureaux; ceux-ci pour- ront avoir la grandeur que l'on voudra partir de l'unité modulaire qui est un cas- de brise-soleil, à vrai dire une loggia, un- véritable loggia.*

*Ainsi se trouve retrouvé l'un des plus a- tiques éléments de l'architecture de tout- les traditions et je m'en trouve ravi : déso- mais, les bureaux seront à l'abri du soleil d- rect et des reflets de la mer aux périod- dangereuses de l'année. Mais il y a dava- tage : le pan de verre peut être nettoyé chaque étage et dans chaque local indépe- damment, à portée de la main. Son occlusi- peut être également obtenue à volonté, s- lon les goûts ou les besoins de chacun sa- qu'il en apparaisse au dehors une impre-*



1.24 Le Corbusier, "Problèmes de l'Ensoleillement: Le Brise-Soleil," from *Techniques et Architecture*, January 1946.

*sion d'anarchie. Et voilà, entrée dans l'architecture d'une manière assez totale, une fonction fondamentale qui a motivé la création d'un organe architectural caractérisé et que l'on est désormais en droit de légitimer.*

*L'ensemble se présentera avec les ressources d'une diversité considérable de brise-soleil dimensionnés selon les locaux à protéger : la plus grande richesse architecturale peut en découler.*

*L'utilisation des locaux pour les besoins les plus modernes est possible en terre d'Afrique; une attitude architecturale en est issue, la fonction est entrée dans l'architecture.*

*Je tiens à indiquer que le ministère des Colonies a jugé intéressant de faire construire une grande maquette de cet édifice pour l'Exposition de la France d'Outremer qui s'ouvrira cet automne à Paris.*

*En conclusion, le dernier schéma semble bien exprimer une vérité architecturale d'aujourd'hui, issue des techniques modernes, acier et ciment armé. Nous voici loin des premiers croquis de cette causerie : le champ est ouvert désormais à l'architecture pour manifester sous une forme nouvelle le rayonnement des formes et des proportions sous la lumière.*

*
**

*Récapitulons et essayons d'aboutir à une conclusion :*

*1° La marche vers la lumière : l'essentiel de la conquête architecturale s'y consacrera; le besoin de lumière se manifeste à toutes les périodes de bien-être, — le Romain, dans sa maison méditerranéenne ou sa villa, avec les grandes baies des atriums qui n'étaient pas munies de verre parce que le climat s'y prêtait et que d'autre part, aucune industrie ne l'autorisait encore. Les Arabes avec leur goût du bien-être et des bienfaits de la vie, ouvrant de grandes baies sur des jardins clos et n'occlusant leurs façades sur rues que pour se protéger des intrus. Puis, la période romane hérissée de difficultés techniques mettant en jeu d'ailleurs un climat tout autre : celui du versant nord de l'Europe.*

*Le jaillissement éblouissant du gothique avec sa croisée d'ogive et ses verrières immenses. N'oublions pas qu'à cette époque, les maisons de bois étaient de véritables pans de verre ou tendaient à l'être : des vestiges le prouvent et les Flamands le montrent bien dans leurs constructions poursuivies au delà de la Renaissance et qui nous sont parvenues intactes : Anvers ou la Grand'Place de Bruxelles; les poteaux de bois y furent remplacés acrobatiquement par des meneaux de pierre, le tout d'une telle légèreté qu'ils donnnnt l'impression intense du pan de verre.*

*On retiendra au passage qu'il s'agit de pays du nord avec des climats brumeux, preuve que le besoin de lumière affecte les gens du nord au même titre que ceux du sud.*

*Vint ensuite une civilisation de plus en plus humanisée de la Renaissance, de la période classique des rois avec une véritable apogée de dimensionnement et de proportionnement sous Louis XV et Louis XVI. Enfin, le bourgeois-roi du XIX^e^ siècle, ce siècle tumultueux si intéressant par tant de côtés où le goût du confort s'empare de toutes les classes, institue une préface au style des villes, aboutit à la solution Haussmann qui, loin d'être méprisable, marque un temps d'arrêt devant le problème de la lumière.*

*Alors, la novation : l'application de l'acier et du ciment armé à l'immeuble commun d'habitation, de bureaux ou de manufactures, aboutissement des techniques, ai-je dit, évolution, révolution même dans l'habitude des hommes : murs portant planchers et qui ne peuvent être troués au delà d'une certaine limite. Des avatars autour de 1900 : voyages des édiles en Angleterre et introduction, dans l'immeuble locatif du boulevard Raspail ou de Passy du bow-window emprunté aux cottages. Tout cela n'est qu'un passage. Déjà Frantz-Jourdain, à la Samaritaine, vers 1905, a triomphalement imposé le pan de verre, mais on a cru à une boutade, on n'a pas vu l'assimilation possible de la solution par la vie domestique.*

*La construction de béton armé se développe, s'épanouit, se précise. Le pan de verre, un beau jour, existe purement et simplement avec toutes ses vertus et avec ses défauts. Mais, nous venons de le voir, l'architecture peut triompher de ses défauts.*

*Cette solution qui s'appelle* « brise-soleil » 22 *porte un nom significatif. En fait, c'est un briseur de toutes sortes de difficultés; on lui adjoindra le « brise-vent » par la possibilité de constituer des parois hermétiques vitrées translucides, transparentes, opaques si l'on veut. Une conquête d'architecture sera faite : l'exploitation du quatrième mur de la chambre. Je m'explique : entre des planchers diversement situés, éclairés par un pan de verre, on voit apparaître des locaux de hauteurs différentes qui sont protégés par un brise-soleil proportionné.*

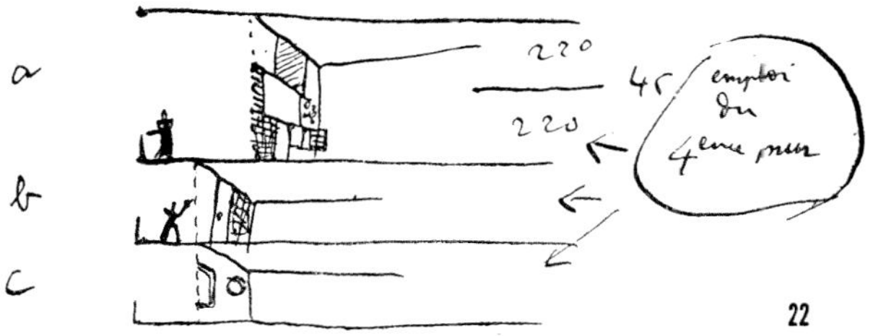


22

22 a

*Par exemple : en a, le local étant très haut, le brise-soleil est plus profond pour qu'il puisse produire son effet. ... ... ...*

22 b

*En* b, *la hauteur étant plus faible, le brise-soleil est réduit proportionnellement. Signaler en passant que l'habitant de* a *ou de* b *nettoie son vitrage à son gré, du dedans ou du dehors.*

22 *En* c, *idem.*

*L'habitant de* a *ou de* b *pourra équiper de manière intéressante la grande surface de son pan de verre, le divisant en panneaux fixes, translucides ou transparents, de verre, de glace, avec parties de vitraux ou de briques de verre. Il pourra aussi faire glisser des écrans de bois coulissant les uns sur les autres et capables de diaphragmer à 30, 60, 100 0/0 les surfaces de verre.*

*Encore ce pan de verre pourra-t-il comporter des éléments meublés, casiers, rayons* 23 *de bibliothèques, panneaux nus ou décorés, etc. Le quatrième mur entre désormais dans la composition de l'intérieur de l'habitation. On pourra, si l'on veut, figurer en* b *par exemple, de la brique de verre, une glace claire, fixe et une porte de sortie sur la loggia extérieure; cette porte de sortie peut devenir un « trou d'homme » avec battement hermétique; désormais, les causes de refroidissement sont diminuées considérablement d'autant plus que cette paroi de verre peut être éventuellement construite en mur « neutralisant », solution de notre invention, pour le Palais des Coopératives à Moscou en 1929, invention rejetée alors, violemment critiquée pour des raisons sentimentales et que Gustave Lyon le physicien, avait estimé être d'importance décisive.*

*Enfin, en* c, *dans un mur de substance translucide ou transparente, en verre ou matière plastique, on pourra ménager un hublot de glace claire permettant de regarder au dehors ou même un simple hublot rond permettant une prise d'air directe, à conjuguer utilement avec les installations d' « air exact » (climatisation). Une souplesse extraordinaire s'offre désormais aux ingénieux et aux imaginatifs.*

*J'ajoute en terminant qu'en* a, b, *ou* c, *les diaphragmes obturateurs pourront être extérieurs ou intérieurs à volonté; le dispositif du brise-soleil est tel, désormais, que l'initiative personnelle peut intervenir sans trouble et sans dommage pour l'attitude extérieure des bâtiments. Un ordre impératif est apporté par le brise-soleil lui-même et derrière lui, la vie peut se dérouler à volonté dans l'infinie variété des goûts et des besoins individuels.*

*Tout cela concerne Rio-de-Janeiro aussi bien que les U.S.A., Barcelone aussi bien qu'Alger, les Flandres aussi bien que Londres, Paris aussi bien que Stockholm ou Moscou. Le problème du soleil est un, il passe d'un extrême à l'autre, selon le jeu des saisons, provoquant tous les nuancements possibles, toutes les solutions adéquates. C'est là qu'un régionalisme authentique a le droit d'intervenir et non pas en prétendant mettre sur l'architecture des « fioritures ». Les techniques sont universelles : acier, ciment armé; le soleil est différent au long de la courbe du méridien, il frappe la croûte terrestre selon des incidences variables.*

*Et c'est là toute la belle et prodigieuse diversité que le Créateur nous a offerte. A nous d'en tirer un parti digne de l'œuvre naturelle.*

LE CORBUSIER.

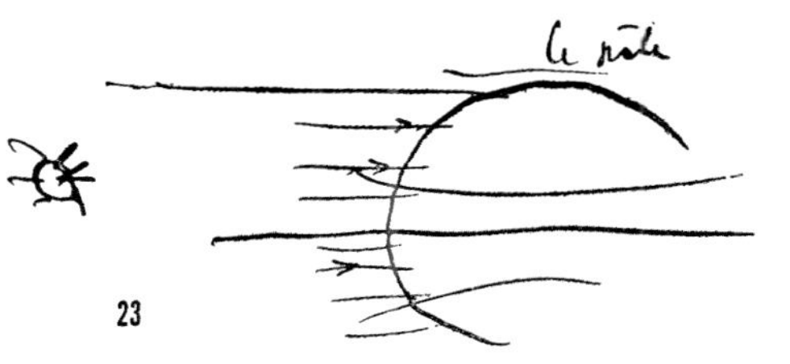

23

« . . . . . . . . . . . . . . . . . . . . . . . . . . . . . . . . . . . .
*Si beaucoup de ceux qui à Paris se disent Architectes n'étaient pas originairement des Margajats de l'espèce de ces hommes dont je vous ai parlé dans ma première lettre, qui n'ont jamais pensé que le Soleil fut nécessaire, l'on ne verrait pas des maisons ni d'autres Bâtimens aussi ridicules que l'on en voit ; comme ces drôles-cy ne sont chez eux que pour y dormir, ils ne connoissent point le Nord, c'est pourquoi, pourveu qu'ils mettent des pierres les unes sur les autres, ils s'applaudissent de leur œuvre et s'embarrassent peu qu'un honnête homme devienne paralytique ou podagre.*
. . . . . . . . . . . . . . . . . . . . . . . . . . . . . . . . . . . . »

FREMIN,
"Mémoires critiques d'Architecture"
(1702)

« . . . . . . . . . . . . . . . . . . . . . . . . . . . . . . . . . . . .
*Certaines règles simples devraient être édictées par le ministre. D'abord le respect du soleil. Le soleil a pris dans la vie actuelle une place particulièrement importante que tous les hygiénistes s'accordent à lui reconnaître, la place capitale qu'on lui donne dans les sanatoria où l'on répare les hommes abîmés par les taudis.*
*Le Ministère doit être armé pour empêcher la construction de maisons dans lesquelles certains appartements ne recevraient pas le soleil.*
*Cela comporte naturellement comme corollaire des règlements sur l'espacement des maisons et sur la nécessité de recevoir le soleil, même l'hiver.* . . . . . . . . . . . . . . . . . . . . . . . . . . . »

Eugène PETIT,
Interpellation à l'Assemblée Constituante
(15 Mars 1946)

# EFFICACITÉ DE L'ENSOLEILLEMENT

Il est généralement admis, aujourd'hui, que les conditions primordiales auxquelles doivent satisfaire les lieux de travail et de résidence des hommes sont le soleil, le grand air et la verdure. Il est donc nécessaire d'assurer à l'architecte les moyens pratiques d'estimer l'efficacité de l'ensoleillement pour les divers partis possibles, au cours de l'élaboration d'un projet.

En réalité cette estimation n'est pas très simple, ce qui explique certaines incertitudes actuelles.

Les facteurs qui interviennent sont multiples, et tous ont leur importance : 1° durée d'ensoleillement de chaque partie des façades ; 2° pénétration du soleil dans les pièces (angle d'incidence) ; 3° énergie du rayonnement solaire (exprimée en calories) ; 4° qualité du rayonnement solaire (composition spectrale importante pour les effets physiologiques et biologiques).

Les deux premiers facteurs sont d'ordre géométrique. Ils peuvent être connus avec précision par les méthodes indiquées dans cet ouvrage ou expérimentalement (par maquettes et héliodon). Le troisième facteur est d'ordre physique. Il mesure la chaleur reçue par un immeuble en chaque instant, valeur qui dépend elle-même des facteurs (1°) et (2°) pour chaque façade. Il est donc important de disposer d'un moyen commode de connaître cette énergie reçue par unité de surface suivant les différentes orientations. Ce qui permettrait, en somme, de faire le bilan énergétique de l'ensoleillement d'un bâtiment ou d'un ensemble (*).

Malheureusement, l'énergie réelle du rayonnement solaire est une quantité essentiellement variable, par suite de l'absorption atmosphérique, qui elle-même dépend de l'altitude, de la hauteur du soleil (heure, saison) et des conditions climatiques locales (nébulosité, etc...).

Nous avons résumé graphiquement, ci-contre, les résultats de mesures émanant de plusieurs sources de documentation : une loi générale se dégage bien de ces cas particuliers, mais les valeurs absolues diffèrent très notablement. Il semblerait donc très souhaitable que des organismes spécialisés puissent fixer les bases d'établissement d'abaque de ce genre, soit théoriques et valables en moyenne pour une certaine latitude, soit expérimentales et valables pour une région déterminée.

Ces données, avec celle du facteur de composition spectrale, (qui serait à préciser d'une manière analogue) permettront à l'architecte de fixer son parti en toute connaissance de cause et de faire intervenir avec certitude l'ensoleillement parmi les critères déterminants de l'architecture.

A. H.

(*) Le Comité Technique du Chauffage et de la Ventilation vient de faire paraître son Rapport N° 5 : « Apports de chaleur par insolation dans les Bâtiments habités », rédigé sous la direction de M. André Nessi.
Simultanément, le Comité Français de l'Eclairage et de Chauffage vient d'aborder ces études et son programme correspond précisément aux questions posées ci-dessus. Nous aurons donc l'occasion de revenir prochainement sur ce sujet.

1

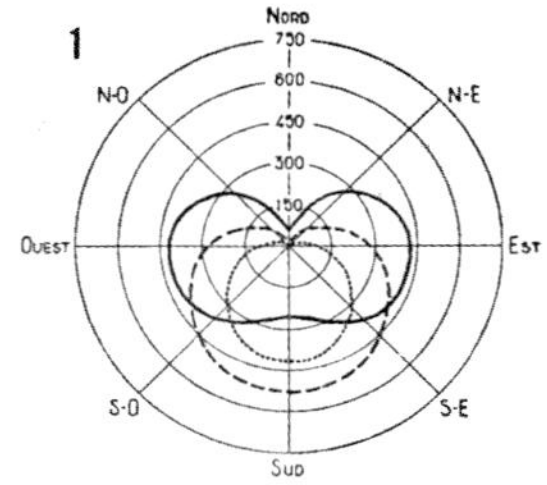


2

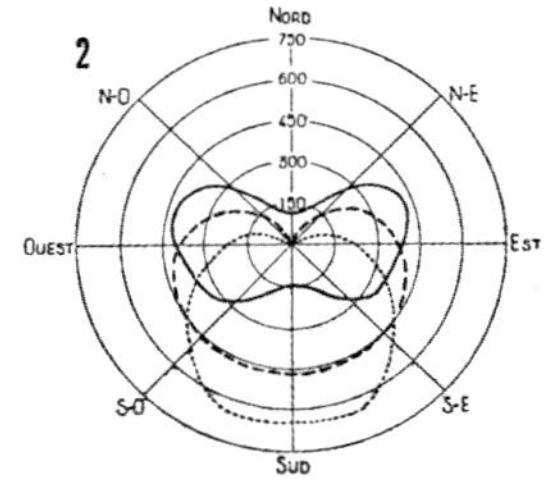


Energie reçue (en calories gr. par jour et par cm² de façade) suivant les diverses orientations aux équinoxes et aux solstices.

1. d'après les sources françaises (tableaux pour la latitude de 49° donnés par F. Marboutin dans la Technique Sanitaire 1931).

2. d'après des sources américaines. (Mesures de l'A.S.H.V.E. pour la latitude de New-York).

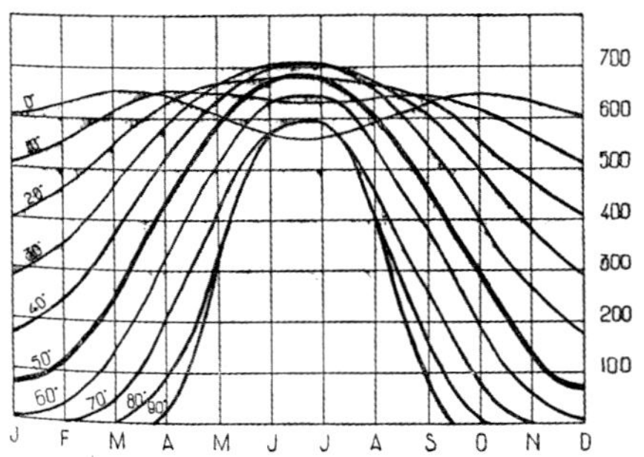


Variations annuelles théoriques de l'énergie solaire reçue chaque jour par la terre, aux diverses latitudes, en cal. gr. par cm² de surface horizontale (D'après les chiffres de Angot reproduits par M. Ch. MAURAIN dans « Etude pratique des Rayonnements », édité par Gauthier Villars — Paris 1937).

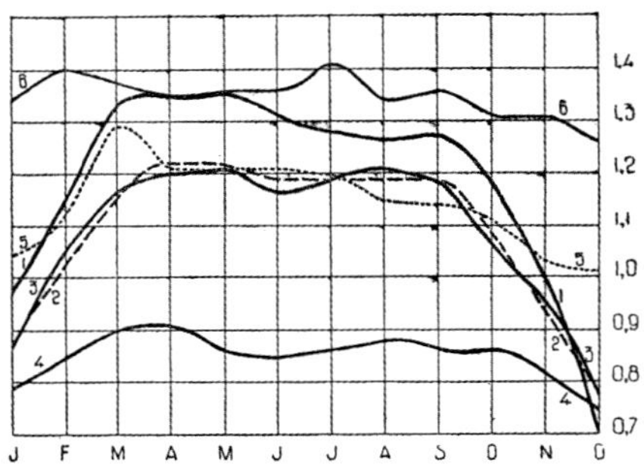


Variations annuelles de l'énergie solaire réellement reçue en différents lie 1° Léningrad, 2° Varsovie, 3° Paris, Parc Saint-Maur, 4° Lausanne, 5° … rence, 6° Antibes (Valeurs à midi, en cal. gr. par cm² de section droite par minute). D'après un tableau du même ouvrage.



1.25 France Fradet, "Table d'Orientation Latitude" and "Réseau des Courbes des Ombres," from *Techniques et Architecture*, January 1946.

La détermination de la direction des ayons solaires en un instant donné eut être faite par des calculs longs t pénibles : c'est la méthode des stronomes, qui ont besoin d'une rande précision...

Pour les études de l'ensoleillement, es méthodes graphiques élémentaires ont suffisantes. Les plus simples de es méthodes semblent être celles baées sur le principe du cadran solaire table horizontale : M. Jean Dournon en a présenté un exemple dans es pages qui précèdent.

Les instruments d'application de ce rincipe peuvent prendre différentes ormes : c'est ainsi que, à la suite de echerches menées indépendamment, Mlle Fradet a mis au point les grahiques que nous présentons ici.

Dans le graphique II, les arcs diures (parcours de l'extrémité de l'omre) sont donnés par les solstices et es équinoxes seulement, mais pour es hauteurs de style échelonnées.

Les lignes radiales représentent la irection des ombres d'une tige verticale : elles ne doivent pas être conondues avec les droites horaires du adran solaire habituel.

N. D. L. R.

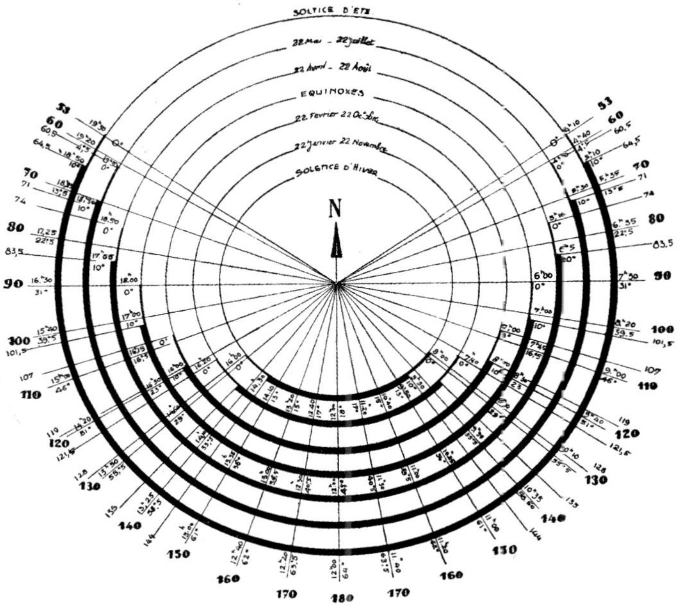


## I. — Table d'orientation (latitude 49°)

**Utilité : Détermination de la durée théorique d'ensoleillement d'une façade — choix d'une exposition assurant une certaine durée théorique d'ensoleillement.**

**Exemple : L'exposition Sud-Est (qui correspond à l'orientation 45o Est — 135o Ouest) assure à la façade les ensoleillements :**

**De 8 heures à 14 heures le 2? décembre ;**
**De 6 heures à 14 h. 30 le 21 mars et le 23 septembre ;**
**De 4 h. 10 à 13 h. 30 le 23 juin.**

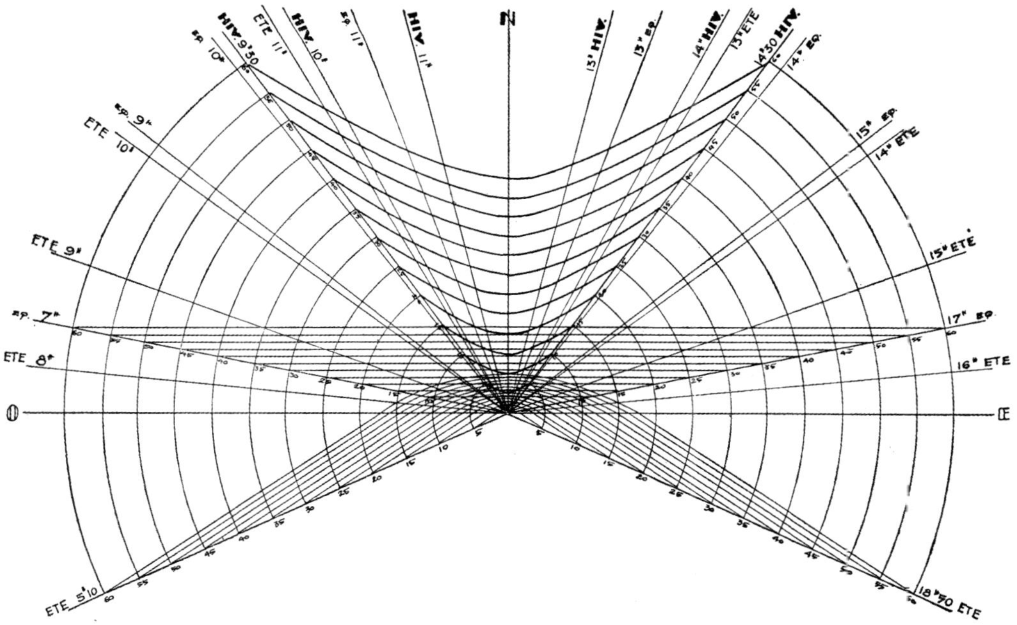


## II. — Réseau des courbes d'ombre (latitude 49°)

**Utilité : tracé de la « Zone de protection d'une façade » : une façade étant destinée à être ensoleillée pendant une certaine période quotidienne, sa zone de protection pour une hauteur d'immeubles H est la région immeuble de hauteur H pour que la façade intéressée jouisse effectivement de l'ensoleillement prévu.**

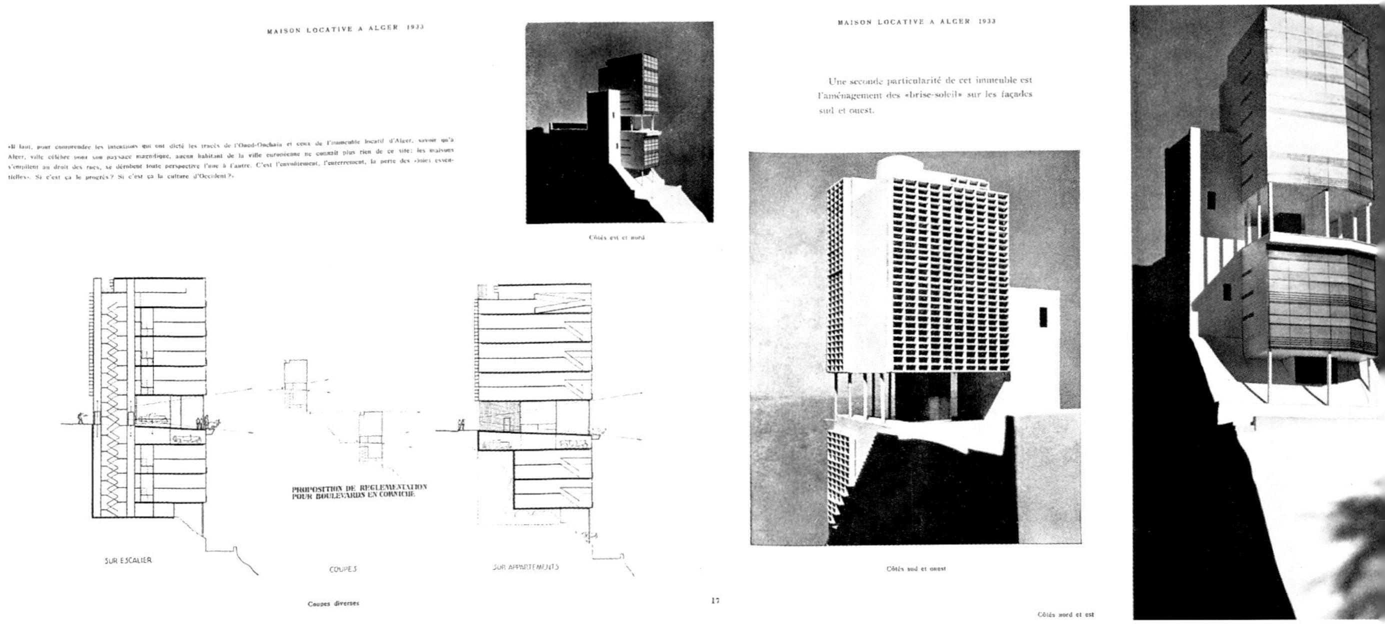


1.26 Le Corbusier, Maison Locative, Algiers, from the *Oeuvre complète, 1929–1934.*

then followed. The science of and the capacity to control *l'ensoleillement* became an important arena for research collaborations between architects, engineers, physicists, and manufacturers.[58] The conference of July 1945 was one of a number of jumping-off points for the integration of scientific knowledge around climate into the architectural strategies of modernism, what we now call the building or architectural sciences—and which have been focused on energy efficiency and climatic performance for the past few decades.

The work and influence of Le Corbusier, especially in his interwar experiments with the *pan de verre* and the brise-soleil that it required, configured architecture as a means for intervening in climatic patterns, and for adjusting the thermal interior according to the relevant details of the atmospheric system, with the façade as a mediating device. The substantive historical legacy, on these terms, was the conception of architecture as a site for the integration of cultural and scientific knowledge: how to build in ways that substantiated a normative perspective on how people want to live.

The events just described, seen from a new perspective, initiate a history of climatic modernism. They open up a different set of legacies and histories that will be explored at length in what follows—in Le Corbusier's relative influence on the shaded modernism of Brazil, in contrast with Neutra's version of climatic adaptability in Puerto Rico, and in the profound influence of the Swiss-French master on the methodological work of Victor and Aladar Olgyay, through to Victor Olgyay's seminal text *Design with Climate: Bioclimatic Approach to Architectural Regionalism*, published in 1963 in a format intended to sit alongside Le Corbusier's *Oeuvre complète* on the architect's bookshelf. This is a different trajectory than has been heretofore elaborated on and will mix with other influences and experiments to provide a robust accounting of a substantive new legacy of modernism—a different past that opens up toward different futures.

The "petit historique" drawing in *Techniques et Architecture*—which was later published in *Architecture d'aujourd'hui* (1947) and reprinted in the Olgyays *Solar Control and Shading Devices* (1957)—serves, in this sense, as a schematic diagram for Le Corbusier's influence on the global expansion of shading systems, for better or worse. It is worth noting that, beyond the evidence presented in the following chapters, there is ample reason to recognize the substantive importance of numerous other architects in the emergence of shading devices. Stamo Papadaki, for example, a Greek architect resident in Brazil from the early 1930s, claimed some primacy in the invention of the modern use of the shading device. His 1928 entry to the Christopher Columbus Memorial Lighthouse competition, a prominent competition that catalyzed the modernization of Latin American architecture, had a south façade of building-length horizontal fins. It is cited by Jeffrey Aronin in the 1950s, by Colin Porteous more recently, and others as the first use of the brise-soleil.[59] Papadaki also built a small house and studio in Athens in 1930 that used a brise-soleil system similar to that adopted by Le Corbusier at the Villa Baizeau. Papadaki later became an influential author and editor, and Aronin and the Olgyays also indicate that Papadaki's books on Le Corbusier and Oscar Niemeyer were central to the global dissemination of the brise-soleil idea.[60]

In any event, the *petit-historique* was seen by Le Corbusier and his acolytes as a record of the development of the brise-soleil and its importance to the global dissemination not only of climatic modernism but of architectural modernism more generally. Interest in the 1940s was particularly focused on a number of projects for Algiers, especially the Maison Locative, of 1933 (figure 1.26). It appears as example #20 in "Problèmes de l'Ensoleillement" (see figure 1.24) in three sketches—a view of the building inserted into a hillside, with different façades reflecting different solar orientations; a midrange view of the solar-exposed northern façade showing the egg-crate shading system, and a close-up of the shaded façade, all keyed to the accompanying text. "On the north, and perhaps on the east, we can simply use a *pan de verre*," Le Corbusier wrote in *Techniques et Architecture*, "but on the south and west, we need to install a brise-soleil . . . these were made of tiny cavities in a box-shape, 80 cm deep and 70 cm in height, capable of making an efficient shadow. The device would be installed a few centimeters in front of the *pan de verre*, and secured by an anchor that stuck out on each floor." Le Corbusier continued, identifying some problems that would become the subject of much analysis by the Olgyays and others:

> The difficulty was in the west because the sun was the most annoying at the hour of sunset when it projected bright horizontal rays—our brise-soleil would have been ineffective and would have needed to be replaced by blades that could be vertical and disposed either perpendicular or oblique to the façade, all of it regulated by the orientation of the façade. The screens we created constituted a significant extension of architecture.[61]

The brise-soleil was seen both as a technical solution—which required significant elaboration in order to accomplish its complex task—and as a design proposal in its own right, subject to a wide range of interventions and innovations.

The Maison Locative has been overshadowed, in the literature, by Le Corbusier's better-known Plan Obus developed for Algiers around the same time—another historiographic obstacle that makes the history of climatic modernism difficult to see (figure 1.27). This urban plan has been celebrated for its integration of housing into the infrastructural element of the elevated roadway. It has also been criticized for its designed omission of the colonized subject: the roadway winds along the coast and then becomes a bridge over the densely populated old town, terminating in the new commercial district. The modernist intervention, however elaborate and overscaled, is also here carefully exclusive.

Perhaps the most scathing criticism of the Plan Obus came from Manfredo Tafuri, in *Architecture and Utopia: Design and Capitalist Development* (first published in Italian in 1973), where he saw it as a potent example of Le Corbusier's remove from the economic conditions of production. Le Corbusier's urban plans in general, Tafuri wrote, were "the most advanced and formally elevated hypotheses of bourgeois culture in the field of architecture and urbanism." In the Algiers case, a further dimension of utopian remove was emphasized by the complete lack of client; the architect "worked in Algiers for four years without an official appointment or compensation. . . . He 'invented' his commission."[62] It is something of a minor point in the midst of the broader argument that Tafuri brings to bear on the project—that, in short, the international forces of corporate capital have removed architecture from the creative engagement with social forces, and placed them in the hands of the developer, as decorators to profit accumulation. As a consequence of this retreat from the "structures of production," or any real attempt to intervene in the social sphere, architecture "hides behind a rediscovered disciplinary autonomy"—thus the importance of Tafuri's general position, however misinterpreted, to the formal autonomy of the 1970s that has significantly conditioned the reception of Le Corbusier, and modernism in general, in the years since.[63]

It is at least symbolically compelling, if perhaps not materially substantive, that the Maison Locative, though unbuilt, and unlike the more

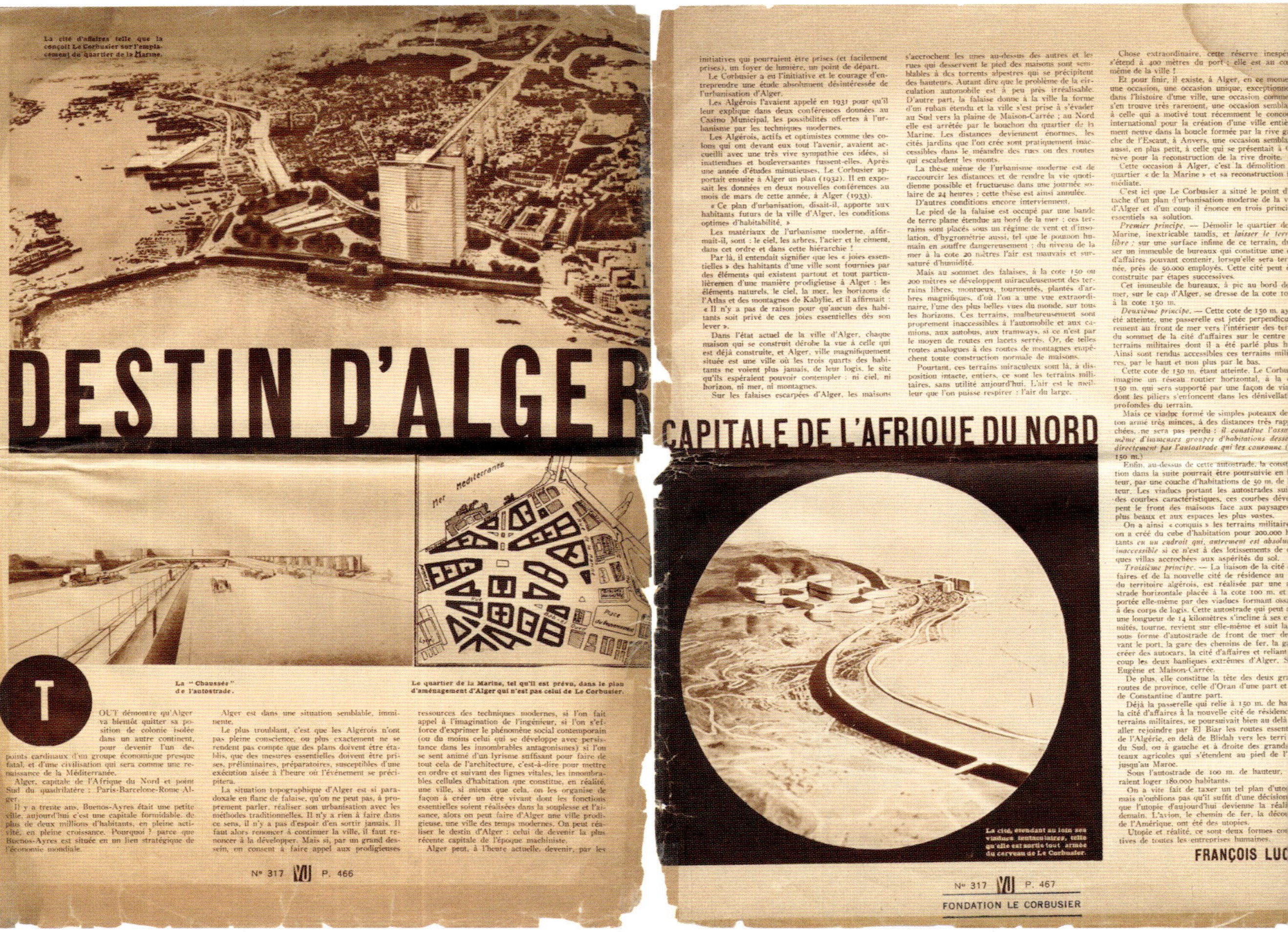


1.27 Le Corbusier, Plan Obus, Algiers, from the September 1932 issue of the industry journal, *Glaces et Verres*.

ambitious Plan Obus, was proposed for an actual site and had an actual client (figure 1.28). It was attempting to innovate in the language of architectural forms insofar as they could reinscribe, through knowledge of environmental conditions, a space for a new kind of socioeconomic effect. It was still framed by the pressures of developer financing—the social actors that might have benefited from the shaded Locative were, presumably, bourgeois office workers. Perhaps rather than a confrontation with the premise of autonomy is a recognition, one that will, again, be played out in what follows, that the planetary interior is also the interior of global capital—it is a space conditioned for the uninterrupted flow of commerce and the architectural management of risk.

Archival photographs show the hillside for which Le Corbusier designed the Maison Locative; other documents detail the complicated relationship with a client that ultimately doomed the project. Much more could be said about the climatic modernism of Le Corbusier—a more extensive examination of his work in India, for example, is warranted, as are his emotional pleas to design according to solar imperatives that some Corbusians would pursue in the 1970s. Perhaps of most interest to the data and aspirations of subsequent climatic modernists is an extensive, unpublished document from Le Corbusier's studio in 1961, just four years before his death, which wrestles with the means by which to calculate a solar azimuth and the relationship of these calculations to articulating a structure with a more

1.28 Le Corbusier, Maison Locative site photographs.

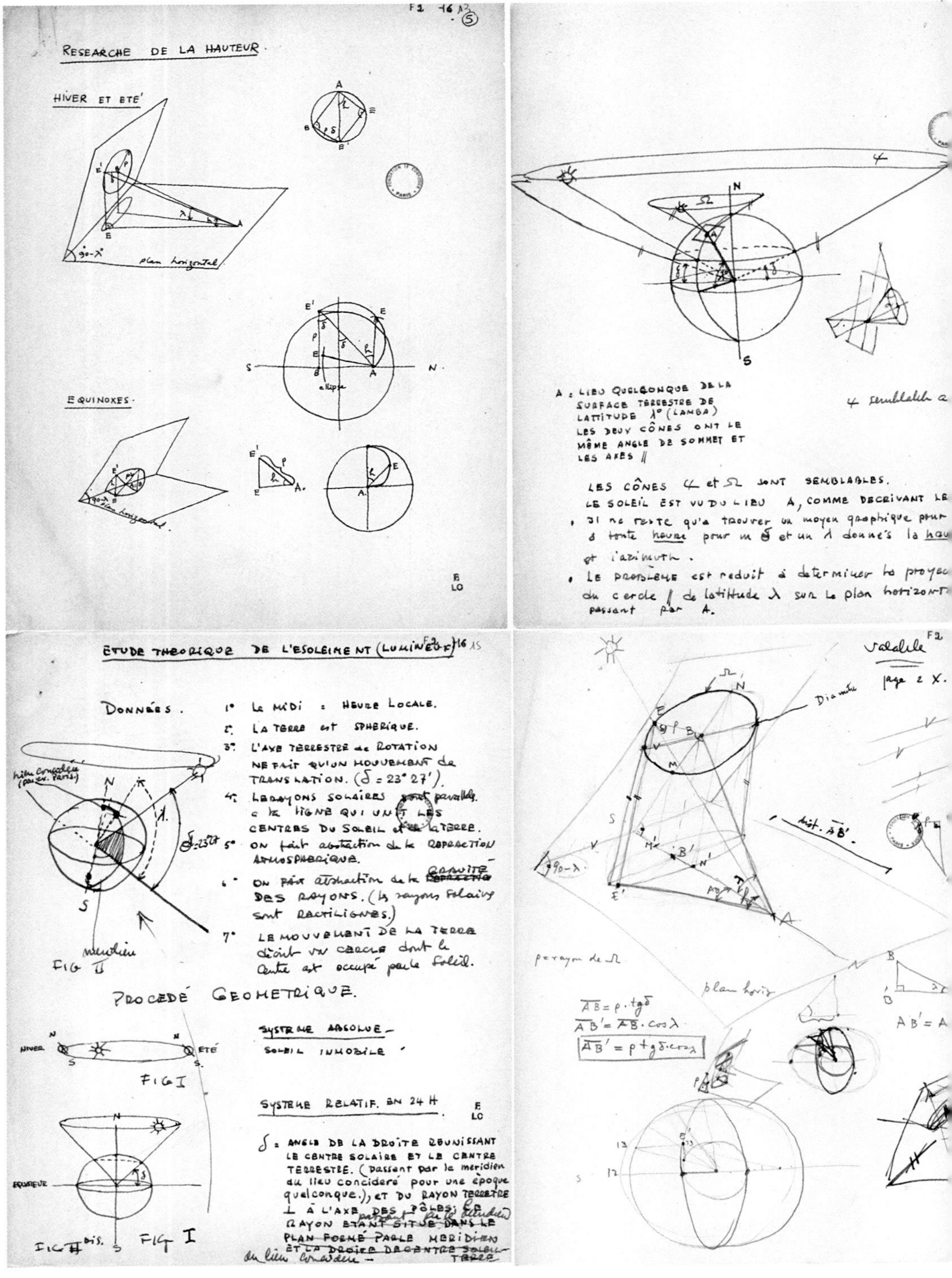

1.29 From the Le Corbusier archive, drawn in his studio, "Etude theorique de l'esoleiment . . ." 1961.

precise climatic optimization (figure 1.29). Next to the calculational methods also under development in the 1950s and '60s, these diagrams are feeble—the baton had been passed from the celebration of shading as a solution to the *pan de verre* to the articulation of a science of climatic-architectural performativity, replete with a new set of variables.

The narratives that follow will not belabor these connective threads to architectural modernism, however evident they may be.[64] Despite the clarity of the title, this book is not about *modernism*; in a significant way, it is not about *architecture* either, at least not in the way these terms are usually understood. Climate-architectural evidence allows for reconfigured perceptions and conceptions of modernization, and of processes of industrialization, in which architecture was involved in numerous and often unexpected ways. Architecture modernized through consumption of fossil fuels, the first phase of which (again, the story of this book) was the rendering thermal of the planetary interior. The planetary interior had to be conceptualized as a thermal space before it could be conditioned by fossil fuels. Once the thermal conditions of the built interior were made available as a conceptual and technological object, they were then made mechanical through heating and cooling systems.

---

This is a story, an image of the world, that sees the thermal interior at the center of an epochal narrative—a story of the ways that life has been lived indoors, with many allusions to how these ways of life have transformed according to the relationship between the planetary interior and the planetary climate. The climate has been and will be warmed, in large part, by changes to the interior—warmed, indeed, by the cooling of the interior, through mechanical means. This is a story of how the world has gotten hotter by cooling itself, or, again, the prelude to it. The project of the rest of this book is to describe how the thermal interior was imagined and built through innovations in architectural methods, *before* it became subject to mechanical conditioning. This discussion highlights possibilities for the future that are embedded in the past.

This book is not about architecture in the sense of trying to preserve something recognizable as *architecture* in the face of the threat or imposition of an environmentalist, activist premise that threatens to disrupt disciplinary and professional norms.[65] It asks, instead, what kind of history informs the challenges to the architecture of the present? It is an attempt to disrupt and reconfigure understandings of architecture and its relationship to the world—of the conditions of the planetary interior, of *how is it conditioned?* as an epochal historical question that, in the early twenty-first century, in the face of increasing climate instability, transforms architecture away from familiar frameworks—in particular formalist frameworks—and explores how architecture has mediated between social and planetary systems.

# 2. Risks

## Insurance

Le Corbusier's Maison Locative was never built, but images of it were widely disseminated. The proposed office building for Algiers was influential less as an icon or an innovation and more as a distillation, a clear and concise vision of ideas about the modern office tower—the scale, the importance of shading, the capacity to articulate a new kind of thermal space in a range of regions, environments, and political contexts. In the 1930s, few such buildings were actually being built. Many of the first attempts to develop an architecture attentive to the changing material possibilities of industrial modernity were built in Brazil. In the 1930s and 1940s Brazil was rapidly industrializing, drawing flows of capital through its cities, and transforming its political structure to attend to the needs of a large, heterogeneous, and geographically extensive population. Climatic modernism emerged as an essential symbolic and material means to communicate the ambitions of and produce the spaces for these new terms for governance.

One of the many buildings that reflects and, in its historical moment, helped to catalyze these changes was the Instituto de Resseguros do Brasil (IRB)—the Brazilian Reinsurance Agency—designed by MM Roberto and built in central Rio in 1936 (figure 2.2). The building is a long rectangular slab—a good deal thicker than the *siedlung* and other bar buildings familiar to the history of interwar modernism, but no less attentive to the principles of the new architecture. The design followed, in general, from the dom-ino premise, stretching up eleven levels of steel frame and concrete floor slab; it rested on pilotis, opening the ground floor to the public as a passageway and reception area; it had a roof garden, designed by Roberto Burle Marx, that took advantage of its bayside location; and its glass façade was covered in louvers, which varied according to the building's different orientations relative to solar incidence.

The IRB housed a reinsurance agency, a conglomerate of Brazilian and international corporations able to secure investments in Brazil's industry. The building initially suggests, and the details of its design and construction will make clear, that modern architecture, as part of the spread of industrialization, was defined by risk. To emerge into modernity at the scale of the nation is to articulate the capacity to manage potential and perceived risk. To enter into the flow of global capital, especially in the period between World Wars I and II, was to encounter the specter of risk—as a means of managing populations amid this transition, as a means of securing financial investment, and as a means of building. The 1930s to the 1950s in Brazil saw the proliferation of shading devices as a strategy to mitigate the potential for discomfort, to take advantage of daylit interiors, and as a means to facilitate a new kind of governmental approach to economic development.[1]

New ways of building, and new ways of conceiving of the sociopolitical valence of the built environment, emerged in the late 1920s and early '30s in the context of dramatic changes to forms of governance and the terms and techniques of social control. *Population* was conceived as an object for political management and optimization, replacing conceptions of the masses, or even the proletariat, as a site for social friction. This transformation was multiply affected far beyond the terms and prospects of the built environment. All the same, by the late 1930s a new role for buildings was being conceptualized, especially in Brazil, concerned with the relationship of design and material strategies to the prospects for the elaboration of modernity, with attendant aspirations toward normalization, management, and experiential conditions of social control.

Modernism flourished first in Brazil—were we to have the capacity to assess the cubic volume enclosed by reinforced concrete, around the world, circa 1945, the largest amount would almost certainly be in Brazil, and most of it in Rio de Janeiro, the cultural and political capital of the country (figure 2.3). And almost all of it would have been subject to a carefully planned shading system. Modernism flourished as a means to build in what

2.1 MMM Roberto, Marques do Herval, Rio de Janeiro, 1952.

was perceived as a challenging climate, relative to an emergent normative model of a temperate global interior. In Brazil the question was how to use modern techniques to allow for adequate daylight and visual access to the stunning surroundings, without overheating the interior.

Modern architecture derived its logic and forms of social rationale in part from the aspiration for and construction of a normative thermal interior. The conception of a norm allowed for innovations that conditioned interiors to conform to it—that, in other words, allowed for innovations in architecture that were focused on the consistency of the planetary interior as a part of the broader set of globalizing effects. The 1930s and '40s saw a rise in standardization around commodities and trade as capital navigated the globe more quickly, and a codification of social norms around the modern subject across a wide geography. Brazil's embrace of climatic modernism, along with its environmental norms, was as an important site for the negotiation of economic, social, and political modernization more generally.[2]

The use of shading systems in Brazil could not be justified, in the period, on purely functional terms and cannot be understood historically on technical terms alone. While shading systems were, to various extents, effective in mitigating the deleterious effects of overheating, and allowed for a technical focus on daylighting, these façades were simultaneously material and symbolic projects—technological attempts to refine architectural design techniques, and formal-monumental expressions of the aspirations of the new forms of governance at play in Brazil. As a regime of building and a regime of representation, they sought to articulate new identities in line with seemingly inevitable processes of development.[3]

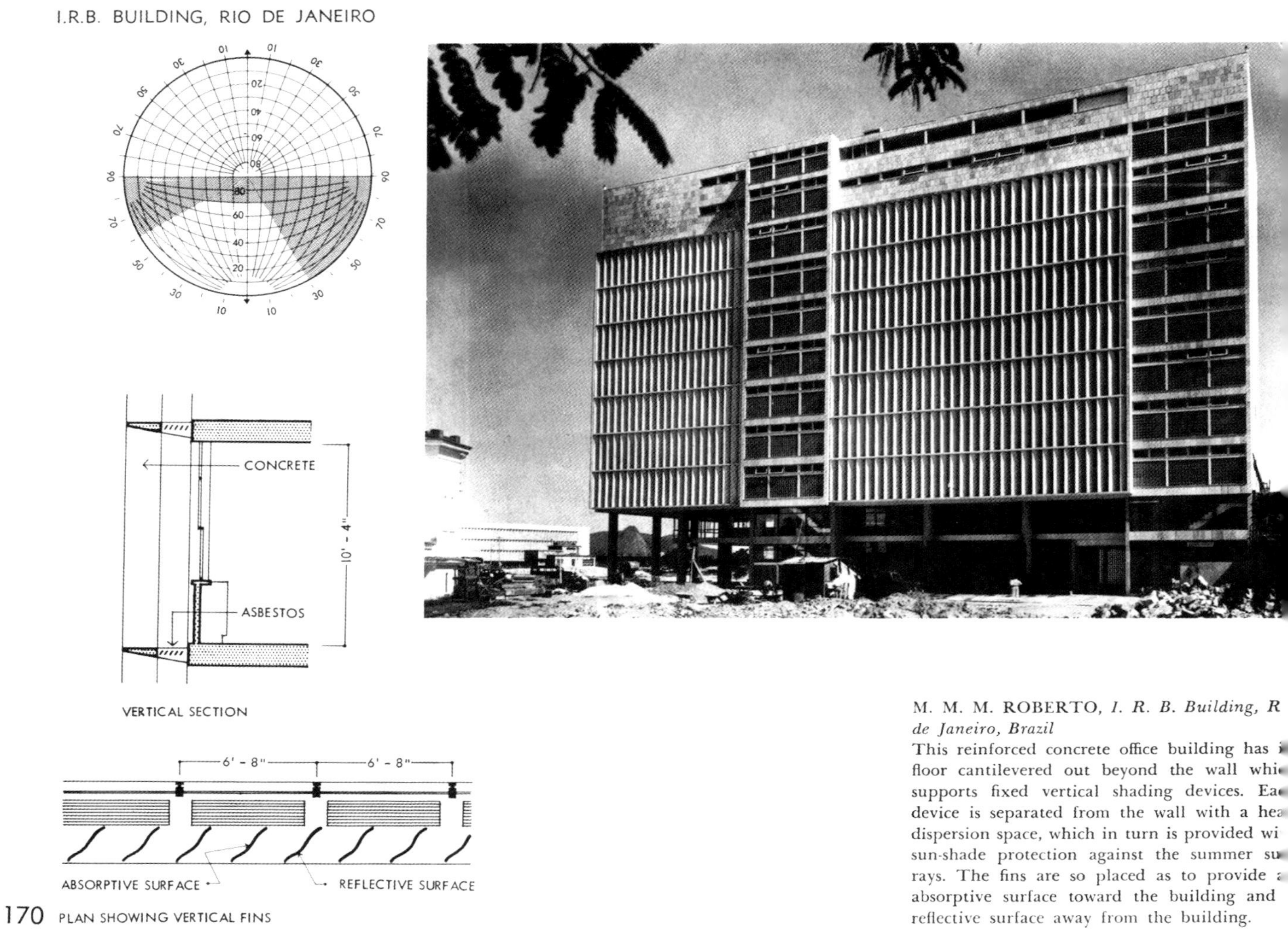
I.R.B. BUILDING, RIO DE JANEIRO



170 PLAN SHOWING VERTICAL FINS

M. M. M. ROBERTO, *I. R. B. Building, R de Janeiro, Brazil*

This reinforced concrete office building has floor cantilevered out beyond the wall whi supports fixed vertical shading devices. Ea device is separated from the wall with a hea dispersion space, which in turn is provided wi sun-shade protection against the summer su rays. The fins are so placed as to provide absorptive surface toward the building and reflective surface away from the building.

2.2 MM Roberto, Instituto de Resseguros do Brasil (IRB), Rio de Janeiro, 1936. North façade and shading analyses from Olgyay and Olgyay, *Solar Control and Shading Devices*.

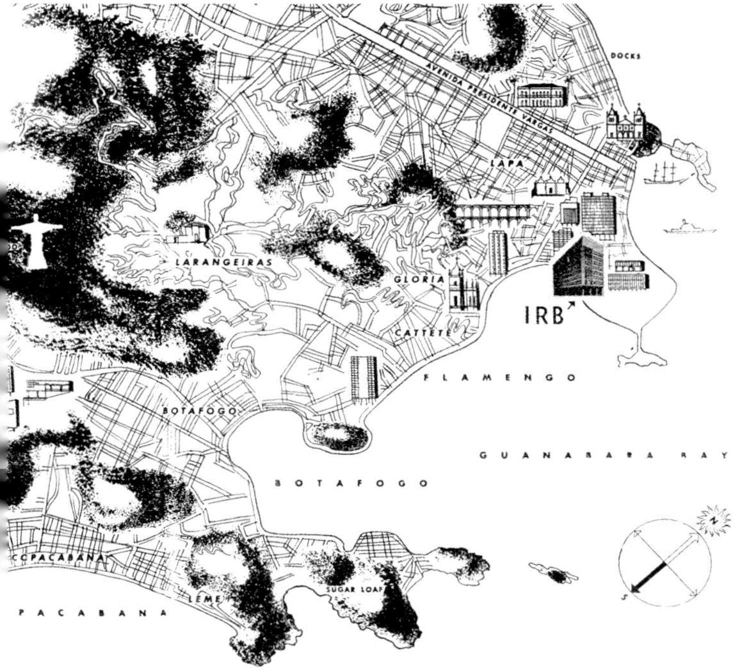


Courtesy: Museum of Modern Art

2.3 Map showing recent modern buildings in Rio, including the IRB, drawn for an issue on Brazil of *Architectural Forum*, August 1944.

A further complication, an allegorical intrusion, helps to tease out how these shaded buildings, and the environmental media that accompanied them, articulate something new. Many of the most elaborate shaded towers in 1940s Rio, and many more elsewhere, were designed and constructed for insurance corporations—or, more precisely, for national and international funds set up to be managed by global insurance corporations as a means to encourage investment in Brazil's developing economy. Design innovation was integrated into a wider range of economic and sociopolitical experiments through these processes of financialization and international development. This confluence of industrialization/development and insurance/risk will be teased out through a number of case studies as a means to explore how the shaded office tower was an architecture of risk management, on a number of scales and with complex resonance into the present.

## Education and Health; or: Another Obstacle

The IRB, as with most of the buildings discussed in this chapter, is largely unknown to the history of modern architecture. The design and construction of the building, however, closely parallels that of one of the best-known buildings in Brazil, and one of the most important modern buildings of the interwar period, the Ministerio da Educação e da Saúde (MES—Ministry of Education and Health), built from 1936 to 1942 (figure 2.4). The MES building draws abstract conceptions of historical change into a concise and poignant case study in architecture, risk, and development. Because it is well known to the history of architecture, it also helps to connect the formal, technological, and sociopolitical specificity of the shaded modernism of Brazil to a more familiar historical narrative. This accounting of the MES allows for a different sense of the contours of architectural history and its relevance—less about the reception of innovative ideas from Europe and more about the emergence of a set of sociopolitical complications. Questions for which a specific kind of building, and a specific treatment to the façade and the interior, were the answer.

The MES was designed by Lúcio Costa, Carlos Leão, Jorge Moreira, Oscar Niemeyer, Affonso Reidy, and Ernâni Vasconcelos beginning in 1936. It is a narrow, tall structure, with an auditorium intersecting the base. Like the IRB, it is the domino diagram repeated, this time up to the height of fifteen stories, with a steel frame and concrete slabs. It stands on pilotis and has two roof gardens (both designed by Roberto Burle Marx). The north, sun-facing exposure is carefully mediated by banks of operable louvers nested in an egg-crate façade; the south-facing façade is a *pan de verre*, open to the sun. The egg crate holds the façade together as a piece, as a monumental

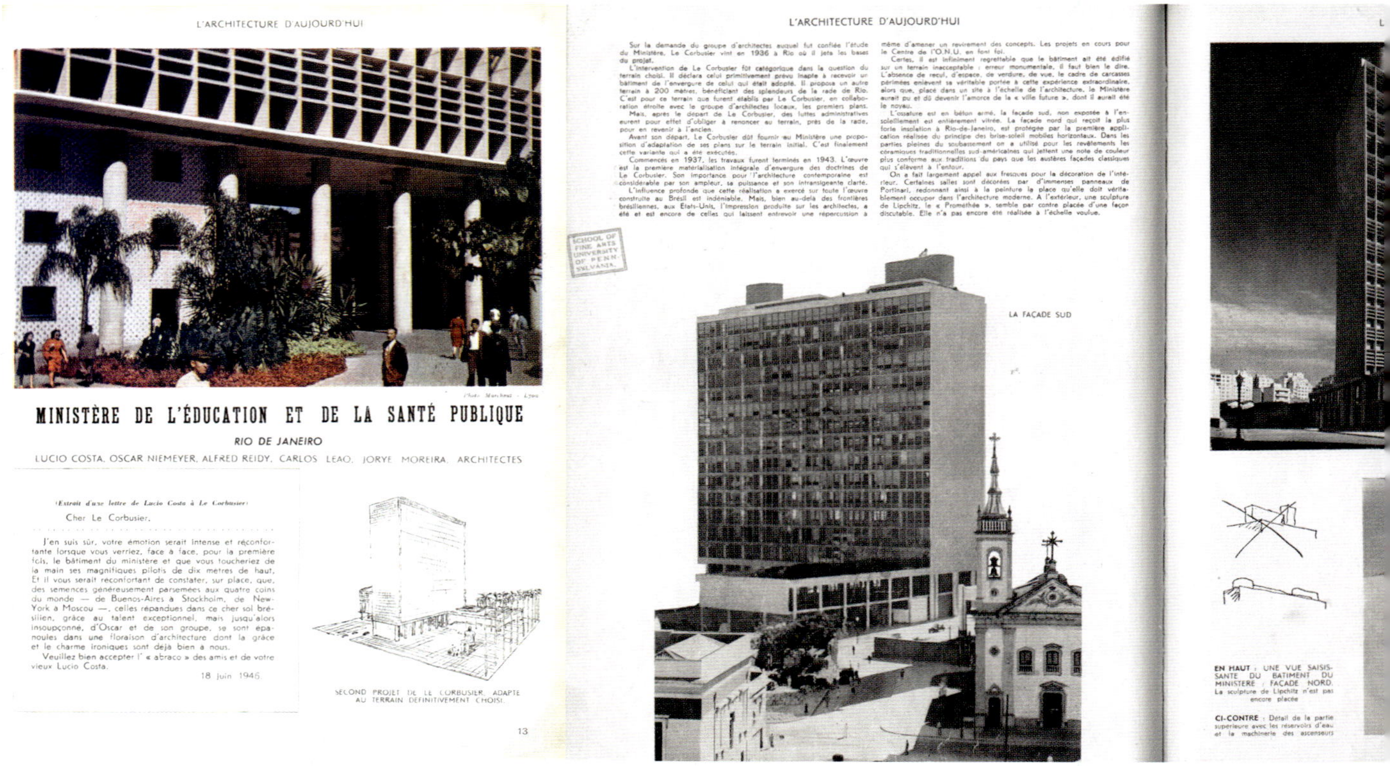

L'ARCHITECTURE D'AUJOURD'HUI

# MINISTÈRE DE L'ÉDUCATION ET DE LA SANTÉ PUBLIQUE

RIO DE JANEIRO

LUCIO COSTA, OSCAR NIEMEYER, ALFRED REIDY, CARLOS LEAO, JORYE MOREIRA, ARCHITECTES

Photo Marchaut - Lyon

(Extrait d'une lettre de Lucio Costa à Le Corbusier)

Cher Le Corbusier,

J'en suis sûr, votre émotion serait intense et réconfortante lorsque vous verriez, face à face, pour la première fois, le bâtiment du ministère et que vous toucheriez de la main ses magnifiques pilotis de dix mètres de haut. Et il vous serait réconfortant de constater, sur place, que, des semences généreusement parsemées aux quatre coins du monde — de Buenos-Aires à Stockholm, de New-York à Moscou —, celles répandues dans ce cher sol brésilien, grâce au talent exceptionnel, mais jusqu'alors insoupçonné, d'Oscar et de son groupe, se sont épanouies dans une floraison d'architecture dont la grâce et le charme ironiques sont déjà bien à nous.

Veuillez bien accepter l' « abraço » des amis et de votre vieux Lucio Costa.

18 juin 1946.

SECOND PROJET DE LE CORBUSIER, ADAPTE AU TERRAIN DEFINITIVEMENT CHOISI.

13

L'ARCHITECTURE D'AUJOURD'HUI

Sur la demande du groupe d'architectes auquel fut confiée l'étude du Ministère, Le Corbusier vint en 1936 à Rio où il jeta les bases du projet.

L'intervention de Le Corbusier fût catégorique dans la question du terrain choisi. Il déclara celui primitivement prévu inapte à recevoir un bâtiment de l'envergure de celui qui était adopté. Il proposa un autre terrain à 200 mètres, bénéficiant des splendeurs de la rade de Rio. C'est pour ce terrain que furent établis par Le Corbusier, en collaboration étroite avec le groupe d'architectes locaux, les premiers plans.

Mais, après le départ de Le Corbusier, des luttes administratives eurent pour effet d'obliger à renoncer au terrain, près de la rade, pour en revenir à l'ancien.

Avant son départ, Le Corbusier dût fournir au Ministère une proposition d'adaptation de ses plans sur le terrain initial. C'est finalement cette variante qui a été exécutée.

Commencés en 1937, les travaux furent terminés en 1943. L'œuvre est la première matérialisation intégrale d'envergure des doctrines de Le Corbusier. Son importance pour l'architecture contemporaine est considérable par son ampleur, sa puissance et son intransigeante clarté.

L'influence profonde que cette réalisation a exercé sur toute l'œuvre construite au Brésil est indéniable. Mais, bien au-delà des frontières brésiliennes, aux États-Unis, l'impression produite sur les architectes, a été et est encore de celles qui laissent entrevoir une répercussion à même d'amener un revirement des concepts. Les projets en cours pour le Centre de l'O.N.U. en font foi.

Certes, il est infiniment regrettable que le bâtiment ait été édifié sur un terrain inacceptable : erreur monumentale, il faut bien le dire. L'absence de recul, d'espace, de verdure, de vue, le cadre de carcasses périmées enlèvent sa véritable portée à cette expérience extraordinaire, alors que, placé dans un site à l'échelle de l'architecture, le Ministère aurait pu et dû devenir l'amorce de la « ville future », dont il aurait été le noyau.

L'ossature est en béton armé, la façade sud, non exposée à l'ensoleillement est entièrement vitrée. La façade nord qui reçoit la plus forte insolation à Rio-de-Janeiro, est protégée par la première application réalisée du principe des brise-soleil mobiles horizontaux. Dans les parties pleines du soubassement on a utilisé pour les revêtements les céramiques traditionnelles sud-américaines qui jettent une note de couleur plus conforme aux traditions du pays que les austères façades classiques qui s'élèvent à l'entour.

On a fait largement appel aux fresques pour la décoration de l'intérieur. Certaines salles sont décorées par d'immenses panneaux de Portinari, redonnant ainsi à la peinture la place qu'elle doit véritablement occuper dans l'architecture moderne. A l'extérieur, une sculpture de Lipchitz, le « Prométhée », semble par contre placée d'une façon discutable. Elle n'a pas encore été réalisée à l'échelle voulue.

LA FAÇADE SUD

EN HAUT : UNE VUE SAISISSANTE DU BATIMENT DU MINISTERE : FAÇADE NORD. La sculpture de Lipchitz n'est pas encore placée

CI-CONTRE : Détail de la partie supérieure avec les réservoirs d'eau et la machinerie des ascenseurs

2.4 Lucio Costa, Oscar Niemeyer, Carlos Leão, Affonso Eduardo Reidy, Ernani Vasconcelos, et al., Ministerio da Educação e da Saúde (MES), Rio de Janeiro, 1936–43, from *L'Architecture d'aujourd'hui*, 1947.

screen, while the variation in each module is visually dynamic and effective as a climate modulation device.

The MES established the basic approach of the shaded office building, produced throughout Brazil and the southern hemisphere more generally—a tall, rectangular tower often with a more free-form addition, usually for public function, at the base.[4] The façade of the MES operates as media, articulating an interface between social practices and geophysical conditions. It offers a precise relationship between the interior and exterior, one that operates materially by adjusting thermal and daylight conditions, and symbolically by making visible the governmental transformations and socioeconomic ambitions of the Brazilian state.

In the early development of the design, Costa made a sectional diagram indicating how the moveable louvers would relate to the diurnal passage of the sun—as the sun reaches different heights, a lever can adjust the angle of the three louvers independently in each egg-crate module, so as to best shade a given room in the interior (figure 2.5). In doing this, he clarified an important principle: physical interaction with the façade is an essential aspect of its shading capacity. In other words, the thermal conditions of the interior are conceptualized in relationship to the physiological presence of a universal subject in a specific space. Such a subject can adjust the lever, moving the louver, to block the sun as it moves across the sky, or to otherwise alter the experience of the interior (figure 2.6). Social practices and embodied habits are essential to the proper functioning of the system.

This is emphasized by the attention paid in the façade section to the capacity for the office worker, at least while standing (as drawn), to view the exterior, and also in relationship to the need, or not, for artificial light in these different states. Artificial illumination is represented in the drawing by the dot just below the ceiling in the iteration of the shaded mechanism represented at the far

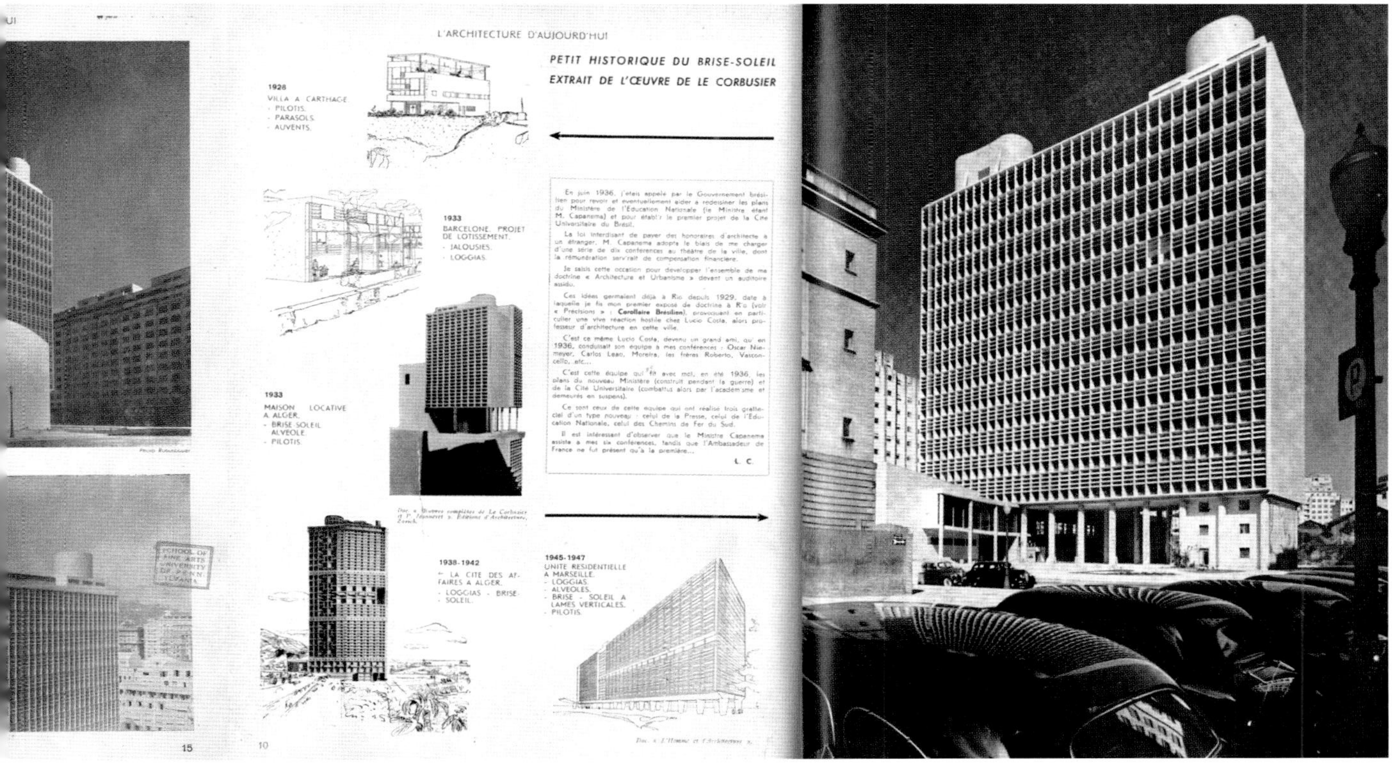

L'ARCHITECTURE D'AUJOURD'HUI

PETIT HISTORIQUE DU BRISE-SOLEIL
EXTRAIT DE L'ŒUVRE DE LE CORBUSIER

1928
VILLA A CARTHAGE.
- PILOTIS.
- PARASOLS.
- AUVENTS.

1933
BARCELONE. PROJET DE LOTISSEMENT.
- JALOUSIES.
- LOGGIAS.

1933
MAISON LOCATIVE A ALGER.
- BRISE-SOLEIL ALVEOLE.
- PILOTIS.

En juin 1936, j'étais appelé par le Gouvernement brésilien pour revoir et éventuellement aider à redessiner les plans du Ministère de l'Éducation Nationale (le Ministre étant M. Capanema) et pour établir le premier projet de la Cité Universitaire du Brésil.

La loi interdisant de payer des honoraires d'architecte à un étranger, M. Capanema adopta le biais de me charger d'une série de dix conférences au théâtre de la ville, dont la rémunération serv'rait de compensation financière.

Je saisis cette occasion pour développer l'ensemble de ma doctrine « Architecture et Urbanisme » devant un auditoire assidu.

Ces idées germaient déjà à Rio depuis 1929, date à laquelle je fis mon premier exposé de doctrine à Rio (voir « Précisions » : **Corollaire Brésilien**), provoquant en particulier une vive réaction hostile chez Lucio Costa, alors professeur d'architecture en cette ville.

C'est ce même Lucio Costa, devenu un grand ami, qui en 1936, conduisait son équipe à mes conférences : Oscar Niemeyer, Carlos Leao, Moreira, les frères Roberto, Vasconcello, etc...

C'est cette équipe qui fit avec moi, en été 1936, les plans du nouveau Ministère (construit pendant la guerre) et de la Cité Universitaire (combattus alors par l'académisme et demeurés en suspens).

Ce sont ceux de cette équipe qui ont réalisé trois gratte-ciel d'un type nouveau : celui de la Presse, celui de l'Education Nationale, celui des Chemins de Fer du Sud.

Il est intéressant d'observer que le Ministre Capanema assiste à mes six conférences, tandis que l'Ambassadeur de France ne fut présent qu'à la première...

L. C.

Doc. « Œuvres complètes de Le Corbusier et P. Jeanneret », Éditions d'Architecture, Zurich.

1938-1942
← LA CITE DES AFFAIRES A ALGER.
- LOGGIAS - BRISE-SOLEIL.

1945-1947
UNITE RESIDENTIELLE A MARSEILLE.
- LOGGIAS.
- ALVEOLES.
- BRISE-SOLEIL A LAMES VERTICALES.
- PILOTIS.

Doc. « L'Homme et l'Architecture ».

10

15

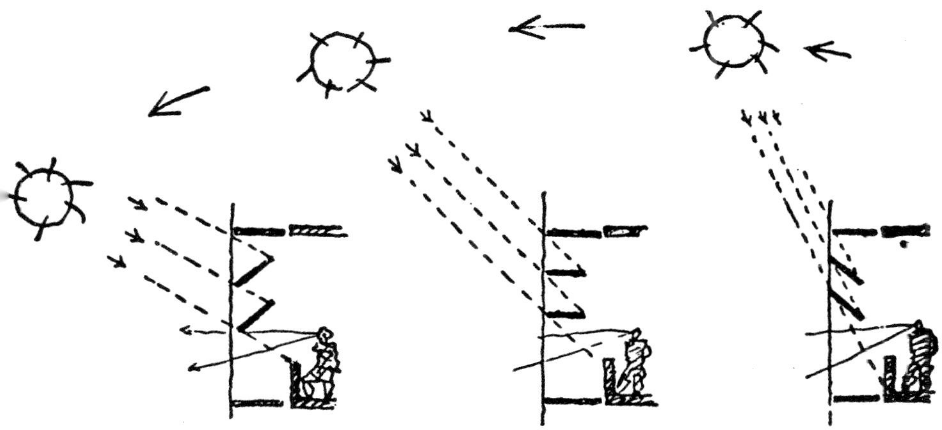

2.5 Lucio Costa, drawing of the daily path of the sun in relationship to the louver system and the daylit conditions of the interior of the MES.

2.6 Louvers and louver-adjustment system at the MES. The building was undergoing renovation at the time of this photograph, and the system was not yet working (again).

right, when less daylight is entering the space. The architecture is eliciting complex forms of behavioral and physiological interaction in order to achieve its designed promise. The MES not only established the active façade as an essential element in a climatic architecture, it also promoted consideration to physical interaction with the façade itself; in both cases new technical images were needed to understand the relations being invoked and manipulated.[5]

The building was an early iteration of the principles of climatic design. In an important way Costa's diagram is more about weather than climate—it does not suggest the complexities of the solar angle as diurnal patterns intersect and develop alongside seasonal patterns. The arc is oversimplified, unidimensional. It was, in this sense, a spark, an instigation to more elaborate discussions around the integration of architectural ideas and the also-emerging contours of scientific knowledge of climate.

The MES is one of the more prominent obstacles to contend with given the historiographic legacy of Le Corbusier. In most accounts, including his own, Le Corbusier is seen to be instrumental to the Brazilian building's design, even though ample evidence suggests otherwise. Certainly the design parameters of the building were conceived in relationship to the influence of European architectural ideas on Brazilian cultural and educational developments. While a general field of influence and counterinfluence is clear—when Le Corbusier first visited Brazil in 1929, he had a strong effect on the work of Costa and many others—it was a two-way street, in which Le Corbusier and his Brazilian colleagues took much from each other in a period when the principles of modernism were undergoing elaboration and refinement (figure 2.7).[6]

The changing political and economic ambitions of the Brazilian state provided a complex context for this architectural elaboration. The Ministry of Education and Health itself—the government agency, that is, not the building—was created ten days into the administration of Getúlio Vargas, in November 1930 (it was initially called the Ministry of Education and *Public* Health—MESP).[7] Vargas had come to power in October through what was effectively a bloodless coup. From Rio Grande do Sul, the southernmost Brazilian state, with the army beside him, Vargas took advantage of alarm over a supposed communist plot in the midst of an election and deposed the democratically elected president.[8]

The Vargas regime, after 1937 referred to as the Estado Novo (new state), was, on the one hand, forward looking—the creation of the MESP (again, the Ministry not the building) suggests the administration's seemingly beneficent approach

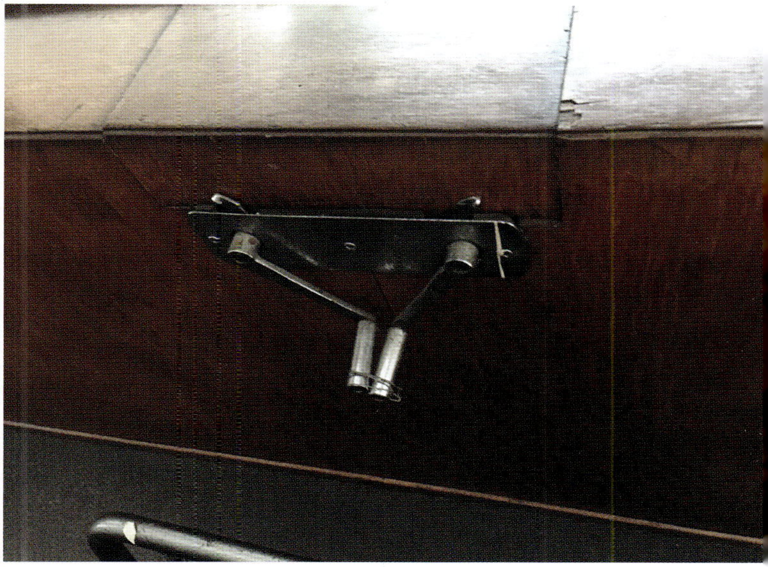

to managing and providing for the body politic. The state, the Ministry suggests, had begun to take on a new kind of responsibility to care for the population, one that was expressed through a regime of managerial imperatives. These new "arts of governance" were focused on how methods of social control infused the daily practices and activities of the population within a given milieu.[9] Diagrammatically, this governmentalized state is concerned with population as an abstract field of individuals; its health and disposition becomes a statistical body that can be optimized according to perceived needs.[10]

The Vargas regime cannot be separated from its authoritarian ambitions. Between 1930 and 1945, Vargas concentrated power in his administration, his confidants, and through the agencies—from the MES to departments for labor, resources, and finance—that he placed under his control. Especially compelling is how the seemingly progressive aesthetics of architectural modernism was embraced by an explicitly authoritarian regime.

The Ministry was, in significant ways, the face—the façade—of this new administration. In 1935, soon after Vargas passed a new constitution, the Minister of Education and Health, Gustavo Capanema, wrote: "Under the provisions laid out in the constitution, the mission of the Ministry of Education, and the government as a whole, can be summed up in one word: culture. Or, perhaps better stated, national culture."[11] The centralized government saw culture as a central aspect of a wide range of social reforms. Active cultural management of the MES was the vehicle through which Vargas aimed to rid the country of what he saw as the misconceptions of his liberal predecessors. The MES developed and managed federal policies that intended to ameliorate the living conditions of the populace while simultaneously increasing the power of the centralized state and also responding to an imperative for change, including dramatic cultural and economic reform.[12]

The Ministry provided a material and symbolic regime of health management, including collective insurance, clinics and vaccines, care around pregnancy and birth, and early education. It symbolized hope for, and established a material trajectory toward, a prosperous Brazilian future. The Ministry, and the Estado Novo more generally, articulated a very specific form of bureaucratized governmental activity focused on the conceptualization of citizens as a population to be optimized. Forms of labor, economic activity, insurance, and growth framed a new approach to the population, alongside techniques, media, and processing systems

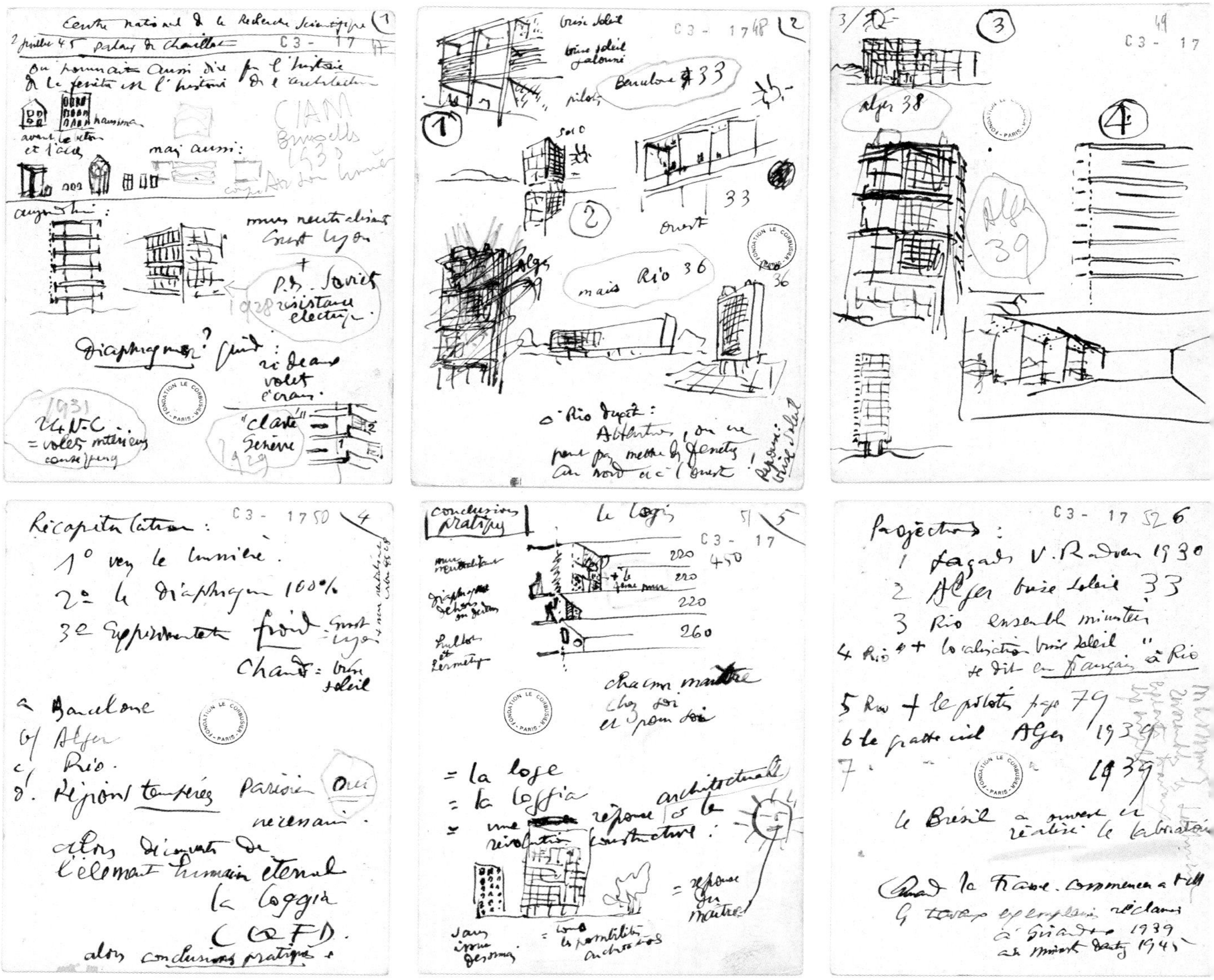

2.7 Le Corbusier, sketches for "Une petite histoire du brise soleil chez Le Corbusier," see figure 1.24.

through which demographic, educational, health, and other population data could be put to work.

The distant Brazilian interior in particular came to be subject to agencies such as the MES as a means of exercising power toward a population seen to be requiring integration into modern ways of life. This included the assessment of health protocols and education benefits through risk calculations, the rapid monetization of the population as a labor force, and the placement of the body politic in a more active and exploitative relationship to natural resources.[13] MES Radio brought entertainment and educational programs to the deep reaches of the interior. Health bulletins and training programs, it was hoped, could help bring the wider population up to a new quality of life standard—better education, improved life expectancy, the eradication of communicable disease.[14] The maintenance of the human mind and body, in other words, was placed in broad relationship to the public—and was integrated, symbolically, into the open entryways, spacious interiors, and carefully articulated, technologically inflected, dynamic façade system for producing the modern interior at the MES and other buildings.

A broad conception of the milieu, at once cultural, technological, and instrumental to economic change, becomes the site for intervention of state power and risk management. Resource, infrastructure, and material conditions of the environment are coextensive with social processes; bureaucratic forms of management and scientific forms of knowledge inform these material conditions and also inform concepts of innovation in architectural practices. Cultural or formal developments in architecture are both cause and effect relative to these tactics of population management and the broader strategies of campaigns, codes, and guidelines.[15]

In other words, the specifics of an architectural approach are reflected in the conditioning of the subject. The *subject*, in this sense, is a subject of politics; of labor, training, and economic integration. The subject is also a participant in a given thermal regime—engaged in the management of shading systems, lights, and ventilation; and itself a generator of heat that needs to be dispersed. The design and production of acclimatized spaces in the urban core has resonance far into the hinterlands insofar is it reflects a range of governmental practices and priorities, and a framing of the subject, individual and collective, as available for optimization according to thermal and other architectural interventions. This sort of people conditioning emerges as a central theme of the political and bureaucratic transformations of Brazil; people conditioning also suggests a more general economic and political disruption as social and economic systems are changing, globalizing, and accommodating themselves to new flows of resources and capital. The geopolitical processes of subject formation begins to pass through thermal interiors, conditioning bodies to experience and engage with specific thermal environments according to physiological norms and expectations geopolitical and geophysical, mediated by the technical systems of the façade.

When Vargas came to power in 1930, he saw a reorientation of national culture as essential to Brazil's industrialization and economic expansion. A week after Vargas started the Ministry of Education and Health, Lucio Costa, then just twenty-eight, was invited by that Ministry to take over the Escola Nacional de Belas Artes (ENBA), the most important school of art and architecture in the country.[16] At the time of his appointment, Costa was best known as an eclectic neocolonialist (on design terms) with an interest in the new ideas informing the field and sensitive to the ways in which architecture was capturing the changing relationship between Brazil and its European former colonial rulers.[17] However delicate his approach, in his appointment at ENBA he sought to expand Brazilian engagement with modern ideas.

The emergence of the new architecture in Brazil in 1930 also circulated around the work of Gregori Warchavchik, a Ukrainian émigré to São Paulo who had studied in Odessa and Rome and worked for Marcello Piacentini in Italy before arriving in Brazil in 1923. His Casa da Rua Santa Cruz (1928) in São Paulo is often celebrated as the first modern building in Brazil, though, as Daniela Sandler has argued, it was a largely superficial approach to modernism, with traditional building techniques covered with a sort of unifying plaster façade.[18] It was a modernism, in a sense, without the benefits of the material possibilities embedded in new technologies and spatial conceptions. It exhibited, however, the relevant cultural effects, encouraging architects and others to reconsider the way they lived in the environment. From 1930, Costa and Warchavchik were in partnership in Rio. The firm employed both Niemeyer and Reidy.[19]

Costa headed ENBA for only ten months—December 1930 to September 1931. Before his tenure, the school had been run following the French Beaux-Arts model, then the standard pedagogical mode—as was also the case with almost every school of architecture in the United States. Costa himself had graduated from ENBA in 1924. His directive at the school was to change the curriculum, in part to bring it into contact with the relatively new Universidade do Rio de Janeiro. He embraced this imperative; however, he had little power to effect change, aside from appointing some colleagues (such as Warchavchik) to teach. An entrenched bureaucracy and faculty stood in his way; the abruptness with which he attempted the shift toward modernism was largely unexpected and was met with alarm. In April 1931, after he had altered the student exhibition system and attempted to transform the curriculum by decree, he was removed from the position. Sympathetic students went on strike; Frank Lloyd Wright, in Rio to give a lecture, made a plea to continue the modernist direction. Costa was pushed out, and ENBA reverted to its previous

2.8 MM Roberto, Associação Brasileira de Imprensa (ABI), Rio de Janeiro, 1936. A collage of the building on site, published in *Arquitetura e Urbanismo* in 1937; the built version in the same journal in December 1940; and a page from an article on the building in *L'Architecture d'aujourd'hui*, 1947.

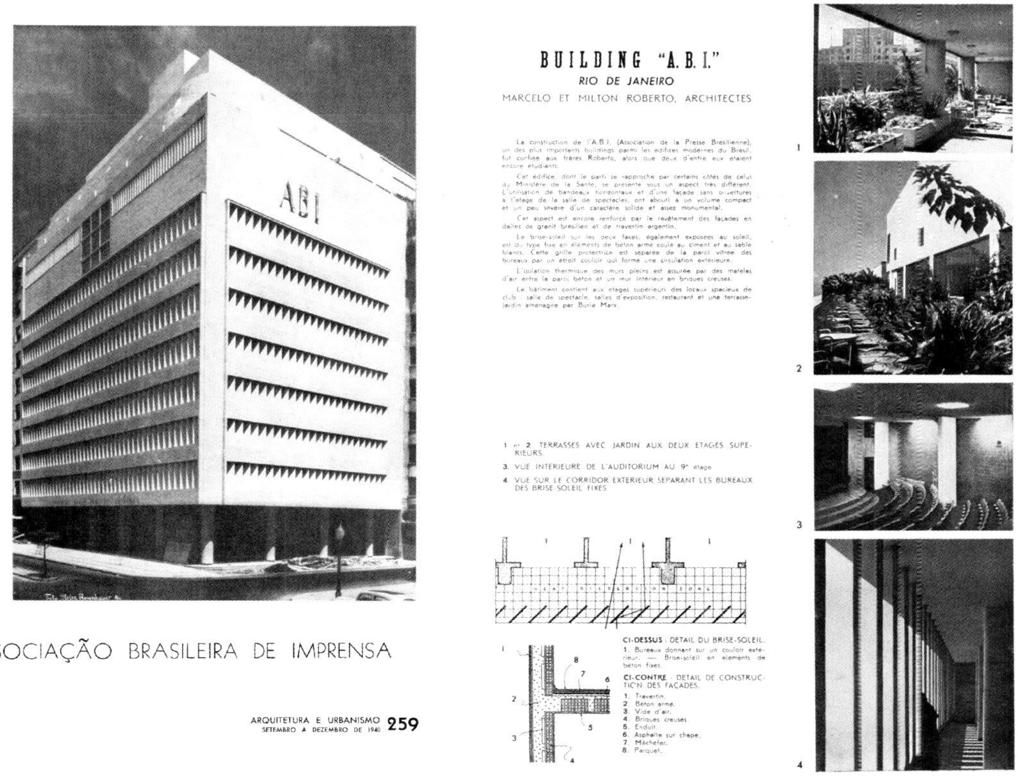


Beaux-Arts focus. In 1945, a second architecture school was founded, the Faculdade Nacional de Arquitetura, which reinstituted a version of Costa's 1931 curricular plan.[20]

Costa was given the MES commission five years later. Almost all members of the team he hired to work on the project were students from his 1930–31 year at ENBA (as was Mauricio Roberto, the youngest brother of the family firm that designed the IRB and many other shaded buildings discussed further on).[21] Costa requested Le Corbusier as a consultant, and the Swiss-French architect returned to Rio in late 1936 by invitation from Gustavo Capanema, the Minister of Education and Health. The authoritarian nature of the Vargas regime made Capanema an ideal client. Such a power formation conformed to the master's ideas about the ruling capacity of the technocratic elite at a time when he was struggling to build at the scale of his ambition.[22]

As it happened, Le Corbusier's main intervention was to propose moving the building from the Distrito Federal in central Rio to a site by Guanabara Bay, which was not available to the Ministry. He drew a low-slung, longer building that he thought more appropriate to the region—it is not unlike, in its general approach, the Museu de Arte Moderna do Rio de Janeiro that Affonso Reidy later built on the same site.[23] As Le Corbusier described it:

> I discovered 200 meters from [the Ministry site], on the coast of the sea, an admirable site; the palace could roll out in front of majestic sites, open its *pan de verre* completely upon an inestimable view. My Brazilian colleagues cried: "You can't orient your façade like that, in Rio de Janeiro!"—"And why not?"—"Because of the sun!" And they explained to me their efforts. I responded: "Don't worry, we will install in front of the *pan de verre* a *brise-soleil*." And I drew on the plan what we were discussing in our proposal for Barcelona and for Algiers.[24]

One assumes that the Brazilians may have explained to him that, by 1936, not only was the IRB building under construction, with various shading schemes, but also the Roberto brothers' Associação Brasileira de Imprensa (ABI—Brazilian Press Association) was already largely complete, with a façade of fixed louvers hung in front of a *pan de verre* (figure 2.8). In the photograph, it is shown

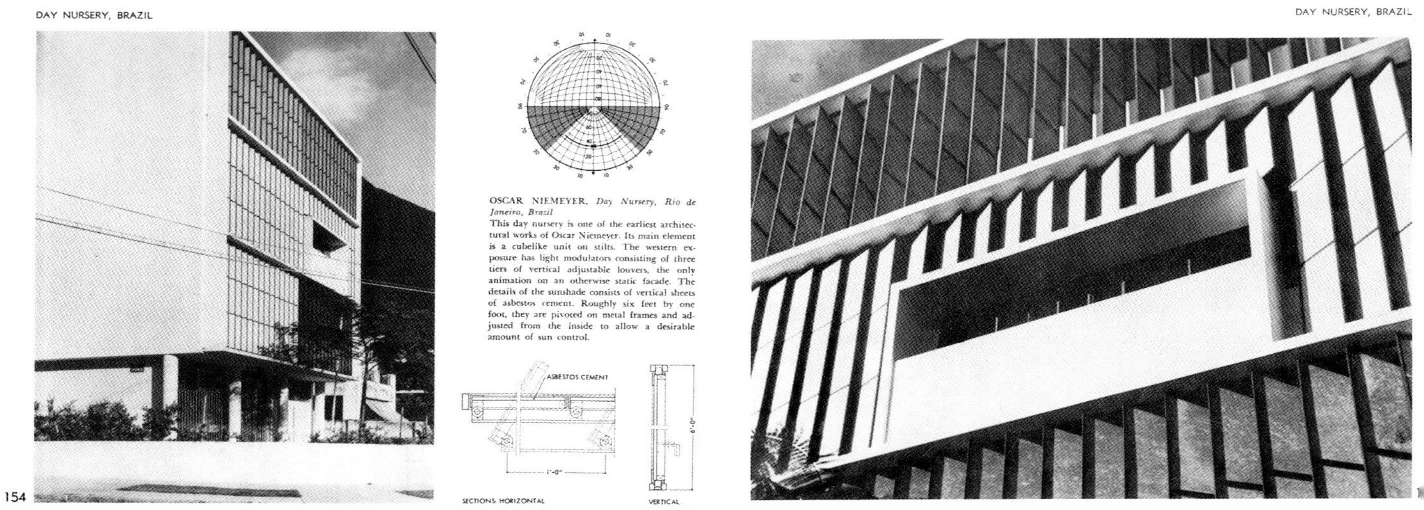


2.9 Oscar Niemeyer, Obra do Berço, Rio de Janeiro, 1935–38; from Olgyay and Olgyay, *Solar Control and Shading Devices*, 1957.

collaged into the existing cityscape, suggesting the cultural disruptions of the modern, thermally attentive style as well as the crucial role of new media practices in articulating it. The ABI was in a prominent site in downtown Rio, just a block from where the Ministry would be built. It was likely the first modern shaded building ever built.[25] The Roberto brothers' passenger terminal for the Aeroporto Santos Dumont and their headquarters for the Instituto de Resseguros do Brasil were also past the design development stage by this time, again in prominent parts of the city and subject to extensive press coverage.[26]

Niemeyer's Obra do Berço, his first commission, was designed in 1935 and was under construction when Le Corbusier arrived in Brazil, it was completed in 1938 (figure 2.9).[27] The Obra do Berço was a small building designed for a foundation that served young children and their mothers in the Lagoa section of Rio. It had three different banks of operable louvers, each level could be adjusted so that light was modulated differently for different uses. By this time Luis Nunes was also building in Recife, in the north of Brazil, constructing small towers with carefully tuned shading mechanisms. The principles that Le Corbusier claimed to be explaining to the Brazilians were, in fact, already part of the architectural culture in Brazil and were being explored as a central aspect of the country's participation in global modernity.[28]

Indeed, the historiographic inflection, once these Corbusian obstacles are overcome, is even more consequential. Recently, the American historian and curator Barry Bergdoll wrote, referencing important buildings of South American modernism in the wartime period, that these buildings "are not the belated reflections of examples set in Europe, but previsions of a modernization to come." A premediation, perhaps: "lessons from the 'underdeveloped' world," Bergdoll continues, were "useful even for the 'developed' world to contemplate."[29] Bergdoll offers a significant historiographic inversion: Brazil was a site of emergence—of production—as much (if not more so) as it was a site for reception of modern architectural ideas. This is especially the case relative to designed engagement with climate. The arrow of history here moves from south to north. The terms on which innovation occurred were relative to the capacity for modern design tropes to be effective as a climatically adaptive, regionally engaged style—expressed, more often than not, through the façade.

Climate was central to many aspects of Brazil's modernization efforts, architectural and otherwise. One of Vargas's primary aspirations was to bring Brazil into a different relationship to geopolitical and geoeconomic systems. Indeed, much of the work of centralizing the government—and of educating the populace—was according to proposals about labor, investment, and other characteristics of the emerging conditions of globalizing capital.[30] Materiality and distance were seen as barriers and opportunities, as the Brazilian government sought to articulate, through buildings and through public policy, a viable, regionally specific approach to industrialization and economic growth. The first Minister of Education and Health, Francisco Campos, saw the project of the Ministry, as one historian recently put it, as that of "rejecting four decades of social engineering informed by pessimistic theories of racial and climatological degeneracy," here Campos is reiterating the premise of climatic determinism that underlay much of the discussion of how to "normalize" the thermal interior.[31]

Climate mitigation in the built interior was a small but significant aspect of the goal of conservative revolutionaries to modernize Brazil through social and economic reforms, and one that implied a convergence of these goals with the promise of modern architecture and a more substantive role of Brazil in global networks. The entanglement of climate and architecture with geopolitics and geophysics, and this sort of subtle panic across the Global South relative to the still persistent theory of climatic determinism, was not exclusive to Brazil. Approaches to architecture and governance, now inflected by the complex shift from colonial conditions of direct control to more complex forms of corporate, pedagogical, and infrastructural management, were essential to reimagining projects and practice of the field.[32]

This represented a fundamental shift from prewar functionalism toward a postwar design operationalism, a transition mapped across these buildings in Brazil, as architectural strategies of climatic adaptability were integrated into processes of modernization. Neocolonial projects across West Africa by Jane Drew and Maxwell Fry and other tropical architects, interpretations of modernism in Singapore and Malaysia, the US Foreign Building Office stipulating shading screens and other recognizably modern interpretations of traditional practices—not to mention the more general use of shading systems and climatic devices in the architecture of American suburbia and in office buildings around the world—begin to suggest the wider dissemination of these strategies in the period, just before air conditioning took command of the building industry and the designers who worked with it.[33]

## The Insurational Imaginary

The Ministry of Education and Health (the Ministry *and* the building) was a sociopolitical assemblage for understanding and managing social risk, for assessing and mediating the uncertainties of the future, and for optimizing the living and working conditions of the populace. Perhaps even more compelling, all the same, than the details of the building itself is the model that it presents—the MES is a concentrated version, in program, façade, and orientation, of a more general and diffuse transformation to Brazil's built environment, and it suggests a different set of prospects for architectural modernity. From the late 1930s, the economic expansion and proliferation of shaded buildings in Brazil was momentous—epochal in defining an approach to architecture and governance, and in opening up the field of architecture to a different framework for assessing the value of a given design. Shaded buildings facilitated the industrialization of Brazil by producing operable and consistent interiors and shepherded the entry of its economy, culture, and people in a new relationship with global flows and patterns.

The firm of MMM Roberto, consisting of the three brothers—Marcelo, Milton, and Mauricio—offers some of the most precise and compelling expressions of the façade as a mediator, conflating thermal, economic, and social conceptions of value. As the authoritarian government saw modernism as a means to move its agenda forward, the Robertos gained favor among the political and economic elite.[34] Their design for the ABI (the Brazilian Press Association), mentioned previously, was their first major commission, awarded by competition and built in Vargas' newly centralized government seat, the Distrito Federal in Rio.[35]

At the ABI, fixed louvers sit at distance from the interior wall across a "heat dispersion zone" that was also a corridor for auxiliary circulation (figure 2.10). The shading panels are angled to block the sun at summer solstice, with a thickness that made the balcony space feel like an interior.[36] Their rigidity and immobility reduced their effectiveness on managing the thermal interior, though it allowed that space, sheathed in glass, to have an open, airy feel. In addition to the shading elements, the building also had a mechanical ventilation system to keep air flowing across the relatively

2.10 Photographs of the interior of the ABI building, 2015.

2.11 Installing the ventilation system at the ABI, from *Arquitetura e Urbanismo*, March/April 1937.

2.12 MM Roberto, Aeroporto Santos Dumont, Rio de Janeiro, 1936–1944, from *L'Architecture d'aujourd'hui*, 1950.

open office floors (figure 2.11). The reception area at the base, under a first floor supported by pilotis, was open to the street, effectively an outdoor space. It was the first modern building in the Distrito Federal.

The Roberto brothers' second commission, also won through a Vargas administration competition, was for the passenger terminal building of the Aeroporto Santos Dumont, begun on a site to the southeast of the Distrito Federal in 1936, completed in 1937 (figure 2.12). It is just across the street, literally, from where the Instituto de Resseguros do Brasil (IRB) would be built starting in 1938. The airport is visible from the open entryway to the IRB, and from its Roberto Burle Marx designed roof terrace (figure 2.13). Today the secondary, regional airport in downtown Rio, Santos Dumont was at the time a central piece of Vargas's modernization project, connecting the growing city to Europe and the United States as well as to São Paulo and the interior. The airport terminal building's large, moveable louvers on the glass façade helped to light and acclimatize the open, high-columned interior. Rio's entry into modernity was one of openness and engagement with the sun. The shading skin was essential, both logistically and symbolically, to bring Brazil onto the world stage.

The liminal condition of the shaded office tower is clearly expressed in the Instituto de Resseguros do Brasil.[37] The building straddled and integrated a range of significant historical passages: from low- to high-rise modern office buildings, from climatic determinism to architectural possibility, and from the social project of the masses to the

2.13 The Roberto Burle Marx designed roof deck of the IRB, with a view to the Aeroporto Santos Dumont.

calculational matrix of the population. Even on strictly formal terms, it was an innovative hybrid, what the editors of *Architectural Forum* described as "a clever blending of the regular, formalist architectural block with ingenious methods of insulation against heat and glare."[38]

The IRB itself—the Institute, not the building—was begun as part of Vargas's initial rise to power in 1930. It was a fund—60 percent from Brazilian government contribution, 40 percent from major global insurers and reinsurers—intended to stabilize the property market and provide capital and coverage for investment in Brazil. It provided life insurance as well as fire, marine, inland, disability, and accident insurance and aviation and shipping insurance. The IRB still operates today, in this same capacity, with funding from the government and reinsurance corporations such as Swiss Re and Lloyds of London.

The building was built on a coastal site that had been a hill but, like much of central Rio, was graded to allow for more buildable space. It was the front door for international capital arriving by plane—from London, New York, Paris, or elsewhere–at the Aeroporto Santos Dumont, entering the Estado Novo to participate in the economic development of Brazil.

The IRB, though mechanically ventilated like the ABI, had an elaborate set of shading mechanisms—it was carefully designed for dynamic interaction with its microclimate. Unlike the ABI, which had the same louver system on both exposed façades, at the IRB the different façades had different treatments, according to their solar exposure. If the ABI was the first shaded tower, the IRB was the first example of what the architects Victor and Aladar Olgyay would later term "bioclimatic" architecture, carefully designed according to precise knowledge of its regional and climatic specificity.[39]

The building presented a stark, rational exterior, solidly built and technologically engaged. The north, sun-facing façade was mostly covered with fixed shading louvers. Two vertical bars of glass bricks provided daylight for two separate circulation systems, one for the public and one for government and corporate access, while also breaking up the consistent plane of the façade. The north façade consisted of a double skin—the first, interior face was about two-thirds glazing, with the second, shading façade hung at a slight distance. The second skin was prefabricated and attached on site in a mere two weeks. The Burle Marx designed roof garden was similar to the contemporaneous one at the MES.

As drawings and photographs indicate, the exterior, second skin contained fixed brise-soleil elements. The Robertos use a range of media to explain the façade details (figure 2.14). The brise-soleil were reinforced concrete louvers formed in

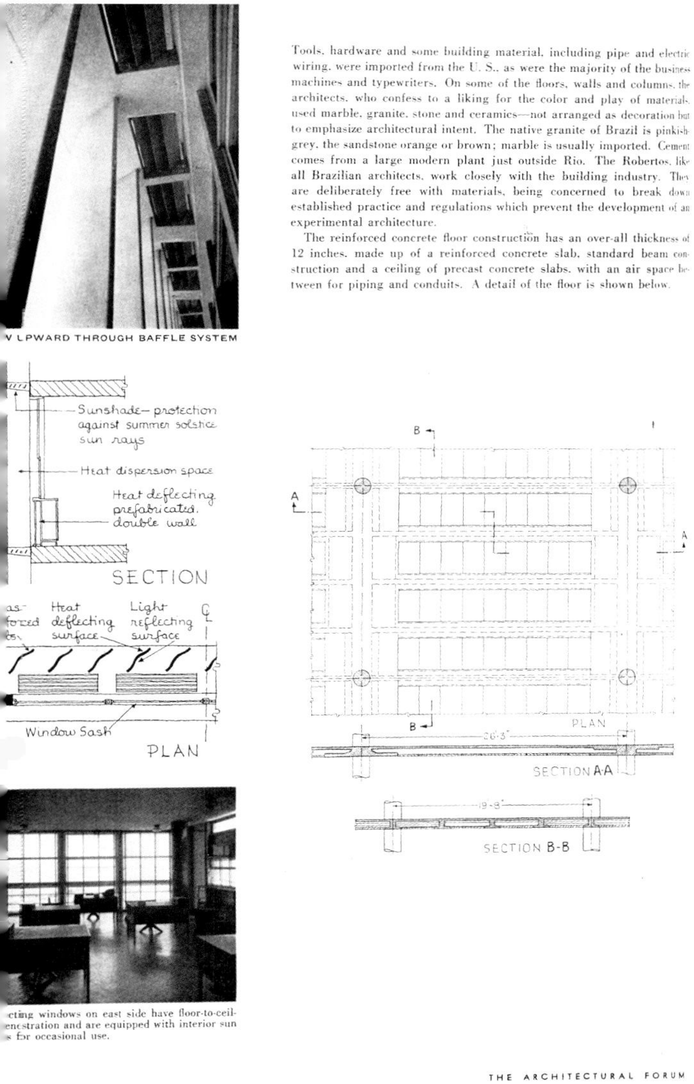

V LPWARD THROUGH BAFFLE SYSTEM



cting windows on east side have floor-to-ceil-
enestration and are equipped with interior sun
s for occasional use.

Tools, hardware and some building material, including pipe and electric wiring, were imported from the U. S., as were the majority of the business machines and typewriters. On some of the floors, walls and columns, the architects, who confess to a liking for the color and play of materials, used marble, granite, stone and ceramics—not arranged as decoration but to emphasize architectural intent. The native granite of Brazil is pinkish-grey, the sandstone orange or brown; marble is usually imported. Cement comes from a large modern plant just outside Rio. The Robertos, like all Brazilian architects, work closely with the building industry. They are deliberately free with materials, being concerned to break down established practice and regulations which prevent the development of an experimental architecture.

The reinforced concrete floor construction has an over-all thickness of 12 inches, made up of a reinforced concrete slab, standard beam construction and a ceiling of precast concrete slabs, with an air space between for piping and conduits. A detail of the floor is shown below.

1. UNE VUE DES BUREAUX, LES CLOISONS VITREES SONT DEMONTABLES ; 2. LE JARDIN DE LA TERRASSE AVEC UN BASSIN ET UNE VEGETATION LUXURIANTE ; 3. VUE INTERIEURE DE LA PAROI NORD AVEC LES BRISE-SOLEIL.

« Les murs extérieurs auraient pu être ainsi..., mais le climat de Rio aurait normalement exigé des surfaces d'éclairage n'excédant pas ces ouvertures...

Néanmoins, le principe de l'éclairage par bandes horizontales est indiscutable pour des bureaux peu profonds. Dans le cas présent, l'éclairage en profondeur n'aurait pas été suffisant.

C'est pourquoi nous avons adopté le principe des deux bandes horizontales éclairant l'une, les surfaces rapprochées de la façade, et l'autre la profondeur des pièces. »

2.14 North façade details of the IRB, from *Architectural Forum*, August 1944; office interior, the Burle Marx roof terrace, a view through *pan de verre* and brise-soleil at the IRB's north (sun-facing) façade from *L'Architecture d'aujourd'hui*, 1950.

2.15 South and east façade of the IRB, with photographs of the interior, *Architectural Forum*, August 1944.

a shallow *S* curve in plan—the outer face of the louver was a "heat-deflecting surface," as this diagram indicates, to block the penetrating rays of the summer sun, while the inner face was "light reflecting," increasing the daylight transmitted to the interior. There was also, as at the ABI, a "heat dispersion space" between the two façade layers, with the shading louvers hung at a short distance from the glazed wall. Unlike at the ABI, the heat dispersion space was not an occupiable balcony. Instead, this space contained a ventilating draw from above—in figure 2.14, the upper left set of semiclosed louvers—to help keep heat away from the glazing. This ventilation element was itself not simply open but contained more louvers, so as to be manipulable and to best seasonally protect the interior from solar radiation. The interior wall, evident in the section, had a thick storage block on the bottom, which was set behind a prefabricated "heat protecting double wall"; above it sat an operable window.

The southern and eastern façades were also activated for their microclimatic positioning (figure 2.15). The banding of the exterior was attuned to solar incidence, allowing the building to further reduce reliance on mechanical systems, even

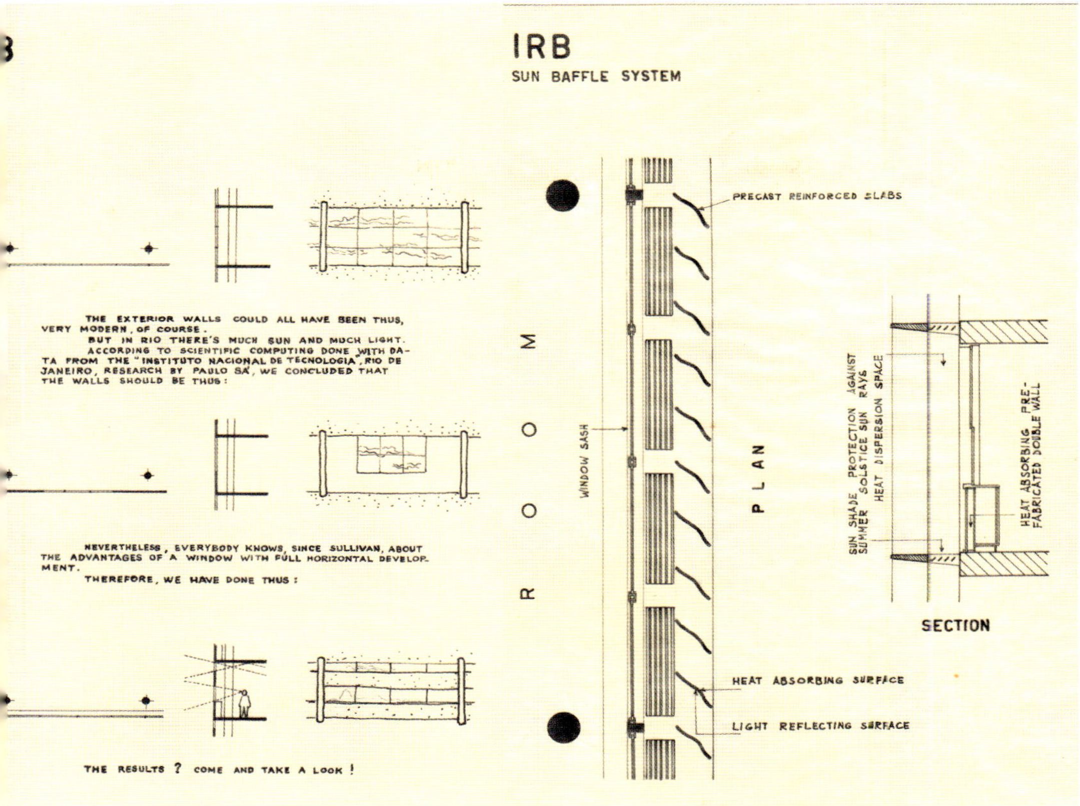


2.16 Diagrams explaining the south-facing (non-sun-exposed) façade at the IRB.

amid seasonal extremes. Milton Roberto played out this intervention in a series of diagrams (figure 2.16). Next to a schematic plan, section, and elevation of an unshaded, glazed wall, he writes: "The exterior walls could all have been thus, very modern, of course. But in Rio there's much sun and much light." Therefore, he continued, "According to scientific computing done with data from the Instituto Nacional de Tecnologia [the National Technology Institute, another Vargas agency], Rio de Janeiro, research by Paulo Sá, we concluded that the walls should be thus." He continued with another set of drawings, of the same façade but with a rectangular window set amid a masonry or concrete wall. "Nevertheless," Milton Roberto continues, with reference to debates in Chicago during the early development of the steel and concrete skyscraper, "everyone knows since [Louis] Sullivan about the advantages of a window with full horizontal development. Therefore we have done thus." The third, and final, series of drawings match the condition of the façade as built, in which bands of windows alternate with concrete—a thin window at the top, to allow light into the room both directly and by reflection off of the ceiling, and a taller window at more or less the height of the inhabitant, able to gaze out comfortably while also allowing light and heat in. "The results?" Roberto concludes, "Come and take a look!"[40]

That these drawings were annotated in English is significant. They were published in *Architectural Forum* and translated into French for *L'Architecture d'aujourd'hui*, in articles discussing the buildings in the larger context of Brazilian modernism—an initial indication of the resonance of these Brazilian experiments across global architectural developments. Further annotations, not published, identified additional complexities. A pair of diagrams that could have replaced the third one already identified indicates that one band of glass at eye level had the disadvantages of poorly lighting the room (without the band at the top to reflect light off the ceiling), the potential for excessive glare, and "not to mention the excessive cost of glass in Brazil." The final drawing, identical to the third, is described differently: "In this way, the whole room is well-lighted. The window has a human scale—and in cold weather the upper part, which is moveable, supplies the ventilation required, while the lower part is used exclusively to provide light and view."[41]

The section of the façade as built (less schematic than the diagrams) also emphasizes the operability of the top windows and, incidentally, the use of thin filing cabinets as an additional thermal buffer (figure 2.17). The proliferation of business machines that were required for processing insurance claims and other data led to the need for elaborate acoustical treatment, including the development of semi-isolated working spaces surrounded by sound-absorbent panels. The façade opened up the interior to extensive daylight, for the open office space and for more intimate meeting spaces, minimizing costs while allowing for programmatic flexibility; it solved some problems and presented others (figure 2.18).

A precise conflation of climate knowledge, thermal design methods, and insurance as part of Brazil's modernization process is expressed in the IRB façade—not precise relative to the history of Brazil but to the relationship between architecture, climate, and prospects for socioenvironmental transformation. Theories of risk, insurance, and security were essential to the conflation of climate knowledge and thermal design methods that were part of Brazil's modernization process. Such a theory of risk as a framework for understanding processes of industrialization and modernization has been well rehearsed.

The writings of the German sociologist Ulrich Beck articulates the complexities of modernization as the entry into a "risk society." The processes of modernization, as he describes them in the 1980s, drew society into a new relationship to unanticipated consequences, one in which knowledge opens up the capacity for understanding risks and threats, for guarding against them, and for recognizing their inevitability. "The concept of 'world risk society,'" Beck wrote, "draws attention to the limited controllability of the dangers we have created for ourselves. The main question is how to take decisions under conditions of manufactured uncertainty, where not only is the knowledge base incomplete, but more and better knowledge often means more uncertainty." Beck proposed that the late stages of capitalism involved the outsourcing of risk from corporations to the public.[42] Bruno Latour has discussed a similar tendency of capitalist systems that allow the social body to become a medium for experimentation—a general notion that resonates across the eventual proliferation of air-conditioned interiors.[43]

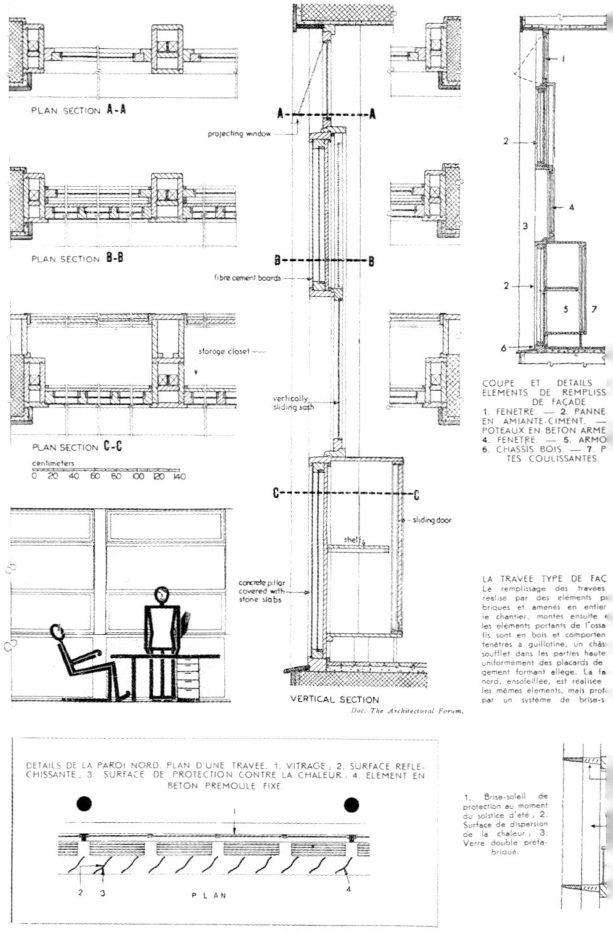


2.17 A detailed section of the IRB's south façade, from *L'Architecture d'aujourd'hui*, 1950.

Beck's framework was ultimately projective and, arguably, overly optimistic. It interfaced with a variety of sociological theories focused on notions of ecological modernization and second industrialization processes.[44] It was grounded, on Beck's terms, in a "reflexive modernity," framing the life-world as a socioindustrial system that had the capacity to learn from itself and improve on its practices, infrastructures, and material dependencies. Implicit in such a positioning is a confrontation with the stark realities of environmental degradation, not yet explicitly operative in the wartime period in Brazil. By using risk as a framework, Beck's notion was that components of the socioindustrial system could recognize and evaluate the harm they were causing—to laborers, to environmental conditions, to the fiber of the society itself—and correct themselves, leading toward a more refined and materially efficient means of

2.18 Interior views of the IRB showing sound-insulated cubicles for processing insurance data, from *Architectural Forum*, August 1944.

attaining familiar lifestyle conditions. The extent of the risk paradigm has increased dramatically in the face of climate change, as modeling risk scenarios became more widely available, albeit unevenly embraced, as tools for policy and as aspects of the global imaginary of possible, if not necessarily desirable, futures.[45]

Beck was also interested in the role of social and cultural movements in determining the future direction of modernization. In the face of a new stage of modernity that was consumed by the environment as a field of political conflict—as the realm in which risk entered the social sphere—sociopolitical change was rooted in arguments over risk distribution. If, in other words, there were unintended, unforeseen hazards caused by the success of science and technology in meeting the material production needs of society, how, Beck asks, could such effects be managed without destabilizing technology's benefits?[46] At stake was the reframing of environmental politics as reflexive and constructive, rather than antimodern, antidevelopment, or antigrowth (as it had heretofore often been seen). Beck's project was to investigate the costs of modernity in order to refine the processes that pertain and to better manage industrial process, so as to reduce harm and derive more benefits. Essential as well was Beck's reliance on what he called "cognitive agents"—experts and counterexperts aware of these complex dynamics and advocating specific positions relative to the application of scientific knowledge in the broad social field.[47] In this sense, again, the shaded buildings of Brazil cannot be explained according to their functional capacities alone but must be understood as material and symbolic gestures expressing conditions of risk and how to manage them. The fact that some of these buildings house insurance corporations is both allegorical and historical.

Risk and insurance can also be seen as a general and even all-encompassing framework for understanding the conditions of the life-world. As Mitchell Dean writes,

> There is no such thing as risk in reality. Risk is a way—or rather, a set of different ways—of ordering reality, of rendering it into a calculable form. It is a way of representing events so they might be made governable in particular ways, with particular techniques, and for particular goals. It is a component of diverse forms of calculative rationality for governing the conduct of individuals, collectivities and populations.[48]

Risk and insurance, in this sense, are of interest as new forms of knowledge that allow novel perspectives to emerge. The carefully shaded buildings for the insurance industry, their planimetric arrangements and protoactive façades, are evidence of a calculational approach to the world that climatic modernism, and technological adaptability, renders in sharp relief.

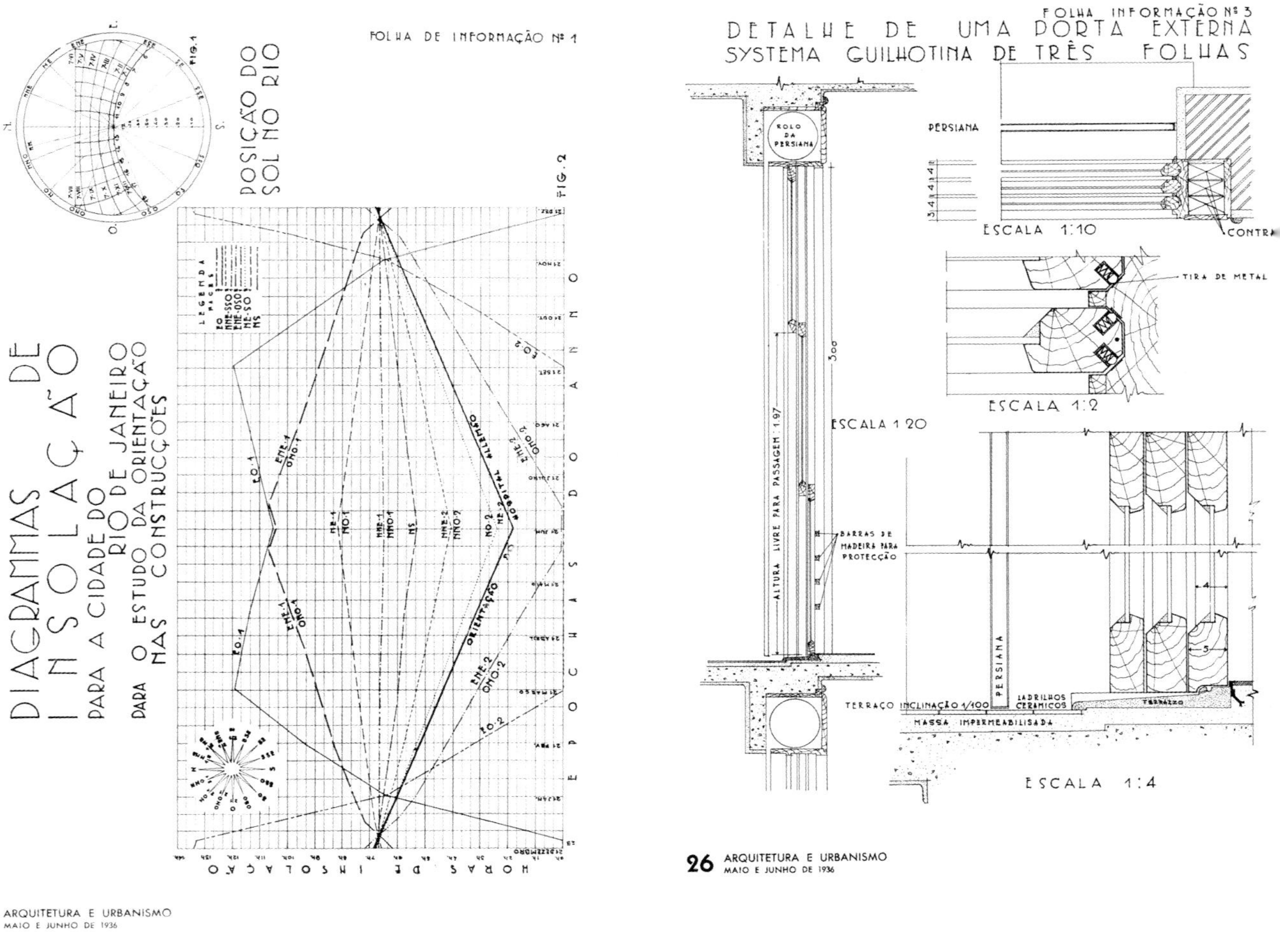


2.19 A diagram of the seasonal radiation patterns for Rio de Janeiro, by Paulo Sá at the Instituto Nacional de Tecnologia and a diagram of a proposed Systema Guilhotina window system, with three collapsing window panes and a built in "Persiana" shade, from *Arquitetura e Urbanismo*, May–June 1936.

Broader claims around the history of insurance examine the "probabilistic revolution" of the mid-sixteenth century, when the French mathematician Pascal used the term "a geometry of hazard" to describe what later came to be seen as the calculations of probabilities that would bring into being an insurable public, subject to rigorous analysis and optimization.[49] Such a geometry does not, as does Beck's theory, cast forward toward a new phase of advanced modernity. Instead, following Francois Ewald (about whom Dean, above, is writing), insurance as protection from risk can be seen as:

> A series of de-centerings, disruptions, destabilizations in the life-world, a sort of pulling through of the masses into a calculational matrix of *population*, of the way one considered people, things, and their relationships, and marks the moment of an approach to *life*—to housing, to public health, to securing future possibilities—that is above all rendered manageable through risk assessment.[50]

In the first instance, insurance and shading devices operate as means to process data toward the care of the population, mediating between social patterns and their potential for aggregate

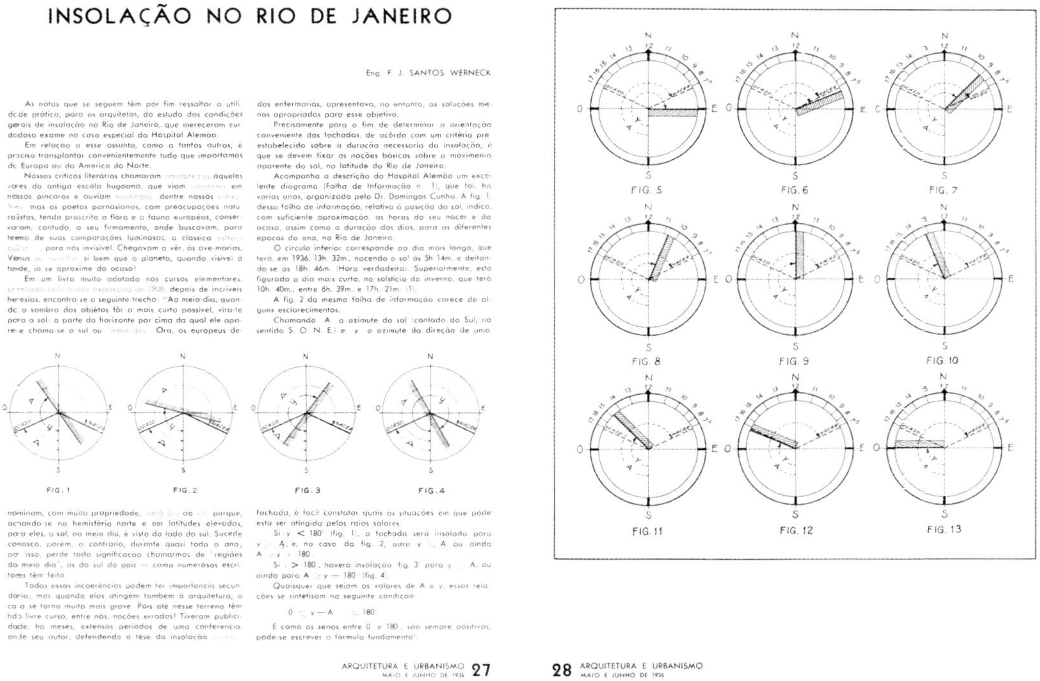

# INSOLAÇÃO NO RIO DE JANEIRO

Eng. F. J. SANTOS WERNECK

As notas que se seguem têm por fim ressaltar a utilidade prática, para os arquitetos, do estudo das condições gerais de insolação no Rio de Janeiro, que mereceram cuidadoso exame no caso especial do Hospital Alemão.

Em relação a esse assunto, como a tantos outros, é preciso transplantar convenientemente tudo que importamos da Europa ou da America do Norte.

Nossos criticos literários chamaram [illegible] áqueles vates da antiga escola hugoana, que viam [illegible] em nossos pincaros e ouviam [illegible] dentre nossos [illegible] mas os poetas parnasianos, com preocupações naturalistas, tendo proscrito a flora e a fauna européas, conservaram, contudo, o seu firmamento, onde buscavam, para termo de suas comparações luminosas, a classica [illegible], para nós invisivel. Chegavam a vêr, ás ave-marias, Venus [illegible] si bem que o planeta, quando visivel á tarde, já se aproxime do ocaso!

Em um livro muito adotado nos cursos elementares, [illegible] depois de incriveis heresias, encontra-se o seguinte trecho: "Ao meio-dia, quando a sombra dos objétos fôr a mais curta possivel, vira-te para o sol: a parte do horizonte por cima da qual ele aparece chama-se o sul ou [illegible]. Ora, os europeus denominam, com muita propriedade, [illegible] ao [illegible], porque, achando-se no hemisfério norte e em latitudes elevadas, para eles, o sol, ao meio dia, é visto do lado do sul. Sucede conosco, porém, o contrario, durante quasi todo o ano; por isso, perde toda significação chamarmos de "regiões do meio dia", as do sul do país — como numerosos escritores têm feito.

Todas essas incoerências podem ter importancia secundaria, mas quando elas atingem tambem a arquitetura, o caso se torna muito mais grave. Pois até nesse terreno têm tido livre curso, entre nós, noções erradas! Tiveram publicidade, ha meses, extensos periodos de uma conferencia, onde seu autor, defendendo a tése da insolação [illegible] dos enfermarias, apresentava, no entanto, as soluções menos apropriadas para esse objetivo.

Precisamente para o fim de determinar a orientação conveniente das fachadas, de acôrdo com um critério pre-estabelecido sobre a duração necessaria da insolação, é que se devem fixar as noções básicas sobre o movimento aparente do sol, na latitude do Rio de Janeiro.

Acompanha a descrição do Hospital Alemão um excelente diagrama (Folha de Informação n. 1), que foi, ha varios anos, organizado pelo Dr. Domingos Cunha. A fig. 1, dessa folha de informação, relativa á posição do sol, indica, com suficiente aproximação, as horas do seu nacer e do ocaso, assim como a duração dos dias, para as diferentes epocas do ano, no Rio de Janeiro.

O circulo inferior corresponde ao dia mais longo, que terá, em 1936, 13h. 32m., nacendo o sol ás 5h 14m. e deitando-se ás 18h. 46m. (Hora verdadeira). Superiormente, está figurado o dia mais curto, no solsticio do inverno, que terá 10h. 40m., entre 6h. 39m. e 17h. 21m. (1).

A fig. 2 da mesma folha de informação carece de alguns esclarecimentos.

Chamando A o azimute do sol (contado do Sul, no sentido S. O. N. E.) e y o azimute da direção de uma

FIG. 1 FIG. 2 FIG. 3 FIG. 4

fachada, é facil constatar quais as situações em que póde esta ser atingida pelos raios solares.

Si y < 180° (fig. 1), a fachada será insolada para y [illegible] A; e, no caso da fig. 2, para y [illegible] A ou ainda A [illegible] y + 180.

Si y > 180, haverá insolação (fig. 3) para y [illegible] A, ou ainda para A [illegible] y — 180 (fig. 4).

Quaisquer que sejam os valores de A e y, essas relações se sintetisam na seguinte condição:

0 < y — A < 180

E como os senos entre 0 e 180, são sempre positivos, póde-se escrever a formula fundamental:

ARQUITETURA E URBANISMO 27
MAIO E JUNHO DE 1936

FIG. 5 FIG. 6 FIG. 7
FIG. 8 FIG. 9 FIG. 10
FIG. 11 FIG. 12 FIG. 13

28 ARQUITETURA E URBANISMO
MAIO E JUNHO DE 1936

2.20 Solar incidence diagrams for Rio de Janeiro by F. J. Santos-Werneck at the Instituto Nacional de Tecnologia, from *Arquitetura e Urbanismo*, May–June 1936.

consequences. In the second instance, insurance emerged as a new form of legal right that devolves not from specific political imperatives, authoritarian or otherwise, but from the "special kind of technological rationality" that insurance, the assessment and social distribution of risk, both requires and allows. In the third instance, of interest is not insurance per se, but the emergence of, again following Ewald, "an insurational imaginary," which came to preoccupy, in his reading, new formations of the state in the early twentieth century (and that are made legible by the manipulations of the thermally attentive façade).[51]

The insurational approach takes on its own "geometry of hazard"—a means of taking care through modernization, and also a sort of hedging against, in which a building is instrumentalized to frame a public and its concerns not only according to regional or nationally specific political imperatives, but relative to general techniques for the regulation, management, and shaping of human conduct, in some cases with direct reference to climate. Ewald's formulation of the insurational imaginary describes the general emergence of risk as a sociopolitical phenomenon and also the specific consequences of relying on the iterative calculations of risk assessment as a means to articulate the prospects of a regionally bounded political economy, and its built environment.[52]

## Collaborations

What could be more calculational than climate? The risk imaginary of the mid-twentieth century involved design and the production of climate knowledge, some of which was specific to the production of buildings. The IRB, as an example of architectural-climate modeling, well clarifies the concerns implicit in interactions between meteorologists, engineers, and architects in Brazil in the 1930s and 1940s. Even basic efforts into mapping the path of the sun required elaborate interpretation and translation into an architectural context. In 1936, journals around the world such as *Architectural Forum* in the United States, *RIBA Journal* in the United Kingdom, and *Arquitetura e Urbanismo* in Brazil began publishing sun-path diagrams and other climate data (figure 2.19; figure 2.20).

This architectural interest in climate, in Brazil in particular, was coincident with scientific and governmental interest in carefully understanding the conditions of the coastal plain on which Rio stood, in order to improve and delineate specific conditions for development. In designing the IRB, the Robertos refer to "computation of Weather Data done at the Instituto Nacional de Tecnologia"; such analyses were being done in both Rio and São Paulo, focused on mapping the specific characteristics of Rio's complex climatic situation so as to best project a built condition of the near future. Rio had been subject to numerous urban restructuring schemes, from the Plan Agache in 1928 to the later intervention of the Boulevard Vargas over the 1940s and '50s. In the late '30s and '40s, as shaded buildings were emerging around the city, knowledge of the climate and geography of Rio was undergoing a dramatic transformation, increasingly crucial to the calculations of the state. Interest in Rio as a body of data, available for scenarios of optimization, further encouraged precise analysis by both architects and climatologists.

Nestled between a thin coast and mountains, wind and wave conditions have a great effect on Rio's microclimate. Climatic analyses took on two basic approaches: first, specific to the region, researchers sought to understand the precise climatic impacts of a given site in Rio; second, analyses focused on the relationship of the body, as generator of heat, to the cooling and ventilation systems that shaded modernism made available. What followed was as a technological trajectory carefully inflected by both these close regional readings and universal species dynamics. Through climatic analysis, architects and climatologists began to understand and express the relationship of the body to the interior, the membrane, and the external climate.

In one foundational article from 1936, Ibrahim Carone asked, "What Is Rio's Healthiest Location?"—an important question for targeted urban development. Rio's urban planners had for centuries been taking down hills and re-routing rivers. For Carone, controlling humidity and insolation was the key to the experience of a comfortable interior. Specific areas of the city were analyzed in terms of general air quality—relative to a sense of "freshness," through proximity to the ocean—than in terms of a concern around pollution. Rio was lauded for an overall lower humidity than most Brazilian urban areas but was too varied for making useful generalizations. Carone discussed the neighborhoods of Tijuca, Copacabana, and Jacarepaguá, and then looked at the Distrito Federal, in the center, which he described as being "ventilated by the south winds" largely due to a stark elevation drop from one side of the occupied coastal plain to the other.[53]

The mechanical system in many of these early modern buildings was focused on ventilation, moving the air around, often in complex collaborative inducement relative to the prevailing winds. The engineer Paulo Sá, quoted by the Robertos, was an expert in understanding the induced experience of ventilation as cooling—"the importance" as he wrote, "of eliminating extra heat produced by the human machine." If the challenge of the global interior was some semblance of consistency across varied regions, in Brazil, the obstacle was the experience of heat, which could be mitigated, even in sweltering weather, by a persistent breeze generated by the ventilation system and induced or distributed through strategic openings throughout the building. "When the air is in motion," Sá summarized, "the layer that was in contact with the body, heated and moistened, is replaced by a fresher and drier one, which increases the feeling of comfort."[54]

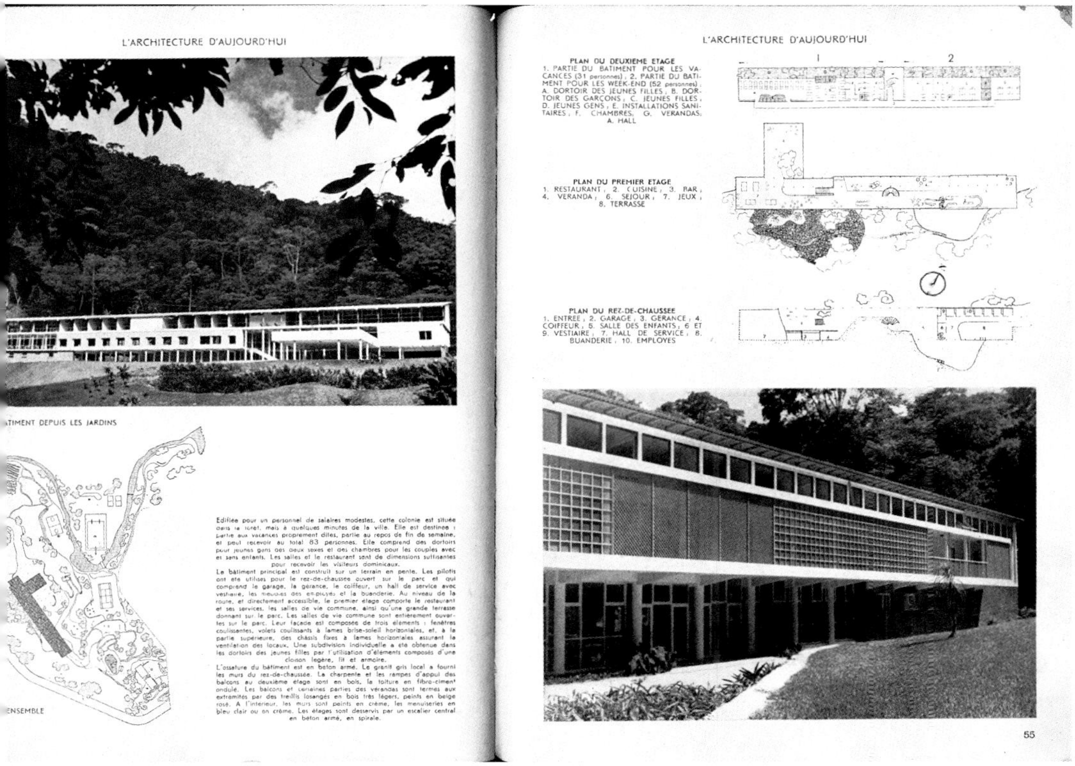

L'ARCHITECTURE D'AUJOURD'HUI

…TIMENT DEPUIS LES JARDINS

…NSEMBLE

Edifiée pour un personnel de salaires modestes, cette colonie est située dans la forêt, mais à quelques minutes de la ville. Elle est destinée : partie aux vacances proprement dites, partie au repos de fin de semaine, et peut recevoir au total 83 personnes. Elle comprend des dortoirs pour jeunes gens des deux sexes et des chambres pour les couples avec et sans enfants. Les salles et le restaurant sont de dimensions suffisantes pour recevoir les visiteurs dominicaux.

Le bâtiment principal est construit sur un terrain en pente. Les pilotis ont été utilisés pour le rez-de-chaussée ouvert sur le parc et qui comprend le garage, la gérance, le coiffeur, un hall de service avec vestiaire, les meubles des employés et la buanderie. Au niveau de la route, et directement accessible, le premier étage comporte le restaurant et ses services, les salles de vie commune, ainsi qu'une grande terrasse donnant sur le parc. Les salles de vie commune sont entièrement ouvertes sur le parc. Leur façade est composée de trois éléments : fenêtres coulissantes, volets coulissants à lames brise-soleil horizontales, et, à la partie supérieure, des châssis fixes à lames horizontales assurent la ventilation des locaux. Une subdivision individuelle a été obtenue dans les dortoirs des jeunes filles par l'utilisation d'éléments composés d'une cloison legère, lit et armoire.

L'ossature du bâtiment est en béton armé. Le granit gris local a fourni les murs du rez-de-chaussée. La charpente et les rampes d'appui des balcons au deuxième étage sont en bois, la toiture en fibro-ciment ondulé. Les balcons et certaines parties des vérandas sont fermés aux extrémités par des treillis losangés en bois très légers, peints en beige rosé. A l'intérieur, les murs sont peints en crème, les menuiseries en bleu clair ou en crème. Les étages sont desservis par un escalier central en béton armé, en spirale.

L'ARCHITECTURE D'AUJOURD'HUI

PLAN DU DEUXIEME ETAGE
1. PARTIE DU BATIMENT POUR LES VACANCES (31 personnes) ; 2. PARTIE DU BATIMENT POUR LES WEEK-END (52 personnes) ; A. DORTOIR DES JEUNES FILLES ; B. DORTOIR DES GARÇONS ; C. JEUNES FILLES ; D. JEUNES GENS ; E. INSTALLATIONS SANITAIRES ; F. CHAMBRES ; G. VERANDAS ; A. HALL

PLAN DU PREMIER ETAGE
1. RESTAURANT ; 2. CUISINE ; 3. BAR ; 4. VERANDA ; 6. SEJOUR ; 7. JEUX ; 8. TERRASSE

PLAN DU REZ-DE-CHAUSSEE
1. ENTREE ; 2. GARAGE ; 3. GERANCE ; 4. COIFFEUR ; 5. SALLE DES ENFANTS ; 6 ET 9. VESTIAIRE ; 7. HALL DE SERVICE ; 8. BUANDERIE ; 10. EMPLOYES

55

2.21 MMM Roberto, Colonia de Ferias do Instituto de Resseguros do Brasil, Boa Vista, Rio de Janeiro, 1943, from *L'Architecture d'aujourd'hui*, 1950.

The analysis of the thermal needs of the body and the satisfaction of these needs through mechanical and architectural means characterizes a thread of architectural developments in this period. In the first part of the twentieth century, factories, large public areas, homes, and office buildings were being analyzed and reconsidered according to their "comfort" conditions, a process that continues and intensifies in the 1950s, as discussed in the second half of this book. Drawing on the work of the French meteorologist André Missenard, who worked closely with Le Corbusier in the development of climate management systems, Sá proposed the adaptation of a coefficient of heat, humidity, and air speed so that this sensation of freshness amid tropical pressure could be codified and regulated.[55] Such a process was not only effective for Rio but could also be extended to "other parts of the territory" and according to "other genres of activities."[56]

The engineers in São Paulo and Rio were struggling to develop visual means to encourage and facilitate architectural engagement with climate. Techniques of data gathering and analysis were brought together with regulations and standards for thermal comfort conditions. The designed interior was a compelling laboratory for the optimization of specific design characteristics in regard to notions of comfort and productivity. The thermal interior in Brazil, and elsewhere, was filled with these multiplistic calculations, subject to manipulation through architectural techniques.

## Proliferations

The façade mechanism of the brise-soleil also marks the intensification of an approach to life—to housing, to public health, to securing future possibilities—that presumes that it can be rendered manageable through risk assessment. Risk in these buildings is the quantitative articulation of possible futures. It represents the capacity for knowledge, and near-term simulation, to shape those futures, as expressed through a precise attention to the façade section. Shading devices and insurance operate as means to process data toward the care of the population, mediating between social patterns and their potential for aggregate consequences, and diagramming the global space of the conditioned interior as one of flow, measurement, and optimization.

A few examples: In the hills west of Rio, MMM Roberto also designed a weekend retreat for IRB workers (figure 2.21).[57] The experience of self-care

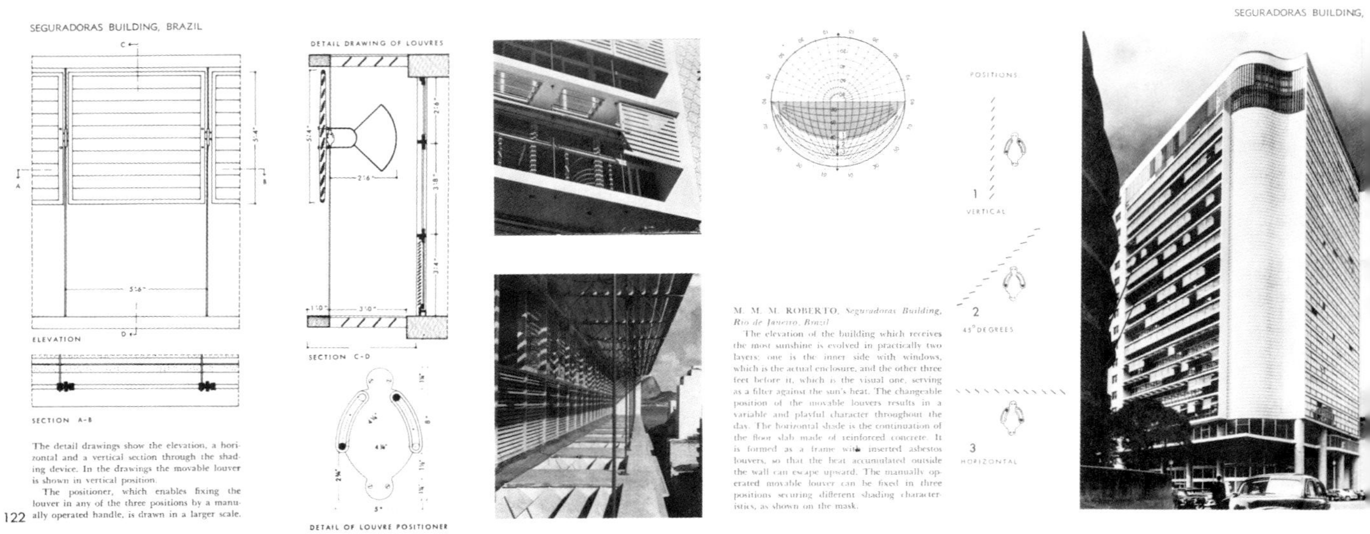


2.22 MMM Roberto, Edifício Seguradoras, Rio de Janeiro, 1949, from Olgyay and Olgyay, *Solar Control and Shading Devices*, 1957.

was part of a system of home, office, and leisure; the weekend colony was a delicate, lengthy building, traversing a small ravine in a larger valley and taking advantage of prevailing breezes. Rio has since become such a beach city that the retreat to the hills for comfort seems anachronistic. Copacabana, at the time of the IRB's construction, was barely developed.[58] The opportunity to escape the city into the countryside was another hallmark of modernity.

The Robertos also designed the Edifício Seguradoras in 1949, a speculative office building for the property insurance industry intended to encourage more foreign investment (figure 2.22). The building had an elaborate set of shading mechanisms. An extrusion on each floor, similar to a balcony, held within it a fixed bank of shading louvers and also supported a device that could be manipulated through controls in the interior—it could rest, as we can see in the diagram and as photographed, at a horizontal, vertical, or a 45-degree-angled condition. The system gave the occupant flexible control over the interior climate, in relation to seasonal and diurnal solar patterns.

These buildings could, at the same time, be placed next to Neutra's Northwestern Mutual Insurance in Los Angeles (1950); Skidmore, Owings & Merrill's building for Pan American Insurance in New Orleans (1952); and Wurdeman and Beckett's less well-known Prudential Building in Los Angeles (1949), showing adaptations to this now quite refined shading style (figures 2.23–2.25). Neutra claimed that his Los Angeles building included the first commercial louver installation in the United States, following his development of shading on a domestic scale at the Kaufmann House in Palm Springs. He noted further that the louver design of the Northwestern Mutual building "became popular for many office buildings."[59] One could even begin to trace a history of the architecture of insurance—back to William Le Baron Jenney's Home Insurance Building in Chicago (1885), the first American building to use structural steel, and forward to Norman Foster's Swiss Re building in London (2001)—to clarify on wider historical terms this relationship between insurance and the means by which architectural agency is sociopolitically conceived.[60]

Attention to the variability of the shading device, the interactivity, the representation of a bodily engagement with climatic conditions through the comfortable experience of the interior and the physical manipulation of the parts of the complex system, indicates a different sort of trajectory of the physiological, the bioclimatic, and the biopolitical, and opens toward a new set of objects of interest to the history of architecture. The obstacles of formalist analysis and the genius of modern masters are cleared away, replaced by the façade as media—mediating between inside and outside,

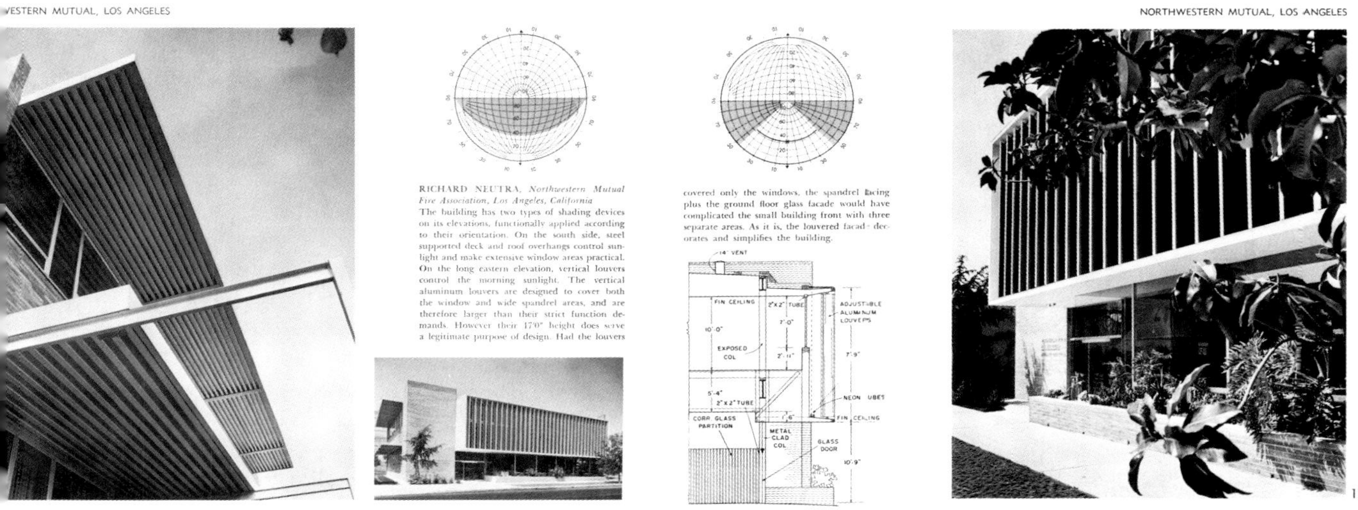

WESTERN MUTUAL, LOS ANGELES

NORTHWESTERN MUTUAL, LOS ANGELES

RICHARD NEUTRA, *Northwestern Mutual Fire Association, Los Angeles, California*
The building has two types of shading devices on its elevations, functionally applied according to their orientation. On the south side, steel supported deck and roof overhangs control sunlight and make extensive window areas practical. On the long eastern elevation, vertical louvers control the morning sunlight. The vertical aluminum louvers are designed to cover both the window and wide spandrel areas, and are therefore larger than their strict function demands. However their 17'0" height does serve a legitimate purpose of design. Had the louvers covered only the windows, the spandrel facing plus the ground floor glass facade would have complicated the small building front with three separate areas. As it is, the louvered facade decorates and simplifies the building.



127

2.23 Richard Neutra, Northwestern Mutual Fire Insurance Building, Los Angeles, 1950, from Olgyay and Olgyay, *Solar Control and Shading Devices*, 1957.

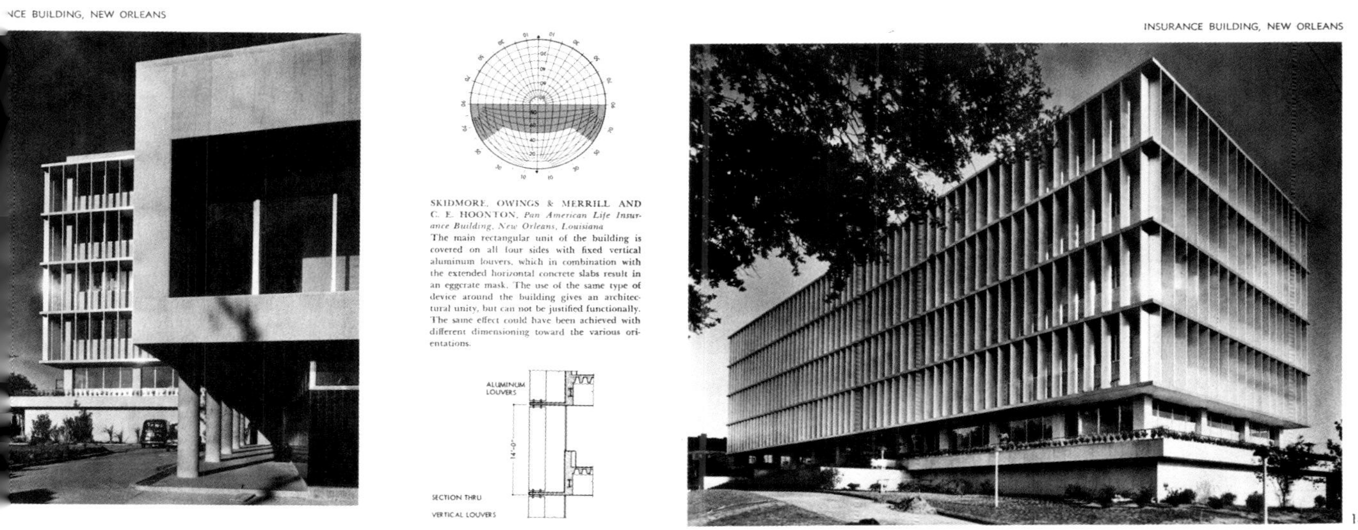

NCE BUILDING, NEW ORLEANS

INSURANCE BUILDING, NEW ORLEANS

SKIDMORE, OWINGS & MERRILL AND C. E. HOONTON, *Pan American Life Insurance Building, New Orleans, Louisiana*
The main rectangular unit of the building is covered on all four sides with fixed vertical aluminum louvers, which in combination with the extended horizontal concrete slabs result in an eggcrate mask. The use of the same type of device around the building gives an architectural unity, but can not be justified functionally. The same effect could have been achieved with different dimensioning toward the various orientations.



143

2.24 Skidmore, Owings & Merrill with C. E. Hoonton, Pan American Life Insurance Building, New Orleans, 1952, from Olgyay and Olgyay, *Solar Control and Shading Devices*, 1957.

PRUDENTIAL BUILDING, LOS ANG

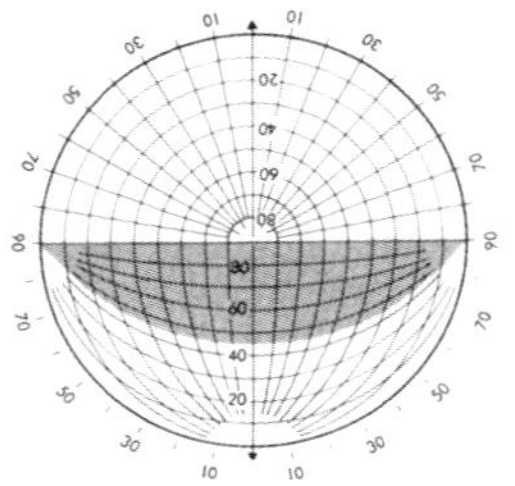

WURDEMAN & BECKET, *Prudential Building, Los Angeles, California*
This elongated office building in Los Angeles faces south, parallel to Wilshire Boulevard. The photograph shows the sun protection afforded the clerical offices, at right angles to the blank service tower wall. The sun-shades are of aluminum and consist of fixed slanted louvers which contrast to the pink terra-cotta spandrels. Despite the sunshades, glare has proved a problem at certain times, so draw curtains were installed on the south windows.

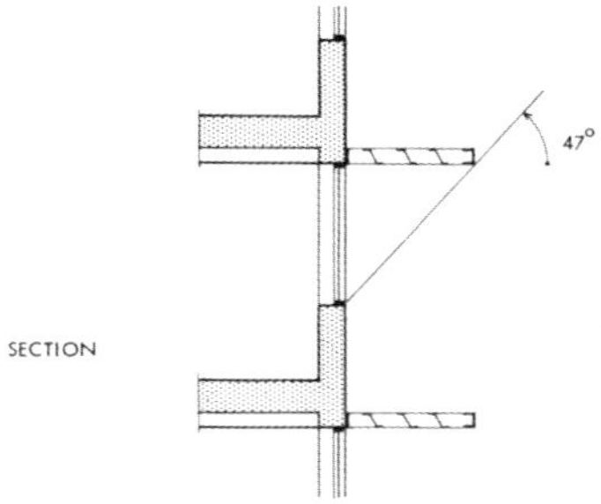

2.25 Wurdeman and Beckett, Prudential Insurance Building, Los Angeles, California, 1949, from Olgyay and Olgyay, *Solar Control and Shading Devices*, 1957.

OFFICE BUILDING IN BAHIA

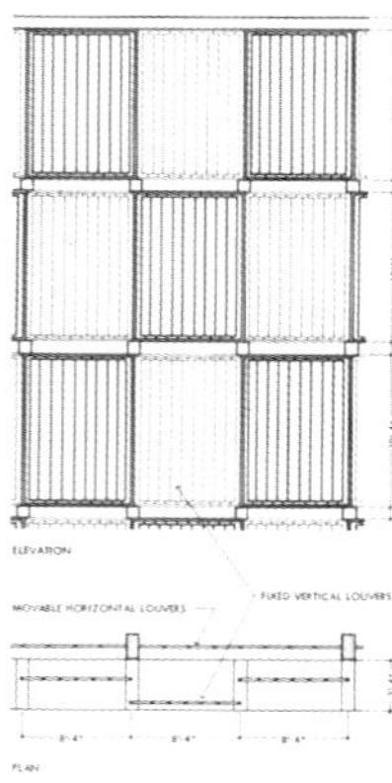

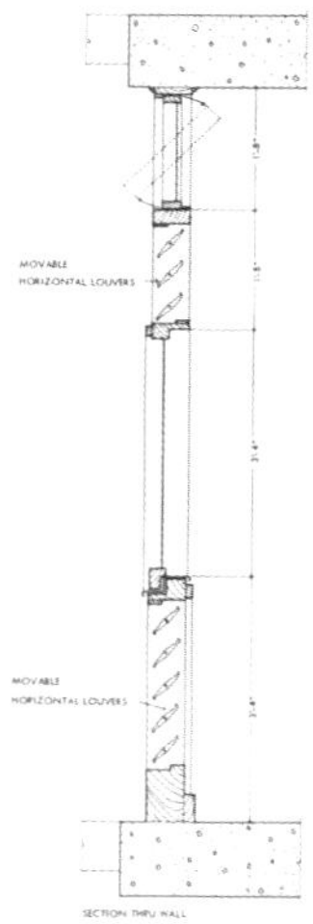

146

OFFICE BUILDING

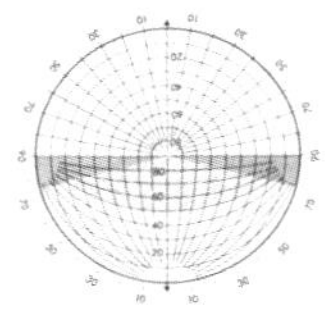

PAULO ANTUNES RIBERO, *Office Building, Bahia, Brazil*
The principal characteristic of this building is in the system of protection from the sun's penetration. The insolation chart showed that two facades receive intense sunlight during the whole day and therefore sun-protection as well as a disagreeable view must be taken care of. The problem was solved by using many stories of sun louvers. The outside vertical louvers are placed on protruding concrete beams on different planes, while horizontal movable wooden blinds are used on the openings of the building.

2.26 Paulo Antunes Ribeiro, Caramuru Office Building, Salvador, Bahia, Brazil, 1946, from Olgyay and Olgyay, *Solar Control and Shading Devices*, 1957.

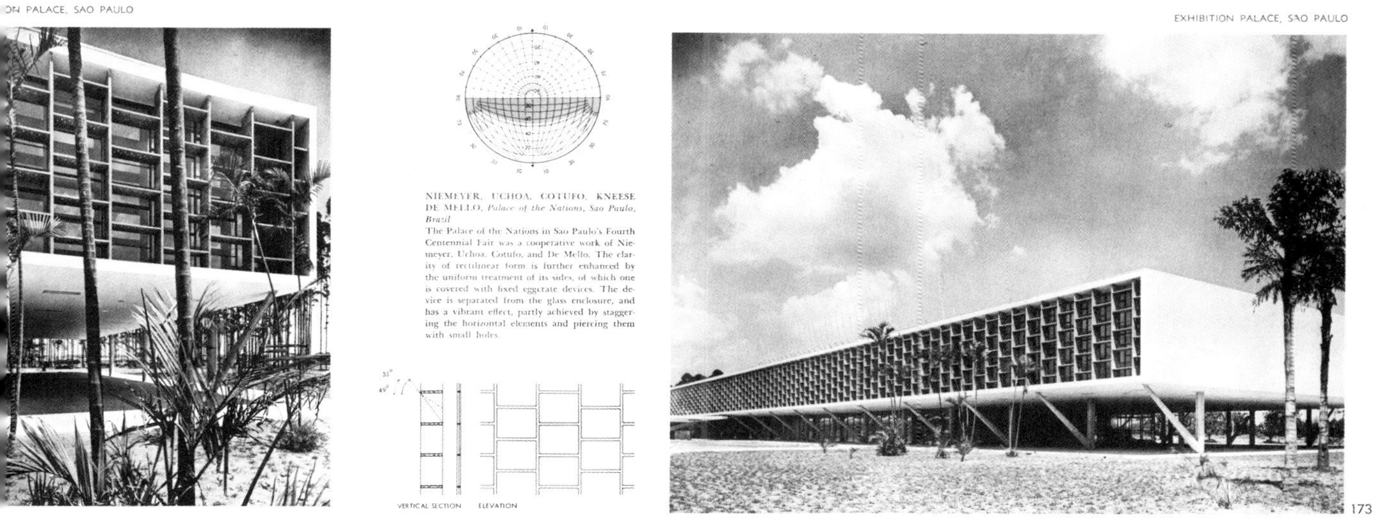


2.27 Oscar Niemeyer, Hélio Uchoa, Rafael Cotufo, and Eduardo Kneese de Mello, Palace of the Nations, São Paulo Fourth Centennial Fair, 1949, from Olgyay and Olgyay, *Solar Control and Shading Devices*, 1957

expressing social commitments through the dynamism of its potential manipulations.

Although these buildings designed for insurance corporations offer a concise indication of the resonance of the brise-soleil, there were many other sites, conditions, and programs in which they were deployed. The majority of these sites continued to reflect the challenges and opportunities of so-called developing economies: how they developed, and for whom. MMM Roberto and many other firms and practitioners in Brazil and across Latin America explored possibilities of façade systems at length. The Robertos designed a headquarters and factory for the Caterpillar corporation, the construction equipment manufacturer. They also designed, as part of yet another Vargas initiative, a number of technical training academies around Rio de Janeiro state, which were focused on improving the knowledge and employability of the workforce under changing economic conditions.[61] There were also prolific designers of shaded middle-class apartment complexes around Copacabana, Ipanema, and Botafogo, many of which are still desirable properties today.

Among the multitude of other shaded buildings are Paulo Antunes Ribeiro's Caramuru Office Building, Salvador, Bahia, Brazil, 1946 (figure 2.26). This building in the north of Brazil uses a system involving three layers of shading. The outer layer is a tic-tac screen of banks of vertical wooden bars resting on protruding concrete beams, just behind which a middle layer of horizontal wooden bars sits on different planes in order to modulate the light and heat that strikes the façades. A third layer consists of movable wooden blinds integrated into the façade. The Palace of Nations at the Fourth Centennial Fair in São Paulo (1949), designed by Oscar Niemeyer, Hélio Uchôa, Rafael Cotufo, and Eduardo Kneese de Mello, was a low, long building with indirect solar exposure (figure 2.27). It has a fixed egg-crate screen, staggered across the façade to visually break up the long span. The horizontal elements of the screen were punctured with small holes to produce a dynamic experience of light in the interior. By this time, void ceramic bricks termed Cobogó had been patented and also proliferated as a shading screen system; projects such as Costa's Parque Guinle would be something of an essay in the use of the exterior ceramic screen as shading device—an exemplary project that masks the wider geographic proliferation, across Brazil's north in particular. These examples only scratch the surface and are still focused on the limited case of Brazil.

2.28 MMM Roberto, Marques do Herval, Rio de Janeiro, 1953. Photographs of the façade; see figure 2.1.

## Habit

MMM Roberto's Marques do Herval (1953) in downtown Rio was a large and somewhat ungainly office building, clearly designed to fill out the lot and maximize rentable space (figure 2.28). The sun-exposed northern façade had a slight curve to break up the plane and to allow for a setback entry at grade; this also resulted in a slight overhang, offering some sun protection on the upper floor. Each floor of the façade had, as was by now usual in the Robertos' work, two shading elements. First, a straightforward horizontal screen with tightly placed metal fins blocked much of the summer heat; second, the same metal fins were collected in a slightly bowed moveable screen operable from the interior. As figure 2.1 shows, this secondary element allowed for extensive adjustments, from fully closed to almost horizontal. Much as one could go and open the window to let in a breeze, or draw an internal shade to block daylight, solar radiation could now be effectively deflected at will. The image of the Roberto brothers operating the shading device, in figure 2.1, is a sort of live-action sectional drawing. It demonstrates the innovation of the system and suggests, given the staging, the importance of media to promoting it as such. The image of an optimized body begins to be articulated as an object of climatic analysis and is increasingly prevalent as a means of defining comfort, for architects and others (figure 2.29).[62]

Another of their projects, and its forms of representation, further emphasizes this physiological conditioning. Here it is less evident through photographs—the section, again, becomes the discursive space for negotiating the relationship of interior to exterior, of climate to body, of past to possible future. The Robertos built the Edifício MMM Roberto, also called the Edifício Mamãe, in 1945 on the Avenida Nossa Senhora da Copacabana, a main thoroughfare just a block from Copacabana beach, an area then undergoing extensive development (figure 2.30). The Edifício Mamãe was one of the first modern buildings on this emerging

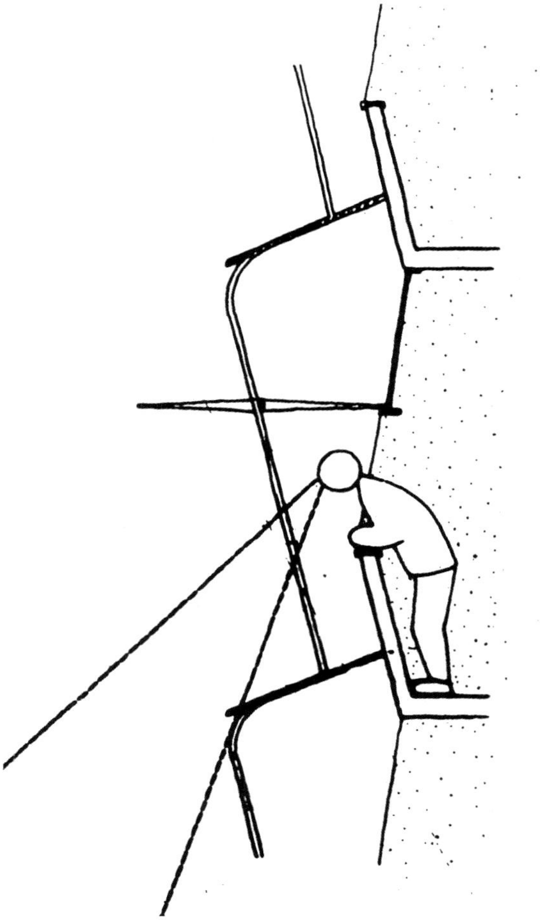

2.29 MMM Roberto, a diagram of the relationship of the inhabitant to the street, by virtue of the open, though protected, façade system.

2.30 MMM Roberto, Edifício Mamãe, Rio de Janeiro, 1945.

strip. It is an apartment building that housed the Robertos' extended family.[63] The façade system of the Edifício Mamãe consisted of egg-crate elements emphasizing vertical fins, with a series of horizontal projections with embedded fixed vanes as well as an adjustable venetian blind integrated into the bottom and top of each egg-crate module. An adjustable screen hung at the end of the horizontal projection, keyed to the evening sun but functional at other times and across seasonal variations. There was an additional fixed shading covering some of the upper floors (figure 2.31).

As at the Marques do Herval, the emphasis at the Edifício Mamãe is on the shading systems on the façade as a designed membrane that simultaneously represents and activates cultural desires for a specific type of habitation—the inhabitant (or more likely, in this case, the domestic help) was free to manipulate the thermal conditions of the interior in concert with the occupation of specific spaces according to diurnal and seasonal patterns. The family's thermal needs were articulated through these interactions and through its mediated effects on the interior. It was an architecture of habits and practices, with complex consequences for concerns over climate.

These buildings are events in the history of a possible future. They are mediatic—the material and infrastructural substrate for the expression and elaboration of social desire. Siegert's insistence on the importance of media as a means of "processing the distinction between inside and outside, between human and nature" is rendered explicit, material even, across the historical gap

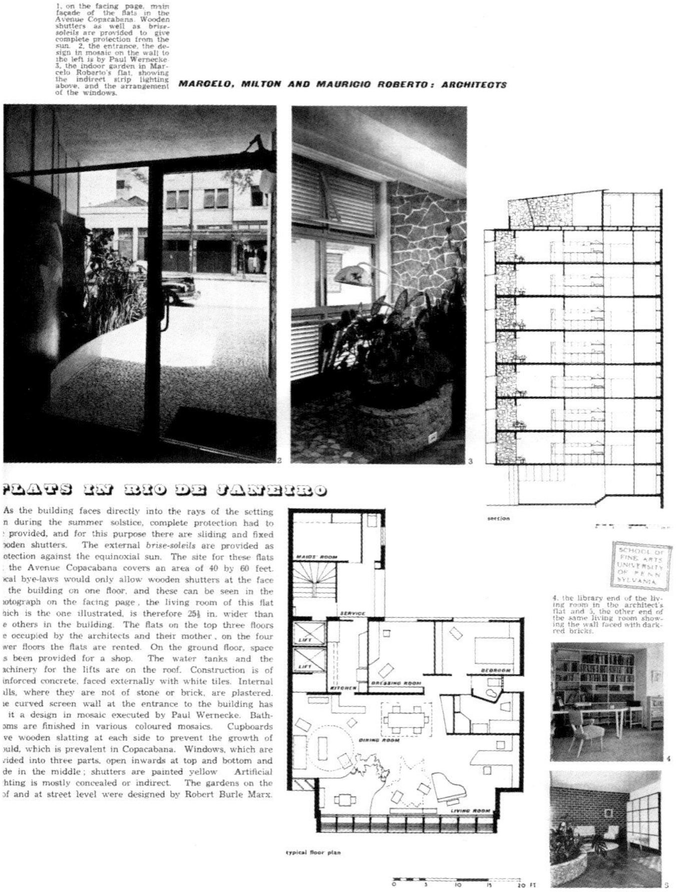


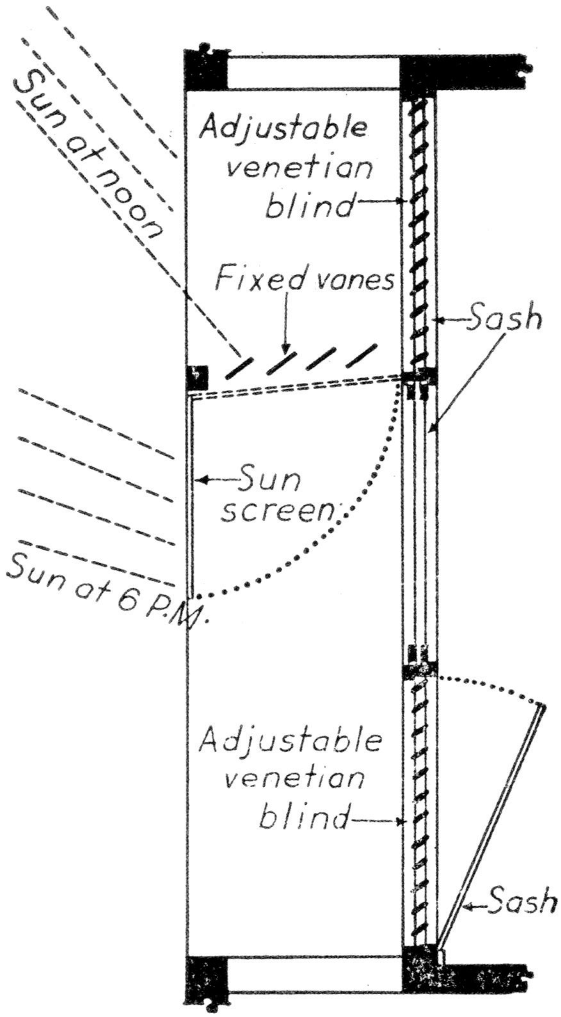


2.31 Plans and sections of the Edifício Mamãe, from *Architectural Forum*, August 1947, and a close-up of the façade section from *Progressive Architecture* in November 1947.

between the initial euphoria of Brazilian modernism and modernization and the mechanical overloads and overcompensations of the present (figure 2.32).[64]

Such distinctions have been collapsing and reconfiguring as the proliferation of air conditioning, in all its shining inefficiency, has become the specific form of this civilizational collapse. This is rendered legible on more contemporary images of the façades of the Marques do Herval and the Seguradoras building, now full of window air-conditioning units (figure 2.33). The reliance, in the twenty-first century in Brazil and elsewhere, on air conditioning obviates the need for social or bodily interaction—such intentions are left to the thermostat.[65] The climatic modernization that arrived did not do so on the terms that reflect the techno-social possibilities embedded within it. These architectural instances can be read as a diagram for a new approach to cultural and climatic contingencies, a new kind of physio-material substrate for processing distinctions between interiors and exteriors, resonating across a wide sociopolitical register.

Here again the IRB represents an interesting inflection of this more general model—it was built to maximize daylight without overheating and to manage internal conditioning without a mechanical cooling system. In the late 1970s, the façade began to sprout in-window air-conditioning units, which eventually took over, one for every office bay (figure 2.34). Two stuck out precariously in the window volume that extended the director's office. In the 2010s, these units were removed as

2.32 The Edifício Mamãe in 2019, with air conditioners.

2.33 At the Seguradoras building, left, the shading system was removed but the framework was repurposed to support air-conditioning units. At the Marques do Herval, right, the entire second façade was removed, and window units inserted.

2.34 The IRB building had window air conditioners installed in the 1990s; since then, as the bottom image shows, the window units have been removed and a low-velocity system installed on the interior.

the building began to use a low-velocity cooling system. While the clarity of the façade returns, the system inside it is now charged with different fuels and holds a different set of values.

The insurational imaginary in Brazil is compelling historiographically for the specifics of the case and more for the diagram it presents. This story is part of a broader narrative that offers, instead of the teleological march of reason, the circular, repetitive patterns of climate—as well as an unexpected corollary in the importance of habit, as a subject and object of design, as a rejoinder to the everywhereness of petroleum and the optimization of the interior.[66] In examining the past for its relevance to the present, nascent moments in the articulation of cultural techniques emerge—techniques that encourage habits of self-care on a societal scale, an agglomerative process of *casual* behaviors that are *causal* as a means of countering logics of insurance and financialization. Causality is here formed, gradually, as the result of habit, not derived according to a probabilistic matrix. "The building" becomes an object of study as a space for habitual engagements with climate, at the intersection of individual actions and corporate or governmental practices, and as a counter-insurational imaginary embedded in design methods and their potential effects. The thermal interior becomes an experiential field for political engagement.

The globalization of the International Style was also the Brazilianization of architecture. After the World's Fair pavilion of 1939 and the MES brought attention to Brazilian modernism, work from the region received increased attention. Much of this story is well known, orbiting around the exhibition and catalog at the Museum of Modern Art in New York, *Brazil Builds*, of 1943.[67] Henrique Mindlin's *Modern Architecture in Brazil* of 1957 was published in English in order to, as Mindlin noted, "provide a more complete picture" of regional projects than the MoMA exhibition had collected—already, that is, resisting the narrative of Brazil receiving a packaged modernism from the Global North. While Mindlin celebrated the Brazilian integration of the brise-soleil into modern design strategies, and acknowledged the influence of Le Corbusier, he indicated that this proliferation was based on "research into the functions of sunlight" in São Paulo engineering schools, and the consequent development of "a scientific basis for the orientation and sunlighting of buildings" in architecture schools. "Easily handled sunlight graphs and tables," Mindlin concluded, had been "in general use by architects for decades now, making it possible to calculate accurately and solve any sunlight problem."[68]

Sigfried Giedion, one of the towering figures in the history and criticism of architecture in the period, wrote the introduction to Mindlin's book, celebrating the dynamism of Brazilian interpretations of the modernist orthodoxies Giedion was everywhere concerned to promote. The widespread publication of Brazilian examples of office towers, houses, and institutional buildings crested like a wave over the architectural press in the early 1950s: Giedion also wrote an introduction to an issue of *L'Architecture d'aujourd'hui* in September 1947 dedicated to recent Brazilian buildings; the journal ran another themed issue in 1952; and *Progressive Architecture* and *Architectural Forum* also had special issues on Brazil in 1947. Stamo Papadaki's book on Oscar Niemeyer was published in 1950.[69]

A recent sociological analysis of modern architects and their networks of influence, while conceding to the importance of Le Corbusier, lists Warchavchik as second, in large part due to his place at the center of a network of Brazilian architects such as Niemeyer, Costa, and the Robertos, and his role connecting these figures to others in schools and journals around the world.[70] Indeed, architects around the world, from Scandinavia to Japan to India to around the United States and Europe, looked to Brazilian examples for technical direction in developing their own façade mechanisms and for a more general cultural approach to imagining the possibilities of architecture as a space of climatic engagement.

Another iconic building in this reconfigured historical landscape is the residential project referred to as Pedregulho, the name of the hill on which it was built—the official name is the Conjunto Residencial Prefeito Mendes de Moraes, after a Rio official close to the Vargas administration (figure 2.35). It was designed by Affonso Eduardo Reidy, who had taught with Costa at ENBA and worked on the MES before becoming part of the city's architectural office. The project, originally within the Distrito Federal, was built for government workers. Although celebrated on completion, lack of maintenance led to the project's slow decline.[71] Around 2008, residents and architects supporting the project began to call for

2.35 Affonso Eduardo Reidy, Conjunto Residencial Prefeito Mendes de Moraes (Pedregulho), Rio de Janeiro, 1947–52.

2.36 Pedregulho's brise-soleil undergoing renovation, 2015.

its restoration.[72] While the renovation covers many aspects of the building, careful attention has been paid to the wooden shading louvers—they have been removed, stripped and retreated, and replaced (figure 2.36). This process of care and the emphasis on refining the effectiveness of the nonmechanical system, rather than retrofitting a more aggressive HVAC system, while largely a consequence of economic constraint and available labor, nonetheless illuminates the negotiations between risk and habit, and past, present, and future, that are evident across the historical span of the shading device as a sociopolitical experiment.

Since the built environment has been overwhelmed by mechanical air conditioning, and since the environment more generally has absorbed the carbon emissions resultant from such a mechanical proliferation, the way that we think about buildings and about how to inhabit them is undergoing stark transformation. The space of the thermal interior, in both domestic and commercial environments, is enacted and emphasized in order to reimagine an embodied relationship to climate. The question becomes: can architecture induce habits that activate a different relationship to fossil fuels? As Wendy Chun writes, "Habit occurs when understanding becomes so strong that it is no longer reflected, when an action is so free that it anticipates and escapes will or consciousness, or when a being's repeated actions assuage its own needs."[73] Habit occurs, at least in some instances, when it becomes spatialized, instantiated, built—in a word, when it becomes architecture.

---

It is, no doubt, too simple of a political program to imagine that an architectural intervention can transform the carbon economy. It is also too simple to rely on individual predilections to aggregate toward a global sociopolitical shift that embraces carbon negativity. Yet, the interior becomes a political object available for manipulation on these terms—or, better, a cultural object that generates not only new desires but also opens up a new space for politics, available for elaboration as a different kind of lived environment.

## Public Interests

Climate was essential to negotiating the role of modernism in the complex geopolitics and development economics of the wartime and postwar period. One hallmark of this period was a changing role for governments and nongovernmental organizations (NGOs), as colonial relations of direct power turned to postcolonial conditions of economic and cultural influence. The built environment took on an even more profound role in the material construction of these new regimes and in their symbolic expression. Again, the façade was an essential mediating agent in this historical transformation. It embodied a system for climatic mitigation that offered to make the planetary interior a space of health and comfort; it also was often deployed as a symbolic screen on which countries and corporations could claim sensitivity and openness to local conditions. A filter, a billboard, and a mask.

This intensification of the geopolitical and geophysical role of the façade is legible in a proliferation of diagrams, perspectives, sections, and explanatory drawings that stand as evidence of architects arguing, through images, for the validity of their interventions. Somewhat suddenly a new question had arisen: how could modern architecture change, and improve, living conditions around the world? In the midst of World War II, concerns about urban and regional organization took on increased urgency relative to the realities of the destruction the war reaped, and in regard to a growing understanding of the interconnections between architecture and governance, on the one hand, and economic systems and ecological conditions, on the other. In concert with seemingly benevolent government and foundation aid programs, modern architecture came to be an essential aspect of global growth, cooperation, and investment intended to increase quality of life in targeted populations. Architecture was configured as a symbol of progressive, democratic values that operated materially as a means to provide spaces for comfortable occupation.

Richard Neutra's climatic experiments for the US government in Puerto Rico reveal emergent conceptions of the global and planetary in this context. The US government's embassy building program across the Middle East and Africa similarly led to a charged mediatic condition for the architectural façade during the Cold War. They both developed in complex relationship not only to economies and ecologies but also to a novel positioning of the public as the client of architecture. Through these tests, the public was envisioned as the beneficiary of design innovation on the specific terms of health and quality of life framed by a developing conception of thermal comfort—though this conception was still quite vague. In each case, albeit unevenly, the design brief was read to include attention to how architecture can instigate a public good amid often conflicting political and economic ambitions and to manipulate the façade both toward relieving the heat on the interior and on projecting a message of conciliation. These projects simultaneously test the material ways that strategies for the built environment can improve living conditions and the subtle and often sublimated means by which political goals could be attained through cultural gestures. Climate, and the technical images that emerge from architectural-climatic analysis, is the intersection, the interface through which these complications become legible.

The social role of the architect was also subject to being tested—at a moment, during the war, when such roles were held in suspension. No longer simply an artist or technocrat, one or the other, the architect's role as a generator of ideas intensified during wartime: ideas about how to live, about how design could elevate the quality of life, about how territories could transform with attention to the liberating potential of industrial modernization and to the felt needs and ambitions of social collectives. The elements Neutra focuses on are not

# 3. Tests

3.1 Richard Neutra, School, outside San Juan, Puerto Rico, with Rexford Tugwell, 1944.

dissimilar from the policy goals and symbolic reach of the Ministry of Education and Health. Ideas about economic patterns, behavioral regimes, and broad sociological and biological knowledge were seen to inform the design process in substantive and determinant ways. Ideas flowed through architecture, technology, and the natural and social sciences to government and corporate discussions, for better or worse, articulating in detail new ways of living and how to construct them. These details were proposed as benevolent, helpful gestures, though they were often couched in a cloying paternalism that was more resonant of colonial ambitions and addressed the inhabitants as a resource to be optimized.

This operational discourse of architecture was related to discussions of regionalism active in the period, and the subject of much debate since, in the form of what is referred to as critical regionalism. In general, such discussions of the regional adaptability of the modern idiom operated on formal terms, while sensitive to the symbolic role of the design, for example, of a government building or other quasi-monumental structure, and often engaged in questions of materials and relationship to site.[1] Concerns over the climatic conditions of a given region are implicit in the premise of a vernacular inflection of the International Style, though they have not been addressed at length in this discourse. The philosopher Paul Ricoeur's 1965 text "Universal Civilization and National Cultures" exerted a substantive influence on these later critical regionalist discussions in a period when the seeming inevitably of the spread of a unified International Style of modernism had significantly waned.[2] Regional considerations were seen to be culturally engaged and to draw from scientific fact, embedded in what Ricoeur called the "scientific spirit" of the "technical civilization," a universality of knowledge embedded in a careful and culturally sensitive treatment of site.[3]

The premise of regionalism herein described was, by contrast, inflected by *planetary* pressures—experiments in how modern architecture could encompass social problems at the scale of the planet and according to the uneven distribution of wealth and opportunity that such an analysis revealed. These were planetary tests of the sociopolitical efficacy of modern architecture as a way of building. They were tests of a global imaginary then developing in a number of contexts, including the changing discussion of meteorology, and general conceptions of economic, social, and environmental systems since. Claims to international styles and universal design methods were couched in theories of relative global consistency. Modern architecture's project was to produce a capacious and flexible system that could normalize interiors across a vast geography while also exploring opportunities for rendering cultural, through building, specific conditions of the site.[4]

3.2 Richard Neutra, Lovell House (Health House), Los Angeles, 1928.

## The Social and the Scientific

In the fall of 1946, the Viennese-American architect Richard Neutra gave a lecture to architecture students in Rio de Janeiro. He was in Rio as part of a US State Department tour of South America, which also included stops in Chile, Bolivia, Ecuador, and Peru. Neutra was president of the US chapter of CIAM (the Congrès Internationaux d'Architecture Moderne) and had just represented that group in the conference that inaugurated the United Nations in San Francisco in the spring of 1945. His visit was part of a larger State Department effort to encourage cultural exchanges with developing economies and to reinforce international institutions—with a particular focus on strengthening the United States' role in South America—as reflected in the Inter-American Affairs Office, then run by Nelson Rockefeller, also a trustee and patron of the New York Museum of Modern Art. MoMA held the *Brazil Builds* exhibition in 1942 and would be central to the promotion of modern, climatic design techniques in US embassy building projects around the world. Neutra also visited São Paulo, Recife, and Belo Horizonte. He met with numerous architects including Costa, Niemeyer, Mindlin, and Warchavchik. Other architects, such as Walter Gropius and the planner Jaqueline Tyrwhitt, would also receive State Department support for international outreach efforts.[5]

"I believe," Neutra said to the students in Rio, "in the social role and contribution of the responsible artist." Neutra argued for the importance of scientific knowledge to the architectural design process—in relationship to the research on Rio's climate discussed in the previous chapter, and in the midst of a cultural milieu in which the relationship of data and applied technology was still undergoing significant transformation. "I have been described to work like an 'engineer,'" Neutra continued, "be that as it may . . . however scientific systematics and information may increase and multiply in scope, there still remains an immense field beyond their fluid boundaries. Chains of essential events and vital parts of our civilization play just in that field beyond."[6] The historical context and the difficulty of Neutra's writing require some translation: at stake, for Neutra and others, was how to recognize and intensify the capacity for an architectural proposal to transform social conditions. In order for design interventions to operate on this social scale, they had to be informed by the sciences.

This was, in some sense, simply an elaboration of familiar modernist principles claiming the importance of technology, or the machine, or science more generally as an input and determinant in the emergence of design style. These founding principles were quickly the subject of critique, most dramatically perhaps by Reyner Banham in the 1950s and 1960s, for their actual relationship to technological potentials.[7] In suggesting a social architecture—as in the title of Neutra's 1947 book, *The Architecture of Social Concern for Regions of Mild Climate*—he was trying to articulate a nuanced pathway for what he called "frozen, rock-rigid data" to have an effect on the formal and affective conditions produced by a given architectural design. It was a period of transition—away from what Banham derisively referred to, in 1955, as "the machine aesthetic" and toward a more nuanced understanding of how a technologically informed design process could refashion the built environment.

Neutra was an important figure in the global spread of modernism, especially in regard to this new imbrication of aesthetics, technology, and

3.3 Richard Neutra, exercise area of the Lovell House (Health House), Los Angeles, 1928.

ways of life. He is best known for his houses in Southern California, beginning with the Lovell Health House, completed in 1928 (figure 3.2). The Lovell House is often celebrated as the first domestic use of structural steel; it is also posed in relationship to the comfortable climate of the region, as sleeping porches and outdoor spaces were essential to its arrangement in both plan and section (figure 3.3). The house itself was a media event. Neutra's client, Dr. Philip Lovell, who wrote a popular column on "The Care of the Body" in the *Los Angeles Times*, opened the home to visitors so they could witness the health advantages of living in a modern house.[8] Thousands walked through the house during the two weekends it was open. Neutra designed a number of similarly intricate houses after World War II, many of them able to open up to the outside—a design approach that took advantage of the fair climate characteristic of the Los Angeles basin.

Neutra presents, as did Le Corbusier, a number of historiographic challenges in order to best understand how climate, and geophysical factors more generally, played a role in the cultural aspirations of the new architecture. Surmounting this obstacle has, again, already been attempted by Banham. In an article in the *Sunday Times Color Supplement* in 1971, "The Master Builders," Banham indicated the nuance with which Neutra's work resonated across familiar historiographic contours. Banham was interested in the importance of the early twentieth-century architects Greene and Greene to the genealogy of California domestic modern designs. Greene and Greene's Gamble House (1909) was unique, he wrote, because it contained an "added architectural dimension that separates their work from their contemporaries" by taking into account "the climate (psychological as much as meteorological) of Southern California."[9] Banham claimed that the Greenes' "four determinants of architecture: Climate, Environment, Materials, and Habits and Tastes" were of significant influence on both Neutra and his fellow Austrian, architect Rudolf Schindler. Neutra and Schindler had both arrived in Los Angeles at a very active time in their careers; both of the émigrés had also studied with Wright.

Of the Schindler/Chace House, designed by Schindler in 1922, Banham wrote that it "seems to take blocks of that climate and fold itself loosely around them" (figure 3.4). The house developed its combination of spaces by resting internal and external partition walls of wood and glass between concrete abutments, using the concrete as "something between an adobe wall and a plank fence." The interior space, with no ceiling under the wood roof and an abundance of clerestory windows, rests within the concrete-defined compound in a porous relationship with the outside (figure 3.5).[10]

The designed ambivalence of the inside and outside is a central trope in the historiography of the modern architecture of California, pronounced in analyses of early experiments of Neutra and Schindler. It was on the basis of this formal-climatic innovation, indeed, that Banham proposed, referring to the purism of Le Corbusier and his colleagues, that Schindler was "inventing 'the white architecture of the Twenties' at the same time as his European contemporaries, and quite independently of them." Writing in the 1970s, Banham supposed that this claim of simultaneous emergence was a scandalous rebuke to an East Coast–based "U.S. architectural history industry," which had yet to take note, at the time of writing, of the California-based developments of modernism, and of Schindler and Neutra in particular.[11]

In the 1950s, Neutra was seen to embody a broad narrative of modern architectural developments. Raised and trained in Europe, though most active after immigrating to the United States, he was regarded, and regarded himself, as a synthesizer of the European (primarily Mies, Wagner, and Loos, but also Gropius and Mendelsohn) and American (Wright, and the knowledge of modern construction he gained while working at the Chicago office of Holabird and Root) traditions.

3.4 Rudolf Schindler, Schindler/
Chace House, Los Angeles, 1922.

3.5 Rudolf Schindler, Schindler/
Chace House, Los Angeles, 1922.

Giedion, in "R. J. Neutra: American and European," is maybe the first to emphasize this synthesis, putting it in terms that recognize the California lifestyle it produced: "what was in the nineteen-twenties architectonic vision—interrelation and penetration of vertical and horizontal, transparent and opaque planes, open radiation into landscape—has become within a quarter century *a form of life*."[12]

His biographer Thomas Hines sees Neutra's two most important early houses as setting up the terms for the conflation of mediatic, lifestyle, and environmental concerns that would follow in the well-known Case Study Houses and become characteristic of this architectural expression of a specific regional culture. Hines proposes a shift to considering this inside/outside dynamic on the terms of communication and, as he puts it, "the commitment to make public, rhetorically and actually, the most traditionally private of architectural genres, the middle-class single-family house."[13] The Lovell Health House was explicitly programmed to model the physician/client's "personification of the Southern California way of life"; its public display was to be an instructive example. The house as technical image? Hines summarized the house: "[Lovell's] clinical reliance on 'body-building, sun-bathing, and vegetarian diet' was reflected in the 'open sleeping porches, commodious swimming pool, and private decks' that Neutra designed."[14] It quickly became an icon in the development of modern architecture, propelling Neutra to international recognition as he used it to illustrate the architecture of the future in his worldwide lecture tour of 1929. Due to the wide publication of the house, and also to Neutra's *Wie Baut Amerika* (1927), *and* to his leadership in the American branch of CIAM, Neutra was received as

3.6 Richard Neutra, Singleton House, Los Angeles, 1956.

a spokesperson of modern architecture not only in Europe but also in Japan and, somewhat later, across Latin America.[15]

Sylvia Lavin's *Form Follows Libido* unsettles this inside/outside discussion somewhat, focusing on the psychological component of Banham's climate distinction while also proposing that a different kind of environment—an "affective environment . . . a saturated plenum"—came to be the determinant factor in Neutra's postwar design practice.[16] More recent interest in California Modern has led to a number of popular histories, ofNeutra and others, and in this material environmental perspectives are more explicitly addressed.[17] Barbara Lamprecht points out in *Neutra* that, if he emphasized the inside/outside relationship it was perhaps because he saw (Lambrecht quoting Neutra's *Nature Near*) "the universe of which we are a part as a dynamic continuum" with "galactic, atmospheric, biospheric, terrestrial . . . molecular and subatomic" interconnections, and the building's envelope as a temporary inflection or mediation of this condition.[18] Thus the expansive use of glass allowed by the steel framing, the "spider leg" extensions of that framing, and pools interpenetrating the glazed envelope all highlight this honed membrane affect (figure 3.6). Lavin's "saturated plenum" is a tightly engineered and distinctively permeable building-membrane, controlling the charged space within as a psychological and technological environment. Neutra is a central figure in the historicization of the California Modern, in whose work one can trace the ambivalent dissolution and affirmation of the formal, mediatic, and climatic envelope.

The historical treatment of Neutra's work represents two challenges. The first is by now familiar: Neutra, in his relative prominence, provides more evidence that attention to climate, even or especially amid the mild weather of regions such as California and Puerto Rico, was central to for-mal innovations in modernism. Second, still implicit, his work indicates that a conception of the globe as a geopolitical and geophysical system was essential to understanding the new world that architects were preparing themselves to encounter. He was certainly not alone in these gestures. Interest in an international approach was elaborated on at length in architectural media in the interwar period. Far beyond the International Style, concepts of the international and the global were essential to the articulation of new methods in architecture. Architects' contributions to the League of Nations, the World Meteorological Society, and any number of global collaborations and ambitions in the period stand as evidence of the consequential trends that led to a more wide-ranging planetary perspective.

This was explicit in the development of CIAM, of which Neutra was a member, even though he represented what was then the peripheral region of the US West Coast.[19] Giorgio Ciucci's article from 1980, "The Invention of the Modern Movement," poses the conundrum of this new internationalism. Ciucci identifies the three years between 1925 and 1928 as those in which an " 'irreversible' transformation had taken place" that expanded interest in modernist architecture from "small avant-garde groups" to the "the public mind in numerous countries." CIAM's global ambitions—largely regarded as parallel to those of Le Corbusier—were explicitly focused on lobbying government agencies to use modern architecture in state building projects, from housing to embassies to headquarters of international institutions.[20] These years were also the beginning of another wave of migrations and exiles that would come to characterize the developments of the field; in particular, 1928 saw the articulation of an internationalist program not only in style, as would be displayed at MoMA four years later in *Modern Architecture: International Exhibition*, but also as a means to establish global flows of social, political, economic, and even biophysical knowledge as they related to architectural methods.[21]

Neutra's conception of the planetary after the war sought to conflate, again, the social and the scientific. The planetary was developed as an epistemological realm in which applied scientific knowledge could improve what was seen as the dismal prospects of the less fortunate; it is a cipher opening up a new role for architectural and other techno-cultural expertise to articulate a field of application that required their services as part of regional economic development. Claiming this planetary perspective identified specific geopolitical territories (usually colonies or former colonies) and specific populations as needing support, support that architects could provide, in the civilizing or development ambitions that were ascribed to them. Neutra's planetary perspective is at once paternalistic, opportunistic, speculative, and benevolent.

Essential to these geo- and biopolitical architectural ambitions—essential, that is, as Giedion put it, to articulating a new, modern, "form of life"—was a novel conception of climate. Climate reiterates the planetary and the specific. Every region has a climate, of course, and thus a method attentive to it can be applied anywhere; each region's climate is specific (at a level of detail that quickly overwhelms the design process, as subsequent chapters will clarify), and demands precise attention and specific design strategies. Climate is a realm of knowledge that explores a local condition in the context of regional and global patterns, a model for conceptions of economic flows and their uneven impact on specific territories and populations. Neutra's conception of the building as a climatic device attempts to respond to and articulate these planetary pressures.

## Reconstructing the Planet

Neutra, as noted, was the US representative for CIAM during the war. Given the turmoil in Europe, he saw himself, and was seen by some others, to be holding down the fort for the forces of architectural modernism.[22] As the CIAM representative, he gave a presentation summarizing material he had just published, in slightly different forms, in *Arts and Architecture* and in the journal of the American Institute of Architects.

In the *Arts and Architecture* article, "Comments on Planetary Reconstruction," Neutra made the rather bold claim that the destructiveness of the war on sites in Europe, Japan, and Africa opened up a more general capacity for rebuilding: "the chance to start from scratch is, or at least could be, a real blessing." This opportunity for reconstruction was physical and psychological. It was not just about cities being relieved of the "those old utility lines [that] have long shackled the living flesh of the city" (that is, a different relationship to infrastructure and resources), but also about the capacity for architecture to facilitate political self-determination and individual growth. As "long suffering peoples of 'possessions' and colonies organize their own successful governments, and demand their post-war share of contemporary improvements," Neutra wrote, architects needed to adapt their skills accordingly.[23]

This emphasis on bringing the technological capacities of modernism into new geographic and social realms was essential to the formulation of the planetary and to conceptualizing architecture as a means to test how design strategies could directly benefit various populations.[24] What is the effect, and how is it measured? "The modern bomb," Neutra wrote, placing this dynamic on rather stark terms, "is much more advanced technically than the houses they have destroyed. Therefore, we must abolish the bombs but maintain the precision and quality level of their manufacture and convert it all to peaceful, planned pursuits."[25] In some ways this again reflects and reproduces the government's ambitions in the establishment of the Ministry of Education and Health in Rio de Janeiro. Neutra's attempt is to direct architectural and technological knowledge, including technologies of social management, toward a wider swath of the population. Yet he articulates a more ambitious positioning for the agency of the architect: as a master of new technologies and their potential application, architects lead the way, helping governments and other institutions understand how to bring the benefits of modernity into a wider social and geographic (if not in fact precisely planetary) context.

In his "Planetary Reconstruction" articles and at the United Nations, Neutra argued for the expansion of the already extant United Nations Relief and Rehabilitation Administration (UNRRA). This agency predated the larger UN organization—it was founded in 1943, in the midst of the war, based on US President Roosevelt's use of the term "United Nations" to apply to the Allied nations fighting against the fascist Axis powers. The UNRRA was later absorbed into numerous UN relief agencies, officially dissolving in 1947.[26] It was focused on aid to countries damaged by war and, as Neutra was suggesting, on providing technocratic expertise to those countries yet to benefit from the processes of industrialization. Such prospective benefits were caught up in institutional, industrial, and ideological conflicts later organized on the terms of the Cold War. That is, reconstruction was necessarily political, despite repeated architectural appeals to universalism or the implicit benevolence of technical application.[27]

Neutra's call for a new UNRRA consisting of "an unbiased international commission of planners, architects, engineers, [and] technological economists" sought to rationalize systems of development and bring them under a general purview of technocratic knowledge. He proposed that such methods required a "sensible interlocking of capital investments" encouraging rich countries to invest in infrastructure, "from dams to hospitals to schools" that would improve quality of life and bring a substantive return on investment—on the terms of the productivity of populations, on the terms of consumer growth.[28] He also proposed to use these infrastructural improvements as a chance to train local personnel and spark competition among aspiring designers. It was an ambitious proposal, and one focused on catalyzing the energy of the international architectural discussion toward development programs.

The organizational and creative center of Neutra's proposed reinvigorated UNRRA was "the American chapter of CIAM for Relief and Reconstruction," of which he was the head. Note the shift, relative to the UNRRA, from "rehabilitation" to "relief and reconstruction," an important and pragmatic indication of the centrality of the design and building industries. The CIAM group would be the catalyst for "immediate action" as the war was ending, "resuming interrupted contacts with all of the national planners and architect chapters in all allied and liberated countries, and aiding the formation of new groups in Latin America, China, Australia, etc.," as Neutra wrote. He continued, the UNRRA "aims to serve as a clearing house between technical research institutions of many kinds and foreign architects and planners, by helping translate their needs to American manufacturers," and applying them throughout the world.[29]

The territorial scale of these ambitions (if again, not quite planetary) was not unknown in Neutra's earlier work. His international reputation was based on, in addition to domestic architecture, the success of the Channel Heights housing project, begun in 1941, as well as the urban ideas embedded in his Rush City Reformed drawings from the late 1920s. Channel Heights was celebrated as a well-designed community and a harbinger of the future. Rush City was true to its name—a linear urban organization based on an interconnected series of super highways, and can be seen as part of a broader discussion of urban organization relative to Le Corbusier's many proposals of the 1920s and '30s as well as Frank Lloyd Wright's Broadacre City, in wide circulation in the late 1930s.[30] Given these urban ambitions and Neutra's CIAM activity, Bruno Zevi, in his immediate postwar text,

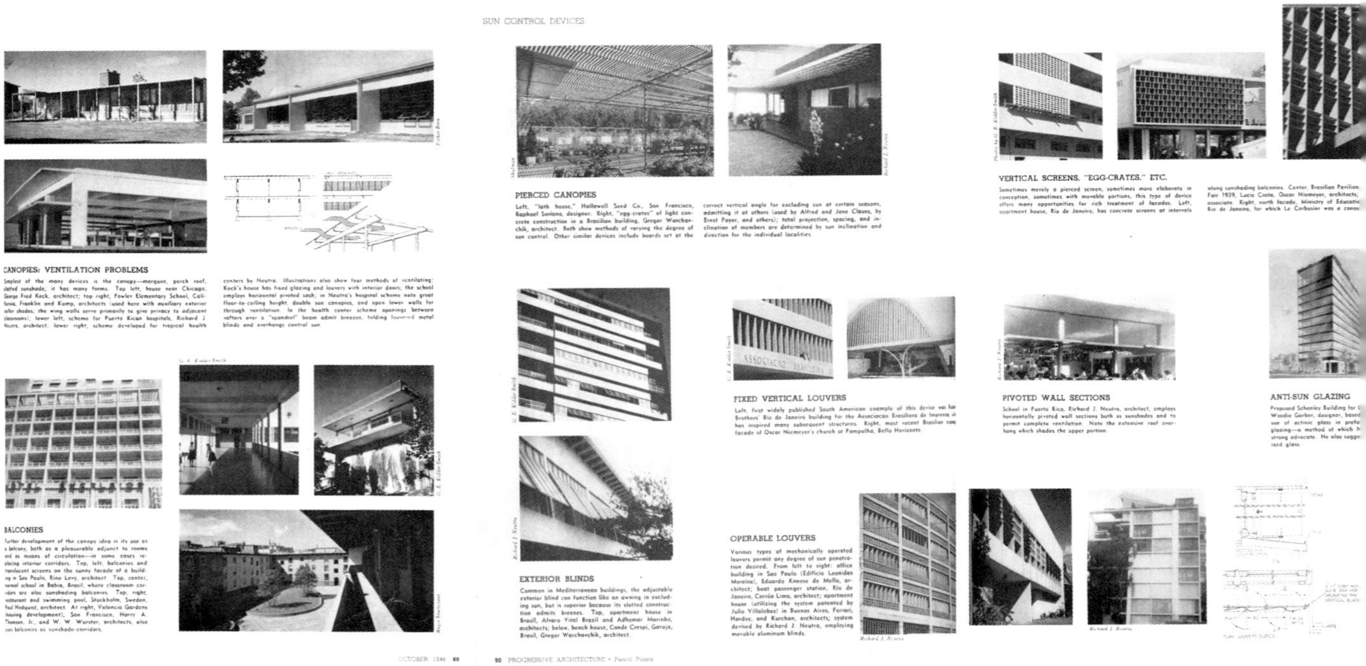

SUN CONTROL DEVICES

CANOPIES: VENTILATION PROBLEMS

Simplest of the many devices is the canopy—marquee, porch roof, slatted sunshade; it has many forms. Top left, house near Chicago, George Fred Keck, architect; top right, Fowler Elementary School, California, Franklin and Kump, architects (used here with auxiliary exterior roller shades; the wing walls serve primarily to give privacy to adjacent classrooms); lower left, scheme for Puerto Rican hospitals, Richard J. Neutra, architect; lower right, scheme developed for tropical health centers by Neutra. Illustrations also show four methods of ventilating: Keck's house has fixed glazing and louvers with interior doors; the school employs horizontal pivoted sash; in Neutra's hospital scheme note great floor-to-ceiling height, double sun canopies, and open lower walls for through ventilation. In the health center scheme openings between rafters over a "spandrel" beam admit breezes, folding louvered metal blinds and overhangs control sun.

BALCONIES

Further development of the canopy idea is its use as a balcony, both as a pleasurable adjunct to rooms and as means of circulation—in some cases replacing interior corridors. Top, left, balconies and translucent screens on the sunny facade of a building in Sao Paulo, Rino Levy, architect. Top, center, normal school in Bahia, Brasil, where classroom corridors are also sunshading balconies. Top, right, restaurant and swimming pool, Stockholm, Sweden, Paul Hedquist, architect. At right, Valencia Gardens (housing development), San Francisco, Harry A. Thomsen, Jr., and W. W. Wurster, architects, also uses balconies as sunshade-corridors.

OCTOBER 1946 89

PIERCED CANOPIES

Left, "lath house," Hallawell Seed Co., San Francisco, Raphael Soriano, designer. Right, "egg-crates" of light concrete construction in a Brasilian building, Gregor Warchavchik, architect. Both show methods of varying the degree of sun control. Other similar devices include boards set at the correct vertical angle for excluding sun at certain seasons, admitting it at others (used by Alfred and Jane Clauss, by Ernst Payer, and others); total projection, spacing, and inclination of members are determined by sun inclination and direction for the individual localities.

EXTERIOR BLINDS

Common in Mediterranean buildings, the adjustable exterior blind can function like an awning in excluding sun, but is superior because its slotted construction admits breezes. Top, apartment house in Brasil, Alvaro Vital Brazil and Adhemar Marinho, architects; below, beach house, Conde Crespi, Garuja, Brasil, Gregor Warchavchik, architect.

90 PROGRESSIVE ARCHITECTURE • Pencil Points

FIXED VERTICAL LOUVERS

Left, first widely published South American example of this device was [...] Brothers' Rio de Janeiro building for the Associacao Brasiliera de Imprensa [...] has inspired many subsequent structures. Right, most recent Brasilian [...] facade of Oscar Niemeyer's church at Pampulha, Bello Horizonte.

OPERABLE LOUVERS

Various types of mechanically operated louvers permit any degree of sun penetration desired. From left to right: office building in Sao Paulo (Edificio Leonidas Moreira), Eduardo Kneese de Mello, architect; boat passenger station, Rio de Janeiro, Corrêa Lima, architect; apartment house (utilizing the system patented by Julio Villalobos) in Buenos Aires, Ferrari, Hardoy, and Kurchan, architects; system devised by Richard J. Neutra, employing movable aluminum blinds.

VERTICAL SCREENS, "EGG-CRATES," ETC.

Sometimes merely a pierced screen, sometimes more elaborate in conception, sometimes with movable portions, this type of device offers many opportunities for rich treatment of facades. Left, apartment house, Rio de Janeiro, has concrete screens at intervals along sunshading balconies. Center, Brasilian Pavilion, [...] Fair 1939, Lucio Costa, Oscar Niemeyer, architects; [...] associate. Right, north facade, Ministry of Educatio[n] [...] Rio de Janeiro, for which Le Corbusier was a consu[ltant]

PIVOTED WALL SECTIONS

School in Puerto Rico, Richard J. Neutra, architect, employs horizontally pivoted wall sections both as sunshades and to permit complete ventilation. Note the extensive roof overhang which shades the upper portion.

ANTI-SUN GLAZING

Proposed Schenley Building for [...] Woodie Garber, designer, based [...] use of actinic glass in prefa[...] glazing—a method of which N[...] strong advocate. He also sugge[sts] ized glass.

3.7 Spread from Richard Neutra, "Sun Control Devices," in *Progressive Architecture*, October 1946.

3.8 Richard Neutra, Kaufmann House, Palm Springs, California, 1946.

*Towards an Organic Architecture*, celebrates the appointment of Neutra to the (non-existent) "Town Planning Board of California" as "reason to hope" that as architects return to work after the war they will "enrich their country with a new and healthy kind of scenery."[31]

There are other substantive aspects implicit in this shift in approach toward thinking about design and the public. Neutra's discussion of reconstruction, and the diagrams, plans, and perspectives that he presented in these articles, of both Rush City Reformed and the Puerto Rico projects, are among a number of indications of the postwar move away from the structured rigor of early modernism toward a different set of proposed relationships: between the architect and forces of government; between the building and the city; between interior space and inhabitant. Rush City was an elaboration on an Athens Charter type of rigid urbanism organized for efficiency, a prospect rejected in the 1940s; instead, an approach more focused on how architects could understand the needs of urban or rural inhabitants, through observation or sociological knowledge, through climate science, came to frame Neutra's endeavors and interventions.

Gregori Warchavchik refers to Neutra's work in Puerto Rico, in 1947, as "an operational architecture, made to fit human concerns, rather than any frozen formalism."[32] The capacity of a building to respond to climate was an essential aspect of this operationalism. In an article on "Sun Control Devices" published in *Progressive Architecture* in October of 1946, Neutra wrote, "No single feature introduced in and by South American architecture has found as much attention as the conspicuous blinds and integrated architectural means of shading on the exterior on window fronts" (figure 3.7). He notes that "fine use has been made of this feature by . . . Roberto Brothers in their Resigures [*sic*] Building and others in Rio. . . . The vertical moveable variety," Neutra concludes, "is particularly intriguing" (he also notes, somewhat dismissively, "I believe Le Corbusier has suggested brise-soleil of a similar type").[33]

In a later archival document—a list of image captions—Neutra wrote in pencil in the corner: "after much experimentation and research, moveable metal louvers were used first in the U.S.A. by Neutra, when he built his desert house." The reference is to the Kaufmann House, built outside Palm Springs in 1944, which as he rightly notes became one of the best-known climatically engaged buildings, internationally (figure 3.8). The louvers are, in fact, shading an outdoor space, reducing direct solar exposure in a relatively comfortable climate. Neutra also claims the installation of movable metal louvers at the Northwestern Insurance headquarters in Los Angeles (1949, see figure 2.23) as the first commercial application, which would go on to be popular in many office buildings in the region.[34]

Neutra's article and comments are yet another object lesson in how significant shading was to the way modern architecture was being viewed in this period. He wrote numerous articles, in American, Spanish, German, and Japanese journals, about climate and its effects. His claims suggest that there was an audience attentive to how and when to deploy climate mitigating devices, and even that, as suggested in the last chapter, experiments in Brazil and elsewhere were seen as seminal events in the development of architectural modernism, influencing the global discussion.

## A "Planetary Test"

"We will all profit by the experiment, no matter where the laboratory area in which it is done," Neutra concluded in his "Comments on Planetary Reconstruction."[35] In late 1943, then with few commissions and teaching at Bennington College in Vermont, Neutra was asked by the US-appointed governor of Puerto Rico, Rexford G. Tugwell, to lead a massive effort for the design and construction of public facilities on the island—particularly houses, schools, and health centers. Neutra had been suggested by a recently formed Committee on Design of Public Works, which selected him in large part because of acclaim for the Channel Heights project.[36] Channel Heights was widely published and was celebrated for its livability as well as for the economy and efficiency of its design. It was also funded by the Federal Works Agency, familiar to New Dealer Tugwell, who established a similar relationship between design and a centralized planning bureaucracy in Puerto Rico.

Tugwell was an economist and a planner; he had been in charge of the Resettlement Association and the development of Greenbelt towns in the early 1930s. In 1936 he became the first head of the New York City Planning Commission, appointed by Mayor Fiorello LaGuardia to increase public housing.[37] In this position he unabashedly embraced large-scale centralized planning as a model for urban growth and social reform. His interpretation of the promise of technical modernity relied on the expertise of urban and economic planners to reduce social inequity through dramatic improvements to the built environment. He approached his work in Puerto Rico as an opportunity to test central planning principles he had developed working with Roosevelt on New Deal programs. Tugwell represented, as one recent article puts it, "the leftmost flank of [the New Deal] 'Brain Trust.' "[38]

Tugwell was appointed governor of Puerto Rico in 1941—the last non-Puerto Rican to serve in that role. He was brought in as the agent of what would be called a "peaceful revolution," the American government having at once conceded that its possessions in the Caribbean were in desperate need of development to decrease economic inequity and increase quality of life, but also hoping to avoid the political upheaval that had played out in other nearby islands.[39] Tugwell's time in the position was largely focused on moving toward a self-governing system for the island, a process reflective of Neutra's interest in "Planetary Reconstruction," in the capacity for self-determination. Neutra shared Tugwell's liberal orientation and his conviction that self-sufficiency could be shepherded by a combination of democratic reforms and a radical transformation to the built environment.[40]

In 1942, Tugwell helped to create the Puerto Rico Planning, Urbanization, and Zoning Board, with the ambition of centrally controlling both economic and physical planning.[41] He filled the board with New Deal planners and others involved in the national resource planning aspects of the war effort.[42] The Committee on Design of Public Works sat under this broader authority. The committee brought in the architect Henry Klumb as director in 1944, in the middle of Neutra's time on the island. Klumb was, like Neutra, a European émigré, and was even more an acolyte of Frank Lloyd Wright. Klumb had worked with Tugwell on the design of three Greenbelt towns built in the 1930s. He would leave the directorship just one year later, in 1945, to join the Puerto Rico Housing Authority, designing a number of significant structures on the island over the next twenty years. He is well known for his own house—an early example of tropical modernism. He also designed the University of Puerto Rico campus in Río Piedras, one of a number of university cities being built across Latin America in the period.[43]

Neutra was only involved in Puerto Rico for a short time—from the end of 1943 to early 1945—and though he produced detailed designs and elaborate rationales for a range of public building types, very little was built. Although they started out by working together, Neutra and Klumb did not get along; the historian Silvia Álvarez-Curbelo refers gently to their "professional incompatibility." Numerous documents in Neutra's archive are less polite. Neutra came to blame Klumb for getting in the way of further realizations of his plans for the island. One imagines they may have been too similar in design approach, vying for dominance in the tight circles of the island's reconstruction.[44]

It was a complicated period on the island—the emergence of a popular party focused on self-governance was disrupting familiar political and industrial networks;[45] the oscillation between central planning and attending to the needs of the people complicated design ambitions; Klumb's entry and then retreat from the directorship of the Committee on the Design of Public Works in particular, it seems, frustrated many of Neutra's efforts. All of these developments would have an impact on the difficult translation of Neutra's plans and drawings to built work.

Alongside this technocratic premise Neutra introduced some more nuanced ideas seemingly resonant with the theories of climatic determinism that informed so many invested in the topic in the period before the war. He does, though, invert the model somewhat, seeing in the less-temperate zones a more appropriate condition for social and intellectual development, as he reveals in an unpublished essay titled "Man's Home Was South," later partially integrated into *Survival through Design*. "The 'ONE WORLD' now expressed by UNESCO is not really a new thing," Neutra began, "it is now assumed that civilization has geographically and psychologically a mild climate origin."[46] He then describes how the challenges of northern architecture, focused on "compensation for thermal deficiency," are irrelevant to designs for a mild climate. Southern inhabitants, furthermore, don't have to negotiate "severe almost 'traumatic' winter memories" that would encourage them to live in small, well-insulated buildings even when the weather is comfortable.

"An architect of tomorrow," Neutra insists, "will be an applied biologist, and this includes all the psychology which branches out from temperature and climate."[47] This tight connection between social structures, the built environment, and individual psychology provides a framework for much of Neutra's work after the war, relative to his intensive engagement with the needs and proclivities of his clients.[48] "Our point," Neutra wrote, on these more general terms, "is that the human abode, the psychology of the family dwelling can never be fully understood by itself. In use and significance it always becomes fully clear only by contrast to and by an appraisal of something external to it."[49] This leads not only to a different climatic attitude on the interior but also to frequent gatherings outside—"differing from the Nordic situation, the individual dwelling is in this climate in psychological contraposition to a daily and perpetual routine assembly outdoors . . . humanity here is in a continuous shindig which *is* the neighborhood."[50]

So, in some sense, by invoking "planetary" ambitions, Neutra sought to elevate the discourse on what is now called the Global South to approach the social and architectural ambitions characteristic of the industrialized north—to use architectural and planning means to draw these regions into a more general global consideration. In particular, he was insistent on the different material and technological requirements for building in different regions, and on the industrial feedback loops that could emerge as populations in warmer climates expressed their need for specific material conditions through consumer spending, thereby encouraging industrial concerns to attend to their specific needs. Neutra's celebration of the planetary was in large part a call for the globalizing flows of capital and industrial production to attend to the material and psychological needs of disparate climatic and geographical regions. In this fashion—that is, by encouraging economic growth in order to accelerate the consumer power of the Global South, as he proposed in numerous places—the economic inequities pervasive in such regions could abate, and the shindig could emerge as a time of celebration and relief from need. The role of architecture was one of facilitation, to use technology and materials to provide a built environment basis for this economic and psychological development. Architecture provided a first phase in settling such populations so that the power of their consumer desires could grow and transform the economic and industrial base accordingly. Neutra concluded "Man's Home Was South" with his typical rhetorical complexity:

> Structural types in the warm climates, as elsewhere, are the outcome of *natural determinants*, which extend from the miles of air over our heads into our inner being and into the minute properties of the human brain, on which responses, conditionings, habits and traditions depend. The physiological and thus the psychological responses to a prevalent climate reach down much beyond sheer physical consequences, and a truly global civilization can well be expected to deviate most interestingly from all its more regional predecessors.[51]

Neutra's efforts on the island, though largely unbuilt, were extensive. Given the initial ambition for 150 schools, the same number of rural health centers, and five large hospitals, Neutra worked out the details of these projects at great length. They were published in most of the major architecture journals—*Progressive Architecture*, *Architecture Forum*, *Arquitetura*, and others—in many cases through issues dedicating

significant space to his work and the project—the April 1952 *L'Architecture d'aujourd'hui*, for example. The material was also collected in the book *Architecture of Social Concern for Regions of Mild Climate*, published in Portuguese and English, with an introduction from Gregori Warchavchik, by a São Paulo publisher in 1948.[52]

There were three major components to the work: schools, health centers, and hospitals. All were intended for construction and use outside the major urban centers on the island and developed in a context of poor infrastructure and little reliable energy availability. Neutra framed this relative to an imperative for the architect to engage "the non-metropolitan world," noting that "the spreading technological situation has not been spreading so well . . . [it] coagulates in a few spots." As a result, "governments must decide to use architects in developing the human resources of the vast hinterlands."[53] Decrying the reliance on monied clients as antagonistic to the development of modernism, the development of new technologies, he wrote, "from window operating hardware, applied finish material, to any material and elements of sensible prefabrication: all of it comes into communal existence only by substantial demand and cannot be developed without mass consumption." Only by reaching out beyond the city, and beyond the upper classes for clients and patrons, could the broader social goals of modernism be reached. The architect, he insisted, should be "*interested in the population of the globe*"—and should express this interest through a certain kind of applied consumerist technics.[54]

Such an interest required careful attention to regional and local distinctions regarding climatic adaptability—the Puerto Rico projects were in this sense a test of the capacity for architects to design with attention to global frameworks and developmental logics, to the possible proliferations of factory production and material wealth, and also according to the specific details of topography, site, and climate.

Neutra's claim that "the architecture to come is of planetary scope" was in this sense distinct from the universalism of Le Corbusier's "every building around the globe" dictum and also from the interest in the International Style symbolized by the eponymous 1932 MoMA exhibition. The planetary approach attended to the climatic and the social according to what was formulated as a universal set of principles and methods, but with a sharp focus on the specifics of site. In Neutra's hands this planetary principle resonated as a sort of salve against the uneven development of infrastructure and of social services, as economic growth restarted after the war.

3.9 Richard Neutra (left) "Typical Classroom Activity Training," from a set of drawings titled Experimental Unit of the Corona Bell School, 1935. Dedicated to his son Richard. (right) Corona School, Bell, CA, 1935.

The design of rural schools was an especially important arena for these complex adjustments to the project of modernism. For Neutra, the school was a place for education, of course, but was also the site for a broader array of social services, such as community centers, health centers, milk dispensaries, demonstration kitchens, loci of water supplies, and a site for lectures on such topics as "housekeeping, wholesome diet and cooking, proper child care and clothing."[55]

Schools were also often the site for the spread of illness and disease. Their design was intended not only to allow for comfortable thermal interiors in this condition of "mild climate" but also to, without mechanical assistance, induce ventilation toward consistent air change. There were two main components to facilitate this imperative: first, Neutra used a hinge door, what he called an "awning type door," that could be opened completely. He had used a similar method for a number of schools near Los Angeles, as part of the Channel Heights development—this door was essential to his work around the island, and presumably a large part of how he was hired (figure 3.9). Paired with strategic openings, it allowed air to flow through the building rather than stagnate.[56] "Even a slow breeze of one mile an hour will change air volume of an open-front classroom five times per minute," Neutra wrote as an annotation to one central drawing, "airborn [*sic*] germs are blown out."[57]

The awning type door also, as this appellation indicates, shaded the interior space. Additionally, the method effectively increased the size of the usable classroom space, framing an indoor/outdoor classroom about 50 percent larger than the room itself. This was seen as an important means to maximize investment in schools on the island, and the square footage figures reflected this expanded area (figure 3.10). The sectional explanations in *L'Architecture d'aujourd'hui* indicate that the building type integrates shading and ventilation while also directing rain runoff into a cistern. The section, and the door/wall it described, embodied and expressed the "principle of flexibility" that was essential to these interventions more generally, any structure designed for only one group of children "*freezes all circumstances about the classroom into one single constellation* [and] is bound sooner or later to be a straight-jacket" (figure 3.11).[58]

This basic built condition underlay Neutra's approach and allowed him to suggest a range of programmatic initiatives—the *Social Concern* at the heart of the project. He designed a number of rural classrooms intended to populate the territory in a distributed fashion, according to need, and also able to aggregate where need proscribed (figure 3.12; figure 3.13). A caption explains the prefabricated elements and strategies for lumber-saving construction—all aspects of the operational approach.

The schools were one element of a village community center, "typically composed of a rural school, a health substation with porch and radio, cistern, village fountain, and dance floor. The entire group," he continued, "is in a way an educational facility." It was envisioned as a sort of annex or continuation of the school, on architectural terms and according to the implicit program of development (figure 3.14). He described the substation as having an educational and public function for "the overcoming of health neglect, of harmful dietetic routine, especially for infants . . . the ignorance of common causes of contagion, etc." Where such instructive measures fell short, architecture would help, constructing an environment, as in the schools, less susceptible to the spread of disease.[59]

After the rural school and the community center, the urban school offered a variation on the rural model with two main differences—a second story, and, ideally, a *J*-shaped occupation of the site allowing for a linear internal courtyard (figure 3.15, figure 3.16). Again, Neutra's drawings were extensive and multifaceted—in *An Architecture of Social Concern* he reproduces plans for each level, numerous perspectives and renderings, including a drawing of the lunchroom. The book also contains a multipage list of "equipment" for the industrial arts classrooms, listing machine shop materials, specialized devices, tools, and furniture. It was an explosion of environmental media—a graphic description of an intense sense of care and organization (figure 3.17). There was also a detailed home economics laboratory, including multiple kitchens, sewing areas, craft and work areas, and a comfortable "Living Room" laboratory that was extendable into the hall. The drawings, plans, diagrams, and equipment lists continued with the hospitals, health centers, rural health centers, rural health subcenters, nurses' dormitories, dining halls, large dining halls with attached kitchens, "homes and car shelter" for a community of "resident physicians," and community centers (figure 3.18). Neutra designed a whole world of health, if not precisely to Dr. Lovell's principles, still as the result of a similar kind of social concern and attuned to the characteristics and presumed prospects of the region.

For these rural and urban health centers, as for the two-story urban schools, the design focus was on ventilation. Neutra developed a device he referred to as the "continuous subsoffit airchange over lowered spandrel" (CSSA/LS) (figure 3.19). By inserting an air space between the ceiling and the roof, for which he coined the multilingual term "ventopenings," breezes could enter into the room above the shaded façade. As this structural frame was continuous through the building the breezes could continuously move air through the rooms and corridors—though as it is schematically rendered, and as he discussed it, it is not clear how this ventilating breeze would circulate within the room, that is, below the lowered spandrel. CSSA/LS was repeated as a motif throughout the book. Although not precisely a façade section, it is a drawing that aims to reveal the building envelope as a site for climatic innovation.

The larger-scale buildings exhibited a different relationship to climate than the small-scale schools and health centers (figure 3.20). The May–June 1946 issue of the French journal *L'Architecture d'aujourd'hui* was dedicated to Neutra's work, published in French and English. It included an interview with Marcel Lods, a number of articles by Neutra detailing his principles and design processes—including a sort of play-by-play "Procedure of the Design Office"—and, for the bulk of the pages, a discussion of his recent buildings. Fourteen private houses were shown, as were a number of apartment buildings and complexes including Channel Heights. The *L'Architecture d'aujourd'hui* issue included an extended twenty-page collection of his work in Puerto Rico, which focused on the larger-scale district hospitals and dormitories. It suggests that this broad approach to climate, though focused on concerns of village development, was also applicable at a larger scale. Indeed, the hospital in particular presented some significant design challenges, notably the isolation of those with communicable diseases, and induced ventilation to reduce the spread of germs in other wards and public spaces. Only surgical suites and certain special service groups had glazed windows and mechanical air conditioning—this mechanical system would have been focused on ventilating more than cooling. The hospital buildings were "extremely narrow, wards are no more than semi-interiors protected from excessive sunshine by moveable blinds and a roof overhang, while non-corrosive screening keeps out insects."[60] Neutra's nuanced approach to a design for development reached an apex here, perhaps, in the

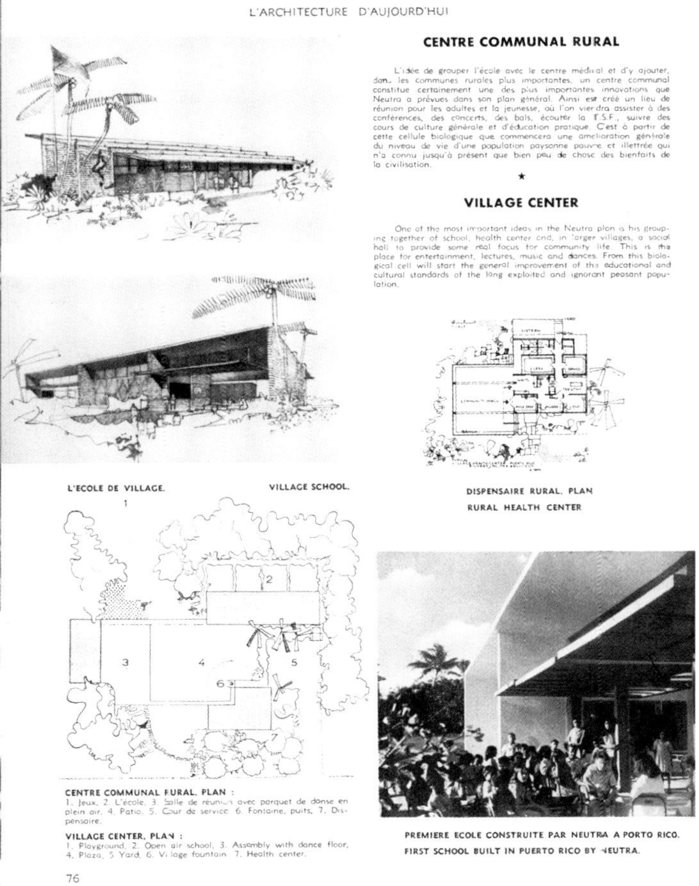

L'ARCHITECTURE D'AUJOURD'HUI

**CENTRE COMMUNAL RURAL**

L'idée de grouper l'école avec le centre médical et d'y ajouter, dans les communes rurales plus importantes, un centre communal constitue certainement une des plus importantes innovations que Neutra a prévues dans son plan général. Ainsi est créé un lieu de réunion pour les adultes et la jeunesse, où l'on viendra assister à des conférences, des concerts, des bals, écouter la T.S.F., suivre des cours de culture générale et d'éducation pratique. C'est à partir de cette cellule biologique que commencera une amélioration générale du niveau de vie d'une population paysanne pauvre et illettrée qui n'a connu jusqu'à présent que bien peu de chose des bienfaits de la civilisation.

★

**VILLAGE CENTER**

One of the most important ideas in the Neutra plan is his grouping together of school, health center and, in larger villages, a social hall to provide some real focus for community life. This is the place for entertainment, lectures, music and dances. From this biological cell will start the general improvement of the educational and cultural standards of the long exploited and ignorant peasant population.

L'ECOLE DE VILLAGE. VILLAGE SCHOOL.

DISPENSAIRE RURAL, PLAN
RURAL HEALTH CENTER

**CENTRE COMMUNAL RURAL, PLAN :**
1. Jeux, 2. L'école, 3. Salle de réunion avec parquet de danse en plein air, 4. Patio, 5. Cour de service 6. Fontaine, puits, 7. Dispensaire.

**VILLAGE CENTER, PLAN :**
1. Playground, 2. Open air school, 3. Assembly with dance floor, 4. Plaza, 5 Yard, 6. Village fountain 7. Health center.

PREMIERE ECOLE CONSTRUITE PAR NEUTRA A PORTO RICO.
FIRST SCHOOL BUILT IN PUERTO RICO BY NEUTRA.

76

3.10 Richard Neutra, School, Puerto Rico, 1944, photograhs and a page from *Architecture d'aujourd'hui*, May-June 1946.

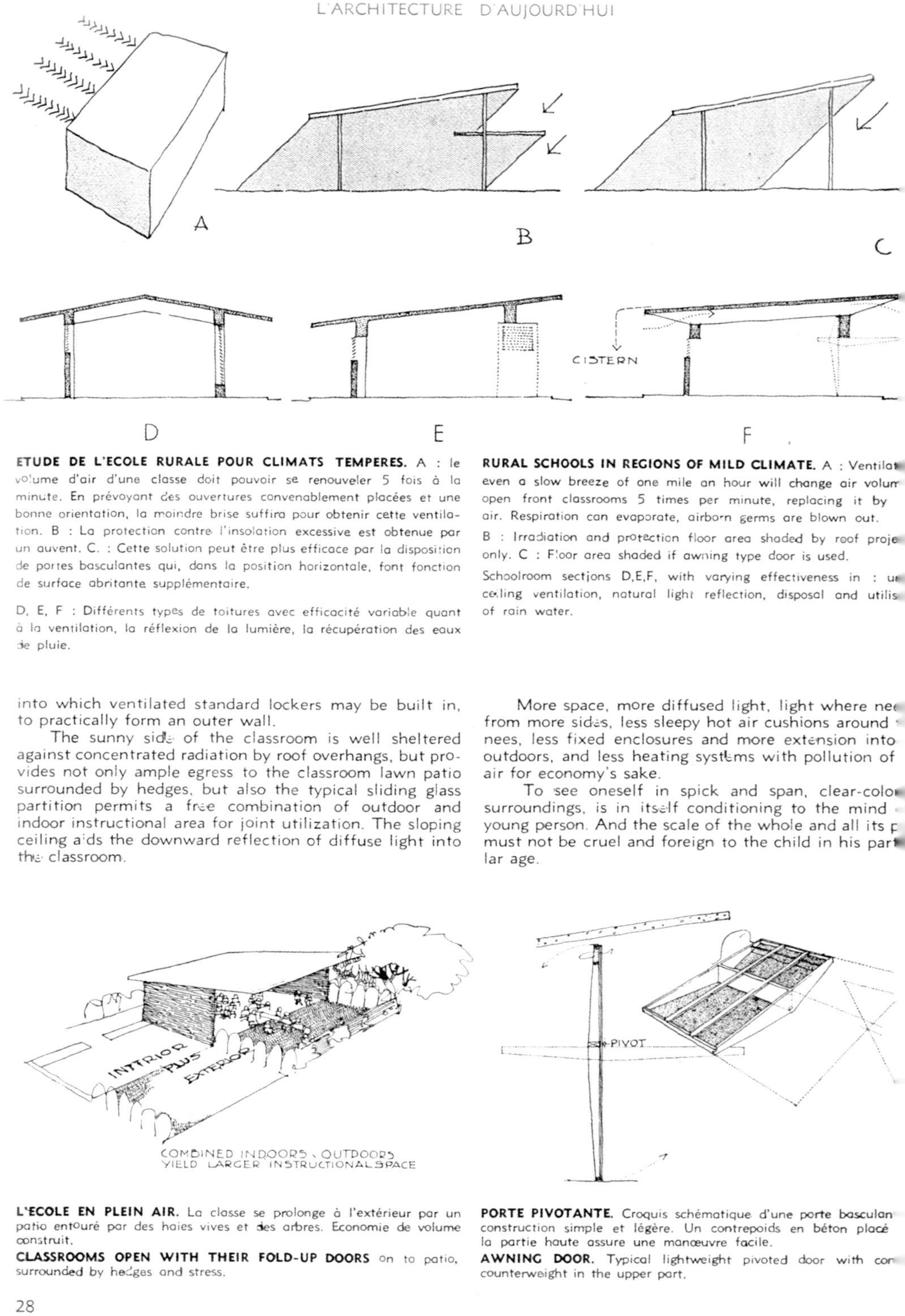

L'ARCHITECTURE D'AUJOURD'HUI



**ETUDE DE L'ECOLE RURALE POUR CLIMATS TEMPERES.** A : le volume d'air d'une classe doit pouvoir se renouveler 5 fois à la minute. En prévoyant des ouvertures convenablement placées et une bonne orientation, la moindre brise suffira pour obtenir cette ventilation. B : La protection contre l'insolation excessive est obtenue par un auvent. C. : Cette solution peut être plus efficace par la disposition de portes basculantes qui, dans la position horizontale, font fonction de surface abritante supplémentaire.

D, E, F : Différents types de toitures avec efficacité variable quant à la ventilation, la réflexion de la lumière, la récupération des eaux de pluie.

**RURAL SCHOOLS IN REGIONS OF MILD CLIMATE.** A : Ventilat even a slow breeze of one mile an hour will change air volum open front classrooms 5 times per minute, replacing it by air. Respiration can evaporate, airborn germs are blown out.

B : Irradiation and protection floor area shaded by roof proje only. C : Floor area shaded if awning type door is used.

Schoolroom sections D,E,F, with varying effectiveness in : u ceiling ventilation, natural light reflection, disposal and utilis of rain water.

into which ventilated standard lockers may be built in, to practically form an outer wall.

The sunny side of the classroom is well sheltered against concentrated radiation by roof overhangs, but provides not only ample egress to the classroom lawn patio surrounded by hedges, but also the typical sliding glass partition permits a free combination of outdoor and indoor instructional area for joint utilization. The sloping ceiling aids the downward reflection of diffuse light into the classroom.

More space, more diffused light, light where ne from more sides, less sleepy hot air cushions around nees, less fixed enclosures and more extension into outdoors, and less heating systems with pollution of air for economy's sake.

To see oneself in spick and span, clear-colo surroundings, is in itself conditioning to the mind young person. And the scale of the whole and all its p must not be cruel and foreign to the child in his part lar age.



**L'ECOLE EN PLEIN AIR.** La classe se prolonge à l'extérieur par un patio entouré par des haies vives et des arbres. Economie de volume construit.

**CLASSROOMS OPEN WITH THEIR FOLD-UP DOORS** on to patio, surrounded by hedges and stress.

**PORTE PIVOTANTE.** Croquis schématique d'une porte basculan construction simple et légère. Un contrepoids en béton placé la partie haute assure une manœuvre facile.

**AWNING DOOR.** Typical lightweight pivoted door with co counterweight in the upper part.

28

3.11 Richard Neutra, Schematic Drawings of Shading Devices, from *Architecture d'aujourd'hui*, May–June 1946.

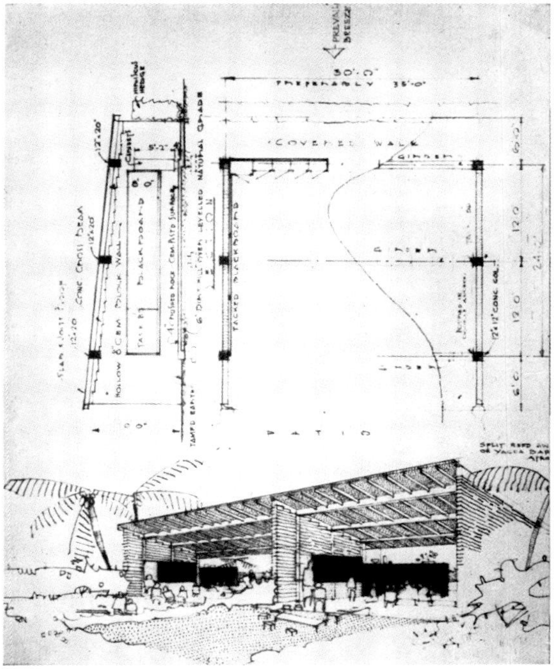

**escola rural,** **tipo semi-prefabricação**

**rural classrooms,** **typical semi-prefabrication**

Para economizar madeira de fôrma, pode-se fabricar blocos de concreto para as paredes transversais das salas de aula. Estuda-se a pre-fabricação de elementos de estrutura do telhado e das vigas, para introduzir uniformidade da qualidade de construção. Porém, o teto liso de construção normal, pode ser superior, do ponto de vista funcional, e economicamente igual, caso se empregue fôrmas de concreto re-usaveis permanentemente.

To save form lumber, hollow concrete blocks may be manufactured for classroom crosswalls. Pre-fabricated roof slab-elements and joists are being studied to introduce uniform quality of construction over a wide area. The unobstructed flush ceiling of normal construction however may prove functionally superior and with permanent reusable formwork equally economical.

**escola rural** — **rural school**

**planta & detalhe da construção** — **plan & structural design**

Cistern — Fossa
Classroom — Sala de aula
Horiz'l. position — Posição horizontal
Section thru swing up patio door — Corte da porta basculante
Vertic'l. position — Posição vertical

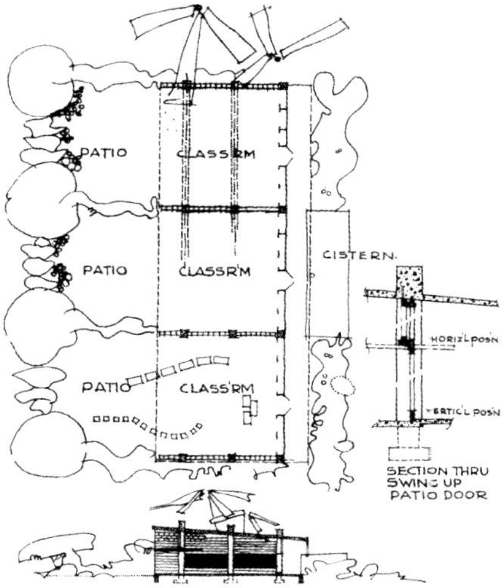


3.12 Richard Neutra, Rural Schools, from *An Architecture of Social Concern for Regions of Mild Climate*, 1947.

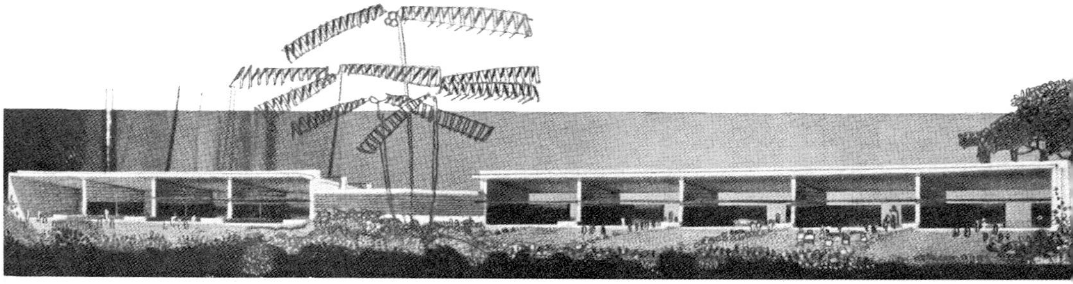

## ÉCOLES POUR PORTO-RICO

Aucune des réalisations envisagées n'est appelée à transformer plus profondément la vie des habitants de Porto-Rico que la construction des écoles, principalement dans les régions rurales. Partant de son école type réalisée déjà en Californie, Neutra a adopté un élément encore simplifié d'unité de classe où le volume construit est réduit au strict minimum. A cet élément qui constitue la cellule de base peuvent s'adjoindre, selon les programmes locaux, d'autres unités plus complexes. Un certain nombre de dispositions type avec équipement spécial est prévu. Tels les quelques exemples reproduits ci-contre. Leur groupement peut se prêter à toutes les variantes en plan.

**PLANS CI-CONTRE : ELEMENTS TYPE**

**1. Classe type - 2. Cantine d'école - 3. Classe d'enseignement ménager - 4. Groupe sanitaire pour garçons et filles.**

★

## SCHOOLS FOR PUERTO-RICO

Of all building projects none will so profoundly change the mode of life of Puerto Ricans as the rural schools. Guided by schools designed for California, Neutra has established a simplified classroom unit complete in itself, with a volume reduced to the minimum. To this basic unit other typical elements with special equipment can be added, in accordance with local needs. (See cut). Grouping can be arranged in innumerable combinations.

**PLANS AT LEFT : TYPICAL UNITS**

**1. Typical classroom - 2. Lunch facilities - 3. Home Economics - 4. Toilets for boys and girls.**

1

2

3

4

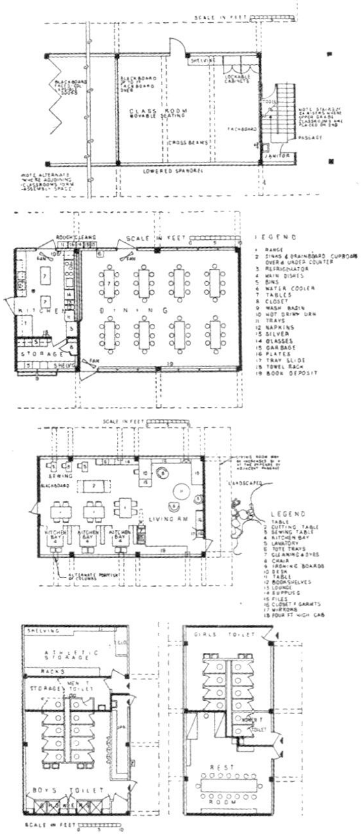

3.13 Richard Neutra, Rural Schools, from *Architecture d'aujourd'hui*, May–June 1946.

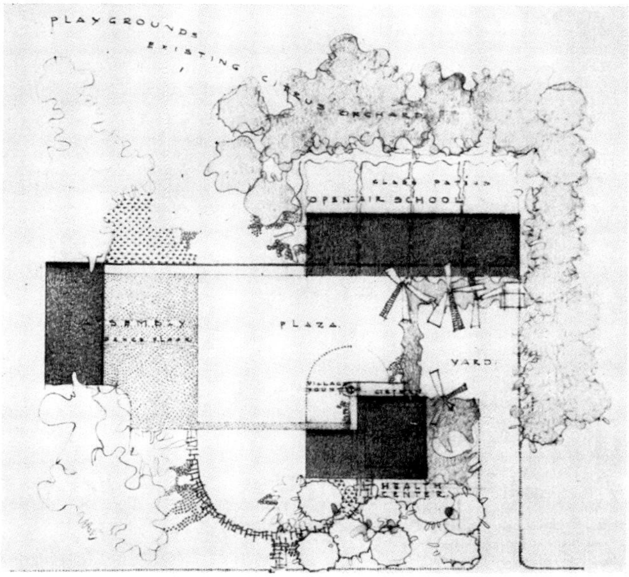


**village community center,** typically composed of a rural school, a health substation with porch and radio, a cistern, village fountain, and dance floor. The entire group is in a way an educational facility.

**centro civico comunal**

com a composição tipica de uma escola rural, um sub-centro de saude, com pateo coberto e radio, com uma fossa de esgotos, um chafariz ou fonte de aldeia e um tablado para dançar.
O agrupamento é organizado no sentido de uma instituição educacional.

3.14 Richard Neutra, Village Community Center, from *An Architecture of Social Concern for Regions of Mild Climate*, 1947.

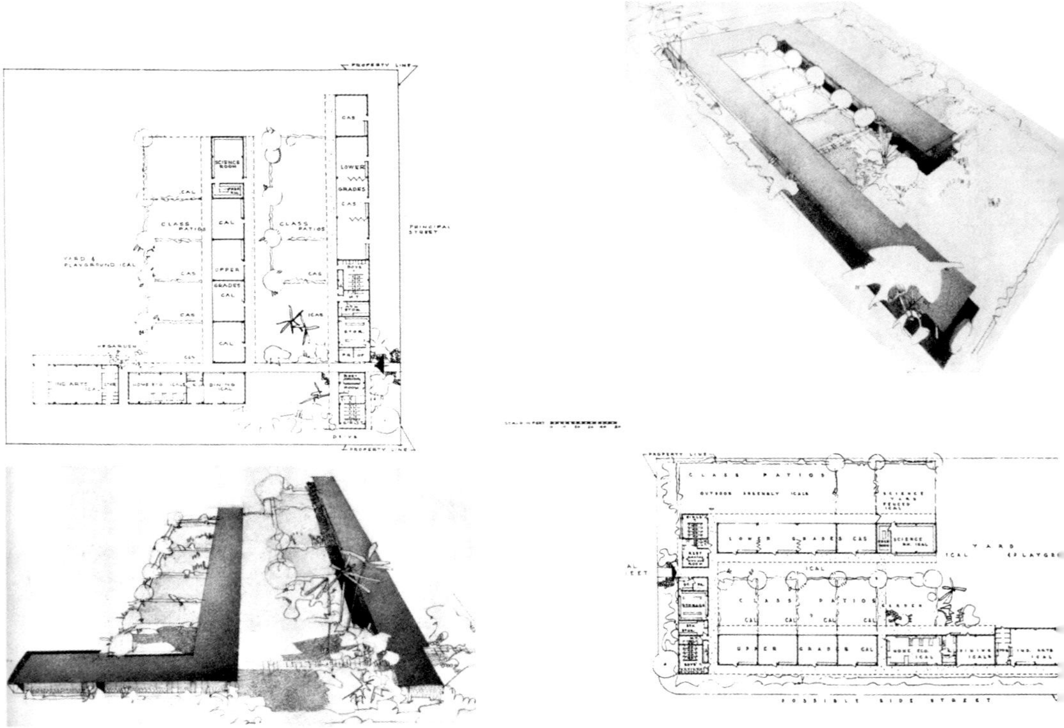

3.15 Richard Neutra, plans and perspectives of urban schools, from *An Architecture of Social Concern for Regions of Mild Climate*, 1947.

3.16 Richard Neutra, lunch room of an urban school, from *An Architecture of Social Concern for Regions of Mild Climate*, 1947.

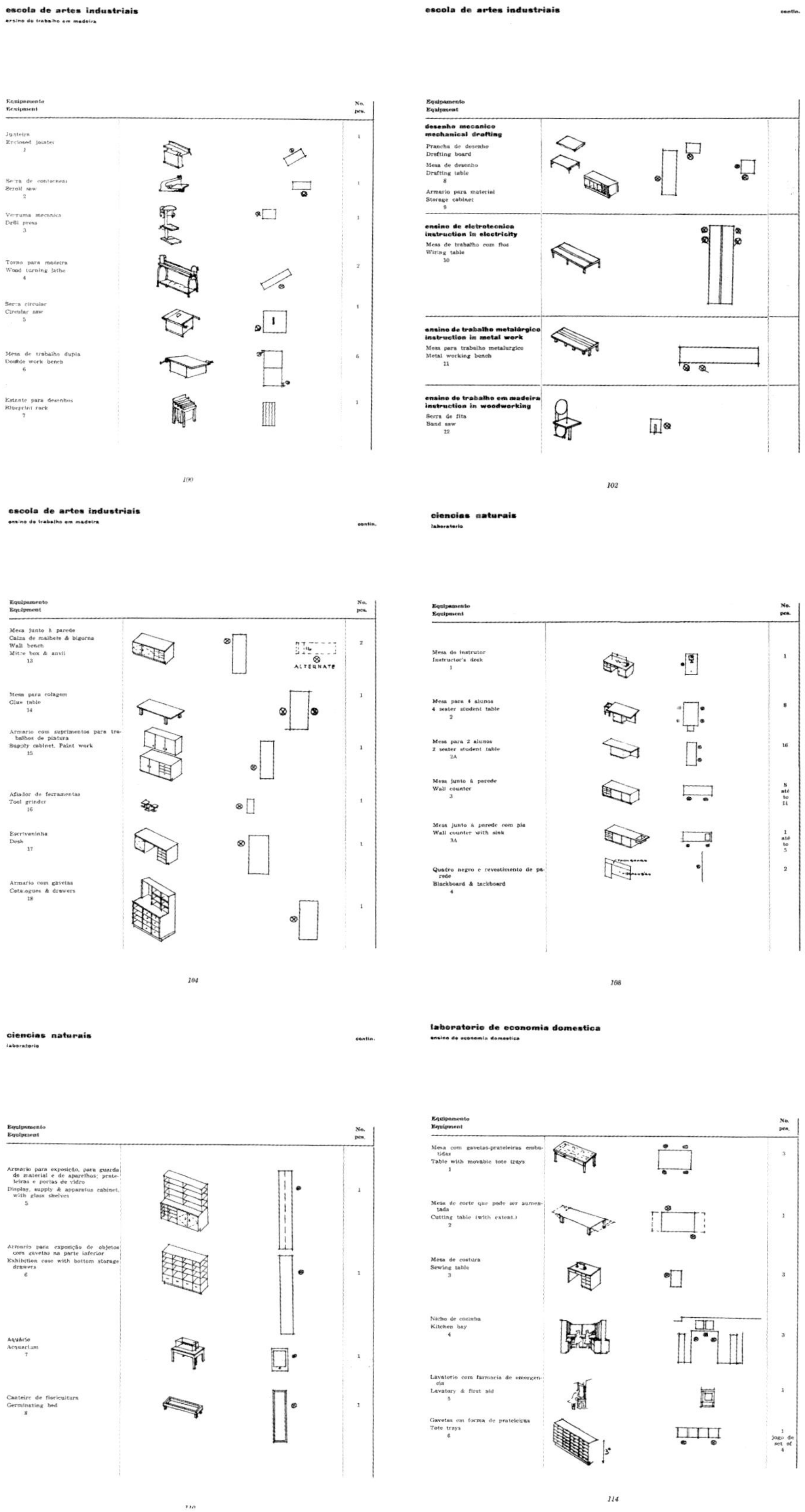

escola de artes industriais
ensino de trabalho em madeira

| Equipamento / Equipment | No. pes. |
|---|---|
| Junteira / Enclosed jointer 1 | 1 |
| Serra de contornear / Scroll saw 2 | 1 |
| Verruma mecanica / Drill press 3 | 1 |
| Torno para madeira / Wood turning lathe 4 | 2 |
| Serra circular / Circular saw 5 | 1 |
| Mesa de trabalho dupla / Double work bench 6 | 6 |
| Estante para desenhos / Blueprint rack 7 | 1 |

100

escola de artes industriais contin.

| Equipamento / Equipment | |
|---|---|
| **desenho mecanico / mechanical drafting** | |
| Prancha de desenho / Drafting board | |
| Mesa de desenho / Drafting table 8 | |
| Armario para material / Storage cabinet 9 | |
| **ensino de eletrotecnica / instruction in electricity** | |
| Mesa de trabalho com fios / Wiring table 10 | |
| **ensino de trabalho metalúrgico / instruction in metal work** | |
| Mesa para trabalho metalurgico / Metal working bench 11 | |
| **ensino de trabalho em madeira / instruction in woodworking** | |
| Serra de fita / Band saw 12 | |

102

escola de artes industriais contin.
ensino de trabalho em madeira

| Equipamento / Equipment | No. pes. |
|---|---|
| Mesa junto à parede / Caixa de malhete & bigorna / Wall bench / Mitre box & anvil 13 | 2 |
| Mesa para colagem / Glue table 14 | 1 |
| Armario com suprimentos para trabalhos de pintura / Supply cabinet. Paint work 15 | 1 |
| Afiador de ferramentas / Tool grinder 16 | 1 |
| Escrivaninha / Desk 17 | 1 |
| Armario com gavetas / Catalogues & drawers 18 | 1 |

104

ciencias naturais
laboratorio

| Equipamento / Equipment | No. pes. |
|---|---|
| Mesa do instrutor / Instructor's desk 1 | 1 |
| Mesa para 4 alunos / 4 seater student table 2 | 8 |
| Mesa para 2 alunos / 2 seater student table 2A | 16 |
| Mesa junto à parede / Wall counter 3 | 5 até to 11 |
| Mesa junto à parede com pia / Wall counter with sink 3A | 1 até to 5 |
| Quadro negro e revestimento de parede / Blackboard & tackboard 4 | 2 |

106

ciencias naturais contin.
laboratorio

| Equipamento / Equipment | No. pes. |
|---|---|
| Armario para exposição, para guarda de material e de aparelhos; prateleiras e portas de vidro / Display, supply & apparatus cabinet, with glass shelves 5 | 1 |
| Armario para exposição de objetos com gavetas na parte inferior / Exhibition case with bottom storage drawers 6 | 1 |
| Aquário / Acquarium 7 | 1 |
| Canteiro de floricultura / Germinating bed 8 | 1 |

110

laboratorio de economia domestica
ensino de economia domestica

| Equipamento / Equipment | No. pes. |
|---|---|
| Mesa com gavetas-prateleiras embutidas / Table with movable tote trays 1 | 3 |
| Mesa de corte que pode ser aumentada / Cutting table (with extent.) 2 | 1 |
| Mesa de costura / Sewing table 3 | 3 |
| Nicho de cozinha / Kitchen bay 4 | 3 |
| Lavatorio com farmacia de emergencia / Lavatory & first aid 5 | 1 |
| Gavetas em forma de prateleiras / Tote trays 6 | 1 jogo de set of 4 |

114

3.17 Richard Neutra, Equipment lists for the Industrial Arts school and the Home Economics Laboratory (partial), from *An Architecture of Social Concern for Regions of Mild Climate*, 1947.

**escola urbana** | **urban school**

laboratorio de economia domestica — home economics lab.
vista total — total view

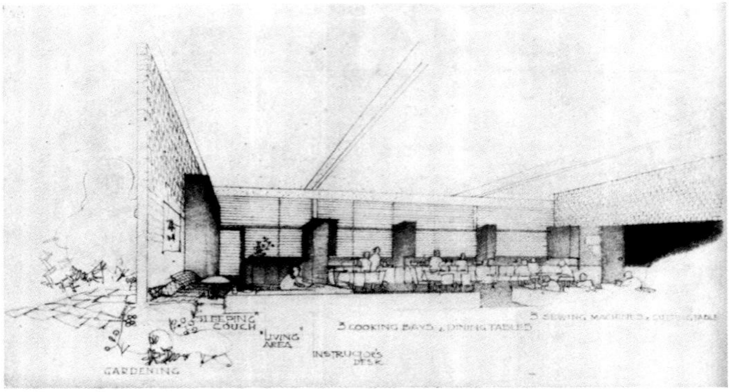


| | | |
|---|---|---|
| 3 cooking bays & dining tables | — | 3 nichos de cozinha e 3 mesas de sala de jantar |
| 3 sewing machines & cutting table | — | 3 maquinas de costura e 1 mesa para cortar fazenda |
| Gardening | — | Jardinagem |
| Instructor's desk | — | Escrevaninha da instrutora |
| Living area | — | Espaço que representa a sala de estar |
| Sleeping couch | — | Sofá-cama |

*112*

**economia domestica** | **home economics**

capacidade para 24 alunas — capacity 24

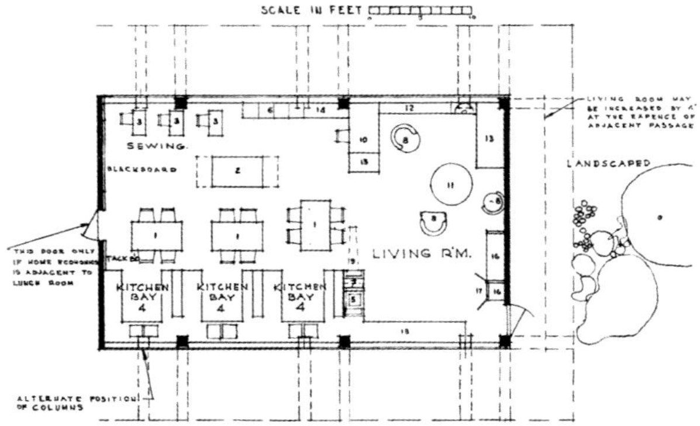


| | | | |
|---|---|---|---|
| 1 | Table | — | Mesa |
| 2 | Cutting table | — | Mesa de corte |
| 3 | Sewing table | — | Mesa de costura |
| 4 | Kitchen bay | — | Nicho de cozinha |
| 5 | Lavatory | — | Lavatorio |
| 6 | Tote trays | — | Gavetas-bandeja num armario |
| 7 | Cleaning & dyes | — | Limpeza & corantes |
| 8 | Chair | — | Cadeira |
| 9 | Ironing boards | — | Tabuas de passar a ferro |
| 10 | Desk | — | Escrevaninha |
| 11 | Table | — | Mesa |
| 12 | Book shelves | — | Estante de livros |
| 13 | Lounge | — | Sofá |
| 14 | Supplies | — | Suprimentos |
| 15 | Files | — | Fichario |
| 16 | Closet for garments | — | Guarda-roupa embutido |
| 17 | Mirrors | — | Espelhos |
| 18 | Four feet high cabinet | — | Armario 1,3 m de altura |

This door only if home economics is adjacent to lunch room

Esta porta sómente em caso de seção de economia domestica ser adjacente ao refeitorio

| | | |
|---|---|---|
| Alternate position of columns | — | Posição alternada de colunas |
| Blackboard | — | Quadro negro |
| Landscaped | — | Ajardinado |
| Sewing | — | Costura |

*113*

3.18 Richard Neutra, Home Economics Laboratory, from *An Architecture of Social Concern for Regions of Mild Climate,* 1947.

**centros de saude urbanos**

**detalhes da estrutura & do teto**

**urban health centers**

**structural design**

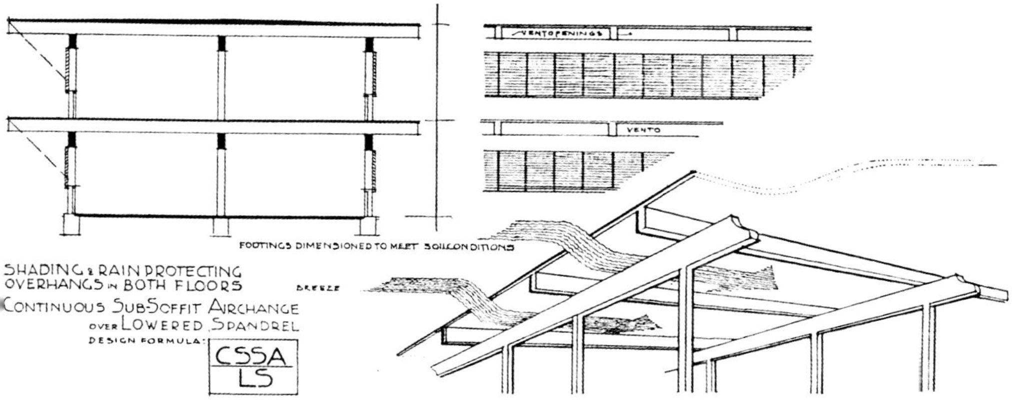


ventopenings
aberturas para ventilação

shading & rain protection overhangs in both floors
saliencias protetoras contra sol & chuva em ambos os andares

footings dimensioned to meet soil conditions
alicerces adaptados às condições do terreno

**CSSA** / **LS** = continuous sub-soffit airchange over lowered spandrel

ventilação contínua entre teto & a viga-mestra abaixada

*126*

3.19 Richard Neutra, "continuous subsoffit airchange over lowered spandrel," from *An Architecture of Social Concern for Regions of Mild Climate*, 1947.

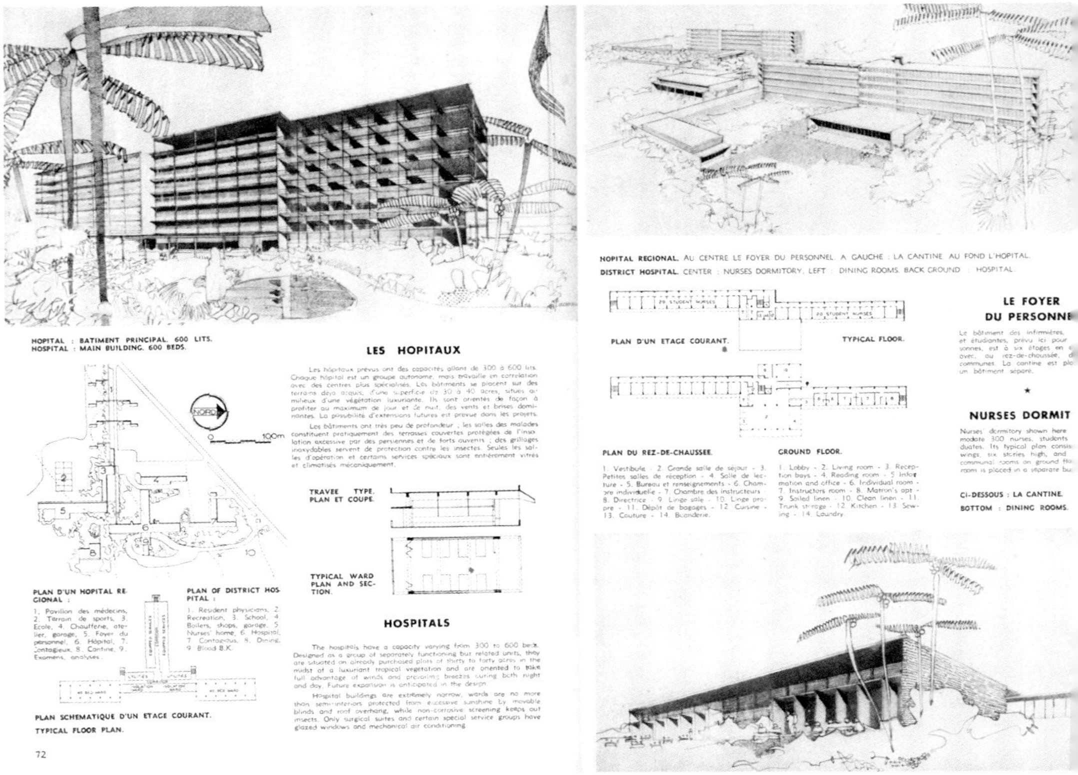


3.20 Richard Neutra, Hospitals and Nurses Dormitory, from *Architecture d'aujourd'hui*, May–June 1946.

ambition for an open-air hospital; none would be built.

## A Test of the Planetary

In the *Architecture of Social Concern* book, and to a lesser extent in the journal publications, Neutra went on to elaborate on the general principles and specific design proposals that would allow these interventions to best realize their broad social purpose. He listed the design attributes of the kitchens, the milk dispensaries, and the industrial arts shop; he insisted on a separation of administrative, faculty, and student restrooms; he identified possible locations where the lunchroom manager could best view the entirety of activities going on in this space. The book included a list of equipment, from coffee urns, to electric ranges, to closets and cabinet hardware, that could be used in these flexible public spaces. He detailed the adjustments to the designs necessary for building a school in a small town or urban condition, especially when a multistory building was preferable. He provided detailed, multiphase instructions of how nurse's aides should engage with patients, with different versions for different age groups. He made administrative "traffic and functional diagrams" to clarify how the management of the school or health center was reflected in its planimetric organization—such charts were distinct for tuberculosis clinics, venereal disease clinics, pediatric clinics, maternity clinics, and the milk dispensary/nutritionist stations that were the quickest and easiest to construct. Plans and perspectival drawings of each type were included in the book, further types were elaborated on in a number of the journal articles published in the late 1940s.

One is struck by the pleading tone of Neutra's writing on this material. He seemed desperate to justify the lengthy elaborations that resulted in significantly less built work than anticipated; he also seemed aware that his pleas for an architecture of development could possibly fall on deaf ears. That he himself turned back, generally speaking, to the design of bespoke private houses, which would propel his career in the 1950s, is perhaps additional evidence of the difficulty with which the architect could be configured as a development expert.

Larger concerns are at stake, having to do with the pace, process, and consequences of "development" as a model for global socioeconomic and political relations, rather than with the potential reconfiguration of architectural expertise. Neutra attempted to model design interventions in Puerto Rico as a radically site-specific means to attend to the needs of a given population—to develop, at least on conceptual terms, a universal method of reconstruction that could flexibly respond to specifics of climate, demographics, and territory, and the relative presence of industry, infrastructure, and economic systems. The goal was less to "raise" Puerto Ricans to a general Western standard and more to improve existing conditions and allow for discrete social collectives to articulate and meet their needs—his approach, however seemingly beneficent, was still determined by factors on which the inhabitants had little influence.

The planetary was in this sense distinct from the internationalism that preceded it and the globalization that would follow. Schematically, internationalism sought to apply a Euro-American model on regions and populations outside these geographic areas, maintaining and indeed reaffirming centers of culture and commerce in the metropoles; it was the "quintessential world-image of colonialism."[61] Globalization, emergent in large part through multinational networks of petroleum distribution and the attendant economic and political effects, reached toward consistency—imagining, and then building, a world where interiors could be sited anywhere. An identical system of production and consumption, backed by global corporations and the economic policies that supported them, enforced a norm through inducing and elaborating on consumer desire. Globalization, while still invested in the importance of a specific center ("global cities") projected a uniform field.

The planetary supposes something else—accounting for the world system of capital and the geophysical dynamics of earth systems, the planetary focuses on the local as a means to also understand how specific sites are integrated in heterogeneous global patterns. It is uneven, inaccurate, and inadequate as a system of corporate optimization or the expansion of government powers; it recognized, perhaps above all, friction—that is, it recognized the social and geophysical conflicts that often emerged. Resource scarcities, carrying capacities, appropriate technologies, and permacultures, for example, inform the conditions on the ground in such a planetary analysis. The planetary is shaped by knowledge from disparate regions and by engaging different versions of the same challenge while focusing on the effects on the immediate, the local, and the communal.

Neutra's designs for Puerto Rico did not exactly embody this ideal articulation of a planetary approach—perhaps his persistent invocation of the island as a "test" indicates the speculative nature of his efforts and his willingness to treat land and people as part of a broader game, a piece of a larger context that could work, or not. In this sense Neutra was looking more at the general system than the details of the project—at least in retrospect. One can also note his interest in pedagogy—in the construction of schools—as being simultaneously elevating of an individual's life possibilities and, in many colonial and neocolonial contexts, oppressive conditions of social normalization. What was being tested, in this sense, was the planetary itself—a nuanced, uneven model for economic and social transformations, attentive to the local in the context of changing geopolitical and geophysical conditions.

It failed, for the most part. Little of value was learned. Knowledge production in design and technology went elsewhere, to conditioned spaces, large-scale electricity infrastructure. According to Tugwell, the lack of realized buildings on the island had the US Congress refusing funding, in part because of the anxiety of politicians on the mainland that political agitation in Puerto Rico was increasingly moving toward forms of self-determination. US concerns over centralized planning in the late 1940s led to the dissolution of the island's planning agency.[62] During the war, it was perhaps a little easier to effect a proposal for territorial transformation that allowed for and focused on such nuanced planetary effects. After the war, with the US government caught up in a range of economic and cultural commitments toward a more assertive global presence, such nuance became an obstacle. By 1947, Operation Bootstrap—a US government program of intensive investment in the island in collaboration with the new governor, Puerto Rican native Luis Muñoz Marín—had begun. It completely changed the scale and significance of the discussion of modernization for Puerto Rico, and for the island as a model and test. Development shifted to cities and coastal areas attractive to tourists, and from agriculture to industry, largely rendering irrelevant the ideas, images, and projects Neutra had proposed.[63]

There were other, dispersed effects of this planetary test. Neutra clearly learned a lot about site and climate and would bring this knowledge into his many houses in the 1950s. He also designed the US embassy in Karachi, Pakistan, with attention to shading and induced ventilation.[64] In part due to the scale of Neutra's own ambition, the Puerto Rico projects were widely published and generally well received. Journals around the world dedicated substantive space not only to the drawings but also to discussing the delicate and environmentally sensitive architecture that carefully facilitated an uneven development model.[65] Neutra smoothed out a pathway for architectural engagement with development programs, as organized by the United Nations or other governmental and nongovernmental agencies, an engagement that, in some iterations, achieved a sensitive approach to the complex relationship of the built environment to the economic and political opportunities of a given population. But by and large, this engagement served the needs of the organization more than those of the population.

Klumb, at the Housing Authority and elsewhere, continued to build with attention to climate and local materials, for a number of decades.[66] Klumb spent time with an Austrian economist named Leopold Kohr—a writer on urbanism, economic growth, and other issues, and a professor of economics and public policy at the University of Puerto Rico from 1955 to 1973. Kohr was focused on producing an economic model that encouraged and allowed for different scales of activity and growth—he is credited, by E. F. Schumacher and others, for developing the term "Small Is Beautiful."[67] The titles of Kohr's books—*The Breakdown of Nations* (1957); *Overdeveloped Nations: Diseconomies of Scale* (first published in Spanish in 1964); and, later, *Development without Aid: The Translucent Society* (1979)—tell some of the story. He also wrote for daily papers in San Juan and elsewhere, collected as *From Mud to Marble: The Inner City*, in the 1980s. Kohr moved from Puerto Rico to Wales, and then back to Austria where he was involved in saving and preserving national forests, and villages, farmland, houses, and institutions within it. In his later life he focused on the revitalization of rural life.[68]

As Ivan Illich put it, rather than an alternative economic model, Kohr "labored to lay down the foundations for an alternative *to* economics" through "a vision of a decent common life [that] was predicated on modesty, not on plenty."[69] Although Kohr's work, as Illich also laments, is largely unknown, it would enter the general discussion of environment and economic growth through the work of Schumacher. The phrase *small is beautiful* soon became a mantra of countercultural movements advocating for alternative lifestyles and for policy makers and technologists proposing self-reliance as essential to the development of the Global South.[70] Kohr and Schumacher's work would circulate as part of the development of environmental economics discussed through the work of Kenneth Boulding and others in the late 1950s. The Center for Alternative Technology, based in Wales, is one of a number of organizations claiming Schumacher's legacy, and one that has focused on architectural means to take advantage of passive solar, thermal materials, and other site-sensitive energy technologies.[71]

## Testing a New Look

Other planetary systems were also being constructed, or reconstructed. As various attempts were made to address the "development challenges" of the Global South, US embassy building projects were organized in Washington, DC, and played out around the world—largely in regions that not only lacked the infrastructure required for mechanical conditioning, but that also were important territories for the ideological battlefield of the Cold War. This led to a different sort of planetary imagination. In these experiments, the connection between geopolitics and geophysics was even more precise. Modern architecture in general, and climatic modernism in particular, came to take on a specific diplomatic, intermediary role. A cultural practice became the mediating device between a shift in governance or policy and its effects on numerous publics. Design absorbed the contradictions and complications.

Cultural and political, the embassy buildings efforts operated at the heart of the American architectural discussion, drawing in the top architects in the field and entering into broader discourse through a series of exhibitions at New York's Museum of Modern Art: *Architecture for the State Department*, of late 1953, and *Architecture for Buildings and Government* in mid-1955. In a letter to the curator of architecture and design at MoMA, Philip Johnson, dated October 2, 1953, the architectural photographer and writer G. E. Kidder Smith reported on a recent discussion he had with Edward Durell Stone. Kidder Smith, it is worth noting, had been the primary photographer for the *Brazil Builds* book and exhibition at MoMA a

3.21 Installation view, "Architecture for the State Department," Museum of Modern Art, October 6–November 2, 1953.

decade earlier and was intimately familiar with historical and contemporary buildings in Brazil, and with their approach to climate.

The conversation with the architect Stone was focused elsewhere: Stone had just submitted a preliminary scheme for his embassy building in New Delhi to the US State Department and shared some disconcerting news. As Kidder Smith wrote:

> It seems that two State Department upper echelon boys . . . (or their wives) do not like modern architecture. Period. And they are fully determined that the State Department will no longer have these glorious United States represented by such "modernistic" clap-trap as is being erected in Stockholm, Athens, etc, . . .
>
> Leland King, who, as you know, is the one man responsible for getting really decent official architecture, being head of Foreign Building Operations, is the man they have to axe. Last week Ed Stone told me they got him. Which means that Ed's New Delhi embassy will never materialize . . . and we shall be represented instead by some fine Colonoid monstrosity. . . . And which also means that the rest of the program all over the world will reverse itself and the columns will sprout.[72]

Kidder Smith goes on to propose that Johnson encourage Alfred Barr, the founding director of MoMA and by then an advisory director, and Nelson Rockefeller, the industrialist and a significant donor to the museum, to get in touch with their fellow "old Princeton man," the new secretary of state John Foster Dulles, and "bring the department to its senses."[73]

The letter was written somewhat after the fact, but it suggests that the MoMA *Architecture for the State Department* was an attempt to do just that. Stone's New Delhi embassy did materialize, as did numerous other State Department commissions by the best-known American and émigré architects—part of the "post-war flowering," to use Johnson's term, of modern architecture in America. *Architecture for the State Department* presented a selection of projects commissioned by the State Department's Office of Foreign Building Operations, known as FBO, from 1948 to 1952. The show was on view from October 6 to November 22, 1953. It was small, taking up only one room, and no catalog was published (figure 3.21). Most of the material listed in the preliminary checklists was also collected in an unsigned article titled "U.S. Architects Abroad" in *Architectural Forum* of March 1953.[74] Johnson declared, in late 1952, that the "battle for modern architecture had long been won"; however, as the exhibition was being planned, the flames of war had been rekindled.[75] Elizabeth Gordon's April 1953 article identifying modern architecture, and MoMA's support of it,

3.22 Harrison and Abramowitz, US embassy, Havana, Cuba, 1952, and Harrison and Abramowitz, US embassy, Rio de Janeiro, Brazil, 1952. From "Architecture for the State Department," 1953.

as a "Threat to the Next America" (discussed in the next chapter) is only the best known of these new fronts.[76]

The exhibition contained nine buildings by four firms: three had been built, four were in construction, and two were still in the project stage. On entering the room at MoMA, turning to the left one saw Harrison and Abramowitz's Havana and Rio de Janeiro embassies, which had been completed in late 1952 (figure 3.22).[77] Both projects demonstrate an affinity to the headquarters for the United Nations, recently completed with Harrison heading an international team of designers to execute Niemeyer's plan.[78] Aside from the glazing resting within a thick façade, allowing for some shading, there is little attention to climate, despite the evident trends in the region. An HVAC plant was added to the Rio embassy in 1964.

Following these two projects was a large horizontal photograph of Perry House, a residential block for embassy staff in Tokyo designed by the firm of Antonin Raymond and L. L. Rado, also finished in 1952 (figure 3.23). The long, low-slung building had deep balconies facing an open garden, with a narrow plan allowing for some seasonal cross ventilation. Raymond's simple drawing of air ventilating across a modern box gave expression as the foundational framework for designing with climate (figure 3.24). Raymond's drawing was published in Fry and Drew, *Village Life in the Tropics* of 1947, referenced in Neutra's articles, and in Victor and Aladar Olgyays' *Solar Control and Shadings Devices* of 1957.

Below the Perry House image were model photographs, plans, and sketches of a prototype for staff housing to be built in the Paris suburbs of Boulogne-sur-Seine and Neuilly-sur-Seine, designed by the relatively unknown architects Ralph Rapson and John van der Meulen. Construction began late in 1953, when the exhibition was running. Rapson had designed Case Study House #4 in 1945, known as the Greenbelt House. It was one of the first to be published in the immediate postwar years and, though never built, had an outsized impact on the discussion of modern residential design.[79] The house consisted of two simple rectangles—one for public spaces: living and dining rooms, and the kitchen; the other for private spaces: bedrooms and family areas. The two were bisected by the "Green Belt," an undesigned, flexible space that the inhabitants, Rapson explained, could use as garden, courtyard,

3.23 Raymond and Rado, Perry House, Tokyo, 1952. From "Architecture for the State Department," 1953.

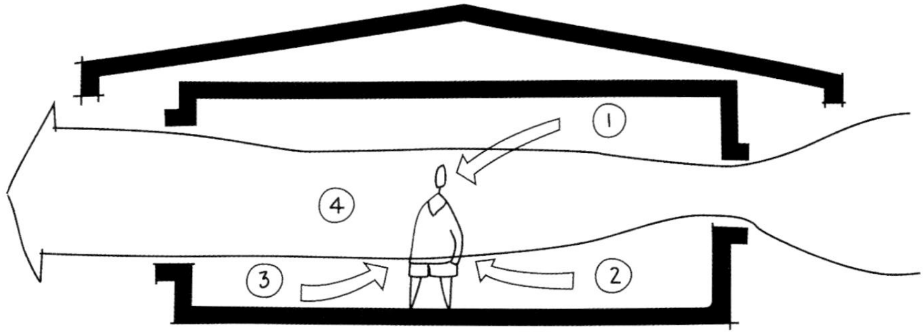


3.24 Antonin Raymond, diagram of tropical design principles, from Fry and Drew, *Village Housing in the Tropics*, 1947.

3.25 Ralph Rapson and John van der Meulen, Consulate Housing, Boulogne, France, 1953.

or play space. Rapson was hired to teach at MIT in 1940 and after a few years there was asked to assist in a number of projects at the FBO, bringing his fellow Cranbrook graduate van der Meulen with him—the two were effectively staff architects of the FBO during the very busy period of 1950–53.[80]

The Boulogne housing blocks consisted of three square apartment buildings (figure 3.25). They had deep balconies that offered sun protection for the main living areas, though there is no evidence that climatic analysis was significant to the design process. Bedrooms and other spaces were of a more exposed façade (figure 3.26). They were followed, in the exhibition, by a model photograph and sketch of Rapson's preliminary scheme for the embassy in Athens, which was not built.[81]

After a large panel with the show title, the exhibition continued with a model and drawings of Skidmore, Owings & Merrill's recently begun Bremen consulate, designed in collaboration with the German architect Otto Apel, followed by—though here the exact sequence is surmised—a plan and model photograph of the Cologne version of the same firm's "Amerika Haus" libraries and information centers proposed for seven cities throughout Germany (figure 3.27). In addition to the Bremen consulate, SOM built consulates in Düsseldorf, Frankfurt, Hamburg, Bremerhaven, Stuttgart, and Munich, and Amerika-häuser in Cologne, Frankfurt, Hamburg, Stuttgart, Berlin,

3.26 Ralph Rapson and John van der Meulen, Consulate Housing, Boulogne, France, 1953.

3.27 Amerika-häuser, Frankfurt, Skidmore, Owings & Merrill, from "Architecture for the State Department," 1953.

3.28 Amerika-häuser, Cologne, Skidmore, Owings & Merrill, from "Architecture for the State Department," 1953.

and Munich. The FBO was a major component of the growth of SOM across the 1950s (figure 3.28).[82]

Finally, there were two projects under construction by Rapson and van der Meulen included in the exhibition but not seen in the installation views: embassies at Stockholm and Copenhagen shown in the project stage, probably with perspective sketches by Rapson (see figures 3.31 and 3.32). Each project was accompanied by wall text outlining the purpose of the various buildings, describing their materials or relationship to the site, and otherwise commending the designers for the excellence and appropriateness of their work. The Bremen consulate, for example, is described as "dignified and sober, with a sparkling elegance not clearly indicated in the model," followed by details of the treatment of the steel structural system members and an explanation of the carefully planned public access to the site.

The exhibition had been organized relatively quickly—in less than six months. The first archived correspondence between Arthur Drexler, the curator of the show, and Leland King, the supervising architect of FBO, dates to May 28, 1953, though it indicates that discussions had already begun. *Architecture for the State Department* was the first architecture exhibition independently curated by Drexler, who had joined the architecture and design department in mid-1951 (and went on to a long career). He had assisted Henry-Russell Hitchcock in the organization of *Built in USA: Post-War Architecture*, which ran from January 20 to March 15, 1953; he also wrote the main essay of the catalog for the exhibition.[83] King, as the handful of letters in the archives indicate, was effectively a co-curator of the State Department exhibition; not only did he suggest and retract possible buildings for inclusion a number of times over the five months of planning, he also acted as de facto editor. All the material from the various firms had first to be sent his office at the State Department, with approved selections sent on to Drexler.[84]

The idea for the exhibition may have originated during Drexler's trip to Japan in February and March 1953. The trip was taken under the auspices of the State Department's Educational Exchange program—a similar program to the one that funded Neutra's trip to Rio de Janeiro and other parts of Latin America.[85] Drexler no doubt saw Raymond and Rado's Perry House while in Tokyo; he likely discussed the foreign building program with the architects and State Department staff.[86] Raymond and Rado's Reader's Digest Building in Tokyo (1951) was one of the first in the region to implement scientific principles of shading (see figure 5.42.) Whether the exhibition originated during this trip to Japan or was one of the reasons for the trip in the first place is not clear. The strong connections between Nelson Rockefeller, patron of the museum, and the State Department in this period are well known, and Rockefeller's promotion of international cultural exchange after the war—evidenced also by his sizable donation to start MoMA's International Program in 1952—likely influenced Drexler.[87]

That was just the beginning. This exhibition of US government buildings abroad was developed in an institutional milieu concerned with the political and the cultural components of America's newfound leadership on the world stage. It was a test, experimenting with how modern architecture could frame and facilitate policy and economic initiatives. The press release for the show opened as follows: "The United States Government is making modern American architecture one of the most convincing demonstrations of the vitality of American culture."[88] The 1953 *Architectural Forum* article on the FBO was even more explicit about placing modern architecture in the context of Cold War tensions, as the editors wrote: "No country can exercise political world leadership without exercising a degree of cultural leadership as well. . . . The FBO is displaying to the rest of the world a colorful picture of a young, progressive, and modern-minded America . . . the lesson will not be lost upon those who have received a different impression from Soviet propaganda."[89] To substantiate this last point, the article was illustrated by comparative images of new American diplomatic projects and their Soviet counterparts in Finland, Germany, and Cuba (figure 3.29).

The FBO, which began operation in 1946, grew dramatically in the following decade.[90] The physical presence of the US government in countries around the world was an important component of emerging Cold War strategies that included financial and military aid, containment, and covert operations of various kinds. The embassies, consulates, office buildings, and United States Information Agency centers built by the FBO were the locus of these activities.

In developing the office, the State Department worked out a crucial arrangement with Congress for acquiring real estate. Most of the host countries were nominally in debt to the United States as a result of Marshall Plan aid or other funding programs, though they were not necessarily expected to repay these debts with currency. The FBO arranged that governments could offset these paper debts by donating land, building materials, and construction services to the production of diplomatic buildings.[91] Thus government buildings abroad were built with little taxpayer expense; this financial independence resulted in a lack of congressional oversight that allowed FBO to respond rapidly to emerging tensions around the world. Indeed, the location and timing of diplomatic building production is a reliable index for identifying hot spots of Cold War tensions.

Around 1950, the design orientation of FBO shifted definitively toward the modernist idiom. The reasons for this shift were overdetermined. It was an expression of Johnson's "post-war flowering" of American modernism that MoMA's *Built in USA: Post-War Architecture* had been concerned to demonstrate—it included work from three of the four firms in the later State Department exhibition.[92] At the same time, some of the basic design principles of modern architecture, such as program separation through volumetric distinction and efficiency in construction, and, most certainly, the building as a cultural and technical response to climate, addressed FBO's challenge of rapidly producing embassy buildings in complicated site and contextual conditions, and also serving the symbolic function identified by the *Architectural Forum* comparisons. King and his staff struggled to balance the symbolic expression of democratic openness with a massive increase in diplomatic workers and a dramatic intensification of security

This, incidentally, is the story of one agency o
Government—the Foreign Buildings Operations
of the Department of State—and its wise decision
the best US architecture and the best US architec
represent us abroad. In more than 50 embass
sulates, information centers and staff quarters no
construction or completed in places as far apart as
and Tokyo, Helsinki and Rio, Berlin and Athe
is displaying to the rest of the world a colorful p
a young, progressive and modern-minded Amer
lesson will not be lost upon those who may have
a different impression from Soviet propaganda.

But this new crop of buildings is likely to be
vanguard of a major "export drive" in America
tecture. Before long, many a US corporation will
ing headquarters overseas—like the *Reader's Dige*
ing in Tokyo (AF, Mar. '52), Ford's offices and pla
Low Countries, US oil companies' structures on the
Gulf and US steel companies' towns on the
And hand-in-hand with such private-enterprise
of American architecture will go technical assis
many foreign countries in need of our building k

Like all sound commerce, in goods as well as ic
will be no one-way street. The more architects ge
to design and construct these buildings, the more
they will be brought in contact with good foreig
tecture and building, and the more good ideas
bring home with them. Undoubtedly there are th
US architects, builders, and manufacturers of
materials can learn from abroad.

The questions raised by FBO's activities, t
are not confined to the most obvious one—i.e. ho
energetic young director, Lee King, managed to
an important and difficult job so very well—t
other questions relating to what US building c
the rest of the world, what it can learn from the re
world, and what US architects and builders wi
against when they work abroad. The story on the
provides some of the answers.

**Finland:** *Preliminary sketches for new U.S. Embassy in Helsinki, by famed Finnish-born modernist Eero Saarinen. Building will overlook Gulf of Finland. Below: The USSR's new Helsinki Embassy.*

**Germany:** *Skidmore, Owings & Merrill's Gordon Bunshaft designed new Bremen Consulate at left. Below: Soviet Monument in Berlin.*

**Architecture makes a good ambassador:**

**Note the pretentious classicism**

**of official Soviet architecture abroad,**

**then compare it with the clean and friendly embassies, consulates, inform**

**Cuba:** *Harrison & Abramovitz just completed the American Embassy in Havana. Right: The Soviet counterpart.*

LIFE: *Rubino*

De C. Arias

**France:** *Rapson & Vandermeulen designed staff apartments for Neuilly.*

Dorsyne

3.29 Comparison of diplomatic buildings from the United States and the USSR, in *Architectural Forum*, March 1953.

provisions across the decade, in part due to the introduction of new "specially trained personnel" of the recently formed Central Intelligence Agency.[93]

SOM's Amerika-häuser operated on a slightly different symbolic register, using the façade to negotiate between the openness of America as the beacon of democratic progress, and an architecture of security endemic to the Cold War (see figures 3.27, 3.28). The distinction between the two volumes that composed the Amerika Haus was extreme. On one side, the type involved a low-slung rectangle with an almost all glass façade that welcomes the visitor into the library and office spaces. This same sort of spread-out, low-volume structure, set back in the woods, would also characterize much of SOM's suburban corporate work in the 1950s, such as the General Life Insurance Company headquarters built in Connecticut in 1955.[94] In the Amerika Haus, these open, almost immaterial spaces were contrasted by the heaviness of the concrete auditorium, sensibly separated by the entryway. The auditoriums were also bomb shelters. SOM, having designed the housing and scientific installations in Oak Ridge, Tennessee, from 1942, had already built a town for nuclear weapons research—the apartments for Oak Ridge were part of the *Exhibition of Recent Buildings by Skidmore, Owings, and Merrill*, on view at MoMA from September 26 to November 5, 1950, and the subject of the MoMA bulletin in the fall of that year. The Amerika Haus's "attractiveness," the bulletin noted, "depends upon the felicity of its fenestration and the purity of proportion," a sort of mild indication of the intensity with which these open and closed façades would be negotiated in the embassy projects.[95]

The design and production of embassy buildings, housing, and Amerika Haus projects were keyed to movements and changes to military, diplomatic, and government personnel. Germany was, in particular, less than a decade after the war, still considered to be at risk relative to the ideological battles of the Cold War and was the site of extensive investment.

It was in part the expansion of global clandestine operations that brought the FBO into climatic regions more susceptible to temperature and humidity variability, thereby necessitating a more robust shaded approach in design and construction. Before 1953, when such clandestine operations were operating on a relatively small scale and required little spatial or technical infrastructure, a compromise between openness and secrecy was often effected in plan rather than section, typically through the repeated approach of a one-story base straddled by a glass and steel or glass and concrete tower.

One of the best examples of this was the embassy building for Stockholm, Sweden, designed by Rapson and van der Meulen. It did not require any sun-shading treatments. The tension between symbolic and programmatic imperatives shimmers in the glass-enclosed staircase, extending up from the center of the visa lobby, almost as an atrium, to the floors above, providing the illusion of access to areas that were actually carefully guarded (figure 3.30; figure 3.31). This base/tower parti pris became something of a formula for embassy and consulate design in the early 1950s, it was used by Rapson and van der Meulen for their proposal for Copenhagen, and also by SOM for all of their embassies and consulates of the period (figure 3.32; figure 3.33). The drawings indicate the isolation of public and secure spaces, much like the Greenbelt House, separating distinct programs and celebrating the distinction with novel architectural spaces.

Eisenhower's entry into the White House in late January 1953—which precipitated the backlash against modern architecture as part of a more general conservative turn—led to a shake-up at the State Department. John Foster Dulles, the new secretary of state, ordered a comprehensive review of FBO in early February, intending to reinstate cost and design oversight.[96] All work was stopped on buildings not already under construction, initiating the crisis later reported by Kidder Smith that was, most likely, already clear to various players at MoMA somewhat earlier in the year. The shake-up was initially ideological on design terms; in early March, King reports being given a "verbal fiat" to replace the plans for Athens, Helsinki, and Jakarta with "Georgian or Venetian designs" and, somewhat contradictorily, to use government buildings in Washington, DC, as a model.[97] The spring and summer of 1953 were consumed by debates over the appropriateness of traditional and modern design to the symbolic and technical concerns of government buildings abroad. Much as Kidder Smith had feared, King was fired on October 1, just five days before the opening of an exhibition based on his organizational accomplishments.

If the politicians in Washington were insistent on changing the symbolic order of the US image

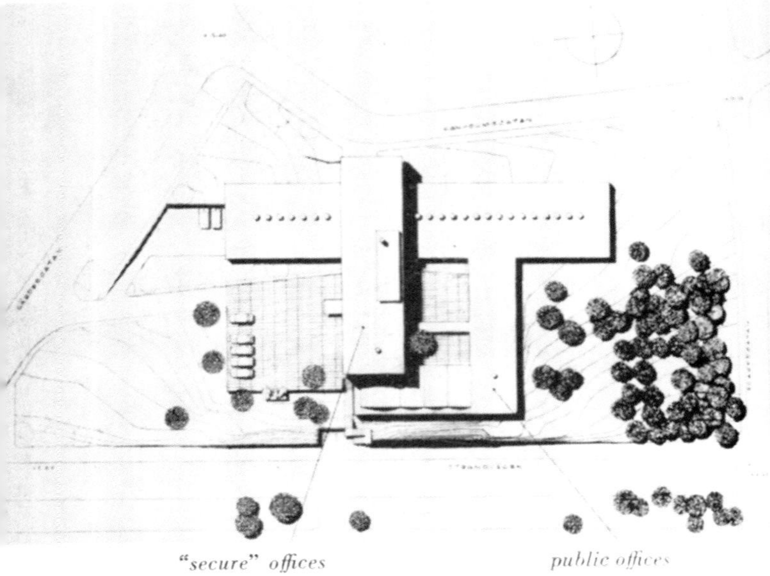


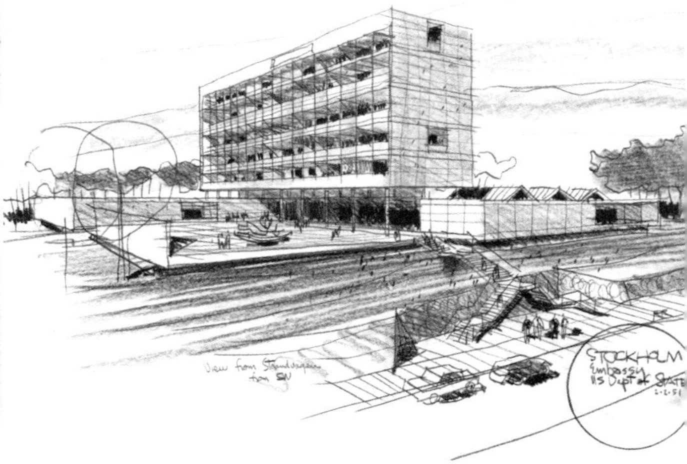


3.30 Ralph Rapson and John van der Meulen, Stockholm embassy, from "Architecture for the State Department," 1953.

3.31 Ralph Rapson and John van der Meulen, Stockholm embassy, from "Architecture for the State Department," 1953.

3.32 Ralph Rapson and John van der Meulen, Copenhagen embassy, from “Architecture for the State Department,” 1953.

**Frankfurt Consulate** *(above and right) is very similar to Bremen scheme on previous page, but has patio-centered lower floor. Composition is not unlike Lever House in Manhattan, by same architects.*

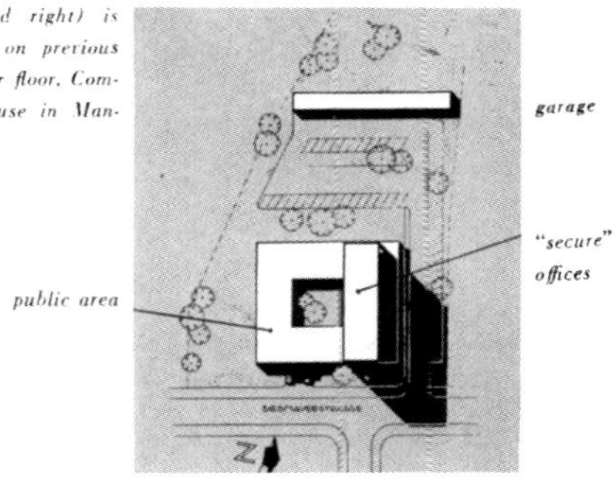


3.33 Frankfurt consulate, Skidmore, Owings & Merrill, from “Architecture for the State Department,” 1953.

abroad, diplomats and agents in the field had a much different, and in the end more influential, opinion of the benefits of modern architecture. In one important instance, CIA agents involved in engineering the May 1953 overthrow of Mohammad Mosaddegh, the popularly elected nationalist leader of Iran, were explicit in faulting the traditional design of the Tehran embassy as frustrating their operational abilities. The Tehran building, designed in 1948 by FBO staff architect Ides van der Grecht, was a bland, neoclassical building with a long open hallway and isolated, but not secured, offices.[98] It provided little separation from public areas, and the agents were forced to organize the coup out of the offices of the Anglo-British Oil Company.[99] The successful overthrow of Mosaddegh, and the subsequent partition of the Iranian oil concession in favor of US corporate involvement, was momentous proof of the effectiveness of covert operations as part of a larger foreign policy strategy.

In January 1954, Secretary Dulles effectively, if obliquely, reinstated modern architecture as the official architecture of US government buildings abroad in announcing what he called, seemingly for nonaesthetic reasons, the New Look in foreign policy. This New Look entailed a shift in defense strategy—away, relatively speaking, from the continued ballooning of standing armed forces and toward the development of massive nuclear strike capability accompanied by an intensification of diplomatic initiatives and financial assistance programs. Dulles had appointed his brother, Allen Dulles, as head of the CIA, and the agency, as is well enough known, became a crucial component of the US foreign policy approach from this period. The New Look inaugurated a golden age if you will, of CIA operations, stretching from 1954 until the Bay of Pigs fiasco in 1961, with major operations not only in Iran but also in Guatemala, the Philippines, Albania, Indonesia, and many other locations.[100]

While the Iran coup had been something of a cowboy operation, executed without much oversight from Washington, the prominent role assigned to the CIA as part of the New Look involved the creation of a bureaucratically complex and technically demanding agency. Loy Henderson, consul to Iran during the coup and head of the FBO from 1955 to 1958, indicated in 1955 that the need had arisen to accommodate the apparatuses of so-called psychological warfare, including "code and cryptographic rooms" and "the installation of air conditioning where windows needed to be kept closed to protect specialized equipment."[101] The private and public separations take on different purposes and become a simple, seemingly benign expression on planimetric terms in most subsequent buildings. See, for example, SOM's Frankfurt consulate (see figure 3.33), which provided a separate entrance for specialized personnel.

Central to this momentous shift in foreign policy was the maintenance of plausible deniability, by which those higher up on the chain of command could convincingly deny any knowledge or involvement in covert activities. Nelson Rockefeller, by this point serving the president as a special assistant for foreign affairs, was instrumental in establishing the so-called Planning Coordination Group, which reviewed possible agency operations and outlined the bureaucratic screening and filtering mechanisms by which the president would be protected from responsibility.[102] At risk of collapsing into conspiracy theory, it is hard not to see these carefully shaded structures as operating across these general diplomatic and clandestine terms, selectively allowing access, both inside and outside. The façade served as a charged plenum in the cultural, diplomatic, economic, and political relations between two countries—and possibly had some beneficent shading effects as well.

It is not surprising, then, that the "post-war flowering" of the CIA corresponds precisely to the most active period of embassy design in the late 1950s. Many of the projects planned or altered as a result of the New Look strategies were under construction or completed in 1956. Many of the best-known architects working in America at midcentury received commissions, including Edward Durell Stone (New Delhi, 1954); Josep Lluís Sert (Baghdad, 1955); Richard Neutra (Karachi, 1955; figure 3.34); Eero Saarinen (Oslo, 1955, and London, 1956); Walter Gropius and The Architect's Collaborative (Athens, 1956), among others. Unbuilt projects by Paul Rudolph (Amman, Jordan, 1954); Mies van der Rohe (São Paulo, 1956); and Louis Kahn (Luanda, Angola, 1960; figure 3.35) were also proposed; some of these are illustrated here. The most obvious result of the new regime at FBO after 1954 was the establishment of a panel of architectural advisors, led for the first five years by MIT dean Pietro Belluschi—a panel that, after 1955, was only allowed to see façade designs, perspective

3.34 Richard Neutra, US embassy, Karachi, Pakistan, 1955 (model).

3.35 Louis Kahn, US embassy, Luanda, Angola, 1955 (unbuilt).

sketches, and diagrammatic presentations of building plans, as the design specifics of the interior remained classified.[103] The FBO program proceeded on the terms of façade analysis.

## Screens

One would strain, nonetheless, to identify the possible influence of the *Architecture for the State Department* exhibition on the triumph of modernism at the Office of Foreign Building Operations. Other factors emerge regarding these clandestine programmatic imperatives, or even to some sort of broader conspiratorial notion of curatorial complicity, though such suspicions appear to be unfounded—or at least not clear from the available evidence. Of interest instead is the role played by the New Look—this dramatic change in foreign policy—in the development of the climatic aptitude of modern architecture. Put simply: when American (often émigré) architects were tasked with designing carefully programmed buildings for US office workers abroad—embassies, consulates, and houses—they relied strongly on the terms and systems developed through the experiments, in architecture and in governance, in Brazil and Puerto Rico. Further, if, indeed, some of the formal experimentation in embassy design of the 1950s was determined in part by the vicissitudes of the turn in foreign policy tactics described, the persistent exhibitions agenda at the Museum of Modern Art—which Alfred Barr had described as "simply the continuous, conscientious, resolute distinction of quality from mediocrity"—naturalized these politically loaded design elements as native to the principles of the evolving International Style.[104]

In order to build diplomatic buildings in regions of concern for the State Department, shading devices were necessary. Most of these shading systems were not attentive in any great detail to precise knowledge about climate—they were not concerned, as the Robertos (for instance) were, with careful details as to the meteorological

3.36 Weed Russell Johnson, US embassy, Kinshasa, Congo, 1954–58.

3.37 Alfred Aydellot, embassy, Manila, the Philippines, 1956–59.

3.38 Mies van der Rohe, US embassy, São Paulo, 1956 (model).

3.39 Harry Weese, US embassy, Accra, Ghana, 1956–59.

conditions of the site. Rather, the systems deployed involved a more general approach—the design of screens, for example, integrated a sense of cultural association with the host country and considerations for how it would affect the light and heat of the interior. In many cases, such screens, flying against emergent bioclimatic principles, were simply four-sided wrappers around an otherwise stoic and eminently modern glass and concrete box.

Buildings designed for the FBO between 1954 and 1958 represent some of the most elaborate experimentation to date of these screen systems. Weed Russell Johnson Associates embassy in Kinshasa, Congo, built between 1954 and 1958, had bands of screening placed in front of a concrete and glass façade (figure 3.36). The screen itself was articulated through an arrangement of rectangular and square holes set in a repeating pattern; there was also a bank of thin columns on each side of the screen, offering additional solar protection. Alfred Aydellot's embassy for Manila, the Philippines, built from 1956 to 1959, was perhaps the most straightforward: a floor to ceiling screen with an ovalesque motif hung at some distance from the glazed façade, identical in each orientation (figure 3.37). Don Hatch's embassy for Haiti, built in Port-au-Prince between 1955 and 1959, also used a bank of thin columns—though here as the screen itself rather than as a vertical accompaniment, and only on the second floor. Paul Rudolph's embassy building for Amman, Jordan, designed in 1964, was not built; neither was Mies van der Rohe's project for the US consulate in São Paulo, drawn in 1956. A stark black box, a sort of truncated Seagram tower, the project likely would have been a haven of air conditioning in a region still largely dependent on architectural shading devices (figure 3.38).

Hugh Stubbins's embassy building in Tangier (1956–59) and Harry Weese's in Accra, Ghana (1956–59) presented wrap-around systems—Weese's was assisted by a roof that extended eaves far over the façade for sun protection; it also sat high up on pilotis to take advantage of prevailing winds for ventilation (figure 3.39). Such an extended roof also characterized the Athens embassy designed by Walter Gropius in 1956, though Gropius inserted a gap at the façade to increase daylighting and did not screen the building.

Josep Lluís Sert's embassy, ambassador's residence, and housing for the diplomatic staff in Baghdad, in construction from 1955 to 1961, was likely the most climatically attuned of these structures.[105] Climate strategies were numerous. On the embassy building itself, there was a double roof to reduce overheating from above, many façade areas were shaded with a tight screen, while windowed areas had both horizontal shades and shutters and sat behind deep eaves. The floors were stepped back so that each provided some shade for those below (figure 3.40). The residence building also had a second roof, more eccentric in form, covering an inhabitable rooftop garden. The thick walls had large blocks of protruding window openings covered in tight grilles, again to provide both shade and privacy (figure 3.41).

3.40 Josep Lluís Sert, US embassy,
Baghdad, Iraq, 1955–61.

Sert's project also demonstrates some important elaborations on the significance of the façade section in conceiving architectural-climatic relationships. As much as the buildings deploy a range of flexible and targeted tactics, his published drawings on the project are hybrids, drawing together a perspective on the interior and the relationship to rays of sunlight, while also clearly articulating the means of shading, screening, and otherwise engaging the path of the sun. The building's climatic operations exceed innovations on the façade itself—the roof, as mentioned, is essential, as are the careful internal volumetric penetrations. A reliance on this compounded drawing suggests the elaboration of climate relevant design techniques (figure 3.42).

Edward Durell Stone's monumental screen for New Delhi expresses the complications and collaborations between architects, the museum, and the State Department, the mutual benefits of climate as a design and diplomatic alibi (figure 3.43). Here again, an extended overhang is deployed, sitting atop thin columns, to provide substantive shading—though it is not keyed, in any precise way, to differing solar angles as they impact the different elevations of the building. A segment of the screen was exhibited at full scale in the Drexler-curated MoMA exhibition *Buildings for Business and Government* in early

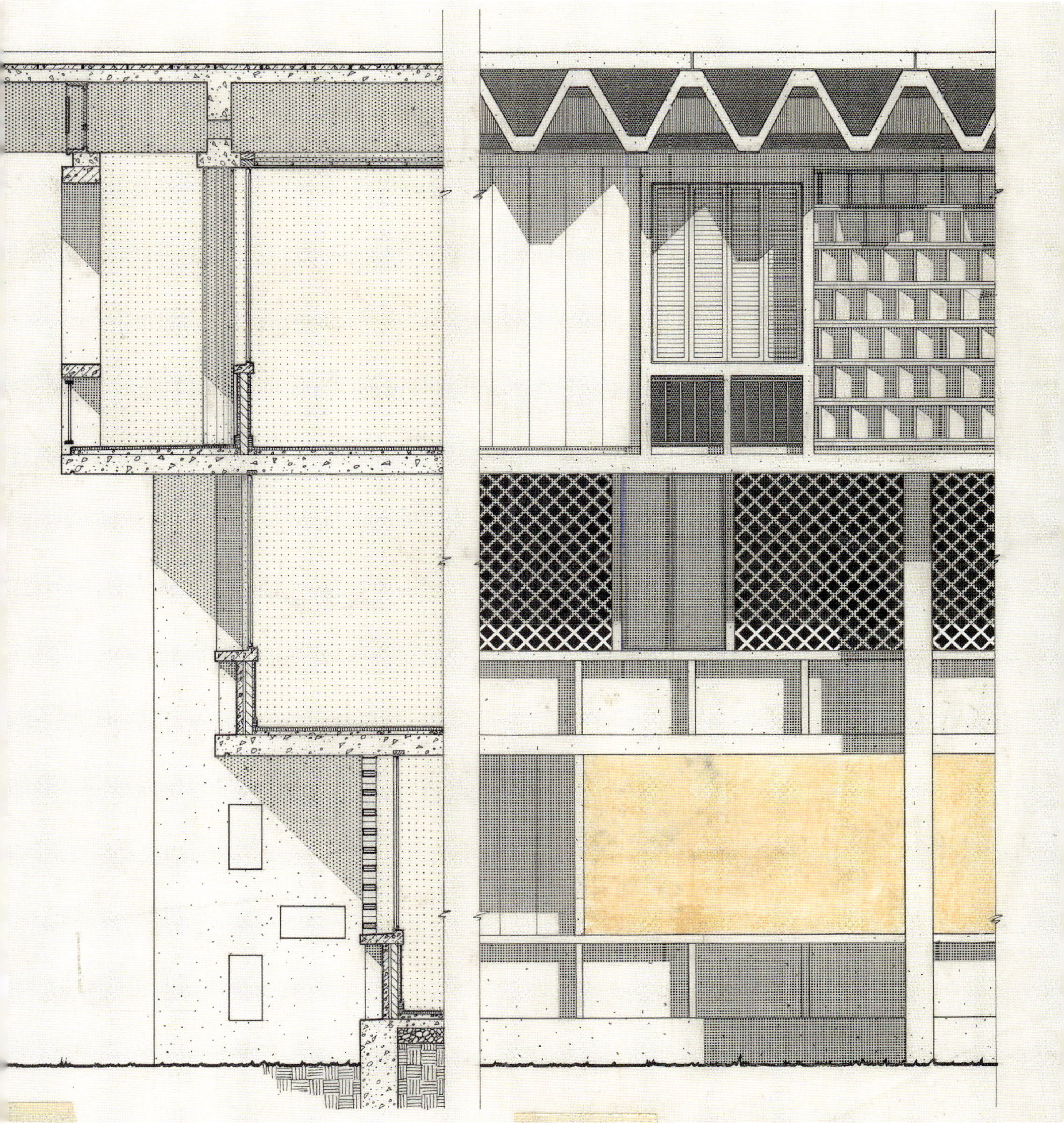

3.40 Josep Lluís Sert, US embassy, Baghdad, Iraq, 1955–61.

3.41 Josep Lluís Sert, US embassy, residence, Baghdad, Iraq, 1955–61.

3.41 Josep Lluís Sert, US embassy, residence, Baghdad, Iraq, 1955–61.

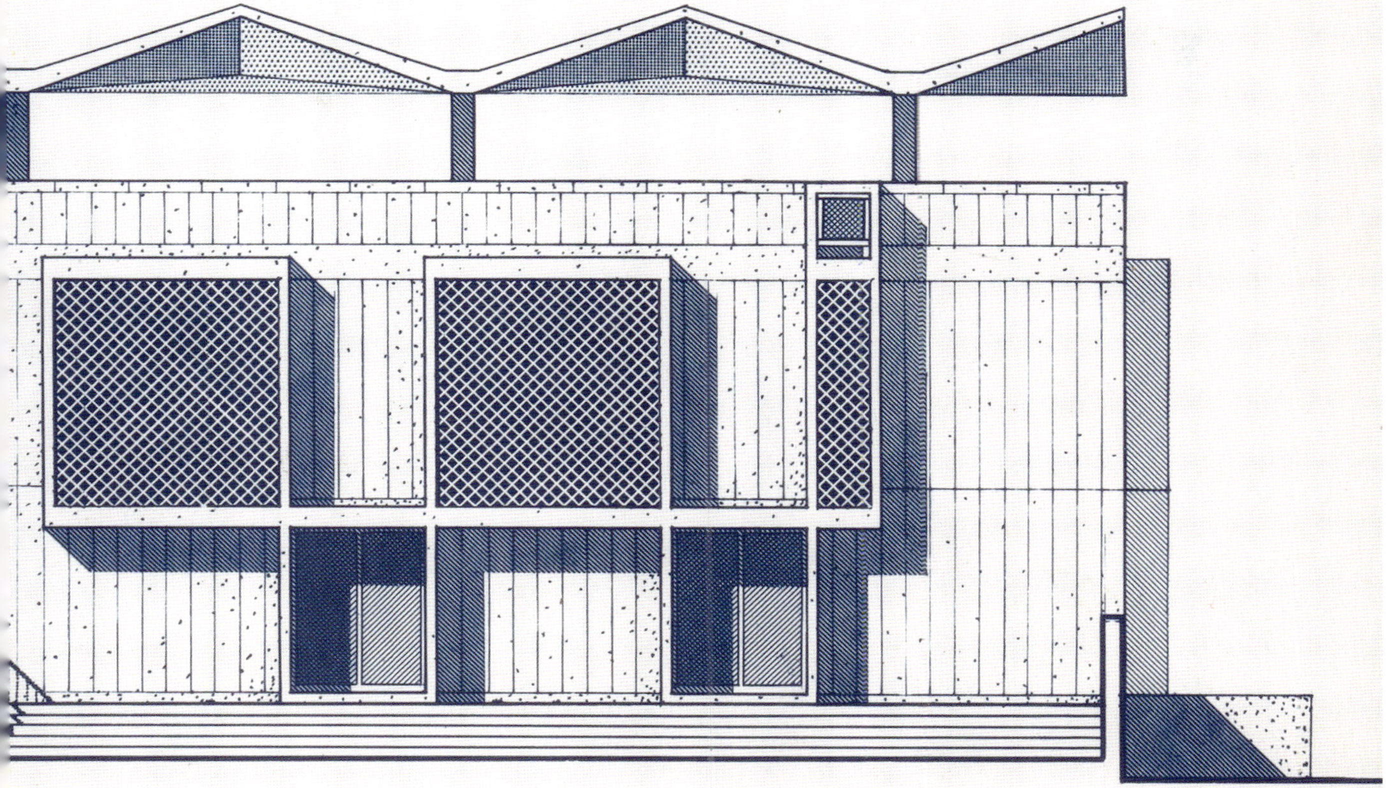

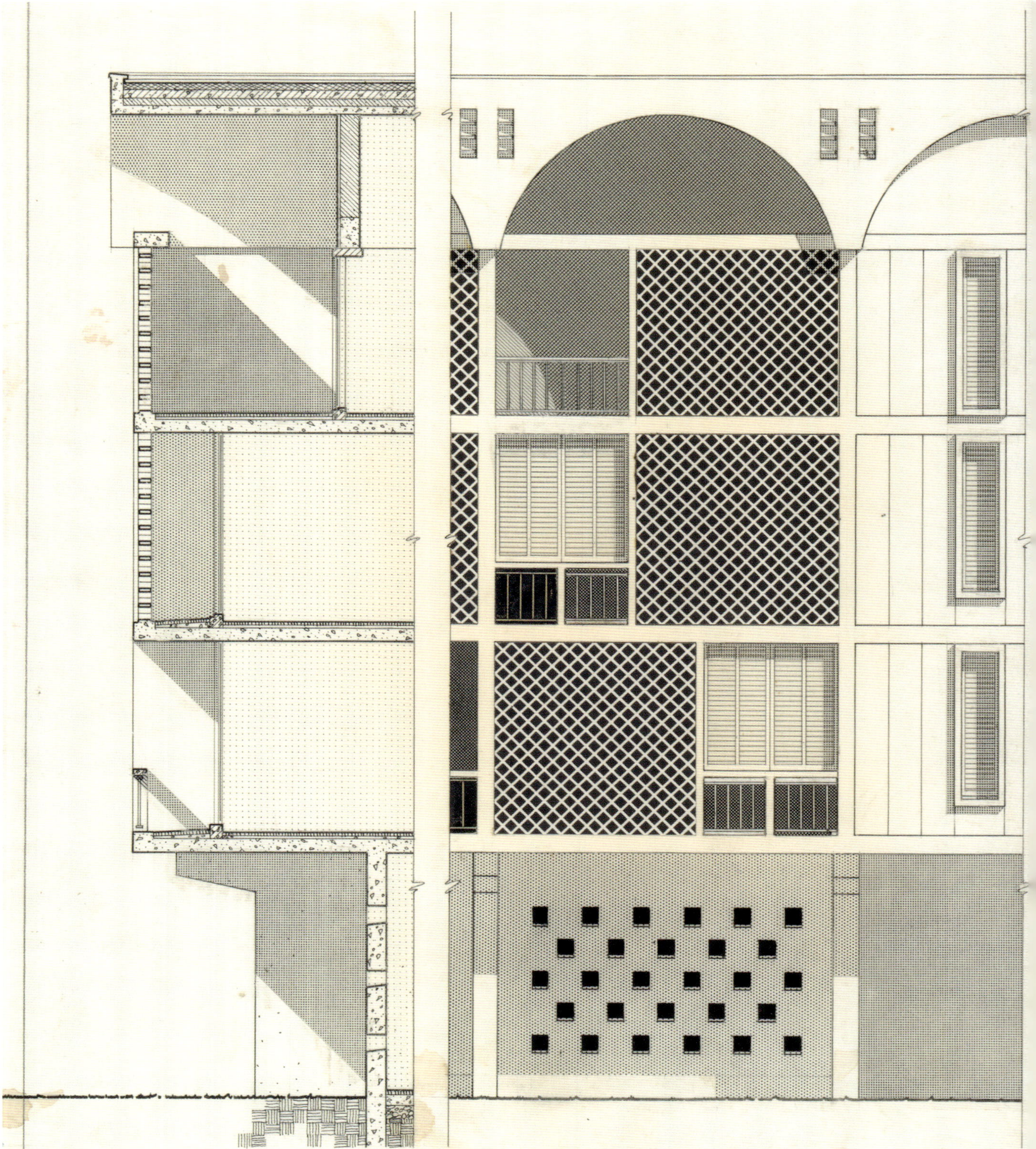

3.42 Josep Lluís Sert, US embassy, staff housing, Baghdad, Iraq, 1955–61.

3.42 Josep Lluís Sert, US embassy, staff housing, Baghdad, Iraq, 1955–61.

3.43 Edward Durell Stone, US embassy, New Delhi, India, 1957 (model [top] and as built).

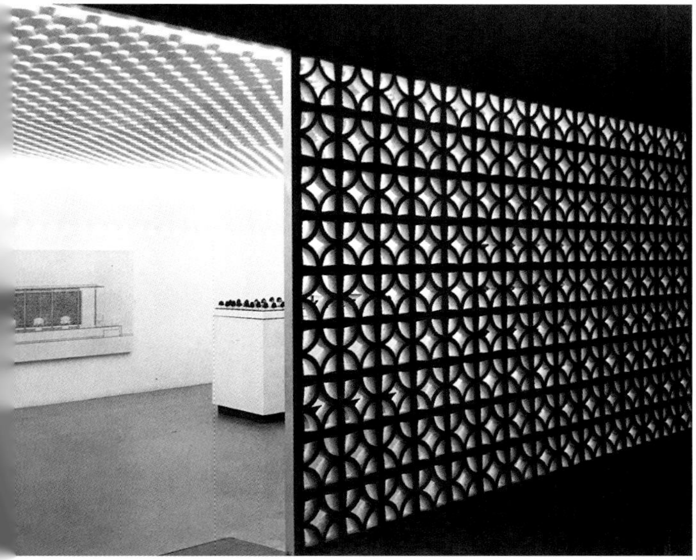

3.44 Edward Durell Stone, US embassy, New Delhi, India, 1957, screen at MoMA during the exhibition *Buildings for Business and Government*.

1957, showing in detail the simple dynamism of the circle in a square pattern (figure 3.44) All the same, the lack of correlated fenestration on the internal glass volume made the shading device largely ineffective for the thermal interior. Another failed test.

As media, it was perhaps more successful as a symbol—of climatic adaptability, of a purported affiliation between American interests and global development, and of an architecture sensitive to its surroundings yet designed according to an increasingly globalizing, purportedly universal method (figure 3.45). Indeed, though it was not acknowledged, the *Buildings for Business and Government* exhibition showed wide climatic variation: Stone's project in New Delhi (the only international project); SOM's Air Force Academy in the Colorado Rockies; Eero Saarinen's General Motors Technical Center in Detroit; two buildings in New York, the Seagram Headquarters (Mies van der Rohe, then under construction) and the Chase Manhattan Bank (SOM); and Helmuth, Yamasaki and Leinweber's airport terminal in Saint Louis (figure 3.46).

3.45 Edward Durell Stone, US embassy, New Delhi, India, 1957, photo exterior and interior.

3.46 Installation view, MoMA exhibition *Buildings for Business and Government*.

## Testing the Planet

Numerous other architects, practices, regions, buildings, and government programs could be drawn on to more comprehensively articulate the globalization of the International Style. All are caught up with transitions from colony to postcolony, from empire to corporate globalizations. Perhaps the most significant omission here is a general discussion of the emergence of Tropical Architecture, as a school (literally) and general disposition first of British architects working in West Africa, and then as a more general discussion of designing in the tropics. This omission is justified by the wealth of literature on the topic emergent in the last decade or so.[106]

Neutra's drawings and ideas circulated in the context of the writings and plans of these practitioners, including especially the extensive work of Jane Drew and Maxwell Fry to establish specific parameters for building in the tropics.[107] Their focus initially was on adapting village structures to embrace modern amenities, and then on the design and production of office buildings, houses,

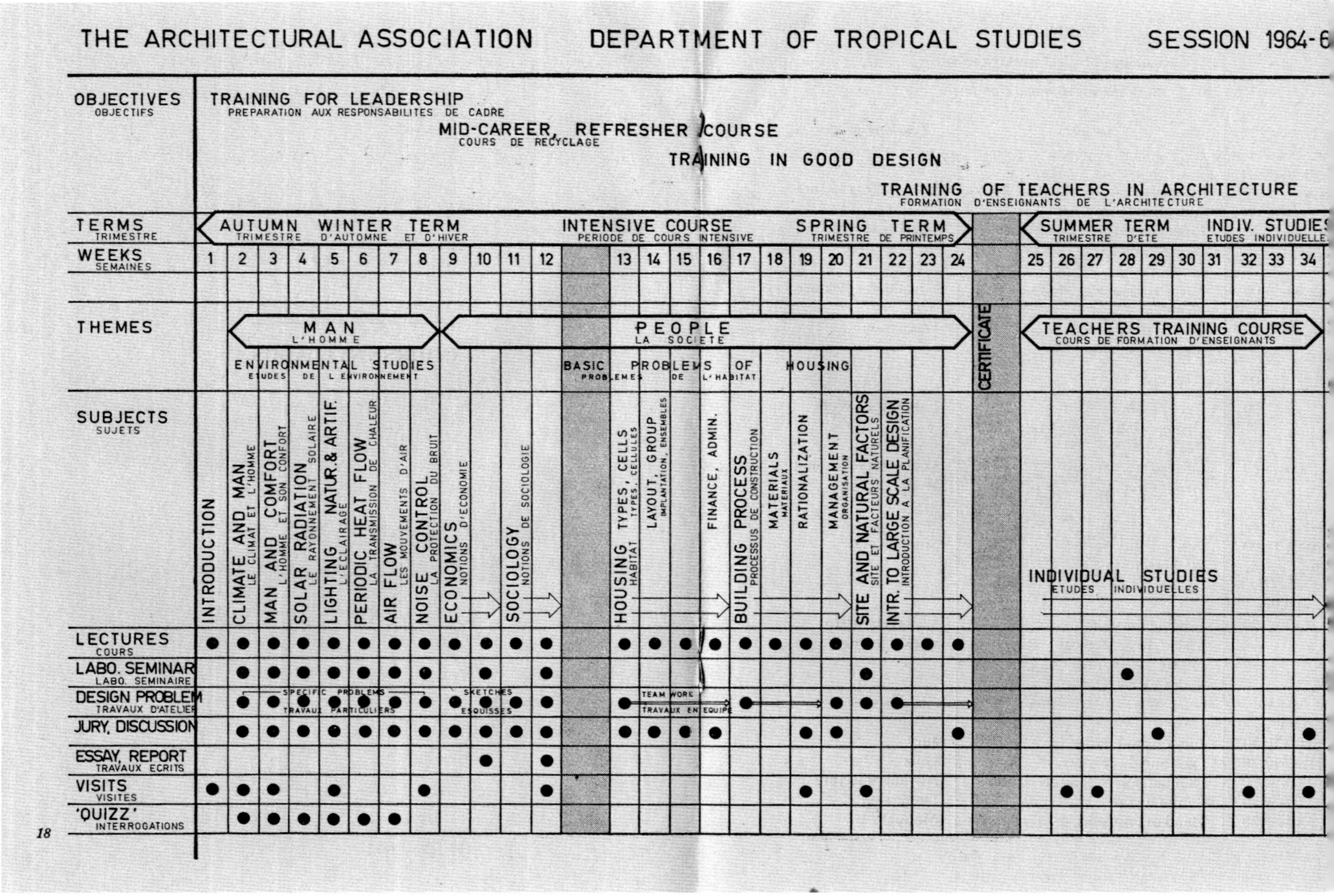


3.47 Otto Keonigsberger et al.,
Tropical Studies curriculum,
Architectural Association, London,
1958.

and other structures for the insertion of corporate networks into these resource-rich areas of the Global South.

The tropical architects were similarly caught in the complexities of the planetary, seeking to provide a certain way of life, according to a presumption of global knowledge and to attention to local conditions.[108] They similarly, at least in some sense, failed; or, better, the apparent good intentions of architects became caught up in a complex array of political and economic systems, as explicitly postcolonial efforts for spreading a technical civilization also participated in the Cold War and the persistent search for oil, among other contexts for labor and territorial exploitation.

Tropical architecture was also developed as a robust pedagogical theme. Fry helped establish the tropical studies department at the Architectural Association (AA) in London in 1955, later run by the German-Indian architect Otto Königsberger (figure 3.47).[109] Königsberger's program involved training the architect as a specialist in economic and territorial development, with concerns not only climatic—not only architectural—but also in sociology and demographics, and in changing political situations, and to means of interpreting local needs in a global context for design and production. Indeed, in 1970 the program left the AA for the Department of Tropical Medicine at the University of London, questions of health management and education overwhelming their potential architectural adjustment. Ideas and designs developed within this potent framework would widely circulate.[110]

---

This range of planetary tests helps to reposition the historical development of architectural modernism in the mid-twentieth century. From Neutra, to Rapson, to Sert, the concern over how to deploy the tools and concepts of modernism was toward improving life conditions and reconceiving geopolitical futures. Was there any architecture, before about 1950, that was not climatic? The answer to this is becoming clear, perhaps, not only through the accumulation of examples but also as one considers the general conditions for building—the infrastructures and materials that were available—in the peripheral regions where modernism was flourishing. The globalization of the International Style occurred by virtue of climatic devices; modern architecture developed, on terms conceptual, territorial, and pragmatic, through its flexible capacity for climatic management. The promise of technology, in this sense, was to render the vernacular into a global condition of relative consistency of interior experience. In architectural terms, a primary effect of modernization was acclimatization, the fashioning of a planetary interior.

# Part II

# The American Acceleration

## Great Accelerations

In the immediate postwar years, architectural strategies aimed to understand and operate on climate, albeit often in ways that were more aspirational than applied. After the war, climate came to be seen as resource and instrument, as an arena for scientific knowledge production and for applied technologies. The discussion of climate in architecture was part of a larger production of knowledge about territories, geographies, cities, and suburbs that conditioned governmental and corporate discussion on environment. After Allied meteorological predictions helped to establish the timing and location of the D-Day assaults that ended World War II, interest in climatic knowledge intensified, and research programs grew dramatically. Climate sciences potentially could contribute to agricultural efficiencies; to organize and regulate the expanding aviation industry; to identify transportation corridors; and to assist the building industry in land use transformation and urban expansion, among many other benefits. Climate was one of a handful of natural sciences slowly transforming to render capital more efficient and to render operational the natural surround.

Most of the climate analyses during this wartime and postwar expansion were at the macrolevel—interest was in the larger patterns of upper atmospheric readings and models, with less attention to lower atmosphere, near-ground complications. At the microlevel, climate was still dizzyingly complex and largely unexamined as an object of knowledge. As architecture encountered climate science, this macrocharacter of the data presented an obstacle. While climatologists (a relatively new breed of research scientists) began to use computers to manage large-scale modeling and increased knowledge of circulation patterns, a computational focus on ground-level dynamics would not develop for another decade. More general developments in biophysical knowledge, the emergence of the planet as an object of study, and the subsequent porosity of local and global knowledge came to be part of how climate was perceived by architects and urbanists—abstractions tied to data rather than the data itself. New and different kinds of media and expertise were needed to understand, process, and analyze planetary and microclimatological conditions and patterns and to understand the connections between them.

The meteorologist Helmut Landsberg made some of the first postwar drawings to depict an architectural conception of climate. Landsberg was an influential figure in statistical meteorology and had been essential to developing military applications for climate statistics during the war (figure 4.2).[1] His March 1947 article "Microclimatology: Facts for Architects, Realtors, and City Planners on Climatic Conditions at the Breathing Line" in *Architectural Forum*, likely co-written with James Marston Fitch, laid out some of the basic principles of the field. More than a catalog of methods that could apply to architecture, it was a sort of interdisciplinary to-do list for how architectural and climatic research could begin to develop shared terms and interests.

An illustrative drawing that is also a diagram, Landsberg's first image shows a lake in the countryside, with elevation lines and prevailing winds marked out. The goal of the drawing was to indicate the importance of taking climate into account in site selection. A number of sketched houses are arrayed around the lake as possible building sites. It reads as a strategic map to help understand the nature of meteorological knowledge and architecture—reliant on new kinds of data, it demonstrated how such knowledge could improve ways of life. Remaining at the schematic level, the image helps to outline a number of parameters and conditions to consider in order to arrive at the best site—it is an indicator of refined and clarified knowledge. Visually, it is striking how the image also reads like a targeting map from the recent war: "poor" sites are eliminated by X's, "fair" sites have the meek outline of a house; while the "good location" is marked with a more detailed image of a house.

Whereas most knowledge production around climate was concerned with the upper atmosphere,

DRAWINGS BY GEORGE COOPER RUDOLPH

Vhen you enter this house, you ›ass through a covered porch hat doubles as extra carport 'or garage at right. Left, be- ›ind fence, is a small garden 'or late, wind-free afternoons. 3eyond, right, is main patio. ?laced so house shields it from ›revailing winds, it yields a ›unny, private outlook—easy o look at, easy to maintain.

Sunny, wind-free, and enclosed. his patio does two important hings. It gives a house a "pri- ›ate climate" which makes out- loor living a comfortable real- ty in a land of marginal weath- er. And it offers the whole ouse a secluded, pleasant fo- us whose beauty no curious ıeighbor or thoughtless passer- y can infringe upon.

***Visit House Beautiful's Pace-Setter houses—on exhibition May 27-Sept. 27***

(Complete details on page 168)

4.1 "The American Style," with Edwin Wadsworth, Pace Setter House of 1950, in *House Beautiful*, June 1950.

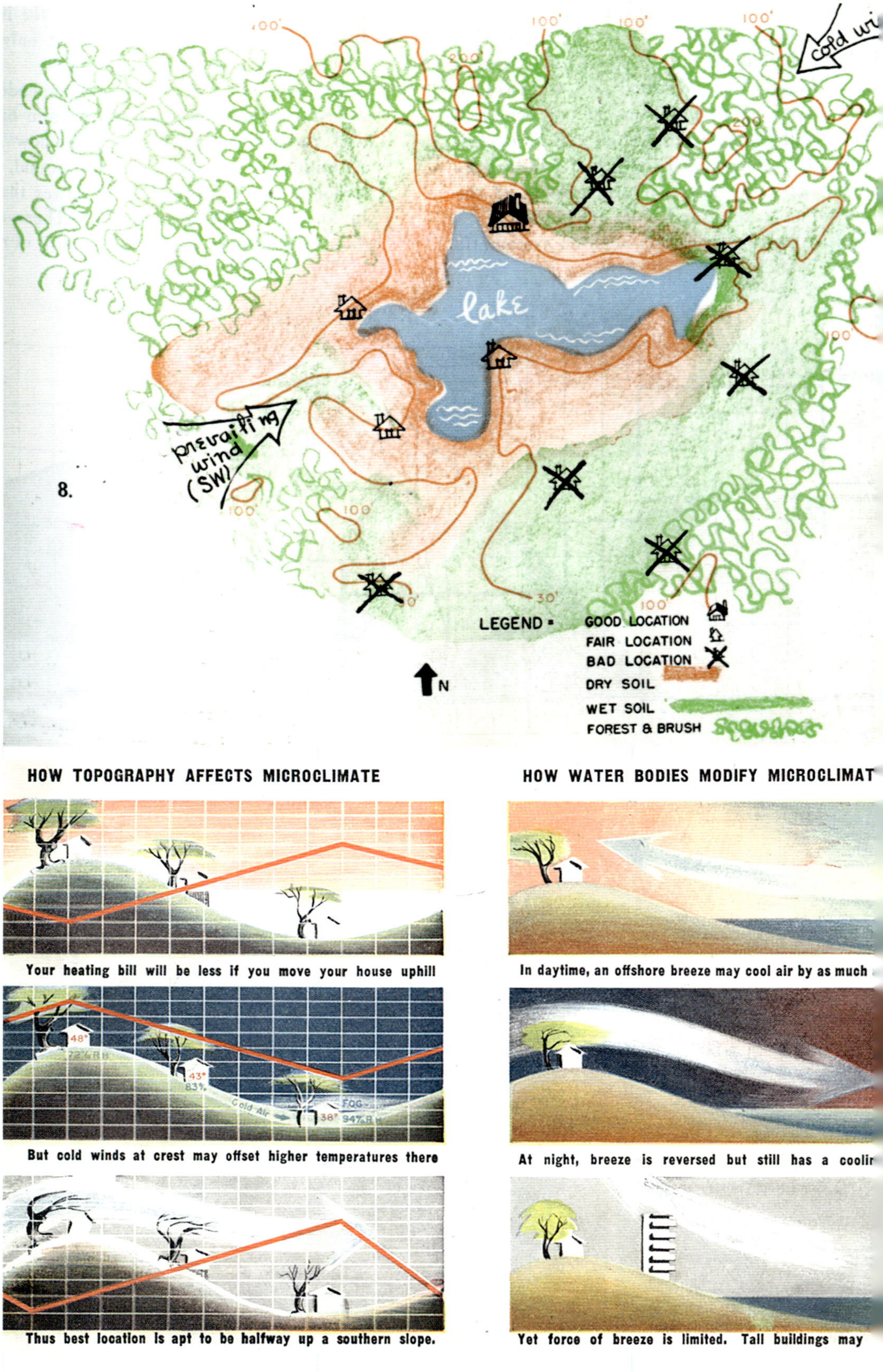


4.2 Climate and site selection, from Helmut Landsberg, "Microclimatology," *Architectural Forum*, March 1947.

Landsberg insisted, "we live close to the ground in a disturbed thin skin of atmosphere which is studded with microclimatic difference."[2] The American suburb, as the targeted realm for economic growth and territorial expansion, emerges here as the subject of methodological inquiry, bringing together the sciences of building, climatology, and physiology. In this initial, immediate postwar foray, it was presumed that some adjustments to the design process and to building strategies could align the conditions of the exterior climate with a specific conception of interior comfort. The first step was positioning the building in a good location.

Landsberg's map in *Forum* is accompanied by a set of drawings intending to explain the principles that are played out in the first illustration. Focused on basic principles in the relationship of prevailing winds to topography and bodies of water, Landsberg explains the consequence of understanding these principles: a reduced heating bill, more comfort at night, and so on. The illustrations proceed in stages, exploring the costs and benefits of different locations on a hillside or near a lake, with some parameters for the ideal possible site. The terms are schematic—"tall buildings may block" the wind; "your house" may find the best temperature "halfway up a southern slope"—as are the images. The tall building illustrated has, in the most general sense, some resonance with the climatic modernism of the Brazilians and Le Corbusier.

At this intersection of architecture and climate in the period right after World War II, reliable information about weather patterns is framed as data to be integrated into the design process, with new ideas about materials, siting, and, of course, shading, now to be considered. Landsberg's drawings are part of a much more elaborate trend of taking climate into account, in which specific, microclimatological knowledge is seen to relate to specific architectural possibilities, thereby intensifying interest in design methods.

A compelling and necessary aspect of this discussion of the façade, around the world as it developed in the period under discussion, is that the specifics of the shading system as an architectural intervention came to be tightly tethered to an intense focus on site—site and façade became accompanying trajectories of technological and professional interventions, focused on specific geographic, political, and cultural knowledge. Patterns of geophysical knowledge became global climate parameters in which architectural variables, largely expressed through brise-soleil, found a space for effect and relevance.

Landsberg's images can also be seen as incitements to action—not quite the military campaign that the targeting diagram suggests, but a no less concerted effort to change how experts think about, plan for, and produce the built environment. Numerous aspects of the landscape are presented, from considering tree cover relative to summer overheating to how to avoid "frost holes" when putting up a retaining wall. The climate-savvy architect faced the daunting task of understanding how all of these tiny forces could aggregate to produce a building that facilitated a more comfortable way of life.

The diagrams set the stage for later developments in many ways, symptomatic of a range of relevant tensions emerging after the war. In the three diagrams on the left, "How Topography Affects Microclimate," Landsberg's images offer a screened landscape, seen through a grid. The image seems to be reflecting a set of *causal* questions about energy, architecture, and climate then being discussed—for instance, the geographical pattern of the hill being traced according to the trajectory of a line on a chart exploring possibilities of growth and decline. The affective positioning of a recognition of patterns, of variability, of ups and downs in the external conditions, suggests a counterpoint in the interior, the capacity for the architect to even out that temperature difference. The importance of three phenomena become paramount—the careful analysis of the building site on climatic terms; the registration of knowledge of resource and climate patterns; and third, that the first two are connected, on global terms and in complex ways. New kinds of image production, a new media practice, are necessary to evaluate the conditions of the climatic surround and its relevance to architecture.

At the same time, a mediatic ambivalence is already registered in Landsberg's drawing. The graphic derivative of the line measures development, production, and growth as it also registers temperature and the indication of wind patterns. This diagrammatic device takes shape in the characteristic curve of the 1940s and 1950s—consumed with the relationship of the unstable present to a range of possible futures. Charts, diagrams, and other technical images focus on the prospects for societies and economies of the future, registering possible (soon seen as anticipated) accelerations. Landsberg's drawing maps these together, allowing one to read, almost too easily, at once the technical premise of the architectural-climatic diagram, an aspirational trajectory of progress, and how the contradictions and complications embedded in this new knowledge inform the schematic nature of the technical image in transition. Both aspirational and information rich, the diagram expresses data and desire simultaneously.

Landsberg's diagrams can be placed next to a number of analytic images attempting to understand the resource conditions of the period. Best known, perhaps, are those of M. King Hubbert in his articulation of the theory of "peak oil," also known as the Hubbert peak, which he defined in 1956 as "the mathematical relations involved in the complete cycle of production of any exhaustible resource"—a maxim that all natural resources would, at some point, run out (figure 4.3).[3] More important than the vagaries with which this proposal was made and received—that is, than the quantifiable details of resource depletion—is a related axiom we could call "Hubbert's pip," recognizing the absolute reliance on oil evident by the late 1940s and the clarity that such a situation could not last forever (figure 4.4). "The consumption of energy from fossil fuels is thus seen to be but a 'pip,' rising sharply from zero to a maximum, and almost as quickly declining, and thus representing but a moment in the total of human history."[4] Hubbert's peak—the peak of fossil fuel availability—has continually moved into the future due to technical innovations, but the general premise remains, and was of concern at the dawn of the fossil fuel age: it won't last forever.

An architectural-environmental imaginary, coalescing from these various media, begins to emerge as a methodological imperative to design with climate. The goal is not only to produce adaptive buildings, but also to make images: to draw a system that will take climate into account in the building process. The climate diagram, in nascent form in Le Corbusier, Marcelo Roberto, and Richard Neutra, here started to mature—in terms of its capacity to clearly articulate scientific knowledge and also in its capacity to suggest new possibilities for the elaboration of architectural techniques in the production of the thermal interior.

These methodological ambitions relied on the technical image for the production of knowledge and for communication. As one of the engineers

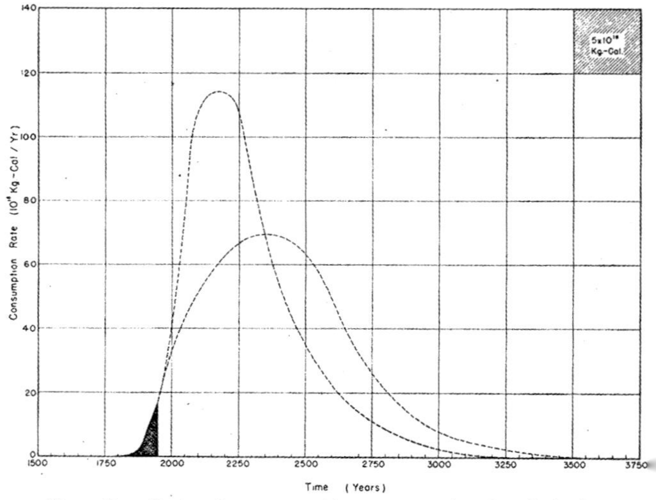


FIG. 6. Rate of consumption curves for fossil fuels.

4.3 M. King Hubbert, "Rate of Consumption Curve for Fossil Fuels," 1949.

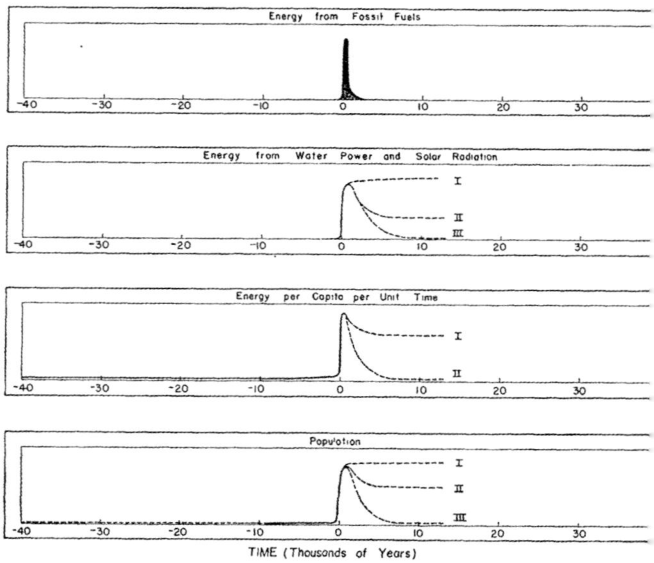


FIG. 8. Human affairs in time perspective.

4.4 M. King Hubbert, "Human Affairs in Time Perspective," 1956.

involved in these immediate postwar discussions, Paul Siple, noted at a government-sponsored conference on Weather and the Building Industry in 1950: "What I visualize are diagrams so clearly depicting [climatic factors] that texts will not be necessary for further interpretation."[5] His goal concisely expressed the environmental media focused on architecture, climate, and the thermal interior in this active period.

Before exploring Siple's own diagrams, made in the context of a number of discussions, conferences, projects, and other efforts, other images need to be examined and understood for the complications they present—in the 1940s architectural discussions in the United States, and in the historiographic patterns that have emerged since. Landsberg had referred, in an article in the same *Architectural Forum*, to "the atmosphere as an underused resource," as a space of scientific, economic, and political development.[6] Taking climate knowledge into account, from this perspective, could help make a number of fields and professions, from agriculture to aviation to architecture, more profitable and efficient. New kinds and data and new kinds of expertise were needed.

In an architectural context, such notions were directly applicable—designing with climate could reduce reliance on heating fuel and electricity for cooling, the designed provision of *comfort* was seen to ameliorate living and working conditions to make them more restorative or productive. As Tomás Maldonado insisted in the 1980s, and many others have since, comfort is a concept long dependent on economic growth and capitalist development—in this sense the twentieth century is a story of increased access to comfort and the design tools and resource costs it entails.[7] Such issues came to the fore in the immediate postwar period just before the American economic engine took off—an engine that involved the expansion of cities and suburbs and a generalized design approach to objects, houses, cities, and infrastructures—that had a pronounced reliance on fossil fuels.

This brief period, right after the war and before economic expansion ramped up, about 1945–52, saw a remarkable transformation not only of architectural ideas about climate but also of a more general conception of the planet as a system—of resources and sinks, of opportunities and potential hazards. It is an *epochal* moment at the beginning of the Great Acceleration. Such is the rough span of this chapter: from Landsberg's article in 1947 to *House Beautiful* editor Elizabeth Gordon's "Threat to the Next America," a xenophobic anticommunist—or really proconsumerist—screed that ended the journal's Climate Control Project in the early 1950s.

These consequential years were also the beginning of the Great Acceleration, a period lasting from 1945 to the present. This period saw the global socioindustrial engine accelerate beyond what was previously imaginable. This period of almost endless economic expansion, consumer growth, and resource exploitation also saw a dramatic increase in the burning of fossil fuels and the emission of carbon. In 2004, geologist Will Steffen, who coined the term, describes the Great Acceleration thus:

> The second half of the twentieth century is unique in the entire history of human existence on Earth. Many human activities reached take-off points sometime in the twentieth century and have accelerated sharply towards the end of the century. The last 50 years have without doubt seen the most rapid transformation of the human relationship with the natural world in the history of humankind.[8]

That architecture has played an essential role in the Great Acceleration is self-evident: today, the built environment, in its construction, operation, and destruction, is cited as producing between 40 and 60 percent of carbon emissions.[9] That is, in the period right after the focus of this chapter, building designs came to be articulated with almost no concern for their reliance on fossil fuels—at a historical moment when there was little knowledge of the damaging consequences of burning oil. These numbers underestimate the role of the design of the built environment, which expanded in relationship to the ways in which architecture and architects facilitated the growth of the fossil-fuel-based economy through urban and suburban expansion, infrastructure, materials innovation, and in many other contexts. Architecture was a cultural catalyst, as much as a technical producer, of fossil-fuel dependence.

Architecture is a process of mediating a specific human relationship to resources and materials. Since about 1952, the connection between architecture and oil has been tight, and difficult to rend asunder. Architecture today is inseparable from petroleum. Or more precisely, able to be separated only through great effort. The climatic methods of the late 1940s clarify the architectural tendencies

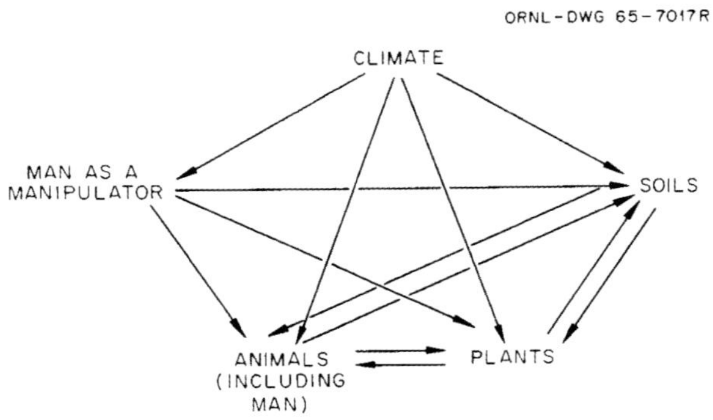


**Fig. 1. An ecosystem is an integrated complex of living and nonliving components. Each componen is influenced by the others, with the possible exception of macroclimate. And now man is on the verge o exerting meaningful influence over macroclimate.**

4.5 George Van Dyne, "Basic Model of an Ecosystem," 1960.

to think about a building in relationship to the interconnected climate/energy system, just before that system was overwhelmed by the global distribution of petroleum.

The architectural mediation of climate shifts around 1952—away from a spectrum across which we can relate climate design techniques to more general tendencies of modern architecture (that is, the concern of part 1), toward a spectrum on which we can relate climate design techniques to a global discussion of earth systems, climate forcings, and other quantifications of living closely with carbon (that is, the concern of part 2). New architectural historical patterns emerge with the Great Acceleration: design ideas reliant on fossil fuels, and, eventually, a design imaginary of how to live in their absence.

Since about 2000, the tenor of the discussion of the postwar world, in the context of energy, environment, technology, and climate, has shifted. The passage toward a new geologic epoch of the Anthropocene is now well established—the epoch in which the human enterprise has a detectable impact on the earth system.[10] Humans have become a force of "telluric amplitude," not simply engaging with biotic systems but having a substantive, determinant role in large-scale nonhuman patterns, such as the climate system.[11] In many ways the idea of the Anthropocene is not new. Bill McKibben wrote of *The End of Nature* in 1989, decrying the fact that human behaviors had by then come to play a role in determining large-scale earth system conditions. As early as 1958 the ecologist George Van Dyne drew one of the seminal diagrams in the emerging ecological sciences, identifying humans as agents both for their biological capacity (as animals like any other) and as "man as manipulator," operating on this system of interactivity (figure 4.5). Van Dyne presciently notes, in the caption, that "man is on the verge of exerting meaningful influence over macroclimate."[12] Of course, humans' deleterious impact on biotic systems has long been known, articulated by both George Perkins Marsh and Alexander von Humboldt in the nineteenth century. The premise of the Anthropocene is that such agency is now more consequential, operating on the time scales of the geologic record and producing forces that cannot easily be reversed.[13]

The precise timing of the emergence of this telluric amplification is not a minor issue—conceptualizing the beginning of a new geologic epoch can facilitate more precise knowledge about its advent and its consequences. While some discussions look to the beginning of the Industrial Revolution, especially given a growing reliance on fossil fuels that characterized the dramatic changes of the late nineteenth century, others focus more directly on the immediate postwar period as the starting point of the Great Acceleration. Alongside a growing capacity to affect the earth system has come the expansion of knowledge about that impact, and in particular about the interrelatedness of human and geophysical activities—a doctrine laid down some decades ago by ecologists, that "everything relates to everything else."[14] But how is everything connected, with what consequences, and what

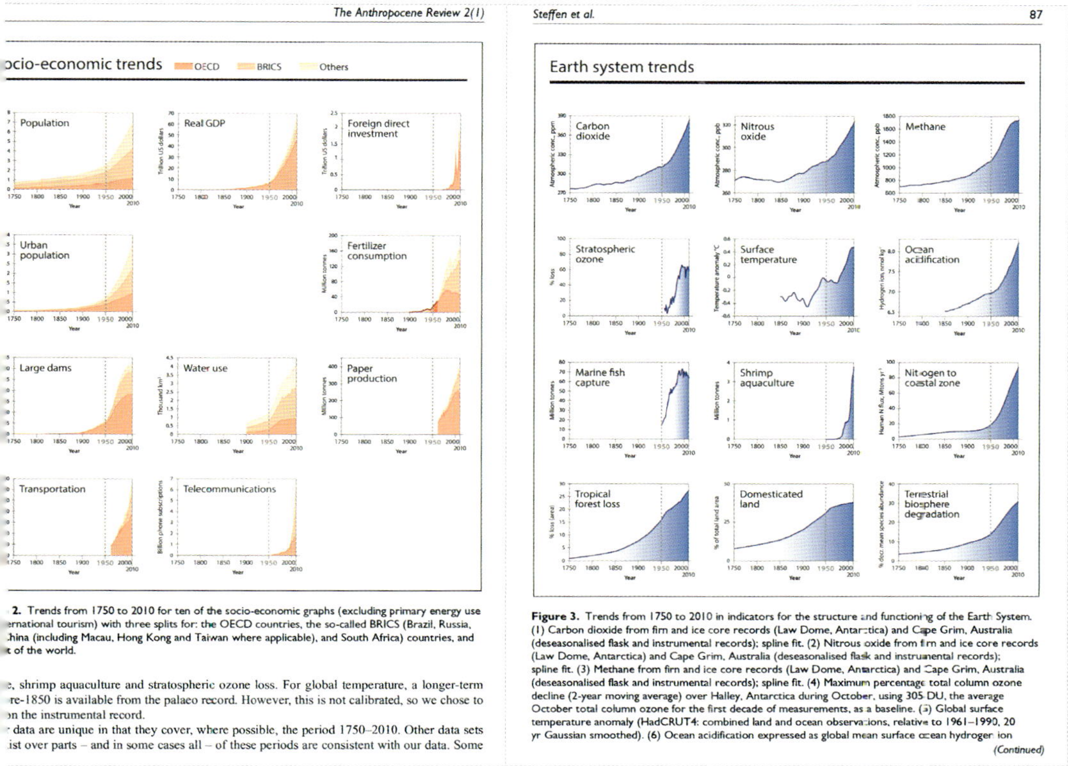


4.6 Will Steffen et al., from "The Trajectory of the Anthropocene," 2015.

are the means of intervening in and operating on those connections?

Geologist Will Steffen and his colleagues have mapped this transformation in a series of charts that show the upward curve of both the biophysical conditions of the earth system and human activities (what they refer to as "the human enterprise") (figure 4.6). The earth system trends that are mapped include ocean acidification, carbon dioxide, domesticated land, surface temperature, and other factors. The human enterprise is seen to approximate social and economic activity indicators. In the graphs these indicators—including water use, primary energy use, population, real GDP, large dams, and others—all increase significantly in the post-1945 period (some, such as telecommunications and international tourism, also effectively start then).[15] Andreas Malm argues that the abstraction of the "human enterprise" is not adequately textured with recognition of the unevenness, across political and class boundaries, of the development of this enterprise and its benefits to different populations—so abstract as to be misleading and to prevent a more nuanced understanding of an appropriate countermeasure.[16]

The Great Acceleration is in this sense a diagram of the specific changes in anthropogenic forces that will lead to climate disruption. It offers a new historical model, a direct reshuffling of periodicity, in history and in architectural history in particular, according to consumption, acceleration, and resource use. The concept encourages us to see how architecture may have changed relative the initial trace of these patterns of growth as they emerged with industrialization and resource exploitation, and how design methods and material considerations changed again in the wave of increased resource availability in the postwar period. Of course, much of this story is how these resources were seen to be available, through what means they would be accessed, and the feedback loops and reinforcing patterns relative to geopolitics, corporate exploitation of oil and other fossil fuels, and consumer behaviors relative to them. This is, twice over, the characteristic curve of the Anthropocene, showing increases in economic activity and increases in environmental degradation, in every possible form.[17] The Great Acceleration is both the historical period in which human capacity to emit carbon becomes the most profound effect of social organization and also a methodological concept that elicits new frameworks and new relationships in our knowledge of the past.

Understanding the contrast and conflation of the human enterprise and the earth system becomes the challenge of the Anthropocene epoch. These are the conditions of interrelation between, on the one side, human societies, however porous a category this may remain, and, on the other, the geophysical systems that allow for life on earth. The built environment, broadly considered, is a mediating device between the human enterprise and the earth system, one that enables humans to adjust geophysical conditions over time. Conceived of in this way, architecture is the space for inquiry about the interrelationship between the human enterprise and earth systems. The built environment is an artifact of that interrelationship, especially relative to its resource demand and its impact on climate.

The graphs of the Great Acceleration line are a visual expression, or mediatic device, of a new realm for historical inquiry. They indicate a metric and a way of knowing—an epistemology—for the relationship of humans to environments, materially and symbolically, as it has changed over time and as it has produced unexpected consequences. Social relationships to resources and sinks, in intricate patterns and occasionally oscillations, are and have been communicated through graphic means as an attempt to understand these phenomena and to incite action relative to them—echoing Siple's imperative for a form of visual explication and clarity that makes other forms of communication unnecessary; a media-based knowledge that directs the relationship of social life to climatic patterns. The figure of the environment, broadly conceived, is a line, indicating a seemingly inexorable uptick in the human enterprise and its earth system effects. It presents the mediatic conditions for collective activity. It is the image that environmentalists hope to affect and adjust, producing social systems that allow for a shifted graphic disposition—a line that, at least, flattens out, and/or opens up to a range of possible futures. Architecture is one of a handful of human induced "forcings"—*forcings* and *flattenings* are debated as means of climate stabilizations, as habits, articulated in aggregate that have produced the unstable conditions of the twenty-first century, and that can operate on them.[18] Architecture is just starting to be seen as a forcing on these terms—a device for changing our relationship to the climate.

The Great Acceleration was largely an American Acceleration, especially in the context of building systems and their mechanization. In Steffen's thorough analysis, OECD (Organization for Economic Cooperation and Development) countries represent the lion's share of the relevant human enterprise, and, at least until about 2000 when China began to dramatically increase energy use, the majority of OECD activity was American economic growth—an even larger amount when aspects such as the Marshall Plan and other US-induced conditions for growth, often based in the spread of petroleum-based systems around the world, are considered.[19] In 1960, most of the world outside Europe and North America used little fossil fuel energy; American energy use accounted for about a third of global energy output in 1965; at the time, American per capita energy consumption was as much as seventy times that of the lowest energy users.[20] If this began to change in the 1980s, if, that is, the energy use of other parts of the world began to catch up to the American Acceleration, this was in part because of the adoption of air-conditioned, fuel-intensive building styles first explored in the United States. The United States was, in this counterintuitive sense, an experimental ground on which energy-intensive lifestyles were developed. These lifestyles were to be exported to other countries as they became economically feasible and politically viable.

The United States was the first and most extensive air-conditioned environment, exporting thermal knowledge through architectural media and through the experience of a conditioned interior. In 1959, the American Society of Heating, Refrigeration and Air-Conditioning Engineers (ASHRAE) was formed out of two related agencies with an explicitly global focus, aiming to facilitate and regulate a planetary interior reliant on fossil-fueled mechanical systems.[21] A conditioned, rather than designed, thermal interior was in this sense a signal characteristic of the Great Acceleration and of contemporary economic life, a signifier of a certain kind of relationship to infrastructure, to energy, to economic possibility, and, perhaps less clearly, to political affiliation with the United States. Control over a building's interior was also the indicator of autonomy from the forces of nature, be they expressed through understanding of regional climate or through determinist bias, and according to a very specific vision of global political and economic collaboration.

Over the period of the Great Acceleration the relationship of earth systems to architecture was constantly changing. In the immediate postwar period, architects experimented with how to design according to microclimatic conditions in order to obviate the need for a mechanical HVAC system at a time when such systems were still relatively expensive and reliant on preexisting robust infrastructure. At the same time, design attention to the thermal interior—that is, attempts to use architectural means to condition interior space—created the physiological and technological parameters for interior spaces that would later be heated and cooled through mechanical systems. By placing the aspiration to design with climate in the context of the American Acceleration it becomes clear how air conditioning became seen as a necessary part of architectural developments, and, also, the precise terms by which this sense of necessity and inevitability was culturally, economically, and politically contingent.

Architectural history is a history of the great acceleration—all buildings, in this sense, are "Anthropocenic" in that they have articulated a specific relationship between the human enterprise and the earth system, even if that articulation was made without adequate knowledge either due to historical contingency or willful ignorance. That architecture in the twenty-first century is still relatively tepid about its approach to reducing fossil fuel use only emphasizes the potency of this claim. What follows is not a history of accelerating per se, but of the spatial and thermal frameworks that gave rise to it—of the planetary interior as the space of, the discursive and material site for, the Great Acceleration.

The climate-informed architectural image became a screen on which ideas about the design of space and the patterns and knowledge of climate could be drawn together. External climate patterns were integrated with attempts to quantify comfort and adjust the conditions of the interior. And there was a wide appeal for more images, a conviction, it seems, that the proliferation of the technical image was a means to *produce* a new thermal environment. Landsberg's formulation of climate as resource was potent, opening an inquiry into a new system of knowledge, and an ambition to reveal the fruits of this knowledge through its application to the built environment. The goal was to produce a new way of living in the American landscape, one supported by scientific knowledge of climate, communicated and promoted through technical images, and designed and built through architectural interventions. The medium for producing climatic effects, for better or worse, was architecture.

## Microclimatic Architecture

The dynamic and multifaceted discussion about architecture and climate right after the war initially played out through the Climate Control Project, a collaboration between the American Institute of Architects and *House Beautiful* magazine. It led to a highly developed notion of how to apply climate knowledge in an architectural context, in concert with materials, site placement, and innovative floor plans to maximize ventilation; it also precipitated a shift away from the open-ended possibilities of the new architecture, and away from the expansion of modern architecture in the United States.

In this immediate postwar moment, when the contours of the postwar reliance on oil were not yet well established, the goal was not so much to make energy use more efficient.[22] It was, rather, to find design methods that could provide the most comfort in a relatively resource-constrained built environment. Architecture was seen as a mechanism to improve quality of life—a principle perhaps taken from a number of interwar modern experiments in Europe and explored in the context of the growing American suburbs.

The *Architectural Forum* article referenced above was co-written by Landsberg and James Marston Fitch and demonstrates an eagerness to outline a specific role for architects in both encouraging and taking advantage of precise climatological data. Fitch, later a strong proponent of historic preservation, was trained as a weather forecaster for the US Air Force during the war and worked closely with Landsberg.[23] Fitch had just published *American Building: The Forces That Shape It*, one of the first architectural histories to appear after the war. It was not just a history. The first half of the book chronicled the development of American building practices from 1620 to the 1940s, examining the materials and cultural influences as well as the geographic, climatic, and industrial terms through which they had developed. The second half, as Fitch reiterated in a preface to the 1972 revised edition, "sought to establish a holistic concept of man/environment relationships—a necessary frame of reference within which building could be fruitfully analyzed and viable goals for its future established."[24] This included analyses of structure, air temperature and quality, noise, and questions of housing policy and planning.

The 1972 preface was also something of a lament, where Fitch expressed his frustration that few had "found it worthwhile to pursue this theoretical line." As a result, Fitch continued, referring to the architecture of the 1970s, "despite its visual novelty and purported modernity, our architecture is on the whole as formalistic in its main configurations—and hence unsatisfactory in its overall performance—as it was half a century ago."[25] Fitch's frustration, though perhaps not widely felt in the early 1970s, clarifies the complications faced at midcentury, when the Climate Control Project sought to bring together the cultural thematics of modernism, the new possibilities introduced by applied science, and the anticipation of a transformed future in the habitation of the American territory.

Fitch's discussion of the building as a climatic system in *American Building* also initiated the rhetoric of a commonsense approach to territorial inhabitation, a sort of plea to the obviousness of using materials and spatial articulations as a means to manage climatic variability (figure 4.7). "Fair and Warmer," one of the first chapters of the second, more operational part of the book, posits a general relationship between the human body, a heat source, and the façade. He explains the different kinds of heat, discusses the importance of thermal continuity—that is, the goal of both *normative* and *consistent* interior conditions—and summarizes the differences in a variety of heating and cooling systems. Radiant heat is his preferred method, with cooling seen to be largely under control through induced ventilation and partially outdoor spaces. "The task of a building," he concludes,

> Is not merely to keep us from freezing or burning to death; not only to maintain conditions which reduce or eliminate the cause of respiratory disease; not even to stop with maintaining comfort conditions for steel worker and stenographer: but to provide the exact thermal environment required by the whole spectrum of modern life.[26]

A broad collection of demographic statistics, weather data, and energy costs informed Fitch's perspective, though his analysis operated at the level of context and background rather than through the precise application of scientific knowledge through design.

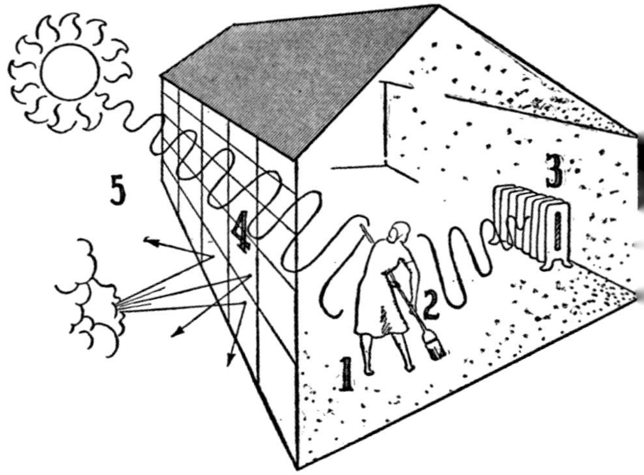


4.7 Explanatory diagram from James Marston Fitch, *American Building: The Forces That Shape It*, 1947.

Fitch also dedicated a chapter to pollution, where a broader conception of climate came into play, and offered a brief diagnosis of upper atmosphere patterns that distribute pollutants in recognizable patterns. Other chapters on daylighting, sound, physiology, and the urban environment intended to open the reader to a new set of environmental inputs for architecture.

In his 1947 article for *Forum*, "Microclimatology," Fitch proposed that the field needed to not only become more aware of regional climatic conditions but also to the specifics of a given building site: "although everyone is aware of the general climate of his locality," Fitch explained, "no one knows much about the climate of his own backyard."[27] Details such as elevation, proximity to water, paving materials, condition of the soil as well as the site's relationship to its urban setting, and a variety of other issues, could all be taken into account to best produce a house adequate to its specific climate.

This initial proliferation of details begins to suggest why the attempt to make microclimate legible to architects was so difficult, and indeed is still complicated today, given the importance of precision and detail to understanding the demands that climate exerts on a site. Fitch and his colleagues attempted to produce a sort of regional assemblage, a conceptual machine that could coordinate a building to climate. But the regional frame was too large, and became just that—a frame within which more precise knowledge of the climate of the building site could be developed. Observation, generalization, triangulation, and estimation characterized the relationship of the climate-design methodological attempts of the late 1940s. Pollution, the grass species of lawns, arrangement and height of hedges, and myriad other factors were discussed in this initial article. Careful placement of trees and other planted elements of landscape were seen to be an especially effective means to influence microclimate.

However, Fitch also understood that the ability of architects to process the complex parameters of climate knowledge were limited. His ambition was less programmatic or operational and more aspirational—to interest architects in climate factors and also to draw the attention of weather analysts to a market for their climate product in architects, developers, and others in the building industry. Landsberg's formulation of the climate as resource was also, as Fitch understood, intended on these commercial terms—that science could mine climatic knowledge in order to provide products appropriate to a range of commercial needs.[28] Architecture was at the top of this list.

Meteorological data gathering had its own trajectories, contours, and accelerations in regard to design. The United States Weather Bureau expanded its weather data gathering significantly in the 1920s, primarily to serve the aviation industry—the wartime aspects of which Fitch had been a part of while in the army. Starting in 1935, Weather Bureau data were also analyzed by the American Society of Heating and Ventilating Engineers (ASHVE), through its Committee on Weather Design Conditions, in order to focus analysis and conclusions on possibilities for the construction industry—including, but at this point only vaguely, the design professions.[29] ASHVE began to monitor the 110 bureau stations in order to assess and summarize climatic data and make it available to its engineers.

Significant developments in atmospheric science were occurring in these same fields after the war. Harry Wexler was a prominent meteorologist who ran the National Weather Service (and may have been involved in Fitch's wartime air force training). Wexler's research focused initially on the circulation of nuclear radioactive waste, one of many reasons that climate patterns were on the minds of the public and of professionals. The stark reality of the planetary effects of radioactive particles cautioned many against the viability of nuclear warfare as assessments of weather patterns, theories of frequency, and possible variations to the circulation system entered into policy discussions.[30]

Modeling tools, rooted in climate knowledge, were being developed to speculate about specific environmental conditions and how to mitigate them. Central to these tools was the development of the computer, in use in particular by a team run by John von Neumann, a Hungarian émigré mathematician who managed the Meteorology Project at the Institute for Advanced Studies at Princeton from 1946 to 1955.[31] It was later absorbed into the army and government agencies for which it was providing forecasts. These early analyses have little in common with the uniform and extensive satellite-based knowledge characteristic of climate sciences later in the century. Climate knowledge had to be produced in very specific ways in which the capacity to gather data and process it went hand in hand.

Wexler, von Neumann, and their associates were focused on numerical climatology that demanded what was, for the time, a lot of computational power. "Primarily engaged with modeling the dynamics of upper air flows," they measured and observed patterns of the upper atmosphere with balloons, and later small rockets, and then analyzed and correlated the data through elaborate computational processing. As one of von Neumann's collaborators put it in 1955, "the machine makes fine forecasts of upper air weather for high-flying aircraft. For ground level weather, it is not yet very good."[32] Understanding these large-scale patterns required a specific system of knowledge and a specific approach to computation, one that was a very different system of knowledge from those of the microclimatic conditions of the building site.

The complexities of climate patterns and the need to establish lengthy computational runs to determine modeling characteristics led to a technological path dependency reliant on processing power that was more amenable to these upper atmospheric systems than occurrences lower to the ground.[33] This numerical climatology, reliant on the increased processing power of ever-expanding computers, eventually flourished at MIT, in the Weather Service, and through the army, using the ENIAC and other computers. These computers were (relatively) fast but required a lot of setup time; that is, they had to be painstakingly programmed in order to be able to process a certain kind of data in a certain way. It was a good system for running models with slight variations, and the computer was seen as a "general purpose machine to solve large systems of equations." Wexler's researchers were, by the late 1940s, successfully running twenty-four-hour forecasts based on actual data and modeling future and past scenarios with some precision. Their success also indicated their limited scope of application. These models intentionally excluded "geography, topography, humidity" and other variables characteristic of terrestrial observations—characteristics that were essential for developing application to design.[34]

The detailed information of the site required different kinds of knowledge, different analytic metrics, the capacity to integrate heterogeneous factors, and the correlation of climatic knowledge with materials. Even here, a number of corollaries could be found in other fields—the promotion of climatic knowledge for highway planning and regional planning for nuclear attack and nuclear waste storage were both active research projects.

Fitch's fine-tuned analysis was an ambitious goal, seeking to inflect the development of knowledge in the burgeoning climate sciences. The expansion of data collection and analysis generally wasn't directly applicable to architectural concerns. Interested parties needed to develop their own analytic framework as well as an avenue for bringing this knowledge to the profession and public. Collaboration was essential, as Fitch well understood. "Cooperation between architects and climatologists," he concluded his 1947 article, "will yield designs better adapted to their environment."[35] Climate was imagined in architecture as a space of cooperation, as an avenue through which architects could work with other experts to improve quality of life.

## The Climate Control Project

Such cooperation was the goal of the Climate Control Project, in which Fitch played a major role, along with *House Beautiful* editor Elizabeth Gordon, after he joined the magazine as architectural editor in 1948. In October 1949, the magazine officially launched the project, a two-and-a-half-year-long series of articles intended to educate architects and their clients to the benefits of designing according to regional and microclimatic knowledge. The project was done in collaboration with the American Institute of Architects (AIA); *House Beautiful* was to "represent the consumer" and demonstrate the ways of living that such climatic adaptation allowed, while the AIA collected, organized, and disseminated relevant technical information to architects.[36]

Gordon had been convinced of the importance of the issue not only by Fitch's article but also through a discussion with the Yale anthropologist Ralph Linton, whose knowledge of Native American building practices, especially at Mesa Verde, had led him to ponder the possibilities of a more climate-responsive architecture across the contemporary American landscape.[37] Linton was appointed by Gordon to be the official director of the Climate Control Project, though he did not have much involvement with the articles and images that the project produced. Economists, geographers, and writers were also included in the team; the primary representative of the architectural profession was Walter A. Taylor, the director of education and research at the American Institute of Architects, who was managing the institute's technical analyses more generally and collaborating with the newly founded Building Research Advisory Board (BRAB), an important government funding source for climatic research in the 1940s and '50s.[38] Siple, an engineer with the Army Corps of Engineers, was the primary scientific consultant. Siple had attained some renown at a young age when, in 1928, he was an Eagle Scout selected to join the Byrd expedition to the South Pole. He later developed and popularized the concept of wind chill.[39] He was invited to join the Climate Control Project by Landsberg, who was working closely with Fitch and the Yale physiologist L. P. Herrington on forming the team of researchers and writers.

The Climate Control Project reveals much that has rested below the surface of the historiography of architectural modernism. It reiterates that climate was a significant though ambivalent factor in American architectural practices of the immediate postwar period. Relative to what was possible after the introduction of the computer in the mid-1950s (in meteorology) and the late 1960s (in thermal interior modeling), these diagrams and drawings are meek and ineffective. The project is interesting as a cultural attempt to bring climate knowledge into the center of architectural considerations, more than as a representation of what remained strained developments in the technological application of that knowledge. At issue was a conception of method, and its illustration—the best way to design in the landscape, how to conduct an architectural practice responsible to the changing needs of the public, and how to frame the architectural profession as a realm of expertise for the mitigation of climatic variability and the mediation of scientific knowledge. Methodological drawings began to expand the purview and the ambitions of architects.

Architecture was a fertile field in which to seed new ideas about how scientific knowledge could change ways of life. European modernism emphasized an objective and rational basis for design methods, even though such a basis was not always realized in built works.[40] A significant aspect of this field of objective analysis was concerned with health, and climate played a major role—perhaps most directly in the design of sanatoriums, hospitals, and schools in northern Europe, where expansive glass façades and engagement with solar patterns were important factors.[41]

The means for dissemination of the project were self-consciously bifurcated, however much they were developed in collaboration and were seen to provide opportunities for further integration of aesthetic and scientific forms of knowledge. The role of architecture and lifestyle journals was also changing in this immediate postwar moment. Perhaps most famously, the Los Angeles–based *Arts and Architecture* had begun, in 1944, the Case Study House program, through which architects were invited to develop a design in the pages of the journal in hopes that they might appeal to the home-buying public. Case Studies emphasized the use of industrial processes and materials as a means to open up new possibilities in residential design. Many such houses were built, including the iconic Eames House (Case Study #9) in 1949.[42]

Other industry journals were similarly reaching beyond the profession to appeal to the prospective architectural client or builder. *Progressive Architecture*, for example, included articles intending to interpret more general public discussions for an architectural audience. *Architectural Forum* published its "House Omnibus" issue in 1945, which reviewed the exploration of new house designs as they were appearing in more popular journals, such as *Better Homes and Gardens*, *McCall's*, *Women's Home Companion*, *House Beautiful*, and others. Such so-called shelter magazines in fact had a long history of engagement with architectural innovations and ideas—*Ladies' Home Journal* in particular had been essential to promoting the work of Frank Lloyd Wright early in the twentieth century.[43] The *Journal* was also, simultaneous to the Climate Control Project, promoting a series of "Victory Houses" as "small but really adequate homes" that could be built affordably across the United States, later shown as part of exhibition *Tomorrow's Small House* at New York's Museum of Modern Art.[44] Many included solar heating and other climatic factors.

*Progressive Architecture* was also focused on developing the technical acumen of the architect in a number of significant issues, articles, and books. The publishers released books collecting articles from their issues, focused on the architect's technical education, including Jeffrey Aronin's 1953 *Climate and Architecture*.[45] *Climate and Architecture* summarized a lot of the material proposed through the Climate Control Project as well as other related developments in the immediate wartime period. *Progressive Architecture* also catalyzed discussions around air conditioning in an issue of 1958, and around the design of nuclear power in 1959.

It was in this dynamic context that *House Beautiful* and the AIA offered the Climate Control Project to architects and clients. In collaboration with the climatologists, physiologists, anthropologists, and others, the AIA elements of the project focused on the technical analysis of the microclimate, and in making that analysis accessible to architects. The Climate Control Project was something of a test case, in the context of the wild proliferation of applied science in the postwar period, for the interrelationship of technical knowledge and cultural effect.

## Fifteen AIA *Bulletins*

A series of fifteen analyses the AIA developed were published as an appendix to the *Bulletin of the American Institute of Architects* every other month from September 1949 to January 1952. Siple, Landsberg, and their colleagues originally intended to demarcate a number of general regions across the continent, and to commission an architect to develop a typical design for each. It soon became clear that there would have had to be "hundreds of zones," because a simplified analysis according to temperature and precipitation ignored too many significant variables—here reiterating the premise of Fitch's 1947 article. Furthermore, Siple "could find no assistance from individuals in the building field who, [he] had hoped, could give criteria that would assure that the zones were significant." In other words, few in the architecture world seemed to care too much about climate, a frustration also oft-repeated in the articles and conferences he participated in. Not only were regional climatic zones too general for relevance to design, but also a stark lack of architectural attention to these problems meant that the specific contours of an architecturally determined climatic region had not yet been conceived of as a possible goal. Architects first needed to be educated as to the value of climatic knowledge, then introduced to its details, only then to begin the process of integrating it into their practices.

The AIA analyses attempted to straddle this contrast between the generalized regional zone and the specifics of microclimatic analysis. Siple and his colleagues decided to focus on fifteen population centers, still aiming to propose a design correlated to each. "From each center," Siple wrote, "we would determine how far away from the site the houses of this design could still be moved before they needed climatically necessitated alterations"; relative boundaries of "few alterations," "minor alterations," and "major alterations" were drawn—thus the enigmatic maps that accompanied each AIA bulletin.[46] The scale of the maps indicated that dramatic changes could be needed across small distances. The Minneapolis example attempts to account for lake effect cold and snow with a rich array of blues (figure 4.8). The New Jersey distinctions were represented with an array of striped, polka-dotted, and hashed areas indicating "5% drier," "less snow," and "July 5% warmer," among others (figure 4.9).[47] This tension between generalizable knowledge and the need, at a given site, to respond to specifics would not be resolved in the project and, indeed, continued to plague architectural climatic analyses for the rest of the decade. Siple admitted that he and the *House Beautiful* staff "were still in a quandary" as to whether the zones were significant architecturally, but they used them all the same.[48]

The fifteen regions analyzed, in order of publication, were: the Mid-Ohio Region; Metropolitan New York and New Jersey; South Florida—Miami; Arid Southwest Area; Mid-Mississippi Basin; Gulf Coast; Chicago Area; Twin City Area; Washington, DC, Area; Boston Area; Pittsburgh Area; Portland, Oregon, Area; Charleston, South Carolina, Area; Albany, New York, Area; and Denver, Colorado, Area. If California is conspicuously absent, this was because of a sense that it presented few climatic challenges and, as Elizabeth Gordon argued in a related context, that architectural trends in California were not seen to be open to this specific kind of scientific intervention. One could place the regions analyzed next to a map of the primary growth centers of suburban expansion in the late 1940s and find much convergence.

The technical secretary of the AIA Department of Education and Research, Theodore Irving Coe, was both self-conscious and celebratory about the necessarily incomplete analysis of the regions when he introduced the project in the *Bulletin* of September 1949: "we and our clients have lazily assumed," he wrote, "that we have four climates, North, South, West and the West Coast, with a few local peculiarities. Actually we have at least 100 climates in the United States and each one is different. . . . This climatological data and its design implications should dispose finally and effectively of the fallacy of an International Style or even of a 'national style.'" Gordon would pursue such a disposal, albeit on slightly different terms, in *House Beautiful* during and after the project.[49]

Each region was given identical treatment. Asserting that "in addition to appearance and livability, a house should be compatible with the environment," Siple broke down this potential compatibility into three factors: "first, the climatic conditions typical of the area; second, the microclimatic factors . . . of the site; and third, exploitation of natural advantages, including such things as surrounding topography, vegetation, geology and materials." Although necessarily partial, the hope was that architects would see the information as instigation to more fully examine, in collaboration with landscape architects and climatologists, the complexity of a site's condition. More than an imperative to directly change how architects designed, the AIA *Bulletins* intended to encourage new kinds of expert collaborations.[50]

The fifteen bulletin appendixes were dedicated to climatic analysis. Again, the analysis proceeded in three parts: a "climatic summary," a "guide" for the region, and "design data" based on thermal analysis in the guide. The first section, the climatic summary, included synopses of temperature averages and extremes, precipitation conditions, and the vicissitudes of topography in the region. Special features of the region were also highlighted: the impact of the great lakes on the precipitation norms in Ohio, the proximity to the Atlantic and its effect on storms in Boston, and elevation differences across the Denver region. A map was

# How to Live with America's Worst Climate

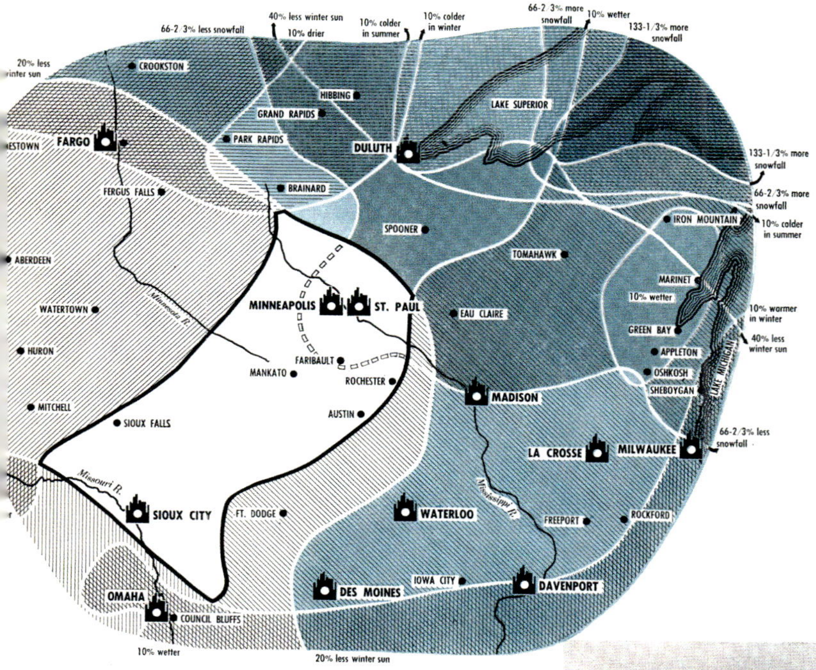


By Dr. Paul A. Siple

House Beautiful's Chief Climatologist

The Minnesota climate zone, described here, obtains in the white area on the map at left. Conditions change as you move out from the white area. To the northeast, winters are colder, cloudier, snowier. Southwest, winters are milder, sunnier, drier. In the Southeast, there's more rain; in the Northwest it's colder, sunnier.

*If you live where there's a big difference between winter and summer, read this story about a place where the difference is biggest of all*

HOUSE BEAUTIFUL'S CLIMATE CONTROL PROJECT

**The scientists who researched Climate Control**

DR. RALPH LINTON
Sterling Professor of Anthropology
Yale University

DR. PAUL SIPLE
Military Geographer,
The General Staff, U. S. Army

4.8 Climate map of the Minneapolis Region, from *House Beautiful*, October 1949.

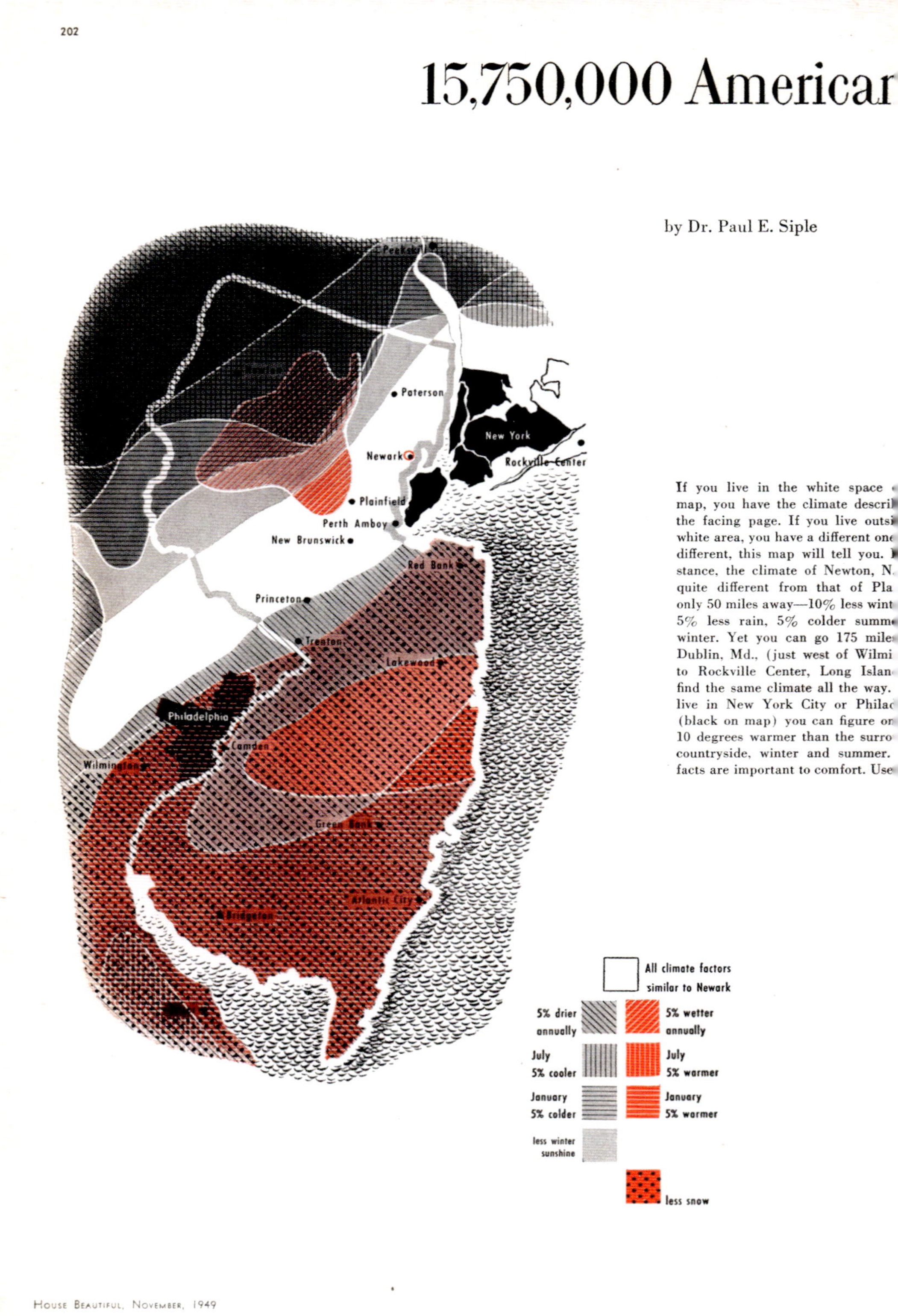

202

# 15,750,000 Americar

by Dr. Paul E. Siple



If you live in the white space
map, you have the climate descri
the facing page. If you live outs
white area, you have a different on
different, this map will tell you.
stance, the climate of Newton, N.
quite different from that of Pla
only 50 miles away—10% less wint
5% less rain, 5% colder summ
winter. Yet you can go 175 mile
Dublin, Md., (just west of Wilmi
to Rockville Center, Long Islan
find the same climate all the way.
live in New York City or Philac
(black on map) you can figure or
10 degrees warmer than the surro
countryside, winter and summer.
facts are important to comfort. Use

House Beautiful, November, 1949

4.9 Climate map of New Jersey, from *House Beautiful*, November 1949.

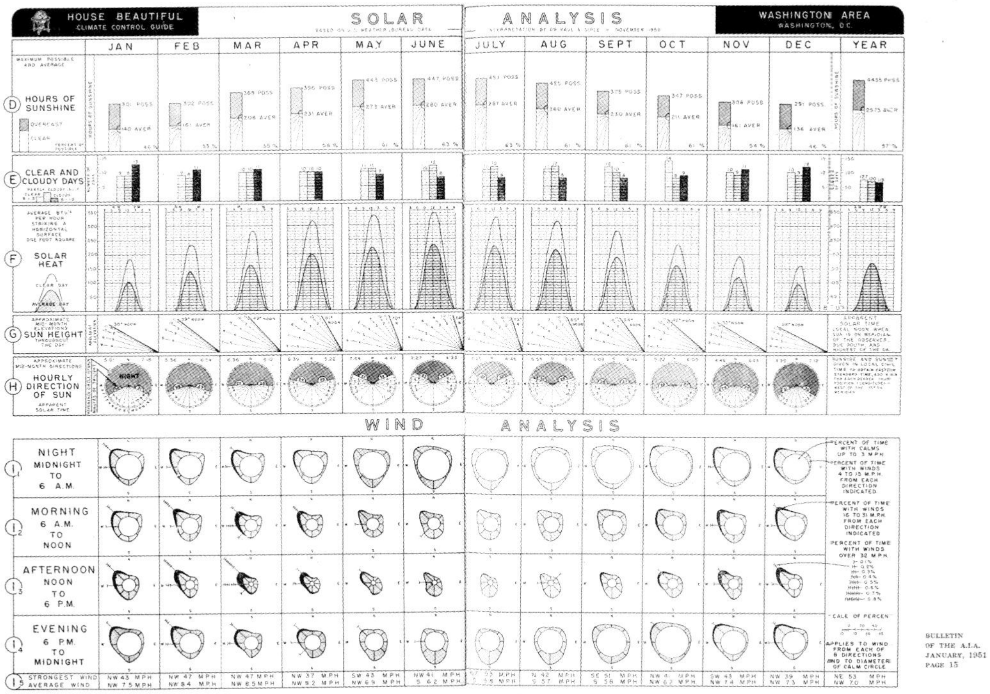


4.10 American Institute of Architects, Solar Analysis, from *AIA Bulletin*, March 1951.

provided, outlining the region in question with its topographic vagaries. By defining climatological rather than cultural outlines, these maps reconsidered what constituted a region on these terms, often crossing state borders and for the most part ignoring regional building types and materials. Most of the summaries were cowritten by Siple and a local architect, or, at least, the architect was invited to comment on the conclusions in the report.

Following the summary was the guide, which detailed a "solar analysis" (figure 4.10) and a "thermal analysis" (figure 4.11). Data for local air and dew-point temperature were plotted across a temperature scale broken down by month, creating a series of arrow or leaf shapes illustrating temperature variation for a given city. The bottom pointed to represent low temperature extremes, the middle widened according to how a normal temperature range expanded across the monthly range, and the top tapered to a thin line to indicate days of especially high heat relative to those norms. Along with these figures of temperature conditions, a bar chart showing the number of "degree days"—in which the daily mean falls below 65—was provided as well as a small chart representing the number of extreme hot and cold days. Together these graphs and diagrams summarized the relative need for climatic alterations or adaptations for buildings—that is, the effects of building for extremes, or managing the middle zones, early hints of adaptive comfort and other theories of adaptability. These "thermal analysis" pages also offered iconic images from the project that were often published in other journals and reports. Presented to architects in a relatively technical form in the *Bulletin* and similar publications, they were also reproduced in *House Beautiful* in more expressive, colorful versions (see figure 4.15).

Thermal analysis pages were followed by a chart of "Design Data Based on Thermal Analysis," one of "Design Data for Precipitation and Humidity" and one of "Design Data Based on Sun and Wind Analysis," which reiterated the summary according to the specific imperatives of the analytic chart (figure 4.12). The chart was pegged to the temperature zones enumerated in the analysis, and specific recommendations were made according to: site and orientation; interior planning; roof, walls, openings, and foundation; and for the use of mechanical systems. In Boston, for example, the insulation and air-tightness of roofs was recommended in order to minimize the impact of summer heat, while it was proposed that research into "quick response heating systems" could help to

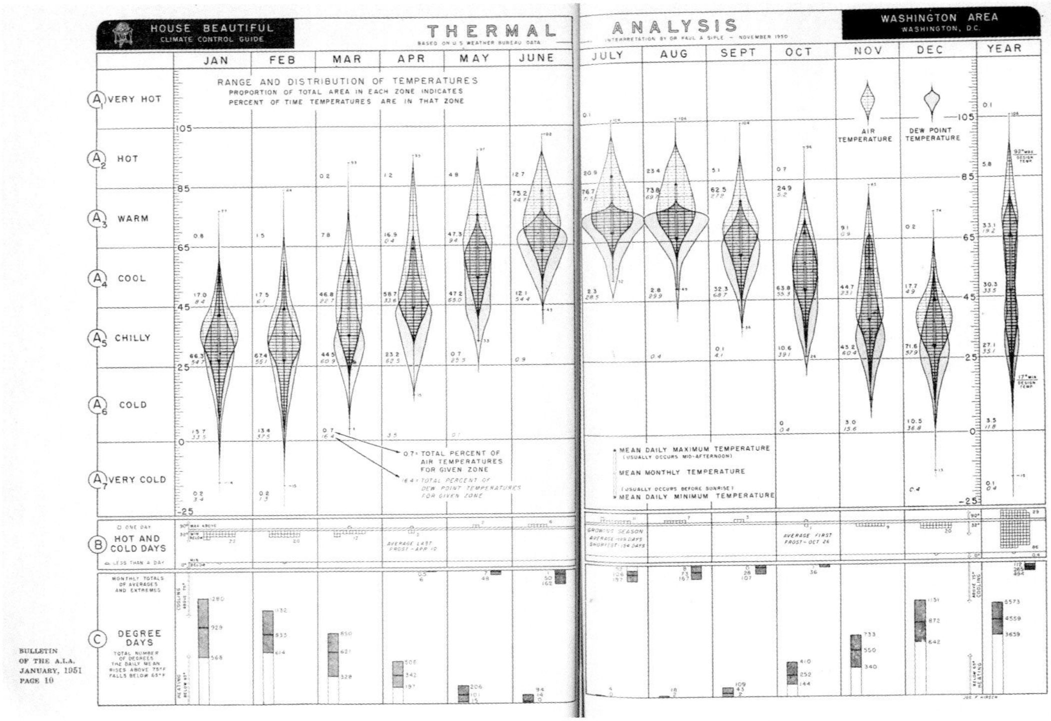


4.11 American Institute of Architects, Thermal Analysis, from *AIA Bulletin*, March 1951.

normalize the fluctuations of "hot and cold days" that were indicated in the analysis to occur in spring and fall.[51] Here again a more general alternative technological trajectory is articulated—one organized to cover extremes with a mechanical system, and the bloated interior on the leaf chart, the majority of climatic demand, through architectural methods. This process of analysis, of correlating recommendations, was repeated for all three Design Data charts.

Even more than the thermal chart, these detailed diagrams provided new information for the architect. But, again, a wider cultural span opens up—Siple continued to recognize a strange hesitance in architects to allow climatic factors to be instrumental to their design thinking. "Some well-known facts," he lamented, such as relative sun angle in summer and winter, "have in many cases been consistently ignored in residential design."[52] Gathering data was important, but of even more concern was how to communicate climatic knowledge to the architectural profession, through the AIA bulletin, and to the consumer, through *House Beautiful*—to make it cultural for these constituencies.

The Climate Control Project was well received by some architects. A review of both the AIA and *House Beautiful* components published in *Progressive Architecture* in February 1950—that is, after only a handful of the analyses had been released—praised Siple and his colleagues: "the data are given in sufficient detail and so weighted that they can be used as design criteria—to decide, for instance, how much to spend on heating or insulation or how to arrange for ventilation . . . whether double glazing or air conditioning is needed, etc." The analytic charts and their accompanying interpretation, the reviewer continued, "outline a complete education in environmental factors affecting design."[53] The author did, however, criticize the project for its exclusive focus on single-family homes rather than apartments, medium-income houses, or schools and other institutions that could be improved through these new design strategies.

The AIA publications of climate analyses were infused with compromise and innovation. The regions could be considered as such only in the sense of a given metropolitan expanse, and not as a more general zone that could be approached according to certain climatic parameters; the readability and applicability of the charts and graphs provided was untested and partial. Although the data were clear, a mechanism for their interpretation into a usable architecture remained wanting—and would be filled largely by the Olgyay brothers, as discussed in the next chapter. Furthermore, climate was only seen

DESIGN DATA BASED ON SUN AND WIND ANALYSIS

| ZONE | GENERAL INTERPRETATION | SITE AND ORIENTATION PLANTING | INTERIOR PLAN | ROOF | WALLS | OPENINGS | FOUNDATIONS & BASEMENT | MECHANICAL |
|---|---|---|---|---|---|---|---|---|
| D<br>HOURS OF SUNSHINE | Days are sunny 58% of time sun is above horizon—varies 49% to 65% annually.<br>Sunshine unevenly distributed throughout yr—av 46% of possible hrs in winter & 63% in summer—or about 4-1/3 hrs/day in winter, 9½ hrs/day in summer. | Sun is major factor in orientation. Plan for max shade in summer & max exposure in winter. | Rooms should be generally shaded in summer, open to sun in winter. However, admission of E sun on summer mornings will help prevent mildew. | Design insulation to deflect summer sun & retain winter interior heat. | E & W walls should be protected from summer sun by overhangs. | Full length screens should be used with venetian blinds to permit opening window top & bottom to form flue effect back of screens. Large openings desirable for ventilation in summer, & light in winter, & solar heat spring & fall. Adjustable blinds or awnings are beneficial. | If possible permit summer sun to enter basement to raise dewpt & prevent mildew. | Provide ample indoor & outdoor electric outlets because of long periods of darkness in winter. |
| E<br>CLEAR & CLOUDY DAYS | Av about 127 clear days, 118 cloudy days, 120 partly cloudy days annually—preponderance of cloudy days in winter. Some tendency to cloudy summer afternoons but not as marked as farther S. This cloudiness may provide shade during period when sun is hottest. | Long periods of cloudiness cause mildew. Luxuriant foliage should not be placed close to openings. | Shallow rather than deep rooms preferable in order to utilize max window area. | Dampproof materials should be used exclusively to avoid fungi & other deterioration. | Smooth, moisture-resistant materials should be used. Paint particularly susceptible to fading & other damage from intense solar radiation. Reduce painted areas on sunstruck sides of buildings. | | | |
| F<br>SOLAR HEAT | Av solar impact about 50 btu's/hr of sunshine on horizontal surface in winter—about 114 btu's/hr of sunshine in summer. Dec & Jan receive least solar heat—av only of 150 btu's/hr. Midsummer impact reaches av max of 1850 btu's/day & 228 btu's/hr.<br>Clear day peaks of 325 btu's/hr & 2720 btu's/day. | Exterior winter solar nooks should be on S, protected from wind.<br>Glass-enclosed solar traps are most effective outdoors since wind tends to maintain air temp & prevents solar build-up.<br>High branching, deciduous trees desirable for summer shade. | Spaces to benefit from solar heating should be oriented toward S. | Inward flow of heat may reach max of 335 btu's/sf/hr on calm day. | In winter more solar heat will strike vertical E, W & S walls than will strike horizontal surfaces. | E & W openings require greater protection from summer sun than S.<br>When storm doors face S provide full glazing to permit occasional use for solar heat, leaving regular door open. | Solar heating in basement during summer may be used to prevent mildew, to bring temp to comfortable level & to reduce RH & condensation.<br>Basement solar heating will rise up thru house reducing mechanical heat requirements. | Flat roof should be specially ventilated or have evaporative cooling in summer.<br>If solar heating devices are used they should be mounted in vertical wall. |
| G<br>SUN HEIGHT<br>&<br>H<br>HOURLY DIRECTION OF SUN | In latter part of Jun, sun is above horizon nearly 15 hrs & reaches max elevation of 74°. In midwinter highest sun is about 28° & length of day only 9½ hrs.<br>Data given on these two graphs is in apparent solar time & should be corrected to local civil or daylight saving time if precise shadows are required at certain hours. | Use diagrams to plan shade patterns of house & landscaping, noting location of solar features. Houses on N-S street, close together, may miss much of winter sun.<br>Fences with either H or V louvers will provide controlled shade & permit breeze access in summer. | Plan rooms for deep sun penetration in winter and min penetration in summer. Watch sun penetration carefully to reduce fading of drapery & upholstery materials.<br>Consider exterior climate control features early in working toward room arrangement. Plan with the climate. | In summer, flat roof gets full solar impact. Try to arrange pitch to N or steeper pitch to avoid normal incidence & secure some reflective effect.<br>When overhangs of adjacent roofs have different pitches junction designs may be awkward & transitional features may be necessary. | | | Consider extensions of S, SE, or SW basement walls beyond foundation lines to permit basement skylights or conservatory arrangement. | |
| I<br>WIND | Because of differences in terrain, wide diversity exists in local variations in wind direction & velocity. High winds infrequent—highest recorded velocity over 5 min is 53 mph, gusts up to 73 mph have been recorded, but are rare.<br>In summer, primary prevailing wind is from S, secondary from NW; in winter NW & W winds predominate with NE & S secondary. Local variations should be checked.<br>Large part of evenings & nights are calm or have very light winds throughout yr but especially in summer. Afternoon is breeziest part of day. Season Oct-Apr, windiest part of yr. | Choice location for relief from summer heat is on edge of E slope, catching down-flow of cool air at night.<br>Protection desirable against strong NW & W winter winds.<br>Fences (which may be opened in summer) make practical windbreak.<br>Porch (including sleeping porch) desirable feature. Location with N-S ventilation desirable—breezeway type especially useful. | Cross ventilation should be planned for N-S (or better, NW-SE) flow in summer.<br>Use of prevailing av wind velocity & direction for planning is fallacy. Analyze wind rose diagrams for other important winds. For example: prevailing S for Jun to Sep does not recognize prominent NW winds. In winter prevailing NW is not all. Frequent S & NE should also be considered. Actual directions always depend on microclimate. | Max probable wind-load not likely to exceed 35-40 mph.<br>Design roofs & building form near entrance to minimize turbulence which will drive rain & snow into these areas. | Wall insulation particularly desirable on N & W sides for winter protection. | Min number & size of windows should be on W, NW & N sides for winter protection.<br>Storm sash will be beneficial on windows facing these directions. | Natural ventilation of basement in summer may merely increase RH & condensation. | Mechanical ventilation particularly desirable for summer nights due to usual calmness. Fan vents should be placed on lee side—should be avoided on N, W & S sides. |

PAGE 16 . JANUARY, 1951 . BULLETIN OF THE AMERICAN INSTITUTE OF ARCHITECTS

BULLETIN OF THE AMERICAN INSTITUTE OF ARCHITECTS . JANUARY, 1951 PAGE 17

4.12 American Institute of Architects, Design Data, from *AIA Bulletin*, March 1951.

as a concern for middle-class suburban homes, not for housing generally, a perspective likely dictated by the audience of both the AIA and *House Beautiful*. The intent to build a test or demonstration house for each metropolitan center, which could have clarified the architectural issues at stake, was not pursued. However, the Pace Setter House, a promotional house program organized by *House Beautiful*, served, in an unsystematic way, to reflect this general goal.

The innovative aspect of the project was in developing new forms for the graphic communication of climatic data—a new kind of media channel that could connect knowledge from the sciences to the design approach of the architect and also, in the *House Beautiful* articles, to a more general interested public. Once familiar with the system, the leaf-shaped figures could provide some crucial temperature information quickly and clearly; similarly, in the sun and wind charts new graphic means were used to easily furnish information for the design interpretations that would follow. Siple's ambition to produce diagrams so clear "that texts will not be necessary" was not exactly realized; they were supplemented with written information.[54] And while Siple's ambitions for a visual language was focused on architects, it was relevant to both aspects of the project. Architects and consumers, the project's editors hoped, could become literate in these new kinds of climatic diagrams, making them increasingly useful in the design decisions that would determine the conditions of the built environment.

The diagram thus sat at the intersection between science and the design professions, and between professional practices and consumer desires. When Siple presented the Climate Control images to climatologists and architects at the

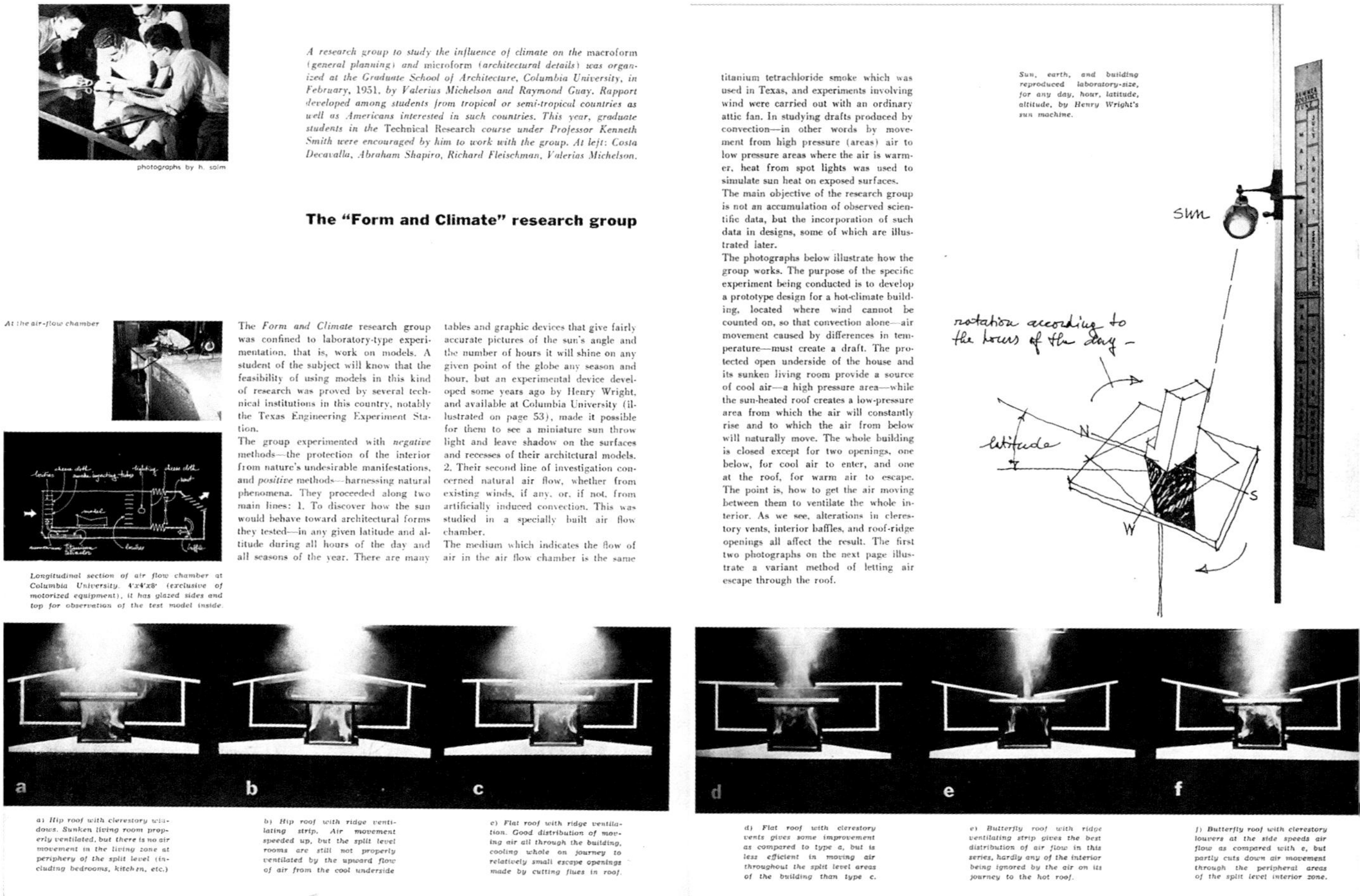

photographs by h. solm

*A research group to study the influence of climate on the* macroform *(general planning)* and microform *(architectural details) was organized at the Graduate School of Architecture, Columbia University, in February,* 1951, *by Valerius Michelson and Raymond Guay. Rapport developed among students from tropical or semi-tropical countries as well as Americans interested in such countries. This year, graduate students in the* Technical Research *course under Professor Kenneth Smith were encouraged by him to work with the group. At left: Costa Decavalla, Abraham Shapiro, Richard Fleischman, Valerias Michelson.*

**The "Form and Climate" research group**

*At the air-flow chamber*

*Longitudinal section of air flow chamber at Columbia University. 4'x4'x8' (exclusive of motorized equipment), it has glazed sides and top for observation of the test model inside.*

The *Form and Climate* research group was confined to laboratory-type experimentation, that is, work on models. A student of the subject will know that the feasibility of using models in this kind of research was proved by several technical institutions in this country, notably the Texas Engineering Experiment Station.

The group experimented with *negative* methods—the protection of the interior from nature's undesirable manifestations, and *positive* methods—harnessing natural phenomena. They proceeded along two main lines: 1. To discover how the sun would behave toward architectural forms they tested—in any given latitude and altitude during all hours of the day and all seasons of the year. There are many tables and graphic devices that give fairly accurate pictures of the sun's angle and the number of hours it will shine on any given point of the globe any season and hour, but an experimental device developed some years ago by Henry Wright, and available at Columbia University (illustrated on page 53), made it possible for them to see a miniature sun throw light and leave shadow on the surfaces and recesses of their architctural models. 2. Their second line of investigation concerned natural air flow, whether from existing winds, if any, or, if not, from artificially induced convection. This was studied in a specially built air flow chamber.

The medium which indicates the flow of air in the air flow chamber is the same titanium tetrachloride smoke which was used in Texas, and experiments involving wind were carried out with an ordinary attic fan. In studying drafts produced by convection—in other words by movement from high pressure (areas) air to low pressure areas where the air is warmer, heat from spot lights was used to simulate sun heat on exposed surfaces.

The main objective of the research group is not an accumulation of observed scientific data, but the incorporation of such data in designs, some of which are illustrated later.

The photographs below illustrate how the group works. The purpose of the specific experiment being conducted is to develop a prototype design for a hot-climate building, located where wind cannot be counted on, so that convection alone—air movement caused by differences in temperature—must create a draft. The protected open underside of the house and its sunken living room provide a source of cool air—a high pressure area—while the sun-heated roof creates a low-pressure area from which the air will constantly rise and to which the air from below will naturally move. The whole building is closed except for two openings, one below, for cool air to enter, and one at the roof, for warm air to escape. The point is, how to get the air moving between them to ventilate the whole interior. As we see, alterations in clerestory vents, interior baffles, and roof-ridge openings all affect the result. The first two photographs on the next page illustrate a variant method of letting air escape through the roof.

*Sun, earth, and building reproduced laboratory-size, for any day, hour, latitude, altitude, by Henry Wright's sun machine.*



*a) Hip roof with clerestory windows. Sunken living room properly ventilated, but there is no air movement in the living zone at periphery of the split level (including bedrooms, kitchen, etc.)*

*b) Hip roof with ridge ventilating strip. Air movement speeded up, but the split level rooms are still not properly ventilated by the upward flow of air from the cool underside*

*c) Flat roof with ridge ventilation. Good distribution of moving air all through the building, cooling whole on journey to relatively small escape openings made by cutting flues in roof.*

*d) Flat roof with clerestory vents gives some improvement as compared to type a, but is less efficient in moving air throughout the split level areas of the building than type c.*

*e) Butterfly roof with ridge ventilating strip gives the best distribution of air flow in this series, hardly any of the interior being ignored by the air on its journey to the hot roof.*

*f) Butterfly roof with clerestory louvers at the side speeds air flow as compared with e, but partly cuts down air movement through the peripheral areas of the split level interior zone.*

4.13 The Form and Climate Research Group, in *Interiors*, August 1953.

January 1950 symposium on "Weather and the Building Industry," sponsored by the Building Research Advisory Board (BRAB) of the National Research Council, issues of translation across fields were placed in the foreground. The conference was billed as a "research correlation conference on climatological research and its impact on building design."[55] Siple introduced his presentation, and the symposium in general, with a focus on collaboration, cautioning his colleagues to "use simple language, understandable to all the represented groups, and to avoid as much as possible the use of specialized terminology."[56] Others reiterated this imperative, and amid numerous technical presentations the primary concern was with how to convince architects and clients that climate was a central component to design.

The BRAB conference is further evidence of the dynamism of the architectural and climate discussion in the years before the flow of oil began to overwhelm the designed rather than mechanical manipulation of the climatic interior. Landsberg, Siple, and Fitch presented papers at the conference, as did the physiologist Herrington; the AIA's Walter Taylor chaired a panel. Numerous engineers from ASHVE and ASRE attended and presented; the anthropologist Linton was there (Gordon's inspiration to initiate the projects), as were the architects Carl Koch and Bedford Pickens.[57] The publication of the proceedings was made possible by a grant from *House Beautiful*.

Numerous other aspects joined these discussions of climate, architecture, and how to build in the suburbs. Journals published by the AIA and a range of scientific and technological societies and agencies focused on the evaluation of climate as a resource for building efficiency and building knowledge. In addition to the *Progressive Architecture* collection, *Architectural Record*

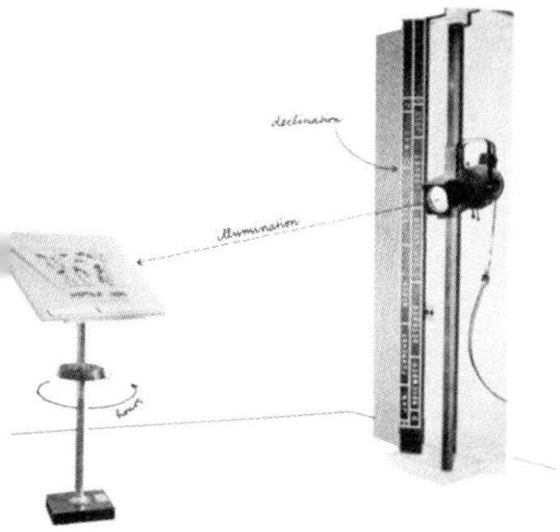

Heliodon at Princeton University.

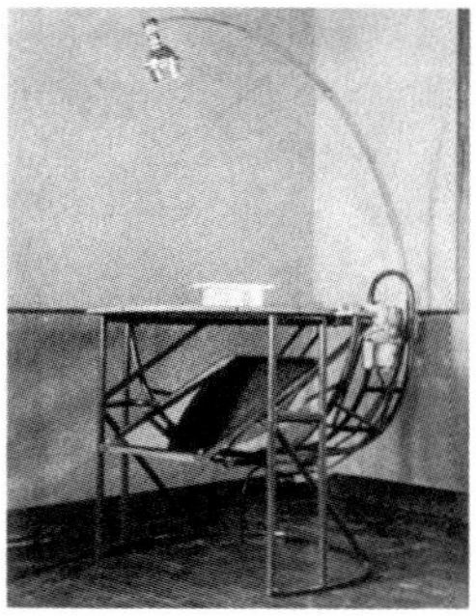

**56.** Sunmachine at University of Kansas.

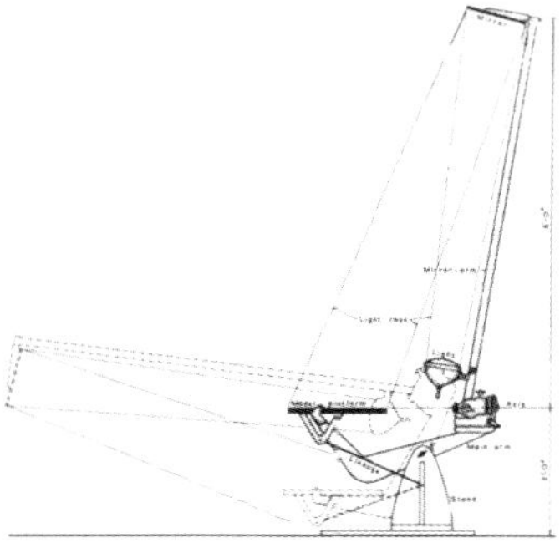

**57.** The Solarscope.

4.14 The Olgyays' Heliodon at Princeton; G. M. Beal's Sunmachine at the University of Kansas, 1954; George Atkinson's Solarscope at the Commonwealth Experimental Building Station, Sydney, Australia, 1955 from Olgyay and Olgyay, *Solar Control and Shading Devices*.

commissioned the book *Design of Insulated Buildings for Various Climates* in 1951.[58] That same year, the Housing and Home Finance Agency published an extensive bibliography on the subject under the title *Climate and Architecture: Selected References in Housing Research*, which included relevant texts from around the world and a list of the *House Beautiful* articles and AIA *Bulletins*; this bibliography was distributed widely as part of AIA and governmental efforts.

Fitch was instrumental in many of these other inquiries. He taught at Columbia University from the late 1940s, and he also helped to facilitate the Form and Climate Research Group, made up of a group of students interested in using new technologies to analyze architecture-climatic relationships. These students were beginning to think about how to model this relationship (figure 4.13).[59] In 1936, the planner Henry Wright, also teaching at Columbia, had built the first heliodon in the United States.[60] It was a relatively simple device: a sun lamp calibrated along the vertical calendar to provide the seasonal height with a model building placed on a platform angled according to latitude. The platform could spin to simulate diurnal patterns relative to the sun's location. Columbia's was built based on designs published by the Royal Institute of British Architects in 1935; it was widely used by Wright in his research for the garden cities he built with Clarence Stein, and also by Raymond Unwin in his planning studios.[61] Other heliodons were built at the University of Kansas, Princeton, and at a number of the tropical building research stations in former British colonies (figure 4.14).[62]

The Form and Climate Research Group imagined the shape of the building as the register of its environmental performance. In addition to the Wright's heliodon, they used a wind tunnel and material tests to model a building's performance and adjusted the proportions and edges to make it more efficient. It was a sort of blatant architecture as media, the shape registering and producing a different relationship to climate—another hint of the computational possibilities to come, and even of the methodological diagrams of later in the decade.

## House Beautiful

At the AIA, and in the interested architectural community more broadly, the primary aim of the Climate Control Project was to collaboratively develop new forms of visualization. This interest in refining the technical image also initially preoccupied the Climate Control articles in *House Beautiful*, though they were soon overwhelmed by a desire to affect the architectural profession more directly and on broader cultural terms. If the AIA *Bulletins* clarify the means by which the technical was seen to offer seemingly objective knowledge to generate new frameworks for practice, the elaboration of the Climate Control Project in *House Beautiful* offers more evident cultural contingencies concerning global debates about economies and cultures, and the architectures appropriate to them.

The Climate Control Project in *House Beautiful* involved about sixty-five articles appearing in the journal from October 1949 until the early 1950s; related articles continued until about 1953, and more infrequently until the early 1960s.[63] In addition to pieces specifically connected to the project, issues around climate-appropriate designs also informed and were used to promote the Pace Setter Homes that the magazine sponsored, again under Gordon's direct leadership, from 1948 to 1955. Taken together, these two projects—the Climate Control Project and the Pace Setter

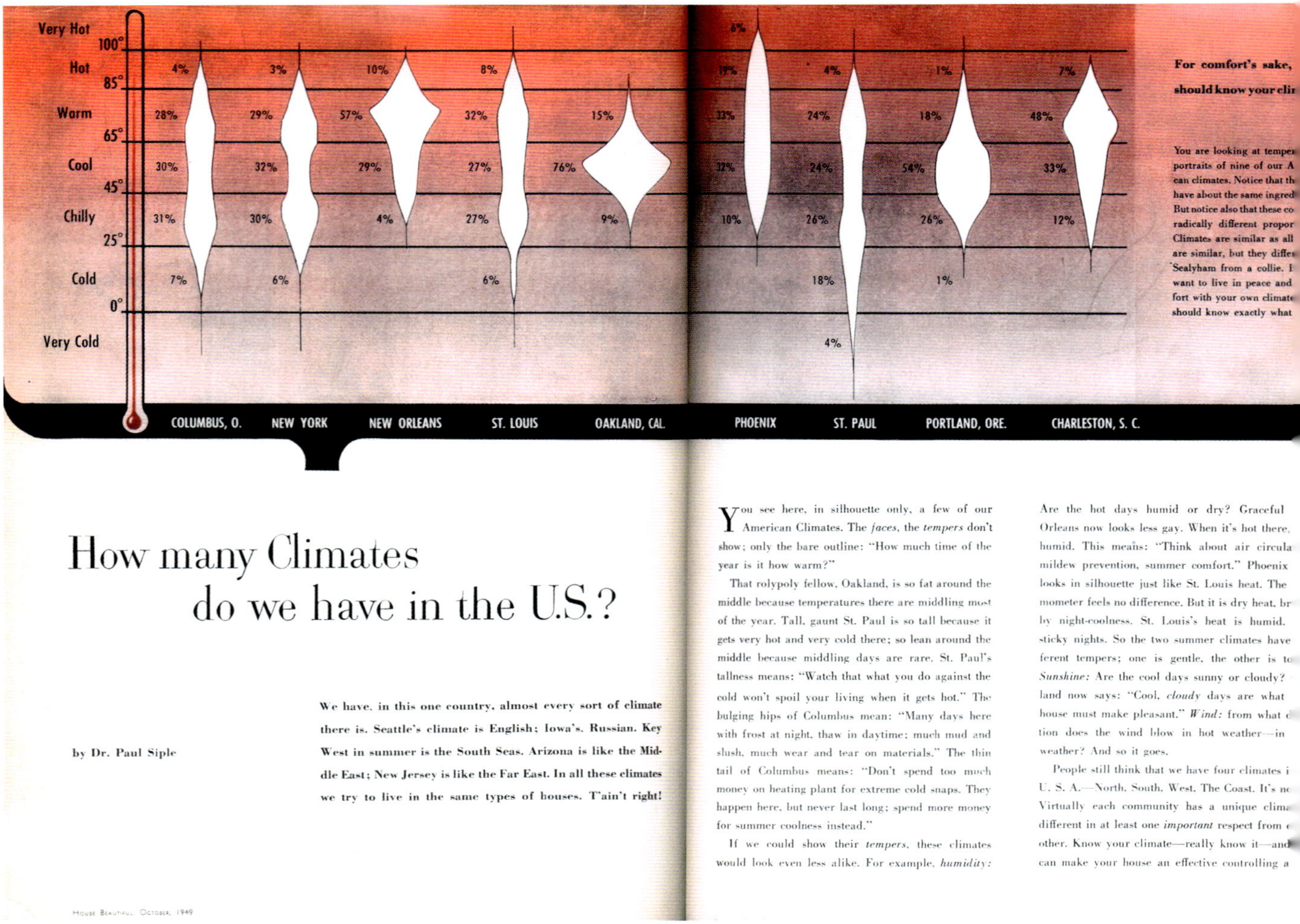


**For comfort's sake, should know your cli**

**You are looking at temper portraits of nine of our A can climates. Notice that th have about the same ingred But notice also that these co radically different propor Climates are similar as all are similar, but they diffe Sealyham from a collie. I want to live in peace and fort with your own climat should know exactly what**

# How many Climates do we have in the U.S.?

by Dr. Paul Siple

**We have, in this one country, almost every sort of climate there is. Seattle's climate is English; Iowa's, Russian. Key West in summer is the South Seas. Arizona is like the Middle East; New Jersey is like the Far East. In all these climates we try to live in the same types of houses. T'ain't right!**

You see here, in silhouette only, a few of our American Climates. The *faces*, the *tempers* don't show; only the bare outline: "How much time of the year is it how warm?"

That rolypoly fellow, Oakland, is so fat around the middle because temperatures there are middling most of the year. Tall, gaunt St. Paul is so tall because it gets very hot and very cold there; so lean around the middle because middling days are rare. St. Paul's tallness means: "Watch that what you do against the cold won't spoil your living when it gets hot." The bulging hips of Columbus mean: "Many days here with frost at night, thaw in daytime; much mud and slush, much wear and tear on materials." The thin tail of Columbus means: "Don't spend too much money on heating plant for extreme cold snaps. They happen here, but never last long; spend more money for summer coolness instead."

If we could show their *tempers*, these climates would look even less alike. For example, *humidity:* Are the hot days humid or dry? Graceful Orleans now looks less gay. When it's hot there, humid. This means: "Think about air circula mildew prevention, summer comfort." Phoenix looks in silhouette just like St. Louis heat. The mometer feels no difference. But it is dry heat, br by night-coolness. St. Louis's heat is humid. sticky nights. So the two summer climates have ferent tempers; one is gentle, the other is t *Sunshine:* Are the cool days sunny or cloudy? land now says: "Cool, *cloudy* days are what house must make pleasant." *Wind:* from what tion does the wind blow in hot weather—in weather? And so it goes.

People still think that we have four climates i U. S. A.—North, South, West. The Coast. It's n Virtually each community has a unique clima different in at least one *important* respect from other. Know your climate—really know it—and can make your house an effective controlling a

House Beautiful, October, 1949

4.15 Paul Siple, "How Many Climates Do We Have in the U.S.?" *House Beautiful*, October 1949.

Homes—represented an intense investment on the part of the journal in promoting a specific kind of architectural disposition.

Climate was at the forefront; it was one of a number of factors that Gordon attempted to harness in order to pursue her agenda for a modified architectural modernism that, as she saw it, better reflected the needs and desires of the American consumer—here, again, at a moment when the geophysical, geopolitical, and geoeconomic impact of exponentially increasing American consumption was only beginning to be understood. While *House Beautiful* was at the center of this emergent network of specialists concerned with designing according to applied scientific knowledge, the editorial direction of the magazine was simultaneously preoccupied with how such issues could be deployed toward more specific ideological goals.

The project was announced in a dedicated issue in October 1949. Gordon wrote the leading article, "What Climate Does to YOU and What You Can Do to CLIMATE"; other articles, by Wolfgang Langewiesche: "So You Think You're Comfortable?"; by Siple: "How Many Climates Do We Have in the U.S.?"; and Fitch: "How You Can Use *House Beautiful*'s Climate Control Project," were all directed at the potential home buyer, intending to educate the consumer to be a well-informed client of architects, landscape architects, and interior designers (figure 4.15). Climate was seen as one of the most important factors in house design as modernism was beginning to be reflected in American architecture, and as metropolitan regions were expanding into the suburbs. Over the

4.16 Cliff May, *House Beautiful* Pace Setter House, February 1948.

next few years the articles examined everything from window curtain material, to urban planning and site selection, to a capsule history of American architecture according to climate innovations.

The tone of the magazine on these issues was a bit admonishing; Langewiesche's December 1949 article "Don't You See?" perhaps renders this most clearly. The article was written in the style of an expert, shocked at the general lack of knowledge of his subject. He was aghast at the readers' purported lack of familiarity with ideas of climate and comfort. "This is the thing I want you to see," Langewiesche wrote. "I have learned to tell one sort of heat or cold from the others, and it helps me to do something about it." This information, it was posed, was available to anyone who took the time to pay attention. In the same article, in a rare populist moment in the journal, Langeswiesche also wrote, "When your Editor first roped me in to do some explaining pieces for HOUSE BEAUTIFUL's Climate Control Project, I thought, 'Sure, I'll tackle it. It's interesting.' Of course, her final aim leaves me rather cold . . . helping some pampered people who own expensive houses to make their precious selves a little more comfortable. That is of no interest to me. In fact, it smacks of Decline and Fall." [64] As other articles emphasized, climate was an issue of comfort and economy.

These writers were optimistic, demonstrating faith in the consumer's capacity to engage new design ideas. An article that appeared in January 1949, a few months before the Climate Control Project's launch, was titled "They Are Open Minded about New Ideas." Describing a small, semicircular vacation home, the author elaborated: "they subscribe to the glass house . . . they believe in radiant heat," and, "they believe in fixed windows." These ideal clients, the article continued, also "go in for much personal comfort . . . believe in effortless house-keeping . . . [and] believe in double purpose furniture."[65] *House Beautiful* sought to capitalize on this apparent willingness by elaborating on additional design possibilities that could emphasize views, outdoor living, privacy, and comfort.

In many ways the project started not in October 1949, but with the publication of the first *House Beautiful* Pace Setter House in February 1948 (figure 4.16). The banner headline for the house designed by Cliff May near Los Angeles was a "house to set the pace . . . in all climates . . . for all budgets."[66] The discussion, in the magazine, of climate was one of a few guiding principles—alongside privacy, and bringing in the outdoors—that was seen to be poised to transform the experience of the suburban landscape and improve, on specific terms, the quality of life of the building's inhabitants. The argument for designing with climate was made as one of common sense, or really, again, as a sort of more than common sense, as the magazine appealed to those with the interest and leisure to peruse it and outlined a seemingly straightforward logic for taking climate into account.

The Pace Setter House, the journal copy cooed, was "so well thought out and soundly executed" that it could be scaled down or adapted; it could "apply to all pocketbooks, to all climates."[67] The house was seen to embody a number of principles—climate sensitivity, affordability, as noted,

How to tame sun, wind and rain

**First, be sure that you know what your awning problem is. Then make certain that the awning can handle *all* the elements it's apt to meet. Use scallops, spears, and frills if you must, but, chances are, they'll add only cost, not beauty**

In a patio like this, wind is not apt to be much of a problem. But the need for sun (when the air is cool) and for shade (when it's hot and glarey) dictates this flexible solution—a series of parallel canvas strips that slide back and forth on pulleys. They permit ventilation but cannot be shower-proof.

Simplest of all awning problems—that of protecting the single window—often fails because awning is too skimpy or unventilated. Be sure awning is wide and deep enough to protect window all day long—not just at noon. To avoid a hot pocket, be sure awning top is mounted some inches away from wall.

House Beautiful, May, 1949

The Garden Room

**—answer to many problems**

The court, snug and private within the heart of a house, is not a new idea. It is found in many countries, in a variety of climates, but never in the United States.

Yet the court offers us many things—now that our national love of the sun is causing us to use more and more glass in our houses.

For, if we turn our back to the street and the neighbors, figuratively speaking, and turn our face inward to a private garden space, we can design with glass with no limitations. Automatically, that garden court becomes another room in the house. But it can also become a sunpocket or a windbreak or both—as it is in this house. It has been proved that if you have an outdoor place that can be quickly and easily manipulated so you may control both sun and wind simultaneously, you can add another two months of outdoor living to those you already have. It can let you be outdoors when your neighbors are driven indoors because they are too hot or too cold.

This fact is so little known, but so far-reaching, that it takes time to grasp it. As we take you through this house we will try to explain what outdoor weather control can mean to homeowners in all climates.

Garden room can be closed in from sun and wind by a canvas sky shade, which pulls horizontally. It is important to day and night lighting.

4.17 Cliff May's Pace Setter "Garden Room" in *House Beautiful*, May 1949.

and also an imperative to live as much of the year as possible in the outdoors. The main intervention May proposed to articulate these new opportunities was an exterior/interior space—what they called a "garden room" (figure 4.17). On the one hand it was typical of many courtyard designs in modern residential architecture; on the other hand the garden room resolved a specific contradiction between the desire for privacy in the suburban home and "our national love of the sun" that is, the copy continued, "causing us to use more and more glass in our houses." "If we turn our face inward to a private garden space," May suggested, "we can design with glass with no limitations."[68]

"Above all," Gordon and her colleagues intoned, "try to visualize the social values that such a house represents. For houses and people are inseparable." The profound conservatism of the project was articulated in direct relationship to other presuppositions about climate, regions, and ways of life. There was, in other words, an ideological framework—less represented in the researchers involved but seemingly a foundation from which the magazine was operating. In a stand-alone image in the introductory issue, six books were arrayed across a lined landscape, with clouds above and a young man, naked above the waist, looking at them as if to receive their knowledge (figure 4.18). Under the image:

> It may be news to you, but a whole literature has developed in recent years. Scientists have studied its effect on man, animals, and plants, on materials and machines. Climatology played a big role in the last war. Its importance to health, industry, and

4.18 "It May Be News to You, But . . ." image of climate-related texts, *House Beautiful*, October 1949.

> agriculture is widely recognized. Now *House Beautiful* applies this science to the job of making your house more comfortable more of the time by making it fit into your climate.[69]

Most of the illustrated texts squarely followed a climate determinist approach, in which cultures emerging in temperate climates were seen to benefit from their geographic conditions in the formation of knowledge and civilized social practices—other cultures, it followed, especially those in the tropics, were on a lower rung of the ladder. Ellsworth Huntington's *Mainsprings of Civilization* (1945)—a follow up to his *Civilization and Climate* (1915) and *The Red Man's Continent* (1927)—was in the illustration and is emblematic here; Huntington saw climate as a sort of filter to assist the process of evolution, with Europeans and Americans made more favorable for selection. Other texts argue similar theses on social and political, rather than biological, terms; a much smaller group of the collected books examined how these broader climatic patterns resonated in building practices—Fitch's *American Building* was illustrated. In identifying climate as a major factor in the comfort of the American home, concerns over race, xenophobia, and cultural elitism were placed in the frame, in ways that were not directly addressed in the initial issues of the project. The project was also, in other words, attempting to intensify the racial disparities implicit in the white migration to the suburbs across the 1950s; concerns over "privacy" in particular can be read as a cipher for white suburbanites' anxiety about adequately distancing themselves from the African American and immigrant populations in city centers.[70]

The garden room was described, instead, according to its benefits of the comfort of the inhabitant. It provided an outdoor space that, because of a pull-over sky shade, could be used longer: "it has been proved," the description concluded, "that if you have an outdoor place that can be quickly and easily manipulated so you can control both sun and wind simultaneously, you can add another two months of living to those you already have." The internal court also allowed for management of solar incidence on the interior of the house—letting the sun into living spaces in the winter, keeping it out in the summer, through shades, plantings, and orientation.[71]

The publication of the first Pace Setter House suggests the struggle to communicate the design and ideological complexity of the project through images alone. Increasingly, as the project proceeded, annotated photographs and diagrams were invoked to educate the reader about climate and also to describe the sorts of design options now available to them.

One central premise that allowed for these more developed technical images was rooting the analysis in a specific site, rather than generalizing about a region. The most substantive article in the October 1949 introductory issue was titled "A Lesson in Climate Control" and entailed an elaborate and multifaceted description of planning "a climate-wise house" for Columbus, Ohio—the house was not a built specimen but was, rather, represented through a range of drawings and diagrams (figure 4.19). The initial lesson was that readers should focus on the principles, not the details of the house: "you get climate control"

4.19 House in Columbus, Ohio, from "A Lesson in Climate Control," in *House Beautiful*, October 1949.

the editors insisted "by understanding—not copying."[72] They sought to portray these principles through plans and renderings and diagrams focused on how the climate behaved with the house.

The Columbus house was a two-story *L*-shaped building on a large lot (figure 4.20). "Fitting the plan to climate," a caption read, "gave us summer breeze and view in all main rooms; winter sun in every room; a covered breezeway for rainproof, insect-free outdoor living; terraces for year-round sunbathing."[73] Sun porches and other penetrations operated as thermal buffers and barriers; many opened up completely in the summer and then insulated the interior in the winter. The house was full of glass—the drawings have a triumphant expansiveness to them, a comfortable, enclosed, shaded space, cared for by climate knowledge, and celebrating a new way of life.

In the extensive discussion of the siting of the house the technical image became essential. Langewiesche's article "How to PICK Your Private Climate" accompanied the spreads on the Columbus house and indicated the importance of climatic analysis of the site in a fashion reminiscent of Landsberg's earlier diagrams (figure 4.21). Antonio Petrucelli's drawing shows a portion of the globe placed floating above the image of a hill in Ohio—"This is the sunshine in the middle of March" floating text reads, with reference to arrowed lines pointing to the wide scale of the globe and to the smaller scale of the hill. "This is the Earth. . . . This is a Hill in Ohio."[74] The image recognized that climate knowledge necessitated taking planetary patterns into account and

4.20 House in Columbus, Ohio, from "A Lesson in Climate Control," in *House Beautiful*, October 1949.

tried to summarize and simplify this knowledge by correlating different slopes of an Ohio hill to global climatic patterns—one side of the slope gets "tropical noon sunshine," the other side gets "Ontario-type noon sunshine."[75]

However overgeneral such a diagram was, the integration of house design into this planetary system perspective represents an important impulse. Images later in the issue exploring the same basic house design and siting used arrows and other diagrams to demonstrate how some simple design adjustments and innovations could dramatically improve the experience of the interior. A number of other, slightly more technical, principles came through in pages at the back of the issue interspersed with advertisements: radiant floor heating, fixed-pane windows with ventilation systems, and the use of vegetation as sun and privacy shade all were seen as means to elaborate on and meet the principles highlighted in the central articles.

In "Climate Control on the Potomac," published in April 1951, Fitch demonstrates how to "make your own private breeze" through the use of an attic fan and "self-closing metal louvers." "If they can be Cool on the Congo," the first line read, "You can be Cool on the Potomac." Thus another sort of technical image, a sort of user-friendly sensible technology for the home, came to inform the consumer about what was possible not only in how a building looked but also in how its systems operated, and, at least symptomatically, in the corrosive ways this relationship extended into developing economies, in colonial and neocolonial aspects of this climatic research (figure 4.22). Fans, shutters, ventilation shafts, and louvers helped to produce a more comfortable interior.

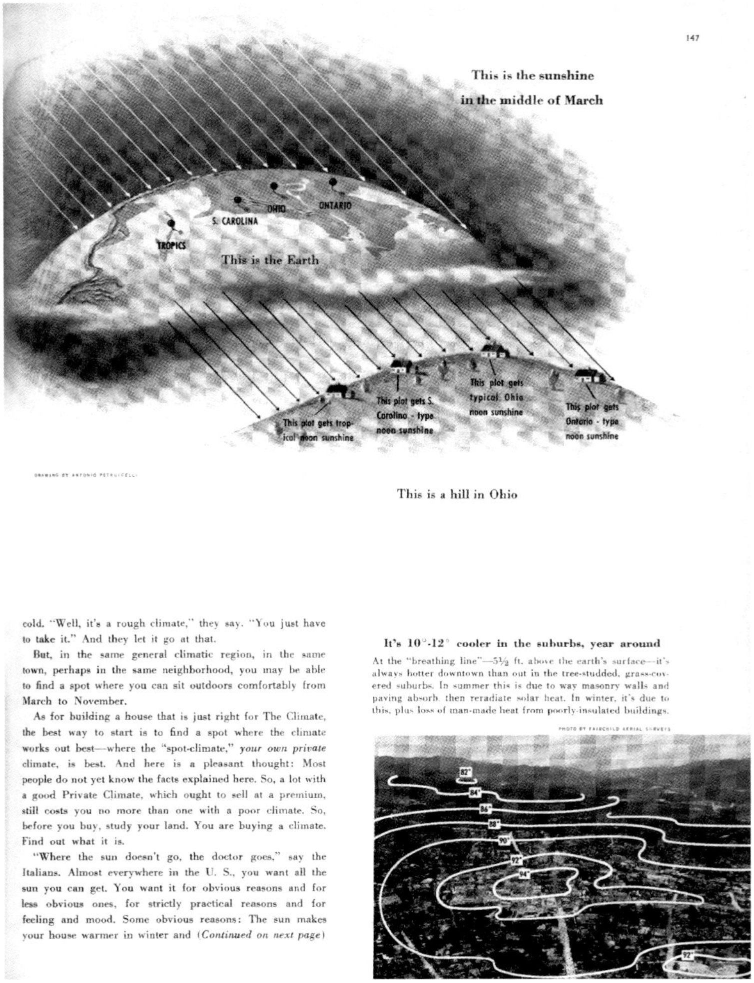


4.21 Antonio Petruccelli, "This Is a Hill in Ohio," illustration from "How to PICK Your Private Climate," in *House Beautiful*, October 1949.

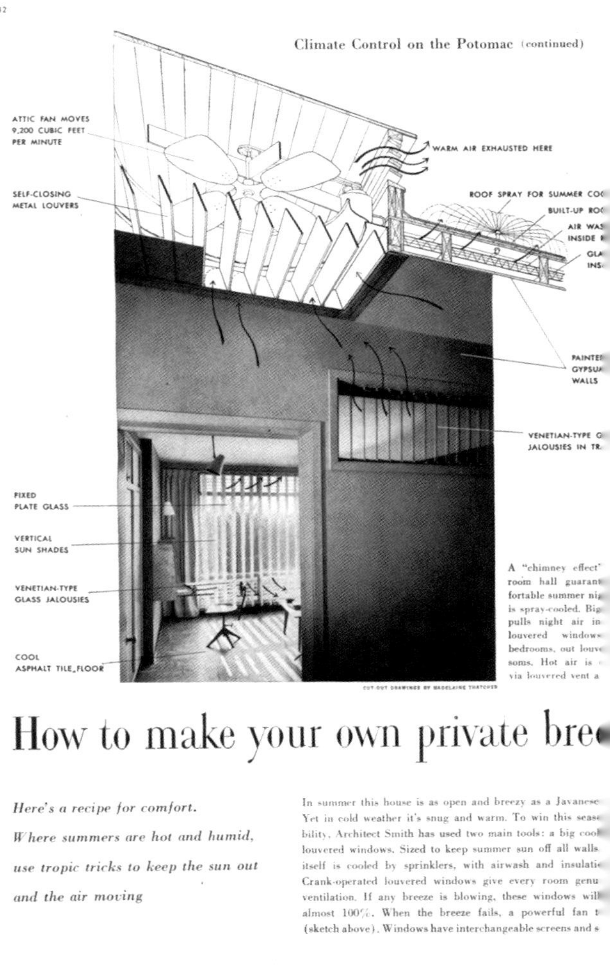


4.22 Schematic of ventilation system from "Climate Control on the Potomac," in *House Beautiful*, April 1951.

Outdoor spaces were carefully shaded and protected from rain. The house was able to celebrate the sun and the elements and articulate a certain way of life, without reliance on mechanical conditioning.[76] It was simultaneously an invocation of climatic inequities relative to political boundaries or class distinctions, and also evidence, if not in fact insistence, that climate-design methods, once identified, approached the universal.

The Climate Control Project produced media that attempted to impart material and symbolic transformations—a new way of living in the landscape, with new principles to underlie this lifestyle. This was evident in what the magazine showed, and the way they showed it. Diagrams negotiated climatic knowledge in a fashion similar to that of the Brazilian façade. As media, the façade was porous and human-focused, seemingly resisting the coming automation of these interiors. The diagrams indicate an attempt to understand the relationship of objective, data-driven knowledge to the production of a built environment framed by ideological and political goals—that is, objective knowledge applied according to subjective, albeit seemingly collective, principles.

In aggregate, the articles intended to provide a robust set of ideas, data, and imperatives for adjusting architectural conditions and daily living patterns to climatic surroundings (figure 4.23). The details of these imperatives were similar to those explained in the AIA *Bulletins*, but the form of communication and the type of imagery was distinct. Siple's "How Many Climates . . . ?" featured a two-page spread of a temperature chart

4.23 "Face Up to the Worst Things in Your Climate . . ." in *House Beautiful*, October 1949.

similar to the one he developed for the AIA, though here with a gradient of deep red to white to visually reinforce the degree scale, and stylized figures of the leaf-shaped temperature distribution (see figure 4.15). In the image, nine cities, not all of which were subject to analysis by the project, were placed in a sequence, demonstrating the differences and similarities in temperature averages in one glance. The interpretive language was markedly different from what was offered in the professional context; regarding the temperature figure for Oakland, for example, Siple wrote, "the roly-poly fellow . . . is so fat around the middle because temperatures are middling most of the year."[77]

Gordon's first article, "What Climate Does to YOU and What You Can Do to CLIMATE," is instructive in its emphasis on the word "YOU" as subject to climatic variability and, if properly educated, able to control it. The increase of consumer knowledge was the goal, so that, as clients, educated consumers could convince architects of the importance of climate, siting, and other factors. In a number of passages and as captions for many illustrations, the intelligence of the reader was praised—while at first this was often a prelude to indicating that new knowledge was needed, this attitude shifted to reinforcing existing knowledge and making it more specific. In a February 1950 article on "The Three Big Ideas of 1950—Climate Control, Privacy, the American Style," readers were first called on to focus their attention on the relevant issues: "the best things in life CAN be enjoyed by most Americans. But they don't fall in your lap. They have to be reached for." And then

4.24 Emil Schmindlin, second Pace Setter House, Orange, New Jersey, in *House Beautiful*, November 1949. The Great Room.

readers were reassured: "It's easy to do. It's all common sense, and you really know it already." This article also made clear that while adjusting to climate was important, this was not to suggest that, in America, climate was a threat or a hindrance to happiness: "in the highly civilized circumstances of a nice suburb . . . we now deal with subtle effects—not with gales and fierce cold and frozen noses, but merely with cold air, a puff of wind, a feeling of chill."[78]

The types of imagery were similarly accessible and aspirational. As many of the ideas were not yet clearly reflected in built houses, pencil drawings of exterior and interior views were used to describe the innovations being discussed. Sometimes these were accompanied by plan views or a sectional cut to clarify how the architectural solution worked. Many of these drawings also had keys or callouts to point to where the specific issues were being addressed.

Additional articles focused on specific climates and houses rather than more general orientations to the implications of scientific knowledge. Fitch's March 1950 essay, "A Good Plan for Climate-Wise Living," looks at a Dallas house designed by local architects Sigman-Ward; though the house was built, many of the illustrations are drawn in pencil in order to emphasize general principles—of wind control, the use of plants, curtains on the interior, and the relationship of rooms. A final drawing places the house in three different plots with different solar and wind exposures, reiterating the general solution it provides.[79] Articles would continue to play out these major themes—in topic, language, and illustration—and expand them with details about a wider range of climatic areas. In some cases, such as an article that accompanied a prelude to the project in May 1949, "How to Tame Sun, Wind, and Rain," plans of the exemplary house under discussion were available for purchase.[80]

The Climate Control Project's initial concept, to design a house for each climate, was not pursued directly. However, another initiative by Gordon helped readers to envision what these climate-adapted houses would actually look like—the Pace Setter Homes. Gordon developed the Pace Setter Homes program in direct opposition to the Case Study Houses then being conceived, promoted, and occasionally built under the auspices of John Entenza at *Arts and Architecture*. Gordon wanted to offer a different version of architectural modernism, one that was less about the integration of objective principles and industrial materials into the domestic sphere, and more about what she considered to be an American type of building, fit to the landscape and the culture of the country.[81] This imperative soon reached an ideological zeal that would dissolve the burgeoning interest in the Climate Control Project.

Cliff May's first Pace Setter in Los Angeles in 1948, despite the exhilarating headlines, in the end only made a nod to climate issues—in large part because of its siting in the mild and agreeable climate of Southern California, which required little treatment. Later houses were more explicit.[82] The second Pace Setter, designed by Emil Schmindlin in Orange, New Jersey, in 1949, demonstrated the sort of ease with which modern tropes of outdoor living, expansive living rooms, and simple materials could be comfortable in climates outside the pleasant West Coast (figure 4.24).[83]

Schmindlin's house, published in a lavish set of spreads just a month after the Climate Control Project was introduced, was directly aimed at improvements to living—"167 pace making ideas . . . including the new field of Climate Control" were shown (figure 4.25). The house used insulated glass on the large south-facing wall, with integrated screens to block the sun in the summer. Ventilation was induced through strategically placed openings, and a large tree was used for seasonal shade. Alongside the extensive photographs of the main living room and its fully glazed façade—in summer, in winter, and night, from inside and out—perspective/plan hybrid diagrams laid out the principles by which eaves, trees, and blinds excluded the sun in the summer and let it in during the winter, while maintaining privacy year-round (figure 4.26).

The main article presenting the house was followed by two additional exercises: first, a spread on "How to Look at a Pace-Setter House" emphasized that the house was made for its specific climate and was "*not a house to copy exactly—ever*." Instead, the reader was to apply the principles of Climate Control to their own condition. This reflected a primary principle for the *House Beautiful* audience: to look beyond familiar aesthetic dispositions and also investigate the "intrinsic performance of a house or its capacity to produce comfort."[84] Second, a piece by Siple, "15,750,000 Americans Live in This Climate," reproduced the climatic map from and summarized the analysis detailed in the AIA *Bulletin* of the same month, which focused on Metropolitan New York and New Jersey (see figure 4.9).

Although not attentive to all of the microclimate issues that Siple and Fitch were promoting, the house represented a significant step in conceiving of the residential design project on climatic terms. Again, the issues were quickly complicated. In the article on "The Three Big Ideas of 1950," Gordon began to lay out a more specific agenda for the American Style. This notion went far beyond the logic of climatic adaptation; it retained the commonsense rhetoric that was typical of the Climate Control Project. The main house presented in the "Three Big Ideas" article was praised for its economy—"it offers better living than many twice as costly"—and its lack of "fuss or feathers." The house "typifies the emerging American Style," Gordon wrote, "by its emphasis on comfort and convenience, by its lack of ostentation and insistence on good design." Other factors that the article lauded were the use of "standard materials, available anywhere," "pleasant to live in and easy to maintain," "easy to look at," and buildable by a "regular merchant builder." Climate control was still paramount and was the main subject of the house's description; indeed, the emphasis of the extended captions to the drawings of the house merged two of the three "big ideas," proposing that the right design focus "gives a house a 'private climate' which makes outdoor living a comfortable reality in a land of marginal weather" (figure 4.27).[85]

"The Three Big Ideas" presented an alternative to what Gordon and others saw as a European-infected modernism focused on stark forms and empty interiors, and attempting to operate as a global norm rather than a local solution. The American Style, by contrast, purported its origins in the work of Frank Lloyd Wright, the Greene brothers, and H. H. Richardson, prominent arts and crafts architects of the early twentieth century. Gordon's position was similar to a number of related publications during and right after the war, most of which, if they appreciated the work of European émigrés, did so because they detected hints of Wright's influence (figure 4.28).[86] Although some historical veracity can be ascribed to such suggestions, by virtue of the popularity of Wright's *Wasmuth Portfolio* among German architects in particular, the pitting of American versus European influences was one-sided and forced.[87] Gordon's version was a not very subtle claim to American exceptionalism, with tropes of pioneer individualism, integrity, and ruggedness presented in opposition to what were seen as empty claims to objectivity characteristic of the interwar European modernists.[88]

4.25 Emil Schmindlin, second Pace Setter House, Orange, New Jersey, in *House Beautiful*, November 1949. Private outdoor space.

4.26 Emil Schmindlin, second Pace Setter House, Orange, New Jersey, in *House Beautiful* ,November 1949. Summer and winter.

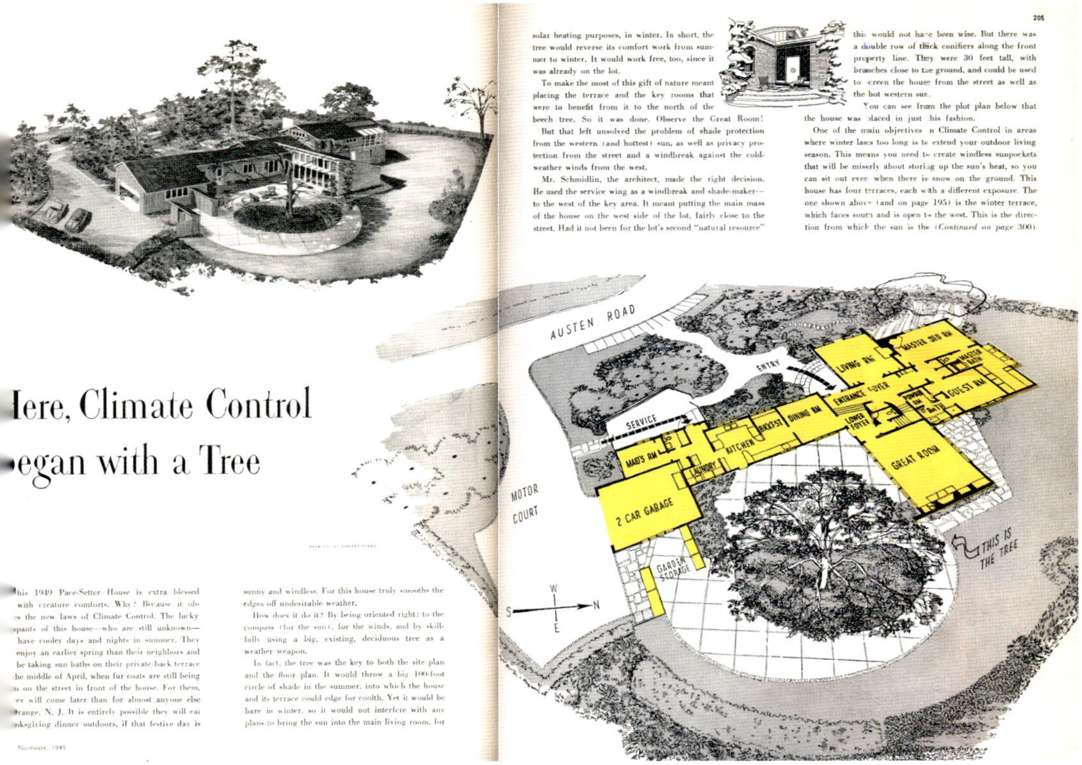


4.27 Emil Schmindlin, second Pace Setter House, Orange, New Jersey, in *House Beautiful*, November 1949. View and plan.

Gordon's focus was, as she saw it, on opening up a new avenue of creativity for architects who felt constrained by purported modernist orthodoxy. She celebrated the provision of amenities and a clean, easy, and casual lifestyle. Technology supported streamlined and efficient kitchens as well as stereos and televisions; open plans embraced family life in both the living and dining room, and playrooms were essential for the kids. Privacy was also essential, represented by the backyard porch that brought the family home into the landscape and simultaneously established their territorial presence. In no small measure, the Climate Control Project emphasized *control*, intending to articulate a new realm of social productivity in the American suburban lifestyle.[89]

## The Next America

Gordon's argument for an American Style reached a turgid pinnacle in her 1953 article, "The Threat to the Next America" (figure 4.29). The gloves were off, so to speak, and the subtleties of climate management and a commonsense approach were replaced with a not so subtle implication of communist architects plotting to destroy the American way of life. Turning away from a considered support of a range of architects and builders seen to be espousing the American Style, Gordon directly addressed European architects and their followers whom she saw as containing "a threat of cultural dictatorship" that was resistant to American consumerism and suburban expansion. Her descriptions of such houses as "barren" and "unlivable," and of the "less is more" modernists "trying to convince you that . . . beauty and comfort are incompatible" were in direct contrast to the designed comfort she had been promoting in the Pace Setter Houses and Climate Control Project. The anticommunist implications, directed at German émigrés in the midst of McCarthyism, were difficult to overlook.

These polemics were not directly engaged with questions of climate. The word *climate* does not appear in the article, and the central articles of the Climate Control Project had ceased two years earlier. However, the basic premise driving the Climate Control Project—that of an educated consumer—was still paramount: "If you are aware of what is happening," Gordon wrote in bold text in "The Threat," "we believe you will be quite competent to handle the matter yourself. We still

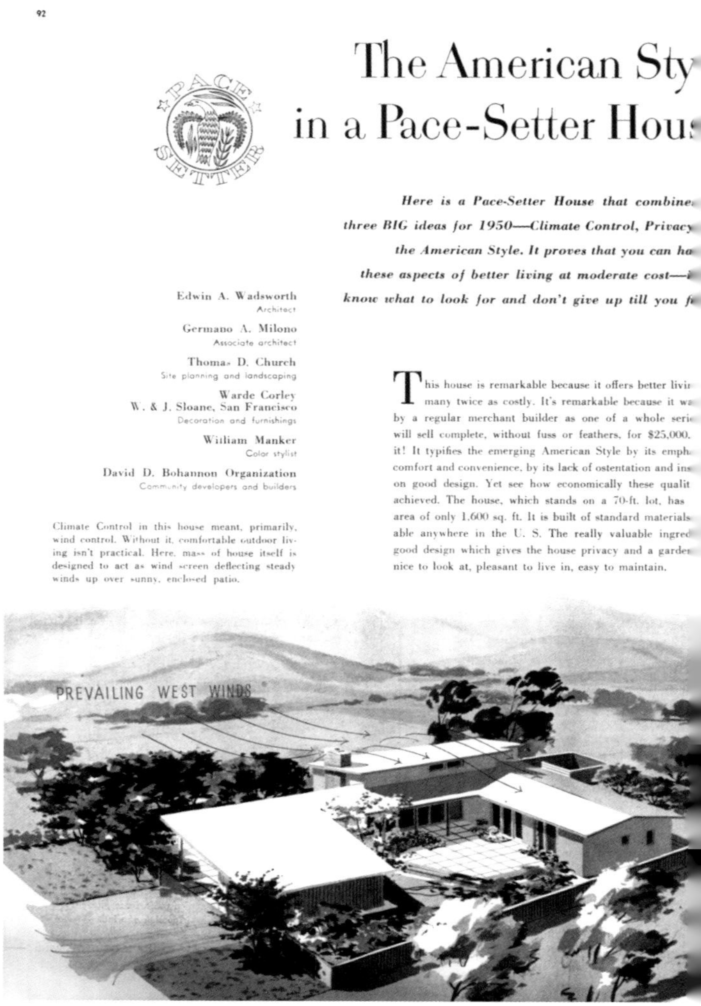

92

The American Sty
in a Pace-Setter Hou

*Here is a Pace-Setter House that combine three BIG ideas for 1950—Climate Control, Privacy the American Style. It proves that you can ha these aspects of better living at moderate cost— know what to look for and don't give up till you f*

Edwin A. Wadsworth
Architect

Germano A. Milono
Associate architect

Thomas D. Church
Site planning and landscaping

Warde Corley
W. & J. Sloane, San Francisco
Decoration and furnishings

William Manker
Color stylist

David D. Bohannon Organization
Community developers and builders

Climate Control in this house meant, primarily, wind control. Without it, comfortable outdoor living isn't practical. Here, mass of house itself is designed to act as wind screen deflecting steady winds up over sunny, enclosed patio.

This house is remarkable because it offers better livi many twice as costly. It's remarkable because it wa by a regular merchant builder as one of a whole seri will sell complete, without fuss or feathers, for $25,000. it! It typifies the emerging American Style by its emph comfort and convenience, by its lack of ostentation and ins on good design. Yet see how economically these qualit achieved. The house, which stands on a 70-ft. lot, has area of only 1,600 sq. ft. It is built of standard materials able anywhere in the U. S. The really valuable ingred good design which gives the house privacy and a garde nice to look at, pleasant to live in, easy to maintain.



4.28 "The American Style," with Edwin Wadsworth, Pace Setter House of 1950, in *House Beautiful*, June 1950.

4.29 Elizabeth Gordon, "The Threat to the Next America," in *House Beautiful*, April 1953.

operate on common sense and reason. We know less is *not* more. It is simply less!"[90]

As Gordon's initial proposal to provide an alternative modernism evolved into a near total rejection of European models and practices, the Climate Control Project was caught in the middle. The 1953 article instigated aggressive opposition by many in the architecture world, including those who had supported the seemingly more innocuous proposal for a specific American building type. In the wake of the article, Fitch resigned from the magazine; while the number of climate articles had already been dwindling, the momentum seems to have collapsed with his departure. Also of significance was the concurrent rise of the air-conditioning industry. One late article recast the Climate Control Project on these terms, exploring design parameters for the most efficient use of mechanical systems.[91]

By contrast, in Siple's presentation at the 1950 "Weather and the Building Industry" meeting, he noted that "although we have made constant improvement in buildings and have many mechanical developments to our credit, we must admit that some of these improvements, such as air-conditioning, have really been developed in order to rectify errors or inadequacies in building."[92] Such nuance was overwhelmed by the ideological imperative to continue to promote a certain kind of building. Although Gordon disappointed many with the "Next America" article, it also brought her closer to Frank Lloyd Wright, reinvigorating for the next few years a call for a specifically American style that was now more about a proscribed political reading of forms and materials than a commonsense approach to climatic adaptation.

If it seems a little too easy to equate Gordon's "Next America" with the America of the Great Acceleration, the evidence is ample enough. The article, and the general disposition of the magazine by the early 1950s, was one of a number of rallying cries for American consumerism—appeals that were well aware of the relationship between economic growth and geopolitical strength. This arc from climate control to uncontrolled consumerism is another recognition that economic expansion was not merely a casual development based on individual desire, but a complex social project—a successful attempt, across a range of

BUILDING IN THE TROPICS

OFFICE BUILDING FOR THE BAHREIN PETROLEUM CO., LTD.
***Bahrein Island, Persian Gulf***
***Chauncey W. Riley, Architect***

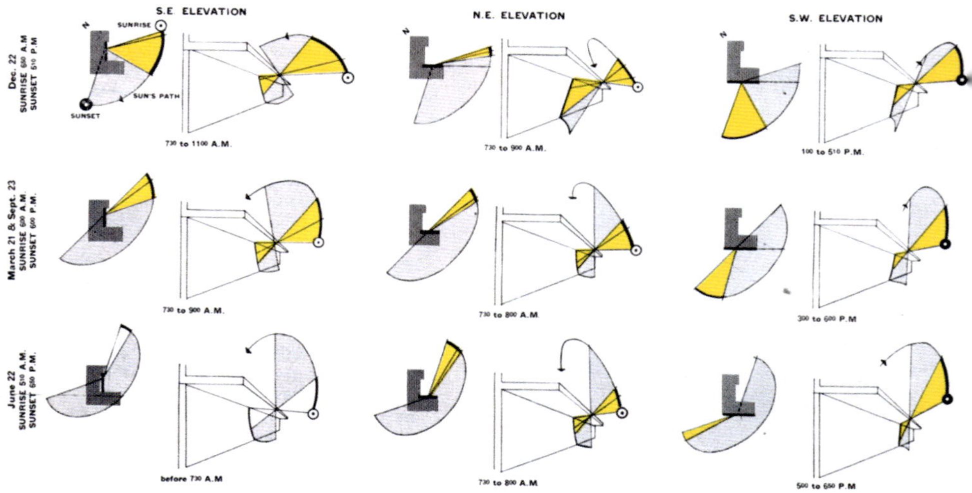


Drawing by Tom Ballenger

*Seasonal sun orientation for determining sunshade designs. Sunshades are of simple construction, designed to relieve the air conditioning load by screening both windows and walls from direct sun during period of greatest build-up of heat in the structure*

4.30 Chauncey W. Riley, office building for the Bahrain Petroleum Company, from "Building in the Tropics," *Architectural Record*, August 1952.

government, corporate, and cultural agents, to engineer American economic power as an engine for geopolitical dominance. The Great Acceleration was very much an intentional project, evidence of a desire to increase ties to a number of different nations and corporations, to place American consumption at the center of a behemoth of empire and corporate agency that sought to define the conditions of life around the world—including the management of air routes, the coordination of infrastructure, and the narrowing of the popular imagination to see a future built only off a single material base; a world designed, that is, according to fossil fuels.[93]

In the context of Gordon's vituperative American exceptionalism, much of the architectural interest in design as a method of climatic management played out on an international scale. That is, claims for the value of American consumer culture had direct manifestations in a range of global architectural strategies. If this was already apparent in the embassy building projects and tropical architectures discussed in the previous chapter, it took on a different valence in the American discussions of the early 1950s. In this sense the Climate Control Project was something of a methodological testing ground for a more expansive approach to how design tools could mediate and mitigate the impact of climate. In particular, the design of offices and housing for American oil corporations—in Lagos, Bahrain, and many other locations—reflected many of the principles of the project; an architecture of access to oil (figure 4.30).

The Climate Control Project made important strides in applying scientific research to building processes and also served to reveal profound tensions in the discourse of American modernism. Above all, the project began a process of using interpretive images and diagrams to translate scientific knowledge onto an architectural register. This new universe of technical images would become increasingly important, not only in the designed provision of climatic adaptation but also in understanding relevant factors of mechanical heating and cooling systems.

---

Since this period, the visual exploration of applying science to an architectural proposal has become an expected aspect of a design project. The climate design methods of Victor and Aladar Olgyay, peripheral to the Climate Control Project but clearly inspired by it, became increasingly sophisticated and visually astute as the decade progressed. The "Next America" article helped to separate modernism from its scientific and technological potentials, and in its wake the progressive veneer of new ways of building collapsed as developer-driven traditional styles took over—*House Beautiful*'s xenophobic turn was just one prominent aspect of a much wider range of causes—economic, policy-oriented, social, and demographic—in this regard.

The AIA's part of the Climate Control Project has resonated across subsequent decades of architectural research. Indeed, the intensity and clarity of the interpretive mechanism presented in the project helped to legitimate the architect as researcher, and also to facilitate the exploration of new ways to design with climate.

## Reception

The Hungarian émigré architects Victor and Aladar Olgyay, twin brothers, came to the United States in 1947 and quickly applied themselves to research on architecture and climate. They are central to the narrative of this book. Much of what has been discussed in previous chapters is also a story of their travels and intellectual development: they were committed Corbusians and admirers of Neutra; the shaded buildings of Brazil were essential to their postwar research; and, they worked closely with Siple while they were collaborating with the Solar Energy Fund at the Massachusetts Institute of Technology. Their research, first at MIT and then at Princeton, represents an apex in the midcentury interest in architecture-climatic design methods—an excited flurry of activity that would soon begin to recede behind formalisms and architectural sciences as they pulled apart. The characteristics of this climatic heyday are evident in their two books, *Solar Control and Shading Devices* (1957) and *Design with Climate: Bioclimatic Approach to Architectural Regionalism* (1963), and in the projects, consultations, diagrams, methods, and devices they pursued.

They are also central to this narrative because, in the Olgyays' work, the diagram becomes a tool of integration. Their early 1950s experiments orbited around a sort of master diagram, the "Method of Climatic Interpretation in Buildings," first drawn in 1952 and reprinted in their books, articles, and conference presentations (figure 5.2). The drawing signaled a shift in methods of designing with climate and its representation. It is at once productive, instrumental, and a sort of map to explain the Olgyays' frustration. Evident initially is the ambition—the desire to develop a universal means to assess a building's microclimate and apply appropriate design strategies—and the cumbersomeness of executing that ambition, the number of steps and analyses it is seen to entail. It has already become clear that addressing microclimate in architecture presents a number of obstacles, on terms of available technology and in relation to historiography. The "Method of Climatic Interpretation in Buildings" diagram, and the Olgyays' work in general, is a concentrated instance of these efforts and their seemingly intractable complications. While the Olgyays designed a number of buildings and consulted on even more, their diagrammatic methodological work was their primary occupation.

Among those complications is the precomputational nature of the drawing and the method it proposed. Although the computer was being used, increasingly across the later period of the Olgyays' activity, to analyze and predict climatic parameters, it would not, generally speaking, be used for architectural design for another decade—not until the 1960s and early 1970s.[1] Victor Olgyay briefly used a FORTRAN computer in 1962 in an attempt to clarify the findings of UN-sponsored research related to his work in Venezuela, but he faced frustrations. The brothers were, in a sense, stuck in an epistemological model rooted in calculations, although the terms they use and the ambitions of their devices can be seen as proto-computational—the diagram represents a sort of analog programming that offers a series of shifting and contingent parameters as a result of precise data entry. It is, as an analog device, unable to effectively manage all of these variables, leading to overdetermined results; its historical weight is as much in its aspirations as what it was able to accomplish.

Some decades later, in the late 1990s, the basic method presented in the diagram would be rendered computational through the design and performance assessment software Eco-tect. The software platform was produced by an Australian architect, Andrew Marsh, who drew directly on the diagram and the Olgyays' method as laid out in *Design with Climate*. A few compelling issues can be found in the development of Eco-tect: that the Olgyays' work continued to be relevant to many architects and engineers long past the rise of air conditioning, and that the capacity for computational knowledge reopened

5.1 Victor and Aladar Olgyay, *Thermoheliodon*, Princeton Architectural Laboratory, 1956, from *Collier's* magazine.

the ambition to carefully adjust a building to its microclimate. This long thread of influence leads to questions about the viability of the diagram and Eco-tect, relative to the more recent emergence of the computer as the site for design integration and experimentation. Eco-tect, in any event, became the industry standard for environmental performance software.[2] In 2008, it was purchased by AutoCAD and is now a part of their broader CAD packages, an integrated element rather than a stand-alone platform, with potential implications for the dissolution of the specificities of climate knowledge as it is, seemingly, seamlessly integrated into the design process.

The Olgyays' ideas, innovations, and designs were generally well received from the 1930s to the 1960s. From the beginning of their career in Hungary, they received prizes, awards, and grants as well as established academic positions and consultations on prominent projects; they were operating in rarefied architectural circles. While physical and meteorological principles were well integrated into their work, the field of climate architecture they pioneered was left fallow as engineering and architecture schools went through a decades-long lull in supporting such collaborations and shared climate knowledge—overwhelmed, as these discussions were, by the end of the 1950s, with HVAC.[3]

Indeed, discussion of the Olgyays' ambitions and methods is almost overwhelmed by the historical contingencies that have since emerged—contingencies relative to the processing power of computers; relative to the relationship between the Great Acceleration and climatic instability; and relative to an increasingly form-focused architectural discussion. Their method was developed at a moment when issues of climate and comfort were seen as an expression of the clarity and brilliance of an architectural idea. This was a moment of excitement over applying scientific knowledge to architecture, long an ambition of modernism, and

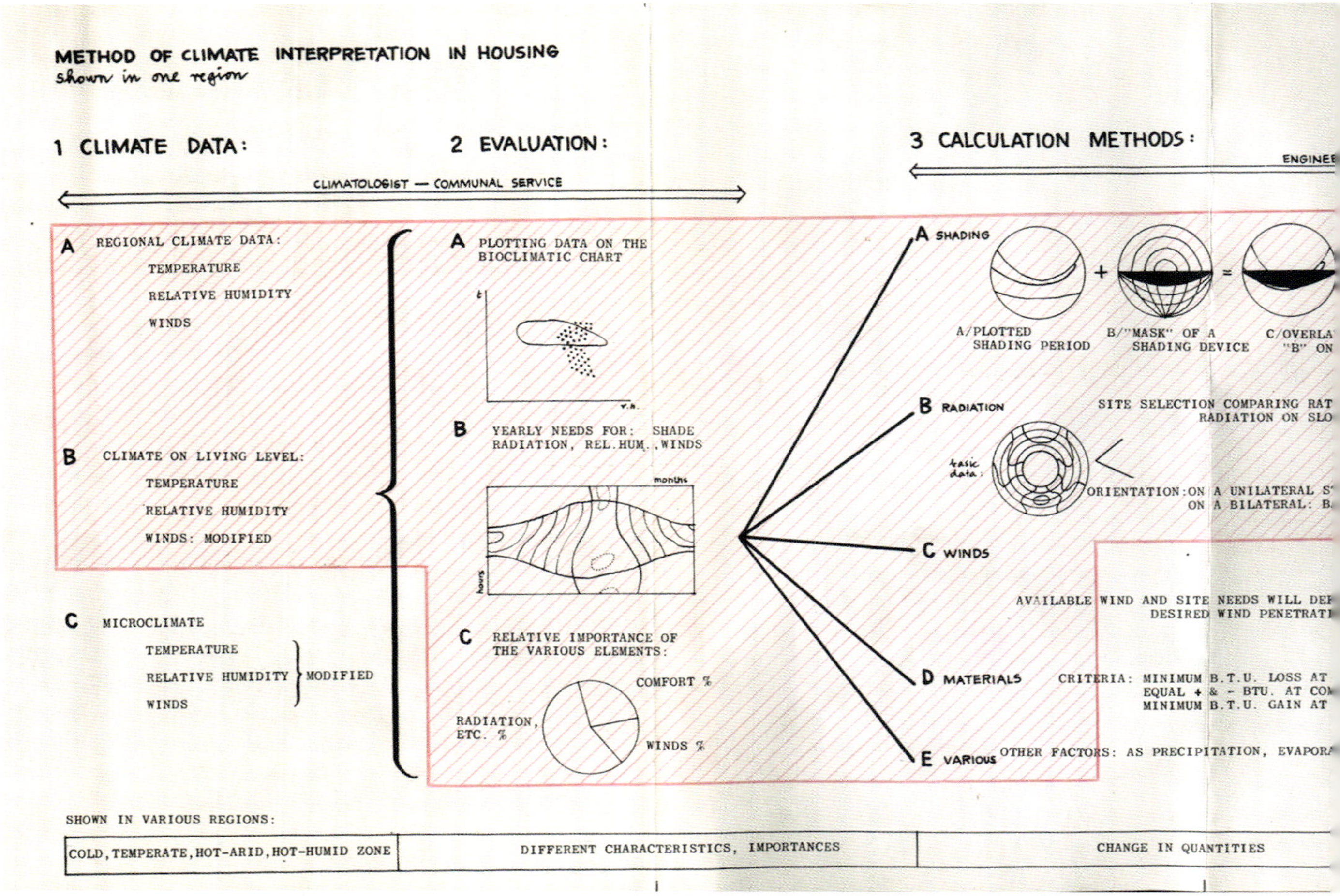


5.2 Victor and Aladar Olgyay, "Method of Climatic Interpretation in Housing," 1952.

essential to its logic of innovation.[4] The architectural manipulation of climate was seen as a means to improve a building's interior, and also to demonstrate the adeptness of a designer who was attentive to specific traditions. Such issues were an aspect of how architecture was valued in the postwar world before it was overwhelmed by oil.

*Comfort* became an essential focus. Climate design methods were seen as a way to codify and regulate the thermal conditions of the interior, before producing them through design means. Comfort was just that—if not quite a luxury, then at least a sign of the relative sophistication of a given culture, a given client, an approach to space and its occupation. It was on these terms that the Olgyays' commissions and consultations for suburban homes, urban towers, and development-aid-based proposals were received and disseminated as finding new means to increase comfort at low cost. Far removed from the condition of the early twenty-first century, where building culture has come to represent the complications of climate, energy, and political economy, their interest in climate was that it provided a medium in which architects could establish a new kind of relevance to the increasingly interdisciplinary analysis of the production of the built environment—a straightforward career opportunity and a robust attempt to completely rethink how architecture operates in defining and designing sociobiotic relationships.

Designing with climate was focused on rendering the thermal interior as a consistent space for social and individual optimization. The comfort zone was above all a space of the *norm*, an absolute and by this time scientifically supported conception of an optimal interior condition, for home life, institutions, or offices. The Olgyays' research developed in tandem with and in relationship to processes of quantification, optimization, regulation, and subjecting the interior to a range of

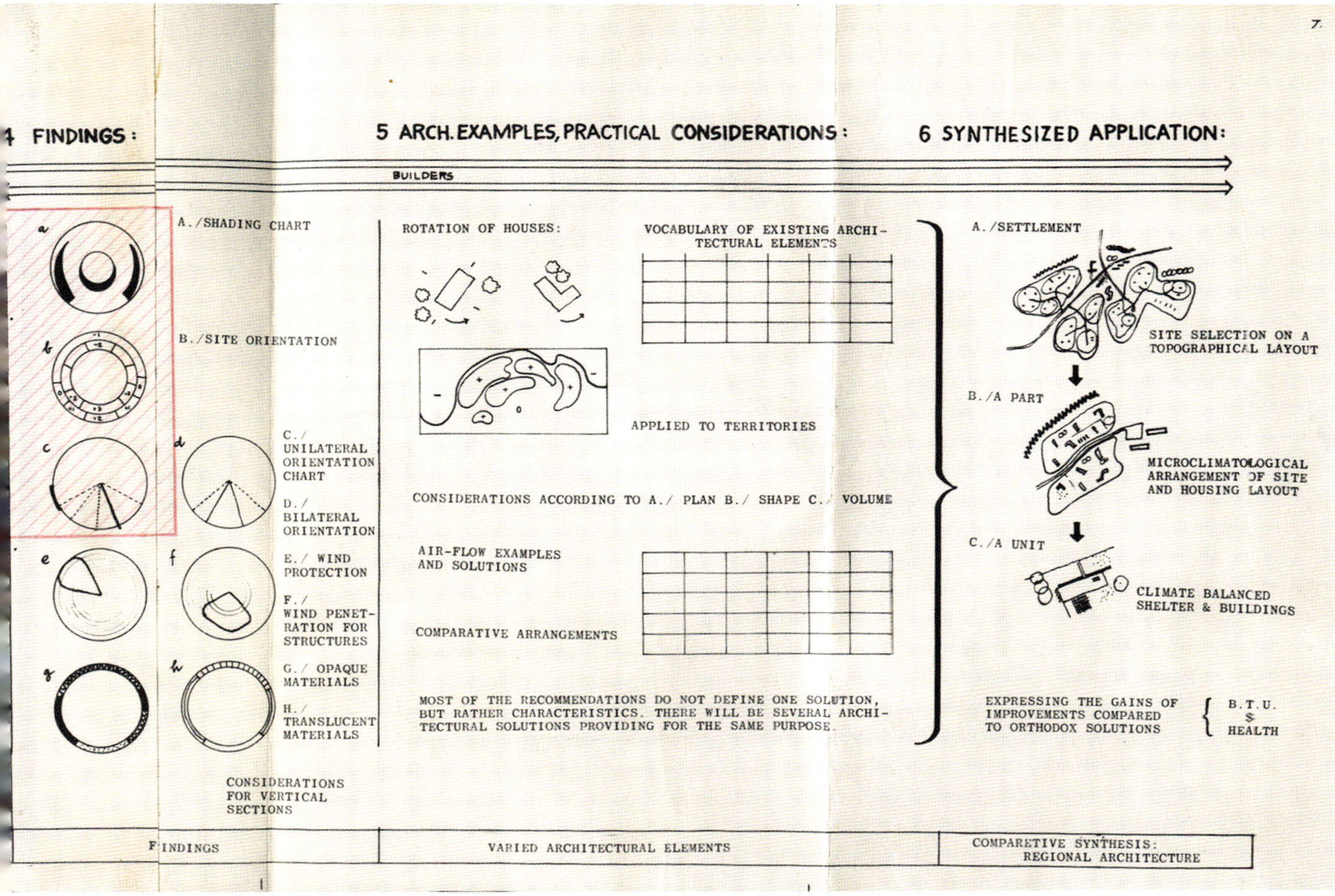


approaches and social ideals that, by the time their work lost its traction in the early 1960s, had come to rely completely on mechanical conditioning. At stake is how their ideas developed in support of conceptualizing the thermal conditions of the planetary interior and also how they offered a counterproposal to how these conditions could be achieved through architecture, rather than air conditioning.

In the twenty-first century, as the development of Eco-tect and other simulation software suggests, the story has changed. The Great Acceleration and its effects have transformed interest in climatic knowledge, in architecture and elsewhere, to one that not only focuses on the provision of comfort but also (in some cases) challenges what that comfort provides, and how. As global circulation systems are increasingly destabilized by the carbon emissions that result from the mechanical provision of an optimized indoor environment, the everywhere twenty-degree-Celsius interior is no longer viable. The carbon emissions resultant from the provision of thermal comfort—the construction of the planetary interior—have also made the planet, in a word, uncomfortable.

And here is the specter that continues to haunt this book: it is not enough to suggest that the Olgyays' method is now, finally, applicable—technically, as a result of digitalization, and socially, given increasing anxiety over climatic instability. It is also clear that the design conditions imagined by the Olgyays and their followers, the forms and urban arrangements they produced, are antagonistic to many conceptions of architectural innovation, both then and now. The Olgyays need to be seen, in this sense, as conservatives amid a progressive tumult of design possibilities. As much as they used new methods, their ambitions were decidedly focused on stability rather than change, on the reification of a standard, universal condition for the interior. In this sense they are following on the Corbusian dictum of a world conditioned to a smooth optimized state. Of course, this vision did not encompass every building, and it entails a gross abstraction toward similarly universal conditions of the human. But it was a resolute conviction in the context of the changing discussion of architecture and climate in the period.

That the Olgyays' most active period was at the Princeton School of Architecture while figures such as Charles Moore and Robert Venturi were beginning to articulate what would soon be celebrated as architectural postmodernism is just one indication of how their projects, ideas, diagrams, and buildings were received. Assessing their work and its potential requires attention to not only the broad socio-environmental challenges of understanding the human enterprise in relationship to earth systems, but also seemingly to smaller-scale complications of how to change the terms by which architectural innovation and excellence are valued. By the early 1960s, in other words, questions around climate were of less interest to the profession at large, increasingly absorbed in formalist debates, yet their methods and their aims persisted in marginalized discussions of architectural science and in schools and venues where collaboration between engineers and architects was more common.[5]

It is not a question of a delayed reception or a return to relevance but one of how to frame a historical accounting of work that is of intense interest sixty years later, but on terms barely recognizable to the conditions of initial production. And, further, how to recognize and emphasize its value according to new and more urgent prospects for application. As a technological system, the insights of the Olgyays have been absorbed into many aspects of contemporary architectural practice, and new kinds of applied scientific knowledge have exceeded their ambitions for the climatic adaptation of a building—or at least for design tools that would make such applications possible. Rather than treat their work on the terms of technical acuity, of interest are the cultural transformations that can be read into their experiments and methods. Their diagrams, in particular, are technical images undergoing a very specific kind of transition in terms of what they are presenting, how they are presenting it, and the assumptions that underlie both form and content.

As with shaded buildings in Brazil, the Olgyays' motivations, challenges, drawings, and methods are not legible by functional considerations alone, however much we can appreciate the vagaries of *function* in this context. Other issues, ideological and disciplinary, need to be explored to understand how and why these ideas emerged and intensified, and when, and why they were difficult to engage.

## Reverse House

Victor and Aladar Olgyay were born in Budapest in 1910 and trained as architects at the Royal Hungarian Polytechnic. They were enthusiasts of the new architecture as it was developing in the 1920s and '30s and won a number of commercial, government, and institutional commissions very early in their careers. In 1935 Victor spent a year at the Scuola Superiore di Architettura di Roma.[6] They then traveled together to London to study housing with the MARS (Modern Architecture Research) group; in the mid-1930s, London was an important arena for new architectural ideas, in part because it served as a way station for many of the European architects fleeing fascism for the United States.[7] In London they met Maxwell Fry and Jane Drew, Walter Gropius, and many other prominent modern architects concerned, to various extents, with how climate related to design. Late in 1936 they were awarded a Kendall Fellowship to study at Columbia University and pursued "special graduate studies" there for a year. They then returned to Budapest, opening an office that quickly became very active for the next eight years. They went back to the United States permanently in 1947, largely as a result of the political uncertainty of Hungary as part of the communist bloc. On their return, they worked with the compatriot Marcel Breuer to publish a collection of their office's work, with an introduction by Peter Blake, as a sort of thick calling card for their new American contacts. It was published by Reinhold in 1952.

In the United States, their first position was at the University of Notre Dame in Indiana; they moved to the Massachusetts Institute of Technology in 1950, through their friend, another Hungarian, the engineer Maria Telkes, who was then deeply involved with solar house design through the Solar Energy Fund at MIT. They worked on a government grant, producing work that would be exhibited and published in

*Architectural Forum* in April 1952 as "The Temperate House." That same year, they were recruited to Princeton by the director of the Princeton School of Architecture, Robert McLaughlin, again, in part, through Telkes's influence. For 1953–54 they were awarded Guggenheim Fellowships in Architecture and Urban Design, which allowed them to fund their research at Princeton and establish an ongoing lab. They also received a number of grants from the National Science Foundation. They stayed at Princeton for the rest of their careers—aside from a number of visiting positions: Aladar at the University of Texas in 1952–54 to study climatology; Victor at the Harvard GSD from 1960 to 1963, and in Venezuela working for the United Nations from 1967 to 1968. They worked in the Princeton Architectural Laboratory, where they trained students in daylighting and elaborated on their diagrammatic design method. Victor designed a number of houses in the Princeton area, while Aladar worked closely with the engineer Telkes on solar house design templates and on developer projects in Texas and upstate New York.[8] They consulted, together, on a wide range of architectural projects. Aladar passed away in 1963, Victor in 1970.[9]

It is likely that they began to aggressively engage the question of architectural relationships to climate at Columbia in the late 1930s. Fitch was not yet teaching there, but the planner Henry Wright, a prominent figure at Columbia in the 1930s, was actively researching the relationship of climatic patterns to the plot organization and design orientation of the garden cities he was designing with Clarence Stein. In 1936, Wright built one of the first heliodons—a device for modeling the solar incidence on a given site (see figures 4.13 and 4.14). It used an adjustable, tilting plane to approximate location and a moveable light to model the sun. Wright's heliodon was built to a design recommended by A .F. Dufton and H. E. Beckett, which was illustrated and explained in the *Journal of the Royal Institute of British Architects* in 1931.[10] It was part of a general interest in solar calibration devices, including examples in Kansas, Australia, Brazil, Puerto Rico, and Singapore, that informed a wealth of climatic research in subsequent decades. We have also already seen the influence of Wright's device on the training of architects at Columbia after the war, through the Form and Climate Research Group; it is likely that it played a role in Fitch's research interests as well.

The Olgyays brought this research into their design practice, Olgyay and Olgyay Architects, when they returned to Hungary in 1939. Experiments in siting, orientation, and shading devices characterized these projects, as did the diagrams that accompanied them. They first garnered some attention with an apartment building in Budapest, referred as the Reverse House, in which they oriented the building to the garden rather than to the city, facing the more prominent façade away from the street (figure 5.3).[11] The project used egg-crate shading frames as part of an extruded, boxed balcony to mediate the entrance of the sun into the interior. This was not done with attention to the details of the local climate, but it benefited from straightforward sun-path analysis that a heliodon provided.

These sun-path readings were essential to the "reverse" move, the building's openness to the garden, rather than the street, maximized winter solar incidence and brought radiation farther into the house. Most press attention to the building emphasized its openness to the parkland behind, as a review in *Domus* indicated: "Every room faces the hill and the big trees in the garden," yet even here the interest was in an attention to new architectural parameters. "Here we see," the review continued, "the creative power of architecture which is able to create something of a new expressive and practical nature."[12] The brothers, in the commentary for a book that was published about their firm, focused on the role of the balcony in shading provision, though they lamented the relative lack of specificity in understanding how the extruded elements performed.[13]

A subsequent commission for the Stühmer Chocolate Factory outside Budapest, in 1941, saw a turn from this more impressionistic approach to a focused climatic engagement—in modeling, experimenting, and calculating to determine a façade system appropriate to the needs of the interior (figure 5.4). The solar architect Donald Watson, prominent in the 1970s, later described the building as "Corbu with numbers . . . [an] architectural design with the tools of the formative science of building climatology."[14] Chocolate production and storage is a temperature-sensitive activity. The Olgyays performed extensive daylighting analysis with a model in order to ascertain where production, storage, and office areas would best be placed in relationship to site and

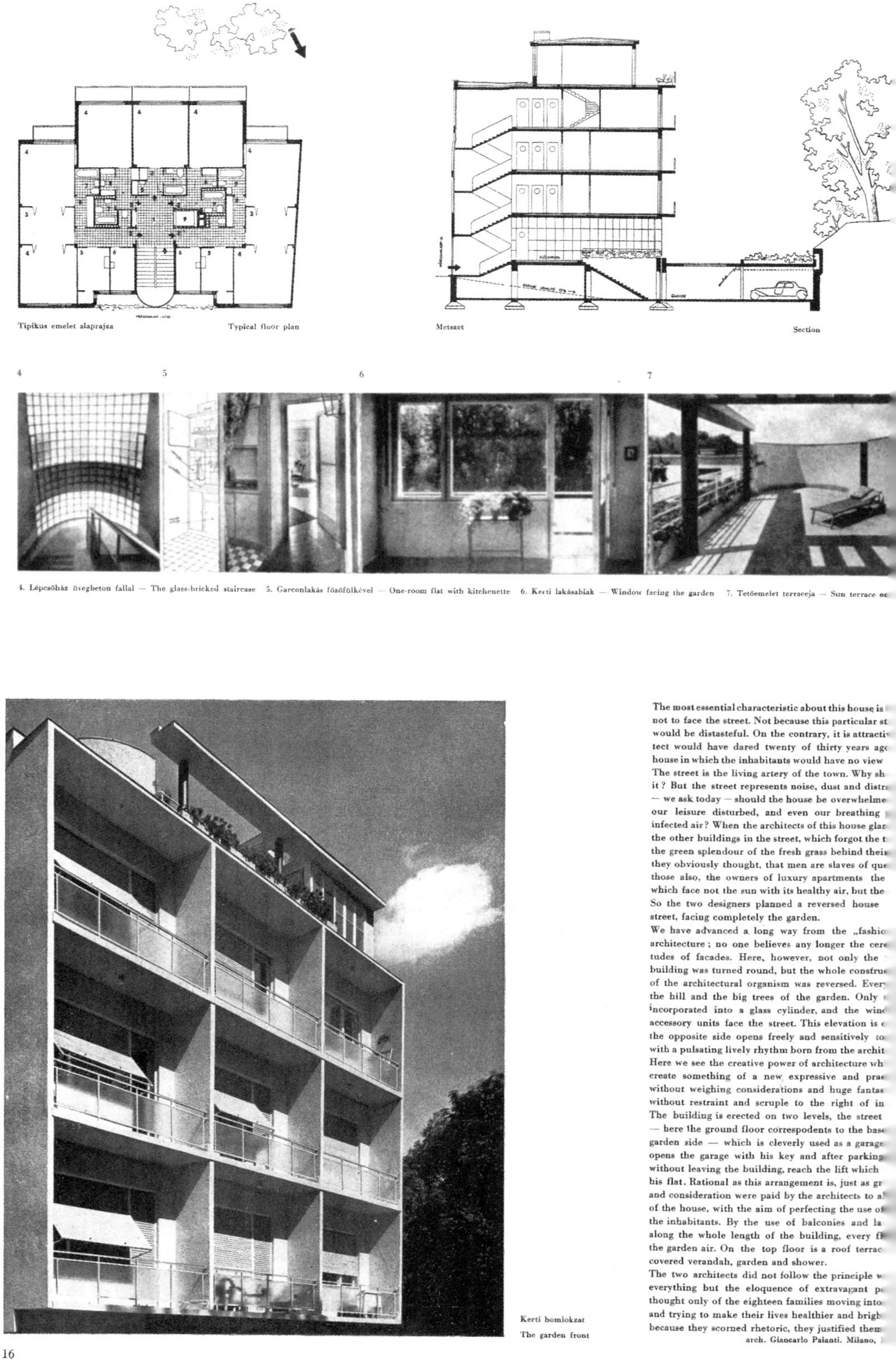

Tipikus emelet alaprajza — Typical floor plan

Metszet — Section

4. Lépcsőház üvegbeton fallal — The glass-bricked staircase 5. Garconlakás főzőfülkével — One-room flat with kitchenette 6. Kerti lakásablak — Window facing the garden 7. Tetőemelet terraceja — Sun terrace or

Kerti homlokzat

The garden front

The most essential characteristic about this house is
not to face the street. Not because this particular st
would be distasteful. On the contrary, it is attracti
tect would have dared twenty of thirty years ag
house in which the inhabitants would have no view
The street is the living artery of the town. Why sh
it? But the street represents noise, dust and distr
— we ask today — should the house be overwhelme
our leisure disturbed, and even our breathing
infected air? When the architects of this house glar
the other buildings in the street, which forgot the t
the green splendour of the fresh grass behind thei
they obviously thought, that men are slaves of que
those also, the owners of luxury apartments the
which face not the sun with its healthy air, but the
So the two designers planned a reversed house
street, facing completely the garden.
We have advanced a long way from the „fashio
architecture; no one believes any longer the cer
tudes of facades. Here, however, not only the
building was turned round, but the whole constru
of the architectural organism was reversed. Ever
the hill and the big trees of the garden. Only
incorporated into a glass cylinder, and the wind
accessory units face the street. This elevation is
the opposite side opens freely and sensitively to
with a pulsating lively rhythm born from the archit
Here we see the creative power of architecture wh
create something of a new expressive and pra
without weighing considerations and huge fantas
without restraint and scruple to the right of in
The building is erected on two levels, the street
— here the ground floor correspodents to the bas
garden side — which is cleverly used as a garage
opens the garage with his key and after parking
without leaving the building, reach the lift which
his flat. Rational as this arrangement is, just as gr
and consideration were paid by the architects to a
of the house, with the aim of perfecting the use o
the inhabitants. By the use of balconies and la
along the whole length of the building, every fl
the garden air. On the top floor is a roof terrac
covered verandah, garden and shower.
The two architects did not follow the principle w
everything but the eloquence of extravagant p
thought only of the eighteen families moving into
and trying to make their lives healthier and brigh
because they scorned rhetoric, they justified them

arch. Giancarlo Palanti. Milano,

16

5.3 Victor and Aladar Olgyay, Reverse House, Budapest, 1939.

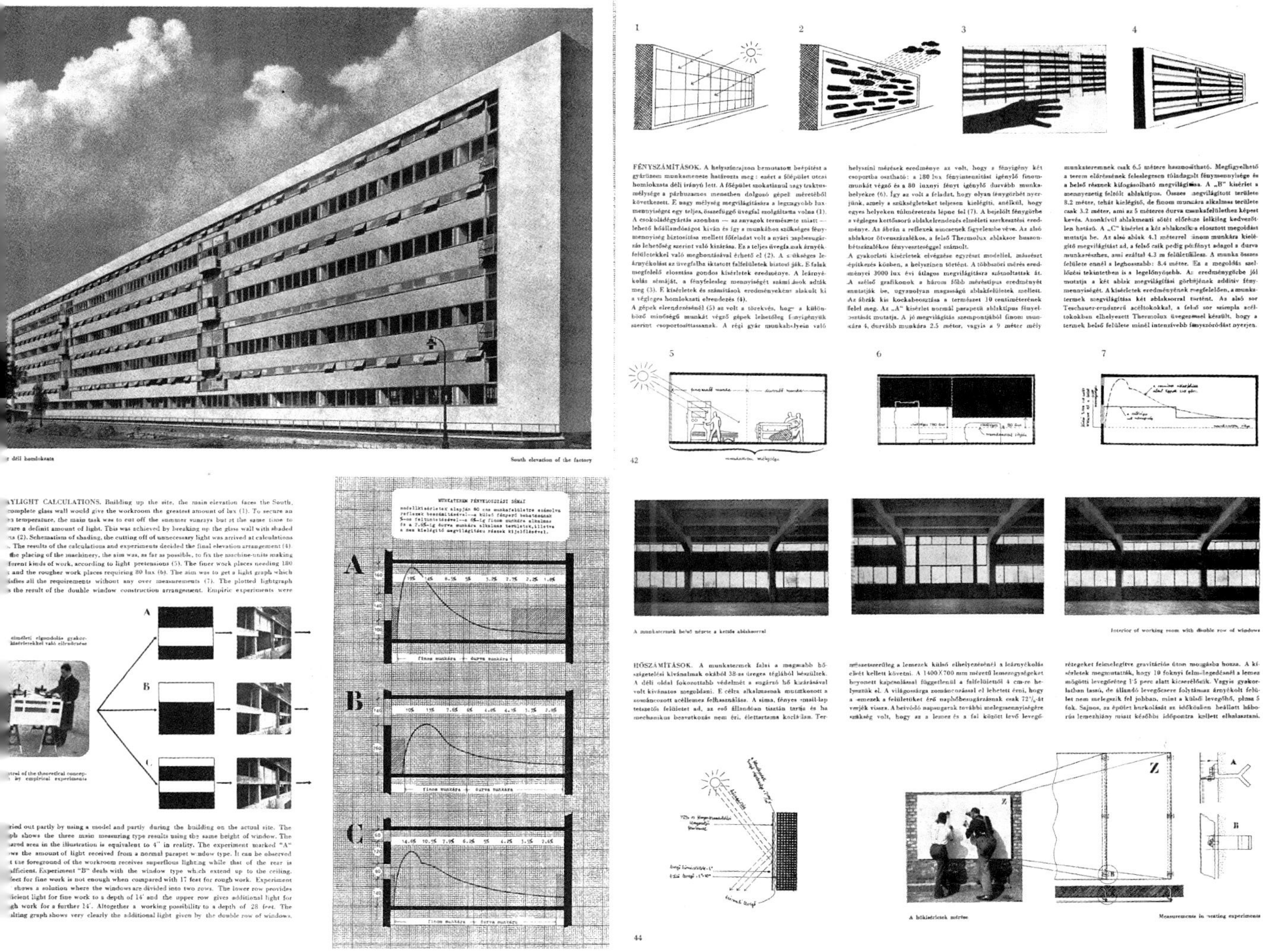

5.4 Victor and Aladar Olgyay, Stühmer Chocolate Factory, outside Budapest, 1941.

orientation. The left side of the bottom image in figure 5.4 shows one of the brothers in a hard-to-understand process of solar analysis, with photographs of the model and diagrams of each banded option, and a series of graphs detailing the daylighting and implied thermal effects. The banded façade resonates with the contemporaneous experiments in Brazil, the banding on the south of the IRB, for example, which allowed daylight in without excessive heat.

This turn toward precision necessitated a different approach to research and the production of new kinds of diagrams—for their own use, as method, and for explaining the virtues of the project to clients and the architectural public. These included a number of drawings indicating how the façade relates to the solar path, and how the specific façade condition proposed changes the thermal experience of the interior. The façade condition was expressed through graphs that indicated periods of overheating; the Olgyays connected this analysis to the size and disposition of the window opening—not unlike Roberto's roughly contemporaneous diagrams for the IRB, walking the reader through their decision to alternate glazing and masonry on the façade.

The banding on the north façade was keyed to mitigate the impact of seasonal heat on the workers and products in the interior. On the south, they proposed a largely glazed façade that was protected by a second skin of enameled steel panels—much of the solar radiation was deflected by these panels, and "the remaining heating power of the sunrays was used up in heating the air between the panel and the wall," air that was exchanged simply by being allowed to rise up and ventilate out of the top of the façade. Because this reduced the air flow into the interior, they also increased the provision for mechanical ventilation. "Experiments showed," they wrote, that "by this slow but continuous change of air, the shaded part [of the interior] does not become warmer than the outside." Because of wartime material needs, the steel skin was not installed until the late 1940s.[15]

Before going back to the United States in 1947, Olgyay and Olgyay designed and built over forty projects in Hungary, buildings that demonstrated, as Victor W. Olgyay (the son of Victor Olgyay) has recently put it, "a gradually increasing level of environmental analysis and application."[16] They discuss, in their 1952 book, the chocolate factory as having benefited from the lessons of their planned, but not built, Statistical Bureau in Budapest—its stark, planar façade didn't allow for substantive shading or directing of sunlight (figure 5.5). The drawing of the façade shows the use of external shading blinds, not well integrated into the architecture. They seemed to take the client and program—offices for statisticians—as an imperative for more effective data analysis: "statistics," the Olgyays wrote,

> achieve results from an accumulation of small impersonal precise records, serving to enlighten the problem produced by life. . . . The plan was made from a row of units in a regular right angular system. The size of the card indexes was considered in the size of the tables, the size of the tables prescribed the size of the rooms, and the room size fixed the pillar span measurement at 11 feet. The multiplication of this measurement gives the whole building size.[17]

For the Stühmer factory and in their subsequent work in Hungary they produced a number of schematic drawings demonstrating the basic principles of solar shading. Already, they were interested in the specifics of the project and in the development of a method. In detailing a housing estate, they essentially reproduced Gropius's "light and air" drawings from the 1930 CIAM conference in Brussels (discussed in chapter 1), relating the height of a mid-rise slab building to seasonal angles of the sun and prevailing wind patterns. While their projects are otherwise difficult to distinguish from many other modern projects of the period, this intensive climate analysis, and the diagrams to support and express it, was distinct.[18]

They also designed the Hungarian pavilion for the 1939 World's Fair in New York. It was this same event that helped introduce Brazilian modernism to the global architectural discussion with the Costa and Niemeyer designed Brazilian pavilion. The Brazilian project glowed with a new approach to familiar principles and prerogatives, while the Hungarian pavilion was a bit more staid.

They came to the United States primarily for political reasons, part of a large migration of Hungarians to the Midwest.[19] The brothers encountered a much larger architectural market and cultural scene in the United States, where they lacked both recognition and prominence. Their building activity waned, and they turned more aggressively toward research and pedagogy. Frustrated at Notre Dame, which then, as now, focused on classical principles, they sought out the engineer Telkes, an émigré with a family prominent in Budapest politics, and who had recently left Cleveland's Westinghouse Corporation to become a research scientist for the Solar Energy Fund at the Massachusetts Institute of Technology. Telkes was working with MIT's Bemis Foundation to develop a grant on climate methods for the Housing and Home Finance Agency (HHFA) that could justify bringing the brothers to MIT; they were also supported by the dean of the School of Architecture, Pietro Belluschi. The HHFA was initiated by the 1949 Housing Act and the parent agency to the Building Research Advisory Board, which would fund conferences and publications on a number of building interests developed out of wartime industrialization and applied scientific knowledge—including prefabrication, solar heating, innovations in mechanical systems, and materials science, and, indeed, "weather and building" as the section relevant to climate was known.

MIT was a vibrant center for integrating technological and design analysis in the years right after the war. Buckminster Fuller was a frequent visitor; Carl Koch's research on the Industrialized House was the subject of a number of design studios. The historian Arindam Dutta has recently identified MIT as the locus of "a second modernism," which he referred to as the techno-social moment: "a *second*, 'systems' based modernism can thus be seen superimposing itself on the first one, affecting a 'research' outlook" that complicated

5.5 Victor and Aladar Olgyay, Statistical Bureau, Budapest, 1941 (unbuilt).

modernism's relationship to aesthetics and other value systems familiar to architecture. Technological acuity was paramount. This second modernism would certainly characterize the Olgyays' work at MIT, and after.[20]

This was also a period of extensive exploration in solar house heating. MIT's first solar house for the Cabot Solar Energy Fund was built in 1947. In late 1949, Telkes engineered the production of a second house, really a shed, to test a chemical salt system for phase-change heat storage system. The system didn't work well and was the ostensible reason for her departure from the MIT Fund. Telkes tried the process again in a house designed with the architect Eleanor Raymond outside of Boston. Telkes and Aladar Olgyay used the phase-change system for a number of projects, including a group of houses outside of Dallas, a subdivision in upstate New York, and an industrial solar research center called Solar Park, built to Telkes's technical specifications and Aladar's design by the Curtiss-Wright Corporation in Princeton in 1955.[21] Aladar also designed a house for Telkes in 1958, which was not built.[22]

The Olgyays attended the "Space Heating with Solar Energy" symposium held at MIT in August 1950. The brothers didn't participate in the conference as speakers, but an exhibition of their research, which was published in *Architectural Forum* in 1951 as "The Temperate House," hung in the hallways, as is visible, in the photograph, behind Telkes, framed by the Libbey-Owens-Ford Solarometer (figure 5.6). Telkes is in between the solar house architect George Fred Keck and MIT architecture professor Lawrence Anderson, who taught a number of studio classes on solar house design in the period.[23] The Olgyays also collaborated, as did Telkes and others, with Paul Siple as he was developing the images and the design parameters for the Climate Control Project. This was the intellectual milieu in which the brothers were researching.

Their grant at MIT, the report for which was published by the HHFA as *Application of Climate Data to House Design* in 1952, established much of the basis for the Olgyays later work: foremost, developing a graphic means to communicate the complexities of climate in an architectural context; secondarily, understanding and refining the experiential conditions of the comfort zone itself. They began to articulate these interests relative to a "Climatic Comfort Zone" in the context of potential "Danger Zones"—of overheating or overly humid conditions. They also articulated a need to focus on "Climate and the Living Level," that is, near the ground—reflecting the concerns of Landsberg, Fitch, and others. As an interim report for the HHFA indicated:

5.6 The Solarometer at the Space Heating with Solar Energy symposium at MIT, August 1950. Maria Telkes, Lawrence Anderson, and George Fred Keck watching W. J. Arner demonstrate the device; Victor Olgyay is in the background, on the left, and images from the Olgyays' "Temperate House" research can be seen behind Telkes.

> During the course of the year, the work became divided into two parts: one that was carried out under the direction of Victor and Aladar Olgyay and was devoted to analysis of climate data evaluated in tabular and graphic form, and the means of using them in design; and another that under the direction of Thomas F. Malone and devoted to the search for quantitative information on the effects of the interior of a dwelling of measures taken to combat exterior climate conditions.[24]

The Olgyays' *Application of Climate Data* study was a first attempt, both cumbersome and ambitious in its claim to rethink the house according to knowledge of climate patterns. It set off in the right direction, but was seen as inadequate by many, largely due to its complexity. The problem of generalization or specificity continued to haunt the interest in clarifying precise climatic imperatives in the design method. As one of the project supervisors, Burnham Kelly, the director of the Bemis Foundation, wrote in a memorandum in early 1952, "The MIT research report will look ridiculous if it uses in the development of methods of application a series of simplified assumptions on which we have been able to make no improvement, especially since the very purpose of the project is to find means of making clear to architects and engineers the scientific facts regarding climate control."[25] Rather than oversimplify drawings, the decision was made to accompany the drawings with extensive textual summaries.

It was also not the first time the opacity of the Olgyays' diagrams would be seen to compromise their broader research goals. In another instance the criticism was determined, in part, by the opinions of Hoyt Hottel, a mechanical engineer at MIT and the director of the institute's Solar Energy Fund, who was angling against Telkes and her allies—out of reasons simultaneously political (the red scare) and gendered (Telkes was the only female researcher or faculty member in the MIT School of Engineering). This was compounded by a general resistance on Hottel's part to the capacity of architects to contribute to the meteorological sciences or their application. This dismissal was, in some ways, similar to the way Siple expressed frustration at the lack of serious interest in climate among the architectural profession. Douglas Lee, an Australian physiologist then at Johns Hopkins, was similarly dismissive of architectural efforts, as he wrote in a review of the published *Application of Climatic Data* volume: "the ideas tend to outrun the details of execution, or at least a clear exposition of the execution, and one is left slightly breathless, more than slightly bewildered, and just a little suspicious that somewhere along the line the argument has been a trifle tenuous," and, relative to the diagrams produced, Lee wrote "as a challenge to seminar students the diagrams are excellent; as a guide for the harassed architect they are hardly appealing."[26]

This is not to say that their research was incomplete or impressionistic; rather, it is symptomatic of the difficulty of integrating scientific knowledge into the architectural design process—obstacles of the Olgyays' training, their formal and programmatic predilections, and the significant institutional barriers to interdisciplinary knowledge production all inform these complications and subvert good intentions. Research, if nothing else, was squarely put on the table as a viable trajectory for career development and influence on the field, in this the brothers were prescient. Their many research projects established a knowledge base and a collaborative infrastructure that remained relevant for decades, and is again today.

## Research

A review of the Olgyays' research projects in this sociotechnical moment, once they were well embedded in the emergent research culture at MIT and Princeton, allows for a more precise consideration of their work and its impact on architectural and climatological knowledge. Their presentations at the 1952 Building Research Advisory Board conference initially allow for a summary of the state of the science of thermal comfort, as to how the built interior was being understood, and as to how that understanding was informing simultaneously an architectural discussion of climate design methods and a discussion based in engineering and industry that was focused on an increased role for air conditioning. In both cases, the discourse was demonstrably more sophisticated and precise than during the more or less contemporaneous Climate Control Project.

The 1952 "Housing and Building in Hot-Humid and Hot-Dry Climates" conference was another of the research conferences organized through BRAB. It took place at the University of Texas at Austin, where Aladar was a visiting research professor. Victor Olgyay presented a paper titled "A Bioclimatic Approach to Architecture"; Aladar presented a supporting argument in "Solar Control and Orientation to Meet Bioclimatic Needs."[27] It was the occasion for a number of firsts—the first use of the term "bioclimatic" in an architectural context; the first presentation of the Olgyays' elaborate biometric charts, which attended to the experience of the inhabitant and applied the term "comfort zone" to the thermal interior; and the first presentation of their "method of climate interpretation in housing," the diagram they continued to discuss, reproduce, and refine in subsequent years (see figure 5.2).

The BRAB conference brought the brothers' research to an interested, specialized audience. Fitch was on the comments panel for Aladar's paper; Douglas Lee also first took notice of their work at this conference, some years before his scathing review quoted above. Einer Engberg, then head of the UN Housing and Town Planning section, was also impressed with the presentations. Representatives from the US Weather Bureau and from a number of climatology research departments interested in housing questions were also present. There were also a few more architects, including Harwell Hamilton Harris and Ralph Walker, who presented on "The Practical Aspects of Tropical Living" in the same panel as Victor Olgyay.[28]

Victor's paper emphasized the brothers' attempts to use an architecturally derived diagrammatic system to present scientific knowledge to a design audience. It was rich in technical images: graphs showed how wind reduces humidity at high temperatures; the effect of winds on vapor pressure across different temperatures; how added moisture increases the effects of heat, and many other factors. All of these factors were discussed in relationship to the designed attainment of what they were calling the *comfort zone*—a term also being used by the HVAC industry at the time, though less consistently than it would be later. The altered bioclimatic chart was presented in two versions—it is subject to more analysis in a later, refined version below. At this stage the chart was essentially an aggregate of the above factors to determine what needed to be adjusted by

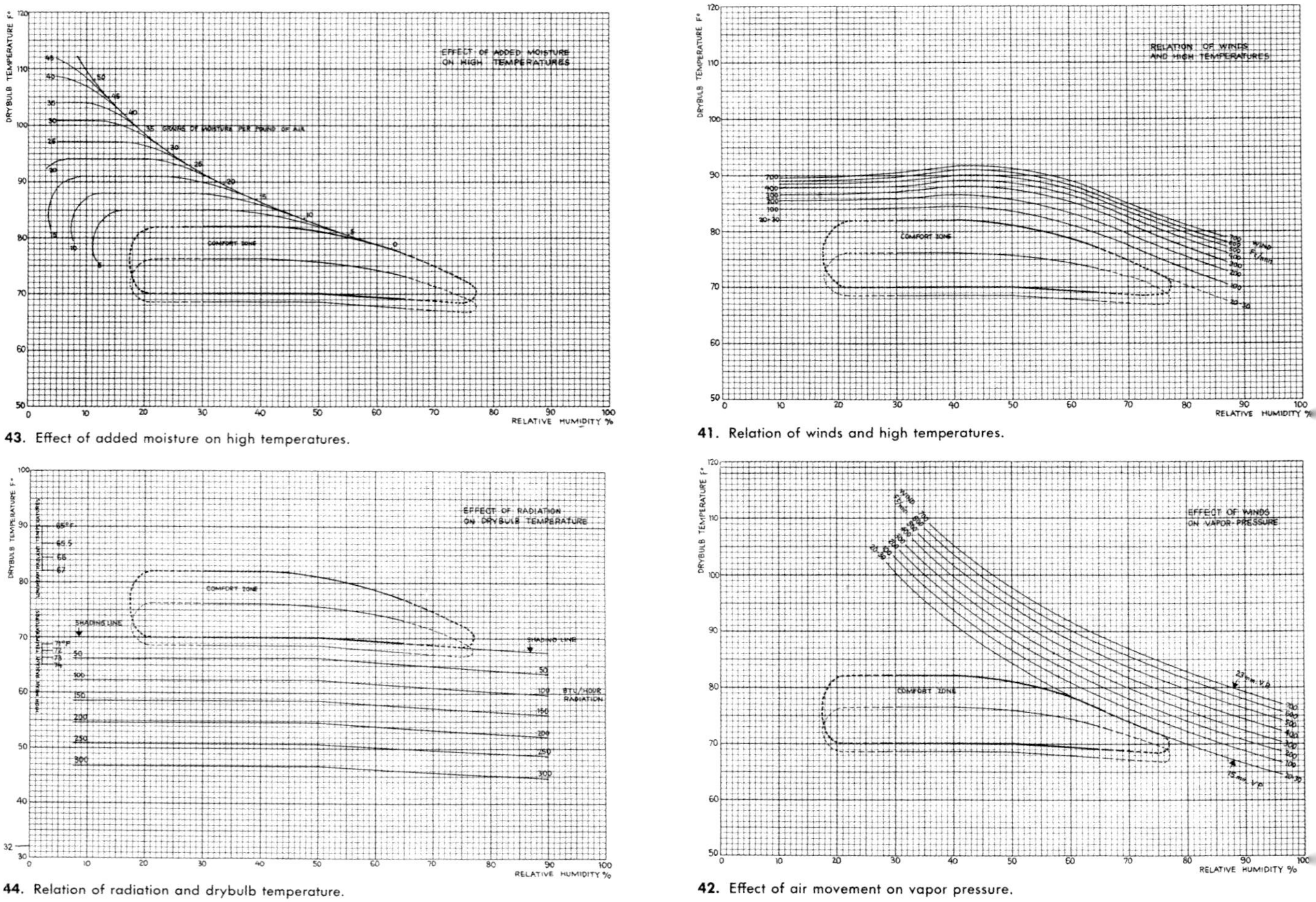


5.7 Victor Olgyay, drawings made for *Application of Climate Data to House Design*, 1954, as they appeared in *Design with Climate*, 1963.

architectural intervention to render the interior thermally normative.

Victor Olgyay summarized the paper as follows:

> Desirable temperature, humidity, and vapor pressure ranges are discussed along with the effects of wind movement, evaporative cooling, and the radiation effects on dry-bulb temperatures. A bioclimatic chart combines these elements so that a determination of a general comfort zone can be made. The chart can be related to any region and climatic conditions, so that for any hour of the day throughout the year the requirements for physical comfort can be generally ascertained.[29]

The paper also reproduced a number of overheating diagrams, showing the times of day that shading was needed, for New Jersey, New Orleans, and Phoenix. He presented a "bioclimatical chart," composed of points and described as an "envisioned surface"—both uniquely available to a visible register, and also modeling a new set of relations. The bioclimatic chart, and the comfort zone it outlines, becomes a technical image in the Olgyays' development and communication of their project.

In relationship to other presentations, Victor's paper stood out for its integrative goals (that is, how to bring together engineering, architectural, climatological, and physiological knowledge) and for its general resistance to assuming that there were "psychological and sociological" factors that could also ameliorate the experience of the interior—factors, in other words, that relied on transformations to the human condition rather than to design and its effects of the interior. The universalism of the premise was key—in "any region" at "any hour" comfort could be attained through his method.

In many other presentations, contingencies of physiology, culture, and habit were paramount to determining comfort. Factors were implicitly related to issues of gender (C. A. Mills: "as anyone knows who has taken a wife [to the tropics]. . . . It hurts the women . . . the women are less active and as a result the tropical heat hurts them") or to more general, climate determinist claims about race (Douglas Lee: "racial differences in heat tolerance are largely attributable to nutrition, health, incentive, and experience in accomplishing work with less expenditure of effort")—in effect, the conceptualization of a comfort zone that recapitulated the inequities embedded in favoring the temperate zones in climatic determinist analyses.[30] The Olgyays' insistence on architectural-technological, rather than social or psychological, solutions to the problem of thermal comfort treated the "human" as a uniform sociophysiological entity—that is, on species terms, reinscribing normative conditions for a specific, unchanging species condition.

Their focus, again, was on outlining a comfort zone—a thermal condition that was the target at which climate design adjustments were aimed. The idea of the comfort zone did not originate in the Olgyays' work but developed out of ASHVE-funded research in the 1920s, carried out by Constantin Yaglou, first in his research position at ASHVE and then as he became a professor at the Harvard School of Public Health. Yaglou was at the 1952 conference. Comfort charts had first been published in 1932, by ASHVE, based on experiments with heat, humidity, and ventilation performed in the medical school at Yale.

Yaglou developed the concept of effective temperature from the 1920s to measure relative heat stress, considering humidity and the movement of air—intending to measure the physical experience of heat. The effective temperature scale was developed by moving test subjects, stripped to the waist, from one conditioned room to another.[31] Effective temperature modeled, somewhat in the negative, a condition for optimized physical activity, focused on how much energy the body has to expend in heating or cooling. Comfort, in other words, was considered as how to best dissipate the heat energy the body is producing, according to different activities and spaces, according to the norms of a given region, and facilitated through ventilation. A comfortable effective temperature was one in which the least amount of physiological adjustments were required.

Such conditions of comfort would continue to be refined. By the 1950s Yaglou and many others, usually working for ASHVE and cooling industry corporations, either directly or through university-based research grants, had developed a very precise means to measure and assess internal environments, using a range of new devices.[32] The Olgyays saw these new parameters as an invitation to determine which architectural elements to adjust in order to reach the optimum state.

Thermal comfort was essentially a measure of relief from overheating. Yaglou expanded on this research in a 1957 paper introducing wet bulb globe temperature as an indicator of heat stress that considered the effect of air temperature, relative humidity, and heat exchange through radiation. It used an emissive globe that radiates much like the human body, thereby improving on effective temperature measurements that had heretofore not been able to take such radiation into account. Ideal conditions were seen to be between 30 percent and 70 percent relative humidity, with an effective temperature range between 63 and 71 degrees Fahrenheit. Further refinements and continued development of devices for monitoring thermal interiors, as well as a plethora of regulatory and metric regimes to determine the working performance of that interior, were under discussion in other papers, indicating the widespread interest in climate, comfort zones, and their attendant methods, measurements, and systems.[33]

There is nothing, really, deterministic about the comfort zone as a concept (figure 5.8). It describes a range of climatic effects—primarily temperature and humidity—as a quantitative goal for architectural-climatic manipulations. The imposition of a stable norm onto this zone is somewhat distinct as a historical phenomenon—that is, it can be keyed to other genders, physiologies, desires, and communities. It operates as the object of architectural optimization. The Olgyays' work is an elaboration of climate design techniques at the last moment this was viable—before computation took over the measurement and production of thermal interiors; before formalist postmodernism took over from a still barely social-focused modernism; and before air conditioning took over everything, leaving the architect and the inhabitant hostage to fossil fuels.

The conditions of knowledge were such that in the published discussion about Victor Olgyay's paper, a number of the nonspecialists in the audience had effective temperature explained to them as a principle that if sweat is induced in a given interior—that is, if the body has an overheating condition to react to—it is not comfortable and requires adjustments.[34] Victor Olgyay later generalized this approach: "maybe [comfort] can be defined negatively as the situation where no discomfort occurs."[35] It was generally assumed that architectural means could hope to reduce heat stress, "producing a tolerable discomfort" if not in fact providing comfortable living and working conditions.[36]

Architectural means were not, even in 1952, the only mechanism to rely on for adjusting the thermal interior. The technical progress of the air-conditioning industry was far beyond what was legible at this conference and in the climate discourse more generally. Because air conditioning was still largely focused on specialized applications of theaters, institutional buildings, and some offices, it had not yet systematically been a subject for architectural discussion. Journals were beginning to talk of mechanical space; electricity was becoming more available and at lower rates and was appropriate for numerous household applications.

Yaglou and others, at Texas in 1952 and in general, were especially concerned with *if*, and if so *how*, design methods on their own could mitigate humidity in particular. If shading systems and attention to site and materials were discussed in many contexts at the conference as an aid to reducing summer insolation—blocking the sun from radiating into the interior, minimizing heat gain—they had almost no role to play in managing humidity. In some cases, and some regions, induced ventilation (increased airflow) could help substantially in the experience of humidity. Indeed, though here and elsewhere one uses the term "air conditioning" to indicate the cooling and de-humidifying of a room or building, the primary aim of the early mechanical air-conditioning systems under discussion was focused almost exclusively on removing humidity from the air.[37]

The first part of the BRAB conference focused on design and material strategies to produce comfortable conditions in hot climates; the second part consisted primarily of HVAC industry representatives discussing the relative benefits of their products in development. Yaglou was not optimistic that nonmechanical strategies had a substantive role to play in attaining comfort: "to get any measure of comfort," he wrote, "we have to have some sort of air-conditioning." While this was generally supported it was also noted that, as a Danish architect in attendance who was working in the tropics put it, while "mechanical cooling can aid in comfort . . . it is all very well and good if you have got the funds," but in most places we "must depend on architectural design more than on the mechanical aids." Fitch stepped in to offer a compromise position: "if architecture doesn't accomplish the job for either minimal or maximal comfort, naturally we draw on technology."[38]

These comments also indicate that, though the conference was expressly focused on hot climates within the United States, many were interested in how the ideas being discussed had relevance elsewhere: "the big show now is in tropical areas," as the UN's Engbert put it in the published comments, and "in the past few months quite a few governments have requested UN to send experts."[39] By the early 1950s, the relationship between architectural and mechanical means to manage climates was transforming the profession globally, and was becoming the realm for an elaborate discourse on climate modeling and architectural management. Le Corbusier's brise-soleil narratives had been published, as had most of the Brazilian work, in American and European journals; Le Corbusier was designing Chandigarh, with Maxwell Fry, Jane Drew, and others, and Fry and Drew were also designing in West Africa and writing about climate in British architectural publications. By 1952 the Tropical Department had started at the Architectural Association. The Texas conference was yet another indication of the bifurcation of technological trajectories across the 1950s—the development of air conditioning in urban centers and large swaths of the Global North, with more reliance on architectural techniques and hybrid approaches across the Global South. But the debate was ongoing, and the approaches coexisted.

Mechanical tools for air conditioning the built interior were, by the early 1950s, relatively sophisticated, though they were also very expensive and generally speaking were only being used on large commercial projects. Pietro Belluschi's office tower for Equitable Savings and Loan, built in Portland, Oregon, from 1944 to 1948, was the first

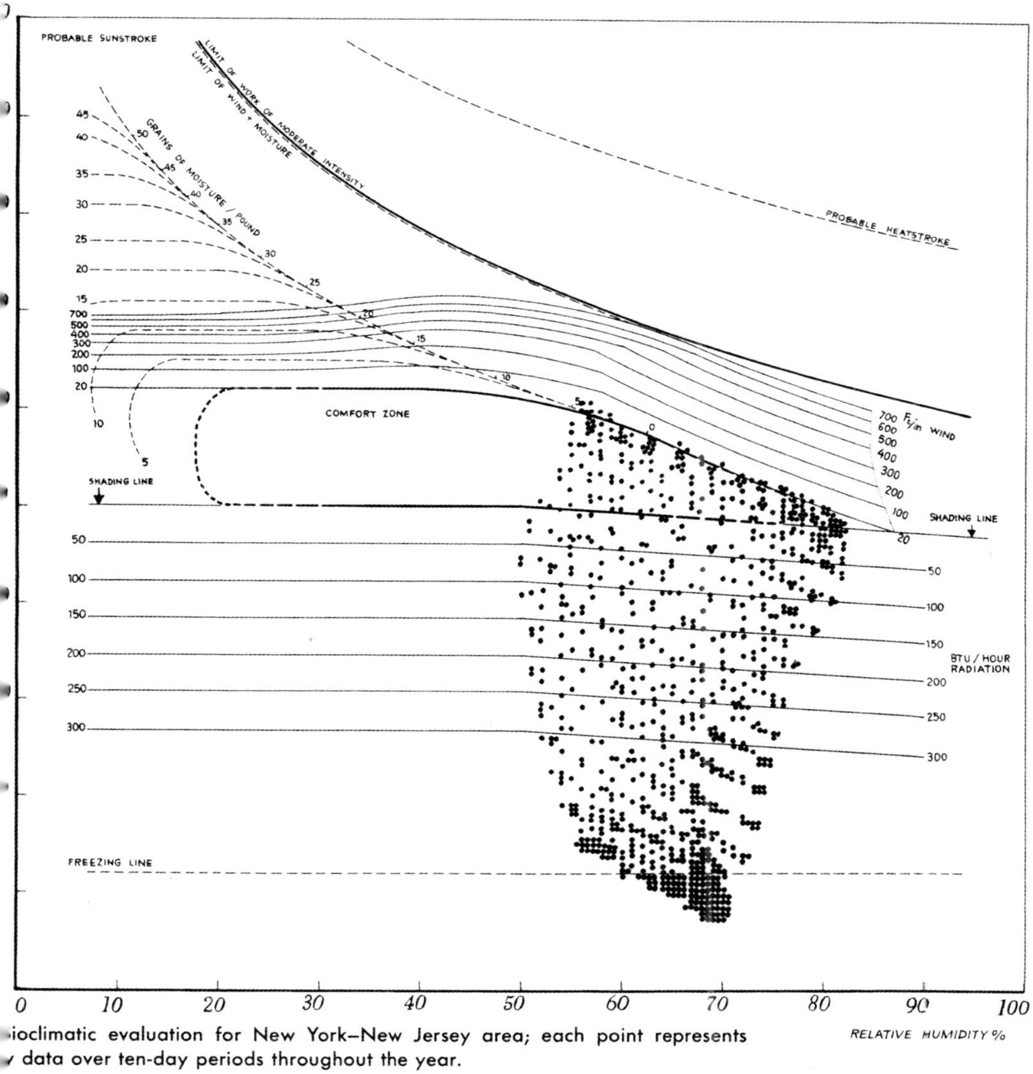


5.8 Victor Olgyay, "bioclimatic evaluation," originally made in "A Bioclimatic Approach to Architecture," as it appeared in *Design with Climate*, 1963.

building to deploy a sealed curtain wall façade and be completely air conditioned by mechanical means.[40] Many others followed. It was certainly not yet clear, in 1952, that the flow of oil from the Gulf of Mexico, the Middle East, and Venezuela would provide enough of an energy base to mechanically condition not only most office towers, but also, eventually, homes and institutional buildings—the Equitable drew its energy from hydroelectric installations on the Columbia River.[41] Part of the intent of the Equitable was to use as much energy as possible—to increase energy demand as a means to increase economic activity; by the mid-1950s, architecture would become a reliable arena for energy intensification, building so as to engineer economic growth, as at the Seagram Park Avenue building and other buildings discussed later in this book.

Simultaneous to the proliferation of the sealed curtain wall, the mid-1950s still harbored some aspirations for using design strategies to produce comfortable conditions—without mechanical assistance. This was less of an ethical goal—that is, a claim to a new set of social obligations for the architect, or even a paean to architectural humanism—than it was an economic advantage, a means of identifying how certain approaches to design could assist mechanical plants through responsive shading devices, reducing the cost of HVAC, increasing access to it, and doing so through well-developed architectural traditions. That is,

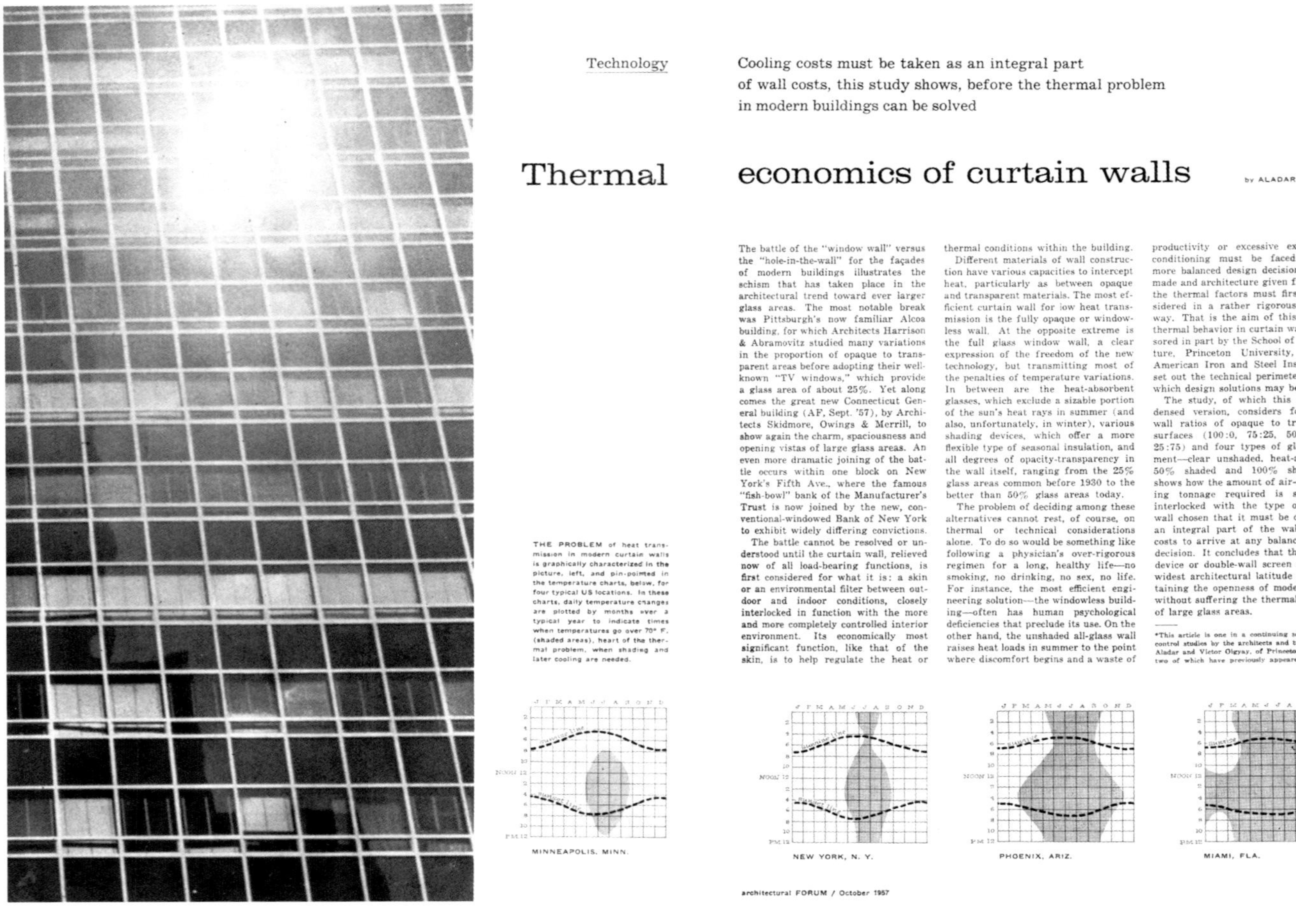

Technology

Cooling costs must be taken as an integral part of wall costs, this study shows, before the thermal problem in modern buildings can be solved

Thermal economics of curtain walls

The battle of the "window wall" versus the "hole-in-the-wall" for the façades of modern buildings illustrates the schism that has taken place in the architectural trend toward ever larger glass areas. The most notable break was Pittsburgh's now familiar Alcoa building, for which Architects Harrison & Abramovitz studied many variations in the proportion of opaque to transparent areas before adopting their well-known "TV windows," which provide a glass area of about 25%. Yet along comes the great new Connecticut General building (AF, Sept. '57), by Architects Skidmore, Owings & Merrill, to show again the charm, spaciousness and opening vistas of large glass areas. An even more dramatic joining of the battle occurs within one block on New York's Fifth Ave., where the famous "fish-bowl" bank of the Manufacturer's Trust is now joined by the new, conventional-windowed Bank of New York to exhibit widely differing convictions.

The battle cannot be resolved or understood until the curtain wall, relieved now of all load-bearing functions, is first considered for what it is: a skin or an environmental filter between outdoor and indoor conditions, closely interlocked in function with the more and more completely controlled interior environment. Its economically most significant function, like that of the skin, is to help regulate the heat or thermal conditions within the building.

Different materials of wall construction have various capacities to intercept heat, particularly as between opaque and transparent materials. The most efficient curtain wall for low heat transmission is the fully opaque or windowless wall. At the opposite extreme is the full glass window wall, a clear expression of the freedom of the new technology, but transmitting most of the penalties of temperature variations. In between are the heat-absorbent glasses, which exclude a sizable portion of the sun's heat rays in summer (and also, unfortunately, in winter), various shading devices, which offer a more flexible type of seasonal insulation, and all degrees of opacity-transparency in the wall itself, ranging from the 25% glass areas common before 1930 to the better than 50% glass areas today.

The problem of deciding among these alternatives cannot rest, of course, on thermal or technical considerations alone. To do so would be something like following a physician's over-rigorous regimen for a long, healthy life—no smoking, no drinking, no sex, no life. For instance, the most efficient engineering solution—the windowless building—often has human psychological deficiencies that preclude its use. On the other hand, the unshaded all-glass wall raises heat loads in summer to the point where discomfort begins and a waste of

THE PROBLEM of heat transmission in modern curtain walls is graphically characterized in the picture, left, and pin-pointed in the temperature charts, below, for four typical US locations. In these charts, daily temperature changes are plotted by months over a typical year to indicate times when temperatures go over 70° F. (shaded areas), heart of the thermal problem, when shading and later cooling are needed.



architectural FORUM / October 1957

5.9 Aladar Olgyay, "Thermal Economics of Curtain Walls," from *Architectural Forum*, October 1957.

design was the key to an efficient, well-designed, comfortable, and affordable future.

The research project that brought the Olgyays to Princeton involved the economic assessment of curtain walls on these terms—how to assess the relative viability of a shaded system versus a sealed system. Robert McLaughlin, then director of the Princeton School of Architecture, was asked by the American Iron and Steel Institute to assess the use of metals, especially stainless steel, in curtain wall production. The project began in 1952. Aladar published "Thermal Economics of Curtain Walls" in *Architectural Forum* in October 1957, summarizing his version of the findings, and a longer report *Thermal Behavior of Metal Curtain Walls in Relation to Cooling Costs and Shading Devices* was submitted to the Institute that same year (figure 5.9).[42]

Glass walls dominated the architecture of the mid-1950s, placing rather than relieving pressure on mechanical systems. Aladar began his article noting an apparent conflict between the all-glass curtain wall then subject to much discussion—again, SOM's Lever House in New York was completed in 1952 and Mies van der Rohe's iconic Seagram Park Avenue tower just opened in 1957; he contrasted these to what he called "hole in the wall façades," which were largely opaque, such as the ALCOA headquarters in Pittsburgh (Harrison and Abramowitz, 1953), which had an aluminum façade with small "TV windows." He placed this building also in contrast to SOM's recently completed headquarters for Connecticut General Life Insurance in Hartford (1957), a low, sprawling suburban complex with, as Aladar put it, "the charm, spaciousness, and opening vistas of all glass areas."[43]

"The battle cannot be resolved," he continued, "or understood until the curtain wall, relieved now of all load-bearing functions, is first considered for what it is: a skin or an environmental filter between

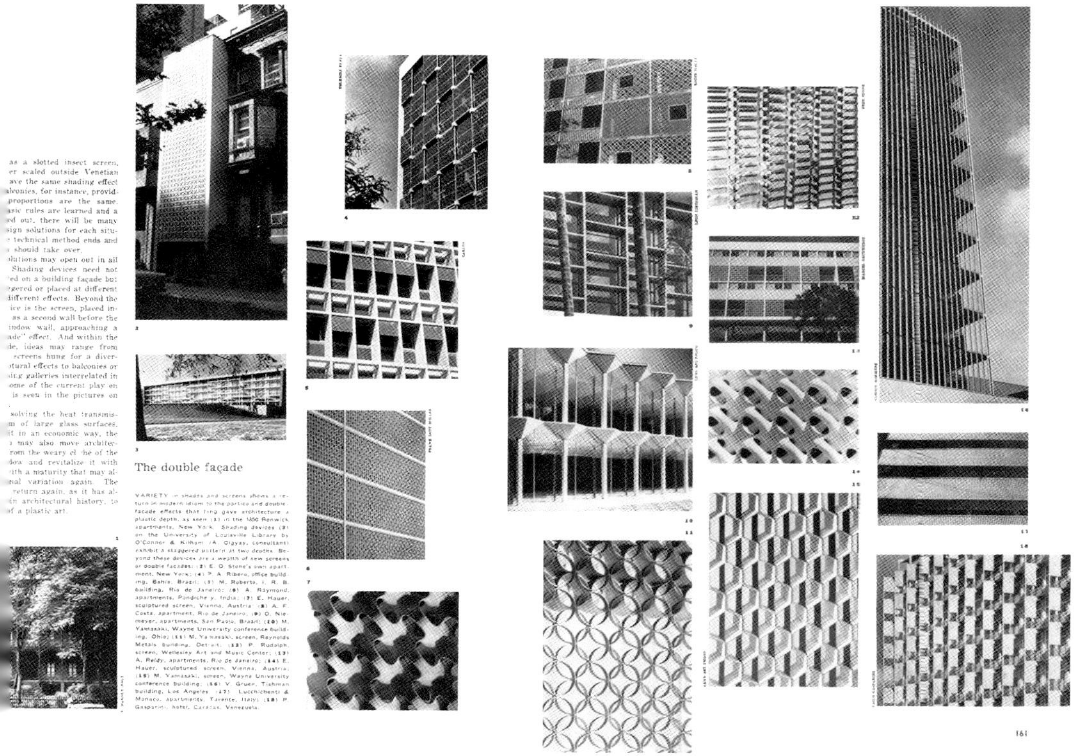


5.10 Aladar Olgyay, "Thermal Economics of Curtain Walls," from *Architectural Forum*, October 1957.

outdoor and indoor conditions, closely interlocked in function with the more and more completely controlled interior environment" (figure 5.10).[44] Thermal factors of the interior, in other words, needed to be taken into consideration when determining the best façade solution for a given building and a given site—first in isolation and then in a more general relationship to cooling costs and other conditioning factors.

In most cases, a glass wall as it was then being manufactured did not hold up well in these analyses. Most of the curtain walls in the period were of single-paned, uninsulated glass—another early indication that a building like the Seagram Headquarters was essentially a transmission center for energy, moving it from resources in the ground, through infrastructures, and to the building, only to be emanated to the exterior through the poorly insulated façade.

Aladar's study, therefore, intended to show "how the amount of air-conditioning tonnage required is so closely interlocked with the type of curtain wall chosen that it must be considered an integral part of the wall and its costs." A double façade, with a glass wall and a second, screening element—that is, neither SOM's naked glass wall nor Harrison and Abramowitz's excessive opacity—was the solution, nor "actually justified economically."[45] Which is to say, if a glass façade relies on a more robust cooling plant, these costs should be seen together; if shading systems can reduce the mechanical requirements in construction and operation, those savings should be reflected in the façade systems analysis. This economic argument was reiterated in many different contexts, including Lewis Mumford's screed against the all glass walls and inadequate shading screens of the UNESCO secretariat.[46]

"To make them function well," Aladar continued, "the architect must know . . . *when* to intercept the sun's rays (the seasonal consideration), *where* to intercept them (the angle of the sun's rays during the desired shading period), and from these, *how* to intercept them by the most suitable designed device."[47] There followed an extensive demonstration of the diagrammatic tools that the Olgyays had been developing to meet these when, where, and how criteria. He illustrated the article with technical diagrams and with a spread of historical precedents, many by now familiar to the reader, that were then also being collected in *Solar Control and Shading Devices*.

McLaughlin supported Aladar Olgyay's general claim about the economic effectiveness of climatic analysis in a 1955 press release detailing the Olgyays' research: "The objective in the develop-

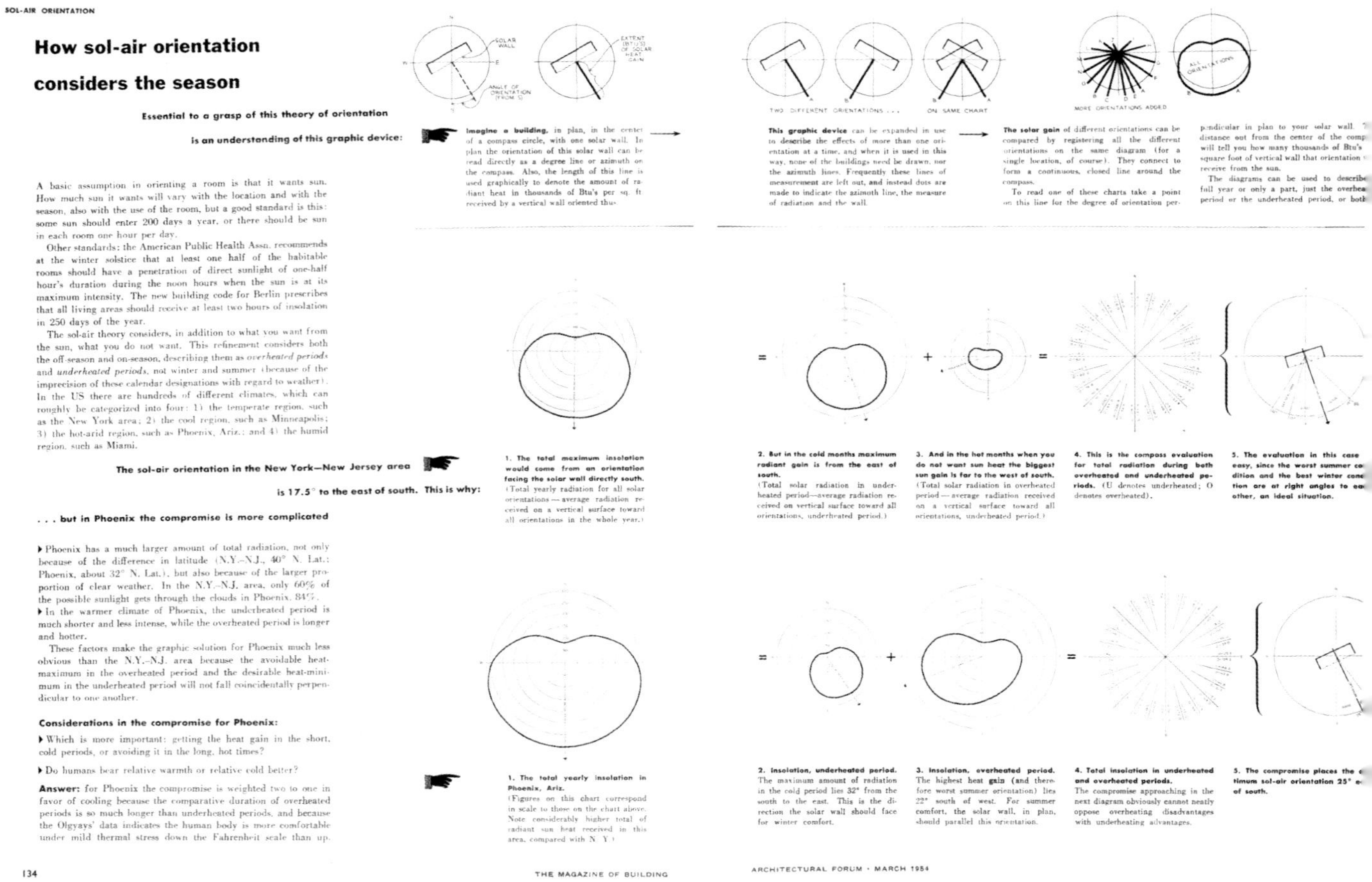

5.11 Victor and Aladar Olgyay, "The Theory of Sol-Air Orientation," from *Architectural Forum*, March 1954.

ment of right-shaped buildings for particular exterior environments will be to combine esthetic appeal with a marked reduction in heating-cooling loads and a corresponding saving of natural resources."[48] Resources themselves were not seen to be scarce, but heating oil in particular was subject to dramatic shifts in cost. Shading systems were a hedge against possible instability. There were, in short, a myriad of reasons to be interested in shading systems in the early 1950s. None of them had to do with carbon emissions, but many related to pressures on economic and resources systems, and many lent themselves to imperatives for efficiency. The interest in shading was focused on careful analysis of region, site, and a range of climatic parameters in order to realize its possibilities.

The Olgyays were at the center of these discussions. They published a number of articles about the topic before bringing their research together for the publication of their jointly authored book, *Solar Control and Shading Devices* (1957). The curtain wall article was part of an extended series for *Forum*, which also included "The Temperate House" (March 1951), "A Theory of Sol-Air Orientation" (March 1954), which laid out a method for induced ventilation; and "Environment and Building Shape" (August 1954) (figure 5.11). The brothers also consulted on a number of buildings in the 1950s. For instance, they developed the shading mechanisms for the American Association for the Advancement of Science building in Washington, DC, with Faulkner, Kingsbury and Stenhouse (1955), it still stands as the US embassy for Tunisia, and will be discussed again in the next chapter (figure 5.12; figure 5.13).[49] They also collaborated with O'Connor and Kilham to design the shading screen for Lehman Hall at

5.12 Faulkner, Kingsbury and Stenhouse with Olgyay and Olgyay consulting, American Association for the Advancement of Science Building, Washington, DC, 1955.

5.13 Faulkner, Kingsbury and Stenhouse with Olgyay and Olgyay consulting, American Association for the Advancement of Science Building, Washington, DC, 1955.

5.14 Josep Lluís Sert, Peabody Terrace, Cambridge, Massachusetts, 1962.

Barnard College, which housed the library until it was torn down in 2016. They worked on Gropius/TAC projects in Baghdad, for Josep Lluís Sert's Peabody Terrace in Cambridge, and a number of other prominent international projects (figure 5.14). Their research, diagrams, and buildings helped to bring together a range of architects and others to clarify how to best develop a design method appropriate to the complexities of climate.

## The Big Picture

Aladar's 1957 article on the thermal dynamics of curtain walls argued a role for shading in the economics of building design and production, largely through diagrams. The diagram was intended to clarify the effectiveness of shading in general—as method—and relative to a specific site, with its façade orientations, programs, and materials. Opening the article, he wrote, referring to the diagram on the bottom of the page in figure 5.9, and clarifying the primacy of a visual language in these discussions: "The problem of heat transmission in modern curtain walls is graphically characterized in the picture, left, and pin-pointed in the temperature charts, below." The diagrams showed a number of hatched areas that indicated overheating, illustrating, through another means of diagrammatic translation, a specific shading intervention. These were divided into regionally adjusted parameters for considering curtain walls and shading systems across the United States. The insufficiency of this regional analysis and the importance of visual material in specifying the prospective applicability of climate design techniques have already been a focus of this book—the Climate Control Project in particular sought to instrumentalize images in such a way that they produced a specific effect.

The Olgyays' diagrams strove to integrate new kinds of knowledge into the design process. Architecture had, in fact, long been a space for such integration. The intersection of architecture and climate was an early arena for the exploration of the role of computation as a tool on these precise terms. Here again the Olgyays work appears pre- or proto-computational—an early use of the computer in architecture, just without a computer. Such a formulation also has a history. In 1917 the amateur climatologist Lewis Fry Richardson designed what he called a "program" for processing climate knowledge, using "computers." Richardson, a Quaker in the Ambulance Corps in World War I, sketched a method, since referred to as the Forecast Factory, that would process existing weather data in relationship to broader patterns in order to predict future behavior (figure 5.15). The proposal was for a spherical room to be constructed, a sort of inverted globe on the inside of which would be rows of cubicles, arranged like box seats in a grand theater. In each cubicle, a group of "computers"—people sharing knowledge, integrating data, and adjusting parameters—would document the conditions of their quadrant and process it in relationship to other quadrants. They were parallel processors, each responsible for their own module in coordinating a larger picture of the future weather. The aggregate capacity of all the computers at once would give the researcher a picture of the state of the climate at a given moment. The process, as it was conceived—it was never built, needless to say—articulated a method for the modeling of climate, one that is in some sense still used today. It was not, though, successful for the prediction of weather, which was Richardson's goal.[50]

It was the first computer model of the atmosphere. The Olgyays were also computing without computers, establishing parameters as variables to model potential performance, producing a dynamic system image. The diagram was a means to engage the world on these computational terms—to bring a series of practices into interrelationship in order to encounter a complex problem. Today's design platforms use climatic data parameters from climatology, engineering, and material behavior to present a picture of a building's performance. In the 1950s, this was not all available at the architect's fingertips, so they needed to talk to and collaborate with climatologists, engineers, materials scientists, and many others. Diagrammatic images were cross-disciplinary platforms to integrate knowledge from a range of perspectives and fields. And once you start collaborating, why not include social scientists, policy makers, developers, research foundations, and others interested in the built environment. The diagram became an essential tool for thinking about building and climate at the same time that it directed this heterogeneity toward a system of normalization.

These imperatives of integration and normalization were diagrammed in Victor Olgyay's "Temperate House" article of 1951 (figure 5.16). In the midst of regional analyses, diagrams of sun paths, overheating charts, and a grid of photographs showed the relationship of a tree to a

5.15 Lewis Fry Richardson's Forecast Factory, c. 1917.

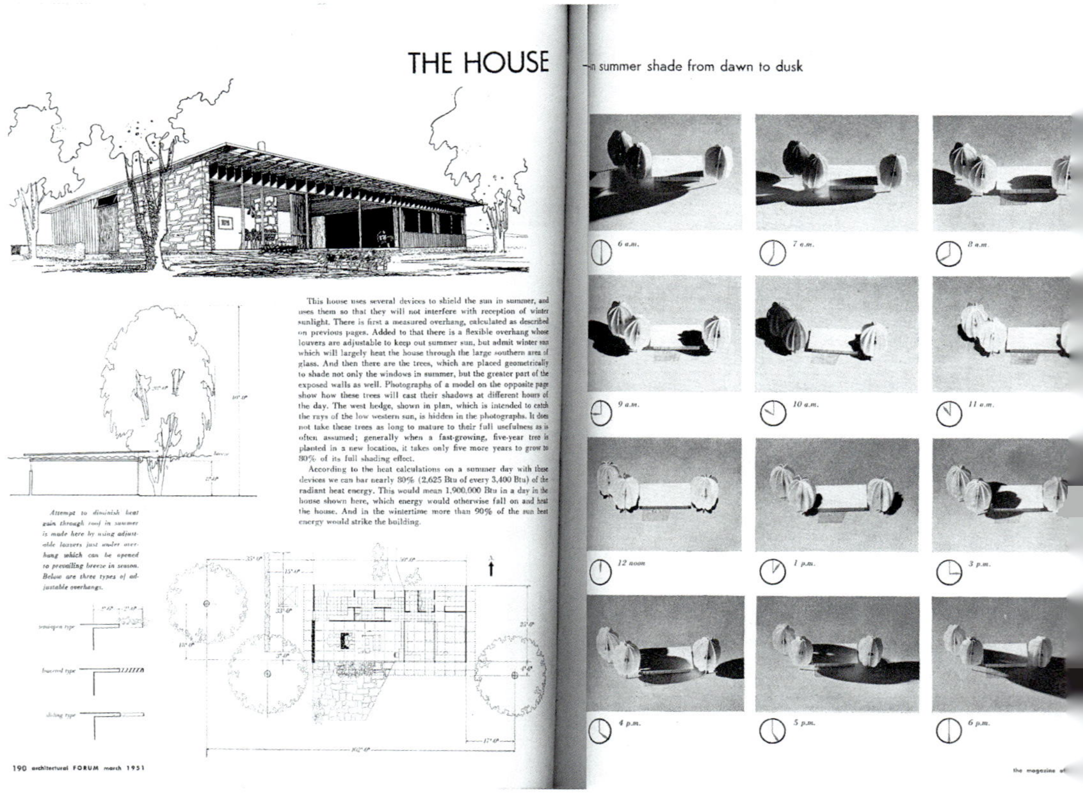

THE HOUSE —in summer shade from dawn to dusk

This house uses several devices to shield the sun in summer, and uses them so that they will not interfere with reception of winter sunlight. There is first a measured overhang, calculated as described on previous pages. Added to that there is a flexible overhang whose louvers are adjustable to keep out summer sun, but admit winter sun which will largely heat the house through the large southern area of glass. And then there are the trees, which are placed geometrically to shade not only the windows in summer, but the greater part of the exposed walls as well. Photographs of a model on the opposite page show how these trees will cast their shadows at different hours of the day. The west hedge, shown in plan, which is intended to catch the rays of the low western sun, is hidden in the photographs. It does not take these trees as long to mature to their full usefulness as is often assumed; generally when a fast-growing, five-year tree is planted in a new location, it takes only five more years to grow to 80% of its full shading effect.

According to the heat calculations on a summer day with these devices we can bar nearly 80% (2,625 Btu of every 3,400 Btu) of the radiant heat energy. This would mean 1,900,000 Btu in a day in the house shown here, which energy would otherwise fall on and heat the house. And in the wintertime more than 90% of the sun heat energy would strike the building.

*Attempt to diminish heat gain through roof in summer is made here by using adjustable louvers just under overhang which can be opened to prevailing breeze in season. Below are three types of adjustable overhangs.*



190 architectural FORUM march 1951

5.16 Victor Olgyay, shading trees from "A Temperate House," 1951.

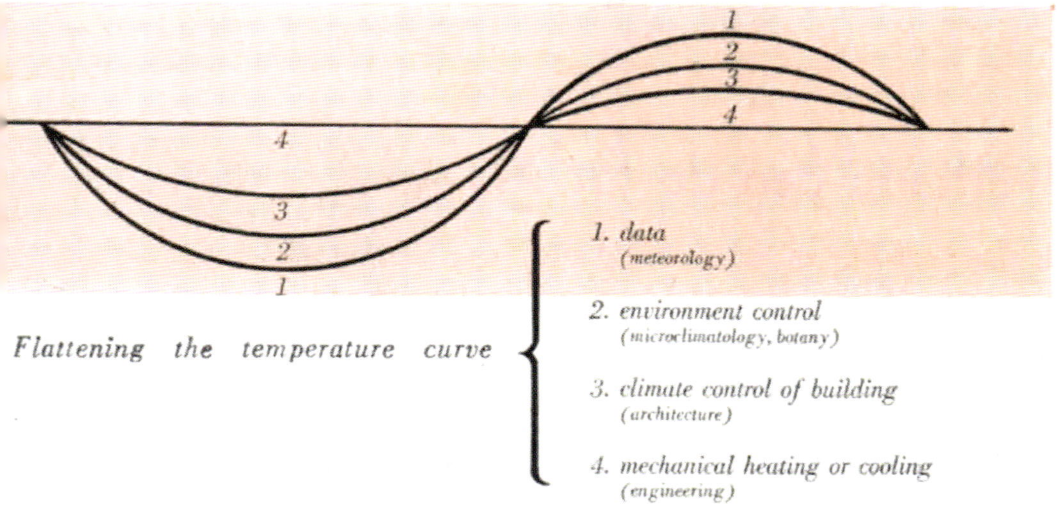


5.17 Victor Olgyay, Flattening the Temperature Curve, from "A Temperate House," in *Architectural Forum*, March 1951.

house under changing solar conditions. Most of the Olgyays technical images operated at this general level, focusing on a specific design problem rather than a specific site or project. Their drawings required extensive context in order to communicate effectively—a discourse of images, as Siple imagined, but one in which the viewer had to be significantly engaged in the relevant terms and methods. The cultivation of an expertise, in other words, and a discourse community reliant on media.

Such expertise was not as yet widespread. Jeffrey Aronin, another integrator of architectural and climate knowledge in the period, wrote of the "Temperate House" charts, graphs, and diagrams that while "there is considerable data here . . . it is unfortunate that their graphs are very difficult to interpret, unless one spends a lot of time on them."[51]

Some were more simple. The "Temperate House" article included the image of an *S*-curve on its side with four different levels of remove from the central line, which was identified as the 70-degree line of comfort (figure 5.17). Each wedge in the diagram represented a specific discipline that would participate in "flattening the temperature curve": "1. Data (meteorology); 2. Environmental control (micro-climatology, botany); 3. climate control of building (architecture); 4. Mechanical heating and cooling (engineering)." It was a clever collection of disciplines and approaches used to imagine the production of a consistent condition of comfort. The diagrams proposed that such a production involved a big-picture understanding of climate; a clear sense of how that plays out on a given site; a sophisticated approach to the architectural tools—in design, materials, and specific devices for shading and ventilation—that would control the climate of a building; and the use of HVAC to cover the rest, making up the difference as Fitch had suggested in Texas.

These diagrams invoke a history of the methodological diagram more broadly in modern architecture. As a category of drawings, the methodological diagram traces a graphic history of framing architecture according to its many interrelationships. The trajectory from the Bauhaus to the Ulm Hochschule für Gestaltung is one iconic arena for such diagrams—the Ulm diagram drawn of Tomás Maldonado's curriculum, in the late 1950s, is especially compelling for visualizing the different systems of thought being brought to bear on the design project (figure 5.18). Media, in the form of film and journalism, and in relationship to contemporary politics, became a critical subject for designers at Ulm, as the diagram indicated. There, media was a device used to think through elements of production and clients, as well as systems and optimization—quite distinct from the pressures exerted and the pedagogical program produced at the Bauhaus some forty years earlier, which seems caught up in familiar disciplines and practices, by comparison.[52] Serge Chermayeff's 1953 drawing, somewhat more abstractly, places design out front in the center, amid technology,

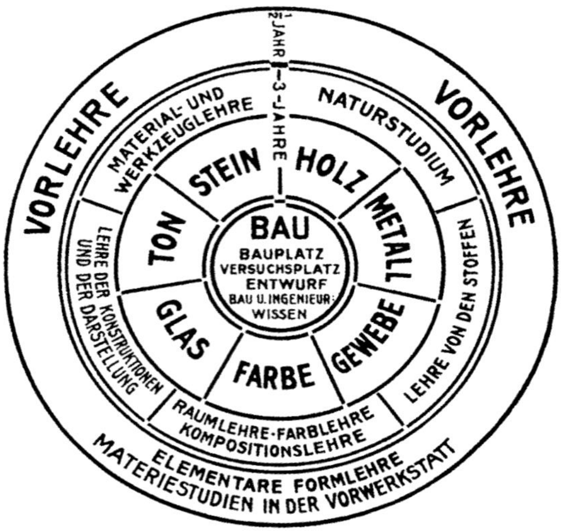


5.18 Walter Gropius et al., course structure at the Bauhaus.

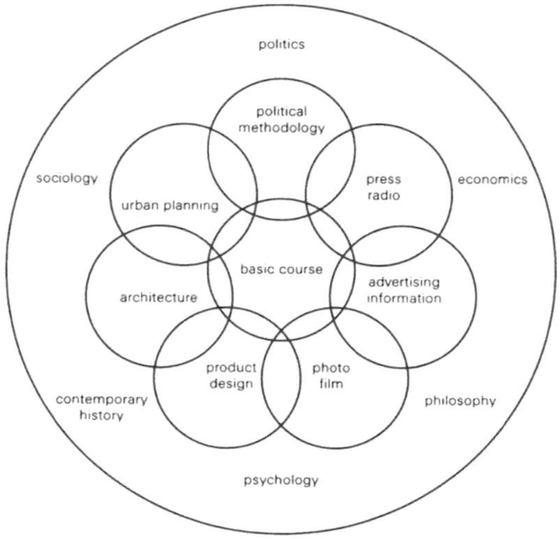


5.18 Tomás Maldonado et al., course structure at the Ulm Hochschule für Gestaltung.

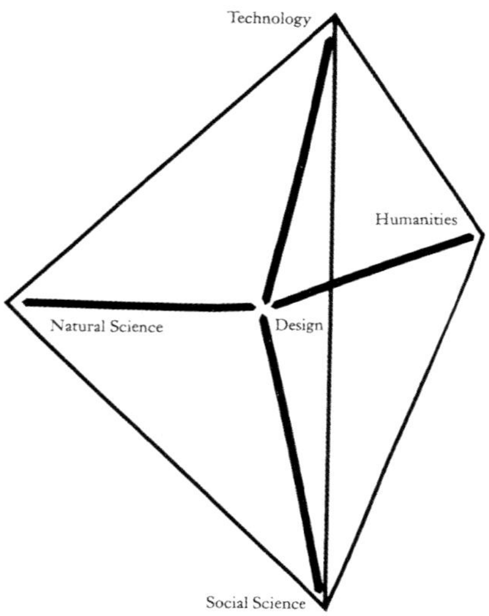


5.19 Serge Chermayeff, design as integration, 1962.

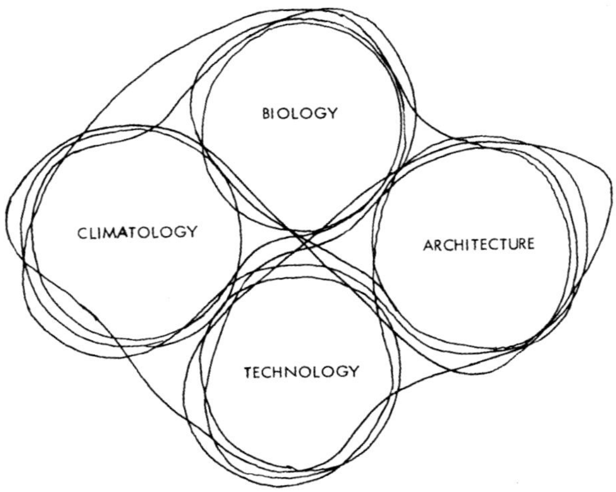


**31. Interlocking fields of climate balance.**

5.20 Victor Olgyay, "Interlocking Fields of Climate Balance," from *Design with Climate*, 1963.

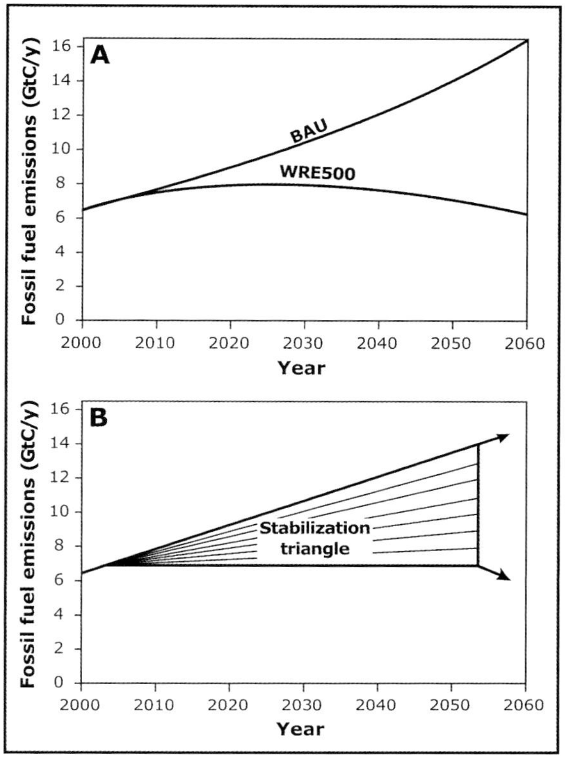


5.21 Stephen Pacala and Rob Socolow, "Stabilization Wedges: Solving the Climate Problem for the Next 50 Years with Current Technologies," 2004.

humanities, and the natural and social sciences (figure 5.19). Again, the project of design is seen to be one of integrating a range of heterogeneous inputs. Victor Olgyay rehearsed a similar set of interdisciplinary integrations in a diagram he titled "Interlocking Fields of Climate Balance," published in a number of contexts from 1955 (figure 5.20).

The 1951 Olgyay drawing, the depiction of flattening the temperature curve, is also visually reminiscent of Le Corbusier's solar path drawings (see figure 1.7), a modeling of the diurnal patterns that was seen to reflect the capacity to design according to these inexorable environmental conditions—"the sun rises, the sun sets." Le Corbusier repeated this image in a wide range of contexts and insisted that such solar patterns determined the context for architectural intervention.

The image also evokes a more recent description of *forcing* and *flattening*, one Robert Socolow and Steven Pacala proposed in 2004 as a means to drastically reduce carbon emissions (figure 5.21). Referred to as the "Stabilization Wedges," the image presents fifteen distinct strategies toward reducing the carbon footprint, all intended to solve "the climate problem for the next fifty years with current technologies." Set inside a graph indicating the increase in fossil fuel emission in a "business as usual" condition, seven out of the fifteen wedges would be needed to flatten out emissions and maintain stability in geophysical systems (and, by extension, social conditions). "Efficient buildings" is one wedge, indicating the need and possibility to "cut carbon emissions by one-fourth in buildings and appliances"; the primary obstacle to this goal is indicated as "weak incentives," which is something of a euphemism for the difficulty in adjusting expectations not only in architecture and the building industry but also among the public—no one is asking to be uncomfortable. Architecture could also be seen as relevant to the increase of photovoltaic solar, another wedge, of which "700 times the current capacity" was called for.[53] In a 2011 update, Socolow indicated that even more wedges would be necessary; one assumes that such an increase has only been exaggerated since.[54]

The stabilization wedges, which were popularized in Al Gore's 2009 film *An Inconvenient Truth* and in Elizabeth Kolbert's *Field Notes from a Catastrophe*, nicely summarize some of the challenges that resonate in analyzing climate-design-methodological images from the 1950s.[55] First, an image is meant to explain a general principle in order to spur *specific action*. It intends to communicate and instigate; as Flusser put it, "images are intended to serve as models for actions. . . . For although they show only the surfaces of things, they still show relationships among things that no one would otherwise suspect. Images don't show matter; they show what matters." Second, the goal of such a proposal is *stabilization*. They seek to maintain the status quo by new means. Flusser again: "If images were to become models for actions, they had to be made accessible, intersubjective, and they had to be stabilized."[56] Through countering a "business as usual" premise, the diagram nonetheless identifies how to keep social systems intact by virtue of technological innovation and application; it eschews any notions that instability, disruption, or other possible conditions of social transformation would have a role to play in climate management. It attempts to model and instigate. This is not to say that climate instability is preferable to such technological solutions.

The technical image becomes paramount in the Olgyays' work by the early 1950s and determines the trajectory of their reception. Much as Paul Siple hoped that the collaboration of the Climate Control Project could produce images that required no explanation for effective use in the design process, so did the Olgyays operate on an assumption that the effective figuration of a problem—in a diagram, on paper—could open up pathways to its eventual resolution in the sociobiotic sphere. Distinct from the diagrams focused on documenting or analyzing a specific architectural-climatic scenario—a graph, for example, that models the overheated periods of a given building's shape and orientation—methodological diagrams sought, however frustratingly, to operate on the profession, to draw together a range of intersubjective and quasi-objective parameters and relationships in order to produce a new approach to architecture in its processes and values.

This kind of image—contestations over the stability of the concept of the human amid a changing relationship to economic and ecological processes—was widespread. In a 1966 essay titled "The Economics of the Coming Spaceship Earth," the economist Kenneth Boulding placed his cultural moment "in the middle of a long process of transition of the nature of the image which man has of himself and his environment."[57] Boulding, who was then working with a think tank called Resources for the Future, was only partially concerned with the kind of drawn technical images of the architectural-climatic methodologists—constructed representations, physically manifest, usually in two dimensions. Such images are cultural objects, historical evidence, documents of intentions to express, engage, critique, or otherwise intervene in cultural practices or social norms. Boulding was interested in something else, a broader sort of media discourse that has been the foundation of a certain kind of environmentalism since.

Boulding's 1957 book *The Image: Knowledge in Life and Society* describes a sense of himself located in space and time (he is at Stanford University, in California, at the western edge of North America):

> I know that beyond the mountains that close my present horizon, there is a broad valley; beyond that a still higher range of mountains; beyond that other mountains, range upon range, until we come to the Rockies; beyond that the Great Plains and the Mississippi; beyond that the Alleghenies; beyond that the eastern seaboard; beyond that the Atlantic Ocean; beyond that is Europe; beyond that is Asia. I know, furthermore, that if I go far enough I have come back to where I am now. In other words, I have a picture of the earth as round. I visualize it as a globe.

He connects this planetary imaginary directly to new kinds of knowledge production, concluding:

> What I have been talking about is knowledge. Knowledge perhaps is not a good word for this. Perhaps one would rather say my *Image* of the world. Knowledge has the implication of validity, of truth. What I am talking about is what I believe to be true; my subjective knowledge. It is this Image that largely governs my behavior . . . *behavior depends on the image*.[58]

This last principle, of the image as guide to behavior, would be developed in the "Spaceship Earth" essay. Boulding discussed contrasting images—of the past and a possible future—that he hoped would condition collective behavior.[59]

The image was the site of ecological contestation. "Early civilizations," Boulding wrote in 1966, "imagined themselves to be living on a virtually illimitable plane." This conception of an endless frontier, where there was always somewhere to go if resources ran out or social structures failed, Boulding termed "the cowboy economy." He placed this in stark contrast to the image of the "spaceman economy," in which, as he wrote, "man has been accustoming himself to the notion of the spherical earth and a closed sphere of human activity," the world as a closed system, "without unlimited reservoirs of anything."[60]

This closed system was most famously imaged in the late 1960s through the so-called Blue Marble photographs taken by Apollo astronauts starting in 1968, looking back at the earth from space. These images were published across the cultural spectrum, from the *Whole Earth Catalog* to *Time* magazine, and they immediately became "symbols of the shared home and fate of all humanity," as a recent historian has put it.[61] What Boulding believed to be true in 1957—his subjective sense of the earth as round—was by 1966 an objective imperative, an instigation for the development of new knowledge about the earth, its social

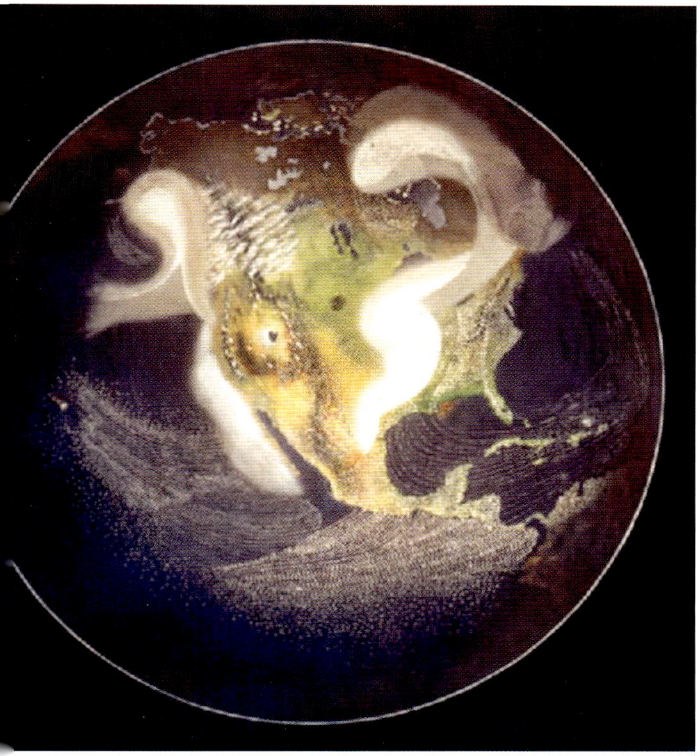

5.22 "A 1954 Color Painting of Weather Systems Viewed from a Future Satellite," commissioned by Henry Wexler, 1954.

and economic systems, and the implications of interconnectivity.

Although scientists had long been producing images to facilitate inquiry into these complex dynamics, in the decades following World War II such efforts intensified, eventually pointing more explicitly to the need to adjust human behaviors toward managing a limited resource condition. The "Spaceship Earth" essay intended to articulate a new approach to how ways of being in the world could reflect this new collective self-conception—both a cultural and a techno-material phenomenon, engaged in the systems of social operations. Images of the globe, mental or physical, were thus also concerned with the "state of the human bodies and minds that are included in the system," as Boulding noted. At stake were the new ideas about the human that these images could invoke and the new social patterns and individual behaviors that they were seen to encourage.[62]

Boulding's call for a new image economy of "man and environment," in both 1957 and 1966, was not articulated on terms directly legible to the Olgyays' research, it resonates across their ambitions. They were also interested in forms of representation that sought to clarify the possible social, material, and economic relationships that would result from these innovations. It was through these images that new design methods attempted to conceptualize relationships and encourage new ideas about how to live. Diagrams were instruments, tools for historical change. Boulding's claim to universality as well as his invocation of the centrality of the figure of "man" in conceiving of this new image would also be expressed in the Olgyays' images and writings.

Concern over the role of images and visual narratives in encouraging socioenvironmental change has again come to the fore. The environmental humanist Rob Nixon, for example, suggests that "climate change, the thawing cryosphere, toxic drift, biomagnification, deforestation, the radioactive aftermath of wars, acidifying oceans, and a host of other slowly unfolding environmental catastrophes present formidable representational obstacles that can hinder our efforts to mobilize and act decisively"; that is, the slow and aggregative nature of these environmental threats are, quite simply, difficult to see, and thus difficult to bring to public attention.[63] Media strategies are required to intervene in this process and make these conditions legible.[64] The terms of the crisis are distinct, yet a similar interest infuses the Olgyays' methodological drawings as they attempted to model, for architects and other interested professionals, the seemingly invisible parameters of climate and the potential for climatic analysis to reimagine the shape of relationships to the natural world—although, like Boulding, the Olgyays' analysis assumed a normalized subject within the planetary interior (figure 5.22).

Boulding's article can be seen as symptomatic of anxieties, then still nascent, about how lifestyles of consumption might negatively affect environmental conditions, limiting the possibility of individual and social development. New ideas about the human necessarily accompanied the widespread interest in exploring the potential for resource transformations through design and building practices—people were being conditioned, first by shading systems, soon by mechanical systems. Images were frequently deployed to encourage new ways of thinking about familiar social patterns.

5.23 Jean Labatut et al., the Princeton Architectural Laboratory, Princeton, New Jersey, 1948, view of the daylighting dome.

5.24 Jean Labatut et al., the Princeton Architectural Laboratory, Princeton, New Jersey, 1948, view of the building with student experiments.

5.25 Jean Labatut et al., the Princeton Architectural Laboratory, Princeton, New Jersey, 1948, louver analyses in The Cage.

5.26 Jean Labatut et al., the Princeton Architectural Laboratory, Princeton, New Jersey, 1948, view of an early model for Fuller's World Game in The Cage.

## The Laboratory and the Method

When the Olgyays were brought to Princeton in 1952, to work on the curtain wall research mentioned previously, they were hired as "research professors." They set up shop at the Princeton Architectural Laboratory (PAL), a small building converted from a horse stable. It sat behind the football field, a ten-minute walk from the School of Architecture. The PAL was designed by the architect and historian Jean Labatut in 1947. He renovated the stables and added a significant annex—a glass cube at one end of the building, appropriate for daylighting studies, known as The Cage (figure 5.23; figure 5.24).[65] The Lab was seen by chair Robert McLaughlin as an important site for all kinds of architectural research, some of which focused on the interest in the environment then emergent—for instance, an early version of R. Buckminster Fuller's World Game was played at the Lab in the mid-1950s. The Lab was the location for the Olgyays' intensive research into climate design methods (figure 5.25; figure 5.26).

The Lab was an essential part of their teaching as well. They argued successfully for the insertion of a Plexiglas dome to increase the Lab's capacity for precise daylighting research, and they also proposed to build a more complex climate modeling device so as to better assess the performative potential of a given design. Victor's teaching in particular focused simultaneously on practical experiments, methodological explorations, and careful reviews of relevant literature. He framed his course Climate and Architectural Regionalism as follows

> The primary task of architecture is to act in man's favor; to interpose itself between man and his natural environment in order to remove the environmental load from his shoulders. The fundamental task of architecture is thus to lighten the very stress of life, to maximize man's energies and permit him to focus on spiritual tasks and aims. The thesis of this course is that this interposition between man and his climatic environment is the physiological basis of health and comfort in architecture.

He continued:

> Man's relationship to his environment is affected in our era by rapid and dramatic changes. Technology, along with physical and cultural communication, transforms the face of the earth; new territories emerge; new countries enter the political theater, awakening hitherto neglected problems, bringing with them a new sense of world-wide interdependence.

The course brief included an extensive collection of mostly technical literature of relevance to the course, what he called "a bibliography of climatic effects."[66]

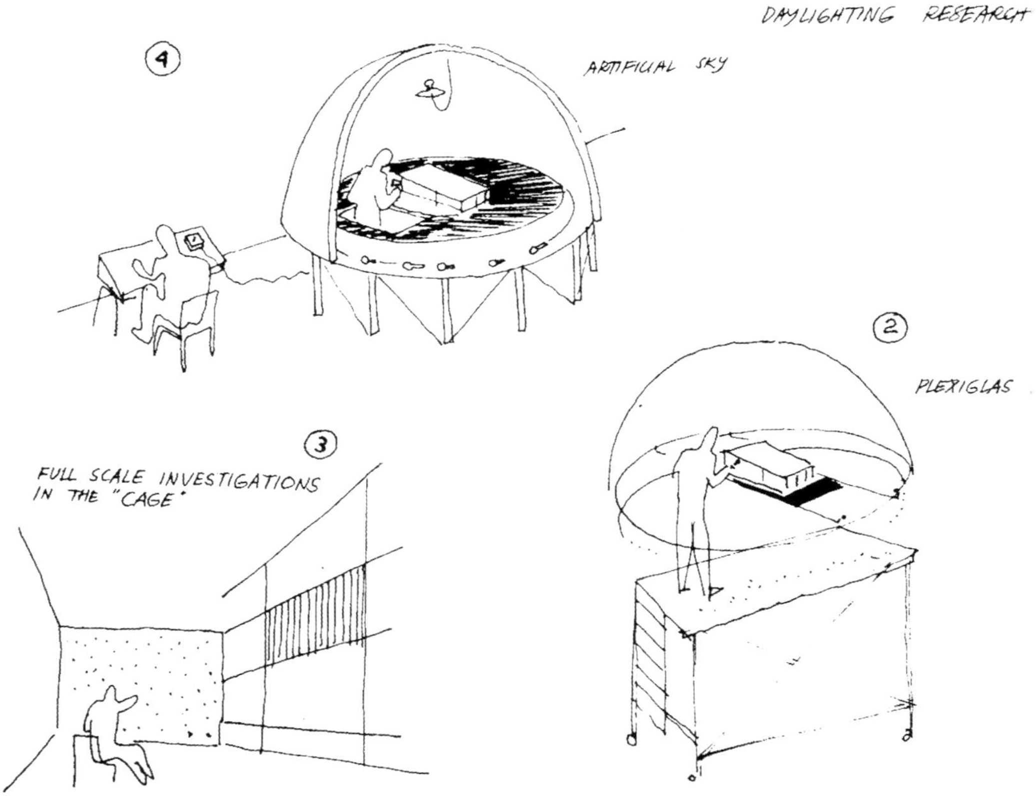


5.27 Olgyay and Olgyay, Daylighting Research from "Preliminary Outline of the Proposed Program at the Architectural Laboratory," 1953.

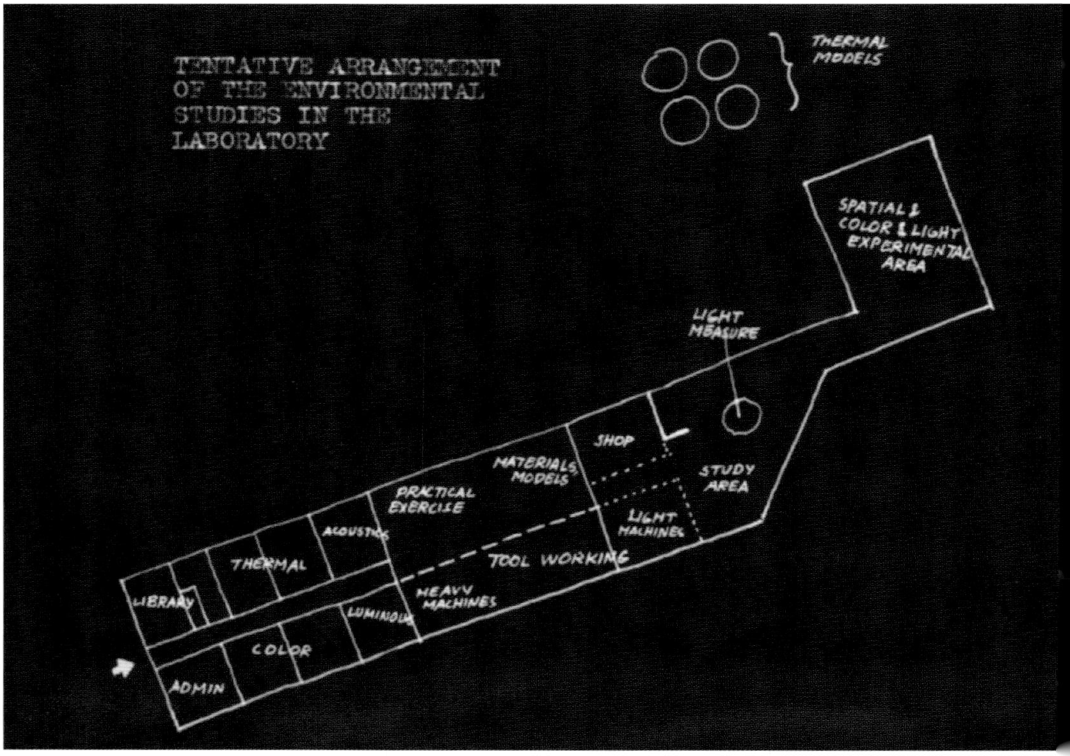


5.28 Olgyay and Olgyay, "Tentative Arrangement of the Environmental Studies in the Laboratory," from "Preliminary Outline of the Proposed Program at the Architectural Laboratory," 1953.

Their proposed program for research, submitted to McLaughlin in 1953, was ambitious (figure 5.27; figure 5.28). On practical terms, it involved integrating daylighting and thermal issues as well as exploring the sonic environment in order to get a fuller picture of how the design interventions they were interested in modeling could be synthesized into a general pedagogical and professional program. On conceptual terms, as they wrote:

> The intention is to develop fully an area of knowledge which heretofore has not been systematically explored: the relationship between Man, his Environment, and Building. Many discursive generalities have been made on the subject, hardly any of them more than intuitive. It is imperative that more basic premises, founded on the results of systematic research, be established in determining the relationships characteristic of Man and Environment; when this is done and made available, we shall have the basic premise for Architecture. From this solid foundation, Architecture will then be in a position to express not only the needs but the aspirations of man.[67]

This proposal document also contained another version of the design method diagram. Needs and aspirations, again, a release from a certain kind of shackled living, a cohabitation with environment that catalyzes a positive transformation to the human.

Working at the Laboratory, the Olgyays produced a complex method to correlate a building to its climatic conditions—one that engaged in a range of innovations in the architectural and environmental sciences, and one that relied on images and diagrams to communicate both fact and aspiration. The Olgyays operated on the premise that Boulding was simultaneously proposing—that the way in which they conceived of, imagined, and represented the relationship between humans and the environment was central to the social patterns, material conditions, and professional processes that would allow individuals to live comfortably within it. Their diagrams provide evidence of an image in transition in form and content, message and medium, while an image of the human was placed in a new relationship to the planet (figure 5.29).

Although concerned with the local and global dynamics of climate patterns, in the plans, diagrams, and methods developed by the Olgyays at the Lab, the figure of the human was central—literally, rendered in the middle of images intending to illustrate the challenges and benefits of a climatic architectural approach; conceptually, as the figure of the new possibilities that these architectures could allow. The example in figure 5.30 draws the human figure surrounded by a range of heterogeneous factors—moral, historical, thermal, sonic, and spatial, among others. The role of architecture, this diagram proposes, was to filter these factors and align them with human needs through new design strategies. "Man," the Olgyays wrote, "with his intimate physical and emotional needs, remains the module—the central measure—in all approaches. The success of every design must be measured by its total effect on the *human* environment."[68] Versions of this diagram accompanied many of their architectural drawings and methodological proposals, serving to illustrate the method itself, and also to clarify that their project was to produce a universal comfort zone, a designed condition seen to be most amenable to human habitation

Also significant in the Olgyays quote is the slippage from "Man . . . and his needs" to "the human environment," a shift that begins to hint at a rhetorical transformation from a gendered though univocal condition of the male subject to a more nuanced consideration of the species—human, anthros—as having identifiable and universal needs. "Man" and "humanism" were ciphers for a much wider reconsideration of the social and technological forces aimed at improving social conditions in the decades following World War II. Indeed, the notion was ubiquitous. Edward Steichen's exhibition on *The Family of Man* was of the most straightforward; opening at the Museum of Modern Art in 1955 and touring globally for the rest of the decade, images of individuals across a geographic and sociocultural spectrum were brought together to affirm a global consistency to the human condition.[69] In a similar vein, the German émigré psychoanalyst Erich Fromm discussed the possibility of a "Science of Man" that, as he saw it, would better realize the potential of the species through "making the world a human one."[70] In the invocations of man, humanism, and the imperatives of human rights, an idea about the human was asserted as able to, through technology or the force of ideas, have an impact on both environmental and social conditions. Images, diagrams, were, again, essential to these possible transformations.

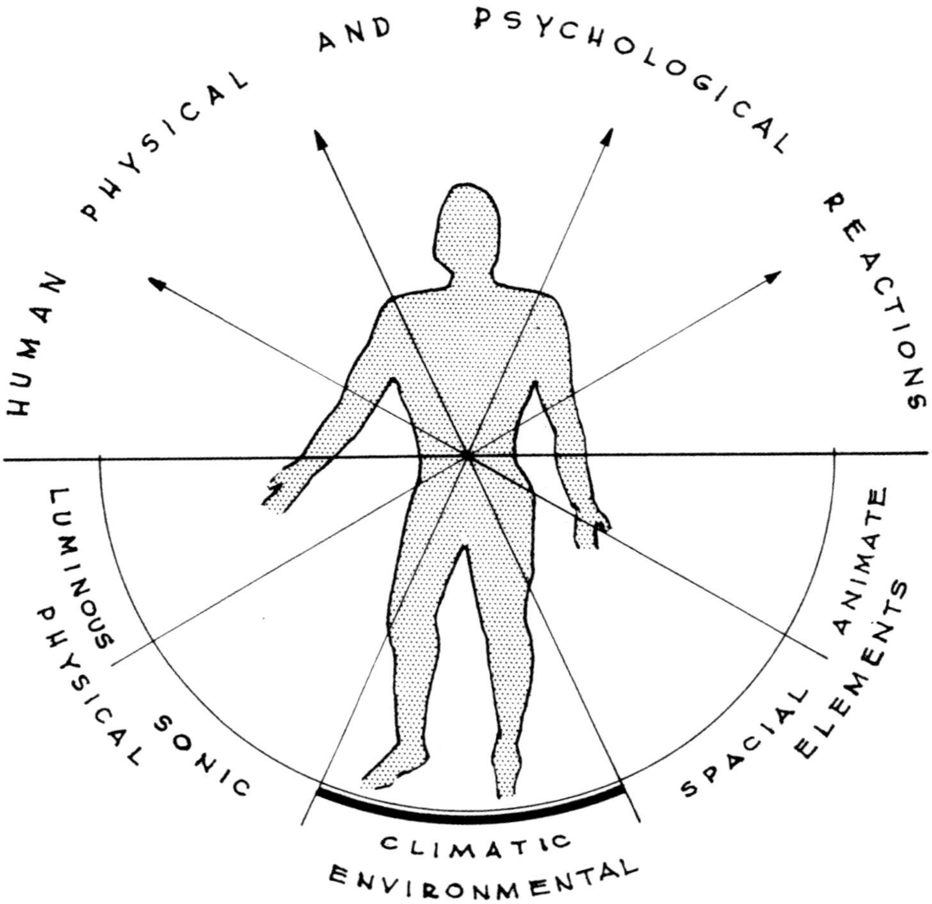


5.29 Victor and Aladar Olgyay, "Man as the Central Measure in Architecture," 1955.

In postwar architectural discussions, this interest in the universal condition of the human, and in how design could improve that condition, was also widespread. The Finnish architect Alvar Aalto spoke of "a broader, new purpose for architecture" focused on the field's capacity to provide a "softening human touch" that could mediate the anxiety of the postwar world in the face of the potentially alienating forces of technology and scientific knowledge (figure 5.31).[71] Rudolf Wittkower's *Architectural Principles in the Age of Humanism* (1952) and Colin Rowe's essay on "The Mathematics of the Ideal Villa" (1949) also appealed to a universal conception of the human, derived from the Renaissance, as a means to encourage new ways of building.[72] Rowe relied on diagrammatic analyses to establish a historical continuity up to the present. Simultaneously, Le Corbusier proposed his *Modulor* system in the late 1940s, updating the Vitruvian man as a framework for modern design.[73] The Olgyays' research into the dynamic between humans and climate participated in this reconstruction of universal architectural principles; Le Corbusier was the touchstone for their figuration of the human and for their climatic architectural techniques.

The Olgyays' images attempted to make the connection between increasingly specific knowledge about regional climate and the direct effect that this analysis could have on the form and orientation of a building (figure 5.32). They considered the relevant solar angles on each possible façade exposure, the use of shade trees, and the capacity of different materials to respond to these conditions in different ways; a shading system was also proposed to compensate for the inevitable

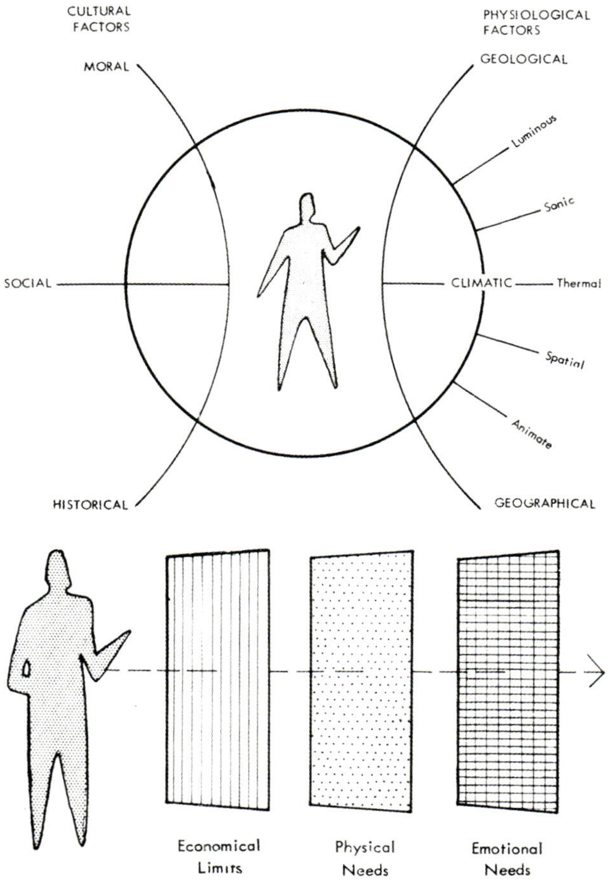


5.30 Victor and Aladar Olgyay, "Factors Influencing Architectural Expression," from *Solar Control and Shading Devices*, 1957.

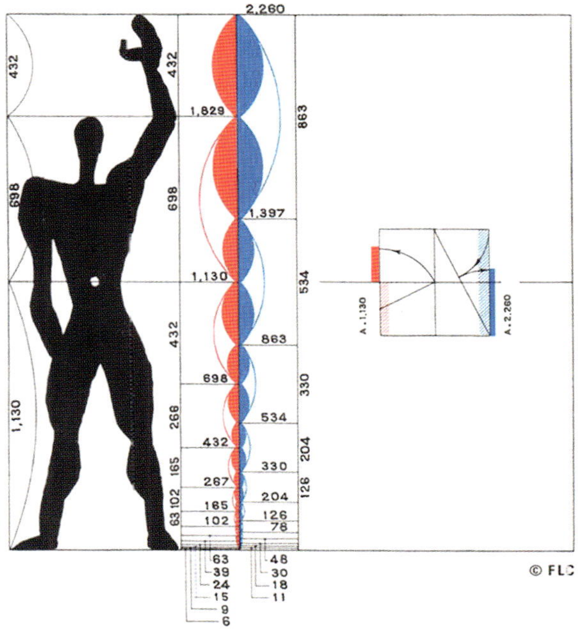


5.31 Le Corbusier, from *The Modulor II*, 1955.

complications amid these numerous factors. This sequential and diagrammatically informed methodological process developed a conception about the human that was at once delicate and static, as a sort of force of stabilization amid the unstable transformation of ideas about the environment.

The basic premise of the method, summarized in the diagram of figure 5.2, was to collect climatic data, evaluate it, integrate it into new diagrammatic representational methods, and then use these intermediate diagrams as parameters for formal, material, and site-related decisions in the design process. There were a number of phases. The first involved contacting climatologists to gather data on the building site in question. The second phase focused on evaluation and new kinds of representational tools.

Of special interest was the "bioclimatic index," which mapped temperature averages and extremes as well as factors of humidity and wind velocity (figure 5.33). The y-axis on the chart represented temperature, the x-axis, humidity; the upper dotted line, angled as it responds to both temperature and humidity, indicated a limit beyond which there is danger of sunstroke; the lower dotted line was simply labeled "freezing line." The center line was speculative, or at least contingent, suggesting how a shading system cut through these extremes and neutralized them—it sat at the bottom of the oddly shaped "comfort zone."

In the "Bioclimatic Registration of Climate Data" we can read some of its instrumental aspirations (figure 5.34). The dots each represented hourly data points, which would be different for each

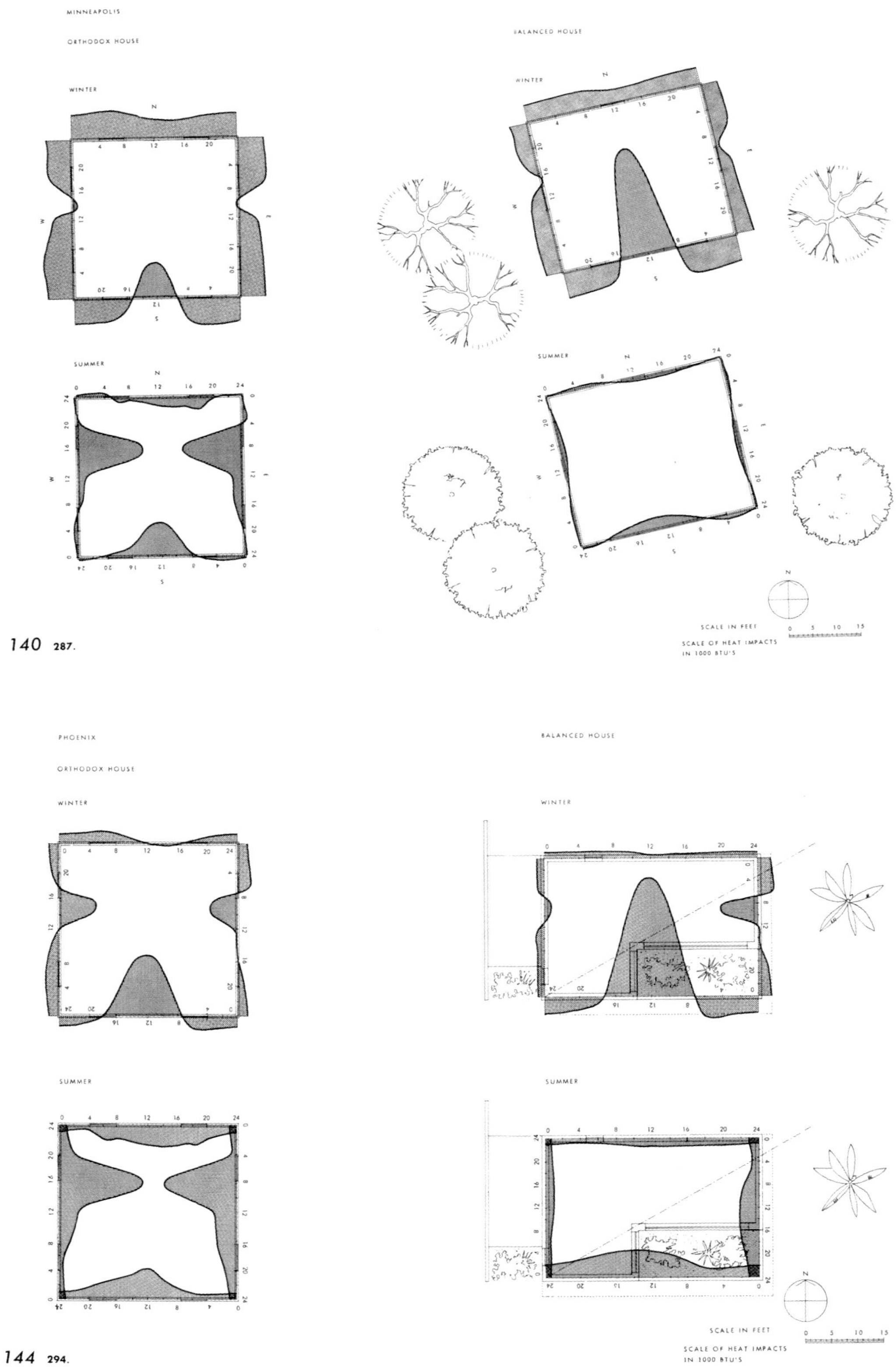


5.32 Victor Olgyay, analysis of "building shape" in Minneapolis and Phoenix; from *Design with Climate*, 1963.

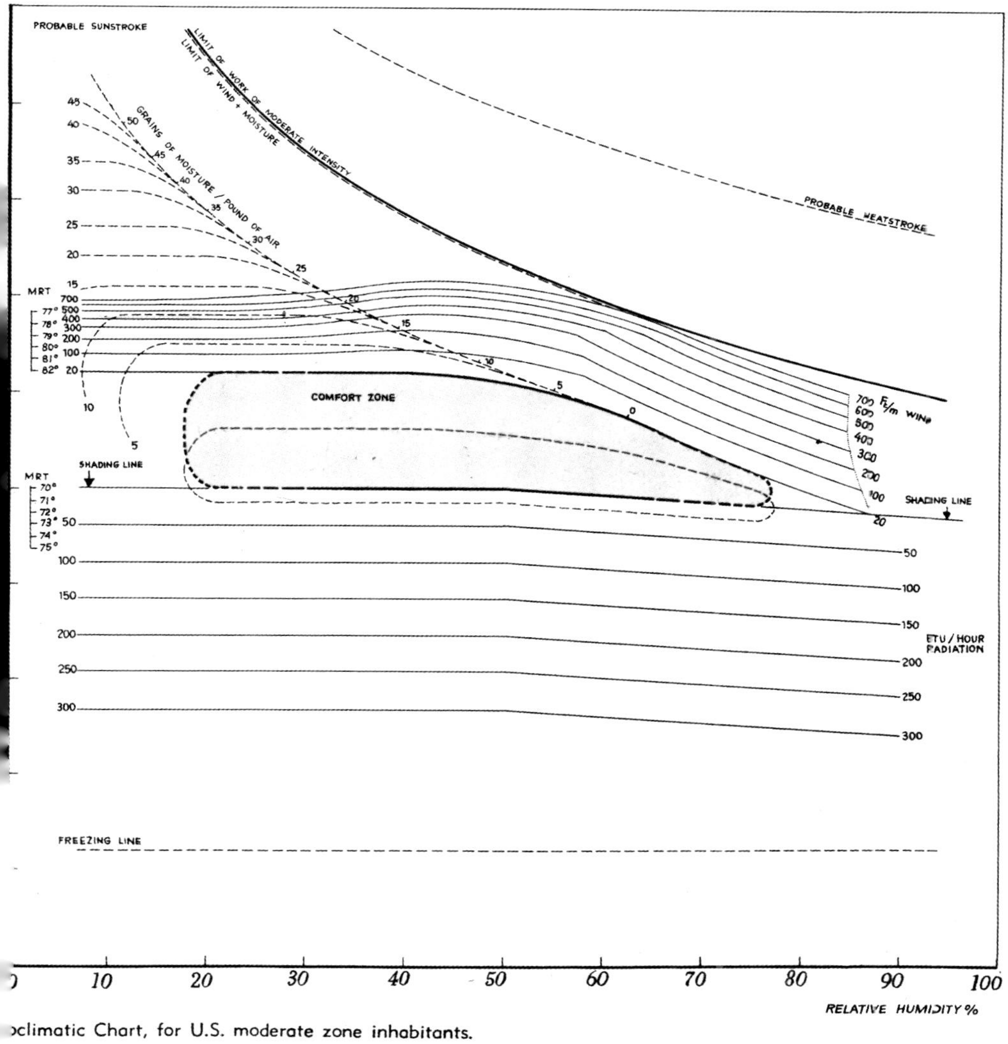


5.33 Victor and Aladar Olgyay, a "bioclimatic index," from *Design with Climate*, 1963.

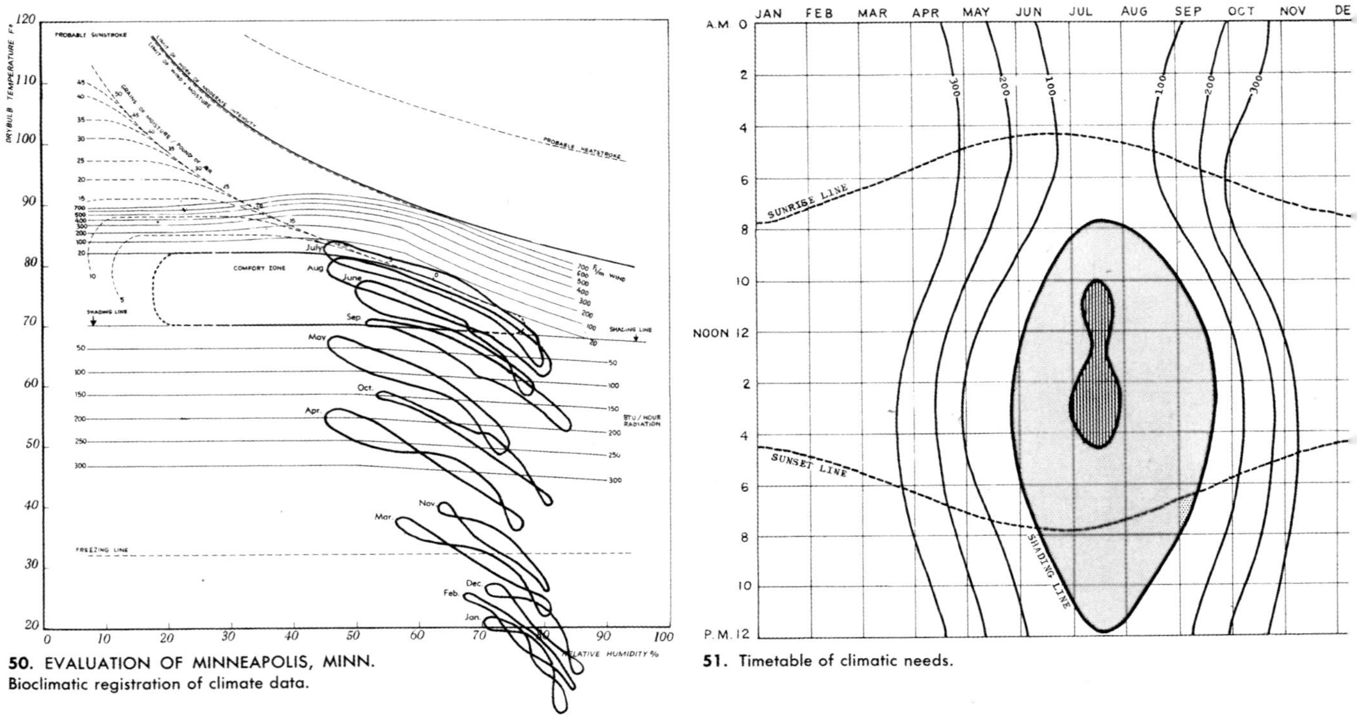


5.34 Victor Olgyay, "Bioclimatic Registration of Climate Data," from *Design with Climate*, 1963.

region. These data points were then translated into drawn shapes for each month, arranged across the graph to show their relative coextension with the comfort zone in a nonmanipulated state. An accompanying drawing interpreted this chart as a "timetable of climatic needs," with the dark areas in the center showing the overheated periods—June to August, not surprisingly—that required a focused shading approach.[74]

The bioclimatic chart was a refined version of the psychrometric charts that had been in use in mechanical comfort analyses from the 1920s, discussed previously in the context of corporate and ASHVE research on air conditioning. The bioclimatic chart focused on relative comfort, and, unlike psychrometric charts, attempted to take radiation effects and wind into account. "This chart shows the comfort zone in the center," the Olgyays wrote in 1963, "the climatic elements around it are shown by means of curves which indicate the nature of corrective measures necessary to restore the feeling of comfort at any point outside the comfort zone."[75] Suggesting the distinction of their research from that of those focused on mechanical systems, they also asserted that while mechanical conditioning was calibrated to the "middle of thermal neutrality," when a building's ambient environment was balanced, "the criterion was adapted that conditions wherein the average person will not experience the feeling of discomfort can constitute the perimeter of the comfort zone."[76] A seeming tautology, but in effect a flexible apparatus of human adaptation and architectural optimization that allows for comfortable inhabitation in a range of climates, according to a dizzying number of factors that their books meticulously lay out.

In the third phase, that of calculation, site-specific shading needs were translated again, this time onto a "sun mask," one of the most recognizable diagram types deployed in their work. This diagram was derived from the relationship, in plan and section, to seasonal solar incidence. Again, the darkened sector of the mask correlated to a specific approach to shading, as suggested in the "Vocabulary of Shading Devices"; each specific site required a specific approach to shading (figure 5.35). One can again detect, in this assembly of charts, a proto-computational system, in which

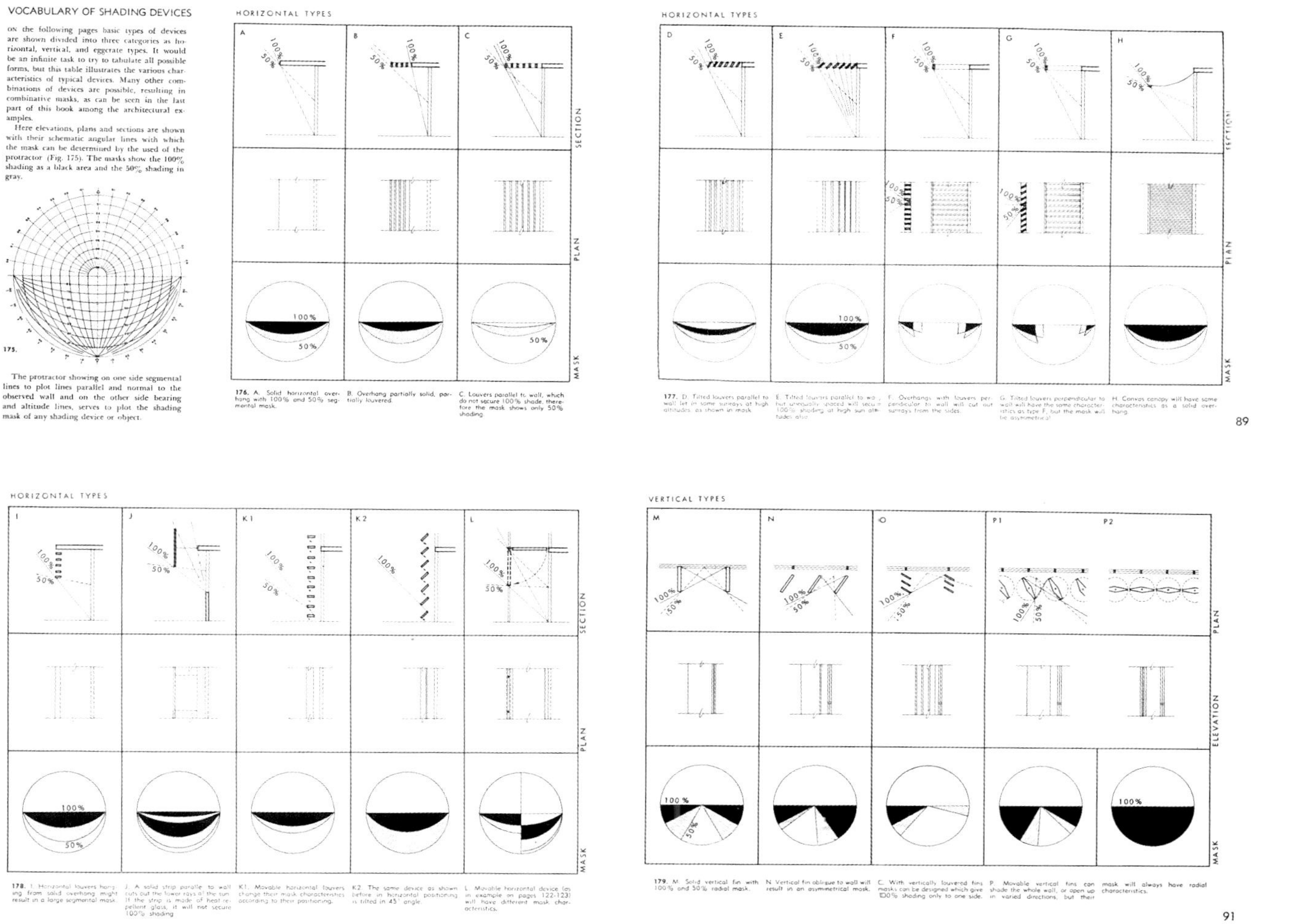


5.35 Victor and Aladar Olgyay, "Vocabulary of Shading Devices," from *Solar Control and Shading Devices*, 1957.

the climate aspects of the site are analyzed and then related to a specific shading treatment.

The third phase also looked at orientation, wind, the effect of different materials on possible overheating, and a number of other issues that the Olgyays played out in detail elsewhere. The fourth phase then explored the findings of the diagrams and image indexes from phase three, and compared them and evaluated the differences through a number of diagramming techniques. For example, the "timetable of climatic needs" could also be mapped onto orientation studies to determine the best building shape—square, a long rectangle, or other variations. In this and other instances, data-driven analysis led directly to formal parameters, sometimes intending to suggest balanced or harmonious patterns, sometimes intended to reflect how specific shapes were appropriate to the specific climate conditions. Finally, the fifth and sixth phases began to lead the architect closer to familiar territory, including careful analysis of the historical examples provided in *Solar Control and Shading Devices*, and a number of analytic diagramming techniques intended to bring all of these factors (and a few others) to bear on the specific design needs of a given project (figure 5.36).

The conceptualization of the comfort zone and the means to attain it through architectural means relied on a research framework for architecture and also on a specific conception of the human—one of stability, normalization, and optimization. In the "Schematic Bioclimatic Index," the human is figured in the center, relaxing on a modern chaise

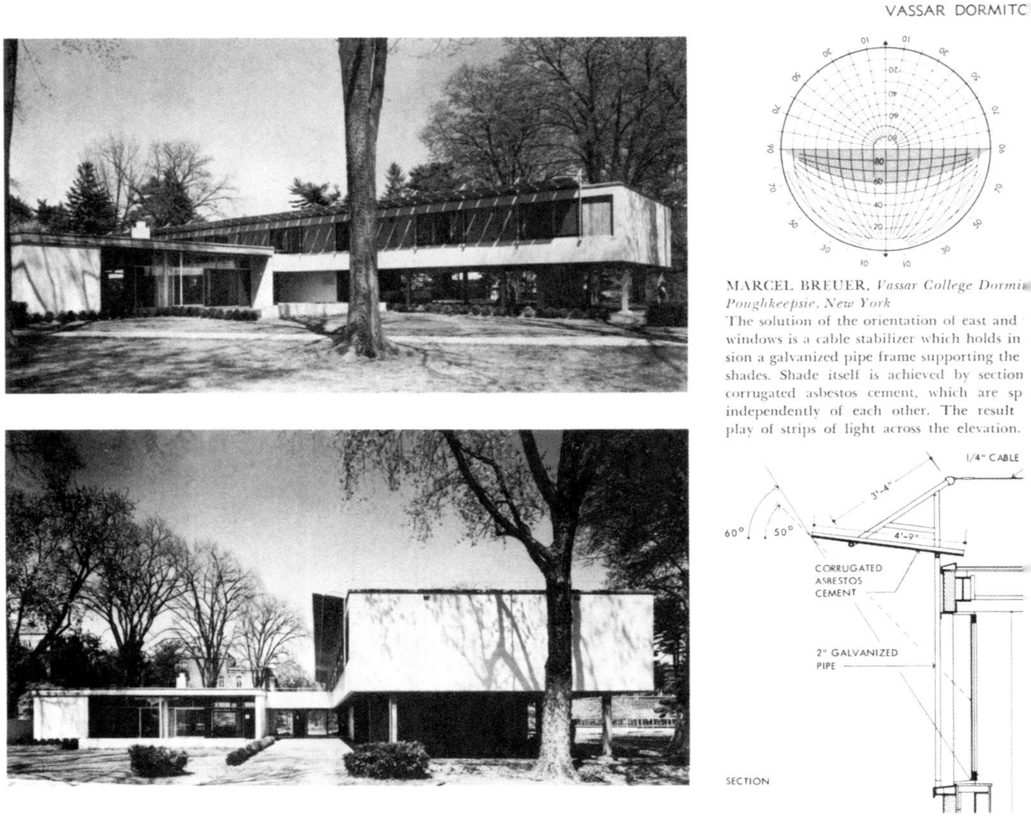


5.36 Marcel Breuer, *Ferry Cooperative Dormitory*, Vassar College, Poughkeepsie, New York, 1951, from Olgyay and Olgyay, *Solar Control and Shading Devices,* 1957.

lounge, smoking a pipe, reading the newspaper and completely at ease—without irritation, without having to experience any of the also possible climatic variables that surround and threaten him (figure 5.37). The human is imaged and imagined as a stable, protected figure. He—it is clearly a male figure—is solid in the experience of well-designed space, consistent across changes in the elements that the past, present, or future can bring. In 1957, this diagram suggests, the image of man's relationship to his environment is more than anything one of stasis—a stasis and position of normativity that was, importantly, constructed through carefully considered architectural methods, and that, even more importantly, would be codified and regulated by the air-conditioning industry and exported to sealed curtain wall buildings around the world.

What should we make of this image of stasis, and its potential effects? First of all, it becomes clear that all of these diagrams were drawn in order to identify and celebrate the new possible conditions for the human that a climate-focused architecture could bring about—a realization of human potential through architecture. On the one hand, a static climatic interior had long been the dream of modern architectural interventions—Le Corbusier's premise, again, of a time when "every building, around the globe, will be 18 degrees."[77] On the other hand, the astounding complexity of the Olgyays' method is indicative of how difficult it was to design such a climate-sensitive interior and to manage thermal comfort in the period before the widespread availability of HVAC systems. Thus also a question to contemporary practice—does the computer allow enough correlative power and flexibility to overcome reliance on fossil fuels?

These diagrams are hybrids, concerned with affect and instrumentality. As methodological diagrams they activate a disciplinary agenda and operate as a means for architecture to navigate and realign a number of analogous relationships: that between the interior of a building and its site, between the inhabitants of a building and the weather outside, between the climatic analysis and architecture (figure 5.38; figure 5.39). These relationships are imagined as a dome of protection—"the project of man's needs" as the caption

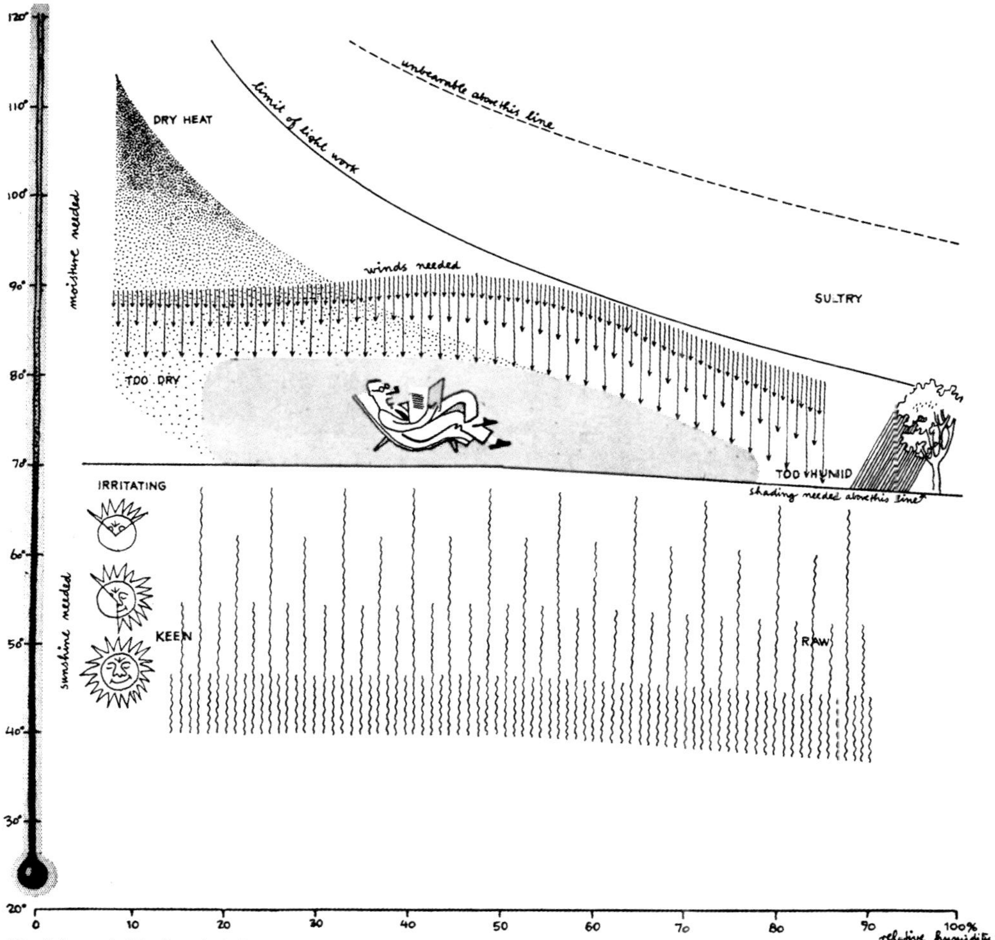


46. Schematic bioclimatic index.

5.37 Victor Olgyay, "Schematic Bioclimatic Index," from *Design with Climate*, 1963.

of figure 5.39 reads, "should be the shelter with calculated surfaces of transmitting, absorbing, filtering or repelling characteristics of the environmental factors," a premise that Victor Olgyay later called the "Theoretical Approach to Balanced Shelter."[78] They were concerned to specify the forms, materials, and orientations that can translate this balanced climatic dome into a real, built condition. The images operate as an appeal to the technological disposition and the aesthetic intentions of midcentury designers, encouraging them to realize the apparent promise of architecture as a shelter in this wide sense: as the provision of comfort that can, in turn, realize the potential of the humans that inhabit it.

This appears at first to be a utopian premise—an argument, in diagrammatic form, for containing the human and isolating the species from the unpredictability of the natural world. Although enmeshed in the pitfalls of a well-meaning humanism, their positioning between the aesthetic, the scientific, and the disciplinary still suggests a profound aspiration for encouraging transformation—for how this new quasi-technical perspective on the parameters of the design process can lead to new kinds of architectural expertise and new modes for inhabiting the globe. But still, what kind of aspiration is at play? What sort of future did these diagrams imagine?

## The Predicament of Mankind

This last question is complicated by the fact that, almost as soon as it was articulated, the Olgyays' specific "image of the relationship between man and his environment" began to fade away. For one thing, their research had a mixed reception in postwar architectural culture; their method

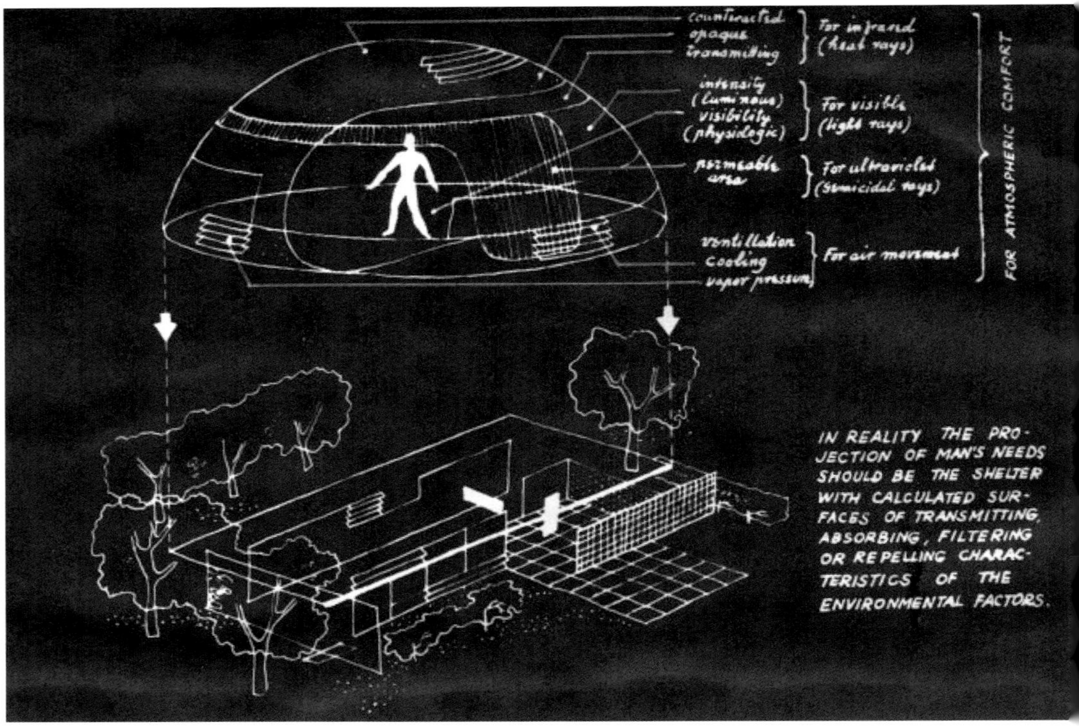


5.38 Victor and Aladar Olgyay, untitled image from "Preliminary Outline of Proposed Program at the Architectural Laboratory," 1953.

was taught in numerous schools, and they were embraced by many prominent architects—as consultants and colleagues. Their influence was limited by a fundamental architectural bias: that the technological determination, under the name of environment, of any aspect of a building design ultimately had the effect of frustrating an architect's expressive voice.[79] The Olgyays were working at Princeton amid an emergent architectural postmodernism in which new forms would be derived from historical examples rather than according to innovations in the understanding of complex building functions. Perhaps of most significance, the convergence of available energy and more efficient and affordable mechanical conditioning technology overwhelmed their delicate attempts at designed transformation.

The Olgyays' focus on design research, all the same, and their ability to garner independent funding from corporations, foundations, and nongovernmental organizations, helped to reposition architecture in relationship to other departments in the university context. This was especially the case as the new field of Architectural Science tried to find a place alongside climatic and environmental research.

Here as well, their fit amid these other fields was awkward; in particular, their apparent dedication to the centralized figure of the human was

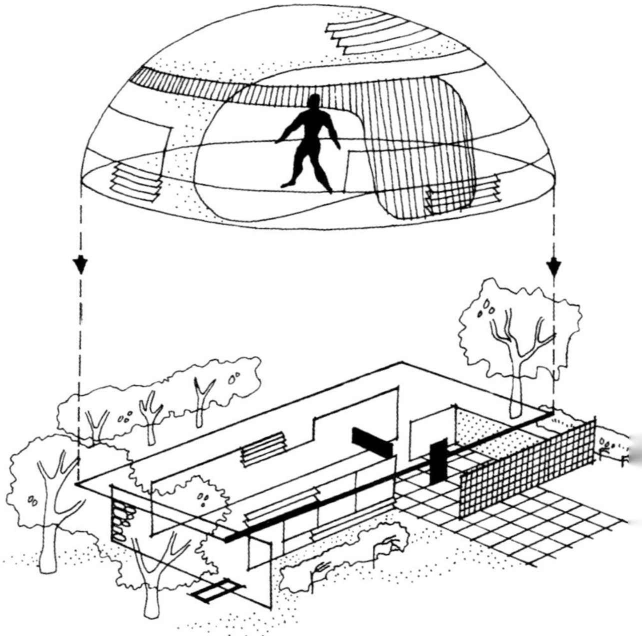

5.39 Victor Olgyay, "Theoretical Approach to Balanced Shelter," from *Design with Climate*, 1963.

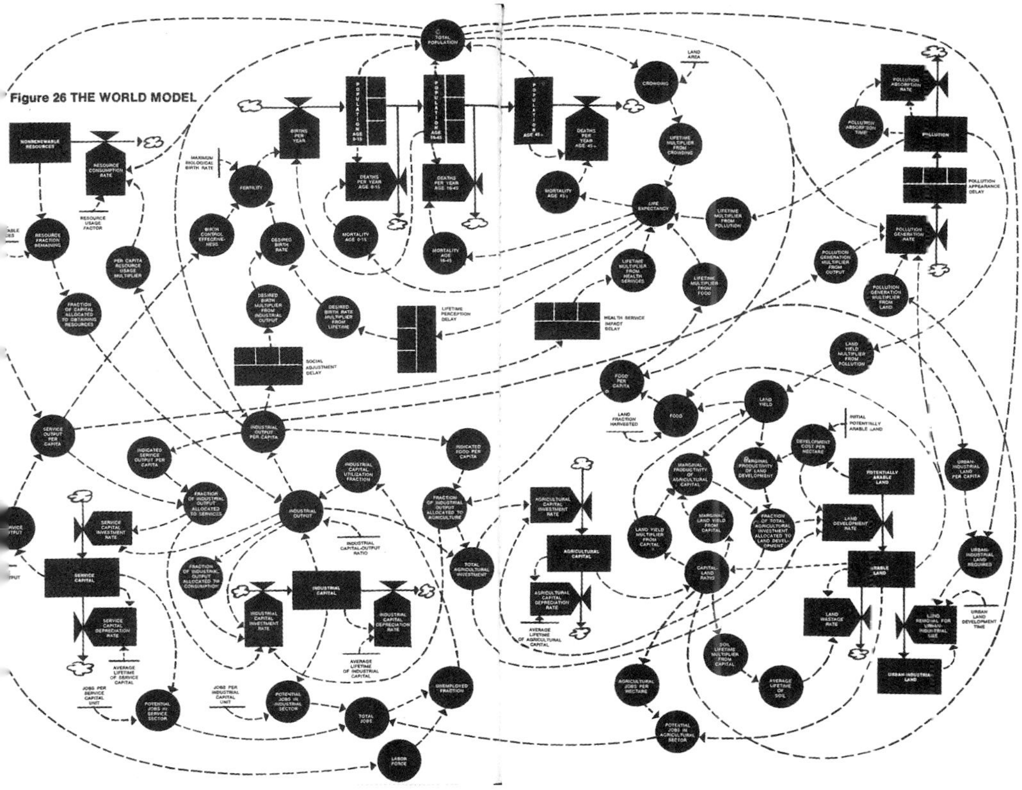


5.40 The "World Model" produced by Donatella Meadows and the "Group for the Study of the Predicament of Mankind" at MIT, 1964–69 (published in *Limits to Growth*, 1971).

soon eclipsed in many adjacent discussions, as technical images proliferated that modeled socio-biotic relationships on different terms. So, another historical misalignment—the comfort zone that the Olgyays articulated, and that simultaneously became the object of ASHRAE research—was rooted in human-to-climate relationship of fixity and centrality rather than flexibility, dynamism, and adaptation; this premise of adaptability was reconfigured almost immediately in the ecological and behavioral sciences, but not embedded in the path dependencies of mechanical cooling.

Just down the street from the Olgyays' lab, at the Princeton Institute for Advanced Study, the Hungarian émigré physicist John von Neumann was running the Meteorology Project, exploring computational methods of weather prediction. Computational, not proto-computational. The project was just beginning to reach an understanding of the complexity of the planetary climate system and the difficulty of representing and modeling it.[80] Von Neumann's computational efforts were facilitated through the increase in climate data that resulted from the International Geophysical Year, a global scientific initiative that, from 1957 to 1959, greatly expanded knowledge of earth, ocean, and atmospheric systems.[81] Related images of the relationship between "man and environment," also reliant on the availability of more and new kinds of data, were being developed in the young science of ecology, as suggested in the painted image of weather patterns discussed previously (see figure 5.22). Ecological analyses were interested in tracing "man's" capacity to disturb an existing set of interconnected energetic pathways. Chains of energy as they flowed through the ecosystem were in part the result of human influence; the effects of these interventions by "man as a manipulator" also affected humans in their animal state, according to their biological needs.[82] Ecology, as it was schematically figured, relied on a dual positioning of "man," now de-centered, and a new image of species relations.

By the early 1960s, new research, based on entering ever more data into increasingly powerful computers, also began to develop alternatives to the premise that all ecosystems inherently work toward a state of balance.[83] Instead of a progression to a peak condition, such models conceived of the world in a state of constant flux and subject to human intervention. The "world model" imaged by the Group for the Study of the Predicament of

Mankind, working with the Systems Dynamics Group at MIT in the 1960s, for example, presented a system of variable inputs and outputs, subject to bottlenecks and stoppages, with complex and, ultimately, unpredictable consequences (figure 5.40).[84] This "limits to growth" model came to maturity simultaneous to, and in dialogue with, Boulding's conception of the closed sphere of spaceship earth; it also came under much scrutiny, largely for implicit assumptions about the technological capacities of emerging economies.[85] It was nonetheless representative of a significant shift, of an environmentalism no longer focused on "the long-lost fellowship and intimacy between man and other living things," and concerned instead with producing models and images of ecological interdependence so as to increase technological efficiencies and, at least in some iterations, reduce social inequity.[86] The world model in fact modeled, in new ways, a political approach—however fraught, partial, and biased—to socioenvironmental problems. Ultimately, much like the Olgyays' figure relaxing on the chaise, the world modelers were working toward their own idealized model of a steady state economy in which intensive government regulation would allow economic expansion to occur in concert with the management of environmental goods and bads.[87]

## Technology and the Ahistorical

Much more could be said about the Olgyays and their legacy—their buildings and consultations, their research for the United Nations, their influence, directly and indirectly, on subsequent generations of practitioners and pedagogues. Victor Olgyay's research in Colombia and Argentina, funded by the Rockefeller Foundation and the United Nations, respectively, allowed him to play out ideas about climate and house design in a tropical region attentive to the needs and technologies of shading—in Buenos Aires he performed climatic analyses on Argentina's regions, and on adapting buildings to them, at the city's Research Center for Building and Housing.[88] The Olgyays also consulted widely with architects and engineers, some already mentioned. Victor Olgyay also helped to frame a new field of study, biometeorology, that was significant in reframing the context for the climate sciences in the early 1960s.[89] Whether the Olgyays were directly involved or more vaguely influential, there is little doubt that their research had an effect at sophisticated levels of the field. Their continued efforts and influence played out, especially after about 1960, in the context of a more general expansion in climatic knowledge and further developments in climate science.[90]

They also were influential, especially due to an appendix in Victor Olgyay's *Design with Climate* of 1963, in codifying climate-based design approaches to subdivision design and organization. This would be influential on a generation of environmentally conscious designers somewhat contradictorily producing the suburbs in the 1950s and '60s. In this territorial approach their work also resonates across that of Ian McHarg, who was developing expansive analytic landscape design strategies at the University of Pennsylvania. Victor produced a series of four models at the Laboratory, referred to as "Architectural Designs for Community Layouts," one each for a "Cool Region" (Minneapolis); "Temperate Region" (New York–New Jersey); "Hot-Arid Region" (Phoenix); and "Hot-Humid Region" (Miami). They attempted to mitigate the deficiencies of overgeneralization with extensive notes and caveats as to how to maximize climatic opportunities in a given climate zone. Each model had the same basic topography so as to most easily compare across climate zones.[91]

One of the Olgyays' main projects at the Princeton Architectural Laboratory, one of their lasting contributions to the history of climate image production, was the Thermoheliodon device (see figure 5.1). It was designed in collaboration with the Princeton engineer Alfred E. Sorenson and was developed through a grant from the National Science Foundation, awarded at $19,100 in 1955—not a small amount at the time and indeed quite remarkable given the limited support for architectural research.[92] "It is expected," the Olgyays wrote in a report on the device in 1957, "that with the use of this empirical technique it will be possible to clarify the fundamental principles involved in the use of a building shell as a modulating factor between the humanly controlled and natural environments." It was to be available as a teaching tool for both architects and engineers to explore and apply the principles of a "climatically balanced house."[93] It was perhaps the apex of their analytic endeavors—the apex of the broader architectural-climatic efforts of the period and also the closest approximation (yet still very far from) of a computational means for climatic design.

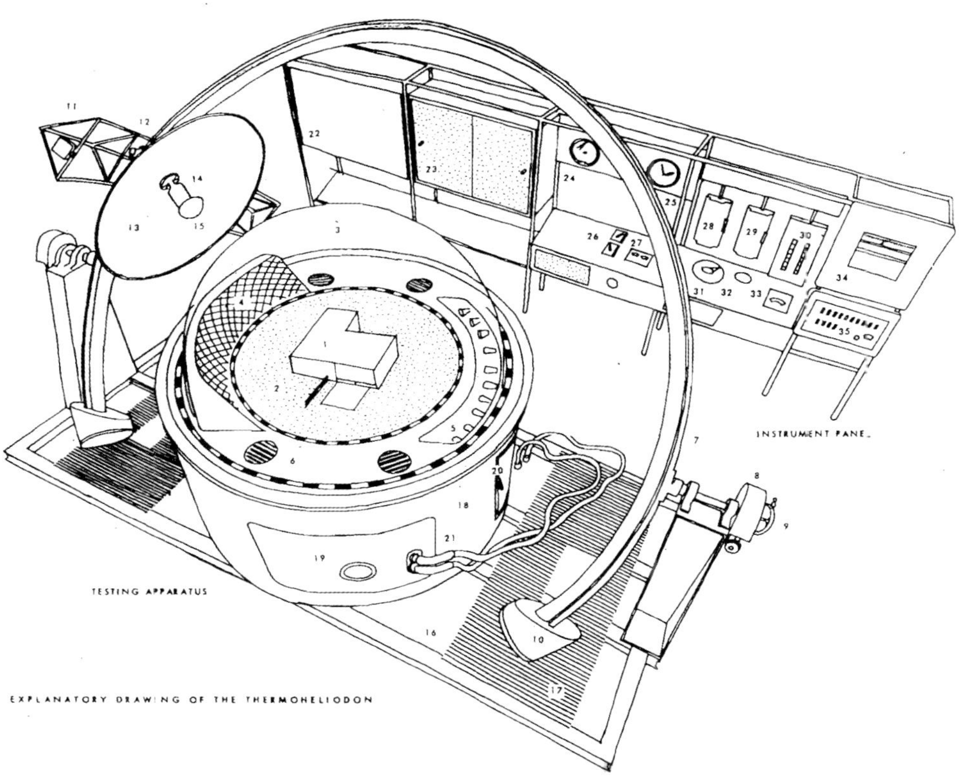


5.41 Victor and Aladar Olgyay, "Explanatory Drawing of the Thermoheliodon Device," from the *Report on the Thermoheliodon*, 1957.

The components of the Thermoheliodon express how climate was defined in the period: the arc of the sun was carefully calibrated; there was an adjustable screen for refining wind direction, and a shallow pit in the middle, where soil from the building site was to be placed; humidity was controlled by jets on the right; and all elements were sealed in a dome that could be induced to approximate larger-scale atmospheric patterns (figure 5.41). There were heating coils and an air outlet to manage temperature. A building model was constructed and placed in the center of the Thermoheliodon device and subjected to a number of tests, based on what was then a remarkable amount of data about a given building site—a day could be simulated in forty minutes, as the "sun" passed over the dome and the thermal conditions inside it changed accordingly. It was proposed that the researcher could analyze "orientation, solar openings, shading devices and overhangs, materials, insulation, desirable shape, and consequences of surroundings" through use of the device.[94] Compared to the heliodons of the period already seen, a significantly more detailed model of the climatic world became available to the designer.

Unfortunately, the device didn't really work—perhaps, again, a sort of limit to precomputational computation. Its claims to exactitude were compromised by some complications in design and assembly that led to leaks, poor connections between controls and the humidity system, and other problems. This is a familiar story of environmental technologies in the period—insightful, even prescient, but unable to technically achieve their experimental goals.

In using the Thermoheliodon, the Olgyays also hit on the complexity of a building's modeled relationship to climate. While a model could be tested for solar angles and the general design parameters relative to them—essentially the function of a heliodon—the understanding of the thermal conditions of the modeled interior was frustrated by lack of a means to scale up the thermal effects of materials. A small brick operates very differently, on thermal terms, than does a large brick. Interior climatic conditions—the comfort zone itself—could not be adequately predicted, or premediated, through this device, because of this difficulty of scaling up the thermal capacity of materials. Air also does not behave consistently within the domed chamber, and they would have had to pres-

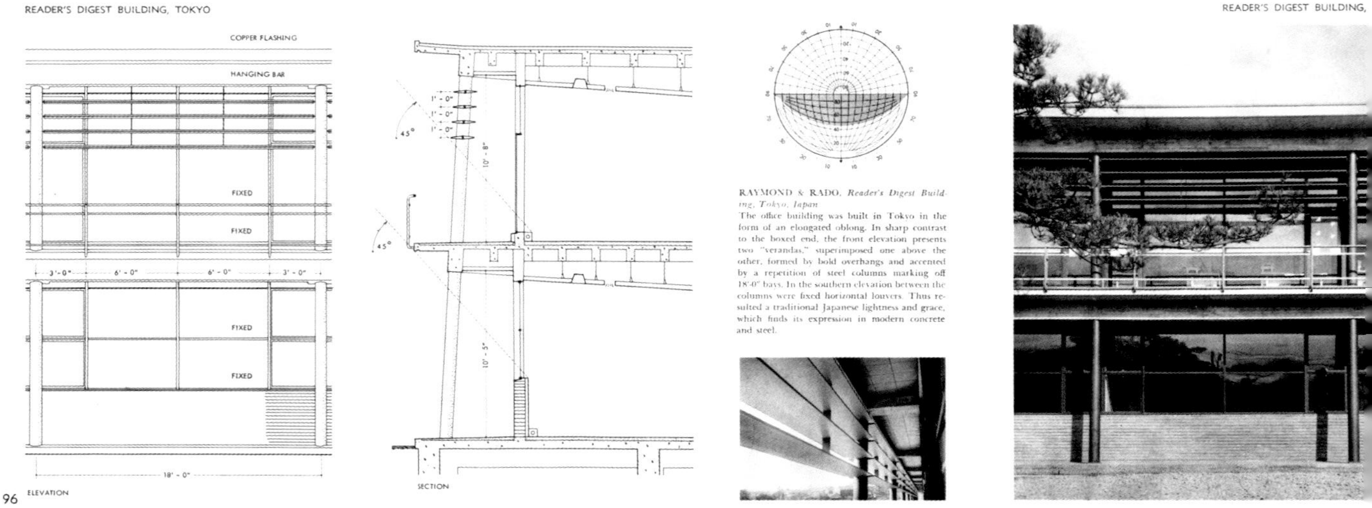


5.42 Raymond and Rado, Reader's Digest Building, Tokyo, Japan, 1951; from Olgyay and Olgyay, *Solar Control and Shading Devices*, 1957.

surize the device, as in a wind tunnel, to achieve workable accuracy. A significant portion of the report they submitted to the National Science Foundation focused on "Scaling Criteria for Heat Transfer in Model Experiments" and plans for pressurization.[95] This report, detailing their attempt to calculate the intermingled impacts of materials, humidity, and heat exchange, read almost as an extended lament expressed in calculus—a longing for a more direct means to predict a building's performance. When seeking additional funding, they proposed to build identical test houses in Princeton, Montreal (at McGill University), and Los Angeles (at the University of Southern California), and to maintain constant data analysis of these three sites, triangulating and constantly adjusting their calculative matrix according to the recent historical record. Their funding was not renewed.

If some of the conditions for the production of knowledge imaged and imagined by the Olgyays did not play out precisely as they had intended, their efforts nonetheless resonate across the architectural and environmental inquiries of subsequent decades, up to the present. The design-technological methods they initiated, or at least intensified, are still struggling to find a place amid the formalist methodologies seen as more native to the field. Yet their initiation (or, again, intensification) of *research* as a viable, fundable pathway for architecture resonates across developments in the field in the second half of the twentieth century and into the twenty-first.[96]

Their legacy is also the repository of knowledge about climate-focused architecture, its history and practices; the 1957 text *Solar Control and Shading Devices* in particular is a tool to use to reconsider historical patterns in the field, and to tell a different story. The extended final section of this book consists of seventy-seven full-page or two-page spread analyses of ninety-seven "Architectural Examples." These constituted the new kind of media practice that architectural-climatic analysis elicited—a building was represented not only by a photograph but also by a sun-path diagram clarifying the specific climatic demands relative to the thermal interior, and, of course, in almost all cases, a façade section as a means to elaborate on the precise technological means to render a specific interior climatically consistent despite the vagaries of the exterior (figure 5.42).

These examples were collected from around the globe—many from Brazil, others from India, West Africa, across Europe and the United States, in Japan and Australia. Far from comprehensive, the collection does not attempt to be a history as such; indeed, there are no dates, the locations are often imprecise, the organization of the examples is not self-evident (figure 5.43). The examples stand instead as a multivalent collection of the recent past—not a history, again, but a reflection on possibilities for the future informed by a survey

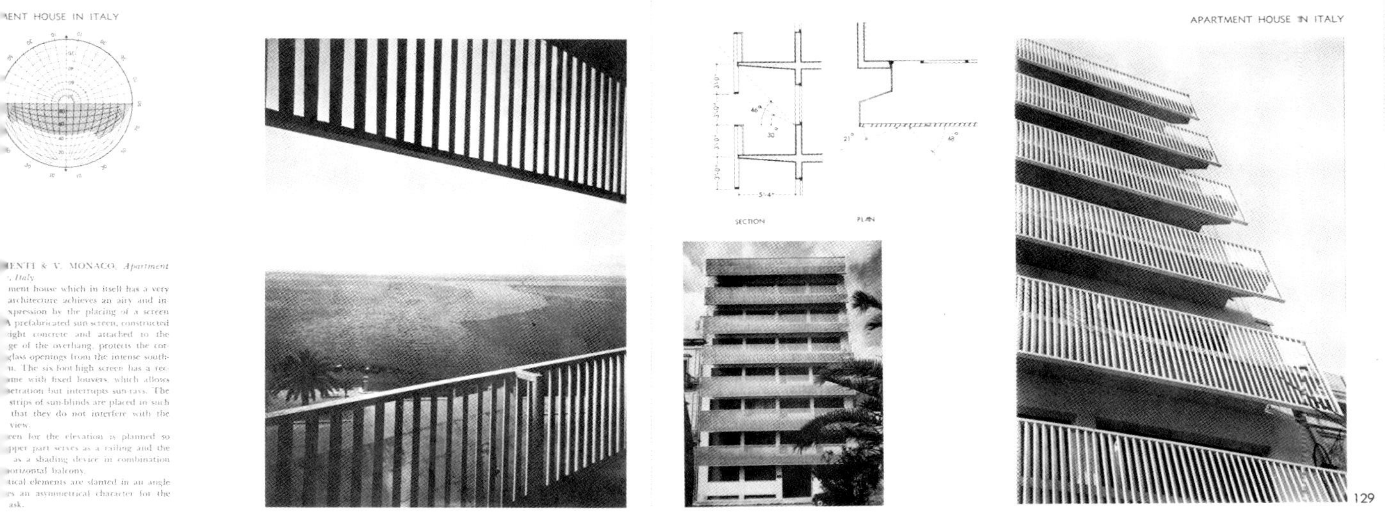


5.43 Luccichenti and Monaco, Apartment Building, Taranto, Italy, c. 1950; from Olgyay and Olgyay, *Solar Control and Shading Devices*, 1957.

of select buildings, techniques, and practices. An instrumentality of history through the diagrammatic image, and one that has a strange resonance across the anxieties and capacities of architecture in the present. While many of the buildings were well known—including the Ministry of Education and Health, the Unite d'Habitation, or Paul Rudolph and Ralph Twitchell's Florida houses, among many others—a surprising number of them are unfamiliar to narratives of modernism, in general not published in other histories written in the period, or about it. Focused on how these techniques could produce a more comfortable interior, the Olgyays' atlas of climatic buildings also begins to translate the social, formal, and technological project of architectural modernism into a method for systematically rethinking the relationship between humans and the environment.

From one perspective we can see the pitfalls of their integrative approach. It stands as a sort of ahistorical presentation of technological facts that is a precursor for any number of more recent published collections of "green," "sustainable," or "eco-buildings" that elaborate on the pictured projects as technological objects, often in isolation. From another perspective, these are documents of a technological history in both form and content—tracing the historical contours of the rise of shading as a viable and, in many instances, vital technique for the recalibration of the architectural project, and tracing that history, presenting these buildings, in a very specific integrative image—one that always includes a façade section as a means to demonstrate relevant innovations. Such a formulation, such a representative strategy, does not only suggest, as has been implicit throughout this book, that technologically minded architects can learn much from this history of the shaded façade for how they approach designing with climate as a social, as much as a technological, project. It also suggests that historians can attend to the technological knowledge embedded in the causal chains of relevance reaching deep into the past. How can we imagine, and write, a history of architecture that is more attentive to the interactions between technological knowledge and design innovation, and that maps, models, and proposes new terms for valuing architectural ideas? Not only as a means to inflect our understanding of architecture but also to insert other factors and other consequences into the framework of architectural knowledge.

Two after-images from this 1950s discourse offer reflections and refractions of these changing ideas and expand on the transitional condition of the perception of the sociobiotic relationship and of the image as instrument. This first is an image produced in the early 1970s by the Centre for Alternative Technology (CAT), one of the many radical "back to the land" collectives of the period (figure 5.44). CAT occupied a quarry in Wales in 1973 and began experiments to, as one of the

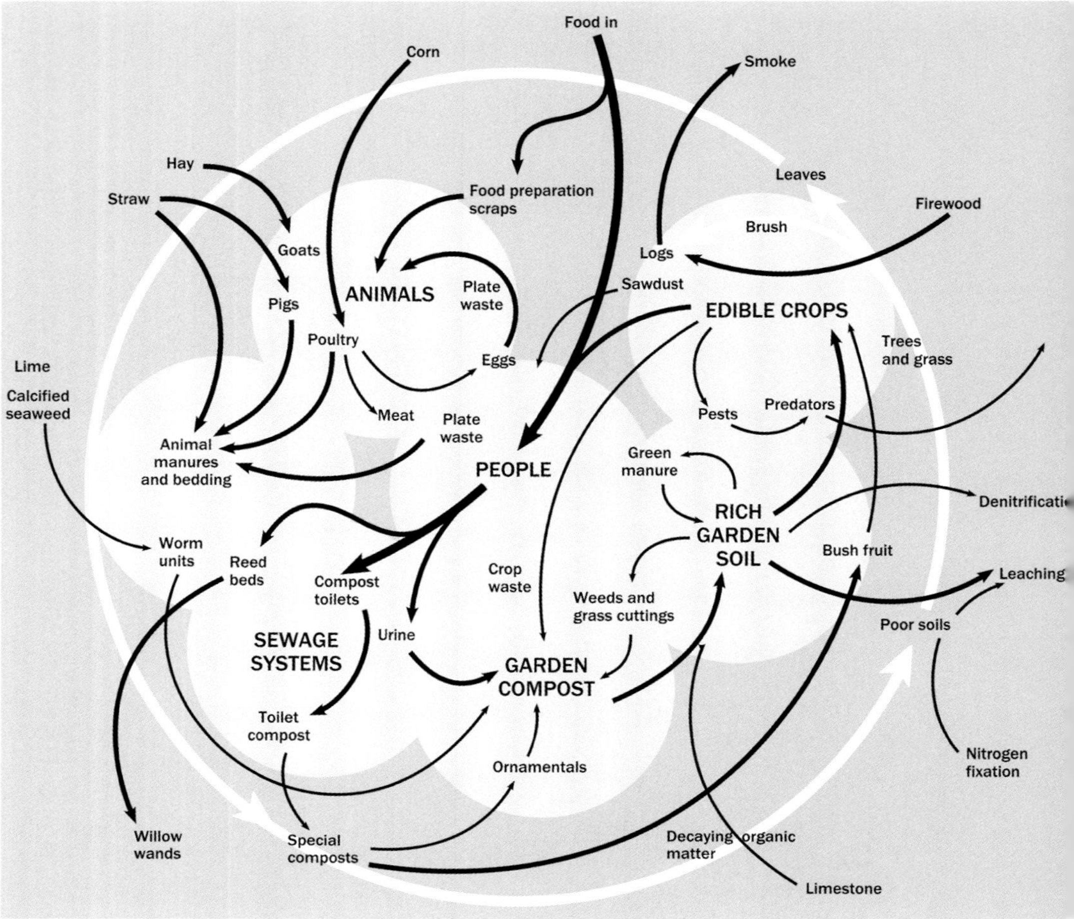


5.44 Centre for Alternative Technology (Wales, United Kingdom), Life Cycles, 1974.

leaders wrote, "show the nature of the problem and show the ways going forward."[97] The diagram attempts both, using the circle to imply a fully closed system, and to refigure connections between humans and their natural and sociopolitical context. There were many others like it, in the 1960s and '70s, as architectural aspects of the global counterculture sought to legitimate and systematize their modes of thought and practice.

The diagram operates as an instrument, but more broadly attempting to influence new social patterns—it does not restrict itself to architecture. Indeed, it implicitly repositions architecture in much the same way that the "limits to growth" model implicitly repositioned technology—it is both nowhere and everywhere, not mentioned in the diagram, but seen by the Centre as the means to attain the goals that the image represents. Amid this dizzying array of inputs into the "Life Cycle"—from pigs to flowers, sunlight to compost, with arrows pointing everywhere—the diagram expands the image of man and environment to contain a much more complex and entangled set of subjects and objects, both human and non-human. A different image of the human-ecology relationship, but one still caught up in a hope for humanistic effects, for the clarity of the image to lead to the relationships it suggests.

The second afterimage is a screen capture from the Eco-tect software, from 2015 (figure 5.45). The program considers climatic and environmental factors of the building site and provides parameters to maximize a building's performance. Which is to say, in part, that the Olgyays' method, incubated in Architectural Science departments for decades, has now been realized as an instrumental design tool in which images are manipulated according to data inputs, material efficiencies, and designed optimizations, sometimes leading to increased energy efficiency in the built environment.[98] At the same time, the figural tension is missing—the computational claim to adequate knowledge of climate systems and of design techniques elides the premise that an architectural,

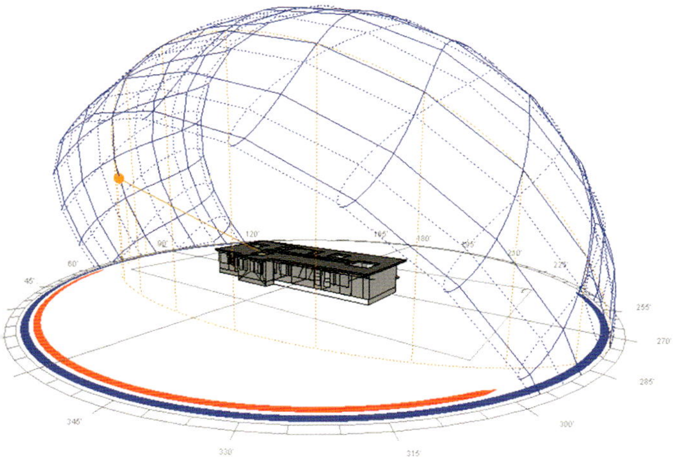

5.45 Screen capture from Autodesk's Eco-tect performance software, c. 2015.

or any other, image can directly influence human behavior. The aspiration is not toward imagining new ways of life, but toward maximizing efficiency. Data overwhelms the entanglement of aesthetic, scientific, and political knowledge, as this imperative for efficiency plays into the urgency of climate change as a technological and sociopolitical issue.

This view frames building efficiency as unproblematically participating in solutions to a global problem—as a stabilization wedge, perhaps, rather than an opportunity to reimagine sociobiotic relationships. The imaged relationship between "man and environment" is flattened on this digital surface, across which "man" is attempting to control all possible factors and to build an environment more precisely reflecting the calculated needs of the species. Which is not to say that such performance software programs are not important tools, but rather that their use can collapse into a form of technological determinism, one that optimizes and normalizes, and in so doing resists other possible futures. Different humans experience climate, and climate change, differently. This is also not to say that the human figure itself needs recovering as an image of environmental health, but rather that the tension between objective knowledge and aspiration, between data and desire, is productive for social change.

---

Data has overtaken the image of the human as the framing mechanism of the architectural-climatic diagram. The Olgyays' diagrams stand as evidence of the difficult passage from one worldview to another—the end point of which we have not, despite the resurgence of relevant imagery, yet managed to approach. Across a broad historical spectrum, the Olgyays' schematic bioclimatic index is an image of species stasis that resisted, rather than facilitated, the transformative potential of socioecological dynamics. In the face of climate change and other environmental threats, questions about how images can affect social patterns are again of great interest. Despite their shortcomings, or, indeed, perhaps because of their inadequacies—their quasi-technical and transitional condition; their inability to effectively draw things together—the Olgyays' diagrams figure human entanglements with the environment as a persistent challenge. By critically analyzing visual rhetoric that claims relevance to environmental change, and by implicitly reframing environmental challenges to recognize the inextricable connections between social patterns, cultural desires, technological possibilities, and climatic effects, these diagrams challenge the seamlessness of data-based architectural-climatic models. These diagrams also suggest that representational strategies can reflect and facilitate new modes of existence, a prospect that will become increasingly vital in the environmentally threatened future.

## Plan B

In January 1959 the American Society of Refrigeration Engineers (ASRE) and the American Society of Heating and Air-Conditioning Engineers (ASHAE) merged to form the American Society of Heating, Refrigeration and Air-Conditioning Engineers (ASHRAE). Although seemingly a simple technocrat maneuver, it was another epochal event. These two associations, when formed in the first decade of the twentieth century, seemed to have little in common; however, by the mid-1920s collaborations had begun in earnest. Only five years earlier, ASHAE had placed "Air-Conditioning" in its name (replacing Ventilating, ASHVE was the acronym until 1954), already seeming to consolidate the importance of refrigeration and air-conditioning mechanisms to their work of managing the planetary interior. ASHAE engineers were increasingly turning to their ASRE counterparts (many engineers were members of both societies) as they used mechanical refrigeration equipment to control humidity (figure 6.2). The slow move from steam or hot water heating to forced air systems (far from universal, but already common in new construction) also encouraged the consideration of heating and air-conditioning functions in one mechanical system.[1]

The standardization of the building interior, through heating, ventilation, and air-conditioning (HVAC) systems, was a primary object of the merger, which further served to develop a regulatory mechanism that could consider the possibilities of conditioning, and de-humidification in particular, in order to conceptualize a thermal interior that could be produced, through mechanical means and a sealed curtain wall, in virtually any climate.

The merger had been tried before; it occurred at this juncture as the result of two distinct trends: first, fuel costs had been reduced to such an extent that air conditioning was now much more widely affordable, especially across the globalizing corporate landscape of Euro-America and relative to its management of the so-called third world; second, ASHVE engineers, drawing on new sensing devices and measurement systems for assessing the thermal interior, had articulated a general, universal standard that provided a clear pathway on which industry could develop.

An indication of the first point requires some elaboration of the various states of the art of interior climatic management. Indeed, there was a complex range of sensors, models, and charts to determine the ideal conditions of the planetary interior and also to mitigate its being affected by climatic extremes. The 1950s was a hybrid, transitional phase where both mechanical cooling plants and the methods and materials of architectural shading engaged the façade as a dynamic membrane, in relationship to the conditioning system—though by now somewhat beyond the façade section, and into the ceiling heights, ventilation shafts, and other arrangements for cooling systems. Generally, over this decade, as a model of architectural practice and aspirations toward a normative condition, the complex dynamism of the shading device was replaced, in design and technological method, with a sealed curtain wall and an interior fully conditioned by a fossil-fuel-driven mechanical heating and cooling system. The standardization and regulation of these systems was the techno-cultural assemblage that precipitated and was, in turn, consolidated by this merger.

Although "American" remained in the name, ASHRAE had an explicitly global agenda. They had already established a system of assessing climatic zones for most appropriate types of HVAC intervention—much later, in 2004, when the ASHRAE "international climate zone map" was simplified to eight general zones (with a few subzones), the association used a database involving thirty-eight zones and detailed information on 240 cities globally. However, most international ASHRAE chapters (aside from Toronto, Montreal, and other Canadian cities that had been active since the 1930s) were not officially established until the 1980s or '90s—

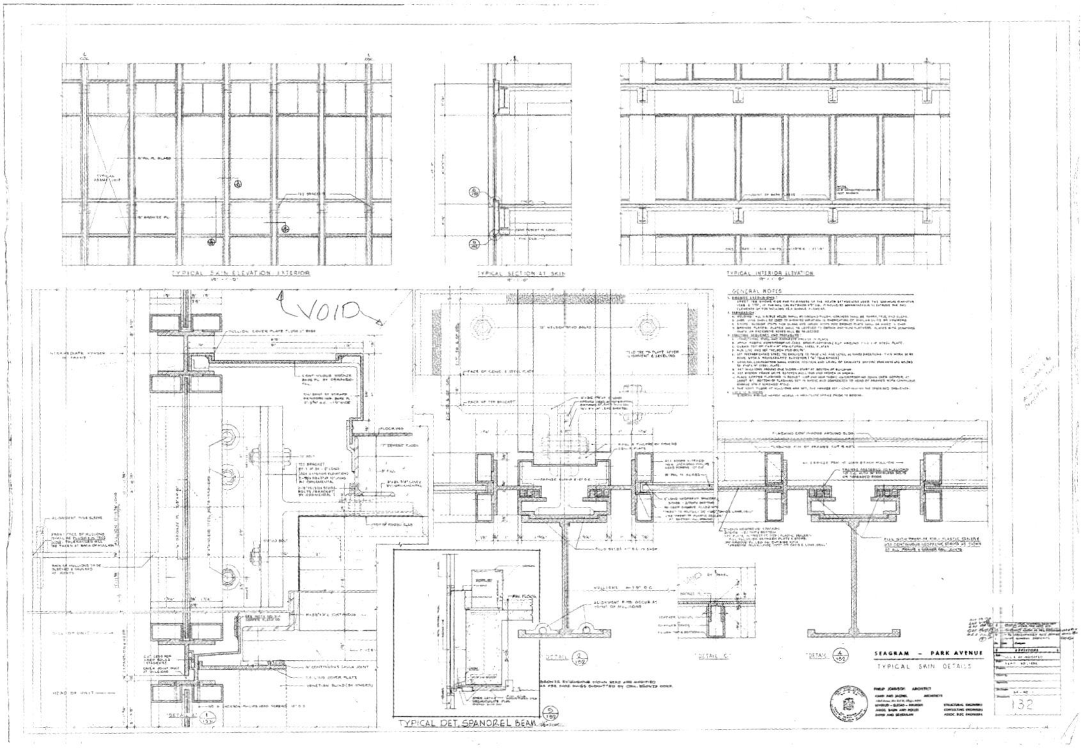



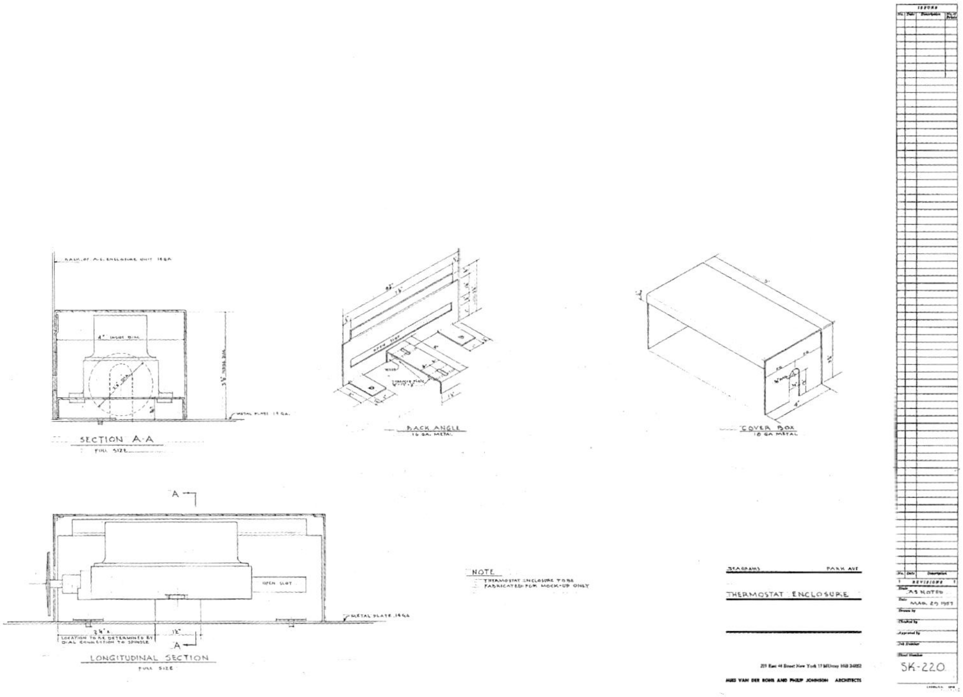



6.1 Mies van der Rohe, Seagram Park Avenue, New York, 1957.

as of today, there are active chapter in 132 nations. Even early on, however, international architects hired to build offices, apartments, hotels, and other buildings around the world brought these standards, and the fossil-fuel systems they required, with them.

Modernist internationalism quickly became planetary conditioning, as building types around the world succumbed to the infrastructural pressures and physiological pleasures of fossil-fueled HVAC. Again, the complexity of political forces, economic inducements, industrial path dependencies, and technological contingencies summed up in the concept of an energy regime are self-evident yet difficult to excavate. An air-conditioned building became a functional means to draw capital across borders—out to various peripheries, in the air conditioning in particular of large cities in the Global South, and also as a means to radically concentrate wealth. A tall, glass and steel forest of office towers is a primary indicator of global financial power, in London, New York, Singapore, Shanghai, Lagos, Rio, or Toronto (or many other places). Even in many countries where air conditioning is not strictly necessary or, in cases, not desired (Italy has a well-known dread of dehumidification), corporate and financial centers, hotels and convention centers, airports and manufacturing showrooms still tend to be conditioned through mechanical systems.

Globalization as a geopolitical and geophysical force was, on the terms of carbon and climate, the spreading of air conditioning around the world. These are also the epochal terms on which the history of modern architecture now resonates. The air conditioning of buildings was an essential cultural and infrastructural force of the Great Acceleration—providing the possibility of conditioned spaces, the technological dependencies and industry infrastructures, and then the cultural desires, if not in fact societal dependence, that air conditioning continues to produce.

This was especially true of large-scale architectural projects—commercial towers, apartment buildings, and institutional and educational campuses, and still with much regional variation. Over time, the premise of the universal overwhelmed these specifics. The conception of the planetary and its corollary in air conditioning, here on corporate-political as much as on resource-earth system terms, became a unified model that could assess and address conditions anywhere on the globe. It overwhelmed the relative adjustments of façade systems to specific time and place. In the accumulation of carbon it doesn't matter where it comes from—the longed-for rendering of modernist interiors as universal was in the end as an air-conditioned architecture, producing the all-over effect of climate instability.

6.2 Image promoting the merger of ASRE and ASHAE into ASHRAE, 1959.

Architectural-climatic analyses changed after air conditioning. The geographers, meteorologists, climatologists, and architects interested in producing planetary interior consistency focused less on a process of detailed site analysis, of integration with modeling devices, or on the production of intricately functional façades, as the protagonists of this book had been working toward and imagining. Rather than specificity of site, the conditioned world was produced through specificity of standards in building systems—fossil-fuel-powered HVAC systems, usually as forced air, filtered and blown through ducts in walls or false ceilings, and cooling, heating, and adjusting the humidity of the interior according to feedback monitoring systems, all within a sealed building. This was how the realm of expertise in design and engineering initially emerged from the mid-century period of designing for climate—not as

6.3 Faulkner, Kingsbury and Stenhouse with Olgyay and Olgyay consulting, American Association for the Advancement of Science Building, Washington, DC, 1955, from *Science*, 1956.

site-specific methodologists, but as experts in the production and effects of air conditioning. An unexpected continuity of knowledge production that of course has taken another unexpected turn.

The 1950s was, again, a period of transition. As late as 1958, an article on "Man-Made Climate" in *Progressive Architecture* outlined the still relatively mild uptake of air conditioning across the built environment generally considered: "Although the full definition of air conditioning—which includes heating, cooling, cleaning, controlling humidity, and moving of air—has been established for at least 30 years, a few architects and the majority of their clients still think of it [only] as the provision of cooling for summer comfort." However, the article continued, "a better understanding of thermodynamics coupled with the advantages of future development of electronics and tomorrow's nuclear resources of power will all contribute to the progressive evolution of our man-made climate."[2] The slow process of adopting air-conditioning systems, the elaboration of this normative interior, continued across the following decades—it still continues on a global scale—as methods and buildings developed around partial and hybrid modes of mechanical HVAC systems.

Hybrid systems suggest that other sorts of interiors and other sorts of mechanisms were still feasible. Although in the 1950s the stakes were seemingly not especially high, the planetary interior was here already emergent as a space of contestation. A large number of the buildings reproduced in the Olgyays', "Architectural Examples" section of *Solar Control and Shading Devices* used a shading device to assist the mechanical air-conditioning system by reducing the requirements being placed on it—by reducing solar radiation and alleviating the need for intensive conditioning.

The relevant debates can be rehearsed by returning to the 1955 American Association for the Advancement of Science building in Washington, DC, by Faulkner, Kingsbury and Stenhouse with Olgyay and Olgyay consulting (see figure 5.13). In a 1956 article in *Science*, Waldron Faulkner, the design principal on the project, described the building, including the shading system and the reasoning behind it (figure 6.3). The AAAS building (which is now the embassy for Tunisia) sits on a prominent site on Massachusetts Avenue, at the southeast curve of Scott Circle. All but the north façade of the building were covered, on the second and third floor, with full-length vertical louvers. As Faulkner described them: "they turn during the day by means of an electric clock mechanism and take certain predetermined positions at definite times." Each façade operated differently, as he continued:

> On the east side of the building the sunshades are closed, or partly closed, early in the morning and open gradually. . . . Their starting position depends on the time of year. On the west side the operation in the afternoon is exactly the reverse of this. The sunshades on the south of the building operate entirely differently . . . [they] are open in early morning and close gradually until noon. At this time they rotate quickly through an angle of

6.4 The president of Barnard College reviewing plans for O'Connor and Killiam with Olgyay and Olgyay consulting, Lehman Hall, 1959.

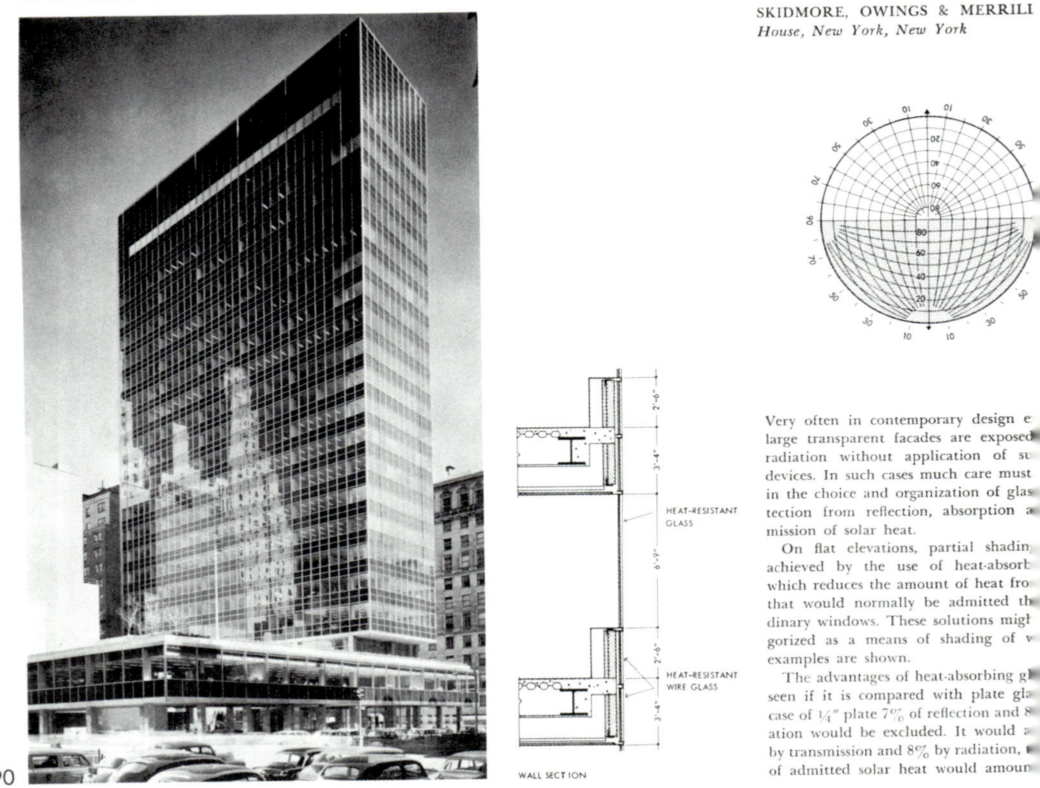

LEVER HOUSE, NEW YORK

SKIDMORE, OWINGS & MERRILI
*House, New York, New York*

HEAT-RESISTANT GLASS

HEAT-RESISTANT WIRE GLASS

WALL SECTION

Very often in contemporary design e
large transparent facades are exposed
radiation without application of su
devices. In such cases much care must
in the choice and organization of glas
tection from reflection, absorption a
mission of solar heat.

On flat elevations, partial shadin
achieved by the use of heat-absorb
which reduces the amount of heat fro
that would normally be admitted th
dinary windows. These solutions migh
gorized as a means of shading of w
examples are shown.

The advantages of heat-absorbing g
seen if it is compared with plate gla
case of 1/4" plate 7% of reflection and 8
ation would be excluded. It would a
by transmission and 8% by radiation,
of admitted solar heat would amoun

190

6.5 Skidmore, Owings & Merrill (Gordon Bunshaft, designer), Lever House, New York City, 1952, from Olgyay and Olgyay, *Solar Control and Shading Devices*, 1957.

> 180 degrees and open gradually in the opposite direction in the afternoon.

He described how workers in the building could organize their lunch breaks according to the movement of the shading system. Faulkner claimed that this was the first use of such a system in DC, though it was based on successful projects in the "Far West" of the United States—Neutra's Northwestern Insurance Building, completed in 1951 and discussed in chapter 2, may have been the precedent he was referring to.[3]

"The starting positions and speeds of operation for this installation," Faulkner wrote, "were determined by A. Olgyay and V. Olgyay of Princeton University."[4] Although they were, at this point, involved in many consultations, the AAAS was a model project for the Olgyays' method—sited with open, varied exposure, and with a client interested in exploring climate-design adjustments for a prominent insertion in the built landscape. The

Table 1. Comparative costs of heating and air-conditioning.

| Item | Plan A ¼ - in. plate glass | | Plan B Double glazing | | Plan C ¼ - in. Solex | |
|---|---|---|---|---|---|---|
| | With Venetian blinds | With outside louvers | With Venetian blinds | With outside louvers | With Venetian blinds | With outside louvers |
| *Installation cost* | | | | | | |
| Refrigeration equipment | $ 61,000 | $ 50,500 | $ 53,900 | $ 50,800 | $ 53,900 | $ 38,500 |
| Boilers | 10,000 | 10,000 | 9,900 | 9,900 | 10,000 | 10,000 |
| Radiation | 12,500 | 12,500 | 10,200 | 10,200 | 12,500 | 12,500 |
| Glass | 12,000 | 12,000 | 32,000 | 32,000 | 16,000 | 16,000 |
| Louvers | | 25,000 | | 25,000 | | 25,000 |
| Venetian blinds | 5,000 | | 5,000 | | 5,000 | |
| Total Installed cost | $100,500 | $98,000 | $111,000 | $107,900 | $97,400 | $102,000 |
| *Annual maintenance cost* | | | | | | |
| Fuel (gas) | 2,940 | 2,940 | 2,360 | 2,360 | 2,360 | 2,940 |
| Maintenance (filters, servicing, electric power, etc.) | 1,540 | 975 | 1,360 | 785 | 1,360 | 975 |
| Total operating cost | $ 4,450 | $ 3,915 | $ 3,720 | $ 3,145 | $ 4,300 | $ 3,915 |
| Depreciation (10 yr) | 10,050 | 9,800 | 11,100 | 10,790 | 9,740 | 10,200 |
| Operating costs per year | 4,480 | 3,915 | 3,720 | 3,145 | 4,300 | 3,913 |
| Total annual cost | $ 14,530 | $ 13,715 | $ 14,820 | $ 13,935 | $ 14,040 | $ 14,113 |

SCIENCE, VOL. 124

6.6 Faulkner, Kingsbury and Stenhouse with Olgyay and Olgyay consulting, American Association for the Advancement of Science Building, Washington, DC, 1955. Comparative costs of heating and air conditioning, from *Science*, 1956.

Olgyays were able to explore in depth the consequences of their calculative method, determining the precise solar angles for each façade, programming the system with multiple daily angles to maximize efficiency. Faulkner celebrated the wisdom of the client—an association dedicated to furthering scientific knowledge and its application. He described how the architects produced a number of presentation drawings, moving from the fully climate-focused version "in graduated steps to more traditional and less exciting treatment," and thereby received approval for the scientifically determined scheme.[5] A counterexample: the 1958 design for the library at Barnard College, Lehman Hall, with the firm O'Connor and Kilham, covered a glass box with a decorated, monumental screen, hung at some distance from the insulated membrane—it was a fixed screen, identical across different exposures, and more decorative than instrumental in adjusting the experience of the interior (figure 6.4).[6]

The AAAS building was not a laboratory experiment. A primary consideration for the use of a shading system was the potential reduction in cost, and the relative importance of the two elements—shading and conditioning—in the design of the thermal interior. "The shades also reduce the heat absorption through the windows," Faulkner noted. "This brings about economies in the operation of the air-conditioning system. It also means the capacity and, therefore, the initial cost of the air-conditioning equipment can be considerably reduced."[7] Faulkner included in his *Science* article a table of "comparative costs of heating and air-conditioning" evaluating the installation and operating costs of using louvers compared to venetian blinds, according to three different types of glazing—they went with a double-glazed glass panel instead of a single-glazed or the use of Solex heat-resisting glass. Solex, it is worth noting, had first been used in the 1930s though it had been popularized by its use at Skidmore, Owings & Merrill's Lever House in New York City, completed in 1952—the iconic green tint on the façade, often seen as in place to reflect the greenish hue of Lever's soap products, was the result of the spectral selectivity required in this early low-emissive glass product (figure 6.5).[8]

The AAAS cost estimate chart is thus a rich piece of historical evidence—perhaps the end of a moment when this careful articulation of how little oil can be used had any relevance to the building industry in the United States. Initially, Faulkner's basic equation seems quite clear: by using louvers, instead of blinds, the cost for the "refrigeration equipment" decreases significantly. However, the price of the louver system makes up for much of that initial savings. The louvers, however, reduce costs significantly more than the use of blinds, by 43 percent for double glazing and by 29 percent for Solex (figure 6.6).

The chosen "Plan B," with double glazing and outside louvers, is not the cheapest option, either in installation cost or maintenance—not only because of the expensive louver installation but also because of the significantly higher cost of the insulated glass. The glass panels do provide a small amount of savings for the furnace of the water-based radiant heating system—the insulated glass keeps the heat in—but Plan B still cost about $10,000 more to build.[9]

This operative cost savings, in Plan B, was due to the general effect of the insulated double-glazed panel: both the blinds and louvers columns in the chart, of the double-glazing option, would reduce fuel consumption, or at least overall fuel cost, by almost 20 percent. Savings also come from the modest reduction in other expenses for the air-conditioning system, identified as "maintenance (filters, servicing, electric power, etc.)." The maintenance costs for the double-glazed, louvered option were listed at $785 per year, a 43 percent savings over the double-glazed version with venetian blinds. These costs were almost exactly half of the most expensive option (single-paned, venetian blinds), and were $190 less than both the Solex version with louvers and the single-paned version with louvers. Although once depreciation was factored in, the single-glazed, louvered version won out, perhaps due to relatively higher depreciation calculations for the still relatively new double-paned insulated glass panel being used, or perhaps due to depreciation assessments of a heating and cooling plant versus metal louvers.[10]

In sum, the cost of the mechanical louvers largely compensated for initial savings in the mechanical plant, and the yearly savings were not insubstantial but also not, it seems, at a level that would induce much fiscal excitement—or widespread use, especially as petroleum became increasingly cheap. Savings in energy costs, in other words, were a factor but not necessarily a primary one, amid assessment of materials (primarily glass, though they also note the use of white gravel rather than black on the roof "to reduce heat loss") and the relative costs for the construction of a given system.[11]

## Hybridity

Energy was cheap—it had been made cheap through numerous initiatives in government support for corporate investment in oil exploration, extraction, and delivery. The Great Acceleration was produced, induced, through subsidies, geophysical assessments, and geopolitical machinations, ossifying into a material and cultural infrastructure of fossil fuel dependence—ossifying, in part, through architecture. Architecture has been, in all but the most exceptional cases, a medium for the *intensification* of energy use.

The internationalism of climatic modernism persisted as a central historiographic figure in this condition of hybridity—two buildings in particular represent, here quite literally, images of hybrid conditioning façades and systems, amid material and symbolic transformations to the energy system—a sort of hybridity as a phase, as a shepherding in of a more resolutely fuel-dependent building. British Petroleum House, or BP House, now Petroleum House, in Lagos, Nigeria, was one of the first air-conditioned buildings in West Africa, completed in 1960 (figure 6.7). It was designed by Fry, Drew, Drake, and Lasdun, something of a triumph of Fry and Drew's later period, working extensively in the former colony. Its imbrication in the oil economy is too obvious; the Niger delta became the primary extractive site in the region for BP. BP House has moveable louvers on the sun-facing façade, operating banks that correspond to interior partitions, and face operable interior windows. It is also cooled mechanically—"fully air conditioned"—thus the louvers operate to minimize the load placed on the mechanical system.[12]

The other representation of this internationalist thread, another sort of apex in the consideration of the *international* as the *project* of modern architecture—the goal of regionally inflected design toward a consistent interior—is the UNESCO building in Paris. The building was designed by an international collaboration among Pier Luigi Nervi, Bernard Zehrfuss, and Marcel Breuer (figure 6.8). A student of the Olgyays, Piotr Kowalski, worked with Breuer on the shading details of the façade.[13] Lewis Mumford's scathing review of the UNESCO building focused in part on the climatic misapprehensions of the curtain wall. "Walls that are windows and windows that are walls," Mumford writes, "cannot fulfill one function [daylight] without spoiling the other [comfort, over-radiation]. The careful disregard of this simple theorem," he continued, "has become almost the equivalent of a diploma in modern design."[14] "On hot, sunny days," he wrote, "the offices, by all accounts, are decidedly uncomfortable."[15] Mumford feigned shock that after what he saw as the disastrous curtain wall of the United Nations Headquarters in New York the complex in Paris was again a glass office building—a somewhat

6.7 Fry, Drake, Drew and Lasdun, British Petroleum Headquarters (BP House), Lagos, Nigeria, 1960.

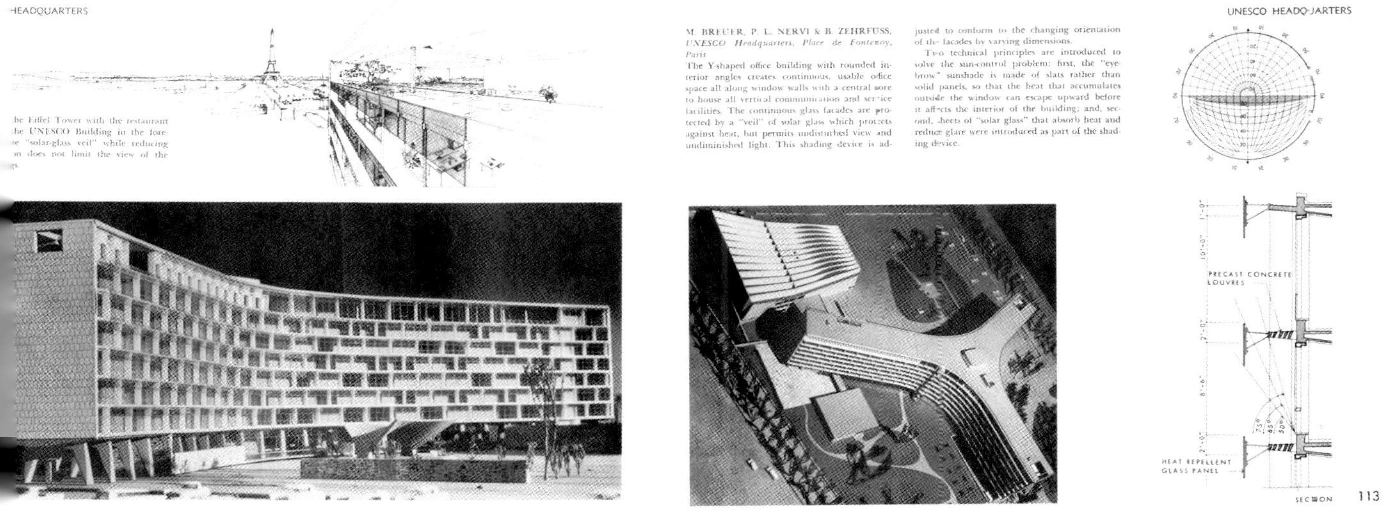


6.8 Marcel Breuer, Bernard Zehrfuss, and Pier Luigi Nervi, UNESCO Secretariat, Paris, 1958, from Olgyay and Olgyay, *Solar Control and Shading Devices*, 1957.

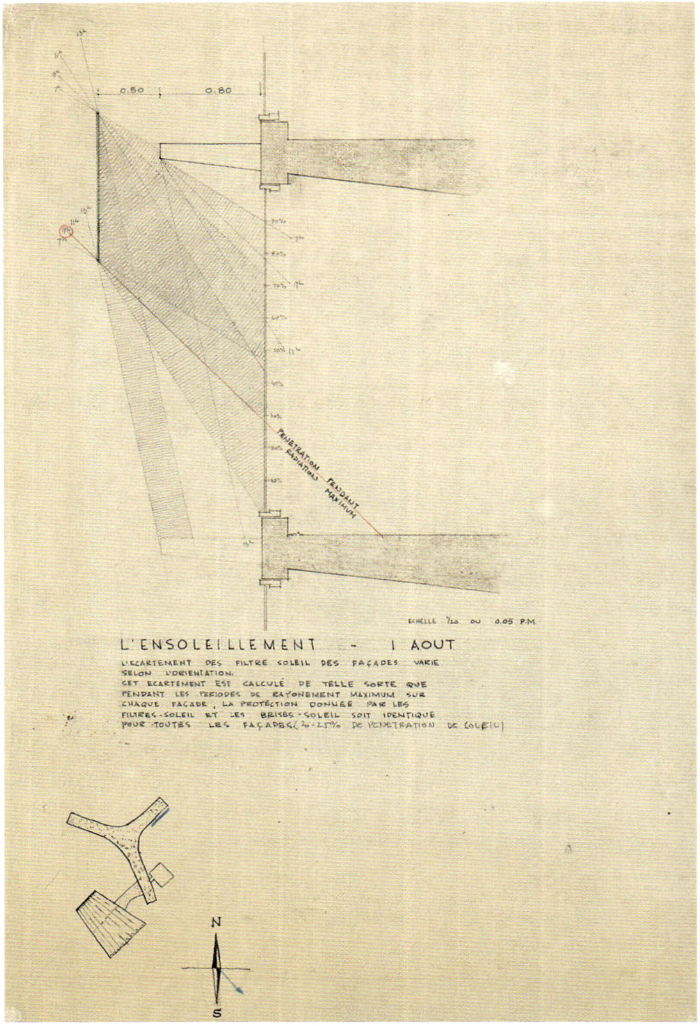


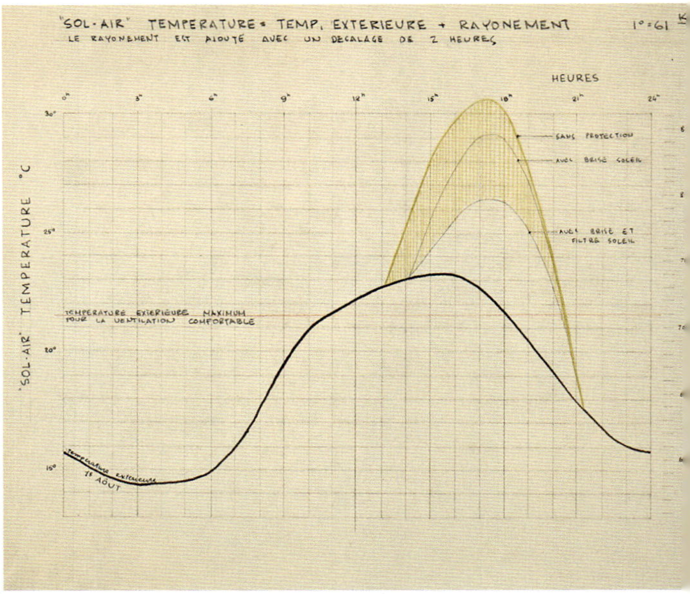


6.9 Marcel Breuer, Bernard Zehrfuss, and Pier Luigi Nervi, UNESCO Secretariat, Paris, 1958. , diagrams of the shading façade and the patterns of solar radiation.

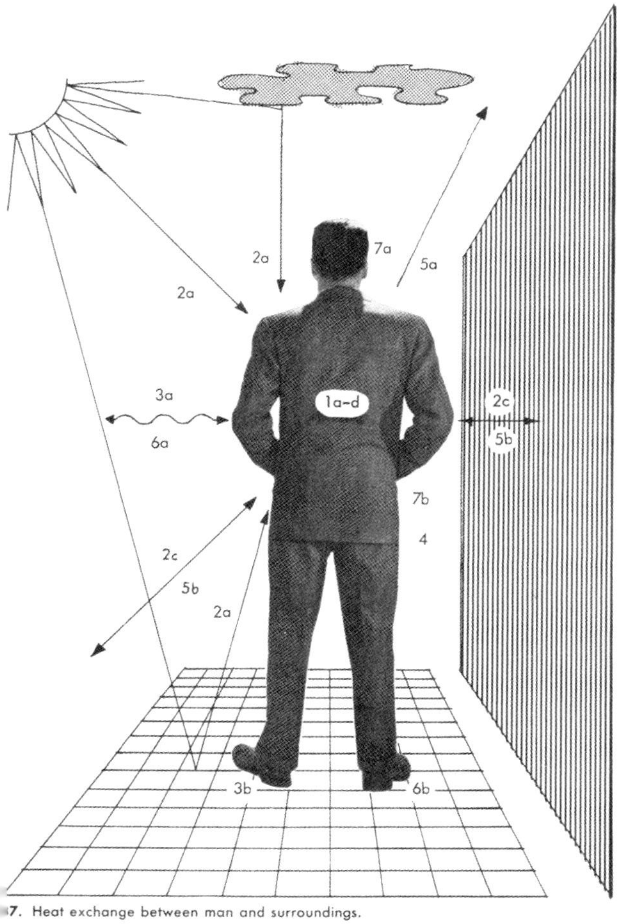


6.10 Victor Olgyay, "Heat Exchange between Man and His Surroundings," from *Design with Climate*, 1963.

distended critique of the use of a corporate façade for a cultural organization.[16]

The UNESCO building was built without air conditioning, relying instead on double skin façade and shading to allow seasonal modulation of the interior (figure 6.9). The *Y*-form of the buildings allowed for numerous solar exposures, the south and west façades had both concrete horizontal louvers and a vertical slab to increase solar protection. Further screening was provided by a tinted glass element, set at a distance from the window openings. Ventilation could be induced through the building due to operable windows and openings above the office doors. The system intentionally ignored temperature extremes, presuming that late afternoon summer sun and the intensity of radiation in August did not need to be mitigated because the building would not be occupied. However, overheating occurred in many other periods; in later years this was exacerbated by the heat generated by computers and other devices. In 2008, a retrofit involved inserting air-conditioning units into the offices, also requiring drop ceilings for duct space. Windows were also replaced.[17] The building's retrofit stands as an indication of the purported viability and insipid hegemony of mechanical systems—even though, in this case, such conditioning was only needed in summer extremes, the entire building was integrated into the carbon economy.

The UNESCO building stands in a consequential relationship to the production of global flows of knowledge.[18] The United Nations, and nongovernmental organizations in general, have come to serve a prominent role in the articulation of limits to fossil-fuel-driven expansion, as much as policies and programs have sought to expand the reach of capital through development. The conditioning of buildings was one of the primary forces of the human enterprise in this radical engagement with the resources and sinks of the earth system.

That architecture has operated in tight connection with the oil economy is self-evident. Since World War II, the typology of the office building in particular has emerged in concert with elaborate geopolitical mechanisms to make fossil fuel available to the West, both eliciting and participating in global patterns of epochal consequence. The need for more energy is constantly being produced through energy-intensive lifestyles and building types, and also through forms of national security, as a means to justify military, diplomatic, and corporate interventions, especially in the Middle East and Venezuela, toward securing energy resources. New modes of political cooperation and American geopolitical dominance followed.[19] Even before the specter of carbon emissions raised its head, oil was implicated in the historical patterns of the twentieth century; office towers in the United States in particular, and the models developed in the United States for export abroad, were its medium of expression, its prospect for cultural relevance and resonance. Living and working conditions have been produced by petroleum.

Alongside the relative marginalization of shading versus mechanical cooling on economic terms (undermining Aladar Olgyays' 1957 argument in the previous chapter) was a robust attempt

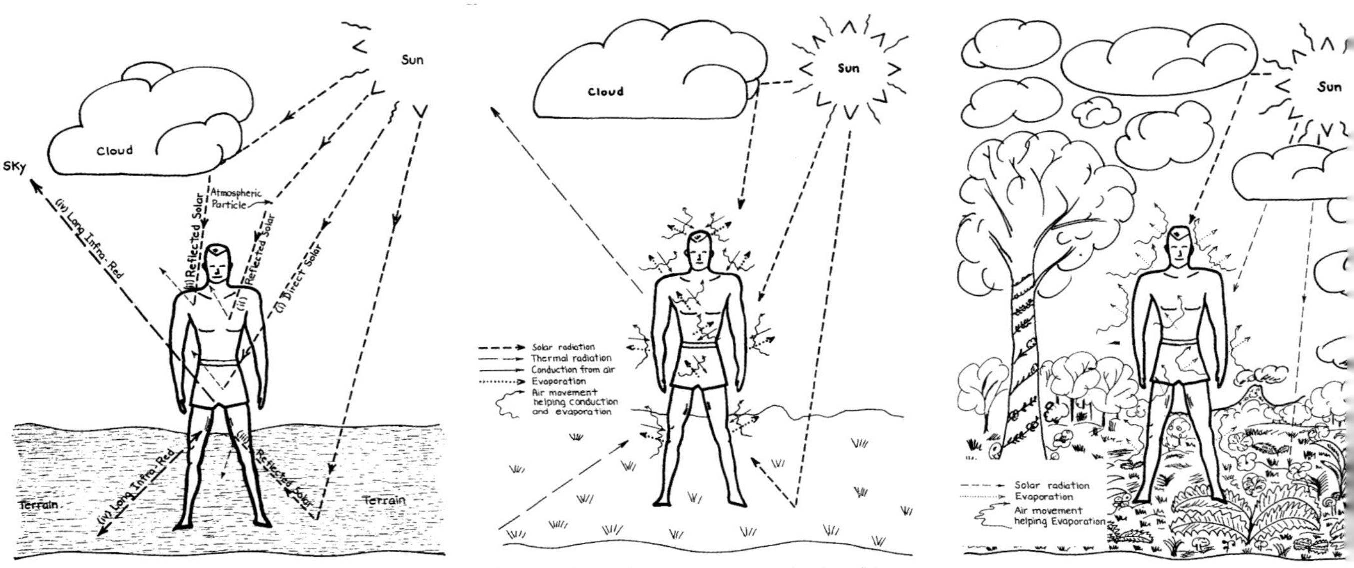


6.11 D.H.K. Lee, diagrammatic analysis of heat exchange in different climates, from *Physiological Objectives in Hot Weather Housing: An Introduction to the Principles of Hot Weather Housing Design*, for the US Housing and Home Finance Agency, 1953.

to sense, monitor, and regulate interior conditions through the work of experimental scientists and refrigeration engineers working under the ASHRE (not quite yet ASHRAE) umbrella in the mid-1950s (figure 6.10). In particular, new sensing devices were becoming widespread. Kata thermometers, in use since the 1930s, could read the conductive, convective, and radiant heat transfer between membranes, objects, and bodies, measuring air speed and humidity to model interior atmosphere. Hollow globe thermometers had also been in widespread use since the 1930s—they were easier to calibrate and more accurate than previous devices, especially relative to heat exchange factors of the body. Debates over the analytic model of thermal measurement persisted, with effective temperature being replaced, through an updated paper from Yaglou in 1956, into a more dynamic reading of mean radiant temperature (MRT) (figure 6.11).[20]

MRT became the standard for the large number of sensing devices and the interiors their data sought to produce. Which is to say, the ASHRAE merger was also about refining and disseminating a series of specific thermal comfort standards, adaptable to any climate around the world, through a new kind of thermal sensing device keyed to the norms it aimed to produce. The first handbook of the ASHRAE standard was published in 1966, with a number of updates since. Their stated goal was to "'provide year-round thermal comfort for most people, normally clothed, engaging in sedentary or near sedentary activities."[21] Many have argued that MRT is not the best means to measure thermal conditions, or, actually, that ASHRAE's use of MRT was based on a flawed set of studies from the 1930s. The path dependencies set out by the AHRAE standards were definitive and absolute.

Other buildings already discussed can be seen to also demonstrate this hybrid, transitional character (figure 6.12). Belluschi's Equitable Building in Portland used low-emissive glass instead of evident shading devices—even interior blinds were eschewed. An earlier sectional drawing by Belluschi developed for the building, as a sort of general model for postwar office building construction in a 1942 *Architectural Forum* issue on "194x," showed "pivoting aluminum louvers" sandwiched between two panes of glass to form a climatically adaptive panel; under it another panel of moveable louvers controlled the air-intake system.[22] Small,

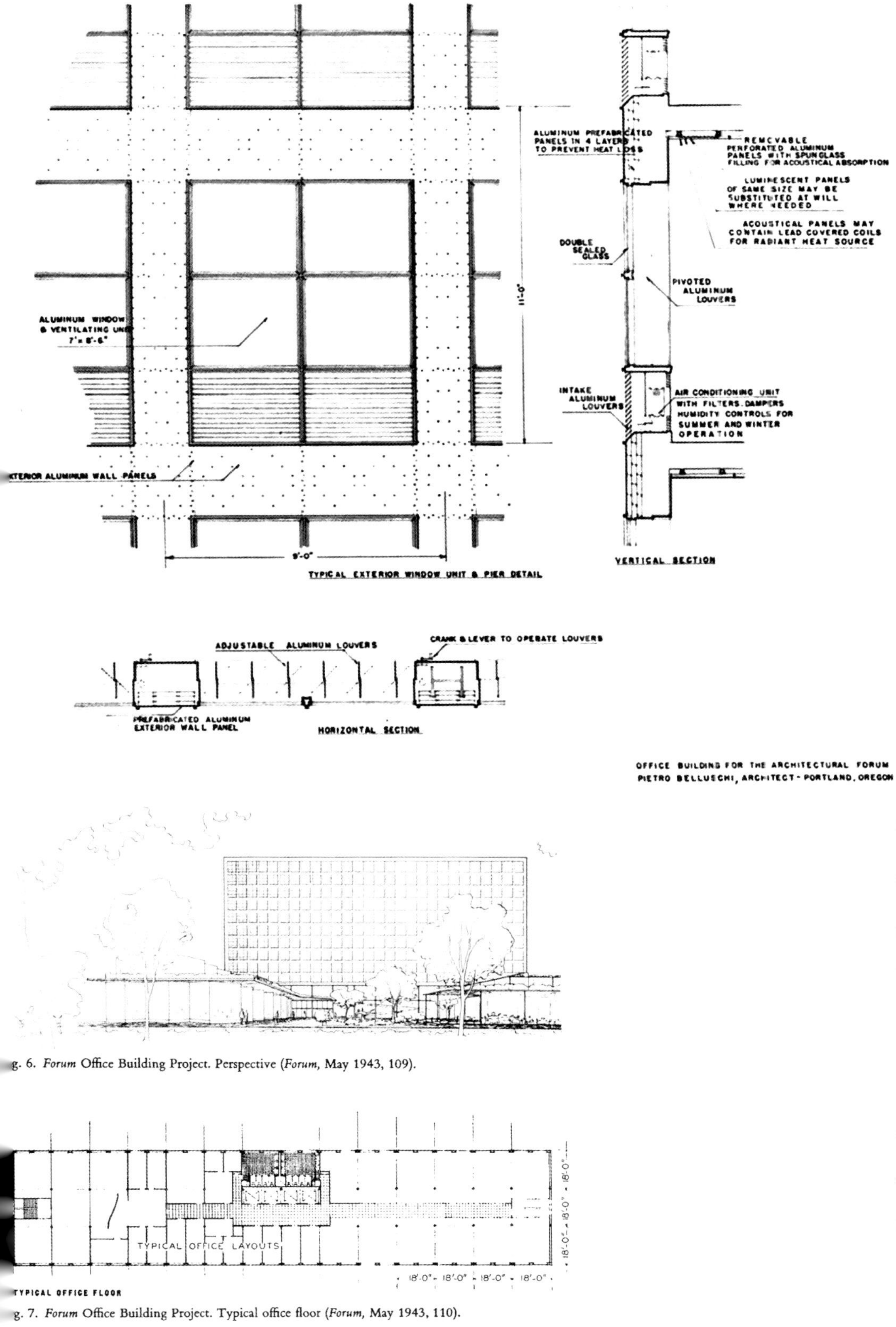


6.12 Pietro Belluschi, "194x—Office Building," from *Architectural Forum*, March 1942.

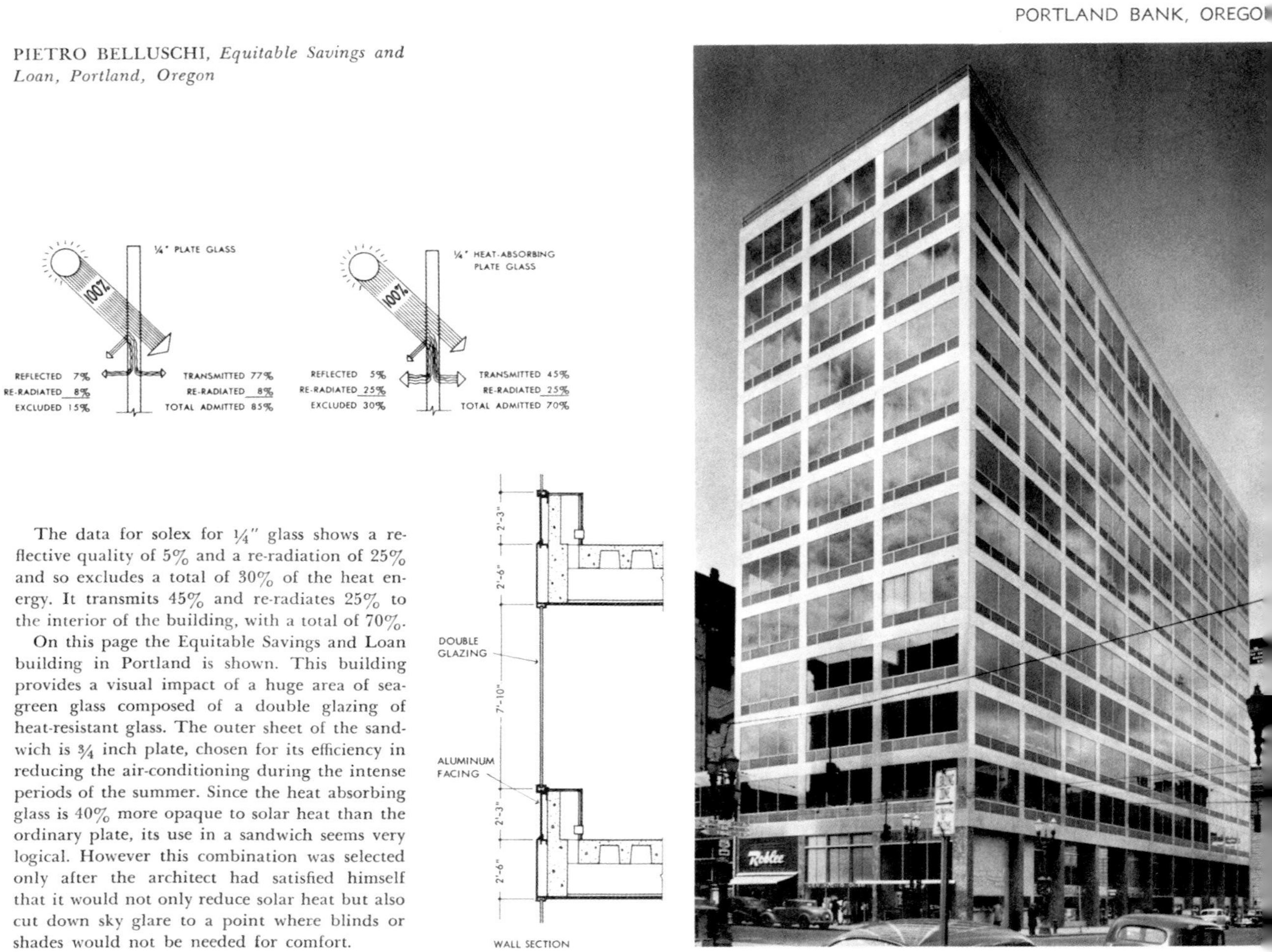
PORTLAND BANK, OREGO

PIETRO BELLUSCHI, *Equitable Savings and Loan, Portland, Oregon*

¼" PLATE GLASS

100%

REFLECTED 7%
RE-RADIATED 8%
EXCLUDED 15%

TRANSMITTED 77%
RE-RADIATED 8%
TOTAL ADMITTED 85%

¼" HEAT-ABSORBING PLATE GLASS

100%

REFLECTED 5%
RE-RADIATED 25%
EXCLUDED 30%

TRANSMITTED 45%
RE-RADIATED 25%
TOTAL ADMITTED 70%

The data for solex for ¼" glass shows a reflective quality of 5% and a re-radiation of 25% and so excludes a total of 30% of the heat energy. It transmits 45% and re-radiates 25% to the interior of the building, with a total of 70%.

On this page the Equitable Savings and Loan building in Portland is shown. This building provides a visual impact of a huge area of sea-green glass composed of a double glazing of heat-resistant glass. The outer sheet of the sandwich is ¾ inch plate, chosen for its efficiency in reducing the air-conditioning during the intense periods of the summer. Since the heat absorbing glass is 40% more opaque to solar heat than the ordinary plate, its use in a sandwich seems very logical. However this combination was selected only after the architect had satisfied himself that it would not only reduce solar heat but also cut down sky glare to a point where blinds or shades would not be needed for comfort.

DOUBLE GLAZING

ALUMINUM FACING

2'-3"
2'-6"
7'-10"
2'-3"
2'-6"

WALL SECTION

6.13 Pietro Belluschi, the Equitable Building, from Olgyay and Olgyay, *Solar Control and Shading Devices*, and an interior view of the Equitable Building, Portland, 1947.

moveable cooling and dehumidifying units could be placed under the window, just next to the lever for adjusting the embedded louvers. When the Equitable Building was built, just a few years later, it was one of the first sealed-curtain wall buildings, as noted. According to Belluschi, "some of the tenants expressed alarm at the lack of shading, but after several months of satisfactory conditions few of them had installed blinds" (figure 6.13).[23]

In general, air conditioning had been an aspect of office building production, however minor initially, since the 1930s, as part of post-Depression recovery. A wide range of technologies—shading, low-e glass, insulated glass panels, and endless proliferation of mullions, sealants, prefabricated windows, and wall units—mitigated some of the most dramatic climatic variations on a given site. Because of this capacity to mitigate and reduce the expense of the mechanical plant, shading served a transitional role in an intricate economic rationale. Eventually, the efficiencies and savings afforded by shading systems could be attained by tightly sealed curtain walls or more efficient cooling plants—air conditioning and the template of the sealed building that accompanied it was made

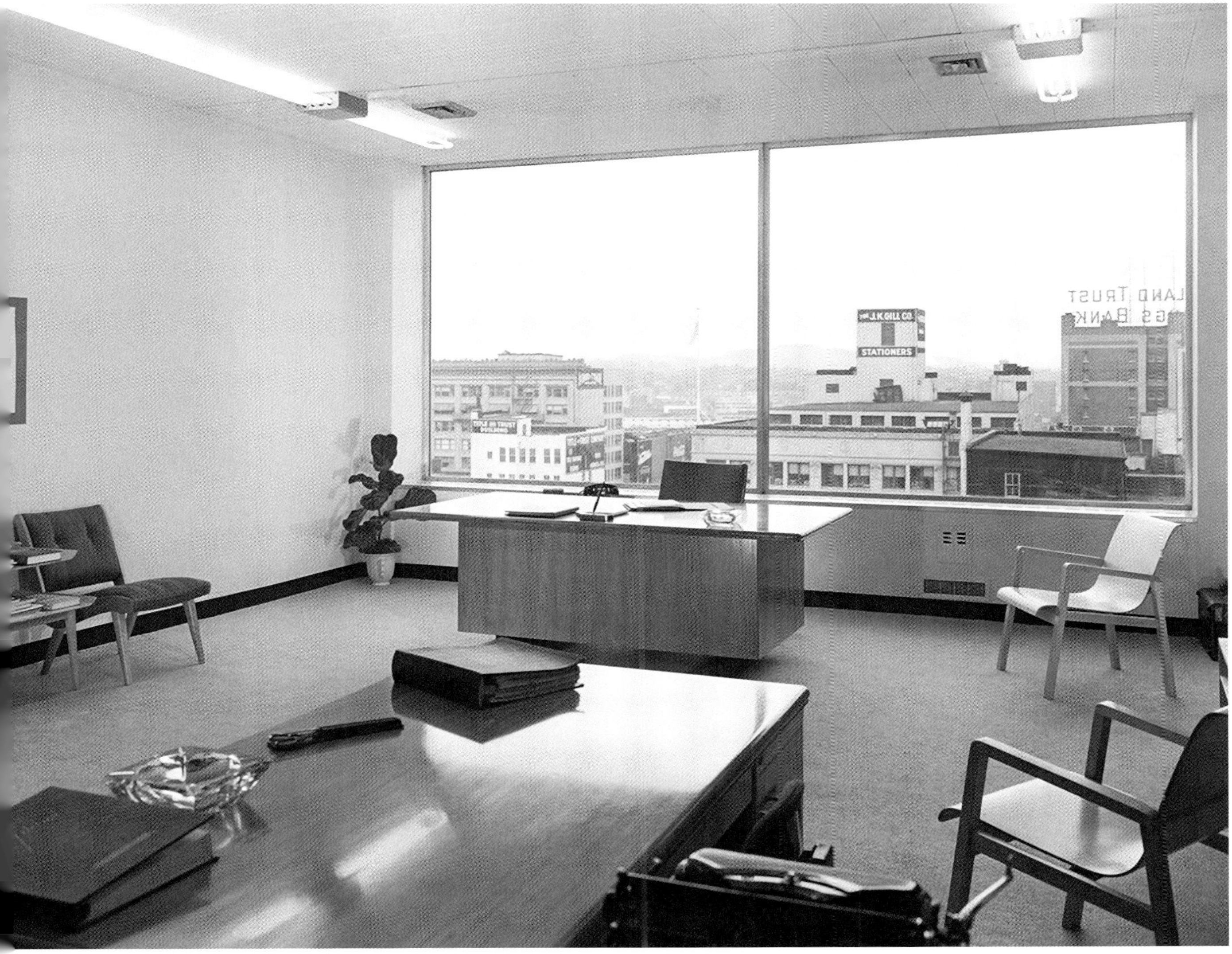


more effective and affordable. Shading devices facilitated investment in what eventually led to a sealed, conditioned tower.

Belluschi developed his first section just discussed relative to an anticipated abundance in aluminum after the war effort wound down; in shifting the balance from more shading/less cooling to less shading/more cooling he noted the preponderance of "cheap power" (largely hydropower) in the northwestern United States.[24] Before the ASHRAE merger and the slow but definitive adaptation of its standards, innovations in HVAC systems proceeded, to some extent, in concert with glass technologies aimed at stopping radiation and increasing insulation and certainly relative to the massive expansion of the engineering expertise in the design and construction of the HVAC systems themselves.

Importantly, low-e glass and attention to the sealed condition of the façade were not always readily visible in a building's façade. This had both material and immaterial effects. By the later 1950s, as these ideas and practices began to circulate outside the increasingly air-conditioned centers of American cities, it was often the case that an all-glass curtain wall similar to the Equitable or Lever façades would be specified alongside significantly less robust performative aspects in the glass treatment and construction, and with inadequate knowledge of the scale of the cooling plants that fed these American buildings. In some cases, such towers were built without adequate floor height in which to insert the ducts and other elements of the cooling system. As a result, many air-conditioned buildings before the wider adoption of ASHRAE standards were uncomfortable and also almost impossible to renovate on thermal terms (it is difficult to add floor height). The United Kingdom was an early adopter of such misapprehended climatic models, and a number of buildings built in London in the late 1950s were demolished the decade after.[25]

Many examples of climatic misapprehension, often more subtle but no less detrimental, follow this general model, all needing to be subject to detailed analysis to determine their relative failings or successes. The United Nations Headquarters, after much wrangling between Wallace Harrison, Le Corbusier, Oscar Niemeyer, and others, decided against brise-soleil in favor of a low-e glass curtain wall with internal blinds and induction coolers—four thousand of the new Carrier Weathermaster units were installed on the interior edge of the façade, leading to extremely high cooling costs (figure 6.14). The system was tested and modeled repeatedly, along the cost/benefit analysis of the AAAS chart, with variables for glazing type, use of shading, and scale of the cooling plant.[26] Results were inconclusive. Individual units led to a difficulty in centralized control and to significant unanticipated costs—some people left the units on when not needed. There were problems as well with the Solex glass panels, some of which cracked under the pressure of the intensive heat differential. Many panels were replaced. A substantive renovation of the building in 2015 added a building-wide system.[27]

Perhaps the most egregious offender in this context is also the most iconic: the Seagram Park Avenue, also in Manhattan, built in 1957 to a design by Mies van der Rohe and Philip Johnson (figure 6.15, see also figure 6.1). The cooling system was similar in principle to that of the United Nations, though the conditioning units were smaller and lower in elevation, in order to maximize the daylight and views from the floor-to-ceiling windows; there was also a cooling vent on the ceiling near the window and a separate system dedicated to the interior core of the building. Drapes were used for relative solar protection; though, as Victor Olgyay was quoted in the introduction to this volume, this was not "the right place": the sun had already warmed the interior. The placement of the window units next to single-paned glass was incredibly inefficient and costly—in effect, the building drew energy

6.14 Adjusting the Weathermaster, at Harrison and Abramowitz, with Oscar Neimeyer et al., United Nations Headquarters, New York, 1952.

6.15 Mies van der Rohe, Philip Johnson et al., Seagram Park Avenue, New York, 1957. Interior with curtains and conditioning units.

through the mechanical system and leaked it out into the atmosphere.

The Seagram tower is a landmark of poor climatic performance. In a recent "energy audit" of midtown Manhattan, office towers were rated for their energy efficiency on a scale of 0 to 100, in order to identify those towers most readily available for effective retrofit and a reduction of midtown's overall energy demand. The Seagram tower came in at a 3—the lowest grade given, by a wide margin.[28] In related press coverage it was noted that "the biggest drain could be the International-style [*sic*] landmark's most lauded features. The Seagram's single-pane glass curtain walls, far less efficient than treated or double-pane windows, and its luminous fluorescent ceilings work against energy conservation."[29] Some of the attributes that have made the building central to the history of modern architecture are also those attributes that make it difficult to retrofit the building for the energy efficient demands of the present—inflected as they are by concerns over carbon emissions resulting from burning fossil fuel, the subsequent instability of the global climate, and the resulting intensification of economic inequality, decimation of territories, threats to nonhuman species, and the specter of global civilizational collapse.

These are just a few of the more prominent examples, which is to say, the beginning of a historical thread of air-conditioned architecture that requires much more substantive elaboration. It would be folly to try to assess the proliferation of conditioned buildings through case-based research—the historical fact of interest is not the building itself but the accumulation of conditioned interiors, the articulation of a new kind of thermal norm conditioned through fossil-fuel systems, regulated by ASHRAE standards, and produced as a matter of course by most architects in most contexts, at least since the Seagram attained prominence on completion in 1957. Indeed, the building was the explicit model for a large number of towers across the United States and around the globe, as the late 1950s and '60s saw the proliferation of fully sealed, single-paned curtain wall towers. This production of a planetary interior also produced a new kind of climatic exterior—the Great Acceleration was intensified through these built objects.

As the Seagram was being designed, in 1955, James Marston Fitch published an article in *Scientific American* on "The Curtain Wall." Describing its technical development, from the Crystal Palace to the UN Secretariat, as a structural triumph, he also sees it as leading to new responsibilities in "controlling the environment within the building." He decries what he calls the "passivity" of the curtain wall as then being used, when it could be "able to intervene actively in the building's struggle to maintain its internal stability." Reiterating the premise in the "Hill in Ohio" image in *House Beautiful* (see figure 4.21), Fitch described how, in the sorts of rectangular, uniformly wrapped curtain walls then being planned and going up in Manhattan, the temperature can be remarkably different across the relatively thin span of the building. He poses a hypothetical scenario: "the south wall, shielded from the north wind and heated by the sun, may have the climate of Charleston, S.C., while the north wall, chilled by the wind and untouched by the sun, may have the climate of Manitoba." "Ideally," Fitch continues, advocating for a more dynamic approach to the curtain wall system—describing, in its most basic formulation, the bioclimatic premise, "the two walls should have quite different properties . . . under different weather conditions the properties of the walls should change to handle the new circumstances." The accompanying drawing shows an abstracted structure breathing in harmony with the varied conditions of the exterior— "coils in the curtain wall," Fitch writes, "will absorb heat on the sunny side and carry it to the cold wall facing north"—perhaps confirming that it was, as Fitch labeled it, a "Design of the Future" (figure 6.16).[30]

Thus did a different kind of façade begin to emerge by the middle of the 1950s, a different kind of screen that expressed something new—to return to Siegert, a different "processing [of] the distinction between inside and outside."[31] From a *dynamic array* of interactive media devices operating on the façade, producing the thermally consistent interior of the comfort zone; to a *regulated formula* involving a sealed, multipaned glass curtain wall with an interior conditioned to a more precise consistency, by fossil-fuel-powered HVAC systems. By the late 1950s, buildings around the world began to adopt the ASHRAE system unevenly. The recurrent publication of new ASHRAE standards has increasingly led to a universal planetary interior, at the level of commercial, institutional, travel, and education, and many residential buildings. Many spaces, regions, cities, and communities that do not have air conditioning desire it. The elaboration of the ASHRAE model was a robust historical process of producing a specific interior effect, a specific atmospheric effect, and a specific species to inhabit it.

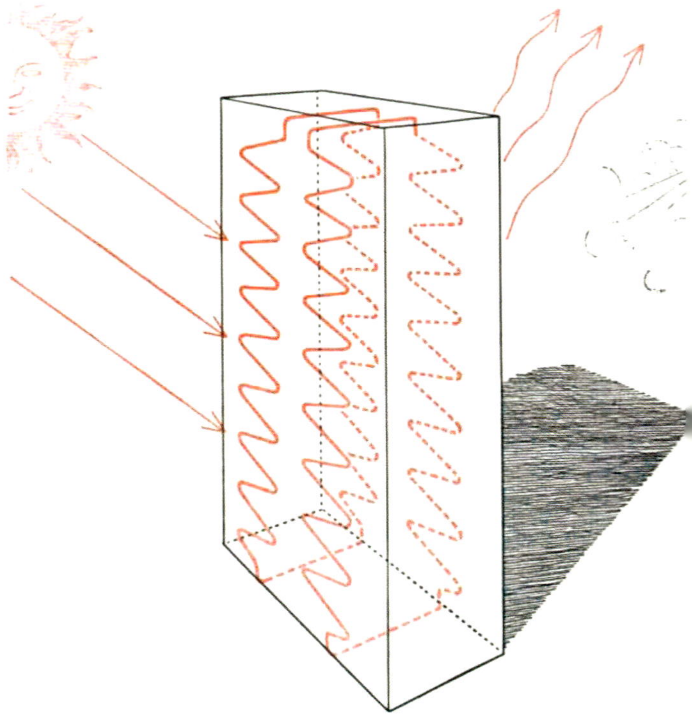

6.16 Design of the Future from James Marston Fitch, "The Curtain Wall," in *Scientific American*, 1955.

## People Conditioning

This vision and production of the air-conditioned future also imagined a specific kind of human, occupant, inhabitant, or user: the insurance processor at the IRB and the active inhabitant of the Edifício Mamãe; Neutra's implicit figuration of the subject in need of care and attention; the Olgyays' sketch of a figure, likely Aladar, relaxing on a Corbusian chaise and smoking a pipe, reading the newspaper, completely at ease. Comfortable. This was a radically racial, gendered, and class-inflected figure of the future human. It was an ode to stability and to comfort as a specific form of economic exclusion, and the consistency of social and infrastructural values, expressed through architecture.

Air conditioning is also people conditioning. In the "comfort zone" and other elocutions, a specific kind of human was imagined to occupy interior space in new ways. Occupants of the planetary interior, which includes most of the readers of this book, have themselves (ourselves) been conditioned, as we have adjusted to anticipate and expect normative conditions in built interiors around the world. This was, it turns out, a profound project of the twentieth century, a restructuring of physiology, the built environment, and energy resources and sinks that have reshaped the physical and social world—with complex resonance up to the present, a resonance that challenges architects to provide different spatial conditions, different interiors, and a different relationship between the human enterprise and the earth system. If humans have been conditioned to enjoy, aspire to, or expect air conditioning, how can we be conditioned otherwise?

An aspect of this problematic has been, again, the increasingly demanding ASHRAE regulations that have been released since the initial publication in 1966. These updates have been informed by sponsored research and have made substantial claims as to the effects of interior space on health and productivity. Although the efficiency of energy use has increased, so have ASHRAE regulations, requiring thermal interiors to be produced to increasingly intensive standards—standards that could only be met through an increasingly efficient HVAC system within a sealed façade.[32] The dynamics have been such that the standards of comfort increase faster than the capacity of

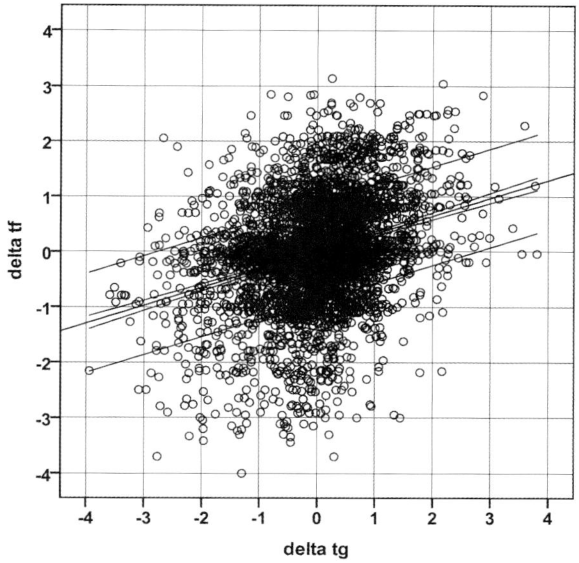


**Fig. 5.** Pooled regression of the day-surveys in the SCATs database. The range of delta tg has been restricted to ±4 K to remove outliers. The outer lines show the residual standard deviation of the ASHRAE scale votes (delta tf). The inner pair of lines show the 95% limits on the placing of the regression line.

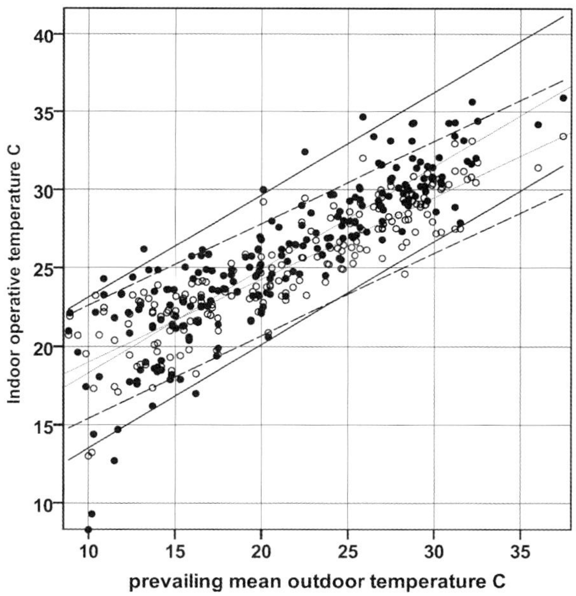


**Fig. 15.** Scatters of neutral temperatures and mean operative temperatures superimposed. The open points are the neutral temperatures and the filled points the mean operative temperatures. The dashed lines delineate the zone in which lie 95% of the neutral temperatures, and the solid lines the equivalent zone for the mean operative temperatures. (FR mode).

6.17 From Humphreys and Hancock, "Do People Like to Feel Neutral?" different means of measuring norms of thermal experience, 2007.

HVAC systems to efficiently meet the new standards—increased energy throughput is almost always required. Even the various global systems intended to measure levels of architectural sustainability generally operate in the amount of carbon being emitted—decreasing this throughput to meet the same comfort standards—rather than eliminating carbon emissions.

From this perspective the challenge of the twenty-first century is, perhaps, less one of improving on the technological efficiency of the HVAC system, of clarifying its regulatory breadth, and more to provide alternatives—alternative spaces, lifestyles, regulatory mechanisms, and metrics, facilitating habits that can depend less on fossil fuels. Is it possible, in other words, to live in discomfort?—on the assumption that discomfort, by virtue of global climatic instability, is likely coming anyway. What are the politics and distribution of this discomfort, how does it operate in relationship to class and race?

Discussions in architecture and engineering have long been attentive to these forms of adjusting regulations, standards, and interiors toward other conceptions of comfort. Theories of adaptive comfort, in particular, abound—proposing that the regulatory systems rely on a too-limited model of human relationship to their thermal environments. The basic premise is that the abstraction of universal comfort is inadequate to encompass the wide range of possibly comfortable conditions. Such adaptive proposals suggest that a hotter, cooler, or more or less humid condition might be acceptable in certain regions or for certain groups, and that regulations and building practices should allow for local differences.[33]

One such study by researchers in the United Kingdom asks, "do people like to feel 'neutral?'" The study's administrators exposed individuals to a variety of spaces and conditions and then questioned the individuals about their comfort. They discovered some variation—"the desired sensation on the ASHRAE scale is often other than 'neutral,' and it differs systematically from person to person—people had different characteristic desires regarding their thermal sensation."[34] There was about a three-degree Celsius variation across the presumed desired temperature. Further indexes were made for regional origin, eating habits, and exercise (figure 6.17). While these findings are significant in their general disruption of the closed feedback loop of ASHRAE regulations, the authors indicate that they are even more relevant to the goal of privileging reduced carbon emissions over comfort. If, as they write, the predominant "assumption that optimal comfort can be equated with thermal neutrality is incorrect, then temperature standards based on the ASHRAE scale will also be to some extent faulty, and faulty assumptions about the required temperatures can lead to erroneous estimates of energy requirement."[35] Such considerations have also led to heating and cooling devices focused on the individual rather than the space, to minimize carbon emissions while attending to these differences.

For the nonspecialist, this study also reveals the reliance of ASHRAE standard derivations on the surveying of inhabitants of different interiors. Individuals are asked to identify their relative comfort across a scale of possible conditions. Leaving aside the social complexities and potential economic and racial stratifications of such a purportedly neutral interrogation, the scale itself is functionally and conceptually inadequate. The authors of the study also indicate that "warm," for example, sometimes indicates comfort and sometimes means too hot.[36]

Another potent example of the design and politics of adaptive comfort involves a relatively well-known, though worth rehearsing, story of the speech delivered by then-US President Jimmy Carter on July 15, 1979—officially titled the "Address to the Nation on Energy and National Goals."[37] In this televised event Carter laid out an ambitious plan for energy efficiency and conservation, based on the principle that "this nation will never use more foreign oil than it did in 1977," a promise that was quickly broken after the election of Ronald Reagan. To achieve his goal of conservation, Carter proposed, while clad in a warm cardigan, that individuals and families change their habits—drive less, lower thermostats, put on a sweater, and other seemingly simple practices that could transform the geopolitics and economics of oil. Carter was not reelected—an indication of, at least, three things: first, that habits are difficult to disrupt; second, that concern over energy efficiency relies on individual behavior, as much as enlightened policy, to manage social and environmental inequity; and third, that broader collective perceptions, such as those of a national identity—which, in the context of Carter's speech, came to associate lowering thermostats with capitulation to foreign pressure—can encourage or discourage specific choices. Policy, and politics, have a role to play, in other words, in framing the thermal experience of the conditioned interior as a site of contestation.

Of course, the larger question is: can design encourage different kinds of cultural aspirations, or at least reflect them? Numerous critics outside the field have illuminated the intensity with which buildings—as cultural as much as technological objects—have come to be seen as obstacles and opportunities toward a collective ambition to reconsider ways of life amid climatic instability. For example, Amitav Ghosh, in his text *The Great Derangement: Climate Change and the Unthinkable*, is interested in clarifying the extent to which our current climate challenge is rooted in culture, and he identifies the importance of buildings early on, in two seminal passages: "Culture generates desires," Ghosh writes, "for vehicles and appliances, for certain kinds of gardens and dwellings—that are among the principle drivers of the carbon economy." A seemingly simple causal imperative that locates design intention as essential to broad social transformations. Focusing even more closely on the cultural dimensions of design and its reception, Ghosh writes, "if contemporary trends in architecture, even in this period of accelerating carbon emissions, favor shiny, glass-and-metal-plated towers, do we not have to ask, What are the patterns of desire that are fed by these gestures?"[38] At stake, for Ghosh, is how new buildings, new narratives, and new cultural practices can adjust such patterns and foster new desires. Ghosh's imperative suggests that we not only need to have the technical tools for producing climate with less reliance on energy but also that the mediatic positioning of the dynamic façade has, perhaps, the capacity, or at least the potential, to induce new patterns of desire in order to open up to other possibilities for change.

The space of the thermal interior, in both domestic and commercial environments, is thus enacted and emphasized in order to reimagine an embodied relationship to climate—a different kind of people conditioning. The question becomes: can architects induce habits that activate a different relationship to fossil fuels? If so, the goal of such architecture, and related scholarship, is to provide a framework in which such patterns of desire can best be enacted.

## The Comfortocene

All the same, in many ways the climatic determinists have long since won the day—a racially, geographically, and gender determined norm for climatic conditions of habitation has spread around the globe, at great cost and with epochal consequence. That air conditioning has also improved health conditions and in many ways increased quality of life is not to be overlooked. "The mansion of modern freedom," as Dipesh Chakrabarty has put it (note the architectural metaphor), "has been built on a base of fossil fuels."[39]

The Anthropocene presents productive challenges for how to encounter changing conceptions of the human. Given the significance of a range of anti- and a-humanisms to critical historical practices over the past few decades, the apparent imperative in Anthropocene discourse to return to a uniform species-being threatens to, at best, temper the further expansion of conditions of freedom. As Chakrabarty, again, has written, "The discipline of history exists on the assumption that our past, present, and future are connected by a certain continuity of human experience."[40] The Anthropocene, and the planetary cautions it brings to the fore, disrupts this sense of continuity. How to confront this new sense of humanity, after decades of disrupting the hegemonic epistemologies of "man"? Humans are simultaneously being placed at the nexus of a causal diagram, in the invocation of "geological agency," and also recognized as relatively impotent in collectively expressing that agency with any clear intentionality. In considering the Anthropocene as a framework for historical scholarship, the imposition of species-being is, rather than an imperative, an opening toward the acknowledgment of diverse ways to life and their different climatic effects.

In the critical discourse on the Anthropocene, careful attention to precisely which humans, which "anthros," are being discussed is of great importance. Insofar as the Anthropocene indicates a material condition—of more carbon in the atmosphere, of fewer trees in the ground or less fish in the sea—these conditions are the result of a wildly uneven process of economic growth across the planetary surface. The British and other imperial powers of western Europe, and then the United States in its manifest push for a paradigm of endless growth, are largely to blame for atmospheric instability. Questions of scientific knowledge, social responsibility, and geopolitical compensations are caught up in this unevenness. The situation is further complicated through the complex means by which so-called developing countries are poised to "catch-up" to levels of industrialization and consumer saturation, but with a changing set of ethical and material ideals. This is manifest in the debates on climate change as they play out at the geopolitical and NGO level, as at the talks in Paris in 2015, and further solicits a need for carefully understanding the history of modernization on these terms. Maintaining a precise, varied, and above all historically and geographically specific understanding of the role of actual humans engaged in these diverse processes is an important task for scholarly inquiry.[41]

Thus another risk—for many advocates of the term, the Anthropocene stands as an opportunity to celebrate the role of human ingenuity and technology in its potential for planetary transformation. This so-called good Anthropocene, perhaps most clearly represented by the *Eco-Modernist Manifesto* published online in 2015, envisions a bright future in which human dominion over the earth is rendered sustainable through a combination of geo- and social engineering.[42] The city is a primary site for these optimistic speculations: in the manifesto this is argued relative to the importance of increased density and enlightened urbanity as a means for rendering more efficient the relationship between social and biotic processes.

This premise is also reflective of the prevalent premise in architectural practice that technological innovation can resolve the sociopolitical challenges seeded by environmental pressures. As the eco-modernists approach it, the goal is to decouple economic growth from environmental damage. The mechanism of this decoupling is technological innovation. The techno-optimisms that have consumed the professional field of architecture beg for a critical-historical apparatus that will temper and at times refute them—to critically address the relationship between changes in the built environment and the myriad potential futures they contain. Rather than technological solutions, alternative people conditioning requires a political debate and the willed desire of collective subjects.[43] Historical artifacts and processes help to shed light on design, among other collective ventures, as a realm rich with discursive and mediatic speculation on these terms.

Rather than a call for disciplinary exceptionalism, this discourse elaborates on the specific contributions that the field of architectural history is poised to make to wider cultural understandings of the Anthropocene: to the slow and accumulative condition of its development, to the profoundly ambivalent prospects it outlines relative to human futures, and to a skeptical though engaged approach to technological innovation and to the role of these new kinds of cultural inquiry in the development of subjectivity. Alternative framings of the Anthropocene epoch—Jason Moore's Capitolocene, Donna Haraway's Chthulucene, Jussi Parikka's Anthrobscene, and many others—help to clarify both the significance of language in these debates, and also how these interventions solicit simultaneous social, political, and material questions.[44] One shudders at the thought of another, but the Comfortocene, or the Air-Conditioned Epoch, highlights the casual ways that mechanical systems have entered, infiltrated, and taken over the prospects for humanity. The cultural techniques and objects that are the subjects of architectural histories serve as mediating devices between collective desire and ecological systems. With these tools and methods in mind, environmental histories of architecture can maintain a potent critical perspective on issues relevant to the discipline while also expanding its field of evidence and scope of resonance.

Interiors are small spaces. Discrete, distinct. Even the largest enclosed stadium is minuscule compared to the cubic volume of the breathable atmosphere. Yet, these small blocks of air are connected by systems, conditioned by fuel, and integrated into a planetary interior. Interiors accumulate; images are needed to visualize, understand, and counter these accumulations. Since the late 1950s, the mechanical conditioning of the built interior has been one of the primary sources of carbon emissions. The current epoch is one of accumulation, not only of capital but also of raw, often unruly material, from plastic in the ocean and carbon in the atmosphere to people, buildings, and cities.[45] Also the accumulation of anxiety and of a recognition of the difficulty of finding effective means for intervening in the behaviors and practices that engender these patterns. Alongside these material accumulations, image-making practices embedded within the disciplines of art and architecture have proven to be fertile, mobile, and capacious. Images of accumulation help open up the climate to cultural inquiry and political mobilization.

This mediatic dynamism operates according to the basic principle that the accumulation of carbon in the atmosphere is invisible, and its myriad systemic impacts difficult to trace. The unspectacular nature of images of accumulation means that environmental challenges are also representation challenges. The relative invisibility of environmental decay, its delayed and dispersed effects, and perhaps most importantly its attritional or agglomerative condition, renders it oblique in cultural discourse.

The difficulty of visualizing climatic instability presents obstacles to collective action and complicates the political resonance of its effects. In a spectacle-infused culture, it can be difficult to bring into relevance the slow accumulations now destabilizing the climate. In order to visualize accumulation, media practitioners are faced with technical challenges not only in image production but also in devising new relationships between representation and knowledge, theory and practice, and data and agency.

Climate is the nexus for social and cultural change relative to the unpredictability of our environmental future. These discussions have become potent sites for the articulation and elaboration of the media of accumulation and for examining the potential resonance of environmental knowledge across social and cultural patterns. As discursive sites, art, architecture, and other creative fields engage in the production of images of accumulation to share knowledge internal to their disciplines and to integrate knowledge across fields, collectively outlining methods for investigating cultural dimensions of the global ecological system. These image-making practices have formed a cultural infrastructure focused on the relationship among humans, other species, and their environments.

## Comfort and Capital

In Tomás Maldonado's 1987 text, "The Idea of Comfort," he clarifies the extent to which the provision of what he calls "livability" operates as an engine for and a consequence of processes of modernization, industrialization, and the financialization of life. "Comfort is a modern idea," Maldonado argues, and one shot through with the inequities of capitalist forms of development. "Before the Industrial Revolution," he explains, "the expectation of comfort . . . was the privilege of the few. But the progressive diffusion of comfort to the masses was not accidental. There is no doubt that it has played, from the beginning, a fundamental role in the task of controlling the social fabric of the nascent capitalist society."[46]

A compelling premise—to map the rise of a socioeconomic system of capital according to the disposition of the thermal interior. Of course, Maldonado is speaking of comfort more broadly, and distinctly across class lines, though it is not difficult to extract the thermally conditioned interior as a symbolic and material realm for the intensification of class difference. Neutra reflected a similar disposition, in his *Architecture of Social Concern*: "there has, of course, always been comfort in the world, reckless comfort, we could say—comfort based on someone else's continuous labors."[47] Together they articulate a broad gesture—to some extent self-evident when one considers the entanglements of histories of architecture, of colonialism and postcolonialism, of wars for oil and corporate-technological advancements in extraction, processing, and the direct utilization of fossil fuels in the conditioning of the built interior—of the importance of thermal conditioning to the emergence of capitalist space. A space of excess, of signification, of expenditure.[48] From this perspective of comfort and the intensification of inequity, it is not enough to map the modern movement in architecture directly along the trajectories and inclines of the Great Acceleration; rather, a more general constellation of built objects, consumer products, the circulation of marketing and media begin to coalesce as a system of carbon production, translating fossil fuels into comfortable environments and luxury objects for the relative few. These consolidations and stratifications are materially produced and are starkly legible in the built environment.

Maldonado was invested in environments, with a range difficult to summarize. A compelling architectural theorist, he ran the Hochschule für Gestaltung at Ulm from 1954 to 1966 and was essential to the development of the Ulm Model, a sort of architectural interpretation of cybernetics, promulgated also by the engineer Abraham Moles. Maldonado described the Model at length in an essay on "Design Education and Social Responsibility," written in 1961 and published in English in 1965, in Gyorgy Kepes's edited volume *Education of Vision*.[49] The Ulm Model involved, in part, the close integration with industry in the formation of development groups, organizing pedagogical and design projects according to agendas laid out by Krups, Lufthansa, and others.

The premise was that the designer could lead industry toward a more developed engagement with society—in terms that resonated with Ulm's claims to be the "postwar Bauhaus" and that also resonate today, across questions of livability and comfort. Maldonado moved to Princeton in 1966. No doubt he would have at least met Victor Olgyays, and perhaps read his book. Maldonado wrote *Design, Nature, and Revolution: Towards a Critical Ecology* in 1972. He aspired to outline what was at once a sort of wild logic for ecological ways of life and a strict rationale for technobureaucratic and social management. It was framed in opposition to the deception and imperialism of the Vietnam War, and in line with a Gramscian praxis or applied ethics of design intervention.[50]

Maldonado's comfort essay appeared, as noted, in 1987—a year after the Bruntland Report's publication of "Our Common Future," largely hailed as the document that inserted the framework of sustainability into the global discussion of environmentalism, and amid a world already deep in the throes of an intensifying neoliberalism and the architectural postmodernisms that expressed and reified it. Maldonado elaborates on the importance of managed and normative internal environments to the conditions of architectural, and more generally economic, production across the Great Acceleration, according to the specifics of the "domestic sphere" that were also the focus of the Olgyays' early work:

> Comfort is seen as a procedure with a compensatory function, that is, a procedure seeking to restore—as much physically as psychologically—the energies consumed in the hostile external world of work. With standards more or less formalized, more or less explicit, comfort serves to structure daily life, to ritualize conduct, especially the attitudes and postures of the body . . . it may well be that comfort expresses, better than any other cultural contrivance, the "techniques of the body" appropriate to modern bourgeois society.[51]

Maldonado was putting back on the table an interest in comfort, in particular the thermal consistency of the interior environment, that had been the subject of much debate until the mid-1960s. So, another period of transition in the mid-1980s, perhaps a more precise one, a sort of reckoning with comfort and its intractability.

Maldonado's appeal to the critique of capital as a means to evaluate the resonance of comfort and design itself resonates strongly with a much better-known analysis of the built interior offered in this same moment—one that suggests a conclusion, on the terms of cultural relationships and environmental change, to this narrative of the

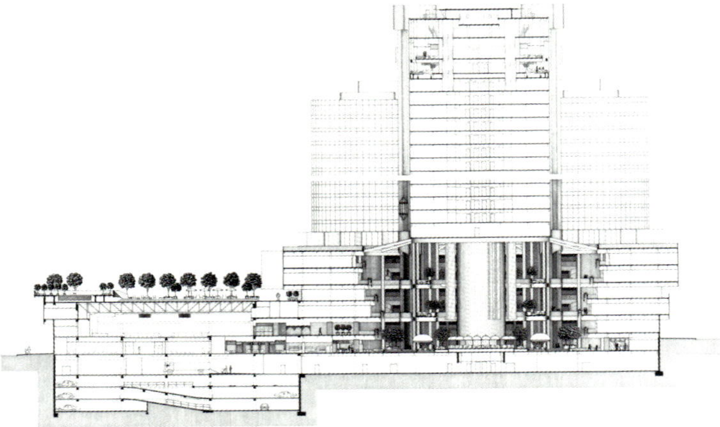

6.18 John Portman, Bonaventure Hotel interior, Los Angeles, 1977.

potential of climatic modernism. Fredric Jameson's article "Postmodernism; or, the Cultural Logic of Late Capitalism" was published in 1984, the book in 1991—the latter ended with, and the former started with, a discussion of John Portman's Bonaventure Hotel in Los Angeles, built in 1977 (figure 6.18). Jameson reads the building's soaring, disorienting interior as symptomatic of the emergence of anyspace, produced through similarity and reflection, both inside and out. "Given the absolute symmetry of the four towers," he initially writes, "it is quite impossible to get your bearings in this lobby."[52] He is consumed with the modes of conveyance, the smoothness of the intersecting flows of elevators and escalators, the openness of the interior hallways and their frank accessibility, the persistence of the cognitive incapacity to locate and relate to these new "spatial mutations." He is commenting obliquely on the atmospheric conditions of the interior, themselves similar, if not identical, to many other thermal spaces around the world, giving Jameson's critique a new aspect. Naming this condition "postmodern hyperspace," Jameson argues for the emergence of a planetary subjectivity: "this latest mutation in space . . . succeeded in transcending the capacities of the individual human body to locate itself, to organize its immediate surroundings perceptually, and cognitively to map its position in a mappable external world." A premise at once similar to and at odds with Kenneth Boulding's invocation of the image of the world. And yet, Jameson decries, this cognitive map, this emergent epistemological shift, faces an "even sharper dilemma which is the incapacity of our minds, at least at present, to map the great global multinational and decentered communicational network in which we find ourselves caught as individual subjects." A techno-mediatic version of the current climatic challenge—incapacitated minds facing the challenges of global accumulation. To insert climate, or oil, or conditioned interiors, or comfort, into these dilemmas and incapacities, into the complexity of a network of economies and ecologies, investments and resources and sinks, insurance and reinsurance, is to recognize the significance of architecture's role in the intensification of a culture of the comfort zone.

The eco-critic Ursula Heise has recently emphasized the importance Jameson also ascribes to Frank Gehry's house in Santa Monica—designed and built in almost exact parallel with the Bonaventure, across 1977–78, a few miles toward the Pacific. In building the house, Gehry applied a second skin on an older building in such a way that spaces, Jameson writes, are "not adequately defined as inside or outside in the traditional sense"; perhaps similar to (though of course also quite distinct from) the sort of atmospheric and climatological ambiguity that Banham had ascribed to Greene and Greene, and Neutra and Schindler, in his article from 1971.[53] This spatial unsettling is seen as indicative of an end to "place . . . in that simpler phenomenological or regional sense. . . . More precisely," Jameson continues, "[space] exists at a much feebler level. . . . As individuals, we are in and out of all these overlapping dimensions all the time."[54]

---

Jameson's analysis of the Bonaventure relies on the hard boundary of its exterior—he describes, in the book, how one does not even enter from the street, does not penetrate the four identical towers, but enters through the car parking lot, below. The screen is absolute in both its material and symbolic capacity: a barrier between internal and external climates, a marker, in its reflectivity, of an isolated interior. But one that also, endlessly, aggregates, accumulates, and produces a planetary effect. The Bonaventure interior is a space of absolute conditioning, treacherous in the simplicity, audacity, and epochal crisis of its ubiquity—of the transformation of selected atmospheric volumes into the global interior of capital, positioned to intensify, simultaneously, the accumulation of both wealth and carbon. Jameson is here describing, in part, the effects of the emergence, solidified by the 1980s perhaps but nascent in the 1950s and '60s, of a normativity and consistency of the planetary interior; he is in this sense on the cusp of a different kind of recognition of the significance of this everyspace, of a cultural conditioning that is also mechanical conditioning and the conditioning, or altering, of the global atmosphere.

## Time and Space

This narrative resists conclusion—it is an account of a historical process that is still ongoing, though transformed. We are now, or soon will be, past air conditioning. Rather than attempt to draw all of these historical threads together, the aim here is to shepherd them along into disparate possible futures; into heterogeneous and even unexpected ways of encountering the problematic of climate and comfort; into cultural and political agitation, to recognition of air conditioning as a space of contestation; and to exploring how design can facilitate social conditions that mitigate the impacts of climate instability. The thermal interior becomes a wildly abstract but remarkably potent site for productive cultural friction—for the production of alternatives, and for speculation on different socioclimatic conditions.

As HVAC took over the conditioning of the interior by the end of the 1950s, the media of architecture and climate also began to shift. Experiments in the contours of climate system knowledge, and in the technologies to understand and communicate it, continued to produce instructive imagery, though it was increasingly marginal to cultural developments in architecture. It was a technical image in the simplest sense: a manual, providing a lesson. Much of this research took place in engineering schools, or in new specialized departments or research streams in schools of architecture that were focused on what had come to be called architectural science. These can be seen in relationship to the Olgyays' self-orientation as researchers, in white coats, working in a laboratory rather than a studio. Many such programs and departments developed institutional means to insulate research on architectural science from the design cultures that surrounded them, intending to free their experiments and explorations from undue influence. This led, in general terms, to deeply entrenched institutional and communicative barriers between engineers and designers, or even between technologically oriented architects and those focused on design. Again, the debates of postmodernism—Eisenman's efforts discussed in chapter 1, and those resonant in Jameson's extended critique, and many others not discussed here—were all a sort of froth on the material transformations and energy infrastructures being developed below, alongside, and at the same time.

The Olgyays, in this sense, were elaborating on a template largely originated by Henry J. Cowan, who occupied the first chair in architectural science at the University of Sydney from the early 1950s. He taught and wrote on the topic for decades, encouraging a robust research culture focused on climate and environment in the region.[1] The research and writings of the Israeli American architect Baruch Givoni followed these leads, later in the 1960s, developing elaborate and more precise means to analyze, evaluate, and produce thermal conditions. Givoni could perhaps best be seen as a second-generation architectural-climate methodologist, no longer caught up, as the Olgyays were, in the travails of how to get the discussion started but, rather, expanding its technical acuity in the context of focused research streams. Cowan's student Steven Szokolay, at the University of Queensland, and the Olgyays' student Jeffrey Cook at Arizona State University, also fit in this category. These figures, their institutional context and the influence of their many students, deserve their own historical treatment. The work of this generation involved, among other developments, extensive elaborations of the bioclimatic chart and more detail on the architectural means to attain the desired thermal conditions, and the methods, diagrams, softwares, and, eventually, diagnostic and sensing devices that accompanied them.[2] Only recently have explicit efforts been made, at Sydney and in many other institutions, to bring these different trajectories of research together.

So while understanding of the relationship of climate patterns to the cycles and patterns of social life persisted in a specialized technical context, and in numerous unaffiliated attempts

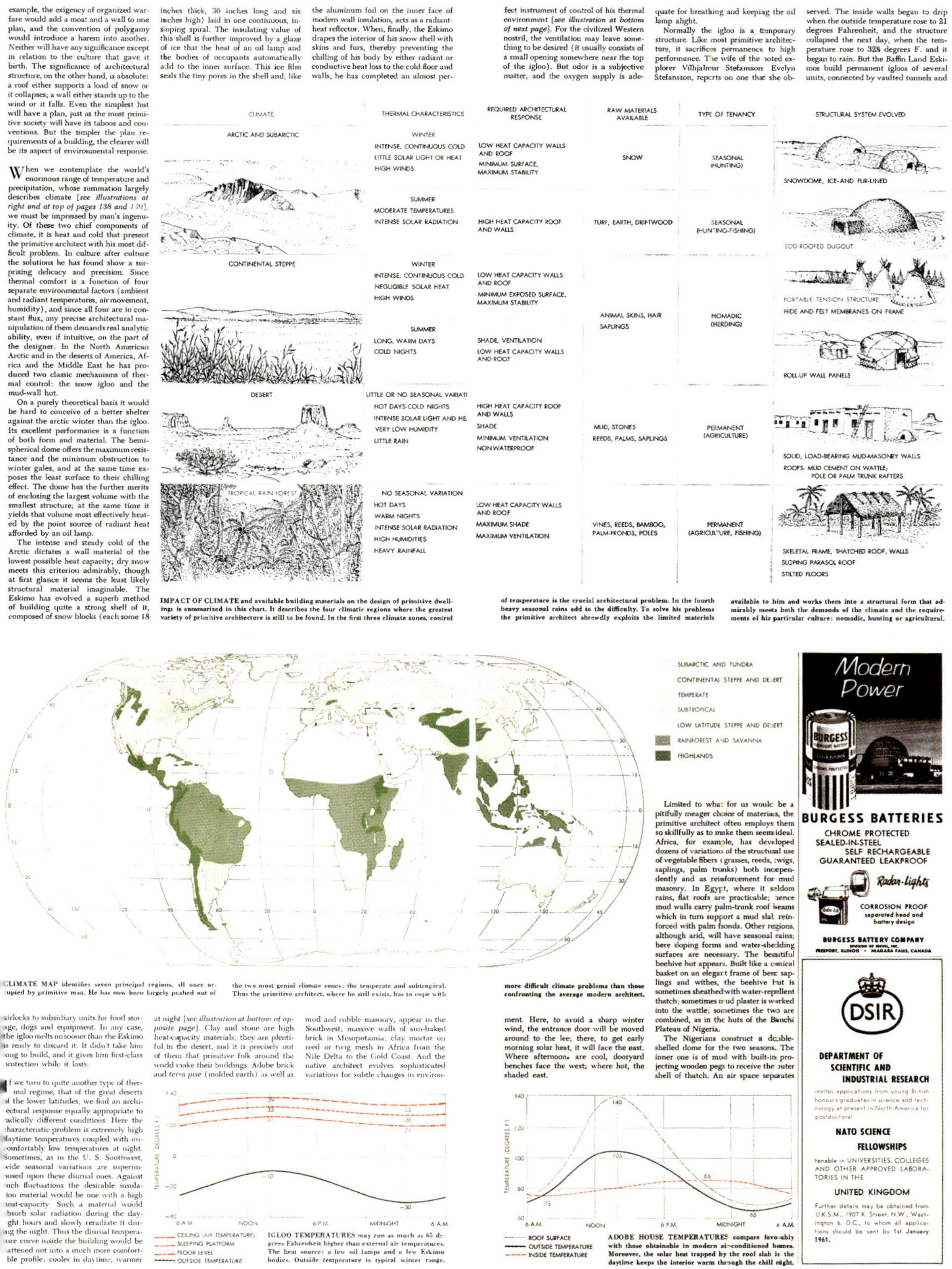

example, the exigency of organized warfare would add a moat and a wall to one plan, and the convention of polygamy would introduce a harem into another. Neither will have any significance except in relation to the culture that gave it birth. The significance of architectural structure, on the other hand, is absolute: a roof either supports a load of snow or it collapses; a wall either stands up to the wind or it falls. Even the simplest hut will have a plan, just as the most primitive society will have its taboos and conventions. But the simpler the plan requirements of a building, the clearer will be its aspect of environmental response.

When we contemplate the world's enormous range of temperature and precipitation, whose summation largely describes climate [*see illustrations at right and at top of pages 138 and 139*], we must be impressed by man's ingenuity. Of these two chief components of climate, it is heat and cold that present the primitive architect with his most difficult problem. In culture after culture the solutions he has found show a surprising delicacy and precision. Since thermal comfort is a function of four separate environmental factors (ambient and radiant temperatures, air movement, humidity), and since all four are in constant flux, any precise architectural manipulation of them demands real analytic ability, even if intuitive, on the part of the designer. In the North American Arctic and in the deserts of America, Africa and the Middle East he has produced two classic mechanisms of thermal control: the snow igloo and the mud-wall hut.

On a purely theoretical basis it would be hard to conceive of a better shelter against the arctic winter than the igloo. Its excellent performance is a function of both form and material. The hemispherical dome offers the maximum resistance and the minimum obstruction to winter gales, and at the same time exposes the least surface to their chilling effect. The dome has the further merits of enclosing the largest volume with the smallest structure; at the same time it yields that volume most effectively heated by the point source of radiant heat afforded by an oil lamp.

The intense and steady cold of the Arctic dictates a wall material of the lowest possible heat capacity; dry snow meets this criterion admirably, though at first glance it seems the least likely structural material imaginable. The Eskimo has evolved a superb method of building quite a strong shell of it, composed of snow blocks (each some 18 inches thick, 36 inches long and six inches high) laid in one continuous, insloping spiral. The insulating value of this shell is further improved by a glaze of ice that the heat of an oil lamp and the bodies of occupants automatically add to the inner surface. This ice film seals the tiny pores in the shell and, like the aluminum foil on the inner face of modern wall insulation, acts as a radiant-heat reflector. When, finally, the Eskimo drapes the interior of his snow shell with skins and furs, thereby preventing the chilling of his body by either radiant or conductive heat loss to the cold floor and walls, he has completed an almost perfect instrument of control of his thermal environment [*see illustration at bottom of next page*]. For the civilized Western nostril, the ventilation may leave something to be desired (it usually consists of a small opening somewhere near the top of the igloo). But odor is a subjective matter, and the oxygen supply is adequate for breathing and keeping the oil lamp alight.

Normally the igloo is a temporary structure. Like most primitive architecture, it sacrifices permanence to high performance. The wife of the noted explorer Vilhjalmur Stefansson, Evelyn Stefansson, reports on one that she observed. The inside walls began to drip when the outside temperature rose to 21 degrees Fahrenheit, and the structure collapsed the next day, when the temperature rose to 32½ degrees F. and it began to rain. But the Baffin Land Eskimos build permanent igloos of several units, connected by vaulted tunnels and airlocks to subsidiary units for food storage, dogs and equipment. In any case, the igloo melts no sooner than the Eskimo is ready to discard it. It didn't take him long to build, and it gives him first-class protection while it lasts.

| CLIMATE | THERMAL CHARACTERISTICS | REQUIRED ARCHITECTURAL RESPONSE | RAW MATERIALS AVAILABLE | TYPE OF TENANCY | STRUCTURAL SYSTEM EVOLVED |
|---|---|---|---|---|---|
| ARCTIC AND SUBARCTIC | WINTER<br>INTENSE, CONTINUOUS COLD<br>LITTLE SOLAR LIGHT OR HEAT<br>HIGH WINDS | LOW HEAT CAPACITY WALLS AND ROOF<br>MINIMUM SURFACE, MAXIMUM STABILITY | SNOW | SEASONAL (HUNTING) | SNOWDOME, ICE- AND FUR-LINED |
| | SUMMER<br>MODERATE TEMPERATURES<br>INTENSE SOLAR RADIATION | HIGH HEAT CAPACITY ROOF AND WALLS | TURF, EARTH, DRIFTWOOD | SEASONAL (HUNTING-FISHING) | SOD-ROOFED DUGOUT |
| CONTINENTAL STEPPE | WINTER<br>INTENSE, CONTINUOUS COLD<br>NEGLIGIBLE SOLAR HEAT<br>HIGH WINDS | LOW HEAT CAPACITY WALLS AND ROOF<br>MINIMUM EXPOSED SURFACE, MAXIMUM STABILITY | ANIMAL SKINS, HAIR SAPLINGS | NOMADIC (HERDING) | PORTABLE TENSION STRUCTURE<br>HIDE AND FELT MEMBRANES ON FRAME |
| | SUMMER<br>LONG, WARM DAYS<br>COLD NIGHTS | SHADE, VENTILATION<br>LOW HEAT CAPACITY WALLS AND ROOF | | | ROLL-UP WALL PANELS |
| DESERT | LITTLE OR NO SEASONAL VARIATI<br>HOT DAYS-COLD NIGHTS<br>INTENSE SOLAR LIGHT AND HE<br>VERY LOW HUMIDITY<br>LITTLE RAIN | HIGH HEAT CAPACITY ROOF AND WALLS<br>SHADE<br>MINIMUM VENTILATION<br>NONWATERPROOF | MUD, STONES<br>REEDS, PALMS, SAPLINGS | PERMANENT (AGRICULTURE) | SOLID, LOAD-BEARING MUD-MASONRY WALLS<br>ROOFS: MUD CEMENT ON WATTLE; POLE OR PALM TRUNK RAFTERS |
| TROPICAL RAIN FOREST | NO SEASONAL VARIATION<br>HOT DAYS<br>WARM NIGHTS<br>INTENSE SOLAR RADIATION<br>HIGH HUMIDITIES<br>HEAVY RAINFALL | LOW HEAT CAPACITY WALLS AND ROOF<br>MAXIMUM SHADE<br>MAXIMUM VENTILATION | VINES, REEDS, BAMBOO, PALM-FRONDS, POLES | PERMANENT (AGRICULTURE, FISHING) | SKELETAL FRAME, THATCHED ROOF, WALLS<br>SLOPING PARASOL ROOF<br>STILTED FLOORS |

**IMPACT OF CLIMATE and available building materials on the design of primitive dwellings is summarized in this chart. It describes the four climatic regions where the greatest variety of primitive architecture is still to be found. In the first three climate zones, control of temperature is the crucial architectural problem. In the fourth heavy seasonal rains add to the difficulty. To solve his problems the primitive architect shrewdly exploits the limited materials available to him and works them into a structural form that admirably meets both the demands of the climate and the requirements of his particular culture: nomadic, hunting or agricultural.**

SUBARCTIC AND TUNDRA
CONTINENTAL STEPPE AND DESERT
TEMPERATE
SUBTROPICAL
LOW LATITUDE STEPPE AND DESERT
RAINFOREST AND SAVANNA
HIGHLANDS

**CLIMATE MAP identifies seven principal regions, all once occupied by primitive man. He has now been largely pushed out of the two most genial climate zones: the temperate and subtropical. Thus the primitive architect, where he still exists, has to cope with more difficult climate problems than those confronting the average modern architect.**

If we turn to quite another type of thermal regime, that of the great deserts of the lower latitudes, we find an architectural response equally appropriate to radically different conditions. Here the characteristic problem is extremely high daytime temperatures coupled with uncomfortably low temperatures at night. Sometimes, as in the U. S. Southwest, wide seasonal variations are superimposed upon these diurnal ones. Against such fluctuations the desirable insulation material would be one with a high heat-capacity. Such a material would absorb solar radiation during the daylight hours and slowly reradiate it during the night. Thus the diurnal temperature curve inside the building would be flattened out into a much more comfortable profile: cooler in daytime, warmer at night [*see illustration at bottom of opposite page*]. Clay and stone are high heat-capacity materials; they are plentiful in the desert, and it is precisely out of them that primitive folk around the world make their buildings. Adobe brick and *terra pise* (molded earth) as well as mud and rubble masonry, appear in the Southwest; massive walls of sun-baked brick in Mesopotamia; clay mortar on reed or twig mesh in Africa from the Nile Delta to the Gold Coast. And the native architect evolves sophisticated variations for subtle changes in environment. Here, to avoid a sharp winter wind, the entrance door will be moved around to the lee; there, to get early morning solar heat, it will face the east. Where afternoons are cool, dooryard benches face the west; where hot, the shaded east.

Limited to what for us would be a pitifully meager choice of materials, the primitive architect often employs them so skillfully as to make them seem ideal. Africa, for example, has developed dozens of variations of the structural use of vegetable fibers (grasses, reeds, twigs, saplings, palm trunks) both independently and as reinforcement for mud masonry. In Egypt, where it seldom rains, flat roofs are practicable; hence mud walls carry palm-trunk roof beams which in turn support a mud slab reinforced with palm fronds. Other regions, although arid, will have seasonal rains; here sloping forms and water-shedding surfaces are necessary. The beautiful beehive hut appears. Built like a conical basket on an elegant frame of bent saplings and withes, the beehive hut is sometimes sheathed with water-repellent thatch; sometimes mud plaster is worked into the wattle; sometimes the two are combined, as in the huts of the Bauchi Plateau of Nigeria.

The Nigerians construct a double-shelled dome for the two seasons. The inner one is of mud with built-in projecting wooden pegs to receive the outer shell of thatch. An air space separates

TEMPERATURE (DEGREES F)
+40
+20
0
–20
–40
6 A.M.
NOON
6 P.M.
MIDNIGHT
6 A.M.
39
33
27
35
28
21
–10
–30
CEILING (AIR TEMPERATURE)
SLEEPING PLATFORM
FLOOR LEVEL
OUTSIDE TEMPERATURE

**IGLOO TEMPERATURES may run as much as 65 degrees Fahrenheit higher than external air temperatures. The heat source: a few oil lamps and a few Eskimo bodies. Outside temperature is typical winter range.**

TEMPERATURE (DEGREES F)
140
120
100
80
60
6 A.M.
NOON
6 P.M.
MIDNIGHT
6 A.M.
140
105
85
75
65
ROOF SURFACE
OUTSIDE TEMPERATURE
INSIDE TEMPERATURE

**ADOBE HOUSE TEMPERATURES compare favorably with those obtainable in modern air-conditioned homes. Moreover, the solar heat trapped by the roof slab in the daytime keeps the interior warm through the chill night.**



7.1 James Marston Fitch and Daniel P. Branch, "Primitive Architecture and Climate," *Scientific American*, 1960.

to experiment with and refine these methods, form and climate did not develop along the implicitly intertwined trajectory described in the preceding chapters. Given the preeminence of HVAC, and of the sealed façade and the fully conditioned interior, interior spaces in industrialized economies (in the United States in particular) became increasingly cut off from the environmental conditions that surrounded them. Architects generally saw no need to understand the principles of climate design methods, or even analysis.[3]

Architectural engagement with the question of how design mediates social and climatic conditions was largely relegated to a kind of nostalgia for so-called primitive cultures that were seen to live in harmony with their environmental surround—intending to serve as both model and object lesson.

James Marston Fitch again provides a cogent example: his 1960 article, "Primitive Architecture and Climate," illustrated by Daniel P. Branch, starts out by indicating that "despite meager resources, primitive people have designed dwellings that successfully meet the severest climate problems. These simple shelters often outperform the structures of present-day architects."[4] Fitch's temporal slippage contrasting the "primitive" to the "present-day," while also indicating that both coexisted in their contemporary time, suggests some of the cultural and racial bias implicit in their project. They provided a chart indexing the design proclivities of different cultures in different climates, a map to locate these different practices geographically, graphs of temperature variation with different building materials, and other analytic visual materials. These sorts of technical images became familiar sites of research communication among historians, preservationists, and some specialist architects but were largely alien to the broader discussion of design—the article was published in *Scientific American* and not, for example, *Architectural Forum*. These images can be seen in concert with a number of contemporaneous interventions questioning the role of the modern architect and traditional practices relative to processes of cultural, economic, and industrial development, including the work of Hassan Fathy, Bernard Rudofsky, and Aldo van Eyck.[5]

Illustrating the article, photographs of village life among Indigenous populations were accompanied by Branch's quasi-technical pencil drawings, intended to show how "primitive" use of materials and design methods could achieve relative comfort. Implicit in these materials and methods was a basic assumption that other aspects of cultural life facilitated the attainment of comfort in challenging climates; that is, it was not only the material characteristics of the igloo or the adobe—as illustrated, mapped, and charted—that was seen to mediate climate extremes. Clothing, rituals, family arrange ments, and other cultural patterns also played a significant role in producing thermal comfort.

The aim of these documented practices was not the same as that of the climatic modernists and their HVAC antecedents—achieving stable temperature and humidity, in all seasons and regions—but, rather, to develop architectural methods and cultural tactics that could mediate climate conditions. Specific, regionally and climatically sensitive forms of collective life were, Fitch's article suggested, as essential as design methods to producing conditions of thermal comfort, or, perhaps more precisely, their analysis sat outside the project of thermal consistency and indicated that climatic variations allowed for precise architectural interventions on regional terms. Inconsistency provides opportunities, not obstacles.

This contrast of images—the technical and the cultural—was also a contrast of approaches to how the past and future of architecture can be imagined, in its intimate relationship to cultural life and economic development. Technical images are now seen in architecture as uncomplicatedly instrumental, focused on *solutions*: enter the right data into the right program and the problem will be solved. A further legacy of the Olgyays and their counterparts, as it played out over subsequent decades, was the reification of the technical fix as the goal of architectural-climatic research. On the other hand, media continues to be focused on *problems*: what are the contingencies that interrupt these instrumental gestures? How do people want to live? Who is included in a given technical solution, and who is not?

Fitch's retreat to the "primitive" in the 1960 article, reflected also in Branch's reliance on traditional forms of representation, is symptomatic of a broader relegation of the *cultural* presence of climate in architecture to designs and ideas that were either historically or regionally distant (or both), rather than as a matter of present concern. In the period since about 1960, in other words, climate was not (generally speaking) a concern for architects; it was instead the object of technical and economic analysis by HVAC consultants, engaged with contractors through relationships that design professionals remain largely tangential to. The rich discussion of climate models and predictions, thorough understandings of the relationship of social and physical health in the context of regional specificity, and many other compelling discussions, proceeded without extensive architectural involvement. When climate was a concern for Fitch, it was often in order to better adjust some of those projects to the conditions of the present—Fitch would become a key player in the expanding discourse on historic preservation and heritage in architecture. This is not to say that the emergence of preservation was reliant on conceptions of the primitive; Fitch's influence and practice were much more wide-ranging.[6] A general tendency, especially from an American perspective, to relegate climate as a specialized interest persisted until the early twenty-first century; the focus was either with the past or on distant isolated areas.

And yet shading devices are everywhere, an essential part of the contemporary built environment. They are even more essential today than they might have been decades ago, as they offer a model and a mechanism for reducing carbon emissions. On a global scale, through the technical experimentation of architectural scientists and the continued interest of some designers, the terms and practices of integrating dynamic shading devices with climate knowledge through building design continued to develop. In both small- and large-scale buildings, from this mid-1950s period to the present, shading devices have been used, often in concert with some sort of conditioning system, to mitigate the vagaries of climate. The façade section still suggests the complexity of these cultural relationships.

As much as it is difficult to summarize the worldwide proliferation of HVAC systems, in case studies, so is it necessary to point toward the sharp increase in shading devices, and more generally the materials and design methods of non-mechanical thermal conditioning, as an important aspect of the architecture of the twenty-first century. To count, or list, such buildings is less important than the recognition that simulation tools and materials are increasingly effective and increasingly engaged in architecture and its frameworks of aesthetic and functional value.

While air conditioning has seemingly taken over the built environment, in many parts of the world, involving tightly sealed and conditioned spaces, there are numerous other means by which architects and others have sought to articulate new methods of shading and new ideas about how to live in a less-than-consistent interior. Which is simply to say: shading devices are still an essential aspect of the built environment, a part of the design and construction of buildings around the planet. This is, or has been, especially the case in those regions where seasonal heat is of concern, and where infrastructural, economic, and cultural barriers to mechanical conditioning exist. The persistence of the dynamic shading device, and of the façade as cultural technique, seems less like an anachronism, or a design reference to a recent past, and more like an outline of methods for the immediate future—a future in which infrastructural, economic, and cultural ambitions may be more likely to play out in compromised, inconsistent, unevenly shaded spaces.

### Business as Usual

The brise-soleil persists, partway into the twenty-first century, haltingly gaining acceptance and interest as a design tool appropriate to the contemporary formal and social milieu. Technical images are everywhere ascendant, determinant relative to the technological present and immediate future, especially in climate discourse.[7] Architects in the period discussed here were still struggling to develop means of graphic representation, illustration, and visualization that could articulate the promise of a given architectural intervention relative to changes to the cultural and technical conditions of the climatic interior. These images have moved far, far beyond the dynamic potential of the façade section that has been essential to the present narrative—perspectives, animations, false color diagrams, and a whole range of photographs, charts, spreadsheets, and other visual material have contributed to the discussion of architecture and climate, as traditional means of plan, section, and elevation, and biometric charts as well, have been overcome by a wide range of computer-assisted drafting programs, visualization methods, and modeling software.

The field of architecture has become one of the primary sites for the production of future imaginaries relative to climate change. Designers are increasingly prolific in the use of images to present, frame, apply, or criticize data.[8] New analytic tools allow for an increasingly precise understanding of climatic patterns in their relationship to materials, technologies, and interior spaces, allowing designers to approach a project with a capacious range of methods and materials for rendering the building as energy efficient as possible.[9] The challenge to architects today, as to society at large, is less about the clarity of the technical image and more about how to overcome cultural barriers to the transformations necessary to radically reduce carbon—how to produce a convincing model of the future attentive to the structural conditions that continue to destabilize the climate.[10]

The issue is this: while numerous innovations in energy efficiency have informed the architecture of the twenty-first century, global fossil fuel emissions are still on the rise. All of the bureaucratic and technocratic efforts toward managing a 1.5-degree Celsius rise have fallen short; as this book was being written, potential US leadership on energy transitions and climatic effects has been put on hold, and other governments are struggling to develop effective means to reduce carbon dependence without exacerbating societal tensions.[11] Even in centers of the proposed energy transition, such as Germany, where high-tech ecological buildings are the norm, the ongoing *energiewende* faces significant political and economic challenges.[12] Despite our collective best intentions, we are not necessarily working toward a reduced carbon future.

Architecture in the twenty-first century engages a spectrum of climate agency. What Socolow called the BAU (business as usual) trajectory is here given a more robust dimension: technological innovation is seen as a means of providing more comfort at less carbon cost (more efficient) and also as a generator of economic growth. That is, even if the fossil-fuel mechanical system can be rendered efficient, the sociotechnical production of new sustainable buildings is founded on a discourse of technological innovation and growth with only marginal impacts on the throughput of fossil fuels (especially when the embodied energy costs are taken into account).[13] In other words, even "green capitalism" assumes economic expansion, leading back to an apparent axiom of industrial modernity: that trajectories of economic growth are coupled with trajectories of environmental damage. If one goes up, so does the other.[14]

Sustainability in architecture tends to be about minimizing carbon emissions, not eliminating or absorbing them.[15] Business as usual. Guidelines for the green building metric active in the United States, LEED (Leadership in Energy and Environmental Design), suggest those buildings aiming for the highest, platinum ranking "add as little as possible to our world's greenhouse gas emissions."[16] There is little discussion of reducing, or even absorbing, carbon.[17] Implicit is an understanding that such a prospect would fundamentally change the means and ends of the architectural profession, in its relationship to culture, policy, and industry, not to mention a more general cultural disruption toward carbon-neutral ways of life. Climate instability presents a challenge not just to certain fields, practices, or lifestyles, but to the social fabric more broadly—dramatic changes to the status quo will occur, either by design or by default.

## The Planetary Interior

All buildings are environmental. Building systems and forms negotiate resources and pollution, capital and comfort; they adjust, decreasing or intensifying specific flows of knowledge and products and ways of life; they articulate a capacious mediating presence as an object, a screen, a space. Buildings are a means to amplify the resonance of new (again) ways of thinking about climate. All buildings are environmental in that they help *produce* the environment, its tangible and atmospheric effects, especially in the Anthropocene; indeed, they are a primary aspect of the material and immaterial condition of the apocalyptic present. The "environment" is not one of a set of issues to take up, to identify this or that project as "environmental" or "green" or "sustainable" or "resilient," it is rather a perspective on the built world in its relationship to the social world and to planetary systems.

One probable effect of architectural-climatic discourse is the reframing of the history of architecture writ large according to an understanding of how issues we now identify as environmental have played a role in the production of buildings, and in the production of the subjects, collectives, and societies that inhabit them. The effects of this climatic discourse are historiographic in the sense described at the beginning of this book, following Isabelle Stengers's concept of the "event" leading to a new understanding of the past so as to imagine a different possible future—new narratives tying together different stories, identifying novel understandings of cause and effect. One could, for example, examine the role of coal availability to the open, uninsulated workshop spaces of the Bauhaus Dessau (designed by Gropius in 1925), or how concerns about population growth informed the Archigram drawings for a "Walking City." Such an effort also involves reconsidering the diagrams, drawings, buildings, and speculations that we gather under the term "architecture" and focusing on it as a medium for reflecting a cultural approach to environment. Architecture is a screen on which to watch socio-environmental transformation as well as a material system from which to produce it.

All modern buildings are environmental because they affect the climate, and they always have; for the last six or seven decades, this effect has intensified dramatically. Before air conditioning, the thermal interior was a space of creativity for designers; since air conditioning, and increasingly in the face of rising emissions, the interior becomes a space of contestation, a space of disruption, a space for assessing and measuring cultural capacity for responsiveness.

The interior is defined by its isolation. It is discrete, distinct, cut off to varying degrees from the vagaries of the increasingly unpredictable exterior climate. However, these millions of interior spaces, all around the planet, aggregate toward a collective impact on geophysical systems. The thermal conditions of the interior are a crucial site for collective engagement, and for a new kind of planetary politics.

The thermal interior became a planetary space—everywhere, but not universal, and with consequences that further complicate local, regional, and global effects. If "planetary" accounts for the world system of capital and also the geophysical dynamics of earth systems, in all of its unevenness, then the *planetary interior* can be conceptualized and analyzed with attention to multiple and varying scales, and according to a new understanding of the causal relationship between the conditions of that discrete interior and, as they accumulate, changes to the atmosphere of the planet. We are, in terms of the causal chain of history, both inside and outside all of the time, producing and reflecting on these distinct but entangled spaces. The thermal interior has both a circuitous and a direct role in determining the future of human life on earth; the media practices of architects and others are increasingly focused on understanding and making tangible these multiscalar and abstract connections. The mediatic and communicative systems of architecture, their technical images—their capacity to express complex knowledge and imagine possible futures—becomes an essential aspect of the field and its contribution to knowledge.

---

The challenge to architects, and to others, is to stay focused on the planetary resonance of these discrete spaces, and how they are designed. Their form, and their climate. Their materials, shapes, and the systems that produce them and make them livable. The challenge is to articulate, through media, the importance of this aggregated space of the planetary interior to the prospects for a new kind of life. Architecture is the interface of a material and a symbolic substrate for a range of new ideas about social engagement with climatic patterns. Collective attention to the thermal conditions of the planetary interior is of increasing urgency. In this sense the challenge to architects is familiar—how can design induce new cultural desires, now also aware of the resulting impact on the global climate? The planetary interior becomes the space for cultivating a planetary imaginary, where the role of climate in design is not an obstacle but an opportunity.

# Acknowlegments

This book has been in development for more than a decade, a period over which I accrued many intellectual and personal debts. I want to thank, first of all, my students at the University of Pennsylvania and Princeton University—the MArch and PhD students in my seminars on Architecture, Media, and Climate at both schools, and the first-year undergraduate students in my Architecture in the Anthropocene seminar at Penn. Their engagement in the material and their questions were invaluable in thinking through these events and their resonance.

Research for this book was supported by a Samuel P. Hays Fellowship from the American Society of Environmental History, by the University of Pennsylvania University Research Fund, by the Graham Foundation for Advanced Studies in the Fine Arts, and by the Alexander von Humboldt Foundation. I also received support from the Andrew Mellon Foundation funded Humanities + Urbanism + Design seminar at Penn, organized by David Brownlee and Genie Birch, as well as the Andrew Mellon Foundation funded Global Architectural History Teaching Collaborative, led by Mark Jarzombek and Vikram Prakash. A generous subvention for image reproduction and permission expenses was provided by the George Howard Bickley Endowment for Architecture Publications through the Dean's Office of the University of Pennsylvania Stuart Weitzman School of Design.

I was fortunate to receive residential fellowships to research and write aspects of this book, first as the Currie C. and Thomas A. Barron Visiting Professor on the Environment and Humanities at the Princeton Environmental Institute, where I was hosted by the Princeton School of Architecture. I'd like to thank Stan Allen, Rob Socolow, Monica Ponce de Leon, and Mario Gandelsonas for their support, and Forrest Meggers, Christine Boyer, Beatriz Colomina, Axel Killian, and Guy Nordenson for engagement and conversations while at Princeton. My time as the Barron Professor was essential to the archival research for *Modern Architecture and Climate*, many thanks to everyone at the PEI for supporting the project. I also received a Fellowship for Advanced Researchers from the Alexander von Humboldt Foundation, and was hosted first by the Rachel Carson Center in Munich and then the Max Planck Institute for the History of Science in Berlin. Jürgen Renn and Christoph Rosol at the MPI, and Christof Mauch at the RCC provided amazing discussions, lectures, conferences, exhibitions, and other events, a rich collegial atmosphere. The book was completed over these Berlin summers, and I am extremely grateful for the writing time the Humboldt Fellowship allowed.

I had the opportunity to present aspects of this research at a number of conferences, symposia, and workshops. I am thankful to all of the colleagues, attendees, and interlocutors that made these experiences productive, including but not limited to: Kevin Bone, Gaia Caramellino, Andrew Cruse, Kenny Cupers, Daniela Fabricius, Orit Halpern, Iain Jackson, Vladimir Jankovic, Lydia Kallipolitti, Janette Kim, Andrew Leach, Caroline Maniaque, Reinhold Martin, Jonathan Massey, Forrest Meggers, Anna-Marie Meister, Whitney Moon, Alona Nitzan-Shiftan, Victor Olgyay, Michael Osman, Charles Rice, Gustavo Rocha-Peixoto, Laurent Stalder, and Lee Stickells.

I am thankful for these and numerous other colleagues for their support, comments, and criticisms. I am especially indebted to: Dorit Aviv, David Benjamin, Etienne Benson, Barry Bergdoll, Dominic Boyer, William Braham, Nerea Calvillo, Jiat-Hwee Chang, Irene Cheng, Peggy Deamer, Isabelle Doucet, Carola Hein, Sophie Hochhaüsl, Andrés Jaque, Ferda Kolatan, Chris Marcinkowski, Kiel Moe, Brendan Moran, Farshid Moussavi, Nicholas Pevsner, Peg Rawes, Eduardo Rega Calvo, Daniel Ryan, Phillip Ryan, Felicity Scott, Anooradha Iyer Siddiqi, John Tresch, Anna Vallye, Mark Wasiuta, Damian White, and Bethany Wiggin, among many others.

Aspects of these chapters were published, in different form, in *Public Culture* (in January 2016), and in the collected volumes *Energy Accounts: Architectural Representations of Energy, Climate, and the Future* (Routledge, 2016), *The Routledge Companion to the Environmental Humanities* (2016), *Architecture/Machine: Programs, Processes, and Performances* (gta Verlag, 2017), and *Climates: Architecture and the Planetary Imaginary* (Lars Müller and Columbia Books on Architecture and the City, 2016).

I am indebted to my research assistants Danielle Lands, Anna Weichsel, Linfan Liu, and especially Taryn Mudge. Their collective thoughtfulness, insight, and organizational acumen were essential to completing the project. Thanks also to my PhD students Dalal Alsayer, German Pallares, Erin Putalik, Taryn again, and Joseph Watson, and at Princeton: Carson Chan, Megan Eardley, and Jessica Ngan, for stimulating discussions and keeping me on my toes. Caitlin Blanchfield provided a careful copyedit and helpful input in the middle stages of the manuscript's development. Victor Olgyay engaged in a number of useful contextual conversations at crucial points and has been very generous in allowing for the reproduction of images of his father's and uncle's work. His contribution to the new edition of *Design with Climate*, alongside contributions of Ken Yeang, John Reynolds, and Donlyn Lyndon, provide a great companion to the Olgyays' research discussed in chapter 5. I am also of course indebted to the anonymous peer reviewers whose feedback was instrumental in giving the book its final shape, and to Michelle Komie, Pamela Weidman, and the editorial team at Princeton University Press.

Isabelle Godineau at the Fondation Le Corbusier was invaluable in her assistance, as was Elvira Ferault at the Cité de l'architecture & du patrimoine, who assisted in the commissioning of the model photographs that open the book. Those photographs were taken by Gaston F. Bergeret. Claudio Muniz Viana at the Núcleo de Pesquisa e Documentação, Faculdade de Arquitetura e Urbanismo, Universidade Federal do Rio de Janeiro (UFRJ) was essential to finding my way through the archive there. Gustavo Rocha-Peixoto was a generous host in Rio, and Erin Putalik a welcome archive companion. Fernando Delgado made a return trip to the archive on my behalf, scanning articles and later photographing the air conditioners in Rio office towers shown at the end of chapter 2. Thanks as well to Danielle Costa for her reading of some of the early versions of that chapter, and translating some of the relevant archival material. The archive staff at the Museum of Modern Art and the American Institute of Architects were generous in their assistance to find the needed images and in attaining permission for publication. Dean Monica Ponce de Leon at Princeton University School of Architecture graciously granted permission for use of images from the school's archive, and also gave me the opportunity to teach a seminar related to the book at the school. Dan Claro and Camn Castens were also very supportive of archival and other issues at Princeton. Dion Neutra facilitated permissions and images from the UCLA archive; I was lucky to have a number of conversations with Dion before he passed away this fall.

I am thankful most of all for the support of my wife Andrea Hornick. This book is dedicated to our children, Felix and Clarissa Daisy. I apologize on behalf of my generation for the mess of a planet we have left you with. I wish I had tools more effective than historical scholarship to help you dig out. I only can hope that this and other writings on the environmental history of architecture might, in some small way, hasten awareness and action.

# Notes

## Introduction: Architecture, Media, and Climate

1. The 1929–34 *Oeuvre complète* dates the project to 1933. Josep Quetglas's document in the archives traces the derivation of the project to 1931, as the Plan Macia was also being developed, and indicates that it was being worked on until 1939, with a small drawing in the 1938–46 *Oeuvre complète* as well. Josep Quetglas, "Lotissement," Archive of the Fondation Le Corbusier, Paris.
2. See, for example, Colin Porteous, *The New Eco-Architecture: Alternatives from the Modern Movement* (London: Taylor and Francis, 2002); Paul Overy, *Light, Air, and Openness: Modern Architecture between the Wars* (London: Thames and Hudson, 2008); Susannah Hagan, *Taking Shape: A New Contract between Architecture and Nature* (London: Architectural Press, 2001), among many other texts that will be discussed further on. See also Daniel Barber, *A House in the Sun: Modern Architecture and Solar Energy in the Cold War* (New York: Oxford University Press, 2016).
3. GATCPAC was the Grup d'Arquitectes i Tècnics Catalans per al Progrés de l'Arquitectura Contemporània, the Catalan version of a number of Spanish collectives operating under the more general GATEPAC. For specific relevance of the group to the Barcelona project, see Jean-François Lejeune, "Madrid versus Barcelona: Two Visions for the Modern City and Block (1929–1936)," *Athens Journal of Architecture* 1, no. 4 (October 2015): 271–95.
4. Victor Olgyay, *Design with Climate: Bioclimatic Approach to Architectural Regionalism* (Princeton, NJ: Princeton University Press, 1963), 14.
5. See Richard A. Grusin, "Premediation," *Criticism* 46, no. 1 (Winter 2004): 17–39; and Richard A. Grusin, "Radical Mediation," *Critical Inquiry* 42, no. 1 (Autumn 2015): 124–48.
6. Dipesh Chakrabarty, "Climate and Capital: On Conjoined Histories," *Critical Inquiry* 41, no. 1 (Autumn 2014): 1–23; J. R. McNeill and Peter Engelke, *The Great Acceleration: An Environmental History of the Anthropocene since 1945* (Cambridge, MA: Belknap Press of Harvard University Press, 2016).
7. Walter Mignolo, *The Darker Side of Western Modernity* (Durham, NC: Duke University Press, 2011).
8. Paul Siple, "Climatic Criteria for Building Construction," *Proceedings of the Research Correlation Conference on Weather and the Building Industry* (Washington, DC: National Academy of Sciences, 1950): 5–22, 7.
9. Reyner Banham, *Architecture of the Well-Tempered Environment* (Chicago: University of Chicago Press, 1976); see also Michael Osman, "Banham's Historical Ecology," in *Neo-Avant-Garde and Postmodern: Postwar Architecture in Britain and Beyond*, ed. Mark Crinson and Claire Zimmerman (New Haven, CT: Yale University Press, 2010), 231–50; and Todd Gannon, *Reyner Banham and the Paradoxes of High-Tech* (Los Angeles: Getty Publications, 2017).
10. See, for example, Dipesh Chakrabarty, "The Climate of History: Four Theses," *Critical Inquiry* 35, no. 2 (Winter 2009): 197–222; Amitav Ghosh, *The Great Derangement: Climate Change and the Unthinkable* (Chicago: University of Chicago Press, 2016); David Armitage and Jo Guldi, *The History Manifesto* (New York: Cambridge University Press, 2014); Christophe Bonneuil and Jean-Baptiste Fressoz, *The Shock of the Anthropocene: The Earth, History, and Us* (New York: Verso, 2017); and Naomi Oreskes and Erik M. Conway, *The Collapse of Western Civilization: A View from the Future* (New York: Columbia University Press, 2014).
11. Isabelle Stengers, *In Catastrophic Times: Resisting the Coming Barbarism* (Ann Arbor, MI: Open Humanities Press, 2015), 39.
12. Eva Horn, "Air as Medium," *Grey Room*, no. 73 (Fall 2018): 6–25.
13. Thomas Nocke and Birgit Schneider, eds., *Image Politics of Climate Change* (Bielefeld, Germany: Transcript Verlag, 2014); Horst Bredekamp, Vera Dunkel, and Birgit Schneider, eds., *The Technical Image: A History of Styles in Technical Imagery* (Chicago: University of Chicago Press, 2015).
14. For a general discussion of the continuity of environmental and climatic concerns, albeit under different names and frameworks, see Fabien Locher and Jean-Baptiste Fressoz, "Modernity's Frail Climate: A Climate History of Environmental Reflexivity," *Critical Inquiry* 38, no. 3 (Spring 2012): 579–98. On a different note, Kevin Bone's seminar and exhibition at the Cooper Union, collected as *Lessons from Modernism*, proposes that early architectural modernists offer robust technical and spatial examples for contemporary designers to follow.
15. For a relatively recent discussion of these trends, see J. R. McNeill, "The State of the Field of Environmental History," *Annual Review of Environment and Resources* 35, no. 1 (2010): 345–74.
16. Patrick Geddes, *Cities in Evolution: An Introduction to the Town Planning Movement and the Study of Civics* (London: Williams and Norgate, 1915), esp. 60–83; Lewis Mumford, *Technics and Civilization* (New York: Harcourt Brace, 1934), esp. 364–83.
17. George Perkins Marsh, *Man and Nature; or, Physical Geography as Modified by Human Action* (New York: Scribner, 1864).
18. Ramachandra Guha and Joan Martinez-Alier, "The Forgotten American Environmentalist," in their *Varieties of Environmentalism: Essays North and South* (New York: Longman, 2002), 185–202, 187; see also the discussion of Marsh in Paul Hawken, *Blessed Unrest: How the Largest Movement Came into Being, and Why No One Saw It Coming* (New York: Viking, 2007). The Marsh quotes are from *Man and Nature*.
19. See Michael G. Barbour, "Ecological Fragmentation in the Fifties," in *Uncommon Ground: Rethinking the Human Place in Nature*, ed. William Cronon (New York: W. W. Norton, 1995), 233–55; and Daniel B. Botkin, *Discordant Harmonies: A New Ecology for the Twenty-First Century* (New York: Oxford University Press, 1990).
20. Guha and Martinez-Alier, "Forgotten American Environmentalist," 200.
21. Sven-Olov Wallenstein, *Biopolitics and the Emergence of Modern Architecture* (New York: Temple Hoyne Buell Center for American Architecture and Princeton Architectural Press, 2009), 20–21.
22. Michel Foucault, *Security, Territory,*

Population: Lectures at the Collège de France, 1977–1978* (New York: Picador, 2003), 366.
23. Foucault, *Security, Territory, Population*, 21.
24. Georges Canguilhem, "The Living and Its Milieu," *Grey Room*, no. 3 (Spring 2001): 6–31, 26–28. It was originally published as *La connaissance de la vie* in 1952, after being presented as a lecture at the Collège de France in 1946–47.
25. Andrew Barry, *Political Machines: Governing a Technological Society* (New York: Athlone Press, 2001).
26. Vilém Flusser, *Into the Universe of Technical Images* (Minneapolis: University of Minnesota Press, 2011), 33 and throughout; and Mark Poster, "An Introduction to Vilém Flusser's *Into the Universe of Technical Images* and *Does Writing Have a Future?*," in Flusser, *Into the Universe of Technical Images*, ix–xvii.
27. Gilles Deleuze, *Foucault* (Minneapolis: University of Minnesota Press, 1986), 57.
28. See Robert Somol and Sarah Whiting, "Notes around the Doppler Effect, and Other Moods of Modernism," *Perspecta* 33 (2002): 73–77.
29. Anthony Vidler, "Diagrams of Diagrams: Architectural Abstraction and Modern Representation," *Representations*, no. 72 (2000): 1–20, 10–11.
30. Wallenstein, *Biopolitics and the Emergence of Modern Architecture*, 23. I will elaborate on Wallenstein's premise in chapter 2.
31. Hyungmin Pai, *The Portfolio and the Diagram: Architecture, Discourse, and Modernity in America* (Cambridge, MA: MIT Press, 2002); Mauro F. Guillén, *The Taylorized Beauty of the Mechanical: Scientific Management and the Rise of Modernist Architecture* (Princeton, NJ: Princeton University Press, 2008).
32. Bruno Latour, "Visualization and Cognition: Drawing Things Together," in *Knowledge and Society: Studies in the Sociology of Culture Past and Present*, ed. Henrika Kuklick and Elizabeth Long (Greenwich, CT: JAI Press, 1986), 1–40; Joy Knoblaugh, "The Work of Diagrams: From Factory to Hospital in Postwar America," *Manifest*, no. 1 (2013): 154–65.
33. Gisela Parak, *Eco-Images: Historical Views and Political Strategies* (Munich: Rachel Carson Center, 2013); Sheila Jasanoff, "Image and Imagination: The Formation of Global Environmental Consciousness," in *Changing the Atmosphere: Expert Knowledge and Environmental Governance*, ed. Clark A. Miller and Paul N. Edwards (Cambridge, MA: MIT Press, 2001), 309–38; see also Sheila Jasanoff, "A New Climate for Society," *Theory Culture Society*, no. 27 (2010): 233–53.
34. Flusser, *Into the Universe of Technical Images*, 11.
35. Bernhard Siegert, "Doors: On the Materiality of the Symbolic," *Grey Room* 47 (Spring 2012): 6–23.
36. There is a long history of architectural considerations of the façade as membrane, in particular the work of Siegfried Ebeling in the late 1920s and then by some of 1960s experiments in inflatable space. See Siegfried Ebeling, *Space as Membrane* (London: Architectural Association, 2010); see Spyros Papapetros's essay in the volume, "Future Skins." On the 1960s inflatables, see Reyner Banham, "Monumental Wind-Bags," *New Society* 11, no. 290 (April 18, 1968): 569–70; and Whitney Moon, "Environmental Wind-Baggery" on the E-Flux Architecture platform. https://www.e-flux.com/architecture/structural-instability/208703/environmental-wind-baggery/. Accessed September 18, 2018.
37. Bernhard Siegert, *Cultural Techniques: Grids, Filters, Doors, and Other Articulations of the Real* (New York: Fordham University Press, 2015), 2, 9; see also Reinhold Martin, "Unfolded, Not Opened: On Bernhard Siegert's *Cultural Techniques*," *Grey Room* 62 (Winter 2016): 102–15.
38. Ursula Heise, *Sense of Place and Sense of Planet: The Environmental Imagination of the Global* (Oxford: Oxford University Press, 2008).
39. Philip Johnson and Henry-Russell Hitchcock, *The International Style: Architecture since 1922* (New York: W. W. Norton, 1932).
40. Paul N. Edwards, *A Vast Machine: Computer Models, Climate Data, and the Politics of Global Warming* (Cambridge, MA: MIT Press, 2010).
41. See Hilde Heynen's interpretation, for an architectural audience, of Marshall Berman's formulation of the distinctions between modernism, modernity, and modernization, in Hilde Heynen, *Architecture and Modernity: A Critique* (Cambridge, MA: MIT Press, 1999).
42. Richard Grove and Vinita Damodaran, "Imperialism, Intellectual Networks, and Environmental Change," *Economic and Political Weekly* (October 14 and 21, 2006): 4345–54; 4497–505; Peder Anker, *Imperial Ecology: Environmental Order in the British Empire, 1895–1945* (Cambridge, MA: Harvard University Press, 2002).

## Chapter 1

1. Recent literature has begun to explore these aspects of Le Corbusier's work. As noted further on, the present chapter seeks less to contribute to the historiography of Le Corbusier and more to see him as a hinge toward a new perspective on the history of architecture and climate more generally. Some examples of this recent literature include Rosa Urbano Gutiérrez, "'Pierre, revoir tout le système fenêtres': Le Corbusier and the Development of Glazing and Air-Conditioning Technology with the Mur Neutralisant (1928–1933)," *Construction History* 27 (2012): 107–28; Colin Porteous, *The New Eco-Architecture: Alternatives from the Modern Movement* (London: Taylor and Francis, 2002); Ignacio Requena-Ruiz, "Building Artificial Climates: Thermal Control and Comfort in Modern Architecture, 1930–1960," *Ambiances* (November 2016): 1–22; Daniel Siret, "Généalogie du brise-soleil dans L'œuvre de Le Corbusier," *Cahiers Thématiques*, no. 4 (2004): 169–81; Daniel Siret, "Rayonnement solaire et environnement urbain: De l'héliotropisme au désenchangtement, histoire et enjeux d'une relation complex," *Développement durable et territoires* 4, no. 2 (July 2013). A previous generation of scholars also explored these themes, largely in response to Reyner Banham's celebration of Le Corbusier's climatic aptitude; see Harris Sobin, "The Role of Regional Vernacular Traditions in the Genesis of Le Corbusier's Brise-Soleil Sun-Shading Techniques," *Traditional Dwellings and Settlements Review* 6, no. 1 (Fall 1994): 80; Fritz Griffin and Marietta Millet, "Shady Aesthetics," *Journal of Architectural Education* 37, no. 3/4 (Spring 1984): 43–60; see also Christopher Mackenzie, "1993 February: Le Corbusier in the Sun," *Architectural Review* (June 20, 2011).
2. Symptomatic of this emphasis is a persistent anxiety about the intrusion of environment-focused practices into this realm of formal virtuosity, perhaps best expressed in the subtitle (if less clearly in the articles) of a recent collection from the Harvard Graduate School of Design: Erika Naginski and Preston Scott Cohen, eds., *The Return of Nature: Sustaining Architecture in the Face of Sustainability* (New York: Routledge, 2014).
3. Peter Eisenman, *The Formal Basis of Modern Architecture* (Zurich: Lars Müller, 2006); see also a series of editorials in the journal *Oppositions* in the 1970s, including Mario Gandelsonas, "Neo-Functionalism," *Oppositions*,

no. 5 (1976); and Peter Eisenman, "Post-Functionalism," *Oppositions*, no. 6 (1977).

4. For a concise explanation of the autonomy thesis, see K. Michael Hays, Introduction to *Architecture Theory since 1968* (Cambridge, MA: MIT Press, 1998), x–xv. See also the articles collected in Michael Osman, Adam Reudig, Matthew Seidel, and Lisa Tilney, eds., *Perspecta 33: Mining Autonomy* (Cambridge, MA: MIT Press, 2002).
5. See Jean-François Lejeune and Michelangelo Sabatino, eds., *Modern Architecture and the Mediterranean: Vernacular Dialogues and Contested Identities* (New York: Routledge, 2010), and Serge Antoine, "Energy, Climate, and Environment in the Mediterranean Basin," *Ekistics* 58, no. 348/349 (August 1991): 124–34.
6. See Mia Fuller, *Moderns Abroad: Architecture, Cities, and Italian Imperialism* (New York: Routledge, 2006).
7. Le Corbusier, "Techniques Are the Very Basis of Poetry," in *Precisions on the Present State of Architecture and Planning with an American Prologue, A Brazilian Corollary Followed by the Temperature of Paris and the Atmosphere of Moscow* (Cambridge, MA: MIT Press, 1991), originally published 1930. 18° Celsius is approximately 64.5° Fahrenheit, still quite cool by contemporary standards of thermal comfort.
8. Article 26 of the Athens Charter: "A minimum number of hours of exposure to the sun must be determined for each dwelling," CIAM, *The Athens Charter* (Paris: CIAM, 1946); it was originally written in 1933 and revised for republication in 1951. See also Christopher Mackenzie, "1993 February: Le Corbusier in the Sun," *Architectural Review* (June 20, 2011): 3.
9. Peter Sloterdijk, *In the World Interior of Capital: Towards a Philosophical Theory of Globalization* (New York: Wiley, 2006).
10. See, for example, Le Corbusier, *La ville radieuse: Éléments d'une doctrine d'urbanisme pour l'équipement de la civilisation machiniste* (Boulogne-sur-Seine: Éditions de l'Architecture d'aujourd'hui, 1935).
11. The Olgyays mentioned the complications of the Unité's orientation in *Solar Control and Shading Devices* (Princeton, NJ: Princeton University Press, 1957), as does Frampton in *Le Corbusier* (New York: Thames and Hudson, 2001). See also Siret, "Généalogie du brise-soleil."
12. Walter Gropius, "Houses, Walk-Ups, or High-Rise Apartment Blocks?" (1931), in *The Scope of Total Architecture: A New Way of Life* (New York: Harper and Row, 1943), 119–35; and CIAM, *Rationelle Bebauungsweisen: Ergebnisse des 3. Internationalen Kongresses für Neues Bauen* (Stuttgart: J. Hoffman, 1931).
13. See Eric Mumford, *The CIAM Discourse on Urbanism, 1928–1960* (Cambridge, MA: MIT Press, 2000).
14. Porteous, *New Eco-Architecture*, 27. Porteous perhaps goes the furthest, in his *The New Eco-Architecture*, in interpreting the pioneering modernist principles of Le Corbusier, Mies van der Rohe, Walter Gropius, and Frank Lloyd Wright, among others, as implicitly environmentalist strategies. See also Kevin Bone, ed., *Lessons from Modernism: Environmental Design Strategies in Architecture, 1925–1970* (New York: Monacelli, 2014), which sees many interwar examples as essential models for design production in the present.
15. This is in distinction from a recent text that ascribes a sort of protoenvironmentalism to Bauhaus émigrés; see Peder Anker, *From Bauhaus to Ecohouse: A History of Ecological Design* (Baton Rouge: Louisiana State University Press, 2010).
16. John Sargent, *Frank Lloyd Wright's Usonian House: The Case for Organic Architecture* (New York: Whitney Library of Design, 1976); Kenneth Frampton, "The Usonian Legacy," *Architectural Review* 182, no. 1090 (1987): 26–31; Reyner Banham, "Frank Lloyd Wright as Environmentalist," *Arts and Architecture*, no. 83 (September 1966): 26–30.
17. For further elaboration on methods of solar absorption in architecture, see Daniel A. Barber, *A House in the Sun: Modern Architecture and Solar Energy in the Cold War* (New York: Oxford University Press, 2016).
18. See Edward Sekler and William Curtis, *Le Corbusier at Work: the Genesis of the Carpenter Center for Visual Arts* (Cambridge, MA: Harvard University Press, 1978).
19. First in his text *La Maison des Hommes* in 1942, and in most developed form in his *Le poème de l'angle droit* in 1947. Le Corbusier and François de Pierrefeu, *La Maison des Hommes* (Paris: Plon, 1947); Le Corbusier, *Le poème de l'angle droit* (Berlin: Hatje Cantz Verlag, 2012); the latter was originally published in 1953.
20. See Stanislaus von Moos, *Le Corbusier: Elements of a Synthesis* (Amsterdam: nai010, 2013).
21. This is distinct from the interpretation offered in Bone, *Lessons from Modernism*, which proposes that the interwar modernists can be seen as examples for practice in the present.
22. Fabien Locher and Jean-Baptiste Fressoz, "Modernity's Frail Climate: A Climate History of Environmental Reflexivity," *Critical Inquiry* 38, no. 3 (Spring 2012).
23. Overy, *Light, Air, and Openness;* Richard Hobday, *The Light Revolution: Health, Architecture, and the Sun* (Forres, Scotland: Findhorn Press, 2007).
24. This generative aspect is foregrounded in aspects of the theory of architectural formalism; see Peter Eisenman, "Aspects of Modernism: Maison Dom-ino and the Self-Referential Sign," *Oppositions*, no. 15/16 (1978); Robert Somol and Sarah Whiting, "Notes around the Doppler Effect and Other Moods of Modernism," *Perspecta* 33 (2002): 72–77. For a rejoinder, exploring other possible speculative and generative aspects of the diagram, see Daniel A. Barber, "Militant Architecture: Destabilizing Architecture's Disciplinarity," *Journal of Architecture* 10, no. 3 (Fall 2005): 245–53.
25. Urbano Gutiérrez, "'Pierre, revoir tout le système fenêtres': Le Corbusier and the Development of Glazing and Air-Conditioning Technology," 132 and throughout.
26. Michelle Murphy, *Sick Building Syndrome and the Problem of Uncertainty: Environmental Politics, Technoscience, and Women Workers* (Durham, NC: Duke University Press, 2006).
27. Jiat-Hwee Chang, "Thermal Comfort and Climate Design in the Tropics: An Historical Critique," *Journal of Architecture* 21, no. 8 (December 2016): 1171–202; Gail Cooper, *Air Conditioning America: Engineers and the Controlled Environment, 1900–1960* (Baltimore: Johns Hopkins University Press, 2002).
28. Le Corbusier, *Towards an Architecture* (Los Angeles: Getty Publications, 2007), 172; originally published in 1923.
29. See in particular Francesco Passanti, "The Vernacular, Modernism, and Le Corbusier," *Journal of the Society of Architectural Historians* 56, no. 4 (December 1997): 438–51.
30. Jiat-Hwee Chang, *A Genealogy of Tropical Architecture: Colonial Networks, Nature, and Technoscience* (New York: Routledge, 2016); Anthony D. King, *The Bungalow: The Production of Global Culture* (New York: Oxford University Press, 1995); Iain Jackson, "Tropical Architecture and the West Indies: From Military Advances and Tropical Medicine, to Robert Gardner-Medwin and the Networks of Tropical Architecture,"

Journal of Architecture 22, no. 4 (2017): 710–38.

31. Kenneth Frampton, *Modern Architecture: A Critical History* (New York: Thames and Hudson, 1986), 224; see also Kenneth Frampton, *Le Corbusier* (New York: Thames and Hudson, 2001), 130–49.
32. Bruno Reichlin, "The Pros and Cons of the Horizontal Window," *Daedalus* 13 (1984); Beatriz Colomina, "Le Corbusier and Photography," *Assemblage* 4 (1987); Beatriz Colomina, "The Split Wall: Domestic Voyeurism," in *Sexuality and Space*, ed. Beatriz Colomina (New York: Princeton Architectural Press, 1992), 73–130; for a discussion of the persistence of these problematics, see Michael Bell and Jannette Kim, eds., *Engineered Transparency: The Technical, Visual, and Spatial Effects of Glass* (New York: Princeton Architectural Press, 2009).
33. Le Corbusier, *Oeuvre complète*, vol. 3, *1934–1938* (Zurich: Éditions Dr. H. Girsberger, 1939), 35; Flora Samuel, *Le Corbusier in Detail* (New York: Routledge, 2007), 78.
34. L. M. Diaz and R. Southall, "Le Corbusier's Cité de Refuge: Historical and Technological Performance of the *air exacte*," in *Le Corbusier: 50 Years Later* (conference proceedings), Universitat Politecnica de Valencia, Spain, November 18–20, 2015. Vanessa Fernandez and Emanuelle Gallo, "The Glass Façade and the Heating System of the Salvation Army 'City of Refuge': From Conception to Restoration," *Actes de la conférence DOCOMOMO Technology "Perceived Technology in the Modern Movement"* (2014): 45–55.
35. Banham, *Architecture of the Well-Tempered Environment*, 158.
36. Frampton, *Le Corbusier*, 133; see also Kenneth Frampton, "Le Corbusier and Oscar Niemeyer: Influence and Counterinfluence, 1929–1965," in *Latin American Architecture, 1929–1969: Contemporary Reflections*, ed. Carlos Brillembourg (New York: Monacelli Press, 2004), 37.
37. The system would be developed in operational capacity after the war through Centre scientifique et technique du bâtiment, 1947. See Isabelle Buttenwieser, *Panorama du techniques des bâtiment, 1947–1997* (Paris: CTSB, 1997).
38. The quote is from a Mr. Still, engineer for the American Blower Corporation (ABC), in Urbano Gutiérrez, "'Pierre, revoir tout le système fenêtres': Le Corbusier and the Development of Glazing and Air-Conditioning Technology," 114.
39. Frampton, *Le Corbusier*, 138.
40. Porteous, *New Eco-Architecture*, 62.
41. Banham, *Architecture of the Well-Tempered Environment*, 158.
42. Banham, *Architecture of the Well-Tempered Environment*, 158. For an attempt to assess the preformative effects of the brise-soleil additions, see Diaz and Southall, "Le Corbusier's Cité de Refuge: Historical and Technological Performance of the *air exacte*."
43. Rosa Urbano Gutiérrez, '*Le Pan de Verre Scientifique*: Le Corbusier and the Saint-Gobain Glass Laboratory Experiments (1931–1932)," *Architecture Research Quarterly (ARQ)* 17, no. 1 (2013): 63–71.
44. Urbano Gutiérrez, "'Pierre, revoir tout le système fenêtres': Le Corbusier and the Development of Glazing and Air-conditioning Technology," 125. She lists the Maison du Brésil, Paris (1957–59) and the Carpenter Center for the Visual Arts at Harvard, Cambridge, Massachusetts (1959–63) as examples of this hybrid approach.
45. Requena-Ruiz, "Building Artificial Climates," 5–7.
46. For a collection of more recent energy efficient buildings that emphasizes this historical legacy, see Kim Tanzer and Rafael Longoria, eds., *The Green Braid: Towards an Architecture of Ecology, Economy, and Equity* (New York: Routledge, 2007); and Catherine Slessor, *Eco-Tech: Sustainable Architecture and High Technology* (New York: Thames and Hudson, 2001).
47. Michel Foucault, Introduction to *The Normal and the Pathological*, by Georges Canguilhem (New York: Zone Books, 1991), 7–25; 12. The Zone publication is a translation of a 1966 French edition with Foucault's introduction.
48. Ellsworth Huntington, *Civilization and Climate* (New Haven, CT: Yale University Press, 1924); see also S. F. Markham, *Climate and the Energy of Nations* (London: Oxford University Press, 1942), 21–31. For an analysis of the role of climatic determinism in the postwar development of tropical architecture, see Chang, "Thermal Comfort and Climatic Design," 1171.
49. Foucault, Introduction, 9; see also quoted in Simon Springer, "Neoliberalism as Discourse: Between Foucauldian Political Economy and Marxian Poststructuralism," *Critical Discourse Studies* 9, no. 2 (May 2012): 133–47.
50. Georges Canguilhem, *The Normal and the Pathological* (New York: Zone Books, 1991), 45, 51.
51. Canguilhem, *Normal and the Pathological*, 77.
52. Lejeune and Sabatino, *Modern Architecture and the Mediterranean*.
53. Archive of the Fondation Le Corbusier, Paris A2-18-33-001.
54. Archive of the Fondation Le Corbusier, Paris A2-18-34-001; Archive of the Fondation Le Corbusier, Paris X1-14-81-001.
55. Le Corbusier, "Problèmes de l'ensoleillement: Le brise soleil,' *Techniques et Architecture* 6, no. 1–2 (January 1946): 25–28.
56. Le Corbusier, "Problèmes," 26.
57. France Fradet, "Efficacité de l'ensoleillement," *Techniques et Architecture* 6, no. 1–2 (January 1946): 28–31.
58. Archive of the Fondation Le Corbusier, Paris B3-9-132-001.
59. Jeffrey Aronin, *Climate and Architecture*, Progressive Architecture (New York: Reinhold, 1953), 27.
60. Papadaki is an interesting and understudied figure, in regard to the expansion of modernism, and climatic modernism, after World War II. He went to the United States right after the war and, as art director at *Progressive Architecture* from 1950, helped to promote Brazilian modernism to the international architectural public. Citing the impact on Brazil of the 1946 *Brazil Builds* exhibition at the Museum of Modern Art in New York, Lucio Cavalcanti claims that early Brazilian architecture was strengthened by a turn away from Europe and toward the United States, and that Brazilian modernism received an international audience largely due to the efforts of American editors such as Papadaki, who were followed by their European counterparts. As Cavalcanti writes, "according to my research, European magazines usually published [Brazilian] projects that had already appeared in American periodicals." See Lauro Cavalcanti, "Architecture, Urbanism, and the Good Neighbor Policy: Brazil and the United States," in *Latin American Architecture, 1929–1969: Contemporary Reflections*, ed. Carlos Brillembourg (New York: Monacelli Press, 2004), 26. See, for example, Stamo Papadaki, *Le Corbusier: The Gradations of Modulor* (Paris: Durisol, 1947); Stamo Papadaki, ed., *Le Corbusier: Architect, Painter, Writer* (New York: Macmillan, 1948); Stamo Papadaki and Lucio Costa, *The Work of Oscar Niemeyer* (New York: Reinhold, 1950); Stamo Papadaki, *Oscar Niemeyer: Works in Progress* (New York: Reinhold, 1956).

61. Le Corbusier, "Problèmes," 27.
62. Manfredo Tafuri, *Architecture and Utopia: Design and Capitalist Development* (Cambridge, MA: MIT Press, 1976), 133–34.
63. Many have argued against this "autonomous" interpretation, see in particular Diane Y. Ghirardo, "Manfredo Tafuri and Architecture Theory in the U.S., 1970–2000," in Osman et al., *Perspecta 33: Mining Autonomy*, 38–47.
64. See, for example, Bone, *Lessons from Modernism*; Porteous, *New Eco-Architecture*; Dean Hawkes, *Architecture and Climate: An Environmental History of British Architecture* (London: Routledge, 2012); and Dean Hawkes, *The Environmental Tradition: Studies in the Architecture of Environment* (London: Taylor and Francis, 2013).
65. For a counterexample, see Naginski and Scott Cohen, *Return of Nature*.

## Chapter 2

1. That such an approach was a nascent form of neoliberalism is perhaps self-evident, offering yet another case of how architectural ideas have been reflected in and inflected by political economic contexts. See Douglas Spencer, *The Architecture of Neoliberalism: How Contemporary Architecture Became an Instrument of Control and Compliance* (London: Bloomsbury Academic, 2016); and Kenny Cupers, Catharina Gabrielsson, and Helena Mattsson, eds., *Neoliberalism: An Architectural History* (Pittsburgh: University of Pittsburgh Press, 2019).
2. One could also look to the *Semana da Arte Moderna*, in São Paulo from February 11–18, 1922, and to Oswaldo de Andrade's *Manifesto Antropofago* (Cannibalistic Manifesto) to substantiate the development of modern tendencies in Brazil, rather than simply as the reception of ideas from Europe.
3. Arturo Escobar, *Encountering Development: The Making and Unmaking of the Third World* (Princeton, NJ: Princeton University Press, 1995), 12.
4. This initial period of shaded modernism for office towers culminates in its inverse—the air-conditioned UN Headquarters in New York (1952) of the same basic formal disposition, designed by Niemeyer and Wallace Harrison—without attention to orientation or a secondary shading façade, which led to significant thermal complications. See George A. Dudley, *A Workshop for Peace: Designing the United Nations Headquarters* (Cambridge, MA: MIT Press, 1994).
5. Frampton, "Le Corbusier and Oscar Niemeyer, 49; Roberto Segre, *Ministério da Educação e da Saúde: Ìcone Urbano da Modernidade Brasileira, 1935–1945* (São Paulo: Romano Guerra, 2013); Mauricio Lissovsky, *Colunas da Educação: A Construção do Ministério da Educação e da Saúde, 1935–1945* (Rio de Janeiro: Ministério da Cultura, Insituto do Patrimônio Histórico e Artístico Nacional, 1996).
6. Frampton, "Le Corbusier and Oscar Niemeyer," 37.
7. Brazil had a legacy of innovation in vaccines and public health, centered on the physician and epidemiologist Oswaldo Cruz and the foundation in his name, in Rio in 1902. See Nancy Stepan, *Beginnings of Brazilian Science: Oswaldo Cruz, Medical Research, and Policy, 1890–1920* (New York: Science History Publications, 1981).
8. Daryle Williams, *Culture Wars in Brazil: The First Vargas Regime, 1930–1945* (Durham, NC: Duke University Press, 2001), 61. See also Thomas Skidmore, *Politics in Brazil, 1930–1964: An Experiment in Democracy* (New York: Oxford University Press, 1967); and Ronald M. Schneider, *"Order and Progress": A Political History of Brazil* (Boulder, CO: Westview Press, 1991).
9. This governmentalized state is, according to Foucault, "a very specific albeit complex form of power, which has as its target population, as its principle form of knowledge political economy, and as its essential technical means apparatuses of security." Foucault, *Security, Territory, Population,* 28; see also Daniel A. Barber, "Environmentalization and Environmentality: Re-conceiving the History of 20th Century Architecture," in *Design Philosophy Papers #5*, ed. Anne-Marie Willis (Ravensbourne, Australia: Team D/E/S Publishers, 2009); and Aggregate Architectural History Collaborative, *Governing by Design: Architecture, Economy, and Politics in the 20th Century* (Pittsburgh: University of Pittsburgh Press, 2012).
10. Foucault, *Security, Territory, Population*, 105.
11. Capanema quoted in Williams, *Culture Wars*, 61; he tried to get the Ministry renamed the Ministry of National Culture.
12. See the bulletins published by the MES from 1931 describing the laws, decrees, and programs initiated by the agency: *Boletim do Ministério da Educação e Saúde Pública*; it became the *Anais do Ministério da Educação e Saúde* in 1942. The general ambition to quantify and refine the health and social ambitions of the population is also evident in the 1942 collection of relevant data, *Educação e Saúde: Comunicados do Órgão Central de Estatística do Ministério da Educação e Saúde* (Rio de Janeiro: Insituto Brasileiro da Geografia e Estatística, 1942); see also Williams, *Culture Wars*, 80.
13. The government-run energy corporation Petrobras was established in 1953, part of a broader attempt to maintain some energy independence, which also included extensive exploitation of natural gas. See Jacqueline Ganzert Ofonso, *Petrobras, ou comment devenir une grande puissance petroliére* (Paris: Éditions Universitaires Européenes, 2015); and Adilson de Oliveira, "Brazil's Petrobras: Strategy and Performance," in *Oil and Governance: State Owned Enterprises and the World Oil Supply*, ed. David G. Victor et al. (New York: Cambridge University Press, 2012).
14. Instituto Nacional de Estudos Pedagogicos, *Outline of Education in Brazil* (Rio de Janeiro: Ministry of Education and Health, 1946); see also Williams, *Culture Wars*, 86.
15. In this regard Foucault identifies the role of government in the formation of famines as a particularly coherent example of the emergence of the governmentalized state. This appears to prefigure the analysis in Mike Davis, *Late Victorian Holocausts: El Niño Famines and the Making of the Third World* (New York: Verso, 2001), which has been influential on a number of recent global histories of the economic and ecological developments; see, for example, Robert B. Marks, *The Origins of the Modern World: A Global and Ecological Narrative* (Lanham, MD: Rowman and Littlefield, 2002).
16. Hugo Segawa, *Architecture of Brazil: 1900–1990* (London: Springer, 2002), 80. See also Williams, *Culture Wars*, 54.
17. Daniela Sandler, "The Other Way Around: The Modernist Movement in Brazil," in *Third World Modernism: Architecture, Development and Identity*, ed. Duanfang Lu (New York: Routledge, 2010), 31–56; and Gaia Piccarolo, "Lucio Costa's Luso-Brazilian Routes: Recalibrating 'Center' and 'Periphery,' " in *Latin American Modern Architectures: Ambiguous Territories*, ed. Patricio del Real and Helen Gygers (New York: Routledge, 2012), 33–52.
18. Sandler, "Other Way Around," 36–37.
19. Lauro Cavalcanti, *When Brazil Was Modern: Guide to Architecture, 1928–1960* (New York: Princeton

Architectural Press, 2003), 348–49; see also Luis E. Carranza and Fernando Luiz Lara, *Modern Architecture in Latin America: Art, Technology, and Utopia* (Austin: University of Texas Press, 2015), 61–63.

20. Carranza and Lara, *Modern Architecture in Latin America*, 63.
21. Luis Felipe Machado Coelho de Souza, *Irmãos Roberto, Arquitetos* (Rio de Janeiro: Rio Books, 2013).
22. Yannis Tsiomis, *Conférences de Rio: Le Corbusier au Brésil, 1936* (Paris: Flammarion, 2006), 27; see also Robert Fishman, *Urban Utopias in the Twentieth Century* (Cambridge, MA: MIT Press, 1982).
23. Patricio del Real, "Paternity Rights: The Brise-Soleil and the Sources of Modernity in the Ministry of Education and Health in Rio de Janeiro, Brazil," *ACSA Proceedings*, Portland, Oregon, 2002; as the title indicates, del Real is concerned with understanding the precise role of Le Corbusier's influence, read through American interest of the building and the *Brazil Builds* exhibition at MoMA in 1943. Much North American research often suggested that Le Corbusier had an important role; see Carlos Ferreira Martins, "Etat, Culture et Nature aux origines de l'architecture moderne au Bresil: Le Corbusier et Lucia Costa 1929–1936," in *Le Corbusier et la Nature*, ed. Maria Bonaiti et al. (Paris: Editions de la Villette, 2004), 195–208; and Elizabeth Davis Harris, "Le Corbusier and the Headquarters of the Brazilian Ministry of Education and Health, 1936–1945" (PhD diss., University of Chicago, 1984). Brazilian historians have more recently downplayed the specific influence of Le Corbusier on the MES while still acknowledging his importance to the culture of architecture in Rio more generally. See, for example, Segawa, *Architecture of Brazil*, 84–87.
24. Le Corbusier, "Problèmes de l'ensoleillement: Le brise soleil," *Techniques et Architecture* 6, no. 1–2 (January 1946): 27 (my translation).
25. Gustavo Rocha-Peixoto, "Prefacio: Rigor Arejado e Solar," in *Irmãos Roberto, Arquitetos*, by Luis Felipe Machado Coelho de Souza (Rio de Janeiro: Rio Books, 2013), 15–25, 15. See also Luis Felipe Machado Coelho de Souza, "Rigor e brutalismo na obra dos Irmãos Roberto," in *X Seminario Docomomo Brasil* (Curitiba, Brazil: Docomomo, 2013). The March/April 1937 issue of *Arquitetura e Urbanismo* (the journal of the Instituto de Arquitetos do Brasil) included an article on the Roberto brothers winning competition entry, which included an egg-crate shading device on the sun-exposed façade rather than the vertical louvers that would, in the built condition, cover the north and east façades in an identical manner. A feature on the completed building's design and construction published in 1940 includes excerpts from the Roberto brothers' correspondence dating from early 1936. See "O Palacio de Imprensa," *Arquitetura e Urbanismo* 3, no. 2 (March/April 1937): 65–72; and "Associação Brasileira de Imprensa," *Arquitetura e Urbanismo* 5, no. 5–6 (September–December 1940): 259–77.
26. Coehlo de Souza, "Rigor e brutalismo," 4–5.
27. Henrique Mindlin, *Modern Architecture in Brazil* (New York: Reinhold, 1957).
28. As the Brazilian historian Henrique Mindlin wrote in 1957, "The brise-soleil (in Portuguese *quebra-sol*, or "sun-breaker," but that the French expression is commonly used indicates its direct derivation from Le Corbusier) has been applied in Brazil in the greatest variety of ways." That the French *brise-soleil* terminology was used in the midcentury period throughout Brazil is suggestive of the importance of this strategy as a symbol of regional interpretation of a seemingly European modernism. Mindlin, *Modern Architecture in Brazil*, 12.
29. Barry Bergdoll, Introduction to *Latin America in Construction, 1955–1980* (New York: MoMA, 2015).
30. Brazil had also just attempted, in 1926, to become a part of the permanent council of the League of Nations. That this prospect was, in the end, and unexpectedly, rejected is seen by some historians as an important push toward the coup that brought Vargas to power. Williams, *Culture Wars*.
31. Williams, *Culture Wars*, 54.
32. See Amy L. S. Staples, *The Birth of Development: How the World Bank, Food and Agriculture Administration, and World Health Organization Have Changed the World* (Kent, OH: Kent State University Press, 2006); Nestor Garcia Canclini, *Hybrid Cultures: Strategies for Entering and Leaving Modernity* (Minneapolis: University of Minnesota Press, 2005); and Eduardo Viveiros de Castro, "Economic Development, Anthropomorphism, and the Principle of Reasonable Sufficiency," in *Protecting Nature, Saving Creation*, ed. Pasquale Gagliardi et al. (New York: Palgrave Macmillan, 2013), 161–80.
33. On tropical architecture see the end of chapter 3 herein.
34. The youngest brother, Mauricio, did not join the firm until late in 1936, after the design for the ABI was complete but while the IRB was still in development. Milton died in 1953, soon after designing the shading system for the Marques do Herval, discussed further on.
35. This Distrito Federal would be moved to Brasilia in the early 1960s, the new city constructed according to Costa's plan.
36. Mindlin, *Modern Architecture in Brazil*, 194; see also "Building A.B.I.," *L'Architecture d'aud'aujourd'hui* 18 (September 1947): 60–61.
37. Mindlin, *Modern Architecture in Brazil*, 202.
38. "I.R.B. Building, Rio de Janeiro, Brazil," *Architectural Forum* 18 (August 1944): 66–77, 67; see also "IRB Building at Rio de Janeiro," *Architectural Record* (January 1948).
39. Victor Olgyay argues that the distinction between a climate-responsive and a bioclimatic building is the attention to the specific dynamics of a given façade. See Olgyay and Olgyay, *Solar Control and Shading Devices*.
40. The drawings were published in most of the European and North American press on the buildings, including in *Architectural Forum* in January 1944, and in "Bâtiment d'administration 'I.R.B.,'" *L'Architecture d'aud'aujourd'hui* 22 (August 1952).
41. MMM Roberto papers, Research and Documentation Center, Universidade Federal do Rio de Janeiro. Item #26758.
42. Ulrich Beck, *World Risk Society* (Cambridge: Polity Press, 1999), 4. See also Ulrich Beck, *Risk Society: Towards a New Modernity* (London: Sage, 1992);, and Ulrich Beck, *Ecological Enlightenment: Essays on the Politics of the Risk Society* (Atlantic Highlands, NJ: Humanities Press, 1995).
43. Bruno Latour, *The Politics of Nature: How to Bring the Sciences into Democracy* (Cambridge, MA: Harvard University Press, 2004). Latour discusses the industrial practices relevant to food production that led to an outbreak, and anxiety around, mad cow disease.
44. Arthur P. J. Mol and Martin Jänicke, "The Origins and Theoretical Foundations of Ecological Modernisation Theory," in *The Ecological Modernisation Reader: Environmental Reform in Theory and Practice*, ed. Arthur P. J. Mol, David A. Sonnenfeld, and Gert Spaargaren (London: Routledge, 2009); see also Arthur P. J. Mol, "Ecological

Modernization and the Global Economy," *Global Environmental Politics* 2, no. 2 (May 2002): 92–115.

45. Ulrich Beck, "Climate for Change; or, How to Create a Green Modernity?" *Theory, Culture, and Society* 27, no. 2–3 (2010): 254–66.
46. Paul Rutherford, "Ecological Modernization and Environmental Risk," in *Discourses on the Environment*, ed. Eric Darier (London: Wiley, 1998), 95–117, 104.
47. Beck, *Risk Society*, 56.
48. Mitchell Dean, "Risk, Calculable and Incalculable," *Sociale Welt* 49 (1998): 25–42, 25.
49. Lorenz Krüger, Lorraine Daston, and Michael Heidelberger, eds., *The Probabilistic Revolution*, vol. 1, *Ideas in History*; and Lorenz Krüger, Gerd Gigerenzer, and Mary S. Morgan, eds., *The Probabilistic Revolution*, vol. 2, *Ideas in the Sciences* (both volumes: Cambridge, MA: MIT Press, 1987); see also Lorraine J. Daston and Peter Galison, *Objectivity* (Cambridge, MA: MIT Press, 2007).
50. François Ewald, "Insurance and Risk," in *The Foucault Effect: Studies in Governmentality*, ed. Graham Burchell, Colin Gordon, and Peter Miller (Chicago: University of Chicago Press, 1991), 197–210; see also Daniel Defert, " 'Popular Life' and Insurance Technology," 211–34, in the same volume; and Ian Hacking, *The Taming of Chance* (Cambridge: Cambridge University Press, 1990). See also Ewald, "The Values of Insurance," *Grey Room*, no. 74 (Winter 2019), with an introduction by Michael C. Behrent. Ewald was an assistant to Foucault in the 1970s and has been instrumental in publishing Foucault's lectures and other late work. Ewald has since moved to the right, becoming something of an apologist for the tight relationship between corporate expansion, insurance, and the welfare state in France. See Michael C. Behrent, "Accidents Happen: François Ewald, the 'Antirevolutionary' Foucault, and the Intellectual Politics of the French Welfare State," *Journal of Modern History* 82 (September 2010): 585–624; and Richard Wolin, *The Wind from the East: French Intellectuals, the Cultural Revolution, and the Legacy of the 1960s* (Princeton, NJ: Princeton University Press, 2010).
51. Ewald, "Insurance and Risk," 201 and throughout.
52. See also Timothy Mitchell, "Fixing the Economy," *Cultural Studies* 12, no. 1 (1998): 82–101.
53. Ibrahim Carone, "Qual a localidade mais sálubre do Rio," *Arquitetura e Urbanismo* (May/June 1936): 60–64.
54. Paulo Sá, "Ventilacao e indices de conforto," *Arquitetura e Urbanismo* (November–December 1936): 194–95.
55. Ignacio Requena-Ruiz, "Building Artificial Climates: Thermal Control and Comfort in Modern Architecture, 1930–1960," *Ambiances* (November 2016): 1–3. See also André Missenard, *L'Homme et le climat* (Paris: Plan, 1936).
56. Sá, "Ventilacao e indices de conforto," 195.
57. Mindlin, *Modern Architecture in Brazil*, 194; "Colonie de vacances a Gavea," *L'Architecture d'aud'aujourd'hui* 18 (September 1947): 60–61—one of the few color photographs in the issue is of the hillside elevation of the main building; it was also published as "Holiday Hostel at Rio de Janeiro," *Architectural Forum* (December 1947): 185–88; and "Small Resort Hotel in Tijuca," *Architectural Review* (November 1947).
58. Bruno Carvalho, "Mapping the Urbanized Beaches of Rio de Janeiro: Modernization, Modernity, and Everyday Life," *Travesia: Journal of Latin American Cultural Studies* 6, no. 3 (2007): 325–39.
59. "Record of Louvers," from the Neutra Archives UCLA. He also cited his use of louvers at the "U.S. Embassy in Pakistan, the Lincoln Memorial Museum on the battlefield of Gettysburg, and in many other celebrated buildings."
60. On Foster's building, see Jonathan Massey, "Risk Design," *Grey Room*, no. 54 (Winter 2014): 6–33.
61. See, for example, the "Vocational School SENAI [1946]," *Architectural Forum* (November 1947); "School for Industrial Apprentices [1953]," in Mindlin, *Modern Architecture in Brazil*, 140, and *Architecture d'aujourd'hui* 22 (August 1952).
62. Mindlin, *Modern Architecture in Brazil*, 274; the photograph of the brothers adjusting the shading device is in Mindlin and is from the archive. The building was not widely published.
63. Mindlin, *Modern Architecture in Brazil*, 194; see also "Flats in Rio de Janeiro" *L'Architecture d'aujourd'hui* 18 (September 1947): 60–61; it is also included in a review of the Roberto brothers' extensive residential work around Rio, in "Edifícios de Apartmentos, Copacabana, Rio," *Habitat* 6 (1956): 6–17.
64. Seigert, *Cultural Techniques*, 76.
65. On the history of the thermostat, see Michael Osman, *Modernism's Visible Hand: Architecture and Regulation in America* (Minneapolis: University of Minnesota Press, 2018), 12 and throughout.
66. Wendy Hui Kyong Chun, "On Hypo-Real Models or Global Climate Change: A Challenge for the Humanities," *Critical Inquiry* 41 (Spring 2015): 675–703; see also Wendy Hui Kyong Chun, "Crisis, Crisis, Crisis, or Sovereignty and Networks," *Theory, Culture, and Society* 28, no. 6 (2011): 91–112.
67. Philip L. Goodwin, *Brazil Builds: Architecture New and Old, 1652–1942* (New York: Museum of Modern Art, 1943); see also Zilah Quezado Deckker, *Brazil Built: The Architecture of the Modern Movement in Brazil* (London: Taylor and Francis, 2013).
68. While Mindlin celebrated the Brazilian integration of the brise-soleil into modern design strategies, and acknowledged the influence of Le Corbusier in this regard, he further claimed that this proliferation was based on "research into the functions of sunlight" in São Paulo engineering schools at the turn of the century, and the consequent development of "a scientific basis for the orientation and sun-lighting of buildings" in architecture schools by the mid-1920s. "Easily handled sunlight graphs and tables," Mindlin concluded, had been "in general use by architects for decades now, making it possible to calculate accurately and solve any sunlight problem," Mindlin, *Modern Architecture in Brazil*, 11.
69. Papadaki had experimented with the brise-soleil and had also written on Le Corbusier. In 1944 he left Brazil for New York and became an editor at *Progressive Architecture*.
70. Randall Collins and Mauro Guillén, "Mutual Halo Effects in Cultural Production: The Case of Modern Architecture," *Theory and Society* 41, no. 6 (November 2012): 527–56.
71. Cavalcanti characterizes this decline as a result of "the desire to improve the poor by placing them in sophisticated residential spaces clashed with the architect's ignorance of the taste and social skills of the inhabitants." Cavalcanti, *When Brazil Was Modern*, 267.
72. Alfredo Britto, *Pedregulho: O sonho pioneiro da habitação popular no Brasil* (Rio de Janeiro: Edições de Janeiro, 2015); see also a discussion of the renovation on the website of the State of Rio de Janeiro, http://www.rj.gov.br/web/seh/exibeconteudo?article-id=2118261, accessed January 4, 2018.
73. Chun, "On Hypo-Real Models," 702.

## Chapter 3

1. Alan Colquhoun, "Critique of Regionalism," *Casabella* (January–February 1996): 50–55; Alan Colquhoun, "The Concepts of Regionalism," in *Postcolonial Space(s)*, ed. Gulsum Baydar Nalbantaglo and Wong Chung Thia (New York: Princeton Architectural Press, 1997), 13–23.
2. Paul Ricoeur, "Universal Civilization and National Cultures," in *History and Truth* (Evanston, IL: Northwestern University Press, 1965); see also Vincent B. Canizaro, ed., *Architectural Regionalism: Collected Writings on Place, Identity, Modernity, and Tradition* (New York: Princeton Architectural Press, 2007).
3. Kenneth Frampton, "Towards a Critical Regionalism: Six Points of an Architecture of Resistance," in *The Anti-Aesthetic: Essays on Post-Modern Culture*, ed. Hal Foster (Port Townsend, WA: Bay Press, 1983), 16–30; Kenneth Frampton, "Critical Regionalism Revisited: Reflections on the Mediatory Potential of Built Form," in *Vernacular Modernism: Heimat, Globalization, and the Built Environment*, ed. Maiken Umbach and Bernd Huppauf (Stanford, CA: Stanford University Press, 2005); Keith Eggener, "Placing Resistance: A Critique of Critical Regionalism," *Journal of Architectural Education* 55, no. 4 (May 2002): 228–37.
4. Gwendolyn Wright, "Global Ambitions and Local Knowledge," in *Modernism and the Middle East: Architecture and Politics in the Twentieth Century*, ed. Sandy Eisenstadt and Kishwar Rizvi (Seattle: University of Washington Press, 2008), 221–54; Daniel Bertrand Monk, et al., "A Discussion on the Global and the Universal," *Grey Room*, no. 61 (Fall 2015): 66–89.
5. José Tavares Correia de Lira, "From Mild Climate's Architecture to 'Third World' Planning: Richard Neutra in Latin America," in *Urban Transformations: Controversies, Contrasts, and Challenges: The IPHS Fourteenth International Conference, Istanbul, 2010* (London: International Planning History Society, 2010), 1–15, 5–6; see also Ursula Prutsch, "Nelson A. Rockefeller's Office of Inter-American Affairs in Brazil," in *¡Americas Unidas!: Nelson A. Rockefeller's Office of Inter-American Affairs, 1940–46*, ed. Gisela Cramer and Ursula Prutsch (Madrid: Iberoamericana Vervuert, 2014); and Jorge F. Liernur, "Vanguardistas versus expertos: Reconstrución Europea, expansión Norte-Americana y Emergencia del Tercer Mundo; Para una relectura del debate arquitectonico en la segunda posguerra (una mirada desde America Latina)," *Block* 6 (2004).
6. Richard Neutra, "To the Students of Art and Architecture in Rio de Janeiro," Dion and Richard Neutra Archive, University of California, Los Angeles (hereafter Neutra Archive), document A-46.
7. Reyner Banham, *Theory and Design in the First Machine Age* (Cambridge, MA: MIT Press, 1960); Reyner Banham, "The Machine Aesthetic," *Architecture Review* (April 1955): 224–28.
8. Philip M. Lovell, "The Home Built for Health," *Los Angeles Times*, December 15, 1939. Lovell had also commissioned Rudolf Schindler to design a beach house for him; Schindler would also write a six-article series for "The Care of the Body" in 1926, focused on architecture and health. See Sarah Schrank, "Naked Houses: The Architecture of Nudism and the Rethinking of the American Suburb," in *Healing Spaces, Modern Architecture, and the Body*, ed. Sarah Schrank and Didem Ekici (New York: Routledge, 2017), 7–31.
9. Reyner Banham, "The Master Builders," *Sunday Times Color Supplement*, August 8, 1971, 19–27.
10. Banham, "Master Builders," 22.
11. Banham, "Master Builders," 24. This gap remains—though Thomas Hines's encyclopedic treatment of Neutra discussed the contours of his career and his prominence in the development of American modernism, the chapter that briefly discusses Puerto Rico is titled "Transition" and is primarily focused on a shift from wood to concrete in Neutra's private houses. Sylvia Lavin has more recently examined the inside/outside dimension of Neutra's design method from a psychoanalytic perspective, expanding the resonance of his post–World War II work in particular. Thomas Hines, *Richard Neutra and the Search for Modern Architecture* (Berkeley: University of California Press, 1982); Sylvia Lavin, *Form Follows Libido: Architecture and Richard Neutra in a Psychoanalytic Culture* (Cambridge, MA: MIT Press, 2004).
12. Sigfried Giedion, "R. J. Neutra: European and American," in *Richard Neutra: Buildings and Projects* (New York: Praeger, 1951), 3–6.
13. Thomas Hines, "Case Study Trouvé: Sources and Precedents, Southern California, 1920–1942," in *Blueprints for Modern Living: History and Legacy of the Case Study Houses*, ed. Elizabeth A. T. Smith (Los Angeles: Museum of Contemporary Art, 1998), 80–88, 83.
14. Hines, "Case Study Trouvé," 86.
15. The international attention given to the Health House was largely by virtue of the domestic use of an industrial steel frame rather than its relation to lifestyle. See Hines, "Case Study Trouvé," 80. See also Jean-Louis Cohen, *Scenes of the World to Come: European Architecture and the American Challenge* (Montreal: CCA, 1995), 100–101.
16. From his early friendship with Ernst Freud to the long, psychologically penetrating discussions he had with his clients, Lavin traces his engagement with psychoanalytic and empathic theories. Much of this emphasis is legible in his 1954 book *Survival through Design*. On this basis, Lavin sees Neutra, for example in the Perkins House (also of 1954), using architecture to reveal inner psychic dimensions. This originated, for Lavin, an architecture of sensation and affect rather than one informed by an analysis of the natural sciences. She sees this focus on affect as the basis of, or the rationale for, design theories and practices in the twenty-first century—a premise that has played out within a culture focused on form, intentionally isolated and insulated from environmental or social concerns. Lavin, *Form Follows Libido*, 3.
17. Lavin's emphasis is on a contemporary architecture, either contemporary to the 1950s or to the present, as "an approach to design and to the duration of design effects," *Form Follows Libido*, 7. See also Richard Neutra, *Survival through Design* (New York: Oxford University Press, 1954).
18. Barbara Lamprecht, *Neutra* (New York: Taschen, 2008), 10; see also Richard Neutra, *Nature Near: The Late Essays of Richard Neutra* (Santa Barbara, CA: Capra Press, 1989); and Esther McCoy, *Richard Neutra* (New York: Braziller, 1960).
19. Giorgio Ciucci, "The Invention of the Modern Movement," *Oppositions*, no. 24 (1981): 68–91, 69.
20. On CIAM, see Eric Mumford, *The CIAM Discourse on Urbanism, 1928–1960* (Cambridge, MA: MIT Press, 2000); on architectural aspects of the League of Nations, see Ciucci, "Invention of the Modern Movement"; and Kenneth Frampton, "The Humanist versus the Utilitarian Ideal," *Architectural Design* 38, no. 3 (March 1968): 134–36. Experimental architectural culture in the later postwar years, it could be argued, came to be defined by this planetary framework—from Archigram's traveling pamphlets, to Doxiadis's and Fuller's attempts to design at the scale of the planet, to the continuous proposals

for methods and parameters of design that sought to treat the globe as a consistent, albeit to varying degrees uneven, entity.

21. Henry-Russell Hitchcock and Philip Johnson, *The International Style: Architecture since 1922* (New York: Museum of Modern Art, 1932).
22. Hines, *Richard Neutra*, 211–43. See also Correia de Lira, "From Mild Climate's Architecture," 3.
23. Richard Neutra, "Comments on Planetary Reconstruction," *Arts and Architecture* 61, no. 12 (December 1944): 21–23, 21.
24. See Ana Maria Leon, "Modern Architecture Will Help You," *Journal of Surrealism and the Americas* 9, no. 1 (2016): 14–39, which plays out similar issues in the context of Peronist Argentina.
25. Neutra, "Comments on Planetary Reconstruction," 23.
26. George Woodbridge, *UNRRA: The History of the United Nations Relief and Rehabilitation Agency* (New York: Columbia University Press, 1950).
27. The debate on the political deployment of technologies has persisted; see Langdon Winner, "Do Artifacts Have Politics?" in his *The Whale and the Reactor: A Search for Limits in an Age of High Technology* (Chicago: University of Chicago Press, 1986); and Albena Yaneva, *Five Ways to Make Architecture Political* (London: Bloomsbury, 2017).
28. Richard Neutra, "Planetary Reconstruction," *Journal of the American Institute of Architects* 3, no. 1 (January 1945): 29–33, 31. See also Richard Neutra, "Peace Can Gain from War's Forced Changes," *New Pencil Points* 23, no. 11 (November 1942): 28–41.
29. Neutra, "Planetary Reconstruction," 33. These themes are developed at length in *Survival through Design*; see also Franca Trubiano, "Re-defining Architectural Performance—*Survival through Design* and the Sentient Environmentalism of Richard Neutra," in *Architecture in an Age of Uncertainty*, ed. Benjamin Flowers (New York: Routledge, 2016), 43–56.
30. On Rush City, see Hines, *Richard Neutra*, 65 and throughout. On the imagined cities of Le Corbusier and Frank Lloyd Wright (and Ebenezer Howard), see Robert Fishman, *Urban Utopias of the Twentieth Century* (Cambridge, MA: MIT Press, 1982).
31. Bruno Zevi, *Towards an Organic Architecture* (New York: Faber and Faber, 1950), 139; it was published in Italian in 1945.
32. Gregori Warchavchik, Introduction to Richard Neutra, *An Architecture of Social Concern for Regions of Mild Climate*, (São Paulo: Gerth Todtmann, 1948).
33. Richard Neutra, "Sun Control Devices," *Progressive Architecture* 27, no. 10 (October 1946): 88–91; a draft in the archive is titled "Anti-Solar Devices."
34. Richard Neutra, "Record of Louvers," n.d., Neutra Archive.
35. Neutra, "Comments on Planetary Reconstruction," 23.
36. Hines, *Richard Neutra*, 195; see also Correia de Lira, "From Mild Climate's Architecture," 5.
37. Garrett Dash Nelson, "Rexford Guy Tugwell and the Case for Big Urbanism," *Places Journal* (January 2018). See also Enrique Lugo-Silva, *The Tugwell Administration in Puerto Rico, 1941–1946* (Río Piedras: University of Puerto Rico Press, 1955); Linda C. Levin, "Midcentury Planning in San Juan, Puerto Rico: Rexford Guy Tugwell, Henry Klumb, and Design for 'Modernization'" (master's thesis, Washington University in Saint Louis, 2013).
38. Nelson, "Rexford Guy Tugwell."
39. Dennis Merrill, *Negotiating Paradise: U.S. Tourism and Empire in 20th Century Latin America* (Chapel Hill: University of North Carolina Press, 2009): 217 and throughout. See also the film *Puerto Rico: The Peaceful Revolution* directed by Henwar Rodakiewicz, 1962.
40. Hines, *Richard Neutra*, 194. Silvia Alvarez-Curbelo, "The Center of Everything: Consumption, Architecture, and City," in *Ever New San Juan: Architecture and Modernization in the 20th Century*, ed. Enrique Vivoni Farage (San Juan: Archivo de Arquitectura y Construcción de la Universidad de Puerto Rico [AACUPR], 2000), 228–75.
41. Rexford G. Tugwell, *The Stricken Land: The Story of Puerto Rico* (New York: Greenwood Press, 1946). Interestingly, there is no mention of Neutra, Klumb, or any of the prominent members of his Puerto Rico office in this lengthy memoir. Another compelling note—in Philip K. Dick's novel *The Man in the High Castle*, Tugwell was imagined as the elected president of the United States, succeeding Roosevelt and somehow both receiving credit for an Allied victory in World War II and managing the postwar tensions in a fashion that replaced the cold war with the USSR with an economic and military struggle between the American and British empires. His recourse to British models of colonial development in *The Stricken Land* perhaps informed Dick's fictional characterizations.
42. Correia de Lira, "From Mild Climate's Architecture," 3.
43. Silvia Álvarez-Curbelo, "The Design of Process: Henry Klumb and the Modernization of Puerto Rico (1944–1948)," in *Klumb: An Architecture of Social Concern*, ed. Enrique Vivoni Farage (Río Piedras: University of Puerto Rico, 2006), 221–53; on the general importance of campuses to developments in Latin American modernism, see Carlos Eduardo Comas, "The Poetics of Development: Notes of Two Brazilian Schools," in *Latin America in Construction: Architecture 1955–1980*, ed. Barry Bergdoll (New York: Museum of Modern Art, 2015), 40–67.
44. Curbelo, "Design of Process," 272.
45. Tugwell supported Luis Muñoz Marín's attempts to establish Puerto Rican independence. Tugwell later went on to teach planning and economics at the University of Chicago, before retiring to Greenbelt, Maryland, which he had helped plan in the late 1930s. Nelson, "Rexford Guy Tugwell."
46. Richard Neutra, "Man's Home Was South," Neutra Archive, n.d., 2; see also Neutra, *Survival through Design*.
47. Neutra, "Man's Home Was South," 1.
48. Lavin, *Form Follows Libido*, 45 and throughout.
49. Neutra, "Man's Home Was South," 11.
50. Neutra, "Man's Home Was South," 9–10.
51. Neutra, "Man's Home Was South," 17–18.
52. According to Correia de Lira, Neutra was frustrated that the Brazilian publisher did not adequately distribute the book on a worldwide scale; Correia de Lira, "From Mild Climate's Architecture," 11.
53. Richard Neutra, *An Architecture of Social Concern for Regions of Mild Climate* (São Paulo: Gerth Todtmann, 1948): 37–38.
54. Neutra, *An Architecture of Social Concern*, 42. He had made a similar claim, relative to the role of the public in economic development and technological trajectories, in a February 1939 article in *Plus*, in which he wrote, "Technology may or may not be the common denominator of building advance. However, regional variation in the consumer's psychology and in his economic opportunity to reap its benefits, gives the true color to this transitory situation, especially in the design of private dwellings." Richard Neutra, "Regionalism in Architecture," *Plus* 2 (February 1939): n.p.
55. Neutra, *An Architecture of Social Concern*, 52.

56. See Paul Overy, *Light, Air, and Openness: Modern Architecture between the Wars* (London: Thames and Hudson, 2008).
57. Neutra, *An Architecture of Social Concern*, 45.
58. Neutra, *An Architecture of Social Concern*, 56.
59. Neutra, *An Architecture of Social Concern*, 52.
60. "Projects for Puerto Rico," *L'Architecture d'aujourd'hui* 10, no. 6 (May 1946): 72. The issue was headed in red text: "Richard Neutra, Architect" (architect in English, rather than *architecte*).
61. Jennifer Wentzel, "Planet vs. Globe," *English Language Notes* 52, no. 1 (Spring/Summer 2014): 19–31; see also Tim Ingold, "Globes and Spheres: The Topology of Environmentalism," in his *The Perception of the Environment: Essays on Livelihood, Dwelling, and Skill* (New York: Routledge, 2000); and Gayatri Chakravorty Spivak, *Imperatives to Reimagine the Planet* (Vienna: Passagen-Verlag, 1999).
62. Tugwell, *Stricken Land*, 7 and throughout.
63. A. W. Maldonado, *Teodoro Moscoso and Puerto Rico's Operation Bootstrap* (Gainesville: University Press of Florida, 1997); Richard Weisskoff, *Factories and Food Stamps: The Puerto Rico Model for Development* (Baltimore: Johns Hopkins University Press, 1985); and somewhat more enigmatically, though with a tangential relationship to broader architectural-historical themes, Mark Jarzombek, "(Un)Designing Mythologies: Puerto Rico and Operation Bootstrap Undone," *Thresholds*, no. 21 (2000): 52–59.
64. Arif Belgaumi, "Legacy of the Cold War: Richard Neutra in Pakistan," *Int-Ar: Interventions Adaptive Reuse* 3 (2012): 83–89.
65. Both the promise and the naivete of this approach can be seen in Cameron Sinclair, *Design Like You Give a Damn: Architectural Responses to Humanitarian Crises* (London: Thames and Hudson, 2006); see also Andres Lepik, *Small Scale, Big Change: New Architectures of Social Engagement* (New York: Museum of Modern Art, 2010), based on the exhibition of the same name; and Benedict Clouette and Marlisa Wise, *Forms of Aid: Architectures of Humanitarian Space* (Basel: Birkhäuser, 2017).
66. Enrique Vivoni Farage, ed., *Klumb: Una arquitectura de impronta social / An Architecture of Social Concern* (Río Piedras: Editorial de Universidad de Puerto Rico, 2006); on Klumb's climatic orientation, see in particular David Leatherbarrow, "Henry Klumb's Works at Work," in *Klumb: An Architecture of Social Concern*, ed. Enrique Vivoni Farage (San Juan: University of Puerto Rico Press, 2006), 143–220; on Klumb's inheritance from and relative integration into international modernism, see Sandy Isenstadt, "Between Worlds: A Place for Modernism," in *Henry Klumb and Modern Architecture in Puerto Rico*, ed. Enrique Vivoni (San Juan: La Editorial Universidad de Puerto Rico, 2007), 221–52.
67. E. F. Schumacher, *Small Is Beautiful: A Study of Economics as if People Mattered* (New York: Harper and Row, 1973).
68. Kohr's writings on San Juan and Puerto Rican development more generally were collected as Leopold Kohr, *The Inner City: From Mud to Marble* (Talybont, Wales: Y Lolfa, 1989); see also Leopold Kohr, *The Breakdown of Nations* (New York: Routledge and K. Paul, 1957); Leopold Kohr, *The Overdeveloped Nations: Diseconomies of Scale* (New York: Schocken Books, 1978); and Leopold Kohr, *Development without Aid: The Translucent Society* (New York: Schocken Books, 1979).
69. Ivan Illich, "The Wisdom of Leopold Kohr," *Bulletin of Science, Technology, and Society* 17, no. 4 (1997): 157–65. The text was based on the annual Schumacher lecture, organized by the Schumacher Center for a New Economics and presented at Yale University in October 1994. I am grateful to my colleague Bill Braham who pointed me to the coincidence of Kohr's work, Illich's interest in it, and Klumb's friendship with both.
70. E. F. Schumacher, *A Guide for the Perplexed* (New York: Harper and Row, 1977).
71. CAT is briefly discussed in Giovanna Borasi and Mirko Zardini, eds., *Sorry, Out of Gas: Architecture's Response to the 1973 Oil Crisis* (Montreal: Canadian Centre for Architecture, 2007). See also Bryce Gilroy-Scott, John Chilton, and Steve Goodhew, "Earth Footprint of the Construction Phase of the Wales Institute for Sustainable Education at the Centre for Alternative Technology," *International Journal of Sustainability Education* 8, no. 2 (2013): 73–91.
72. G. E. Kidder Smith to Philip Johnson; letter in Museum of Modern Art Archives, curatorial folder for Exhibition 548: "Architecture for the State Department."
73. Kidder Smith, letter.
74. "U.S. Architecture Abroad: Modern Design at Its Best Now Represents This Country in Foreign Lands," *Architectural Forum* 98, no. 3 (March 1953): 101–15; all of the work in the October show at MoMA was in this fourteen-page spread, as was Eero Saarinen's Helsinki project—initially also intended to be included in the exhibition—and Leon Stynen's Brussels embassy of 1951. See also "Architecture for the State Department," *Arts and Architecture* (November 1953): 16–24.
75. Philip Johnson, Preface to *Built in USA: Post-War Architecture* (New York: Museum of Modern Art / Simon and Schuster), 1952.
76. Elizabeth Gordon, "The Threat to the Next America," *House Beautiful* 95, no. 4 (April 1953): 126–30, 250.
77. In 1945, Wallace Harrison had been asked by Nelson Rockefeller to be the head of cultural affairs at the State Department's Office of Inter-American Affairs, and it was likely through this connection that his firm received these early commissions—though the positive reception, at least in diplomatic circles, of their recently completed UN Building must also be acknowledged. See Jane C. Loeffler, *The Architecture of Diplomacy: Building America's Embassies* (New York: Princeton Architectural Press, 1998), 61.
78. On the details of the UN project, see *Report to the General Assembly of the United Nations by the Secretary General on the Permanent Headquarters of the United Nations* (Lake Success, NY: United Nations, 1947).
79. On Rapson, see also Elizabeth A. T. Smith, *Blueprints for Modern Living: History and Legacy of the Case Study Houses* (Cambridge, MA: MIT Press, 1999); Daniel A. Barber, *A House in the Sun: Modern Architecture and Solar Energy in the Cold War* (New York: Oxford University Press, 2016), 37 and throughout; Sarah Bonnemaison and Christine Macy, *Architecture and Nature: Creating the American Landscape* (New York: Routledge, 2003).
80. Rapson was recruited to the FBO over the phone. In addition to the Case Study project and his teaching at MIT, Rapson had worked with Moholy-Nagy on a number of industrial design projects and had worked with the sculptor Harry Bertoia on some furniture and then directly with Knoll. At MIT, he had been design architect for the well-received Eastgate Apartments in Cambridge, in collaboration with William Wurster, Vernon DeMars, and others. On his return from Europe and working with the FBO in late 1953, he taught at MIT one more semester and then went home

to Minneapolis to take over the University of Minnesota School of Architecture, where he was director for thirty-five years. See Jane King Hession et al., *Ralph Rapson: Sixty Years of Modern Design Afton* (Minnesota: Afton Historical Society Press, 1999).

81. Much to Rapson's frustration, this scheme was later taken as the template for a well-known project designed by Gropius and The Architect's Collaborative (TAC), completed in 1956. See Hession, *Ralph Rapson*, 56.
82. See Hyun Tae Jung, "Organization and Abstraction: The Architecture of Skidmore, Owings and Merrill, 1936–1956" (PhD diss., Columbia University, 2011); Gwendolyn Wright, *USA: Modern Architectures in History* (London: Reaktion Books, 2008), 181–82.
83. Drexler had assisted Henry-Russell Hitchcock in the organization of *Built in USA: Post-War Architecture*, which ran from January 20 to March 15, 1953; he also wrote the main essay of the catalog for the exhibition.
84. King insisted that all materials go through him for security reasons, noting that Rapson was actually employed by the State Department and could not release any materials on his own accord. King to Drexler, July 1, 1953, in MoMA curatorial folder for exhibition 543. The early notes also include Saarinen's planned Helsinki consulate and residence, which was not included as it was dropped in the middle of 1953. See letters in the curatorial folder 543.
85. See letter from State Department to Drexler, June 25, 1953, discussing reimbursing Drexler for his expenses abroad, in the MoMA archives.
86. Drexler had, in any event, been in communication with Rado in 1952 while assisting Henry-Russell Hitchcock on the *Built in USA: Post-War Architecture* exhibition, which was hanging at the museum while he was in Japan. Raymond and Rado's Electrolux Building, in Old Greenwich, Connecticut (1950), didn't make it into the 1952 show.
87. The specifics of the connections between MoMA and the State Department after the war and those of the relationship between Nelson Rockefeller, René d'Harnoncourt, and the Office of Inter-American Affairs is of special interest relative to the development and maintenance of postwar global alliances and the importance of the representation of Latin America and South America in the museum. Nelson Rockefeller was an advisor to Truman on inter-American affairs and was central to developing the educational and cultural exchange programs such as the one that had funded Drexler's Japan trip. His influence increased when Eisenhower became president in 1953. Nelson Rockefeller had also been instrumental in developing the traveling exhibition programs and the International Council at MoMA, a significant part not only of the "cultural cold war" but also of more general developments of the internationalization of the art world right after the war. See Frances Stonor Saunders, *The Cultural Cold War: The CIA and the World of Arts and Letters* (New York: New Press, 2001); Patricio del Real, "Building a Continent: MoMA's *Latin American Architecture since 1945* Exhibition," *Journal of Latin American Cultural Studies* 16, no. 1 (2007): 95–110.
88. Press release, "Architecture for the State Department," MoMA Archive.
89. "US Architects Abroad," 103.
90. See "US Architects Abroad"; and Loeffler, *Architecture of Diplomacy*, 38. Loeffler gives ample room to the specific debates in administrative and legislative committees and assigns significant agency to King as the proponent of modernism at State, largely based on interviews and his personal archive.
91. In most cases this meant that the building site and most materials were provided by the host country, a system that often led to serious design constraints but also, at times, opportunities. An extreme example involved the use of Marshall Plan credits to import Italian travertine marble for the H+A embassies in Rio and Havana. Some projects were instigated by foreign governments as a way to eliminate debt burden. In 1951, a lump appropriation of $90 million in credits was authorized, allowing the FBO to operate at least semi-independently for almost a decade. See Loeffler, *Architecture of Diplomacy*, 27.
92. Arthur Drexler and Henry-Russell Hitchcock, *Built in USA: Post-War Architecture* (New York: MoMA, 1952). SOM was represented by Lever House, Harrison and Abramowitz by the UN building, and Rapson through his work on the Eastgate Apartments; Raymond and Rado were also considered for the show. Drexler wrote the main text for the catalog, a ten-page essay outlining the importance of Le Corbusier, Gropius, and Mies for this new generation of American architects. The show proved contentious relative to the conservative cultural backlash against modern architecture spearheaded by Elizabeth Gordon. Hitchcock wrote the introduction and Johnson the preface; both referred to the show as the twentieth anniversary of the 1932 *Modern Architecture: An International Exhibition*.
93. See John Rannelagh, *The Agency: The Rise and Fall of the CIA* (New York: Simon and Schuster, 1986); and David F. Rudgers, *Creating the Secret State: the Origins of the Central Intelligence Agency, 1943–1947* (Lawrence: University Press of Kansas, 2000).
94. Louise A. Mozingo, *Pastoral Capitalism: A History of Suburban Corporate Landscapes* (Cambridge, MA: MIT Press, 2014).
95. "Skidmore Owings & Merrill," *Bulletin of the Museum of Modern Art* 18, no. 1 (Autumn 1950): 4–21; 15. The exhibition also included SOM's unbuilt town for oil refinery workers in Venezuela.
96. This massive State Department shake-up cut back on staff (mostly in the home office at Foggy Bottom, as staff abroad continued to grow) and thus on expenses while increasing effectiveness—a streamlining that completely changed the nature of foreign relations, giving agents in the field policy-making influence. See Rhodri Jeffreys-Jones, *The CIA and American Democracy* (New Haven, CT: Yale University Press, 1989).
97. King quoted in Loeffler, *Architecture of Diplomacy*, 67.
98. Indeed, over twenty-five years later, during the takeover of the Iranian embassy by students in 1979, the so-called den of thieves that they discovered demonstrated this architectural inflexibility—the CIA communications experts operated much of their equipment in a concrete bunker "hidden in plain sight," in an agricultural storage facility.
99. Ervand Abrahamian, "The 1953 Coup in Iran," *Science and Society* 65, no. 2 (2001): 185–215. The story, starring Kermit Roosevelt, is recounted in Steven Kizner, *All the Shah's Men: An American Coup and the Roots of Middle East Terror* (Hoboken, NJ: John Wiley and Sons, 2003); see also, for a more scholarly account, Mary Ann Heiss, *Empire and Nationhood: The United States, Great Britain, and Iranian Oil, 1950–1954* (New York: Columbia University Press, 1997).
100. The New Look was marketed primarily as a support system for the production of nuclear arms; it was not until the mid-1960s that the level of Eisenhower's and Dulles's dependence on the CIA to form and operate foreign policy became clear.

Congressional inquiries after the Bay of Pigs, in mid-April 1961, began to turn things around, in many ways sending the clandestine apparatus deeper under diplomatic and corporate cover. See John Lewis Gaddis, *Strategies of Containment: A Critical Appraisal of American National Security Policy during the Cold War* (New York: Oxford University Press, 2005); and William Blum, *Killing Hope: U.S. Military and CIA Interventions since World War II* (San Francisco: Common Courage Press, 1995).

101. Henderson was a central architect of the postwar CIA and other departments at State. An expert in the Middle East, he believed the future of foreign relations lay in friendship with Arabs, and for this reason opposed Israel. See Loeffler, *Architecture of Diplomacy*, 128; and H. W. Brands, *Inside the Cold War: Loy Henderson and the Rise of the American Empire, 1918–1961* (New York: Oxford University Press, 1991).
102. Brands, *Inside the Cold War*, 223. Brands also demonstrates that Henderson was crucial to approving and facilitating the overthrow of Mosaddegh.
103. Loeffler, *Building Diplomacy*.
104. Johnson quotes this phrase from Barr in his preface to *Built in USA: Post-War Architecture*.
105. For a discussion of Sert's Baghdad complex, see Samuel Isenstadt, "'Faith in a Better Future': Josep Lluís Sert's American Embassy in Baghdad," *Journal of Architectural Education* 50, no. 3 (February 1997): 172–88.
106. Chang, *A Genealogy of Tropical Architecture;* Hannah Le Roux, "The Networks of Tropical Architecture," *Journal of Architecture* 8, no. 3 (2003): 337–54; Mark Crinson, *Modern Architecture and the End of Empire* (Burlington, VT: Ashgate, 2013), 127.
107. Jane Drew and Maxwell Fry, *Village Housing in the Tropics* (London: Humphries, 1947); Jane Drew and Maxwell Fry, *Tropical Architecture in the Dry and Humid Zones* (Huntington, NY: Krieger Publications, 1957); Iain Jackson, *The Architecture of Edwin Maxwell Fry and Jane Drew* (London: Ashgate, 2014).
108. For context, see Douglas H. K. Lee, *Climate and Development in the Tropics* (New York: Harper and Brothers, 1957)—a text that is still profoundly caught up in the racial and climatic determinism of the prewar period.
109. Rachel Lee, "Otto Koenigsberger: Transcultural Practice and the Tropical Third Space," *OASE*, no. 95 (2015): 60–72. Rachel Lee, "Negotiating Modernities: Otto Koenigsberger's Works and Network in Exile (1933–1951)" (PhD diss., Berlin University of Technology, 2014).
110. Asseel Al-Ragan, "Critical Nostalgia: Kuwait Urban Modernity and Alison and Peter Smithons's Kuwait Urban Study and Mat Building," *Journal of Architecture* 20, no. 1 (February 2015): 1–20; and Vandana Baweja, "Otto Koenigsberger and the Tropicalization of British Architectural Culture," in *Third World Modernism: Architecture, Development, and Identity*, ed. Duangfang Lu (New York: Routledge, 2011), 236–54.

## Chapter 4

1. Statistical meteorology can be contrasted to numerical meteorology, the latter reliant on computation to process the data and equations necessary to approximate climate patterns and make forecasts. Landsberg was in this sense a transitional figure—essential to the development of statistical methods before the war, he remained a prominent figure in a field whose techniques had, generally speaking, moved on. See, for example, Helmut E. Landsberg, *Physical Climatology* (State College, PA: School of Mines, 1941); Helmut E. Landsberg, *Geophysics and Warfare* (Washington, DC: Office of the Assistant Secretary of Defense, 1954); and Helmut E. Landsberg, *The Urban Climate* (New York: Academic Press, 1981). See also the festschrift, Ferdinand Baer et al., eds., *Climate in Human Perspective: A Tribute to Helmut E. Landsberg* (Boston: Kluwer Academic, 1991). On Landsberg's later work on urban climate: Michael Hebbert and Vladimir Jankovic, "Cities and Climate Change: The Precedents and Why They Matter," *Urban Studies*, special issue, *Cities, Urbanization, and Climate Change* 50, no. 7 (May 2013): 1332–47, and, from a more applied perspective, Michael Hebbert, Vladimir Jankovic, and Brian Webb, eds., *City Weathers: Meteorology and Urban Design, 1950–2010* (Manchester: Manchester Architecture Research Centre, 2011). Landsberg would also be influential in the development of biometeorology, an emergent field that also briefly embraced the work of the Olgyay brothers.
2. Helmut E. Landsberg, "Microclimatology: Facts for Architects, Realtors, and City Planners on Climatic Conditions at the Breathing Line," *Architectural Forum* 86, no. 3 (March 1947): 119. The article is published under Fitch's name in Martica Sawin, ed., *James Marston Fitch: Selected Writings on Architecture, Preservation and the Built Environment* (New York: Norton, 2007), where it is erroneously indicated to have appeared in the March 1947 issue of *Forum*.
3. M. King Hubbert, "Nuclear Energy and the Fossil Fuels," in *Drilling and Production Practice* (Washington, DC: American Petroleum Institute, 1956).
4. M. King Hubbert, "Energy from Fossil Fuels," *Science* 109, no. 2823 (February 4, 1949): 103–9, 108.
5. Paul Siple, "Climatic Criteria for Building Construction," *Proceedings of the Research Correlation Conference on Weather and the Building Industry* (Washington, DC: National Academy of Sciences, 1950), 5–22, 14.
6. Helmut E. Landsberg, "Climate as a Natural Resource," *Scientific Monthly* 63, no. 4 (October 1946): 293–98; see also Vladimir Jankovic, "Working with the Weather: Atmospheric Resources, Climate Variability, and the Rise of Industrial Meteorology, 1950–2000," *History of Meteorology* 7 (2015): 98–116, 100.
7. Tomás Maldonado, "The Idea of Comfort," *Design Issues* 8, no. 1 (Autumn 1991): 35–43, 35. The article was originally published in Maldonado, *Il Futuro del Modernita* (Milan: Feltrinelli, 1987).
8. Will Steffen et al., *Global Change and the Earth System: A Planet under Pressure* (New York: Springer Verlag, 2004), 131. As he describes elsewhere: "The term 'Great Acceleration' was first used in a working group of a 2005 Dahlem Conference on the history of the human-environment relationship. . . . The term echoed Karl Polanyi's phrase 'The Great Transformation,' and in his book by the same name . . . Polanyi put forward a holistic understanding of the nature of modern societies, including mentality, behavior, structure and more. In a similar vein, the term 'Great Acceleration' aims to capture the holistic, comprehensive, and interlinked nature of the post-1950 changes simultaneously sweeping across the socio-economic and biophysical spheres of the Earth System, encompassing far more than climate change." Will Steffen, Wendy Broadgate, and Lisa Deutsch, "The Trajectory of the Anthropocene: The Great Acceleration," in *Anthropocene Review* 2, no. 1 (2015): 81–98, 83.
9. One of the many projects for reducing

carbon use in buildings, the Architecture 2030 Challenge, indicates that buildings emitted 47.6 percent of US carbon in 2013. See http://architecture2030.org/buildings.problem.why/.

10. Paul J. Crutzen and Eugene F. Stoermer, "The 'Anthropocene,'" *Global Change Newsletter* 41 (May 2000): 17–18.
11. Christophe Bonneuil and Jean-Baptiste Fressoz, *The Shock of the Anthropocene: The Earth, History, and Us* (New York: Verso, 2015).
12. Bill McKibben, *The End of Nature* (New York: Random House, 1989); George M. Van Dyne, *Ecosystems, Systems Ecology, and Systems Ecologists* (Oak Ridge, TN: Oak Ridge National Laboratory/Union Carbide Corporation /Atomic Energy Commission, June 1966); he notes his earlier development of these diagrams in the late 1950s.
13. George Perkins Marsh, *Man and Nature; or, Physical Geography as Modified by Human Action* (New York: Scribner, 1864); Alexander von Humboldt, *Cosmos* (New York: George Bell, 1883).
14. This was one of Barry Commoner's "Four Laws of Ecology," which also included "Everything must go somewhere," "Nature knows best," and "There is no such thing as a free lunch." See Barry Commoner, *The Closing Circle: Man, Nature, and Technology* (New York: Random House, 1971).
15. Steffen, Broadgate, and Deutsch, "Trajectory of the Anthropocene," 83.
16. Andreas Malm, *Fossil Capital* (New York: Verso, 2016).
17. On what I am calling the *characteristic curve*, see Reinhold Martin, "Visualizing Change: The Line of the Anthropocene," in *Energy Accounts: Architectural Representations of Energy, Climate, and the Future*, ed. Dan Willis, William Braham, Katsuhiko Muramoto, and Daniel A. Barber (New York: Routledge, 2016), 42–47.
18. One of the more familiar attempts to encourage social, industrial, and political action on climate change are the "Stabilization Wedges," in Stephen Pacala and Rob Socolow, "Stabilization Wedges: Solving the Climate Problem for the Next 50 Years with Current Technologies," *Science* 305, no. 5686 (August 13, 2004): 968–72. Discussed at more length in chapter 5 herein. It was popularized in Al Gore's film *An Inconvenient Truth* (2006), and in Elizabeth Kolbert, *Field Notes from a Catastrophe* (New York: Bloomsbury, 2006), among other places.
19. Steffen, Broadgate, and Deutsch, "Trajectory of the Anthropocene," 84; David Painter, *Oil and the American Century* (Baltimore: Johns Hopkins University Press, 1986); see also my discussion of oil and American energy ambitions in an architectural context in Barber, *A House in the Sun*, especially chapter 3: "Discovering Renewable Resources," 63–88.
20. Steffen, Broadgate, and Deutsch, "Trajectory of the Anthropocene," 90. This 2015 article republished the Great Acceleration charts originally published in 2004 (in Steffen et al., *Global Change and the Earth System*) because, as they wrote in 2015, "strong equity issues are masked by considering global aggregates" rather than breaking out differences according to the unevenness of economic development.
21. This was following the merger of the American Society of Heating and Ventilating Engineers (ASHVE) and the American Society of Refrigeration Engineers (ASRE) into AHRAE; see Frank H. Faust, "The Merger of ASHVE and ASRE," *ASHRAE Insights* 11, no. 3 (May 1992): 92–122. The March 1958 issue of *Progressive Architecture* was dedicated to the exploration of air conditioning, in recognition of the impending merger. See chapter 6.
22. See my discussion of "the first postwar oil crisis" regarding how an unexpected scarcity of heating oil in 1947–48 led to a general panic around energy resources in the years that followed. Barber, *A House in the Sun*, 147.
23. It is possible he also came into contact with Henry Wexler, discussed further on, who was involved in training new meteorologists during the war.
24. James Marston Fitch, *American Building and the Environmental Forces That Shape It* (New York: Schocken Books, 1972), vii. This was the second volume of what was originally published as *American Building: The Forces That Shape It* (Boston: Houghton Mifflin, 1947). References are to the 1972 edition.
25. Fitch, *American Building*, vii.
26. Fitch, *American Building*, 198.
27. Landsberg [and Fitch], "Microclimatology," 18; see also George Manley, "Microclimatology: Local Variations of Climate Likely to Affect the Design and Siting of Buildings," *RIBA Journal* (May 1949): 317–23; W. E. Graham, "The Influence of Micro-Climate on Planning," *Planning Outlook* (March 1949): 40–52. See also Rudolf Geiger, *The Climate Near the Ground* (New York: Rowman and Littlefield, 2009 [1941]).
28. Vladimir Jankovic, "Working with the Weather: Atmospheric Resources, Climate Variability, and the Rise of Industrial Meteorology, 1950–2000," *History of Meteorology* 7 (2015): 98–116, 101.
29. Walter A. Taylor and Theodore Irving Coe, "Regional Climatic Analysis and Design Data," *Bulletin of the American Institute of Architects* (September 1949): 15.
30. James Fleming, *Inventing Atmospheric Science: Bjerknes, Rossby, Wexler, and the Foundations of Modern Meteorology* (Cambridge, MA: MIT Press, 2016).
31. See John von Neumann, *The Computer and the Brain* (New Haven, CT: Yale University Press, 2012); John von Neumann et al., eds., "The Dynamics of Climate: Conference on the Application of Numerical Integration Techniques to the Problem of General Circulation" (Princeton, NJ: Institute for Advanced Study, 1955); William Aspray, *John von Neumann and the Origins of Modern Computing* (Cambridge, MA: MIT Press, 1990).
32. Fleming, *Inventing Atmospheric Science*, 140; see also Frederik Nebeker, *Calculating the Weather: Meteorology in the 20th Century* (New York: Elsevier, 1995), 156.
33. Paul N. Edwards, *A Vast Machine: Computer Models, Climate Data, and the Politics of Global Warming* (Cambridge, MA: MIT Press, 2010).
34. Fleming, *Inventing Atmospheric Science*, 156–58.
35. Landsberg [and Fitch], "Microclimatology," 21.
36. Taylor and Coe, "Regional Climatic Analysis," 15.
37. Siple, "Climatic Criteria," 7.
38. James Marston Fitch, "The Scientists behind Climate Control," *House Beautiful* 91, no. 10 (October 1949): 144.
39. Paul Siple, *A Boy Scout with Byrd* (New York: Putnam and Sons, 1937); and Siple, *90 Degrees South: The Story of the American South Pole Conquest* (New York: Putnam and Sons, 1959).
40. Reyner Banham, "The Machine Aesthetic," *Architectural Review* 117 (April 1955): 225.
41. Paul Overy, *Light, Air and Openness: Modern Architecture between the Wars* (London: Thames and Hudson, 2008); Colin Porteous, *The New Eco-Architecture: Alternatives from the Modern Movement* (London: Taylor and Francis, 2002).
42. See Esther McCoy, *Case Study Houses, 1945–1962* (Los Angeles: Hennessy and Ingalls, 1977); and Beatriz Colomina, *Domesticity at War* (Cambridge, MA: MIT Press, 2007).

43. Frank Lloyd Wright, "A Home in a Prairie Town," *Ladies Home Journal*, February 1901, one of a number of such articles by or about the architect in the first decade of the century; see also David Shi, "Edward Bok and the Simple Life," *American Heritage* 36, no. 1 (December 1984), discussing the *Journal* editor Bok, who was a strong supporter of Wright's work.
44. Elizabeth Mock and Richard Pratt, "Tomorrow's Small House, Models and Plans," *Bulletin of the Museum of Modern Art* 8, no. 5 (May 1945). See also numerous issues of *Ladies Home Journal* from 1944 to 1946. See also Barber, *A House in the Sun*, esp. 33–63.
45. Jeffrey Ellis Aronin, *Climate and Architecture: A Progressive Architecture Book* (New York: Reinhold, 1952).
46. "Regional Climatic Analyses and Design Data: X. Boston Area," in *Bulletin of the American Institute of Architects* (March 1951): 5.
47. Paul Siple, "15,750,000 Americans Live in This Climate," *House Beautiful* (November 1949): 202–3; see also Paul Siple, "American Climates," *AIA Bulletin* (September 1949): 16–18.
48. Siple, "Climatic Criteria," 8.
49. Taylor and Coe, "Regional Analyses," 16.
50. Siple, "Climatic Criteria," 6.
51. "Regional Climatic Analyses and Design Data: X. Boston Area," in *Bulletin of the American Institute of Architects* (March 1951): 5.
52. Siple, "Climate Criteria," 8.
53. John Rannells, "Technical Press: Climate Control," *Progressive Architecture* (February 1950): 99–102.
54. Siple, "Climatic Criteria," 14.
55. Building Research Advisory Board, *Weather and the Building Industry: A Research Correlation Conference on Climatological Research and Its Impact on Building Design, Construction, Materials, and Equipment* (Washington, DC: National Research Council, 1950).
56. Siple, "Climatic Criteria," 12.
57. Building Research Advisory Board, *Weather and the Building Industry*, 4. See also Carl Koch, *At Home with Tomorrow* (New York: Rinehart, 1958).
58. Tyler S. Rodgers, *Design of Insulated Buildings for Various Climates* (New York: Roberts Publishing, 1951).
59. "The Form and Climate Research Group," *Interiors* 112, no. 7 (August 1953): 52; James Marston Fitch interview with Suzanne O'Keefe, 1978, James Marston Fitch papers, Department of Drawings and Archives, Avery Architectural and Fine Arts Library, Columbia University.
60. Olgyay and Olgyay, *Solar Control and Shading Devices*, 37.
61. See "Heliodon Installed by Architecture Students for Aid in Building Design," *Columbia Spectator* (October 12, 1936): 4; and A. F. Dufton and H. E. Beckett, "Orientation of Buildings—Sun Planning by Means of Models," *RIBA Journal* (May 1931): 509 and throughout; a general discussion of early devices can also be found in George Malcolm Beal, *Natural Light and the Inside-Outside Heliodon* (Lawrence: University Press of Kansas, 1957), esp. 12–17.
62. George Atkinson, "Building in the Tropics: Research into Housing in Tropical Countries, Especially in the Commonwealth," *RIBA Journal* (June 1950): 313–20.
63. A list of the forty-two Climate Control articles in *House Beautiful* up to 1951 can be found in Marie G. Abbrussese and Ruth L. Mishabac, *Climate and Architecture: Selected References* (Washington, DC: Housing and Home Finance Agency, 1951), which also included references to the AIA pamphlets, a list of relevant climatological and anthropological literature, and sections on regional analyses for sixteen states.
64. Wolfgang Langewiesche, "Don't You See?" *House Beautiful* (December 1949): 167–74, 167.
65. "They Are Open Minded about New Ideas," *House Beautiful* (January 1949): 80–86.
66. "A house to set the pace . . . in all climates . . . for all budgets," *House Beautiful* 90, no. 2 (February 1948): 61–66.
67. "A house to set the pace . . ." 64.
68. "A house to set the pace . . ." 63.
69. "It May Be News to You, But . . ." *House Beautiful* 91, no. 10 (October 1949): 142.
70. See Dianne Harris, *Little White Houses: How the Postwar Home Constructed Race in America* (Minneapolis: University of Minnesota Press, 2012), and, for example, Andrew Weise, "'The House I Live In': Race, Class, and African American Suburban Dreams in the Postwar United States," in *The New Suburban History*, ed. Kevin M. Kruse and Thomas J. Sugrue (Chicago: University of Chicago Press, 2006), among the many other interesting essays in this potent volume.
71. "A house to set the pace . . ." 63.
72. James Marston Fitch and Wolfgang Langewiesche, "A Lesson in Climate Control," *House Beautiful* 91, no. 10 (October 1949): 164–72, 164.
73. Fitch and Langewiesche, "A Lesson in Climate Control," 164.
74. Wolfgang Langewiesche, "How to FIX Your Private Climate," *House Beautiful* 91, no. 10 (October 1949): 151–55.
75. Wolfgang Langewiesche, "How to PICK Your Private Climate," *House Beautiful* 91, no. 10 (October 1949): 146–51.
76. James Marston Fitch, "Climate Control on the Potomac," *House Beautiful* 93, no. 4 (April 1951): 129–45, 130–31.
77. Paul A. Siple, "How Many Climates Do We Have in the U.S.?" *House Beautiful* 91, no. 10 (October 1949): 128–29.
78. "The Three Big Ideas of 1950: Climate Control, Privacy, the American Style," *House Beautiful* 92, no. 6 (June 1950): 85–90.
79. James Marston Fitch, "A Good Plan for Climate-Wise Living," *House Beautiful* 92, no. 3 (March 1950): 68–74.
80. "How to Tame Sun, Wind, and Rain," *House Beautiful* 91, no. 5 (May 1949): 132–35,; 224–26; and "This House Won't Be Obsolete 10 Years from Now—Ready-to-Build House #36," *House Beautiful* 91, no. 5 (May 1949): 150–53.
81. Monica Penick, "The Pace Setter Houses: Livable Modernism in Postwar America" (PhD diss., University of Texas at Austin, 2007), 82; Monica Penick, *Tastemaker: Elizabeth Gordon, House Beautiful, and the Postwar American Home* (New Haven, CT: Yale University Press, 2017); see also Beatriz Colomina, "The Exhibitionist House," in *At the End of the Century: One Hundred Years of Architecture*, ed. Richard Koshaleck and Elizabeth A. T. Smith (Los Angeles: Museum of Contemporary Art, 1998), 126–65.
82. "A house to set the pace . . ." 61–66.
83. "Presenting *House Beautiful*'s Pace-Setter House for 1949," *House Beautiful* 91, no. 11 (November 1949): 195–201.
84. "How to Look at a Pace Setter House," *House Beautiful* 91, no. 11 (November 1949): 200–201.
85. "Three Big Ideas," 90.
86. James Ford and Katherine Morrow Ford, *The Modern House in America* (New York: Architectural Book Publishing, 1940); see also Jill Pearlman, *Inventing American Modernism: Joseph Hudnut, Walter Gropius, and the Bauhaus Legacy at Harvard* (Charlottesville: University of Virginia Press, 2007); and Anthony Alofsin, *The Struggle for Modernism: Architecture, Landscape Architecture, and City Planning at Harvard* (New York: W. W. Norton, 2002).
87. Frank Lloyd Wright, *Ausgeführte*

*Bauten* (Berlin: Verlegt bei Ernst Wasmuth, 1911); H. Th. Wijdeveld, ed., *Frank Lloyd Wright: The Life-Work of the American Architect Frank Lloyd Wright* (Santpoort, the Netherlands: C. A. Mees, 1925), which includes articles by Wright, Lewis Mumford, Louis Sullivan, J.J.P. Oud, H. P. Berlage, Erich Mendelsohn, and others; and Anthony Alofisn, "Wright, Influence, and the World at Large," in *Frank Lloyd Wright: Europe and Beyond*, ed. Anthony Alofsin (Berkeley: University of California Press, 1999), 1–17.

88. Penick, "Pace Setter Houses," 88.
89. "The Station Wagon Way of Life," *House Beautiful* 92, no. 6 (June 1950): 103–10; see also Monica Penick, "Marketing Modernism: *House Beautiful* and the Station Wagon Way of Life," *Working Papers on Design* 4 (2010).
90. Elizabeth Gordon, "The Threat to the Next America," *House Beautiful* 95, no. 4 (April 1953): 126–31, 250–51; see also Katherine LaMoine Corbett, "Tilting at Modern: Elizabeth Gordon's 'Threat to the Next America'" (PhD diss., University of California at Berkeley, 2010). Gordon's subtitle was borrowed from Lyman Bryson, *The Next America: Prophecy and Faith* (New York: Harper, 1952), who also wrote an article in the issue. Bryson identified democracy and consumer choice as the central tenets of American life.
91. Curtis Besinger, "A Sensible Way to Control Climate," *House Beautiful* 106, no. 8 (August 1964): 67–75, 132.
92. Siple, "Climate Criteria," 17.
93. See Michelle Murphy, *The Economization of Life* (Durham, NC: Duke University Press, 2017).

## Chapter 5

1. Historical interest in the emergence of the computer as a design tool has increased dramatically in the past decade. See, for example, Molly Wright Steenson, *Architectural Intelligence: How Designers and Architects Created the Digital Landscape* (Cambridge, MA: MIT Press, 2017); and Olga Touloumi and Theodora Vardouli, eds., *Computer Architectures: Constructing a Common Ground* (New York: Routledge, 2019).
2. Another popular performance software is Energy Plus, created through the Department of Energy in 1997.
3. See John Reynolds, "The Roots of Bioclimatic Design," in *Design with Climate: Bioclimatic Approach to Architectural Regionalism*, by Victor Olgyay (Princeton, NJ: Princeton University Press, 2015): ix–xi, xi. Reynolds writes: "Ten years after Victor Olgyay's death, the widely used Wiley textbook *Mechanical and Electrical Equipment for Buildings, 6th Edition* featured Olgyay's map of the US' four climate regions, and his recommended plan volume and shape characteristics for buildings in those four regions."
4. See, among many other possible examples, Walter Gropius's essay from 1937, "Is There a Science to Design?" (published in *The Scope of Total Architecture* in 1954). Much of the behavioralist tendencies of the 1960s and '70s would also claim a scientific basis for their purported effects.
5. See Avigail Sachs, *Environmental Design: Architecture, Politics, and Science in Postwar America* (Charlottesville: University of Virginia Press, 2018).
6. Victor Olgyay Jr., "A Rational Regionalism," in *Design with Climate: Bioclimatic Approach to Bioclimatic Regionalism*, by Victor Olgyay (Princeton, NJ: Princeton University Press, 2015), xii–xv.
7. Peder Anker, *From Bauhaus to Ecohouse: A History of Ecological Design* (Baton Rouge: Louisiana State University Press, 2010).
8. On Aladar's collaborations with Telkes, see Barber, *A House in the Sun*, 121.
9. Biographical details are taken from the Olgyay collection at the Library of the Design School at Arizona State University; see also Victor Olgyay Jr., "Rational Regionalism," xii–xv. Victor passed away on the first Earth Day—April 22, 1970.
10. H. E. Beckett, "Orientation of Buildings," *Journal of the Royal Institute of British Architects* 40 (1933): 61–65; and P. J. Waldram, "Universal Diagrams," *Journal of the Royal Institute of British Architects* 40 (1933): 50–55. See also George Malcolm Beal, *Natural Light and the Inside-Outside Heliodon* (Lawrence: University Press of Kansas, 1957), 12; Howard T. Fisher, "A Rapid Method for Determining Sunlight on Buildings," *Architectural Record* 12 (December 1931): 445–54. See also Waclaw Turner-Szymanowski, "A Rapid Method for Predicting the Distribution of Daylight in Buildings," *University of Michigan Engineering Research Bulletin* 17 (January 1931).
11. *The Work of Architects Olgyay and Olgyay*, with a preface by Marcel Breuer and an introduction by Peter Blake (New York: Reinhold, 1952). The cover was designed by Gyorgy Kepes.
12. Giancarlo Palanti in *Domus*, 1942, quoted in *The Work of Architects Olgyay and Olgyay*.
13. *The Work of Architects Olgyay and Olgyay*, 16.
14. Donald Watson, "Who Was the First Solar Architect?" in *Environmentally Friendly Cities: Proceedings of the PLEA 1998, Passive and Low Energy Architecture, Lisbon Portugal, 1998*, ed. Eduardo Maldonado (London: Routledge, 2014): 213–16, 216; see also Donald Watson, *Designing and Building a Solar House: Your Place in the Sun* (North Adams, MA: Garden Way Publishing, 1977).
15. *Work of Architects Olgyay and Olgyay*, 45.
16. Olgyay Jr., "Rational Regionalism," xiv.
17. *Work of Architects Olgyay and Olgyay*, 32.
18. *Work of Architects Olgyay and Olgyay*, 42; and Olgyay Jr., "Rational Regionalism." The younger Victor writes, "The factory design coordinates the operational needs of the facility with optimal environmental conditions; for example, storage is put in dark areas, and tasks requiring brighter light are located in brighter areas" (xii). On Gropius's diagrams, see Gropius, "Houses, Walk-ups, or High- Rise Apartment Blocks?" 119–35; and CIAM, *Rationelle Bebauungsweisen: Ergebnisse des 3. Internationalen Kongresses für Neues Bauen* (Stuttgart: J. Hoffman, 1931).
19. Cleveland, Ohio, in particular, was a center for Hungarian émigrés well into the latter half of the twentieth century.
20. Arindam Dutta, "Linguistics, not Grammatology: Architecture's a porioris and Architecture's Priorities," in *A Second Modernism: MIT, Architecture, and the "Techno-Social" Moment*, ed. Arindam Dutta (Cambridge, MA: MIT Press, 2013), 1–71, 6.
21. Telkes is an essential figure in *A House in the Sun*, 134 and throughout.
22. They were not, as far as I have been able to tell, romantically involved. Aladar was married to a Hungarian countess, Elizabeth Andrassy, whom he met while they were at Notre Dame. Telkes was a monumental figure in the midcentury solar research community.
23. See Richard W. Hamilton, ed., *Space Heating with Solar Energy: Proceedings of a Course-Symposium Held at the Massachusetts Institute of Technology, August 21–26, 1950* (Cambridge, MA: Massachusetts Institute of Technology / Bemis Foundation, 1954). One of Anderson's students rebuilt Telkes's first chemical storage system house with a water

storage system, under a bank of collectors on the roof, and it was occupied by a young family.

24. *Application of Climate Data to House Design* (Washington, DC: Home and House Financing Agency, 1954). Malone was an MIT meteorologist who edited the book *Compendium of Meteorology* (Boston: American Meteorological Society, 1951), which was essential to the expansion of a public interest in weather systems; he later had a prominent career as a science administrator at the national level. The project originally developed as a grant proposal written by the Olgyays in 1951 as a proposal for coming to MIT, "Outline of a Research Program for Methods for Applying Climatological Data in Dwelling Design, Site Selection, and Planning," dated September 1951.
25. Burnham Kelly, Memorandum to Project Members, Climate Project, March 19, 1952. MIT Archive.
26. See Douglas H. K. Lee, "Review: Application of Climatic Data to House Design," *Geographical Review* 45, no. 2 (April 1955): 307–9. He also notes that "desk computations, however elegant, are rapidly being replaced in [meteorological] practice by the operations of analog computers."
27. Both are published in Building Research Advisory Board, *Research Conference Report #5: Housing and Building in Hot-Humid and Hot-Dry Climates, November 18 and 19, 1952* (Washington, DC: National Academy of Sciences, 1953).
28. Harris, who lived in Texas, was a panelist. Walker, a principal at the New York firm Voorhees, Walker, Foley and Smith (now HLW), was also a member of the Building Research Advisory Board.
29. Victor Olgyay, *Design with Climate: Bioclimatic Approach to Architectural Regionalism*, 1.
30. C. A. Mills and D.H.K Lee, in the Panel Discussion for "Living in Hot Environments," Building Research Advisory Board, *Research Conference Report #5: November 18 and 19, 1952* (Washington, DC: National Academy of Sciences, 1953), 30.
31. F. C. Houghten and Constantin Yagloglou (later Yaglou), "Determination of the Comfort Zone," *Transactions of the American Society of Heating and Ventilating Engineers* 29 (1923); F. C. Houghten and C. P. Yagloglou, "Determining Lines of Equal Comfort," *Transactions of the American Society of Heating and Ventilating Engineers* 29 (1923): 165–76; *American Society of Heating and Ventilating Engineers Guide*, 1935 (New York: ASHVE, 1935), 39. See also Jiat-Hwee Chang and Tim Winter, "Thermal Modernity and Architecture," *Journal of Architecture* 20, no. 1 (2015): 92–121.
32. Michelle Murphy, *Sick Building Syndrome and the Problem of Uncertainty: Environmental Politics, Technoscience, and Women Workers* (Durham, NC: Duke University Press, 2006); Jiat-Hwee Chang, "Thermal Comfort and Climate Design in the Tropics: An Historical Critique," *Journal of Architecture* 21, no. 8 (2016): 1171–202. For a more general history of mechanical air conditioning, see Marsha E. Ackermann, *Cool Comfort: America's Romance with Air-Conditioning* (Washington, DC: Smithsonian Institution Press, 2002); Elizabeth Shove, *Comfort, Cleanliness, and Convenience: The Social Organization of Normality* (Oxford, Berg, 2003); Gail Cooper, *Air-Conditioning America: Engineers and the Controlled Environment, 1900–1960* (Baltimore: Johns Hopkins University Press, 1998); and Adam Rome, *The Bulldozer in the Countryside: Suburban Sprawl and the Rise of American Environmentalism* (New York: Cambridge University Press, 2001).
33. The literature is summarized and referenced in Victor Olgyay, *Design with Climate: Bioclimatic Approach to Architectural Regionalism*, 17–24.
34. Panel Discussion for "Living in Hot Environments," 31.
35. Victor Olgyay, *Design with Climate*, 18.
36. Panel Discussion for "Living in Hot Environments," 32.
37. One could note many other factors, see Murphy, *Sick Building Syndrome*, 22.
38. Panel Discussion for "Living in Hot Environments," 33.
39. Panel Discussion for "Living in Hot Environments," 33. G. Anthony Atkinson, of the UK government's Building Research Stations, who presented research from India and Australia, also gave a presentation.
40. Jo Stubblebine, ed., *The Northwest Architecture of Pietro Belluschi* (New York: F. W. Dodge, 1953), 41.
41. Barber, *A House in the Sun*, 77; Timothy Mitchell, *Carbon Democracy: Political Power in the Age of Oil* (New York: Verso, 2011); Rome, *Bulldozer in the Countryside*.
42. Aladar Olgyay, *Thermal Behavior of Metal Curtain Walls in Relation to Cooling Costs and Shading Devices* (Princeton, NJ: Princeton School of Architecture, 1957). The book is indicated as "Study no. 6 in the investigation of the use of Stainless Steel in the Curtain Wall Construction." It was submitted by Aladar Olgyay, Wayne F. Koppes, John Hancock Callender, and Robert V. McLaughlin in June 1957. The research was funded by the American Iron and Steel Institute, which was itself largely funded by ALCOA. See also William Dudley Hunt, *The Contemporary Curtain Wall: Its Design, Fabrication, and Erection* (New York: F. W. Dodge, 1958).
43. Aladar Olgyay, "Thermal Economics of Curtain Walls," *Architectural Forum* 106, no. 10 (October 1957): 154–64. I note in passing the apparent symbolic relevance of the ALCOA façade to the argument made in Reinhold Martin, "Atrocities; or, Curtain Wall as Mass Medium," *Perspecta* 32, *Resurfacing Modernism* (2001): 66–75. Martin refers to another of the studies of the reports in the McLaughlin research: "*Curtain Walls of Stainless Steel Construction*, School of Architecture, Princeton University, Princeton, New Jersey, 1955, prepared for the Committee of Stainless Steel Producers, American Iron and Steel Institute. The subsequent (1956) American Building Research Institute conference on the same topic is cited in Ian McCallum, ed., "Machine Made America," *Architectural Review* 121 (May 1957): 299. The curtain wall classifications appear on 299–300. See also, for example, "High Rise Office Buildings," *Progressive Architecture* 38 (June 1957): 159.
44. Olgyay, "Thermal Economics of Curtain Walls."
45. Olgyay, "Thermal Economics of Curtain Walls."
46. Lewis Mumford, "UNESCO House: Out, Damned Cliché!" (1960) in *The Highway and the City*, ed. Lewis Mumford (New York: New Architectural Library, 1964), 79–91, 74. Only the ground floor of the building was air conditioned. See also the brief discussion of the UNESCO headquarters in the next chapter herein.
47. Olgyay, "Thermal Economics of Curtain Walls"; see also "Thermal Behavior of Metal Curtain Walls in Relation to Cooling Costs and Shading Devices."
48. Robert McLaughlin, quoted in a press release for the Thermoheliodon, January 1955. Princeton archive, 1.
49. Waldron Faulkner, "An Architect Reviews His Files," *Science* 124, no. 3224 (October 12, 1956): 659–63.
50. Lewis Fry Richardson, *Weather Prediction by Numerical Process* (New York: Cambridge University Press, 2007), originally published in 1922; Frederik Nebeker, *Calculating the Weather: Meteorology in the 20th Century* (New York: Academic Press, 1995), 64; Edwards, *A Vast*

*Machine*, 94–96.

51. Aronin, *Climate and Architecture*; see also Groff Conklin, *The Weather-Conditioned House* (New York: Reinhold, 1958).
52. See Herbert Lindinger, ed., *Ulm Design: The Morality of Objects* (Cambridge, MA: MIT Press, 1990); and René Spitz, *HfG Ulm: The View behind the Foreground: The Political History of the Ulm School of Design, 1953–1968* (Stuttgart: Edition Axel Menges, 2002).
53. Steven Pacala and Robert Socolow, "Stabilization Wedges: Solving the Climate Problem over the Next 50 Years with Current Technology," *Science* 305, no. 5686 (August 13, 2004): 968–72.
54. Robert Socolow, "Wedges Re-affirmed," *Bulletin of the Atomic Scientists* (September 27, 2011), https://thebulletin.org/2011/09/wedges-reaffirmed/, accessed July 17, 2017.
55. Elizabeth Kolbert, *Field Notes from a Catastrophe* (New York: Bloomsbury, 2004).
56. Flusser, *Into the Universe of Technical Images*, 11.
57. Kenneth Boulding, "The Economics of the Coming Spaceship Earth," in *Environmental Quality in a Growing Economy*, ed. H. Jarrett (Baltimore: Johns Hopkins University Press), 3–14, 3.
58. Kenneth Boulding, *The Image: Knowledge in Life and Society* (Ann Arbor: University of Michigan Press, 1957), 6; see also David Woodward, "The Image of the Spherical Earth," *Perspecta*, no. 25 (1989): 2–15, 4.
59. In this sense Boulding appears to have been building on, though without attribution, Walter Lippmann's notion of the "pseudoenvironment," a term he used to describe the discrepancy between the world outside and the image in one's head in *Public Opinion* (New York: Harcourt, Brace, 1922).
60. Boulding, "Economics of the Coming Spaceship Earth," 4. Boulding was not the only one to use the term "spaceship earth"—it was invoked almost simultaneously by the economist Barbara Ward and then US ambassador to the United Nations Adlai Stevenson; later by U Thant, the secretary-general of the United Nations; and by R. Buckminster Fuller. See Barbara Ward, *Spaceship Earth* (New York: Columbia University Press, 1966); R. Buckminster Fuller, *Operating Manual for Spaceship Earth* (New York: E. P. Dutton, 1969); see also Felicity Scott, "Fluid Geographies: Politics and the Revolution by Design," in *New Views on R. Buckminster Fuller*, ed. Roberto G. Trujillo and Hsiao-Yun Chu (Stanford, CA: Stanford University Press, 2006); and Sabine Höhler, *Spaceship Earth in the Environmental Age, 1960–1990* (New York: Routledge, 2015).
61. Robin Kelsey, "Reverse Shot: Earthrise and Blue Marble in the American Imagination," *New Geographies*, no. 4 (2011): 10–16, 12; see also Sheila Jasanoff, "Image and Imagination: The Formation of Global Environmental Consciousness," in *Changing the Atmosphere: Expert Knowledge and Environmental Governance*, ed. Clark A. Miller and Paul N. Edwards (Cambridge, MA: MIT Press, 2001).
62. Boulding, "Economics of the Coming Spaceship Earth," 4. That new ideas about historical change also invoke new concepts of the human was one of the most potent insights in Chakrabarty, "The Climate of History" (2009).
63. Rob Nixon, *Slow Violence and the Environmentalism of the Poor* (Cambridge, MA: Harvard University Press, 2011), 6; see also Alison Caruth and Robert P. Marzec, "Environmental Visualization in the Anthropocene: Technologies, Aesthetics, Ethics," *Public Culture* 26, no. 2 (2014): 205–13.
64. Daniel A. Barber, Nick Axel, and Nikolaus Hirsch, "Images of Accumulation," *e-flux architecture* (2017).
65. Matthew F. Clarke, "Jean Labatut and *Éducation à pied d'œuvre*: The Princeton Architectural Laboratory," *Princeton University Library Chronicle* 74, no. 2 (2013): 178–209; see also Scott, "Fluid Geographies," and Mark Wigley, *Bucky, Inc.: Architecture in the Age of Radio* (Zurich: Lars Müller, 2015).
66. Victor Olgyay, "Architecture 516: Climate and Architectural Regionalism," Princeton University Archive. It is worth noting that there were some misgivings about the Olgyays performance as teachers, relative to some challenges with effective communication in English and a tendency for the brothers to bicker, and in one instance even come to fisticuffs in front of the students.
67. Victor and Aladar Olgyay, "Preliminary Outline of the Proposed Program at the Architectural Laboratory, School of Architecture, Princeton University, on the Human Environmental Approach to Architecture," n.d. (1953), Princeton University Archives.
68. Olgyay and Olgyay, *Solar Control and Shading Devices*, 5.
69. Edward Steichen, *The Family of Man: The Greatest Photographic Exhibition of All Time—503 Pictures from 68 Countries* (New York: Museum of Modern Art, 1955); see also Fred Turner, "*The Family of Man* and the Politics of Attention in Cold War America," *Public Culture* 24, no. 1 (2012): 55–84.
70. Erich Fromm, *The Sane Society* (New York: Reinhold, 1955), 25.
71. Alvar Aalto, "The Human Side as a Political Option for the Western World" (1950), in *Alvar Aalto: In His Own Words*, ed. Goran Schildt (New York: Rizzoli), 113–15, 113.
72. Rudolf Wittkower, *Architectural Principles in the Age of Humanism* (London: A. Tiranti, 1952); Colin Rowe, *The Mathematics of the Ideal Villa* (Cambridge, MA: MIT Press), 1976.
73. Le Corbusier, *Le Modulor 2* (London: Faber and Faber, 1955); Olivier Cinqualbre and Frédéric Migayrou, eds., *Le Corbusier: The Measures of Man* (Chicago: University of Chicago Press, 2015).
74. Olgyay and Olgyay, *Solar Control and Shading Devices*, 81.
75. Olgyay, *Design with Climate*, 22.
76. Olgyay, *Design with Climate*, 18.
77. Le Corbusier, *Precisions*, 66.
78. Olgyay, *Design with Climate*, 76.
79. Neutra, letter to V. Olgyay, 1959. Princeton Archives (Mudd).
80. Nebeker, *Calculating the Weather*, 135 and throughout; Edwards, *A Vast Machine*, 113–15. The Meteorology Project ended in 1956, largely due to von Neumann's failing health and his involvement with the Atomic Energy Commission; many of the more prominent researchers went to MIT, where they worked with Jay Forrester and others, such as the "Limits to Growth" group, who were interested in using computation to model systems dynamics.
81. The now well-known Keeling curve, based on carbon monitoring at a Hawaiʻi observatory that began during the International Geophysical Year, tracks the increase of carbon particulates from this period.
82. George van Dyne, *Ecosystems, Systems Ecology, and Systems Ecologists* (Oak Ridge, TN: Oak Ridge National Laboratory, 1966), 3.
83. Michael G. Barbour, "Ecological Fragmentation in the Fifties," in *Uncommon Ground: Rethinking the Human Place in Nature*, ed. William Cronon (New York: Norton, 1996), 233–55.
84. Donatella Meadows et al., *The Limits to Growth: A Report for the Club of Rome's Project on the Predicament of Mankind* (New York: Universal, 1974).
85. See *The Eco-Modernist Manifesto*

and its many critiques; see also Peter Taylor and Frederick Buttel, "How Do We Know We Have Global Environmental Problems? Science and the Globalization of Environmental Discourse," *Geoforum* 23, no.3 (1992): 405–16; Felicity Scott, *Outlaw Territories: Environments of Insecurity/ Architectures of Counterinsurgency* (Cambridge, MA: MIT Press, 2016).

86. Donald Worster, *Nature's Economy: The Roots of Ecology* (San Francisco: Sierra Club Books, 1977), 15.
87. Herman Daly, *Steady State Economics* (Washington, DC: Island Press, 1977).
88. See "Memorial Resolution at Faculty Meeting, September 14, 1970, Princeton University," Princeton Archives (Mudd).
89. Victor Olgyay, "Bioclimatic Evaluation Method for Architectural Application," in *Biometeorology: Proceedings of the Second International Bioclimatological Congress* (New York: Pergamon Press, 1962), 264–61. Baruch Givoni, whose 1969 text *Man, Architecture, and Climate,* became influential in relevant circles across the 1970s and '80s, was also at the conference, presenting a paper on the same panel: "the Effect of Roof Construction upon Indoor Temperatures" (237–45).
90. Fleming, *Inventing Atmospheric Science*; see also *Changes of Climate: Proceedings of the Rome Symposium Organized by UNESCO and the World Meteorological Organization* (Paris: UNESCO, 1963), which brought together recent developments in the historical understanding of how climates changed, and how societies adapted.
91. Olgyay, *Design with Climate*, 153–77. The original models were found in the Lab during a recent renovation and are in the process of being conserved.
92. Press release detailing the Thermoheliodon grant award from the National Science Foundation, Princeton School of Architecture, January 27, 1955. Princeton University Archives.
93. Victor Olgyay, *Report on the Thermoheliodon: Laboratory Machine for the Testing of Thermal Behavior through Model Structures* (Princeton, NJ: Princeton School of Architecture, 1957), 5.
94. Olgyay, *Report on the Thermoheliodon*, 7.
95. Olgyay, *Report on the Thermoheliodon*, 39 and throughout.
96. Sachs, *Environmental Design*.
97. CAT (Centre for Alternative Technology), 2015. "How CAT Started," content.cat.org.uk/index.php/how-cat-started, accessed January 15, 2015.
98. Steven V. Szokolay, "Bioclimatic Architecture and Solar Energy, ' in *Human Bioclimatology*, ed. Andris Auliciems (Berlin: Springer Verlag, 1998), 111–13. Andrew Marsh's development of Ecotec is summarized here: http://andrewmarsh.com/about.

## Chapter 6

1. B. J. Spanos, *Proclaiming the Truth: An Illustrated History of the American Society of Heating, Refrigeration, and Air-Conditioning Engineers, Inc.* (Washington, DC: AHRAE, 1996). According to the author, in 1956 'about 60% of activity in each society was devoted to air-conditioning," 72.
2. "Man-Made Climate," *Progressive Architecture* (March 1958): 111.
3. Faulkner, "The Architect Reviews His Files," 659.
4. Faulkner, "The Architect Reviews His Files," 660.
5. Faulkner, "The Architect Reviews His Files," 663.
6. O'Connor and Kilham were specialists in academic libraries, having designed such buildings for Smith College and, in the 1930s, for Princeton O'Connor was a Princeton grad and trustee, perhaps through these avenues aware of the Olgyays' research.
7. Faulkner, "The Architect Reviews His Files," 659.
8. Solex was also used at Belluschi's Equitable Building and at the United Nations Headquarters. SOM also used Solex on the Inland Steel Building in Chicago, completed in 1958. When the Lever House curtain wall was replaced by SOM in 2001, they used Solexia, an updated version of the product.
9. Faulkner, "The Architect Reviews His Files," 660.
10. Faulkner, "The Architect Reviews His Files," 660.
11. Faulkner, "The Architect Reviews His Files," 660.
12. Jackson, *The Architecture of Edwin Maxwell Fry and Jane Drew*; Ola Uduku and Alfred B. Zack-Williams, *Africa beyond the Post-Colonial: Political and Socio-Cultural Identities* (New York: Routledge, 2004); Crinson *Modern Architecture and the End of Empire*.
13. Vanessa Fernandez, "Preservation of Modern-Era Office Buildings and Their Environmental Controls," *Association for Preservation Technology Bulletin* 42, no. 2/3 (2011): 21–26.
14. Mumford, "UNESCO House," 69.
15. Mumford, "UNESCO House," 75.
16. S. E. Graham, "The (Real)politiks of Culture: U.S. Cultural Diplomacy in UNESCO, 1946–1954," *Diplomatic History* 30, no. 2 (April 2006): 231–53.
17. Fernandez, "Preservation of Modern-Era Office Buildings," 26.
18. See Christopher E. M. Pearson, *Designing UNESCO: Art, Architecture, and Politics at Mid-Century* (New York: Routledge, 2010), and Lucia Allais, "Architecture and Mediocracy at UNESCO House," in *Marcel Breuer: Building Global Institutions*, ed. Barry Bergdoll and Jonathan Massey (Zurich: Lars Müller, 2018).
19. Mitchell, *Carbon Democracy*; Stephanie LeMenager, *Living Oil* (New York: Oxford University Press, 2013); Imre Szeman, Jennifer Wenzel, and Patricia Yeager, eds., *Fueling Culture: 101 Words for Energy and Environment* (New York: Fordham University Press, 2016); Karen Pinkus, *Fuel: A Speculative Dictionary* (Minneapolis: University of Minnesota Press, 2016). For a more general accounting of the importance of oil to twentieth-century politics, see Daniel Yergin, *The Prize: The Epic Quest for Oil, Money, and Power* (New York: Free Press, 2008); and Daniel Yergin, *The Quest: Energy, Security, and the Remaking of the Modern World* (New York: Penguin, 2012).
20. Constantin Yaglou et al., "Control of Heat Casualties at Military Training Centers," *American Medical Association Architectural Industrial Health* (1956): 1–11.
21. ASHRAE Standard 55 (1956). I am grateful to Hongshan Guo, a PhD student in architecture and technology at Princeton University, for sharing her insights on these matters.
22. Pietro Belluschi, "New Buildings for 194x: Office Building," *Architectural Forum* (May 1943): 108; see also Andrew M. Shanken, *194x: Architecture, Planning, and Consumer Culture on the American Home Front* (Minneapolis: University of Minnesota Press, 2009), 32.
23. Belluschi quoted in Jurgen Joedicke, *Office Buildings* (London: Crosby Lockwood and Son, 1962).
24. Meredith L. Clausen, "Belluschi and the Equitable Building in History," *Journal of the Society of Architectural Historians* 50, no. 2 (June 1991): 109–29.
25. David Arnold, "Air Conditioning in Office Buildings after World War II," *ASHRAE Journal* (July 1999): 33–40; see also Jeodicke, *Office Buildings*, 56 and throughout.
26. "United Nations Headquarters," *Architectural Record* (July 1952); Victoria Newhouse, *Wallace K. Harrison, Architect* (New York: Rizzoli, 1989); Dudley, *A Workshop for Peace*.
27. Thomas Jester, ed., *Twentieth-Century Building Materials* (New York: McGraw-Hill, 1995), 145.

28. PLANYC, *New York City Local Law Benchmarking Report* (New York: Office of the Mayor, 2013).
29. Mireya Navarro, "City's Law Tracking Energy Use Yields Some Surprises," *New York Times*, December 24, 2012, https://www.nytimes.com/2012/12/25/science/earth/new-york-citys-effort-to-track-energy-efficiency-yields-some-surprises.html, accessed October 4, 2018.
30. James Marston Fitch, "The Curtain Wall," *Scientific American* 192, no. 3 (March 1955): 45–49.
31. Siegert, *Cultural Techniques*, 11.
32. Reinhold Martin, "Risk: Excerpts from the Environmental Division of Labor," in *Climates: Architecture and the Planetary Imaginary*, ed. James Graham et al., Columbia Books on Architecture and the City (Zurich: Lars Müller Publishers, 2016), 349–60. The paper was originally presented at the symposium *After the Spectacular Image: Art, Architecture, and the Media of Climate Change*, organized by Daniel Barber at the Princeton University School of Architecture, sponsored by the Princeton Environmental Institute, February 2016.
33. See the data presented and argument made in Fergus Nicol and Fionn Stevenson, "Adaptive Comfort in an Unpredictable World," *Building Research and Information* 41, no. 3 (2013): 255–58.
34. Michael A. Humphreys and Mary Hancock, "Do People Like to Feel 'Neutral'? Exploring the Variation of the Desired Thermal Sensation on the ASHRAE Scale," *Energy and Buildings* 39 (2007): 867–74, 873.
35. Humphreys and Hancock, "Do People Like to Feel 'Neutral'?," 868.
36. Humphreys and Hancock, "Do People Like to Feel 'Neutral'?," 868.
37. The full text is available online as part of the University of California at Santa Barbara's American Presidency Project: https://www.presidency.ucsb.edu/documents/address-the-nation-energy-and-national-goals-the-malaise-speech, accessed January 15, 2018.
38. Amitav Ghosh, *The Great Derangement: Climate Change and the Unthinkable* (Chicago: University of Chicago Press, 2016), 9–10, 11.
39. Chakrabarty, "The Climate of History," 212.
40. Chakrabarty, "Climate of History," 215.
41. Details of this encounter have played out around Chakrabarty's texts. See Ian Baucom, "History 4º: Postcolonial Method and Anthropocene Time," *Cambridge Journal of Postcolonial Literary Inquiry* 1, no. 1 (March 2014): 123–42; and Karen Pinkus, "Search for a Language" *Cambridge Journal of Postcolonial Literary Inquiry* 1, no. 2 (September 2014): 251–57.
42. www.ecomodernism.org/manifesto.
43. Eileen Crist, "The Reaches of Freedom: A Response to the Eco-Modernist Manifesto," *Environmental Humanities* 7 (2015): 245–54.
44. Jason W. Moore, ed., *Anthropocene or Capitalocene: Nature, History, and the Crisis of Capitalism* (Oakland, CA: PM Press, 2016), which includes Moore's own position as well as articles by Crist, Haraway, and others; see also Donna Haraway, *Staying with the Trouble: Making Kin in the Chthulucene* (Durham, NC: Duke University Press, 2016); and Jussi Parikka, *The Anthrobscene* (Minneapolis: University of Minnesota Press, 2014).
45. Reza Negarestani, *Cyclonopedia: Complicity with Autonomous Materials* (Melbourne: re.press, 2008).
46. Maldonado, "The Idea of Comfort," 43.
47. Neutra, *Architecture of Social Concern in Regions of Mild Climate*, 201. Neutra was also, it is worth noting, not optimistic about the application of mechanical conditioning devices in the Global South, writing, "perhaps even in five hundred years 'weather-maker installations' for all humanly consumed interiors will not yet be standard in the teeming moist-hot countries." Richard Neutra, "Man's Home Was South," Neutra Archive, n.d.
48. Fredric Jameson, "Postmodernism; or, the Cultural Logic of Late Capitalism," *New Left Review* 1, no. 146 (July–August 1984): 53–93. See also Fredric Jameson, *Postmodernism; or, the Cultural Logic of Late Capitalism* (Durham, NC: Duke University Press, 1991). On the logic of expenditure, see Georges Bataille, *The Accursed Share: Essays on General Economy* (New York: Zone, 1991); and Allan Stoekl, *Bataille's Peak: Energy, Religion, and Post-Sustainability* (Minneapolis: University of Minnesota Press, 2007).
49. Tomás Maldonado, "Design Education and Social Responsibility," in *The Education of Vision*, ed. Gyorgy Kepes (New York: Braziller, 1965).
50. Tomás Maldonado, *Design, Nature, and Revolution: Towards a Critical Ecology* (New York: Harper and Row, 1972). See also Simon Sadler, "A Container and Its Contents: Rereading Tomás Maldonado's *Design, Nature, and Revolution: Towards a Critical Ecology*," in *Room One Thousand* (2013).
51. Maldonado, "The Idea of Comfort," 36.
52. Jameson, "Postmodernism," 155. For the more general discussion, in human geography, of postmodern placelessness, see Marc Augé, *Non-Places: An Introduction to Supermodernity* (New York: Verso, 2009).
53. Banham, "The Master Builders," 19.
54. Jameson, "Postmodernism," 157; Ursula K. Heise, "Journeys through the Offset World: Global Travel Narratives and Environmental Crisis," *SubStance* 41, no. 1 (2012): 61–77.

## The Planetary Interior

1. Henry J. Cowan, *An Historical Outline of Architectural Science* (New York: Elsevier, 1966); and Cowan, *The Master Builders: A History of Structural and Environmental Design from Ancient Egypt to the Nineteenth Century* (New York: Wiley, 1977). Cowan's student, Steven Szokolay, wrote a prominent textbook: *Introduction to Architectural Science: The Basis of Sustainable Design* (Boston: Elsevier, 2008); he recently retired from the University of Queensland. See also a recent historical treatment of the role of architectural science at the University of Sydney, Daniel Ryan, "Architects in White Coats," in *The Sydney School: Formative Moments in Architecture, Design, and Planning at Sydney University*, ed. Andrew Leach and Lee Stickells (Sydney: Uro Publications, 2018). On contemporary approaches, see Gerhard Hausladen, Petra Liedl, and Michael de Saldana, eds., *Building to Suit the Climate: A Handbook* (Basel: Birkhauser, 2012); Peter F. Smith, *Architecture in a Climate of Change* (New York: Elsevier Architectural Press, 2005); and Henk Ovink and Jelte Boeijenga, *Too Big: Rebuild by Design; A Transformative Approach to Climate Change* (Rotterdam: nai010 publishers, 2018).
2. Baruch Givoni, *Man, Climate, and Architecture* (New York: Elsevier Architectural Science Series, 1969); the book series was edited by Cowan.
3. This was not the case, it should be noted, for landscape architecture, which by the mid-1950s was increasingly focused on ecological knowledge, including climate analyses, as an instigation for a nuanced territorial approach. Ian McHarg was the towering figure here, in his books, television shows, and institution building of the late 1960s; see Ian McHarg, *Design with Nature* (Garden City, NY:

Doubleday/Natural History Museum Press, 1969).

4. James Marston Fitch and Daniel P. Branch, "Primitive Architecture and Climate," *Scientific American* 203, no. 6 (December 1960): 134–45.
5. See, for example, Hassan Fathy, *Architecture for the Poor: An Experiment in Rural Egypt* (Chicago: University of Chicago Press, 1976); Bernard Rudofsky, *Architecture without Architects: A Short Introduction to Non-Pedigreed Architecture* (New York: Museum of Modern Art, 1964); Aldo van Eyck, "Architecture of the Dogon," *Architectural Forum* 115 (1961): 116–21; on the relationship of these developments to new media practices, see Karin Jaschke, "Aldo van Eyck and the 'Dogon Image,'" in *Architect's Journeys: Building, Travelling, Thinking*, ed. Craig Buckley and Pollyanna Rhee (New York: Columbia University Books on Architecture and the City, 2011), 72–103; and Felicity D. Scott, *Disorientation: Bernard Rudofsky in the Empire of Signs* (Stuttgart: Sternberg Press, 2016).
6. See James Marston Fitch, *Historic Preservation: Curatorial Management of the Built World* (New York: McGraw-Hill, 1982).
7. See, for example, Birgit Schneider, "Climate Model Simulation Visualization from a Visual Studies Perspective," *WIREs Climate Change* 3 (2012): 185–93; John May, "Everything Is Already an Image," *Log*, no. 40 (Spring/Summer 2017); and the ongoing series on "Accumulation" on the *e-flux architecture* online platform.
8. See, for example, Barry Bergdoll, ed., *Rising Currents: Projects for New York's Waterfront* (New York: Museum of Modern Art, 2011); Rania Ghosn and El Hadi Jazairy, *Geostories: Another Architecture for the Environment* (New York: Actar, 2018); Lola Sheppard and Mason White, *Many Norths: Spatial Practice in a Polar Territory* (New York: Actar, 2017), among many others.
9. Ladybug Tools is one of the more creative: www.ladybug.tools.
10. Orit Halpern, "Hopeful Resistance," part of the Accumulation series on *e-flux architecture* (2017), http://www.e-flux.com/architecture/accumulation/96421/hopeful-resilience/, accessed December 18, 2018.
11. Daniel A. Barber, "How Can Architecture Respond to the 1.5°C Imperative?" on *Archinect*, November 2, 2018; https://archinect.com/features/article/150093748/how-can-architecture-respond-to-the-1-5-c-imperative, accessed December 18, 2018.
12. See Christina Newinger, Christina Geyer, and Sarah Kellberg, eds., *Energiewenden: Energy Transitions as a Chance and Challenge for Our Time* (Munich: Deutsches Museum, 2017); see, for example, Tobias Haas and Hendrik Sander, "Shortcoming and Perspectives of the German Energiewende," *Socialism and Democracy* 30, no. 2 (2016): 121–43.
13. David Benjamin, ed., *Embodied Energy and Design: Making Architecture between Metrics and Narratives*, Columbia Books on Architecture and the City (New York: Lars Müller, 2017).
14. See the dossier of responses to the "ecomodernist manifesto," by Bruno Latour, Eileen Crist, Bronislaw Szerszynski, and others in *Environmental Humanities* 7, no. 1 (2016).
15. Philip Oldfield, Dario Trabucco, and Antony Wood, "Five Energy Generations of Tall Buildings: An Historical Analysis of Energy Consumption in High-Rise Buildings," *Journal of Architecture* 14, no. 5 (September 2009): 591–613.
16. Taryn Holowka, "Tackling Climate Change through LEED," https://www.usgbc.org/articles/tackling-climate-change-through-leed, accessed October 19, 2018.
17. See, for example, the Living Building Challenge, https://living-future.org/lbc/, accessed October 19, 2018.

## Archival Sources


Archive and Documentation Center. Universidade Federal do Rio de Janeiro, Brazil.

Fitch, James Marston. Papers. Department of Drawings and Archives, Avery Architectural and Fine Arts Library, Columbia University.

Institute Archives. Massachusetts Institute of Technology, Cambridge, MA.

Le Corbusier Archive. Fondation Le Corbusier, Paris.

Museum of Modern Art Exhibition Archives, New York.

Neutra, Richard and Dion. Papers. Special Collections, University of California at Los Angeles.

Olgyay, Aladar and Victor. Papers. Seely G. Mudd Archives, Princeton University, Princeton, NJ.

Olgyay Victor. Papers. Design Archives, School of Design, Arizona State University, Tempe, AZ.


## Published Sources


Abbrussese, Marie G., and Ruth L. Mishabac. *Climate and Architecture: Selected References*. Washington, DC: Housing and Home Finance Agency, 1951.

Abrahamian, Ervand. "The 1953 Coup in Iran." *Science and Society* 65, no. 2 (2001): 185–215.

Ackermann, Marsha E. *Cool Comfort: America's Romance with Air-Conditioning*. Washington, DC: Smithsonian Institution Press, 2002.

Aggregate Architectural History Collaborative. *Governing by Design: Architecture, Economy, and Politics in the 20th Century*. Pittsburgh: Pittsburgh University Press, 2012.

Agrawal, Arun. *Environmentality: Technologies of Government and the Making of Subjects*. Durham, NC: Duke University Press, 2005.

Aleksandrowicz, Or. *Daring the Shutter: The Tel-Aviv Idiom of Solar Protections*. Tel Aviv: Public School Editions, 2015.

Alofsin, Anthony. *The Struggle for Modernism: Architecture, Landscape Architecture, and City Planning at Harvard*. New York: W. W. Norton, 2002.

Alofsin, Anthony, ed. *Frank Lloyd Wright: Europe and Beyond*. Berkeley: University of California Press, 1999.

Al-Ragam, Asseel. "Critical Nostalgia: Kuwait Urban Modernity and Alison and Peter Smithson's Kuwait Urban Study and Mat-Building." *Journal of Architecture* 20, no. 1 (February 2015): 1–20.

Alvarez-Curbelo, Silvia. "The Center of Everything: Consumption, Architecture, and City." In *Ever New San Juan: Architecture and Modernization in the 20th Century*, edited by Enrique Vivoni Farage (San Juan: Archivo de Arquitectura y Construcción de la Universidad de Puerto Rico [AACUPR], 2000), 228–75.

Anker, Peder. *From Bauhaus to Ecohouse: A History of Ecological Design*. Baton Rouge: Louisiana State University Press, 2010.

———. *Imperial Ecology: Environmental Order in the British Empire, 1895–1945*. Cambridge, MA: Harvard University Press, 2001.

Antoine, Serge. "Energy, Climate, and Environment in the Mediterranean Basin." *Ekistics* 58, no. 348/349 (August 1991): 124–34.

Apter, Emily. "Planetary Dysphoria." *Third Text* 27, no. 1 (2013): 131–40.

Armitage, David, and Jo Guldi. *The History Manifesto*. Cambridge: Cambridge University Press, 2014.

Arnold, David. "Air Conditioning in Office Buildings after World War II." *ASHRAE Journal* (July 1999): 33–40.

———. *The Problem of Nature: Environment, Culture, and European Expansion*. Oxford: Blackwell, 1996.

Aronin, Jeffrey. *Climate and Architecture*. New York: Reinhold, 1953.

Aspray, William. *John von Neumann and the Origins of Modern Computing*. Cambridge, MA: MIT Press, 1990.

Badiou, Alain. "Is There a Theory of the Subject in Georges Canguilhem?" *Economy and Society* 27, no. 2/3 (May 1998): 225–33.

Baer, Ferdinand, et al., eds. *Climate in Human Perspective: A Tribute to Helmut E. Landsberg*. Boston: Kluwer Academic, 1991.

Bakke, Gretchen. *The Grid: The Fraying Wires between Americans and Our Energy Future*. New York: Bloomsbury, 2017.

Balibar, Etienne. "Racism as Universalism." *New Political Science* 8, no. 1–2 (1989): 9–22.

Banham, Reyner. *The Architecture of the Well-Tempered Environment*. Chicago: University of Chicago Press, 1969.

———. "Frank Lloyd Wright as Environmentalist." *Arts and Architecture*, no. 83 (September 1966): 26–30.

———. "Klarheit, Ehrlichkeit, Einfachkeit . . . and Wit, Too! The Case Study House Program in the World's Eyes." In *Blueprints for Modern Living: The History and Legacy of the Case Study Houses*, edited by Elizabeth A. T. Smith, 183–96. Los Angeles: Museum of Contemporary Art, 1989.

———. "The Machine Aesthetic." *Architecture Review* (April 1955): 224–28.

———. *Theory and Design in the First Machine Age*. Cambridge, MA: MIT Press, 1960.

Barber, Daniel A. "Environmentalization and Environmentality: Re-conceiving the History of 20th Century Architecture." In *Design Philosophy Papers #5*, edited by Anne-Marie Willis. Ravensbourne, Australia: Team D/E/S Publishers, 2009.

———. *A House in the Sun: Modern Architecture and Solar Energy in the Cold War*. New York: Oxford University Press, 2016.

———. "Le Corbusier, the Brise-Soleil, and the Socio-Climatic Legacy of Modern Architecture." *Thresholds*, no. 40 (Summer 2012): 21–32.

———. "Militant Architecture: Destabilizing Architecture's Disciplinarity." *Journal of Architecture* 10, no. 3 (Fall 2005): 245–23.

Barbour, Michael G. "Ecological Fragmentation in the Fifties." In *Uncommon Ground: Rethinking the Human Place in Nature*, edited by William Cronon, 233–55. New York: Norton, 1996.

Barry, Andrew. *Political Machines: Governing a Technological Society*. New York: Athlone Press, 2001.

———. "Technological Zones." *European Journal of Social Theory* 9, no. 2 (2006): 239–53.

———. "Thermodynamics, Matter, Politics." *Distinktion: Journal of Social Theory* 16, no. 1 (2015): 110–25.

Beck, Ulrich. "Climate for Change; or, How to Create a Green Modernity?" *Theory, Culture, and Society* 27, no. 2/3 (2010): 254–66.


# Bibliography

———. *Ecological Enlightenment: Essays on the Politics of the Risk Society*. Atlantic Highlands, NJ: Humanities Press, 1995.
———. "Living in the World Risk Society." *Economy and Society* 35, no. 3 (August 2006): 329–45.
———. *Revisiting Risk Society: A Conversation with Ulrich Beck*. Rachel Carson Perspectives. Munich: Rachel Carson Center for Environment and Society, 2011.
———. *Risk Society: Towards a New Modernity*. London: Sage, 1992.
———. *World Risk Society*. Cambridge: Polity Press, 1999.
Behrent, Michael C. "Accidents Happen: François Ewald, the Antirevolutionary Foucault, and the Intellectual Politics of the French Welfare State." *Journal of Modern History* 82, no. 3 (September 2010): 585–624.
Behringer, Wolfgang. *A Cultural History of Climate*. Malden, MA: Polity, 2010.
Belguami, Arif. "Legacy of the Cold War: Richard Neutra in Pakistan." *Int-Er* 8 (March 2012): 83–88.
Bergdoll, Barry, et al., eds. *Frank Lloyd Wright: Unpacking the Archive*. New York: Museum of Modern Art, 2017.
———. *Latin America in Construction: Architecture, 1955–1980*. New York: Museum of Modern Art, 2015.
Blaut, James M. "Environmentalism and Eurocentrism." *Geographical Review* 89, no. 3 (July 1999): 391–408.
Blum, William. *Killing Hope: U.S. Military and CIA Interventions since World War II*. San Francisco: Common Courage Press, 1995.
Bocking, Stephen. *Ecologists and Environmental Politics: A History of Contemporary Ecology*. New Haven, CT: Yale University Press, 1997.
Bone, Kevin, ed. *Lessons from Modernism*. New York: Monacelli, 2014.
Bonnemaison, Sarah, and Christine Macy. *Architecture and Nature: Creating the American Landscape*. New York: Routledge, 2003.
Bonneuil, Christophe, and Jean-Baptiste Fressoz. *The Shock of the Anthropocene: The Earth, History, and Us*. New York: Verso, 2017.
Borasi, Giovanna, and Mirko Zardini, eds. *Sorry, Out of Gas: Architecture's Response to the 1973 Oil Crisis*. Montreal: Canadian Centre for Architecture, 2007.
Botkin, Daniel B. *Discordant Harmonies: A New Ecology for the Twenty-First Century*. New York: Oxford University Press, 1990.
Boulding, Kenneth. "The Economics of the Coming Spaceship Earth." In *Environmental Quality in a Growing Economy*, edited by H. Jarrett, 3–14. Resources for the Future Forum. Baltimore: Johns Hopkins University Press, 1966.
———. *The Image: Knowledge in Life and Society*. Ann Arbor: University of Michigan Press, 1957.
Brands, H. W. *Inside the Cold War: Loy Henderson and the Rise of the American Empire, 1918–1961*. New York: Oxford University Press, 1991.
Bredekamp, Horst, Vera Dunkel, and Birgit Schneider, eds. *The Technical Image: A History of Styles in Technical Imagery*. Chicago: University of Chicago Press, 2015.
Britto, Alfredo. *Pedregulho: O sonho pioneiro da habitação popular no Brasil*. Rio de Janeiro: Edições Rio de Janeiro, 2015.
Buchanan, Peter. *Ten Shades of Green*. New York: Architectural League and W. W. Norton, 2005.
Building Research Advisory Board. *Weather and the Building Industry: A Research Correlation Conference on Climatological Research and Its Impact on Building Design, Construction, Materials, and Equipment*. Washington, DC: National Research Council, 1950.
Burchell, Graham, Colin Gordon, and Peter Miller, eds. *The Foucault Effect: Studies in Governmentality—with Two Lectures and an Interview with Michel Foucault*. Chicago: University of Chicago Press, 1991.
Burnett, D. Graham. "The Bonds of Catastrophe." *Cabinet*, no. 57 (Spring 2015): 1–9.
Buttel, F. H. "Ecological Modernization as Social Theory." *Geoforum* 31 (2000): 57–65.
Canclini, Nestor Garcia. *Hybrid Cultures: Strategies for Entering and Leaving Modernity*. Minneapolis: University of Minnesota Press, 2005.
Canguilhem, Georges. "The Decline of the Idea of Progress." *Economy and Society* 27, no. 2/3 (May 1998): 313–29.
———. "The Living and Its Milieu." *Grey Room*, no. 3 (2001): 6–31.
———. *Machine and Organism*. New York: Zone Books, 1992.
———. *The Normal and the Pathological*. New York: Zone Books, 1991.
Canizaro, Vincent B., ed. *Architectural Regionalism: Collected Writings on Place, Identity, Modernity, and Tradition*. New York: Princeton Architectural Press, 2007.
Carlucci, Salvatore. *Thermal Comfort Assessment of Buildings*. Milan: Springer Milan, 2013.
Carone, Ibrahim. "What Is Rio's Healthiest Location?" *Revista Arquitetura e Urbanismo* (June 1936) 60–61.
Carranza, Luis E., and Fernando Luiz Lara. *Modern Architecture in Latin America: Art, Technology, and Utopia*. Austin: University of Texas Press, 2015.
Carruth, Alison, and R. P. Mazrec. "Environmental Visualization and the Anthropocene: Technologies, Aesthetics, Ethics." *Public Culture* 26, no. 2 (2014): 205–11.
Carvalho, Bruno. "Mapping the Urbanized Beaches of Rio de Janeiro: Modernization, Modernity, and Everyday Life." *Journal of Latin American Cultural Studies* 16, no. 3 (2007): 325–39.
Cavalcanti, Lauro. *When Brazil Was Modern: Guide to Architecture, 1928–1960*. New York: Princeton Architectural Press, 2003.
Çelik, Zeynep. "Le Corbusier, Orientalism, Colonialism." *Assemblage*, no. 17 (April 1992): 58–77.
Chakrabarty, Dipesh. "Climate and Capital: On Conjoined Histories." *Critical Inquiry* 41, no. 1 (Autumn 2014): 1–23.
———. "The Climate of History: Four Theses." *Critical Inquiry* 35, no. 2 (Winter 2009): 197–222.
Chambers, David Wade, and Richard Gillespie. "Locality in the History of Science: Colonial Science, Technoscience, and Indigenous Knowledge." *Osiris* 15 (2000): 221–40.
Chang, Jiat-Hwee. *A Genealogy of Tropical Architecture: Colonial Networks, Nature, and Technoscience*. New York: Routledge, 2016.
———. "Thermal Comfort and Climate Design in the Tropics: An Historical Critique." *Journal of Architecture* 21, no. 8 (December 2016): 1171–202.
Chang, Jiat-Hwee, and Tim Winter. "Thermal Modernity and Architecture." *Journal of Architecture* 20, no. 1 (2015): 92–121.
Chapman, Sidney. *IGY: The Year of Discovery, the Story of the International Geophysical Year*. Ann Arbor: University of Michigan Press, 1959.
Chun, Wendy Hui Kyong. "Crisis, Crisis, Crisis, or Sovereignty and Networks." *Theory, Culture, and Society* 23, no. 6 (2011): 91–112.
———. "On Hypo-Real Models or Climate Change: A Challenge for the Humanities." *Critical Inquiry* 41, no. 3 (Spring 2015): 675–703.
CIAM. *The Athens Charter*. Paris: CIAM, 1946.
———. *Rationelle Bebauungsweisen: Ergebnisse des 3. Internationalen Kongresses für Neues Bauen*. Stuttgart: J. Hoffman, 1931.
Ciucci, Giorgio. "The Invention of the Modern Movement." *Oppositions*, no. 24 (Spring 1981): 68–91.
Clarke, Matthew F. "Jean Labatut and Éducation à pied d'œuvre: The Princeton Architectural Laboratory." *Princeton University Library Chronicle*

74, no. 2 (2013): 178–209.
Clausen, Meredith L. "Belluschi and the Equitable Building in History." *Journal of the Society of Architectural Historians* 50, no. 2 (June 1991): 109–29.
Clouette, Benedict, and Marlisa Wise. *Forms of Aid: Architectures of Humanitarian Space*. Basel: Birkhäuser, 2017.
Coelho de Souza, Luiz Felipe Machado. *Irmãos Roberto, Arquitetos*. Rio de Janeiro: Rio Books, 2013.
———. "Rigor e Brutalismo No Obra Dos Irmãos Roberto." *Docomomo* (2013).
Cohen, Jean-Louis. *Scenes of the World to Come: European Architecture and the American Challenge*. Montreal: Canadian Center for Architecture, 1995.
Collins, Randall, and Mauro Guillén. "Mutual Halo Effects in Cultural Production: The Case of Modern Architecture." *Theory and Society* 41, no. 6 (October 2012): 527–56.
Colomina, Beatriz. *Domesticity at War*. Cambridge, MA: MIT Press, 2007.
———. "The Private Life of Modern Architecture." *Journal of the Society of Architectural Historians* 58, no. 3 (September 1999): 462–71.
Colquhoun, Alan. "The Concepts of Regionalism." In *Postcolonial Space(s)*, edited by Gulsum Baydar Nalbantaglo and Wong Chung Thia, 13–23. New York: Princeton Architectural Press, 1997.
———. "Critique of Regionalism." *Casabella* (January–February 1996): 50–55.
Comas, Carlos Eduardo. "Modern Architecture, Brazilian Corollary." *AA Files*, no. 36 (Summer 1998): 3–13.
Commoner, Barry. *The Closing Circle: Man, Nature, and Technology*. New York: Random House, 1971.
*Conference on Tropical Architecture: A Report on the Proceedings of the Conference Held at University College, London, March, 1953*. London: Allen and Unwin, 1954.
Cook, Jeffrey. "Review: Architecture and Technology." *Journal of the Society of Architectural Historians* 37, no. 3 (October 1978): 220–22.
Cooper, Gail. *Air Conditioning America: Engineers and the Controlled Environment, 1900–1960*. Baltimore: Johns Hopkins University Press, 2002.
Corbett, Kathleen LaMoine. "Tilting at Modern: Elizabeth Gordon's 'The Threat to Next America.'" PhD diss., University of California, Berkeley, 2010.
Correia de Lira, José Tavares. "From Mild Climate's Architecture to 'Third World' Planning: Richard Neutra in Latin America." In *Proceedings of the 14th International Planning History Conference: Controversies, Contrasts and Challenges*, 1–15. Istanbul, 2010.
Cowan, Henry J. *An Historical Outline of Architectural Science*. New York: Elsevier, 1966.
———. *The Master Builders: A History of Structural and Environmental Design from Ancient Egypt to the Nineteenth Century*. New York: Wiley, 1977.
Crinson, Mark. *Modern Architecture and the End of Empire*. Burlington, VT: Ashgate, 2002.
Crist, Eileen. "The Poverty of Our Nomenclature." *Environmental Humanities* 3 (2013): 129–47.
———. "The Reaches of Freedom: A Response to the Eco-Modernist Manifesto." *Environmental Humanities* 7 (2015): 245–54.
Crutzen, Paul J., and Eugene F. Stoermer. "The 'Anthropocene.'" *Global Change Newsletter* 41 (May 2000): 17–18.
Daly, Herman. *Steady State Economics*. Washington, DC: Island Press, 1977.
Daston, Lorraine. "What Is an Insurable Risk? Swiss Re and Atomic Reactor Insurance." In *Managing Risk in Reinsurance*, edited by Niels Viggo Haueter and Geoffrey Jones, 230–47. Oxford: Oxford University Press, 2016.
Daston, Lorraine J., and Peter Galison. *Objectivity*. Cambridge, MA: MIT Press, 2007.
D'Auria, Viviana. "In the Laboratory and in the Field: Hybrid Housing Design for the African City in Late-Colonial and Decolonising Ghana (1945–57)." *Journal of Architecture* 19, no. 3 (2014): 329–56.
Davis, Mike. *Late Victorian Holocausts: El Niño Famines and the Making of the Third World*. New York: Verso, 2001.
Dean, Mitchell. "Risk, Calculable and Incalculable." *Soziale Welt* 49, no. 1 (1998): 25–42.
Deckker, Zilah Quezado. *Brazil Built: The Architecture of the Modern Movement in Brazil*. London: Spon Press, 2001.
Delaporte, François. "Foucault, Epistemology, and History." *Economy and Society* 27, no. 2/3 (May 1998): 285–97.
Deleuze, Gilles. *Foucault*. Minneapolis: University of Minnesota Press, 1986.
De Monchaux, Nicholas. *Spacesuit: Fashioning Apollo*. Cambridge, MA: MIT Press, 2011.
"Department of Tropical Studies: A Cross-Section of Recent Work and Teaching Methods." *AA Journal* (April 1963): 302–9.
"Design Problems in the Tropics." *Interiors* 121 (May 1962): 94–95, 107.
Deyong, Sarah. "The Creative Simulacrum in Architecture: Megastructure, 1953–1972." PhD diss., Princeton University, 2008.
Drew, Jane, and Maxwell Fry. *Architecture and the Environment*. London: Allen and Unwin, 1975.
———. *Tropical Architecture in the Dry and Humid Zones*. Huntington, NY: Krieger, 1957.
———. *Village Housing in the Tropics*. London: L. Humphries, 1947.
Drexler, Arthur, and Henry-Russell Hitchcock. *Built in USA: Post-War Architecture*. New York: Museum of Modern Art, 1952.
Dudley, George A. *A Workshop for Peace: Designing the United Nations Headquarters*. Cambridge, MA: MIT Press, 1994.
Dutta, Arindam. "Modern Architecture and the End of Empire by Mark Crinson." *Journal of the Society of Architectural Historians* 67, no. 2 (June 2008): 292–93.
Easterling, Keller. "The Wrong Story." *Perspecta* 41 (2008): 74–82.
Edwards, Paul. "Meteorology as Infrastructural Globalism." *Osiris* 21 (2006): 229–50.
———. *A Vast Machine: Computer Models, Climate Data, and the Politics of Global Warming*. Cambridge, MA: MIT Press, 2010.
Eggener, Keith. "Placing Resistance: A Critique of Critical Regionalism." *Journal of Architectural Education* 55, no. 4 (May 2002): 228–37.
Eisenman, Peter. "Aspects of Modernism: Maison Dom-ino and the Self-Referential Sign." *Oppositions*, no. 15/16 (1978).
———. *The Formal Basis of Modern Architecture*. Zurich: Lars Müller, 2006.
———. "Post-Functionalism." *Oppositions*, no. 6 (1977).
Endfield, Georgina. "Reculturing and Particularizing Climate Discourses: Weather, Identity, and the Work of George Manley." *Osiris* 26, no. 1 (2011): 142–62.
Eriksdotter, Gunhild. "Did the Little Ice Age Affect Indoor and Outdoor Climate? Re-Theorizing Climate History and Architecture from the Early Modern Period." *Journal for Early Modern Cultural Studies* 13, no. 2 (Spring 2013): 24–42.
Ewald, François. "Insurance and Risk." In *The Foucault Effect: Studies in Governmentality*, edited by Graham Burchell, Colin Gordon, and Peter Miller 197–210. Chicago: University of Chicago Press, 1991.
———. "Philosophie de La précaution." *L'Année Sociologique* 46, no. 2 (1996): 382–412.
———. "The Return of the Crafty Genius: An Outline of a Philosophy of Precaution." *Connecticut Insurance Law Journal* 6, no. 1 (2000): 47–79.
———. "Risk in Contemporary Society." *Connecticut Insurance Law Journal* 6,

no. 2 (2000): 364–79.
Farage, Enrique Vivoni, ed. *Klumb: An Architecture of Social Concern*. Río Piedras: University of Puerto Rico, 2006.
Faust, Frank H. "The Merger of ASHVE and ASRE." *ASHRAE Insights* 11, no. 3 (May 1992): 92–122.
Fernandez, Vanessa. "Preservation of Modern-Era Office Buildings and Their Environmental Controls." *APT Bulletin: Journal of Preservation Technology* 42, no. 2/3 (2011): 21–26.
Fishman, Robert. *Urban Utopias of the Twentieth Century*. Cambridge, MA: MIT Press, 1982.
Fitch, James Marston. *American Building and the Environmental Forces That Shape It*. New York: Schocken Books, 1972.
———. *American Building: The Forces That Shape It*. Boston: Houghton Mifflin, 1947.
———. "Microclimatology." *Architectural Forum* 36, no. 2 (February 1947): 18–22.
Fleming, James Rodger. *Inventing Atmospheric Science: Bjerknes, Rossby, Wexler, and the Foundations of Modern Meteorology*. Cambridge, MA: MIT Press, 2016.
———. "A 1954 Color Painting of Weather Systems Viewed from a Future Satellite." *Bulletin of the American Meteorological Society* (2007): 1525–27.
Fleming, James Rodger, and Vladimir Jankovic. "Revisiting Klima." *Osiris* 26, no. 1 (2011): 1–15.
Flueckiger, Urs Peter. *How Much House? Thoreau, Le Corbusier, and the Sustainable Cabin*. Basel: Birkhauser, 2016.
Flusser, Vilém. *Into the Universe of Technical Images*. Minneapolis: University of Minnesota Press, 2011.
Ford, James, and Katherine Morrow Ford. *The Modern House in America*. New York: Architectural Book Publishing, 1940.
Forsyth, Tim. *Critical Political Ecology: The Politics of Environmental Science*. New York: Routledge, 2003.
Foucault, Michel. *Security, Territory, Population: Lectures at the Collège de France, 1977–1978*. New York: Picador, 2003.
Frampton, Kenneth. "Critical Regionalism Revisited: Reflections on the Mediatory Potential of Built Form." In *Vernacular Modernism: Heimat, Globalization, and the Built Environment*, edited by Maiken Umbach and Bernd Huppauf. Stanford, CA: Stanford University Press, 2005.
———. "The Humanist versus the Utilitarian Ideal." *Architectural Design* 38, no. 3 (March 1968): 134–36.
———. *Le Corbusier*. New York: Thames and Hudson, 2001.
———. "Le Corbusier and Oscar Niemeyer: Influence and Counterinfluence, 1929–1965." In *Latin American Architecture, 1929–1969: Contemporary Reflections*, edited by Carlos Brillembourg. New York: Monacelli Press, 2004.
———. "Towards a Critical Regionalism: Six Points of an Architecture of Resistance." In *The Anti-Aesthetic: Essays on Post-Modern Culture*, edited by Hal Foster, 16–30. Port Townsend, WA: Bay Press, 1983.
———. "The Usonian Legacy." *Architectural Review* 182, no. 1090 (1987): 26–31.
Fuller, Mia. *Moderns Abroad: Architecture, Cities, and Italian Imperialism*. New York: Routledge, 2006.
Fuller, R. Buckminster. "U.S. Industrialization." *Fortune* 21, no. 2 (1940).
Gaddis, John Lewis. *Strategies of Containment: A Critical Appraisal of American National Security Policy during the Cold War*. New York: Oxford University Press, 2005.
Galison, Peter. "War against the Center." *Grey Room* 4 (2001): 7–33.
Gandelsonas, Mario. "Neo-Functionalism." *Oppositions*, no. 5 (1976).
Gannon, Todd. *Reyner Banham and the Paradoxes of High-Tech*. Los Angeles: Getty Publications, 2017.
Geddes, Patrick. *Cities in Evolution: An Introduction to the Town Planning Movement and the Study of Civics*. London: Williams and Norgate, 1915.
Geiger, Rudolf. *The Climate Near the Ground*. New York: Rowman and Littlefield, 2009 (1941).
Ghirardo, Diane Y. "Manfredo Tafuri and Architecture Theory in the U.S., 1970–2000." *Perspecta—Mining Autonomy* 33, edited by Osman et al. (2002): 38–47.
Ghosh, Amitav. *The Great Derangement: Climate Change and the Unthinkable*. Chicago: University of Chicago Press, 2016.
———. *Incendiary Circumstances: A Chronicle of the Turmoil of Our Time*. Boston: Houghton Mifflin, 2006.
Godard, Olivier. "De l'imposture au sophisme, la science du climat vue par Claude Allègre, François Ewald et quelques autres." *Esprit* 364, no. 5 (May 2010): 26–43.
González de Canales, Francisco. *Experiments with Life Itself: Radical Domestic Architectures between 1937 and 1959*. Barcelona: Actar, 2013.
Goodrich, Leland M. "San Francisco in Retrospect." *International Journal* 25, no. 2 (Spring 1970): 239–60.
Goodwin, Philip L. *Brazil Builds: Architecture New and Old, 1652–1942*. New York: Museum of Modern Art, 1943.
Goody, Richard. "Observing and Thinking about the Atmosphere." *Annual Review of Energy and Environment* 27 (2002): 1–20.
Griffin, Fritz, and Marietta Millet. "Shady Aesthetics." *Journal of Architectural Education* 37, no. 3/4 (Spring–Summer 1984): 43–60.
Gropius, Walter. *The Scope of Total Architecture: A New Way of Life*. New York: Harper and Row, 1943.
Grove, Richard. "The Origins of Environmentalism." *Nature* 345 (May 1990): 11–15.
Grove, Richard, and Vinita Damodaran. "Imperialism, Intellectual Networks, and Environmental Change." *Economic and Political Weekly* (October 14 and 21, 2006): 4345–54, 4497–505.
Grusin, Richard A. "Premediation." *Criticism* 46, no. 1 (Winter 2004): 17–39.
———. "Radical Mediation." *Critical Inquiry* 42, no. 1 (Autumn 2015): 124–48.
*GSW Headquarters Berlin: Sauerbruch Hutton Architects*. Vienna: Lars Müller, 2000.
Guha, Ramachandra. *Environmentalism: A Global History*. New York: Longman, 2002.
Guha, Ramachandra, and Joan Martinez-Alier. *Varieties of Environmentalism: Essays North and South*. New York: Longman, 2002.
Guillén, Mauro F. *The Taylorized Beauty of the Mechanical: Scientific Management and the Rise of Modernist Architecture*. Princeton, NJ: Princeton University Press, 2008.
Hacking, Ian. "Canguilhem Amid the Cyborgs." *Economy and Society* 27, no. 2/3 (May 1998): 202–16.
———. *The Taming of Chance*. Cambridge: Cambridge University Press, 1990.
Hagan, Susannah. "Performance and Style." *Architectural Research Quarterly* 18, no. 3 (September 2014): 197–203.
———. *Taking Shape: A New Contract between Architecture and Nature*. London: Architectural Press, 2001.
Hales, Peter B. "The Atomic Sublime." *American Studies* 32, no. 1 (1991): 5–31.
Halpern, Orit. *Beautiful Data: A History of Vision and Reason since 1945*. Durham, NC: Duke University Press, 2014.
Hardin, Garrett. "Tragedy of the Commons." *Science* 162 (1968): 1243–48.
Harris, Elizabeth Davis. "Le Corbusier and the Headquarters of the Brazilian

Ministry of Education and Health, 1936–1945." PhD diss., University of Chicago, 1984.
Hawkes, Dean. *Architecture and Climate: An Environmental History of British Architecture*. London: Routledge, 2012.
———. *The Environmental Tradition: Studies in the Architecture of Environment*. London: Taylor and Francis, 2013.
Hays, K. Michael. Introduction to *Architecture Theory since 1968*. Cambridge, MA: MIT Press, 1998.
Hebbert, Michael, and Vladimir Jankovic. "Cities and Climate Change: The Precedents and Why They Matter." *Urban Studies*, special issue, *Cities, Urbanization, and Climate Change* 50, no. 7 (May 2013): 1332–47.
Hebbert, Michael, Vladimir Jankovic, and Brian Webb, eds. *City Weathers: Meteorology and Urban Design, 1950–2010*. Manchester: Manchester Architecture Research Centre, 2011.
Heise, Ursula. "Journeys through the Offset World: Global Travel Narratives and Environmental Crisis." *SubStance* 41, no. 1 (2012): 61–77.
———. "Local Rock and Global Plastic: World Ecology and the Experience of Space." *Comparative Literature Studies* 41, no. 1 (2004): 126–52.
———. "Martian Ecologies and the Future of Nature." *Twentieth Century Literature* 7, no. 3/4 (Fall/Winter 2011): 447–71.
———. *Sense of Place and Sense of Planet: The Environmental Imagination of the Global*. Oxford: Oxford University Press, 2008.
Heiss, Mary Ann. *Empire and Nationhood: The United States, Great Britain, and Iranian Oil, 1950–1954*. New York: Columbia University Press, 1997.
Hensel, Michael, Rumi Kubokawa, and Oscar Niemeyer. "Building Brazil, Part 1: 1900–1964." *AA Files*, no. 37 (Autumn 1998): 48–54.
Hession, Jane King, et al. *Ralph Rapson: Sixty Years of Modern Design Afton*. Minnesota: Afton Historical Society Press, 1999.
Heyken, Richard. "Richard Neutras Soziale Architektur." *Neue Stadt* 4, no. 7 (July 1950): 276.
Heynen, Hilde. *Architecture and Modernity: A Critique*. Cambridge, MA: MIT Press, 1999.
Hines, Thomas. "Case Study Trouvé: Sources and Precedents, Southern California, 1920–1942." In *Blueprints for Modern Living: History and Legacy of the Case Study Houses*, edited by Elizabeth A. T. Smith, 80–88. Los Angeles: Museum of Contemporary Art, 1998.
———. *Richard Neutra and the Search for Modern Architecture*. Berkeley: University of California Press, 1982.
Hitchcock, Henry-Russell, and Philip Johnson. *The International Style: Architecture since 1922*. New York: Museum of Modern Art, 1932.
Hobday, Richard. *The Light Revolution: Health, Architecture, and the Sun*. Forres, Scotland: Findhorn Press, 2007.
Hooper-Lane, Elizabeth. "*House Beautiful*'s Victory Home as Propaganda Tool." *Home Cultures* 9, no. 1 (2012): 5–34.
Houghten, F. C., and Constantin Yagloglou (later Yaglou). "Determining Lines of Equal Comfort." *Transactions of the American Society of Heating and Ventilating Engineers* 29 (1923): 165–76.
Howkins, Adrian. "Political Meteorology: Weather, Climate, and the Contest for Antarctic Sovereignty." *History of Meteorology* 4 (2008): 27–40.
Hubbert, M. King. "Nuclear Energy and the Fossil Fuels." In *Drilling and Production Practice*. Washington, DC: American Petroleum Institute, 1956.
———. "Energy from Fossil Fuels." *Science* 109, no. 2823 (February 4, 1949): 103–9, 108.
Hughes, Richard. "Interview with Richard J. Neutra." *Transition*, no. 29 (March 1967): 22–34.
Hulme, Mike. "Reducing the Future to Climate: A Story of Climate Determinism and Reductionism." *Osiris* 26, no. 1 (2011): 245–66.
Humphreys, Michael A., and Mary Hancock. "Do People Like to Feel 'Neutral'? Exploring the Variation of the Desired Thermal Sensation on the ASHRAE Scale." *Energy and Buildings* 39 (2007): 867–74.
Huntington, Ellsworth. "The Adaptability of the White Man to Tropical America." *Journal of Race Development* 5, no. 2 (1914): 185–211.
———. *Civilization and Climate*. New Haven, CT: Yale University Press, 1924.
Illich, Ivan. "The Wisdom of Leopold Kohr." *Bulletin of Science, Technology, and Society* 17, no. 4 (1997): 157–65.
Isenstadt, Samuel. "'Faith in a Better Future': Josep Lluís Sert's American Embassy in Baghdad." *Journal of Architectural Education* 50, no. 3 (February 1997): 172–88.
Jackson, Iain, and Jessica Holland. *The Architecture of Edwin Maxwell Fry and Jane Drew: Twentieth Century Architecture, Pioneer Modernism, and the Tropics*. London: Routledge, 2014.
Jackson, Neil. "Metal-Frame Houses of the Modern Movement in Los Angeles, Part I: Developing a Regional Tradition." *Architectural History* 32 (1989): 152–72.
Jameson, Fredric. "Notes on Globalization as a Philosophical Issue." In *The Cultures of Globalization*, edited by Fredric Jameson and Masao Miyoshi, 54–76. Durham, NC: Duke University Press, 1998.
Jankovic, Vladimir. "Working with the Weather: Atmospheric Resources, Climate Variability, and the Rise of Industrial Meteorology, 1950–2000." *History of Meteorology* 7 (2015): 98–116.
Jarvis, Darryl S. L. "Theorizing Risk: Ulrich Beck, Globalization, and the Rise of the Risk Society." National University of Singapore, n.d.
Jarzombek, Mark. "Corridor Spaces." *Critical Inquiry* 36, no. 4 (Summer 2010): 728–70.
———. "(Un)Designing Mythologies: Puerto Rico and Operation Bootstrap Undone." *Thresholds*, no. 21 (2000): 52–59.
Jasanoff, Sheila. "Image and Imagination: The Formation of Global Environmental Consciousness." In *Changing the Atmosphere: Expert Knowledge and Environmental Governance*, edited by Clark A. Miller and Paul N. Edwards, 309–38. Cambridge, MA: MIT Press, 2001.
———. "A New Climate for Society." *Theory Culture Society*, no. 27 (2010): 233–53.
Jeffreys-Jones, Rhodri. *The CIA and American Democracy*. New Haven, CT: Yale University Press, 1989.
Joedicke, Jürgen. *Office Buildings*. London: Crosby, Lockwood, and Son, 1962.
Johnstone, William C. "The San Francisco Conference." *Pacific Affairs* 18, no. 3 (September 1945): 213–28.
Jonsson, Fredrik Albritton. "Abundance and Scarcity in Geological Time, 1784–1844." In *Nature, Action and the Future: Political Thought and the Environment*, edited by Katrina Forrester and Sophie Smith. Cambridge: Cambridge University Press, 2018.
———. "Review Article: The Industrial Revolution in the Anthropocene." *Journal of Modern History* 84, no. 3 (September 2013): 679–96.
Jung, Hyun Tae. "Organization and Abstraction: The Architecture of Skidmore, Owings and Merrill, 1936–1956." PhD diss., Columbia University, 2011.
Kelsey, Robin. "Reverse Shot: Earthrise and Blue Marble in the American Imagination." *New Geographies*, no. 4 (2011): 10–16.
Kidder Smith, G. E. "The Architecture of North Africa." *AA Journal* (August 1951): 38–48.
Kim, Jeannie. "C. A. Doxiadis and the Ford Foundation." *Hunch* 13 (2010): 78–91.

King, Anthony. *The Bungalow: The Production of a Global Culture*. London: Routledge, 1984.
Kittler, Friedrich. "The City Is a Medium." *New Literary History* 27, no. 4 (Autumn 1996): 717–29.
———. *Gramophone, Film, Typewriter*. Stanford, CA: Stanford University Press, 1999.
Kizner, Steven. *All the Shah's Men: An American Coup and the Roots of Middle East Terror*. Hoboken, NJ: John Wiley and Sons, 2003.
Knoblaugh, Joy. "The Work of Diagrams: From Factory to Hospital in Postwar America." *Manifest*, no. 1 (2013): 154–65.
Koch, Carl. *At Home with Tomorrow*. New York: Rinehart, 1958.
Kohr, Leopold. *The Breakdown of Nations*. New York: Routledge and K. Paul, 1957.
———. *Development without Aid: The Translucent Society*. New York: Schocken Books, 1979.
———. *The Inner City: From Mud to Marble*. Talybont, Wales: Y Lolfa, 1989.
———. *The Overdeveloped Nations: The Diseconomies of Scale*. New York: Schocken Books, 1978.
Kolbert, Elizabeth. *Field Notes from a Catastrophe*. New York: Bloomsbury, 2006.
Kreutzmann, Hermann. "Ellsworth Huntington and His Perspective on Central Asia: Great Game Experiences and Their Influence on Development Thought." *GeoJournal* 59, no. 1 (2004): 27–31.
Krüger, Lorenz, Lorraine Daston, and Michael Heidelberger, eds. *The Probabilistic Revolution*. Vol. 1, *Ideas in History*. Cambridge, MA: MIT Press, 1987.
Krüger, Lorenz, Gerd Gigerenzer, and Mary S. Morgan, eds. *The Probabilistic Revolution*. Vol. 2, *Ideas in the Sciences*. Cambridge, MA: MIT Press, 1987.
Kury, Lorelai. "La nature de la nation: Le climat et les gens du Brésil (1780–1836)." *Annales Historiques de La Révolution Française* 365 (September 2011): 129–52.
Lahoud, Adrian. "Architecture, the City, and Its Scale: Oscar Niemeyer in Tripoli, Lebanon." *Journal of Architecture* 18, no. 6 (2013): 809–34.
Lamprakos, Michele. "Le Corbusier and Algiers: The Plan Obus as Colonial Urbanism." *Traditional Dwellings and Settlements Review* 2, no. 1 (Fall 1990): 45.
Lamprecht, Barbara. "From Neutra in Japan, 1930, to His European Audiences and Southern California Work." *Southern California Quarterly* 92, no. 3 (Fall 2010): 215–42.
———. *Neutra*. New York: Taschen, 2008.
Landsberg, Helmut E. "Atmospheric Variability and Climatic Determinism." *Yearbook of the Association of Pacific Coast Geographers* 30 (1968): 13–23.
———. "Climate and Planning of Settlements." *Bulletin of the American Institute of Architects* (January 1951): 22.
———. "Climate as a Natural Resource." *Scientific Monthly* 63, no. 4 (October 1946): 293–98.
———. *Geophysics and Warfare*. Washington, DC: Office of the Assistant Secretary of Defense, 1954.
———. "Microclimatology: Facts for Architects, Realtors, and City Planners on Climatic Conditions at the Breathing Line." *Architectural Forum* 86, no. 3 (March 1947): 114–18.
———. *Physical Climatology*. State College, PA: School of Mines, 1941.
———. *The Urban Climate*. New York: Academic Press, 1981.
Langer, Karl. *Sub-Tropical Housing*. 7th ed. Vol. 1. University of Queensland Papers. Brisbane: Faculty of Engineering, 1944.
Lara, Fernando Luis. "Introduction: Brazilian Contemporary Architecture between Centripetal and Centrifugal Forces." In *Architectural Guide: Brazil*, edited by Laurence Kimmel, Bruno Santa Cecilia, and Anke Tiggemann, 13–19. Berlin: Dom Publishers, 2015.
———. "Modernism Made Vernacular: The Brazilian Case." *Journal of Architectural Education* (2009): 41–52.
———. *The Rise of Popular Modernist Architecture in Brazil*. Gainesville: University Press of Florida, 2008
Latour, Bruno. *The Politics of Nature: How to Bring the Sciences into Democracy*. Cambridge, MA: Harvard University Press, 2004.
———. "Visualization and Cognition: Drawing Things Together." In *Knowledge and Society: Studies in the Sociology of Culture Past and Present*, edited by Henrika Kuklick and Elizabeth Long. Greenwich, CT: JAI Press, 1986.
Lavin, Sylvia. *Form Follows Libido: Architecture and Richard Neutra in a Psychoanalytic Culture*. Cambridge, MA: MIT Press, 2004.
Le Corbusier. *Oeuvre complète*. Vol. 3, *1934–1938*. Zurich: Éditions Dr. H. Girsberger, 1939.
———. *Le poème de l'angle droit*. Berlin: Hatje Cantz Verlag, 2012.
———. *Precisions on the Present State of Architecture and City Planning*. Cambridge, MA: MIT Press, 1991.
———. "Problèmes de l'ensoleillement: Le brise soleil." *Techniques et Architecture* 6, no. 1 (January 1946).
———. *Towards an Architecture*. Los Angeles: Getty Publications, 2007.
———. *La ville radieuse: Éléments d'une doctrine d'urbanisme pour l'équipement de la civilisation machiniste*. Boulogne-sur-Seine: Éditions de L'Architecture d'aujourd'hui, 1935.
Le Corbusier, and François de Pierrefeu. *La Maison des Hommes*. Paris: Plon, 1947.
Lee, Douglas H. K. *A Basis for the Study of Man's Reaction to Tropical Climates*. University of Sydney, Australia, 1940.
———. "Biometeorological Consequences of Environmental Controls: Overview." *Environmental Health Perspectives* 10 (April 1975): 183–96.
———. "The Human Organism and Hot Environments." *Transactions of the Royal Society of Tropical Medicine and Hygiene* 29, no. 1 (1935): 7–30.
Lee, Rachel. "Constructing a Shared Vision: Otto Koengsberger and Tata & Sons." *ABE Journal* 2 (2012): 1–26.
———. "Otto Koenigsberger: Transcultural Practice and the Tropical Third Space." *OASE*, no. 95 (2015): 60–72.
Lehmann, Steffen. "An Environmental and Social Approach in the Modern Architecture of Brazil: The Work of Lina Bo Bardi." *City, Culture, and Society* 7 (2016): 169–85.
Lejeune, Jean-François. "Madrid versus Barcelona: Two Visions for the Modern City and Block (1929–1936)." *Athens Journal of Architecture* 1, no. 4 (October 2015): 271–95.
Lejeune, Jean-François, and Michelangelo Sabatino, eds. *Modern Architecture and the Mediterranean: Vernacular Dialogues and Contested Identities*. New York: Routledge, 2010.
LeMenager, Stephanie. *Living Oil*. New York: Oxford University Press, 2013.
Leon, Ana Maria. "Modern Architecture Will Help You." *Journal of Surrealism and the Americas* 9, no. 1 (2016): 14–39.
Lepik, Andres. *Small Scale, Big Change: New Architectures of Social Engagement*. New York: Museum of Modern Art, 2010.
Le Roux, Hannah. "Building on the Boundary: Modern Architecture in the Tropics." *Social Identities* 10, no. 4 (2004): 439–55.
———. "Modern Architecture in Post-Colonial Ghana and Nigeria." *Architectural History* 47 (2004): 361–92.
———. "The Networks of Tropical Architecture." *Journal of Architecture* 8, no. 3 (2003): 337–54.
Leroux, Robert. "El partido constructivo: Punto de vista del ingeniero acerca de una racionalización del 'habitat' humano." *Arquitectura Mexico* (March 1957): 35–40.
Lesser, Jeffrey. "A Better Brazil." *História,*

*Ciências, Saúde–Manguinhos* (2013).
Levin, Linda C. "Midcentury Planning in San Juan, Puerto Rico: Rexford Guy Tugwell, Henry Klumb, and Design for 'Modernization.'" Master's thesis (architectural studies), Washington University in Saint Louis, 2013.
Lewthwaite, Gordon R. "Environmentalism and Determinism: A Search for Clarification." *Annals of the Association of American Geographers* 56, no. 1 (March 1966): 1–24.
Liernur, Jorge F. "Vanguardistas versus expertos: Reconstrución Europea, Expansión Norteamericana y Emergencia del Tercer Mundo; para una relectura del debate arquitectonico en la segunda posguerra (una mirada desde America Latina)." *Block* 6 (2004).
Liscombe, Rhodri Windsor. "In-Dependence: Otto Koenigsberger and Modernist Urban Resettlement in India." *Planning Perspectives* 21 (April 2006): 157–78.
Lissovsky, Mauricio. *Colunas da Educação: A Construção do Ministério da Educação e da Saúde, 1935–1945*. Rio de Janeiro: Ministério da Cultura, Instituto do Patrimônio Histórico e Artístico Nacional, 1996.
Locher, Fabien, and Jean-Baptiste Fressoz. "Modernity's Frail Climate: A Climate History of Environmental Reflexivity." *Critical Inquiry* 38, no. 3 (Spring 2012): 579–98.
Loeffler, Jane C. *The Architecture of Diplomacy: Building America's Embassies*. New York: Princeton Architectural Press, 1998.
Lovins, Amory. *Natural Capitalism: The Next Industrial Revolution*. Washington, DC: US Green Building Council, 2000.
Lowry, William P. *Weather and Life: An Introduction to Biometeorology*. New York: Academic Press, 1969.
Lu, Duangfang, ed. *Third World Modernism: Architecture, Development, and Identity*. New York: Routledge, 2011.
Lugo-Silva, Enrique. *The Tugwell Administration in Puerto Rico, 1941–1946*. Río Piedras: University of Puerto Rico Press, 1955.
Luke, Timothy W. *Ecocritique: Contesting the Politics of Nature*. Minneapolis: University of Minnesota Press, 1997.
Lyndon, Donlyn. "Learning to Design with Climate." In *Design with Climate: Bioclimatic Approach to Architectural Regionalism*. Princeton, NJ: Princeton University Press, 2016.
Mackenzie, Christopher. "1993 February: Le Corbusier in the Sun." *Architectural Review* (June 20, 2011).
Maldonado, A. W. *Teodoro Moscoso and Puerto Rico's Operation Bootstrap*. Gainesville: University Press of Florida, 1997.
Maldonado, Tomás. "The Idea of Comfort." *Design Issues* 8, no. 1 (Autumn 1991): 35–43.
Malm, Andreas. *Fossil Capital: The Rise of Steam Power and the Roots of Global Warming*. New York: Verso, 2016.
———. *The Progress of This Storm*. New York: Verso, 2018.
Manley, Gordon. "Microclimatology—Local Variations of Climate Likely to Affect the Design and Siting of Buildings." *RIBA Journal* (May 1949): 317–23.
———. "The Revival of Climatic Determinism." *Geographical Review* 48, no. 1 (January 1958): 98–105.
Manovich, Lev. "The Practice of Everyday (Media) Life: From Mass Consumption to Mass Cultural Production?" *Critical Inquiry* 35, no. 2 (Winter 2009): 319–31.
Markham, S. F. *Climate and the Energy of Nations*. London: Oxford University Press, 1942.
Marks, Robert B. *The Origins of the Modern World: A Global and Ecological Narrative*. Lanham, MD: Rowman and Littlefield, 2002.
Marsh, George Perkins. *Man and Nature; or, Physical Geography as Modified by Human Action*. New York: Scribner, 1864.
Marshall, Kate. *Corridor: Media Architectures in American Fiction*. Minneapolis: University of Minnesota Press, 2013.
Martin, Reinhold. "Unfolded, Not Opened: On Bernhard Siegert's *Cultural Techniques*." *Grey Room*, no. 62 (Winter 2016): 102–15.
———. "Visualizing Change: The Line of the Anthropocene." In *Energy Accounts: Architectural Representations of Energy, Climate, and the Future*, edited by Dan Willis, William Braham, Katsuhiko Muramoto, and Daniel A. Barber, 42–47. New York: Routledge, 2016.
Martin, Reinhold, Isabelle Graw, and André Rottman. "Do Media Determine Our Situation? Reflections on the Transatlantic Reception of Friedrich Kittler by Isabelle Graw, Reinhold Martin, and André Rottman." *Texte Zur Kunst*, no. 98 (June 2015).
Martins, Carlos Ferreira. "Etat, Culture et Nature aux origines de l'architecture moderne au Bresil: Le Corbusier et Lucia Costa, 1929–1936." In *Le Corbusier et la nature*, edited by Maria Bonaiti et al., 195–208. Paris: Editions de la Villette, 2004.
Masci, Pietro. "Insurance Market Development and Entrepreneurship, with a Focus on Latin America and Brazil." PhD diss., George Mason University, 2013.
Masco, Joseph. "Bad Weather: On Planetary Crisis." *Social Studies of Science* 40, no. 1 (February 2010): 7–40.
———. "The End of Ends." *Anthropological Quarterly* 85, no. 4 (Fall 2012): 1107–24.
Massey, Jonathan, "Risk Design." *Grey Room*, no. 54 (Winter 2014): 6–33.
McCoy, Esther. "Letters between R. M. Schindler and Richard Neutra, 1914–1924." *Journal of the Society of Architectural Historians* 33, no. 3 (October 1974): 219–24.
———. *Richard Neutra*. New York: Braziller, 1960.
McKibben, Bill. *The End of Nature*. New York: Random House, 1989.
McNeill, J. R., and Peter Engelke. *The Great Acceleration: An Environmental History of the Anthropocene since 1945*. Cambridge, MA: Belknap Press of Harvard University Press, 2016.
Meadows, Donatella, et al. *The Limits to Growth: A Report for the Club of Rome's Project on the Predicament of Mankind*. New York: Universal, 1974.
Merrill, Dennis. *Negotiating Paradise: U.S. Tourism and Empire in 20th Century Latin America*. Chapel Hill: University of North Carolina Press, 2009.
Miller, Clark A. "'An Effective Instrument of Peace': Scientific Cooperation as an Instrument of U.S. Foreign Policy, 1938–1950." *Osiris* 21 (2006): 133–60.
Mindlin, Henrique. *Modern Architecture in Brazil*. New York: Reinhold, 1956.
Mirzoeff, Nicholas. "The Clash of Visualizations: Counterinsurgency and Climate Change." *Social Research* 78, no. 4 (Winter 2011): 1185–210.
Missenard, André. *L'Homme et le climat*. Paris: Librairie Plon, 1936.
———. *À la recherche du temps et du rythme*. Paris: Librairie Plon, 1940.
Mitchell, Timothy. *Carbon Democracy: Political Power in the Age of Oil*. New York: Verso, 2011.
———. "Economentality: How the Future Entered Government." *Critical Inquiry* 40, no. 4 (Summer 2014): 479–507.
———. "Fixing the Economy." *Cultural Studies* 12, no. 1 (1998): 82–101.
Mock, Elizabeth, and Richard Pratt. "Tomorrow's Small House, Models, and Plans." *Bulletin of the Museum of Modern Art* 8, no. 5 (May 1945).
Modisette, Eldon. "The Legitimation of Modern American Architecture." *Journal of Aesthetics and Art Criticism* 20, no. 3 (Spring 1962): 251–61.
Mol, Annemarie. "Lived Reality and the Multiplicity of Norms: A Critical Tribute to Georges Canguilhem." *Economy and Society* 27, no. 2/3 (May 1998): 274–84.

Mol, Arthur P. J. "Ecological Modernization and the Global Economy." *Global Environmental Politics* 2, no. 2 (May 2002): 92–115.

Mol, Arthur P. J., and Martin Jänicke, "The Origins and Theoretical Foundations of Ecological Modernisation Theory." In *The Ecological Modernisation Reader: Environmental Reform in Theory and Practice*, edited by Arthur P. J. Mol, David A. Sonnenfeld, and Gert Spaargaren. London: Routledge, 2009.

Monk, Daniel Bertrand, et al. "A Discussion on the Global and the Universal." *Grey Room*, no. 61 (Fall 2015): 66–89.

Moos, Stanislaus von. *Le Corbusier: Elements of a Synthesis*. Amsterdam: nai010, 2013.

Morris, E. B. "Twenty-Five Hundred Miles without Climate: Air Conditioning." *Federal Architect* 7, no. 10 (October 1936): 35–44.

Morton, Timothy. *Ecology without Nature: Rethinking Environmental Aesthetics*. Cambridge, MA: Harvard University Press, 2011.

Mozingo, Louise A. *Pastoral Capitalism: A History of Suburban Corporate Landscapes*. Cambridge, MA: MIT Press, 2014.

Mumford, Eric. *The CIAM Discourse on Urbanism, 1928–1960*. Cambridge, MA: MIT Press, 2000.

Mumford, Lewis. *Technics and Civilization*. New York: Harcourt Brace, 1934.

Murphy, Michelle. *The Economization of Life*. Durham, NC: Duke University Press, 2017.

———. *Sick Building Syndrome and the Problem of Uncertainty: Environmental Politics, Technoscience, and Women Workers*. Durham, NC: Duke University Press, 2006.

Muzaffar, M. Ijlal. "The Periphery Within: Modern Architecture and the Making of the Third World." PhD diss., MIT, 2007.

Naginski, Erika, and Preston Scott Cohen, eds. *The Return of Nature: Sustaining Architecture in the Face of Sustainability*. New York: Routledge, 2014.

Nebeker, Frederik. *Calculating the Weather: Meteorology in the 20th Century*. New York: Elsevier, 1995.

———. "A History of Calculating Aids in Meteorology." In *Historical Essays on Meteorology, 1919–1995*, edited by James Rodger Fleming, 157–78. London: Springer, 1995.

Negarestani, Reza. *Cyclonopedia: Complicity with Anonymous Materials*. New York: re.press, 2008.

Nelson, Garrett Dash. "Rexford Guy Tugwell and the Case for Big Urbanism." *Places Journal* (January 2018).

Neutra, Richard. *Architecture of Social Concern in Regions of Mild Climate*. São Paulo: Gerth Todtmann, 1948.

———. "Comments on Planetary Reconstruction." *Arts and Architecture* 61, no. 12 (December 1944): 21–29.

———. "Europe Rebuilds." *Progressive Architecture* 30, no. 6 (June 1946): 20, 22, 24, 26.

———. "How America Builds, 1937–38: Influences on the Trend of Building Design." *Architectural Record* 83, no. 1 (January 1938): 60–63.

———. "The Modern Health Center Design for Regions of Mild Climate." *Modern Hospital* 66, no. 2 (February 1946): 46–54, 46.

———. *Nature Near: The Late Essays of Richard Neutra*. Santa Barbara, CA: Capra Press, 1989.

———. "Nouvelles écoles é émentaire pour l'amérique." *L'Architecture d'aujourd'hui* 7, no. 5 (May 1936): 49–55.

———. "Observations on Latin America." *Progressive Architecture* 27, no. 5 (May 1946): 67–72.

———. "Planetary Reconstruction." *Journal of the American Institute of Architects* 3, no. 1 (January 1945): 29–33.

———. "Pseudo-ciencia y arte en la arquitectura." *Arquitectura* 15, no. 4 (April 1947): 135.

———. "Puerto Rico." *Architectural Forum* 82, no. 3 (January 1945): 119–32.

———. "Regionalism in Architecture." *Plus*, no. 2 (February 1939): 35–45.

———. "A Revision of the Concept of the School Building: A New Plan for California Schools." *Architect and Engineer* 123, no. 12 (December 1935): 29–33.

———. "Sun Control Devices." *Progressive Architecture* 27, no. 10 (October 1946): 88–91.

———. *Survival through Design*. New York: Oxford University Press, 1954.

Newell, Peter. "New Environmental Architectures and the Search for Effectiveness." *Global Environmental Politics* 1, no. 1 (February 2001): 35–46.

Nicodemo, Thiago Lima. "State-Sponsored Avant-Garde and Brazil's Cultural Policy in the 1940s: Candido Portinari and Gilberto Freyre in the USA." *Revista Landa* 5, no. 1 (2016): 350–80.

Nixon, Rob. *Slow Violence and the Environmentalism of the Poor*. Cambridge, MA: Harvard University Press, 2011.

Nocke, Thomas, and Birgit Schneider, eds. *Image Politics of Climate Change*. Bielefeld, Germany: Transcript Verlag, 2014.

Ofonso, Jacqueline Ganzert. *Petrobras, ou comment devenir une grande puissance petroliére*. Paris: Éditions Universitaires Européenes, 2015.

Ogura, Nobuyuki, David Leonides, T. Yap, and Kenichi Tanoue. "Modern Architecture in the Philippines and the Quest for Filipino Style." *Journal of Asian Architecture and Building Engineering* 1, no. 2 (November 2002): 233–38.

Oldfield, Philip, Dario Trabucco, and Antony Wood. "Five Energy Generations of Tall Buildings: An Historical Analysis of Energy Consumption in High-Rise Buildings." *Journal of Architecture* 14, no. 5 (2009): 591–615.

Olgyay, Aladar. "Economics of Curtain Walls." *Architectural Forum* (October 1957): 154–62, 168.

———. *Thermal Behavior of Metal Curtain Walls in Relation to Cooling Costs and Shading Devices*. Princeton, NJ: Princeton University School of Architecture, 1957.

Olgyay, Aladar, and Victor Olgyay. "Partitions Function as Columns in Scheme for Apartment Buildings." *Architectural Record* (January 1951): 134–39.

———. "Report on the Thermoheliodon: Laboratory Machine for Testing Thermal Behavior of Buildings through Model Structures." Princeton University School of Architecture and School of Engineering, June 1956.

———. *Solar Control and Shading Devices*. Princeton, NJ: Princeton University Press, 1957.

———. *The Work of Architects Olgyay and Olgyay*. New York: Reinhold, 1952.

Olgyay, Victor. "Contribution to a Study of Biometeorology." *Proceedings of the First Annual Conference on Biometeorology*. London: University College, London, 1961.

———. "Description and Preliminary Calculations for the 'Sun Conditioned' House System." Princeton University School of Architecture, 1956.

———. *Design with Climate: Bioclimatic Approach to Architectural Regionalism*. Princeton, NJ: Princeton University Press, 2016.

———. "Human Environmental Approach to Architecture: Preliminary Outline of Proposed Program at the Architectural Laboratory, School of Architecture, Princeton University." Princeton University School of Architecture, 1952.

———. "The Temperate House." *Architectural Forum* 94, no. 3 (March 1951): 180–89.

Oliveira, Adilson de. "Brazil's Petrobras: Strategy and Performance." In *Oil and Governance: State Owned Enterprises and the World Oil Supply*, edited by David G. Victor et al. New York: Cambridge University Press, 2012.

Omidfar, Azedeh, and Dan Weissman. "Design with Climate: The Role of Digital Tools in Computational Analysis of Site-Specific Architecture." In *Interdisciplinary Design*, edited by Hanif Kara and Andreas Georgoulias. New York: Actar, 2012.

Oreskes, Naomi, and Erik M. Conway. *The Collapse of Western Civilization: A View from the Future*. New York: Columbia University Press, 2014.

Osborne, Michael A. "Acclimatizing the World: A History of the Paradigmatic Colonial Science." *Osiris* 15 (2000): 135–51.

Osman, Michael. "Banham's Historical Ecology." In *Neo-Avant-Garde and Postmodern: Postwar Architecture in Britain and Beyond*, edited by Mark Crinson and Claire Zimmerman. New Haven, CT: Yale University Press, 2010.

———. *Modernism's Visible Hand: Architecture and Regulation in America*. Minneapolis: University of Minnesota Press, 2018.

Overy, Paul. *Light, Air, and Openness: Modern Architecture between the Wars*. London: Thames and Hudson, 2008.

Owen, David. "The Efficiency Dilemma." *New Yorker*, December 20, 2010, 78–84.

Pacala, Stephen, and Rob Socolow. "Stabilization Wedges: Solving the Climate Problem for the Next 50 Years with Current Technologies." *Science* 305, no. 5686 (August 13, 2004): 968–72.

Pai, Hyungmin. *The Portfolio and the Diagram: Architecture, Discourse, and Modernity in America*. Cambridge, MA: MIT Press, 2002.

Painter, David. *Oil and the American Century*. Baltimore: Johns Hopkins University Press, 1986.

Papadaki, Stamo. *Le Corbusier: The Gradations of Modulor*. Paris: Durisol, 1947.

———. *Oscar Niemeyer: Works in Progress*. New York: Reinhold, 1956.

Papadaki, Stamo, ed. *Le Corbusier: Architect, Painter, Writer*. New York: Macmillan, 1948.

Papadaki, Stamo, and Lucio Costa. *The Work of Oscar Niemeyer*. New York: Reinhold, 1950.

Parak, Gisela, ed. *Eco-Images: Historical Views and Political Strategies*. Munich: Rachel Carson Center and Deutsches Museum, 2013.

Passanti, Francesco. "The Vernacular, Modernism, and Le Corbusier." *Journal of the Society of Architectural Historians* 56, no. 4 (December 1997): 438–51.

Paton, Bruce C. "Paul Siple and the Origin of Windchill." *Wilderness and Environmental Medicine* 10 (1999): 174–75.

Pearlman, Jill. *Inventing American Modernism: Joseph Hudnut, Walter Gropius, and the Bauhaus Legacy at Harvard*. Charlottesville: University of Virginia Press, 2007.

Penick, Monica. "Marketing Modernism: House Beautiful and the Station Wagon Way of Life." *Working Papers on Design* 4 (2010): 1–16.

———. "The Pace Setter Houses: Livable Modernism in Postwar America." PhD diss., University of Texas at Austin, 2007.

———. *Tastemaker: Elizabeth Gordon,* House Beautiful, *and the Postwar House*. New Haven, CT: Yale University Press, 2017.

Pereira, Claudio Calovi. "O pórtico clássico como terminal aéreo: Os projetos dos irmãos Roberto para o aeroporto Santos Dumont." *Arq Texto* 3, no. 4 (2003): 122–36.

Piccarolo, Gaia. "Lucio Costa's Luso-Brasilian Routes: Recalibrating 'Center' and 'Periphery.'" In *Latin American Modern Architectures: Ambiguous Territories*, edited by Patricio del Real and Helen Gyger, 33–52. New York: Routledge, 2012.

Pinkus, Karen. *Fuel: A Speculative Dictionary*. Minneapolis: University of Minnesota Press, 2016.

———. "Search for a Language." *Cambridge Journal of Postcolonial Literary Inquiry* 1, no. 2 (September 2014): 251–57.

*Planet Earth: The Mystery with 100,000 Clues*. Washington, DC: National Academy of Sciences, 1958.

Polanyi, Karl. *The Great Transformation: The Political and Economic Origins of Our Times*. Boston: Beacon Press, 1944.

Pollmann, Inga. "Invisible Worlds, Visible: Uexküll's *Umwelt*, Film and Film Theory." *Critical Inquiry* 39, no. 4 (Summer 2013): 777–816.

Porteous, Colin. *The New Eco-Architecture: Alternatives from the Modern Movement*. London: Taylor and Francis, 2002.

Postal, Matthew A. "'Toward a Democratic Esthetic?': The Modern House in America, 1932–1955." PhD diss., City University of New York, 1998.

Prutsch, Ursula. "Nelson A. Rockefeller's Office of Inter-American Affairs in Brazil." In *¡Américas unidas!: Nelson A. Rockefeller's Office of Inter-American Affairs, 1940–46*, edited by Gisela Cramer and Ursula Prutsch. Madrid: Iberoamericana Vervuert, 2014.

Rabinow, Paul. "French Enlightenment: Truth and Life." *Economy and Society* 27, no. 2/3 (May 1998): 193–201.

Rannelagh. John. *The Agency: The Rise and Fall of the CIA*. New York: Simon and Schuster, 1986.

Rannells, John. "Building in the Tropics: An Approach to the Study of Building Types Suitable for Tropical Climates." *Architectural Record* (August 1952): 153–81.

———. "Technical Press: Climate Control." *Progressive Architecture* (February 1950): 99–101.

Real, Patricio del. "Building a Continent: MoMA's *Latin American Architecture since 1945* Exhibition." *Journal of Latin American Cultural Studies* 16, no. 1 (2007).

———. "Paternity Rights: The Brise-Soleil and the Sources of Modernism in the Ministry of Education and Health in Rio de Janeiro, Brazil." *ACSA Proceedings* (2002): 199–207.

*Report to the General Assembly of the United Nations by the Secretary General on the Permanent Headquarters of the United Nations*. Lake Success, NY: United Nations, 1947.

Requena-Ruiz, Ignacio. "Building Artificial Climates: Thermal Control and Comfort in Modern Architecture, 1930–1960." *Ambiances* (November 2016): 1–22.

Reynolds, John. "The Roots of Bioclimatic Design." In *Design with Climate: Bioclimatic Approach to Architectural Regionalism*, by Victor Olgyay. Princeton, NJ: Princeton University Press, 2016.

Ricoeur, Paul. "Universal Civilization and National Cultures." In *History and Truth*. Evanston, IL: Northwestern University Press, 1965.

Roberto, Milton, and Vinicius de Moraes. "Dix années d'architecture." *L'Architecture d'aujourd'hui* 23, no. 42 (1952): 26–28.

Rocha-Peixoto, Gustavo. "Prefacio: Rigor Arejado e Solar." In *Irmãos Roberto, Arquitetos*, by Luiz Felipe Machado Coelho de Souza. Rio de Janeiro: Rio Books, 2013.

Rodgers, Tyler S. *Design of Insulated Buildings for Various Climates*. New York: Roberts Publishing, 1951.

Rome, Adam. *The Bulldozer in the Countryside: Suburban Sprawl and the Rise of American Environmentalism*. New York: Cambridge University Press, 2001.

Rose, Nikolas. "Life, Reason, and History: Reading Georges Canguilhem Today." *Economy and Society* 27, no. 2/3 (May 1998): 154–79.

Rosler, Martha. "Bringing the War Home: *House Beautiful* 1967–1972 new series 2004." *Rethinking Marxism* 18, no. 1 (2006): 100–119.

Ross, John F. "Pascal's Legacy." *European Molecular Biology Organization Reports* 5, no. 1 (October 2004): 7–10.

Rowe, Colin, and Robert Slutsky. "Transparency: Literal and

Phenomenal, Part II." *Perspecta* 13/14 (1971): 287–301.
Rudgers, David F. *Creating the Secret State: The Origins of the Central Intelligence Agency, 1943–1947*. Lawrence: University Press of Kansas, 2000.
Rutherford, Paul. "Ecological Modernization and Environmental Risk." In *Discourses on the Environment*, edited by Eric Darier, 95–117. London: Wiley, 1998.
Ryan, Daniel J. "Architects in White Coats." In *The Sydney School: Formative Moments in Architecture, Design, and Planning at Sydney University*, edited by Andrew Leach and Lee Stickells. Sydney: Uro Publications, 2018.
———. "Civilizing Comfort: 1914–1945." *Proceedings of the 7th Windsor Conference: The Changing Context of Comfort in an Unpredictable World*, 1–12. London: Network for Energy Use in Buildings, 2012.
Sá, Paulo. "Ventilation and Comfort Levels." *Revista Arquitetura e Urbanismo* (June 1936): 194–95.
Samuel, Flora. *Le Corbusier in Detail*. New York: Routledge, 2007.
Sandler, Daniela. "The Other Way Around: The Modernist Movement in Brazil." In *Third World Modernism: Architecture, Development, and Identity*, edited by Duanfang Lu, 31–56. New York: Routledge, 2010.
Sargent, John. *Frank Lloyd Wright's Usonian House: The Case for Organic Architecture*. New York: Whitney Library of Design, 1976.
Saunders, Frances Stonor. *The Cultural Cold War: The CIA and the World of Arts and Letters*. New York: New Press, 2001.
Schirato, Tony, and Jen Webb. "The Idea of Globalization." In their *Understanding Globalization*, 3–20. London: Sage Publications, 2003.
Schmindlin, Emil. "Presenting *House Beautiful*'s Pace-Setter House for 1949." *House Beautiful* (November 1949).
Schneider, Birgit. "Climate Model Simulation Visualization from a Visual Studies Perspective." *WIREs Climate Change* 3 (2012): 185–93.
Schneider, Ronald M. *"Order and Progress": A Political History of Brazil*. Boulder, CO: Westview Press, 1991.
Schrank, Sarah. "Naked Houses: The Architecture of Nudism and the Rethinking of the American Suburb." In *Healing Spaces, Modern Architecture, and the Body*, edited by Sarah Schrank and Didem Ekici, 7–31. New York: Routledge, 2017.
Schumacher, E. F. *Small Is Beautiful: A Study of Economics as if People Mattered*. New York: Harper and Row, 1973.
Segawa, Hugo. *Architecture of Brazil: 1900–1990*. New York: Springer Verlag, 2012.
Segre, Roberto. *Ministério da Educação e da Saúde: Ícone Urbano da Modernidade Brasileira, 1935–1945*. São Paulo: Romano Guerra, 2013.
Sekler, Edward, and William Curtis. *Le Corbusier at Work: The Genesis of the Carpenter Center for Visual Arts*. Cambridge, MA: Harvard University Press, 1978.
Shanken, Andrew M. *194x: Architecture, Planning, and Consumer Culture on the American Home Front*. Minneapolis: University of Minnesota Press, 2009.
Shi, David. "Edward Bok and the Simple Life." *American Heritage* 36, no. 1 (December 1984).
Shove, Elizabeth. *Comfort, Cleanliness, and Convenience: The Social Organization of Normality*. Oxford: Berg, 2003.
Siegert, Bernhard. *Cultural Techniques: Grids, Filters, Doors, and Other Articulations of the Modern*. New York: Fordham University Press, 2015.
Sinclair, Cameron. *Design Like You Give a Damn: Architectural Responses to Humanitarian Crises*. London: Thames and Hudson, 2006.
Siret, Daniel. "Généalogie du brise-soleil dans l'œuvre de Le Corbusier." *Cahiers Thématiques*, no. 4 (2004): 169–81.
Skidmore, Thomas. *Politics in Brazil, 1930–1964: An Experiment in Democracy*. New York: Oxford University Press, 1967.
Sloterdijk, Peter. *In the World Interior of Capital: Towards a Philosophical Theory of Globalization*. Malden, MA: Polity Press, 2013.
———. *Terror from the Air*. Cambridge, MA: Semiotext(e), 2009.
Sobin, Harris. "The Role of Regional Vernacular Traditions in the Genesis of Le Corbusier's Brise-Soleil Sun-Shading Techniques." *Traditional Dwellings and Settlements Review* 6, no. 1 (Fall 1994): 80.
———. "Veils and Shadows: Le Corbusier in North Africa, 1928–1936." *Proceedings of the Meeting of the French Colonial Historical Society* 19 (1994): 187–99.
Somol, Robert, and Sarah Whiting. "Notes around the Doppler Effect, and Other Moods of Modernism." *Perspecta* 33 (2002): 73–77.
Spanos, B. J. *Proclaiming the Truth: An Illustrated History of the American Society of Heating, Refrigeration, and Air-Conditioning Engineers, Inc.* Washington, DC: AHRAE, 1996.
Spence, J. McKay. "The New Role of the Architect in the Tropics." *AA Journal* (August 1955): 56–60.
Spencer, Douglas. *The Architecture of Neoliberalism: How Contemporary Architecture Became an Instrument of Control and Compliance*. London: Bloomsbury Academic, 2016
Springer, Simon. "Neoliberalism as Discourse: Between Foucauldian Political Economy and Marxian Poststructuralism." *Critical Discourse Studies* 9, no. 2 (May 2012): 133–47.
Staples, Amy L. S. *The Birth of Development: How the World Bank, Food and Agriculture Administration, and World Health Organization Have Changed the World*. Kent, OH: Kent State University Press, 2006.
Steffen, Will, Wendy Broadgate, and Lisa Deutsch. "The Trajectory of the Anthropocene: The Great Acceleration." *Anthropocene Review* 2, no. 1 (2015): 81–98.
Steffen, Will, et al. *Global Change and the Earth System: A Planet under Pressure*. New York: Springer Verlag, 2004.
Steiner, Hadas. "Life at the Threshold." *October*, no. 136 (Spring 2011): 133–55.
Stengers, Isabelle. *In Catastrophic Times: Resisting the Coming Barbarism*. Ann Arbor, MI: Open Humanities Press, 2015.
Stepan, Nancy. *Beginnings of Brazilian Science: Oswaldo Cruz, Medical Research, and Policy, 1890–1920*. New York: Science History Publications, 1981.
Sullivan, Walter. *Assault on the Unknown: The International Geophysical Year*. New York: McGraw-Hill, 1961.
Swyngedouw, Eric. "Apocalypse Forever? Post-Political Populism and the Spectre of Climate Change." *Theory, Culture, and Society* 27, no. 2/3 (2010): 213–32.
Tafuri, Manfredo. *Architecture and Utopia: Design and Capitalist Development*. Cambridge, MA: MIT Press, 1976.
Taylor, Peter J. "How Do We Know We Have Global Environmental Problems? Undifferentiated Science-Politics and Its Potential Reconstruction." In *Changing Life: Genomes-Ecologies-Bodies-Commodities*, edited by Peter J. Taylor, Saul Halfon, and Paul Edwards, 149–74. Minneapolis: University of Minnesota Press, 1997.
Taylor, Walter A., and Theodore Irving Coe. "Regional Climate Analyses and Design Data." *Bulletin of the American Institute of Architects* (September 1949): 15.
Silva, Theodoro Jitomir da. "Rino Levi and the Evolution of Brazilian Modernism." *AA Files* 17 (Spring 1989): 24–30.
Trubiano, Franca. "Re-defining Architectural Performance—*Survival through Design* and the Sentient

Environmentalism of Richard Neutra." In *Architecture in an Age of Uncertainty*, edited by Benjamin Flowers, 43–56. New York: Routledge, 2016.
Tsiomis, Yannis. "Le Corbusier au Brésil." In *Conférences de Rio*. Paris: Flammarion, 2006.
Tugwell, Rexford G. *The Stricken Land: The Story of Puerto Rico*. 1946; New York: Greenwood Press, 1968.
Turner, Roger. "Weathering Heights: The Emergence of Aeronautical Meteorology as an Infrastructural Science." PhD diss., University of Pennsylvania, 2010.
Tzonis, Alexander, ed. *Tropical Architecture: Critical Regionalism in the Age of Globalization*. New York: Wiley, 2001.
Udovicki-Selb, Danilo. "Le Corbusier and the Paris Exhibition of 1937: The Temps Nouveaux Pavilion." *Journal of the Society of Architectural Historians* 56, no. 1 (March 1997): 42–63.
Uduko, Ola. "Modernist Architecture the 'Tropical' in West Africa: The Tropical Architecture Movement in West Africa, 1948–1970." *Habitat International* 30 (2006): 396–411.
"The United Nations Meeting." *Chronology of International Events and Documents* 2, no. 4 (February 4, 1946): 105–20.
"The United States and the United Nations: Chronology." *World Affairs* 109, no. 4 (December 1946): 254–56.
Van Dyne, George M., *Ecosystems, Systems Ecology, and Systems Ecologists*. Oak Ridge, TN: Oak Ridge National Laboratory / Union Carbide Corporation / Atomic Energy Commission, 1966.
Vidler, Anthony. "Diagrams of Diagrams: Architectural Abstraction and Modern Representation." *Representations*, no. 72 (Fall 2000): 1–20.
Vitalis, Robert. "Black Gold, White Crude: An Essay on American Exceptionalism, Hierarchy, and Hegemony in the Gulf." *Diplomatic History* 26, no. 2 (Spring 2002): 185–214.
Viveiros de Castro, Eduardo. "Economic Development, Anthropomorphism, and the Principle of Reasonable Sufficiency." In *Protecting Nature, Saving Creation*, edited by Pasquale Gagliardi et al., 161–80. New York: Palgrave Macmillan, 2013.
Von Neumann, John. *The Computer and the Brain*. New Haven, CT: Yale University Press, 2012.
Von Neumann, John, et al., eds. "The Dynamics of Climate: Conference on the Application of Numerical Integration Techniques to the Problem of General Circulation." Princeton, NJ: Institute for Advanced Study, 1955.
Wallenstein, Sven-Olov. *Biopolitics and the Emergence of Modern Architecture*. New York: Temple Hoyne Buell Center for American Architecture and Princeton Architectural Press, 2009.
Wark, McKenzie. *Molecular Red: Theory for the Anthropocene*. New York: Verso, 2015.
Watts, Michael. "Resource Curse? Governmentality, Oil, and Power in the Niger Delta, Nigeria." In *The Geopolitics of Resource Wars: Resource Dependence, Governance, and Violence*, edited by Philippe Le Billon, 50–82. New York: Routledge, 2007.
Weber, Samuel. "Bare Life and Life in General." *Grey Room*, no. 46 (Winter 2012): 6–12.
Weisskoff, Richard. *Factories and Food Stamps: The Puerto Rico Model for Development*. Baltimore: Johns Hopkins University Press, 1985.
Werneck, F. J. Santos. "Insolation in Rio de Janeiro." *Revista Arquitetura e Urbanismo* (June 1936).
Wigley, Mark. *Bucky, Inc.: Architecture in the Age of Radio*. Zurich: Lars Müller, 2015.
Wijdeveld, H. Th., ed. *Frank Lloyd Wright: The Life-Work of the American Architect Frank Lloyd Wright*. Santpoort, the Netherlands: C. A. Mees, 1925.
Williams, Daryle. *Culture Wars in Brazil: The First Vargas Regime, 1930–1945*. Durham, NC: Duke University Press, 2001.
Winner, Langdon. *The Whale and the Reactor: A Search for Limits in an Age of High Technology*. Chicago: University of Chicago Press, 1986.
Winslow, C.-E. A., and L. P. Herrington. *Temperature and Human Life*. Princeton, NJ: Princeton University Press, 1949.
Wolin, Richard. *The Wind from the East: French Intellectuals, the Cultural Revolution, and the Legacy of the 1960s*. Princeton, NJ: Princeton University Press, 2010.
Woodbridge, George. *UNRRA: The History of the United Nations Relief and Rehabilitation Agency*. New York: Columbia University Press, 1950.
Woodward, David. "The Image of the Spherical Earth." *Perspecta*, no. 25 (1989): 2–15.
Worster, Donald. "The Ecology of Order and Chaos." In *Out of the Woods: Essays in Environmental History*, edited by Char Miller and Hal Rothman, 1–16. Pittsburgh: University of Pittsburgh Press, 1997.
———. *Nature's Economy: History of Ecological Ideas*. San Francisco: Sierra Club, 1977.
———. "The Shaky Ground of Sustainability." In *Global Ecology: A New Arena of Political Conflict*, edited by Wolfgang Sachs, 132–45. Atlantic Highlands, NJ: Zed Books, 1993.
Wright, Frank Lloyd. *Ausgeführte Bauten*. Berlin: Verlegt bei Ernst Wasmuth, 1911.
Wright, Gwendolyn. "Global Ambitions and Local Knowledge." In *Modernism and the Middle East: Architecture and Politics in the Twentieth Century*, edited by Sandy Eisenstadt and Kishwar Rizvi, 221–254. Seattle: University of Washington Press, 2008.
———. *USA: Modern Architectures in History*. London: Reaktion Books, 2008.
Yaglou, Constantin, et al. "Control of Heat Casualties at Military Training Centers." *American Medical Association Architectural Industrial Health* (1956): 1–11.
Yaneva, Albena. *Five Ways to Make Architecture Political*. London: Bloomsbury, 2017.
Yeang, Ken. "From Bioclimatic Design to Eco Design." In Victor Olgyay, *Design with Climate: Bioclimatic Approach to Architectural Regionalism*. Princeton, NJ: Princeton University Press, 2016.
Yergin, Daniel. *The Prize: The Epic Quest for Oil, Money, and Power*. New York: Free Press, 2008.
———. *The Quest: Energy, Security, and the Remaking of the Modern World*. New York: Penguin, 2012.
Yusoff, Kathryn. "Geologic Life: Prehistory, Climate, Futures in the Anthropocene." *Environment and Planning D: Society and Space* 31 (2013): 779–95.
Zevi, Bruno. *Towards an Organic Architecture*. New York: Faber and Faber, 1950.
Žižek, Slavoj. *Living in End Times*. New York: Verso, 2010.
Zylinska, Joanna. *Minimal Ethics for the Anthropocene*. Ann Arbor, MI: Open Humanities Press, 2014.

# Index

Reproduced with permission of the American Institute of Architects, 1735 New York Ave. NW, Washington, DC: 4.8, 4.10–4.12

*Architectural Forum*, reproduced with permission: 5.9–5.11, 5.16

Photographed by Daniel A. Barber: 2.9, 2.35–38

© Gaston Bergeret, 2019: 0.1

© BP plc, courtesy the BP Archive: 6.7

*Collier's*, reproduced with permission: 5.1

Photographed by Fernando Delgado: 2.32–34

© FLC/ADAGP, Paris / Artists Rights Society (ARS), New York, 2019: 0.1–0.6, 1.1–1.3, 1.7–1.12, 1.14–1.22, 1.24, 1.26–1.29, 2.7, 5.31

Interior photographed by Alexandre Georges: 6.18

© J. Paul Getty Trust. Getty Research Institute, Los Angeles (2004.R.10): 3.4–3.6, 3.8

Courtesy of Amrita Ghosh: 5.45

Courtesy of the Frances Loeb Library, Harvard University Graduate School of Design: 3.40–3.42, 5.14

Redrawn by Stinson Lenz, 2019; reproduced with permission: 5.21 (*Science*), 5.44 (Centre for Alternative Technology), 6.6 (*Science*)

Drawing photographed by Marshall D. Meyers: 3.38

Courtesy Museum of Modern Art, New York, © Art Resource, 2019: 3.21–3.23, 3.25–3.28, 3.30–3.33, 3.38, 3.43, 3.44, 3.46, 6.1

Courtesy Dion Neutra, Architect © and Richard and Dion Neutra Papers, Department of Special Collections, Charles E. Young Research Library, UCLA: 3.1–3.3, 3.7–3.20, 3.34

Courtesy of the Núcleo de Pesquisa e Documentação, Faculdade de Arquitetura e Urbanismo, Univesidade Federal do Rio de Janeiro: 2.1, 2.13, 2.16, 2.28, 2.30

Victor and Aladar Olgyay, reproduced with permission: 5.1–5.5, 5.29, 5.38

Photographed by Sebastien Perez-Duarte: 1.4

Robert Geddes Papers, reproduced with permission from Princeton University: 5.23–5.28

Princeton University School of Architecture and School of Engineering, reproduced with permission: 5.41

Princeton University Press, reproduced with permission: 1.13, 2.9, 2.22–2.27, 5.7, 5.8, 5.30, 5.35, 5.36, 5.42, 5.43, 6.3, 6.5, 6.8

Copyright © 1963 and 1991 by Princeton University Press/Author. Reprinted by permission: 5.20, 5.32, 5.33, 5.34, 5.37, 5.39, 6.10

Photograph by Louis Reens: 3.43

Lewis Fry Richardson's Forecast Factory, reproduced with permission: 5.15

Photograph by Julius Shulman: 3.4–5, 3.8

© Ezra Stoller/Esto: 1.6, 6.13b, 6.15

Courtesy Marcel Breuer Papers, Special Collections Research Center, Syracuse University Libraries: 6.9

© UN Photo/MB: 6.14

Courtesy of the University of Pennsylvania Architectural Archives: 1.7

Courtesy of Louis I. Kahn Collection, University of Pennsylvania and the Pennsylvania Historical and Museum Commission: 3.35

Westin Bonaventure Collection, the Portman Archives: 6.19

# Credits

Published by Princeton University Press, 41 William Street, Princeton, New Jersey 08540

In the United Kingdom: Princeton University Press, 99 Banbury Road, Oxford OX2 6JX

press.princeton.edu

Cover art courtesy of the Frances Loeb Library, Harvard University Graduate School of Design



First Paperback Printing, 2023
Paper ISBN: 978-0-691-24865-3
Cloth ISBN: 978-0-691-17003-9

The Library of Congress has cataloged the cloth edition as follows:
Names: Barber, Daniel A., author.
Title: Modern architecture and climate: design before air conditioning / Daniel A. Barber.
Description: Princeton: Princeton University Press, [2020] | Includes bibliographical references and index.
Identifiers: LCCN 2019052840 (print) | LCCN 2019052841 (ebook) | ISBN 9780691170039 (hardcover) | ISBN 9780691204949 (ebook)
Subjects: LCSH: Architecture and climate. | Architecture, Modern—20th century—Themes, motives.
Classification: LCC NA2541 .B37 2020 (print) | LCC NA2541 (ebook) | DDC 724/.6—dc23
LC record available at https://lccn.loc.gov/2019052840
LC ebook record available at https://lccn.loc.gov/2019052841

British Library Cataloging-in-Publication Data is available

Image reproduction was supported by generous grants from The Graham Foundation for Advanced Studies in the Fine Arts and the George Howard Bickley Endowment for Architecture Publications of the University of Pennsylvania Weitzman School of Design

Design: Office of Luke Bulman

This book has been composed in Untitled Sans

Printed in China